Prince of Tricksters

Prince of Tricksters

THE INCREDIBLE TRUE STORY OF
NETLEY LUCAS, GENTLEMAN CROOK

Matt Houlbrook

University of Chicago Press CHICAGO & LONDON

MATT HOULBROOK is professor of cultural history at the University of Birmingham.

The University of Chicago Press, Chicago 60637
The University of Chicago Press, Ltd., London
© 2016 by The University of Chicago
All rights reserved. Published 2016.
Printed in the United States of America

25 24 23 22 21 20 19 18 17 16   1 2 3 4 5

ISBN-13: 978-0-226-13315-7 (cloth)
ISBN-13: 978-0-226-13329-4 (e-book)
DOI: 10.7208/chicago/9780226133294.001.0001

Library of Congress Cataloging-in-Publication Data
Names: Houlbrook, Matt, author.
Title: Prince of tricksters : the incredible true story of Netley Lucas, gentleman crook /
Matt Houlbrook.
Description: Chicago ; London : University of Chicago Press, 2016. |
Includes bibliographical references and index.
Identifiers: LCCN 2015042768| ISBN 9780226133157 (cloth : alk. paper) |
ISBN 9780226133294 (e-book)
Subjects: LCSH: Lucas, Netley. | Swindlers and swindling–England–Biography. |
Criminals–England–Biography. | Authors, English–Biography. | Biographers–England–
Biography. | England–Intellectual life–20th century. | Popular literature–England–
20th century–History and criticism.
Classification: LCC HV6692.L83 H68 2016 | DDC 364.16/3092–dc23 LC record available at
http://lccn.loc.gov/2015042768

♾ This paper meets the requirements of ANSI/NISO Z39.48-1992
(Permanence of Paper).

I mistrust all frank and simple people, especially when their stories hold together.

ERNEST HEMINGWAY, *The Sun Also Rises* (1926)

CONTENTS

ACKNOWLEDGMENTS

This book has been a long time coming. Writing about a confidence trickster has been a way of working through my own professional crisis of confidence. All historical writing is autobiographical in some way.

All historical writing is also cowriting. The single name on the cover belies how this book could not exist without the rich scholarship on which I have been able to draw. Nor could it exist without the intellectual, professional, and personal support that has sustained me over the years. Acknowledging my debts here is a rare privilege.

It is not always easy to find someone given to telling stories and changing names. My research was made simpler than it might have been by those who gave up their time and shared their knowledge when I asked for help. More than most, I have relied on the kindness of academic strangers. Brenda Roberts and Gina Worboys of the Old Bedfordians Club passed on Bedford School records. Steve Holland and Mike Ashley were generous with their remarkable knowledge of 1920s and 1930s popular magazines. Archivists and librarians patiently answered my questions and helped me find material. The list is long, but in Britain it includes Carole Jones at the Modern Records Centre, University of Warwick; Helen Broderick at the British Library's Modern Literary Manuscripts collection; Frances Pattman at the Archives and Corporate Records Services of King's College London; Howard Greenwood at the Records Management Branch of the Metropolitan Police; Madelin Terrazas at the Churchill Archives Centre, Churchill College, Cambridge; Matthew Piggott at the Surrey History Centre; and Lorna Standen at Herefordshire Record Office. Pamela Clark and her colleagues at the Royal Archives, Windsor

Castle, identified rich material in their collections and painstakingly corrected the mistakes in my transcriptions; this material appears here thanks to the permission of Her Majesty Queen Elizabeth II.

Following someone across national borders has left me further indebted to archivists, librarians, and others across the world. In the United States I have benefited from the help of David Kessler at the Bancroft Library, University of California, Berkeley; Sigrid Pohl Perry and Scott Kraftt at Northwestern University Library; Susan Halpert and Heather Cole at the Houghton Library, Harvard University; Mary Robertson at the Huntington Library; and Elspeth Healey at the Harry Ransom Center, University of Texas at Austin. Stephen Maynard and Christine Grandy kindly took time out from their research to search Canadian newspapers and the City of Toronto and Ontario Archives. Kate Gleeson, Bridget Griffen-Foley, and John Tebbutt; Sally Jackson, Mary-anne Doyle, and Angus Johnstone at the National Film and Sound Archive of Australia; and David Kidd at Radio Station 2GB helped me to track down the script of an obscure 1950s radio play. Sometimes my questions quickly reached a dead end; more often I found surprises and exciting lines of inquiry.

It is inevitable that parts of this book have appeared behind different names and other masks over the past ten years. I am grateful to the publishers and editors who have allowed me to reproduce bits and pieces in the pages that follow. These include Manchester University Press for permission to use parts of "Thinking Queer: The Social and the Sexual in Interwar Britain," first published in *British Queer History: New Approaches and Perspectives*, ed. Brian Lewis (Manchester, UK: Manchester University Press, 2013); and Oxford University Press for permission to use revised fragments of "Fashioning an Ex-Crook Self: Citizenship and Criminality in the Work of Netley Lucas," *Twentieth Century British History* 24, no. 1 (2013). Portions of part 2 appeared as "Commodifying the Self Within: Ghosts, Libels, and the Crook Life-Story in Interwar Britain," *Journal of Modern History* 85, no. 2 (2013), © 2013 by the University of Chicago.

The institutions I have worked at have given me intellectual stimulation and the time and space to be a historian. I started this book at the University of Liverpool, struggled on at Oxford, and finally finished the manuscript at the University of Birmingham. It has been my good fortune to work with engaged and passionate undergraduate historians throughout this period. My students have been among my most strident critics and the most important influence on how I think about modern Britain. In humoring my obsessions, they have also been skeptical enough to ask the hardest question you can pose to a historian: so what? Fingers crossed, I have managed to give a decent answer.

The manuscript would never have been completed without a period of research leave provided by a British Academy Mid-career Fellowship: the reminder that I am getting older is a small price to pay for its generous support. Aileen Mooney and Craig Clunas at Oxford, and Sally Baggott at Birmingham provided constructive criticism that made my funding application more convincing than I could. As well as being a meticulous copyeditor, Sally has an intuitive and enviable grasp of what a research project is really about. Moving to Birmingham came at exactly the right time to reinvigorate my intellectual and professional life. It is an exciting place to be a historian, and my colleagues in the Department of History and Centre for Modern British Studies have created an environment that is stimulating and supportive in equal measure. Thank you, in particular, to Nick Crowson, David Gange, Matthew Hilton, Simon Jackson, Chris Moores, Sadiah Qureshi, Corey Ross, Gavin Schaffer, and Kate Smith. I am indebted to Corey, Michael Whitby, and the School of History and Cultures for further financial support.

I have been lucky enough to work with an inspiring group of doctoral students over the course of my career. They have set the standard to which I aspire through their exemplary scholarship, and enriched my understanding of the practice of cultural history through our ongoing conversations. I suspect I've learned far more from Samuel Hyde, Matthew Hollow, Sarah Newman, Charlotte Greenhalgh, Eloise Moss, Simeon Koole, Ellis Stacey, and Laura Sefton than they have from me. Eloise and Sim, together with Bonnie Burke, provided professional, energetic, and imaginative research assistance. Andrew Jones showed the same qualities in securing the images for the book.

Over the ten years since I started this project, I have lost count of the places where I have shared ideas and the people whose insights and questions have shaped my thinking. The list cannot be exhaustive, but I owe thanks to Guy Beiner, Kate Bradley, Stephen Brooke, Quentin Colville, Pam Cox, Andrew Davies, Alex Drace-Francis, Simon Gunn, Rob Priest, Lyndal Roper, Claire Squires, Nick Stargardt, Marc Stein, Florence Tamagne, Chris Waters, and Mark Williams. The 20s30sNetwork provided a vital (and fun) interdisciplinary and collaborative environment in which to explore new ways of thinking about 1920s and 1930s Britain: I am particularly grateful to Elizabeth Darling, David Hendy, Richard Hornsey, Claire Langhamer, Lawrence Napper, and Tamson Pietsch. The manuscript finally came together during a month as a visiting scholar at the University of California, Berkeley, and a few days in Chicago on the way home. For the opportunity to try out ideas in workshops at Berkeley, the University of Chicago, Northwestern University, and the British History Seminar at the Newberry Library, and for their critically serious engagement with my arguments, I thank Dan Blanton, Michael Saler, Jane Shaw, and James Vernon, and Deborah Cohen, Fredrik Albritton Jonsson, and Alex Owen.

This book has been a long time coming because I struggled for so many years to write it. I have tried to be open about this in my blog *The Trickster Prince*. What began as an exercise in forcing myself to get words on-screen has become a way of exploring my own difficulties and demons and the process of writing a book from behind the scenes. It has been one of the most rewarding projects of my professional career. In challenging times for the modern university, the ongoing social media conversations around the practice of history and the virtual community of #twitterstorians allow us to explore new ways of working and writing together, and of doing history in public. I am indebted to all those who have engaged with my work online, but particularly to the creative originality of Joanne Bailey, Cath Feely, Rachel Moss, Will Pooley, and Helen Rogers.

I used to think I knew what it meant to be a historian. I was wrong. Working on this book has taught me the dangers of hubris and the importance of reflecting critically on how and why we write about the past. I have relearned how to be a historian in conversation with talented scholars and great friends. Chris Hilliard and James Vernon provided models of good history in their work and sharpened my ideas in reading a draft section of this book. Deborah Cohen and Max Jones read the whole thing. Their generosity, insight, and imagination made the manuscript better, just as their support made me believe I could finish it. I have spent so long talking about history with Laura Doan and Seth Koven that I now hear their voices in my head as I write. Laura's provocative critical historical thinking has transformed my sense of what history might be. Seth has shown me how telling stories about individual lives can provide compelling ways of exploring British society and culture. Their work is very different, but both have inspired me with their passion for the study of the past and commitment to exploring new ways of doing history. So, too, has Erika Hanna, who lived with this project (and me) for the most important part of its life. She is one of the smartest historians I know and a wonderful friend. All these scholars set the benchmark I have aimed for in this book. If it falls short, it's my fault.

It was long ago that I started thinking about Douglas Mitchell as a friend rather than a publisher. We have talked about books and ideas, but also about food and films, beards and bicycles, and shiny green drums for many years. Doug's support has been unstinting. His humor, energy, and intelligence have sustained me and animated this book. Alongside his day job in publishing, Tim

McGovern offered creative thoughts about writing and cycling and an epic two-wheeled tour of the microbreweries of Illinois, Indiana, and Michigan. Thank you also to everyone at the University of Chicago Press who worked so hard to make this book what it has become, in particular to Kyle Wagner and Susan Cohan.

If any of my friends thought I was a fraud, they managed to hide it. That is worth thanks in itself, but I owe them much more for everything else they have done for me. Thank you to Dan and Julia (and Callum, Elspeth, and Flora), Martin, Ann and Michelle, Rachel and Jen, and Eamon and Michael. I have often left writing behind to head out into the hills on my bike. On my own, I have found escape, peace, and a different way of seeing the world. In company, I have found good friends who are annoyingly fast: thanks to Ben, Dave, Hannah, Mark, and Roger. As with cycling, no one writes a book on *pan y agua*: West's Wines and Spirits in Williamstown, Muree at the Offie in Leicester, and Jas, Kal, and Roberto at Cotteridge Wines in Birmingham have all kept me going. Thank you, above all, to my family—to Sarah, for making life better in all ways; to Adam, for being both my brother and my best friend, and Christine, for managing the change from colleague to sister-in-law; to Mum and Dad, for far more than I can say here. You all had confidence, even when I did not.

ABBREVIATIONS

BOOKS BY NETLEY LUCAS
(IN CHRONOLOGICAL ORDER)

Autobiography	Netley Lucas, *The Autobiography of a Crook* (London: T. Fisher Unwin, 1924).
Crooks: Confessions	Netley Lucas, *Crooks: Confessions* (London: Hurst and Blackett, 1925).
Criminal Paris	Netley Lucas, *Criminal Paris* (London: Hurst and Blackett, 1926).
London and Its Criminals	Netley Lucas, *London and Its Criminals* (London: Williams and Norgate, 1926).
Crook Janes	Netley Lucas, *Crook Janes: A Study of the Woman Criminal the World Over* (London: Stanley Paul, 1926).
Red Stranger	Netley Lucas, *The Red Stranger* (London: Stanley Paul, 1927).
My Selves	Netley Lucas and Evelyn Graham, *My Selves* (London: Arthur Barron, 1934).

ARCHIVES AND LIBRARIES

BAN: Bancroft Library, University of California, Berkeley

BI: Bishopsgate Institute, London

BL: British Library, Modern Literary Manuscripts

BLAS: Bedfordshire and Luton Archive Services

BSA: Bedford School Archives

CHAR: Churchill Archives Centre, Churchill College, Cambridge

HL: Houghton Library, Harvard University

HRC: Harry Ransom Center, University of Texas at Austin

HRO: Herefordshire Record Office

KCLMA: King's College London, Liddell Hart Centre for Military Archives

LMA: London Metropolitan Archive

MRC: Modern Records Centre, University of Warwick

NFSA: National Film and Sound Archive of Australia

NLA: National Library of Australia

ODNB: *Oxford Dictionary of National Biography*

ONT: Ontario Archives

RA: Royal Archives, Windsor Castle

RMM: Royal Marines Museum, Portsmouth

SHC: History Centre Surrey

SOA: Society of Authors

TORONTO: City of Toronto Archives

TNA: National Archives of the United Kingdom

WEST: City of Westminster Archives Service

FIGURE 1. Mr. Netley Lucas. From Netley Lucas, "The Only Way to Reform Criminals," *Humanist* (July 1926): 242. Published courtesy of The Bodleian Libraries, The University of Oxford, per. 24724 c. 4, vol. 3, July 1926, p. 242.

Gambit

I'm telling you stories. Trust me.

JEANETTE WINTERSON, *The Passion* (1987)

Like all good mystery stories, this one starts with a death. A death in a smolder-
ing fire of a man's own making. A death timeless in its tragedy yet entirely of
its moment. Early one morning in June 1940, the man neighbors know as Robert Tracy is found on a Chesterfield sofa in a large house in Surrey. Crumpled
and ungainly, he is surrounded by empty bottles and glasses, an overflowing ashtray, a mess of books and papers; at his feet are the broken pieces of a
typewriter from the desk before him; the room is thick with smoke. He no
longer writes, but lies still among the detritus of a life in turmoil. This is what
his wife, Mavis, sees when she opens the door. Robert Tracy has had other
names—many others. As police, a doctor, and journalists arrive at the house,
and as Mavis talks haltingly through her tears, and they ignore the bruise
around her eye, the stories unfold one upon the other. Though only thirty-six,
he has been a naval officer, a decorated war hero, a gentleman, a lord; he has
been a servant of empire, a journalist and crime writer, a publisher and famous
royal biographer. He has also been a confidence trickster and thief, a writer
of fake news and bogus biographies, a convicted criminal, a down-and-out.
There are too many names to comprehend at this stage—perhaps there are
forty, though no one is sure—but when newspapers note "Trickster Prince's
Fate in Fire," and when the coroner reports on this death, they call the man
on the Chesterfield sofa by the name he returned to most often in life: Netley
Lucas.

As one man dies at home, many others are dying or about to die on the bat-
tlefields of Europe, in the skies and on the seas, and in towns and cities coming under attack from the air. Newspapers that document the British army's

evacuation from Dunkirk and the growing threat of invasion still find time to report this death. That is not quite right. Journalists note the circumstances of Lucas's fate, but are more interested in his extraordinary lives. In June 1940 the faded headlines of a faint remembered past are resurrected one last time. Lucas reappears as a ghost from an earlier moment. Today he is all but forgotten: a bit-part character in the lives of others, an obscure source for the title of a cabaret about Weimar Berlin. In his time, however, Netley Lucas was famous, even notorious. Colorful and scandalous, he was still a characteristic figure of the 1920s and 1930s.[1]

HISTORIES AND STORIES

This is a book about a prolific storyteller, and the power of his stories to both evoke and unsettle the world in which he told them. Stories were the fabric of Netley Lucas's lives. In the years after the Great War, he told tall tales of his aristocratic status, military record, and wealth to shopkeepers and socialites. Turning their confidence into credit, he enjoyed the life of a young gentleman-about-town in London and beyond. Storytelling could be lucrative but was also dangerous. By 1924 Lucas had been convicted for thefts and crimes of confidence five times and spent months in juvenile reformatories and prisons. Fleeting success gave way to sensational trials and newspaper headlines that secured his notoriety as a gentleman crook. Eventually prison prompted a change of gear. Taking up his pen in the mid-1920s, Lucas described how he was reformed and remade as an ex-crook. Now he sold firsthand accounts of crime and the underworld to newspapers and magazines; he wrote five books, including the best-selling *Autobiography of a Crook*, and a novel; he became a crime reporter and criminologist. Telling stories about telling stories, Lucas rewrote himself into an aristocrat of crooks and expert on crime. Scandal again followed success: discredited and humiliated when journalists identified his exclusive news reports as "fake," he changed direction and took new names. For three years a publisher and writer worked in tandem, industriously producing biographies of British and European royalty. Literary success was entwined with growing scandal. In 1931 a biography factory was exposed as a criminal fraud, and a famous writer went to prison. The stories slowed after a final autobiography in 1934 but did not stop until Lucas's death.

This is also a book about Britain in the 1920s and 1930s, and how Lucas's stories offer a guide—unreliable, yet more revealing for that—to a world undergoing far-reaching change. Stories make lives. Looking back, they give meaning to the passage of time and weave the threads of experiences into a sense of self.

Looking forward, they are purposeful and creative. Lucas knew better than most how stories could bring advancement, affording ways of remaking his lives just as he tried to make sense of them. The stories he could tell and the circumstances in he which narrated them were contingent and constrained. A confidence man's grandiose claims, just like an ex-crook's life-writing and journalism, were historically specific both in how they were elicited and in the social, economic, cultural, and political conditions that made them possible. This is what made Lucas's stories evocative of a time and of a place.[2]

The gentleman crook relied upon charm and self-possession; the freelance writer secured their reputation through imagination and ambition—and, perhaps, by cutting corners and pulling scams. Rather than foreground Lucas's personal qualities, however, we might also treat his storytelling as part of the fabric of the world in which it took shape. The successful crook was an acute observer of the conventions of social interaction, an accomplished mimic of the minute codes of accent and manner that shaped how his contemporaries understood social class. Persuasive stories were parsed into profit because of the cultures of deference and credit governing upscale consumerism in London's West End, and the modern tailoring techniques that made the look of Savile Row available on the cheap. Rather than timeless, the gentleman's charm was a particular cluster of emotional styles and ways of being. Lucas's ambition might have betrayed nagging personal anxieties but also expressed the ambiguous position of someone of his class and education, the cachet of military rank around the Great War, and the Society gossip that prompted one observer to talk of the "Lordolatry" of the 1920s and 1930s. Lucas's crimes were unusual, but his aspirations echoed those of countless ordinary men and women in a period when advertising encouraged dreamlike fantasies of social mobility.[3]

An ex-crook's remaking as a freelance writer was similarly bound up with the transformation of journalism and commercial publishing. Lucas's stories were about markets and professional networks, emerging audiences and forms of cultural production, as much as they were about his own creative imagination. Personal connections and cultural capital eased his pathway into a literary career, but Lucas also exploited the growing news value of crime, and demand for the "authentic" inside story in journalism and biography. The dramatic stories Lucas told about his scams were brought into being through the characteristic practices of the modern newspaper and shaped by changing styles of reporting and crime writing. His claims to professional respectability betrayed his continued efforts to rise in the world, the renewed emphasis on reform in Britain's prison system, and the expert's growing authority in public life. As a publisher and biographer, Lucas found lucrative opportunities as monarchy was refashioned to meet the demands of a modern mass democracy. At the same time as they reinvigorated older forms of social distinction, the particularities of 1920s and 1930s mass culture allowed Lucas to make new claims to status. His idiomatic storytelling interwove the rich threads provided by the most banal and everyday realms of the culture he inhabited. This is a book about the ordinariness of flamboyant stories, the everyday resonance of extraordinary lives.

Whether told in print or in person, about his lives or others', Lucas's stories posed a dilemma: how do you know when to trust someone or something? This is a recurrent ethical question. Yet it is also a historical question, and the ways it can be answered reflect tacit conventions shaped by social relations and cultural forms that are time- and place-specific.[4] It became a compelling question in the 1920s and 1930s. The unsettling legacies of the Great War, shifting relations of class, gender, and race, and new forms of mass democracy and culture disrupted how Britons interacted with institutions and one another. Confidence and authenticity were increasingly prominent yet precarious values. As technologies like the wireless or telephone made social and political life more mediated, new or more pressing conflicts emerged around who or what could be properly known. The claims of scientific expertise suggest how this fluidity also created opportunities to forge new forms of knowledge of self and society. Whether experienced as peril or possibility, the disruptions of war and the transformations of peace raised unsettling questions. How could the "authentic" be identified amid such flux? Who or what could claim public confidence?[5]

Lucas traded in confidence. A charming aristocrat invited hotel managers to accept his bona fides; an ex-crook known to boast of his scams brazenly asked publishers and readers to believe his firsthand tales of the underworlds of London and Paris. To understand how Lucas secured the trust of those he addressed is also to understand how confidence could be claimed, and authenticity was defined, in the 1920s and 1930s. When a gentleman was exposed as a fraud, a news report revealed as a lie, and a biography of a queen shown to be fake, the difficulties of knowing whom or what to trust were rendered starkly. Lucas's storytelling repeatedly exposed how confidence—in society, culture, or politics—could never be more than precarious. This disquieting message was enhanced because neither he nor his stories were unique. Contemporaries worried that Britain was suffering an "epidemic of bogus honourables," and the prevalence of crimes of confidence meant that detectives, journalists, and criminologists identified the trickster as a pressing modern problem. Lucas was an archetypal figure, comparable to the unemployed ex-serviceman or flapper as one of what the poet James Laver called the "people of the aftermath."[6]

We might pursue this argument through a kind of deep cultural anthropology of the trickster—teasing out the conditions and significance of such individuals' tales across different times and places. It is easy to find figures like Lucas elsewhere. The global networks of trade and empire along which people and goods moved from the sixteenth century, the expanding cities of the modern United States, and the turmoil of the new Soviet Union: in each of these contexts, the confidence trickster was identified as archetypal. Mobility and anonymity provided opportunities for personal reinvention and social advancement. They also allowed fakes and frauds to flourish, and created intense anxieties about the difficulties of trusting those one met. Britain's bogus honorable and Weimar Germany's *Hochstapler*; Herman Melville's Confidence-Man; Al-Hasan al-Wazzan and Martin Guerre; Felix Krull and Ostap Bender; Netley Lucas. Tricksters paradoxically seemed both universal and exemplary of their time and place.[7]

Perhaps we might also think of Lucas's stories as bound up with what the historian James Vernon calls societies of distant strangers. Resonant of the conditions of modern life, they echoed dilemmas of confidence that reoccurred in Britain from the 1840s, and persisted long after Lucas's death.[8] In this sense, Lucas exemplified the theatrical social relations that the sociologist Erving Goffman saw as characteristically modern. In a world where everyone was acting, tricksters were different in degree rather than kind, distinguished only by their command of the skills necessary to navigate everyday life.[9]

Yet I am most interested in what happens when we situate Lucas's storytelling in a time and a place—approaching it within the specific social worlds through which he moved, and the particular cultural forms through which he told his tales. If Lucas's stories repeated the question of when to extend trust, they also rephrased it, and changed the ways it could be answered. Most of those who identified the confidence trick as a pressing problem after the Great War knew that Lucas and his like could be found elsewhere, but we should still take seriously their sense that such practices were of their time. Britain in the 1920s and 1930s was not unique, but confronted a crisis of confidence that was particularly marked, or at least marked in particular ways.

Why were dilemmas of confidence rendered particularly vividly after the Great War? Lucas's notoriety and the "epidemic of bogus honourables" were animated by the changing preoccupations of the Metropolitan Police, and the news value of crime. His mobilities depended on particular social, economic, and cultural conditions: the penetration of consumer markets by transnational capital; the growth of mass consumption; the movement of populations through war and empire. The upheaval of war, and the explosive class and racial conflicts of its aftermath, gave concerns about the stability of social hierarchies greater resonance. Britons experienced the war differently, but there was a widespread sense that boundaries between classes, genders, and races on which the nation's stability depended had been thrown into crisis. Moving across a postwar landscape often characterized as rootless, the chameleon-like trickster was an unnerving reminder that no one was necessarily what he or she seemed.[10]

Public discussions of the confidence trick were bound up with the process of remembering the war and debates about the future of a nation rushing hell-bent into a strange new world. The accelerating pace of peacetime change fueled these concerns. For those with enough money, cinemas and department stores represented a reinvigorated consumer culture often thought to threaten visible differences of class. The smart domestic servant was indistinguishable from her mistress; a sharp suit and cultivated accent could make the crook a gentleman. Ostensibly modern forms of mass consumerism and communication gave new life to the patterns and possibilities of social distinction. In topsy-turvy times, the trickster was an exemplary figure.[11]

These tensions were echoed in growing unease around the kinds of popular journalism and publishing through which Lucas made his names. If the millions of women and working-class men who gained the vote under the Representation of the People Act in 1918 signaled a challenge to older ideas of citizenship and authority, so did a burgeoning mass media and culture. That readers and cinemagoers were also voters meant the influence of newspapers or films gave new cause for concern. The effects of commercial culture on public taste and the relationship between class and the hierarchical "brows" around which cultural life was notionally organized prompted renewed concern in the 1920s and 1930s. New forms of biography and personal journalism amplified older debates about the ethics of literary and newspaper culture and, in particular, the boundaries between "truth" and "fiction." Demand for "the real thing" in journalism and publishing sustained an elaborate "culture of the factitious" and the proliferation of shady practices like ghostwriting. As a confessing ex-crook and biographer, Lucas quickly found that the lucrative first-person voice could be ventriloquized; an "ersatz facsimile" could be good enough. When publishing and journalism were changing rapidly, the scandals over his fake news and bogus biographies threatened to reveal the deceptions of commercial mass culture, and eroded the confidence of readers. Lucas's incendiary stories fueled the volatile politics of popular culture and energetic attempts to separate the fake from the real.[12]

The restless ambition that took Lucas beyond the face-to-face gambits of the trickster allows us to see how the drama of the confidence trick encapsulated the fraught nature of personal interaction in a society of strangers, and the precariousness of truth in a mediated mass culture and politics. In 1934 the criminologist Henry Rhodes argued that there "is . . . as much difference between the literary forger and the manipulator of cheques as there is between the pickpocket and the murderer." Rhodes was usually an insightful observer, but he had clearly not met Lucas. Lucas forged checks and charmed strangers; he also blurred "fact" and "fiction" in his scandalous writing. Astounding contemporaries and confounding social boundaries, his picaresque lives gestured toward the process through which a crime becomes a cliché: focus of sensational trials and "true crime" writing, the confidence trick was also a metaphor that could be deployed in political debate, as a critique of advertising or public relations, or in discussions of speculative investment in a capitalist economy.[13]

Lucas embodied a broader awareness of the deceptive surfaces that characterized what the contemporary historians Robert Graves and Alan Hodge called the "age of disguise."[14] Synthetic materials, fashionable interior design, and "painting plaster to look like pickled oak" meant "nothing was what it seemed."[15] Cross-dressers and bigamists, tricksters and masqueraders, and aspirational social climbers rubbed shoulders with flamboyant figures like Trebitsch Lincoln, Liberal MP, German spy, and Buddhist monk.[16] Agatha Christie's novels, Noël Coward's plays, and films like Alfred Hitchcock's *Rich and Strange* (1931) explored the theatricality of social life and played with the difficulties of knowing whether someone was who they claimed to be. There was both comedy and drama in the uncertain borderlands where ambition became delusion and striving turned into snobbery.[17] Where Lucas found opportunities, others worried society was a game, and newspapers and politics a racket. Railing against the "imitations and substitutes" of a "very shoddy age," the journal *John Bull* sought to reestablish confidence throughout public life. Writing as "A Man with a Duster," the critic Harold Begbie argued: "Fakes and make-believe, falseness and hypocrisy, are eating the heart of the British nation." Women wearing makeup and deceitful politicians were "red lights along the road to national decay." Begbie's apocalyptic and eccentric conclusion underscored how the question of whom to trust was mundane yet freighted.[18]

Telling stories about a prolific storyteller breaks apart the frameworks within which historians have understood the 1920s and 1930s. The historian

Joan Scott notes how focusing upon individual lives "challenges . . . the orthodox categories of current historiography: surprising them, throwing them off their guard."[19] Lucas's peripatetic movements between criminal underworld, popular journalism and publishing, and patrician Society suggest how ideas of confidence abraded boundaries between society, culture, and politics, and reshaped relationships between citizen, state, and market. His mobilities suggest surprising resonances between crime, mass culture, and monarchy, and between popular, middlebrow, and high culture. Dilemmas of confidence played out across public and private life. The question of whom or what to trust was phrased differently when posed by a charming stranger or reading a sensational newspaper; what was at stake in getting the answer right changed; Lucas's storytelling ensured it would not go away. Neither idiosyncratic nor accidental, the connections established through his extraordinary lives were symptomatic of a pervasive crisis of confidence.

The inequalities of British society in the 1920s and 1930s are evident in the stark and reoccurring images of mass unemployment and poverty. Lucas's storytelling often depended upon the material privileges of class and social capital he could claim. While his stories were braced by hierarchies of class and status, then, they cannot be understood primarily in those terms. Lucas suggests ways of understanding self and society that were shaped by cultural forms that moved across class lines. His relentless pursuit of advancement echoed the ways in which the cinema or advertising transformed the aspirations of ordinary men and women. Just as Lucas moved between ostensibly discrete worlds, so the stories he told in print cut across genres and media. New ways of imagining and narrating selfhood, pleasure cultures of crime and criminology, and notions of a modern monarchy all traversed hierarchical social structures and cultural forms. The relationship between classes and cultures was never as stable nor as self-evident as some historians have assumed. Following a gentlemanly trickster's inveterate claims to distinction paradoxically throws into relief the limits of class as a category through which to understand the 1920s and 1930s.[20]

Lucas also confounded national borders. His careers encompassed Britain and its empire, Europe, and North America; his crimes took him between London, the French Riviera, and Toronto; he was deported from Canada, discredited in New York; his crime writing and biographies were read across the English-speaking world. These surprising geographical mobilities often provided Lucas with opportunities to tell different stories. They also highlight the transnational networks that shaped popular cultures of crime and debates over journalism and life-writing. Rather than turning inward in response to the horrors of war, Lucas suggests postwar Britain's cosmopolitanism and draws attention to the points of convergence and divergence between forms of mass culture often seen as universal. The meanings of confidence and authenticity shifted across borders. Lucas found that the pace of global communication made confidence increasingly problematic, but also central to ideas of national culture and difference.[21]

Exchanging names and stories, crossing lines of class and nation, blurring "fact" and "fiction" in firsthand accounts of the underworld: Lucas is George Orwell's shadow. Orwell has come to stand for the character of the 1920s and 1930s, and for a certain kind of ethnographic writing—realist in effects and leftist in politics. His *Down and Out in Paris and London* (1933) moved through urban worlds that Lucas had explored several years earlier. The West End was the trickster's natural habitat; the successful writer inhabited prestigious residential neighborhoods off Piccadilly. Lucas's lives also took him through prison and Borstal, lodging houses, and public spaces where men slept rough. He drew on these experiences in his writing, just as he later turned a visit to Paris into a novel and a firsthand description of *Criminal Paris* (1926).[22] Orwell and Lucas translated personal experience into the authority to speak about contemporary social conditions, cultivating the confidence of publishers and readers by fashioning compelling effects of authenticity. Orwell was impassioned; Lucas, self-serving. Lucas wrote to scandalize rather than mobilize public opinion. He could present his task as educating readers about the "truth" of crime but was usually more interested in entertaining; he mimicked Orwell's sincerity, mocked his seriousness.[23] Looking at Lucas and Orwell together suggests how authenticity's value transcended different forms of writing and could be harnessed to the demands of the market and progressive political reform. The names the men lived and wrote under—Orwell and Eric Blair, Lucas and Evelyn Graham—underscored how identities were purposeful and fictive. While the creative fictions of a mercenary ex-crook caused scandal, Orwell's were accepted as political necessity or expressions of literary genius.[24]

Viewing Lucas alongside Orwell suggests new ways of thinking about the relationship between society, culture, and politics, and about the historical moment they shared. Like many contemporaries, Orwell often dismissed the kinds of popular writing Lucas exemplified as frivolous. Yet Lucas's storytelling carried challenges that echoed, and sometimes exceeded, more familiar forms of radical politics. At a time when many commentators thought established elites were under threat, his pursuit of distinction exposed the fragility of social hierarchies. Ferocious debates over the management of crime and prison reform informed, and were informed by, an ex-crook's writing. Concerns over the effects of the market on journalism and publishing, and commercial culture's damaging effects on the citizens of a nascent democracy, were sharpened by the scandals prompted by a duplicitous writer. The transformation of monarchical authority created opportunities for a royal biographer and publisher, who then punctured the establishment's authority and revealed the limits of Britain's democracy. Unruly and inconsistent, he embodied the demotic politics of commercial culture: ordinary, but no less powerful for that.[25]

Lucas's stories mattered because, as the film historian Lawrence Napper reminds us, "it is easy to forget . . . quite how much of the fabric of British life was unfamiliar, in doubt, or (at the very least) in the process of establishing itself" in the 1920s and 1930s. We should not think of this as the period "between the wars," the "long weekend," or a hiatus between the supposedly more significant historical events that came before and after. Such terms cannot accommodate the far-reaching processes through which Britain was transformed, and within which Lucas's lives took shape. Nor should we fall back on easy shorthands like the "Roaring Twenties" and "Hungry Thirties," as evocative as they might be. What I have called a crisis of confidence encapsulated the tensions of a world in the remaking. Anxieties were tempered by opportunities; challenges, by creative possibilities that ensured the "at-stakeness" of Lucas's stories. His genius was that he understood how to get ahead in uncertain times; his challenge was that he exposed the manifold deceptions underpinning that process.[26]

TRUTH IS STRANGER THAN FICTION

I should tell you more about Netley Lucas—the mundane biographical details of his parents, birth, and childhood—but he is elusive and hard to find. He moved between names, changing stories depending on when and where he recounted them. Different versions of his lives accreted one upon the other. He was slipshod with dates and played havoc with time. Writing as a confessed trickster, he demanded a confidence from readers that his status belied and that he playfully questioned in his particular kind of postwar picaresque.[27] Above all, his tales were calculated to cultivate confidence or excite interest. In Lucas's life stories, remembering his childhood was subordinated to the more pressing task of explaining why he had turned to crime, or enhancing the drama of his deceptions.[28]

The Autobiography of a Crook began with an epigraph: "Truth is stranger than fiction, Netley Lucas is stranger than both!" The disclaimer was necessary because Lucas's outline of his background might have stretched readers' credulity. His family was affluent, perhaps aristocratic, he hinted. He was born in the stateroom of the steam yacht *Scorpion*, anchored off the village of Netley in Southampton Water. Such details suggested wealth, but the circumstances were tragic: his mother died in childbirth, and his grief-stricken father embarked on a drunken spree that culminated in his murder in Paris. The orphan's childhood was traumatic. Little wonder he ran away from a prestigious public school at fourteen.[29]

Do you believe him? The most unlikely claim finds archival echo; simple details remain uncertain. In July 1903 a birth certificate recorded the birth of Netley Evelyn "on Yacht 'Scorpion.'" The yacht was much smaller than Lucas claimed (20 tonnes rather than 650) and had no stateroom, but it existed. His father visited the registrar, giving the name Herbert Evelyn and his occupation as actor; the death of Ellen Evelyn, born Ellen Williams twenty-six years earlier, was recorded around the same time. Beyond this, I know nothing about Lucas's mother. Nor, I suspect, did he.[30] He wrote nothing to suggest he met his father, either: "From the day of my birth he hated and detested me . . . for separating him from his year old bride."[31] Evelyn disappeared. Two months later, the *Scorpion* was towed into Portsmouth "with bowsprit, foremast head, and taffrail broken" after "one of the fiercest gales of modern times." It was beyond repair, and its hull was sold at auction the next spring.[32]

Lucas insisted he was born a gentleman—"the first member to disgrace an old and honourable family." The phrasing implied lineage and landed estates, though his father's family was wealthy rather than aristocratic.[33] His paternal grandfather, Alfred Hubert Lucas, was a stockbroker and officer in the Bedfordshire Regiment. Having served in India, by the 1880s he had risen to the rank of colonel, attending levees at St. James's Palace, where he was presented to the Prince of Wales. He had offices in the City, lived with his wife, Alice, in grand houses in Chelsea, and had a country home by the Thames in Great Marlow. Alfred Lucas's finances were not straightforward (he was declared bankrupt in 1905), but everything suggests the family was prosperous.[34]

When Lucas called himself the first to disgrace his family, he glossed over his father's checkered career. He described him as a gentleman and never mentioned he had been an actor. Yet Hubert Evelyn Bernard Lucas had toured with traveling companies since 1890, and Hubert Evelyn was a stage name. He met the actor Mina Cresswell during a successful production of *La Tosca*, in which his Baron Searpia received plaudits. They married in 1892, when he was twenty-one, but divorced acrimoniously four years later.[35] Evelyn was never a leading man but performed in London and New York and was well known

FIGURE 2. Hubert Evelyn Lucas and the child who "appeared to be the object of its father's hatred." From "Tragedy-Romance of an English Actor-Sailor Found Dead in the Seine," *Daily Mirror*, 5 February 1907. Published courtesy of Mirrorpix.com and The British Library Board.

enough to appear in Sybil Verinder's account of her "adventures in a travelling theatrical company" in *Home Circle* in 1902.[36]

Despite his privileged background, Evelyn was "wild from boyhood." After he ran away to sea, the *Nottingham Evening Post* claimed, Evelyn was "unsettled . . . for life ashore," returning to London "a regular buccaneer."[37] In the 1890s and early 1900s, we catch glimpses of his hedonism. He appeared in court, then was declared bankrupt, after running up huge debts; he was disinherited by his father.[38] He drank enough to be nicknamed "Soaky Lucas" and for the *Daily Chronicle* to describe him as "addicted to drink." "Eccentric to the verge of insanity," he increasingly pursued a nomadic existence on a houseboat or cruising the southern coast.[39] After Ellen's death, Evelyn became more reckless. Pursued by creditors and police, he lived with his spaniel Charlie and a young woman who called herself Jessie Lucas, a barmaid he met in the West End, on a ramshackle yawl named the *Seashell*. They crossed the English Channel and explored the rivers of France and Belgium. The story of their exploits, noted the *Daily Mirror*, "reads like a saga of old."[40]

In Lucas's melodramatic account, Evelyn embarked upon a "long orgy of drunkenness and reckless dissipation" after Ellen's death until "one dark night he was foully murdered in Paris and his body flung into the Seine."[41] He was not exaggerating: in February 1907 the "Tragedy-Romance of Actor-Sailor" was headline news (fig. 2). Evelyn had disappeared after an argument with bargemen at Saint-Denis. When the river was dredged, his body was found under a barge. Police suggested this was an accident—it had snowed, Evelyn was drunk, and slipped crossing the plank to his boat—but it was rumored he had been murdered.[42] Journalists reported the "mournful procession" that made its way along snowy roads to the cemetery, headed by Jessie and Alice Lucas, and Jessie's tears as the coffin was lowered.[43]

Those tears seem unlikely to me. Newspapers noted how Jessie's face gave "the impression that . . . she has experienced much hardship," using Evelyn's death as an opportunity to recount their abusive relationship.[44] When Mina Cresswell sued Evelyn for divorce in 1896, she described how he had threatened and strangled her.[45] Now another relationship was marked by violence. On the night Evelyn disappeared, Jessie sought refuge in a café, explaining how he was "given to drink, and was very violent when he was intoxicated."[46] A year earlier, the suffragette Mrs. Juson Kerr was forced to intervene to save a dying child and ill-treated mother when the *Seashell* appeared in St. Margaret's Bay. Like Netley Lucas, this three-month-old boy was born at sea but rejected by his father. The situation was so desperate, Kerr told journalists, that it was reported to the Society for the Prevention of Cruelty to Children.[47] The *Daily Mirror* published a photograph of the child who was the "object of its father's hatred." It was not of Netley Lucas, but the crying infant invites us to imagine the effects of physical and emotional neglect (fig. 2).[48] For this boy, at least, there was a positive resolution. "He's a jolly little fellow now," Kerr noted, "adopted by some quite good people" in Cumberland.[49] Another life would begin in difficult circumstances, however. In July 1907, five months after Evelyn's death, Jessie Lucas had another son at the run-down Lying In Hospital, on London's Endell Street; she called him Hubert. I do not think he knew it, but Lucas probably had two half brothers.[50]

In all these accounts, Ellen Evelyn was only mentioned once. The *Daily Mirror* reported that when Hubert Evelyn went to sea, he "had with him a companion—a girl who died at sea, and was taken ashore at Southampton and buried." There was no mention of Lucas's birth, nor any suggestion Hubert and Ellen were married. Most reports wrote Ellen and Netley Lucas out of history.[51] Faced with these silences, we might tease out the contradictions of the names linked to Lucas in his childhood. In his final autobiography, Lucas introduced himself as "I—Netley Evelyn Lucas."[52] Yet his birth certificate identified him as Netley Evelyn. "My father had christened me Netley, after my birthplace, and Evelyn, after my mother," he explained, even though Evelyn was his father's stage name.[53]

I think this evasiveness was one way in which Lucas effaced his father's disreputable association with the stage to secure his own gentility. It betrayed an apparent compulsion to explain his unusual name. "Netley" was distinctive enough for some observers to suggest it was a pseudonym, its owner a fiction. Lucas later speculated he was named in a "spirit of revenge," his father marking him with a name that carried the suggestion of illegitimacy. Lucas's insistence that his parents married might have been defensive: I have found no record of their wedding.[54] His birth certificate includes none of the telltale signs of illegitimacy, however. Lucas's mother and father appear under the same surname; Ellen is described as "formerly Williams" rather than with the coded "otherwise" used to signal someone using a name to which he or she was not legally entitled. Officials could only register births based on information they were given, however, and this created opportunities to manipulate the official record. In a period when illegitimacy carried considerable stigma, and an expanding state created growing demand for documentary proof of identity, many parents exploited these opportunities. The private circumstances of birth were a matter of public knowledge, and there were good reasons why Lucas's birth certificate carried the impress of legitimacy.[55]

The sensation of Evelyn's death makes it easy to trace his life after 1903. It is harder to know what happened to his son: the archival record is fragmented and contradictory. In some accounts Lucas was cared for by servants or foster parents; in others he was brought up by grandparents in Great Marlow until he went to Bedford School. This was the story Lucas usually told, claiming his grandparents died around this time and he was sponsored by the Duke of Bedford, a fellow officer of Alfred Lucas.[56] I am not sure. Alice Lucas died in August 1910—she was living in Paris—but Alfred was alive when Lucas arrived at Bedford in January 1911. The school's admission registers identified him as Lucas's guardian.[57] The 1911 census listed Lucas among twenty-three boys living in Alfred Tearle's house, in the grand building called Castleside. Lucas said little about this period, but it must have been a daunting experience. Most of his housemates were twelve or thirteen while he was only seven. Many were children of empire, returning from Shanghai or Calcutta to be educated in Britain, while he was there for different reasons.[58] Lucas claimed he ran away from Bedford after six years, but school records suggest he was only there for five terms. His progress was limited. Lucas entered the sixth set of the first form. He had moved up to the fifth set by the autumn of 1911 but was still there when he left Bedford in the spring of 1912.[59]

I do not know where Lucas went or what he was doing for five years between April 1912 and December 1917. The one archival flash confuses rather than clarifies: Lucas's enigmatic birth certificate was altered a decade after he was born. While changing a certificate was illegal, registrars could add marginal corrections, but only if information was proved wrong. Herbert Lucas (probably an alternative version of Alfred Lucas's name) and Elizabeth Squires visited the registrar in May 1913. I cannot tell who Squires was. After their "statutory declaration," the official added a handwritten annotation to Lucas's birth certificate: "Col.4 before 'Herbert Evelyn' read 'Herbert Evelyn Bernard Lucas otherwise' and in Col.5 for 'Ellen Evelyn' read 'Catherine Ellen Lucas (otherwise Evelyn).'" Lucas's father was no longer identified by his stage name, but his mother's name became more uncertain. Why was the correction added? Alfred Lucas, then eighty-two, died several months later. It is possible he was putting his affairs in order and ensuring his grandson was provided for. Whatever the reason, Netley Evelyn Lucas was ten before he was confirmed in the name he claimed from birth, and to which he returned most often in life.[60] Orphaned by the time he was four, by ten he had lost his grandparents and guardians. As we lose sight of him, he was alone, perhaps conscious of the "absence of a mother's guiding hand and love [and] the advice and comradeship of a father."[61]

STORIES AND HISTORIES

In the life stories he later told, Lucas often returned to his childhood. Sometimes he characterized his background as privileged—a point of contrast in unlikely stories of the public-school boy turned crook. Sometimes he presented childhood as the tragedy that explained his character. The contradictions encapsulate the difficulties he creates for historians. The ambiguities of his birth certificate were echoed in records of other rites of passage: there are different names on his birth certificate, two marriage certificates, and his death certificate. While the identity documents through which the modern state tracked citizens from birth to death created the illusion of ordered knowledge, Lucas and others frustrated that process by changing names and telling stories to civil servants. If even the official "truth" of registers and forms was a precarious fiction, then our knowledge of the past has shaky foundations.[62]

The elusive trickster confronts us with the limits of what we can know. Facing subjects given to tall tales, historians and biographers have often likened themselves to detectives, their painstaking research removing the "masks" concealing the "truth."[63] Such histories can be a compelling intellectual puzzle. Maybe I could tell that story here, but despite all the years I have pursued Lucas through libraries and archives, I am less sure in my abilities. Faced with proliferating stories and uncertain sources, the moment we embark on the task of finding the "real" individual, we are doomed to failure. Rather than pursue certainty, I am interested in what happens when we embrace "an irreducible dimension of opacity" and not-knowing about the past. Lucas demands a different kind of practice—a way of writing history that is readier to admit its limits, more open-ended in its conclusions, deliberately less confident.[64]

Sometimes this book gets biographical. Acting with what Carolyn Steedman calls the "overweening arrogance of the historian," I use my sources to make "some kind of 'life' for [Lucas]," and then use those lives to frame the stories I tell.[65] I give Lucas substance by placing his stories in the social, cultural, economic, and political conditions that made them possible, and against what I know of his personal circumstances. In so doing, I suggest ways in which we might understand his restless path through the 1920s and 1930s. The lives I make for Lucas are also rooted in the professional and personal networks he moved through. He was married twice—to Elsie Liggins in 1925 and Mavis Cox in 1938—but boasted of his infidelities. He crossed paths with criminals, journalists, and agents but described few significant friendships, other than his partner in crime and literary endeavor after 1923, the enigmatic Guy Hart.

Teasing out these connections allows us to understand the worlds Lucas inhabited. Viewing him alongside those he knew (or could have known) gives him the illusion of substance. In the lives of others, we might find plausible stories when the threads of his lives turn to dust. This is why I often return to the alluring Josephine O'Dare, a social climber who captivated journalists and was imprisoned for forgery with her lover, Charles Hellier, in 1927. Lucas and O'Dare were friends—some said lovers; she was Guy Hart's friend and partner in crime; she became a compelling subject for Lucas's journalism. O'Dare's and Lucas's lives were entwined, and the rich archival traces she has left provide alternative perspectives on his criminal and literary careers. Too often, however, we only see those Lucas knew through his eyes. They are creations of his storytelling, ciphers for his self-promotion. Everything I know I share with you, but Liggins, Cox, and Hart remain elusive.

Lucas made many lives and left them open-ended. That is how I have left the lives I make for him, treating his mutable selves as something to understand on their own terms rather than a problem to overcome. Storytelling was the substance of Lucas's lives, not something he hid behind. Names and stories were deliberate, contingent on when and where he asked others to consider the demands on their confidence. Like the historian Stephanie Newell, I do not try to "unmask a liar," but focus on the conditions of Lucas's storytelling, the resonances of his stories, the work they might have done.[66] Scrutinizing the competing accounts created by or about a compulsive storyteller brings its own pleasures, but doing so in search of biographical "truth" shuts down rather than opens productive lines of inquiry. Following Kali Israel, I approach Lucas not simply as a "story of a remarkable individual," nor a "set of representations to be 'read through' for the revelation of a real self," but as "exceptionally useful material for considering the relationship between lives, images and stories." I cannot resist making lives for Lucas, but I am just as concerned with the terrain on which those lives took shape—how they might stand in for broader patterns of cultural life and self-making in an "age of disguise." Instead of a mask, Lucas's storytelling made mirrors in which we might see reflected the worlds through which he moved.[67]

Throughout this book, I call my subject by the different names under which he moved. The Honorable Basil Vaughan, Charlotte Cavendish, Lieutenant Francis Deligny: each was equally sincere and disingenuous; together they captured his bewildering multiplicity.[68] "What does it matter who one is?" asks the cultural theorist Lauren Berlant. As historians, we know that it *does* matter: the when, how, and why of our writing shapes the stories we tell about the past; our politics and fantasies mark our histories. We might also ask this question of the individuals we write about. The relationship between what we know and the case studies we draw upon is fragile. Arguments work because they can account for a particular case: change the subject of that case and the edifice threatens to break apart.[69] In following Lucas between stories, I have tried to leave the who of my writing uncertain, and accept that the subject of my account of the 1920s and 1930s is strange and changeable. Making this effort—pressing against the generic conventions of biography—draws attention to points where analytic structures are not quite working and suggests the limits of what we can know. Taking seriously subjects who are neither bounded nor knowable questions the frameworks through which we have sought to understand the past.

This book starts with a death, but the four parts move through successive phases of the lives of a gentleman crook, crime writer, and royal biographer, carrying an implicit chronology that loops back to Robert Tracy's death in 1940. As well as evoking the biographical passage of a life, this movement underscores the scales across which questions of confidence reoccurred. Lucas's crimes between 1917 and 1924 are a limit case for the everyday dilemmas of trust in a society of strangers. His prolific output as a crime writer between 1922 and 1928 suggests how ideas of authenticity were fetishized yet compromised across cultural forms and brows; the scandals when his journalism and biographies were identified as "fake" revealed the deceptions of cultural life. His misadventures in royal biography between 1928 and 1931 suggest how debates around the authorized life story and the representation of established elites exposed the limits of Britain's democracy.

In echoing the chronologies of Lucas's lives, the book moves across the intersecting realms of society, culture, and politics. The idea that those lives can be understood around such neat phases is a necessary fiction that I rely on but unravel at the same time. Lucas's writing often depended upon sharp practices analogous to his confidence tricks. Tracing his criminal scams means setting police and court records, and contemporary newspaper reports, along- side firsthand accounts written in the mid-1920s or early 1930s. Those later accounts betrayed the demands of when they were written as much as those of the period they notionally described. Storytelling was an ongoing conversation between past, present, and future.

I have told stories about Lucas to think through Alun Munslow's injunction that history itself is a "form of narrative making—a fictive undertaking" with its own disciplinary conventions. Time becomes autobiography through narra- tive; the past becomes history through stories we tell, and decisions we make about how to order those stories.[70] Throughout this book, I draw attention to the process of my own storytelling. I show you the authorial acts I have un- dertaken, and those moments when interpretation and speculation elide; I ac- knowledge the limits of my arguments, and the creative expediencies on which they rest. Like Lucas, I try out different ways of telling stories. This book is a "dogged effort to explore the border of the unknowable territory" of the past. Caution has often got the better of me, but it is also a dogged effort to explore how other kinds of narrative nonfiction might convey meaning and interpre- tation.[71] Sometimes I reach for the rhythms of melodrama, romantic fiction, screenplay, or gossip to suggest the timbre of Lucas's lives. I move between voices, and leave frayed edges that invite you to scrutinize the expediencies of writing history. Telling stories seems an appropriate way of evoking differ- ent perspectives on the lives of a prolific storyteller. As the geographer Fraser MacDonald reminds us, analysis "does not always declare itself as such. It can find expression in allegory and be tucked away in the shadows of significant narrative detail."[72]

I know the improprieties of *Prince of Tricksters* place demands on your confidence. This book has as many faces as its subject does names. In fol- lowing Lucas, it makes surprising moves between different worlds, changes complexion depending on your point of view. Sometimes I tell stories rather than set out arguments, suggest lines of thought I do not pursue, present plau- sible alternatives and invite you to make up your mind. My writing echoes the uncertainties of Lucas's lives. Perhaps I have never gone so far as to fabricate sources, but my stories often play with the boundaries between "fact" and "fiction." If this makes you uncomfortable, I offer no apology: that is how I have felt pursuing my impossible subject. The historian as trickster—a charlatan, of a certain kind, hiding among the masks and mirrors of proper scholarship.[73] Can I trust his word? What weight can the sources bear? Little I say can be more than provisional. To pretend otherwise would be hubris, flattening out Lucas's lives and the process through which this book came into being. Joan Scott observes that critical history "ought to make us uncomfortable," historicizing ways of thinking about society and selfhood that appear outside time, troubling notions of authenticity and "truth."[74] In moving between the familiar tropes of academic history and different forms of storytelling, my aim is to trouble the "apparent coherence and ultimate 'given-ness'" of much historical writing, to think critically about how the discipline of history works, and how it might be made differently. If it means you think about what we can know of the past, how we might know it, and what history might be, then I want this book to make you feel uncomfortable.[75]

THE POSSIBILITIES OF PLAUSIBILITY

When contemporaries tried to evoke Lucas's storytelling, they often returned to the idea that he could be described as *plausible*. The word was familiar, repeatedly used to characterize the confidence trickster and gentleman crook. In the hands of journalists and detectives, plausibility provided a way of making sense of the stories in which Lucas and his like consisted. It was a containing term that denoted a distrust of surfaces and the impossibility of classification. While apparently convincing, plausible rogues were never quite what they seemed. Intriguing and disturbing, plausibility evoked the tricksters' dangerous charms, the mobilities their stories enabled, and the insecure effects of authenticity that underpinned journalism and publishing. The idea of plausibility crystallized the social practices and cultural forms that made Lucas's lives possible. To be plausible was to live through front and illusion. It was a practice for modern life.[76]

Let me be clear: plausibility did not signal a move across boundaries between real and fake. Nor did it signal a kind of passing in which tricksters masqueraded as something they were not. No—plausibility gestured toward the incoherence of identification and the authenticity effects of mass culture. It resonates with the writer Neil Bartlett's notion of forgery: "to make a copy, a fake which, when detected, alarmingly reveals that a fake has just as much life, as much validity, as the real thing."[77] The possibilities of being plausible disrupted social hierarchies and drew attention to the absence of fixed boundaries, which included those between fake and real. Despite the rhetoric of exposure within which the scandals around Lucas were figured, it was often impossible to establish who he was or what he had done. Gentleman crook, criminologist, and royal biographer: each demonstrated that status claims were precarious, class and character could be arbitrary and attainable, and familiar cultural forms depended upon shabby compromises and tricks. Lucas was defined by the unlikely mobilities that rendered him unknowable to contemporaries and encapsulated a pervasive crisis of confidence.[78]

That newspapers reported Robert Tracy's death in 1940 suggests how Lucas's lives were considered remarkable and newsworthy. By then he had been a titled aristocrat and convicted con man; a well-known crime writer, best-selling biographer, and discredited fraud. At times, he faded from view. At other times, success and scandal made him headline news. The rich public traces of his lives consisted in his life-writing, journalism, and fiction; in newspaper discussion of him and his work; in the files documenting his encounters with the state. His private correspondence bound him to celebrated novelists and actors, detectives and murderers, politicians, courtiers, and monarchs. I have stopped thinking of this as unusual: little Lucas does surprises me now. A seventeen-year-old convinced shopkeepers he was a decorated officer; a parvenu publisher published a groundbreaking German graphic novel; an ex-crook launched a criminology journal; a Borstal boy and royal biographer coauthored an autobiography. Of course they did, as you will see. Lucas's lives were extraordinary; he worked hard to secure this illusion in everything he wrote and much of what he did. Yet he was ordinary in his aspirations and anxieties. The stories he told, and the conditions that made them possible, were the warp and weft of everyday life. I would never claim the Prince of Tricksters was representative. I only hope to tell plausible stories of how he might be symptomatic of 1920s and 1930s Britain.

A LETTER OF LOVE TO MY IMPOSSIBLE SUBJECT

I remember exactly where I was when I first saw you, Netley. From that seat in that library—the leaves were beginning to turn, but you could not have seen them in a room without windows—I caught a glimpse of you, handsome, well dressed, mysterious. I must have known even then: I wrote about it at the time. As I read those notes now, my excitement is betrayed by capital letters, exclamation marks, emotional excess. There have been many moments since—fleeting, intense, compelling—but that is the one that sticks with me.[79] It is strange how we have met so often in libraries and archives. There our encounters have felt illicit, because they are not meant to happen in this way. A glimpse, hesitation, feverish yearning visceral and embodied. I have wondered about that scar on your thumb. I have looked into your eyes hoping for clues: What is he like? What is he thinking? When you have looked back, it has been only to taunt: forever inscrutable. I have run my fingers over the curves of your signature. I have traced the outline of your name—yours of many—in a bound register. I have felt the dust of you on my skin and in my eyes and mouth and nostrils. Always I have hoped no one is watching. Libraries and archives are never quite as virtuous as they are supposed to be.[80]

I remember exactly where I was when I first saw you. That is long ago now. Still I feel compelled to pursue you, laboring under the illusion that somehow I might become close to you. That demands a certain kind of willful deception on my part—a confidence trick in which I am both grifter and mug. We do not come from the same worlds, you and I. Time brings distance; time breaks off your past from my present; time makes us strangers. Everything I have read tells me that I need you to be distant: that is the basis of my credibility and authority as a historian. Without distance between us, I cannot rely on you to tell me anything about the world from which you come. That is what I need you for the most, isn't it? Certainly not for the desires you might sate, or the anxieties I might explore with and through you.[81]

When I see you, Netley, everything I know threatens to break apart. I understand that I cannot know you. You are too elusive, too distant, too strange—a temporary figment of my imagination, an artifact of the stories I can tell about you. None of that stops me creating the conditions in which I can savor the exquisite pleasures of being with you. Frank Ankersmit talks about the sense of loss when we realize the past has gone, and contrasts this to our desperate attempts to bring it back, "transcending again the barriers between past and present" in what he calls "the moment of desire or of love." Discovery and recovery, loss and love, pain and pleasure, you and I: this makes our historical experience sublime.[82] I do not think I agree with all of this, but it feels like one way of explaining why I have followed you for so long. In pursuing you, my fantasies of you and of me and the accumulating details of a lost world have overwhelmed the distance between us and created the strange intimacy in which (I hope) we have lived together.[83]

This is all I am left with: an unrealizable fantasy of knowing my impossible subject. Here is my letter of love to you, Netley.

* 1 *

Telling Stories: Crime and Confidence after the Great War

CHAPTER 1

The Aristocrat of Crooks

INTRODUCTION

Netley Lucas was "the outstanding example of the gentlemanly confidence trickster."[1] Embarking on an audacious and spectacular criminal career in 1917, over the next seven years he masqueraded as a naval officer, war hero, and aristocrat, constantly changing names and stories. Fraud and false pretenses sustained a hedonistic lifestyle in London, Toronto, and, perhaps, the French Riviera and New York. The summer of 1920 found him in London's West End. Debonair and charming, he moved through this exclusive world with the manners and mien of the right honorable gentleman. Telling stories to shopkeepers and Society brought their confidence, and with that came credit, reward, and privilege. "Crowding a year of glorious life into a week," he stayed in fashionable hotels and went joyriding in a hired motorcar. Yet mobility was never one-directional. Regularly falling foul of the law, the parvenu trickster was put in his place through sensational trials that tried yet failed to establish the "truth" of his identity: he was arrested and imprisoned four times. In court he "stood self-possessed and dressed with perfect correctness": his deceptions exposed, the gentleman crook still remained plausible.[2]

Lucas's exploits were far from unique. In the 1920s the trickster—gentlemanly or otherwise—became ubiquitous in police and court files, popular and scientific crime writing, and the press. In his reminiscence *Con Man* (1938), Detective Inspector Percy Smith reflected:

When I returned from the war the aristocrat of criminals was finding London a happy hunting ground. Officers were at a loose end with fat gratuities, war profiteers were careless with their easy-gotten wealth, Americans and other visitors were flocking to the metropolis, which had become a centre of gaiety and activity after the grim years of uncertainty. . . . The lambs paraded themselves for a season of fleecing. The confidence tricksters swooped down to reap their harvest.[3]

The armistice heralded the start of the trickster's "boom years" and "palmy days": as part of the Metropolitan Police's new "confidence squad," Smith spent much of his career tackling this problem.[4] Reported in the press, the exploits of Lucas and his like prompted debate about the significance of their deceptions. Whether portrayed as a timeless drama or uniquely modern problem, the confidence trick was marked by intrigue and anxiety that were time- and place-specific.

Why did this happen? In *The Criminals We Deserve* (1937), the criminologist Henry Rhodes reflected on the relationship between crime and society. "The criminal and his crimes are social phenomena," Rhodes argued, so that the "kind of crime committed at any particular stage of social development is an index of the social phase." He offered a simple dictum: "Show me your crimes, and I will show you the nature of your society."[5] If crime and the criminal were "social phenomena," they could be understood as historically specific, providing an "index" of the "phase" in which they took shape. Noting the "alarming" increase in crimes of confidence after the war, Rhodes argued that it was "not accidental that crimes of fraud preponderate in our modern world," since a burgeoning consumer culture provided opportunities and temptations for the energetic crook.[6] Lucas's exploits gave journalists rich material for sensation, but Rhodes was concerned with their broader significance: "As a personality, the confidence trickster is interesting, but he is more interesting as an economic and historical event."[7]

Why did the 1920s deserve Netley Lucas? Showing you his lies and lives is a way of understanding the conditions that made them possible as a "historical event." The stories Lucas could tell about his military exploits and aristocratic lineage, and the attention they drew, were shaped by the legacies of war and the challenges of peace. Set against the perception that the Great War had disrupted relations of class, gender, and race, the trickster embodied a pervasive sense of uncertainty. Set against the "gaiety" of the postwar reaction, his deceptions prompted contemporaries to reflect on questions of national character and the responsibility to honor the memory of the dead. Masquerading as the suave Basil Vaughan depended upon the growth of mass consumption and the West End's transformation into a demotic realm of commercialized leisure.

Lucas was unusual, but his desire for advancement and the ways he achieved it were braced by the everyday possibilities of new forms of mass culture.

The ways in which Lucas presented himself to the world contributed to a paradoxical reconfiguration of the meanings of selfhood in the period between the 1890s and the 1920s. Rather than stable and discernible, subjectivity was increasingly presented as fashioned through self-perception, facade, and careful engagement with consumer culture. Having obtained credit at an upscale outfitters, Lucas's suited and booted appearance as a fashionable man-about-town embodied a kind of aspirational dreaming that epitomized the newly fictive qualities of selfhood. Advertising traded in the possibilities of personal transformation, selling commodities like the powder compact as a way of achieving the illusion of fashionable beauty. Young women enacted their utopian desires to become "as glorious as Theda Bara."[8] Just as films and gossip columns made the gentleman a familiar figure, so Lucas claimed the privileges of elite status through stories told about his estates and through his tailored suits and polished demeanor. Advertising was often presented as a confidence trick on consumers, but identities of gender and class could themselves be seen as analogous to the deceptions of men like Lucas.

Henry Rhodes also understood crimes of confidence as a "significant study in social ethics."[9] The forms of consumerist self-fashioning embodied by the Right Honorable Netley Lucas mattered because they crystallized at a moment of considerable anxiety regarding the stability of social elites and class relations. Setting reports of Lucas's exploits alongside debates over the wartime "temporary gentleman" and the "Society racket" of the 1920s suggests how the plausible rogue compromised the status he claimed and exposed gentlemanliness as a fiction. As the disruptions of war, new regimes of taxation, and democratic political reform challenged established forms of social leadership, so Lucas's ability to induce the confidence of those he met revealed the everyday difficulties of knowing whom or what to trust. Moving between names and stories, existing within putatively discrete social worlds, he drew attention to the porousness of Society, the insecurity of elite status, and the impossibility of social classification. Such deceptions had material effects. While patrician cultures of credit based on deference and trust persisted after the war, they were undermined by new economic imperatives emblematized by Lucas and his like. The penurious aristocrat and plausible swindler probed away at the fissures in traditional cultures of consumption in ways that shaped the emergence of an anonymous modern marketplace.

The gentlemanly trickster exploited and exposed a broader crisis of confidence in everyday social relations. Existing in perpetual motion, constantly switching identities, Lucas embodied the power of a plausible story and the precariousness of trust in a society of strangers. His exploits carried a troubling message resonant of Albert Einstein's theory of relativity, which entered public consciousness around the same time. Announced in Britain in November 1919, relativity, noted Robert Graves and Alan Hodge, suggested that "solidity" was "merely a subjective sensation."[10] Here was a ready metaphor for the uncertainties of modern life. "Solidity" and "matter" were illusory; individuals were "peripatetic points of view"; how was it possible to retain any sense of the fixed moorings necessary for an ordered society? When the social commentator Patrick Balfour described the "rootless, restless social world" of the 1920s, he turned the emphasis on "energy" characteristic of the new physics into a vivid image of a society in motion. Relativity unsettled ideas of space, time, and matter; the peripatetic trickster unsettled everyday social relations. Each dramatized the precariousness of confidence as a problem of "social ethics" in a period when social boundaries were in flux.[11]

AN OFFICER AND A GENTLEMAN

Netley Lucas first came to attention in December 1917, when he was charged at Westminster Police Court with obtaining money by false pretenses. It is difficult to trace his path to the dock. I have found no sign of him between the note of his departure from Bedford School in 1912 and the handwritten entries in a court register and remand home's admissions records five years later. Nor was his trial reported in the press. The Westminster magistrate Cecil Chapman described him as the "so-called 'young midshipman,'" suggesting the case had some notoriety, but the exigencies of war and paper rationing apparently precluded giving a fourteen-year-old's deceptions any space.[12]

Written over a decade apart, the *Autobiography* and *My Selves* told stories similar in outline if not detail. Lucas described how he absconded from Bedford during 1917 (itself a problematic claim). Returning to London, he worked as a page at a Park Lane house before following the well-trodden path of Victorian slummers to the dockside neighborhoods of the East End. This was a drama of downward social mobility, and the public-school boy found himself working as a stevedore unloading ships, sleeping at the Sailors' Home on Well Street, and exploring the cosmopolitan pleasures of docklands life. A desire for adventure, Lucas claimed, prompted him to sign on as a pantryman on the *Kenilworth Castle*, a liner plying the dangerous route from London to Cape Town, carrying the soldiers of empire to and from war. One observer suggested that Lucas disappeared before making the voyage, but he described himself as a "pantryman" when arrested, so his claims seem plausible.[13]

Lucas attributed his turn to crime to two meetings on the voyage to Cape Town. His interest piqued by a newspaper report of a man masquerading in officer's uniform, he then befriended a South African midshipman called Gerald Chilfont, who was returning home after convalescing from wounds. Lucas learned the details of his life and war record, and an idea took form: here was an "ideal subject for impersonation." Lucas ensured that: "I 'got' Chilfont, personality, outlook, ambitions."[14] When Lucas returned from Cape Town, he invested in a smart naval uniform. "Gerald Chilfont" arrived in London "outwardly a respectable member of the Senior Service but secretly a thief and a trickster looking always for an opportunity to enrich myself at the expense of others."[15]

It was not only Lucas who assumed unauthorized military status. A growing number of men were exposed wearing uniforms, badges of rank, or medals to which they were not entitled: enlisted men posed as officers; infantry soldiers turned themselves into members of the Royal Flying Corps.[16] Being in the armed forces brought admiration and philanthropy; rank brought prestige; these were dangerous temptations. The prison chaplain Reverend Eustace Jervis, who met Lucas as a "rosy-cheeked boy of fourteen," attributed his impersonation to "war fever," a common ailment contracted after "seeing so many others in uniform and reading of all the wonderful things that were being done."[17] Lucas's choice of masquerade was more deliberate. He later wrote about his youthful interest in a naval career, and his decision was carefully calibrated along axes of age and class. Lucas claimed he could pass as older, but observers often remarked on his boyishness. An officer yet not quite a man, poised on the brink of adulthood, the midshipman or "snotty" was a plausible figure to emulate. Above all, a midshipman's uniform carried powerful messages about its wearer's class. Naval uniforms were integral to a sense of corporate identity and discipline, but were also designed as a material sign of the upper- or upper-middle-class backgrounds from which officers were usually drawn. In cut and fit, the dark blue uniform Lucas acquired was patterned on the gentleman's suit. Combined with the necessary social skills, uniform was "an active component in the creation of the gentleman officer."[18]

The social power of the midshipman's uniform was confirmed because it was prohibitively expensive and could only be acquired through demanding social rituals. Fashionable menswear became more affordable and accessible in the early twentieth century. A naval officer's uniform, by contrast, usually required a personal fitting at an outfitters like Gieves and Company. Lucas did not mention where he bought his uniform, but he had the money after signing off from the *Kenilworth Castle*. Somehow, perhaps, he negotiated the scrutiny of an experienced tailor, telling the plausible story necessary to establish confidence in his claims.[19] As the war progressed, civil and military authorities became increasingly concerned that access to officers' uniforms was not being rigorously policed. In 1918, having interviewed several outfitters, the *Empire News* reached a troubling conclusion: while the "law provides penalties for any unauthorised wearing of military apparel, it does not empower a tailor to demand the credentials of a man applying for the provision of uniform and kit of an officer." Hierarchies of class and rank made deferential tailors reluctant to risk offending customers. Rank and its rewards might be available to anyone with money: "There was nothing to prevent a man in mufti one moment emerging from the establishment 'an officer' a few moments later." As Lucas exploited these opportunities, his near-instant transformation questioned the officer's status.[20]

Midshipman Chilfont found his way to King George and Queen Mary's Club in Westminster, one of several philanthropic institutions providing accommodation for dominion soldiers in London.[21] His uniform and good looks attracted the interest of one of the aristocratic women doing their bit for the war. Through her he was introduced to a glittering social round.[22] Passing from the East End to Mayfair, Lucas suggested, reflected the confidence with which he told his stories. An effortless chameleon, he was "adaptable to my surroundings," and "readily taken for what I represented myself to be." Securing trust was easy with "sufficient nerve to bluff things out and a tongue sufficiently glib to tell a convincing story."[23] Those stories were made more powerful by the wartime context in which he told them. A sense of living for the moment and the constant movement of men through London meant "old social barriers were broken down [and the] critical faculties of those who, in ordinary times, were 'rather particular, don't you know' about whom they 'took up', were numbed."[24]

Here was Lucas's opportunity. Overwhelmed with "invitations from perfect strangers to dinners, theatres, lunches and week-end parties," he accepted them "diffidently and with genuine gratitude." He recalled how "people whose names and titles are quite well known recommended me to tailors, motor-car hirers, and restaurants, where . . . I found obsequious persons ready . . . to give me credit." Uniform and a well-judged story brought friendship. Once Lucas was introduced into this charmed circle, his social rise was eased through networks of patronage and clientelism that created opportunities for luxury and the credit to pay for it. With the confidence of shopkeepers, Lucas elaborated his performance. He added "uniforms of irreproachable cut and fit" to "the trappings and accessories proper to a gentleman of means and position"; he frequented country house parties and upscale hotels. While staying at officers' clubs, he borrowed money from new friends, claiming that he had lost his kit at the Battle of Jutland.[25] Exploiting his "manly appearance and expression of guileless innocence," Lucas, noted the *News of the World*, "carried off the 'young officer on leave' idea with perfection."[26]

Social success was short-lived. Reckless borrowing and unpaid bills drew suspicion from fellow officers and club officials.[27] After a complaint from a man he defrauded at the South African Officers' Club in Grosvenor Square, Lucas was arrested in December 1917. From Westminster's juvenile court, he was admitted to the Pentonville Remand Home. In the register's "Condition on admission" column, a clerk scribbled "mid naval uniform": he still looked like the smart midshipman.[28] Lucas was placed on probation for twelve months. Chapman saw a "chance of saving what looked like an innocent boy" and sent him to West Drayton Reformatory, an institution dedicated to reforming the juvenile delinquent, to be restored to the responsibilities of citizenship.[29]

Chapman's faith was misplaced. Within days a new annotation was added to the remand home's register: Lucas had "Absconded."[30] Without money or uniform, Lucas entered a different world. For several weeks over the cold winter of 1917–18, he eked out a "bare existence" in the roads and arches around Villiers Street. Running alongside Charing Cross Station from the Strand down to the Thames Embankment, this was a notorious red-light district— Lucas called it the "worst street in the Metropolis"—haunt of pleasure-seekers, prostitutes, and cruising men, site of rough pubs, and hotels and lodging houses that let rooms by the hour, and a gathering point for London's homeless. Lucas presented this as necessary rather than a thrilling adventure:

> I, Netley Lucas, public schoolboy—scion of an ancient family . . . became a *gamin* of the London streets. I consorted with the lowest types of prostitute, carried parcels and bags from the Underground Station to Charing Cross Station, and occasionally picked a pocket.

Despite the weather, Lucas was "not unhappy" with his "free vagabond existence" among the "petty crooks and down and outs." When he had money, he stayed at a Rowton House south of the river; at other times, "I had to 'do a starry' and sleep out on the Embankment, or under the Adelphi Arches."[31]

PORTRAITS OF PERSONS WANTED—*contd.*

SUSSEX (EAST).

55.—**Hastings** (Boro.).—**Robert Bernard Belfour Clarke,** Case No. 15, 19-3-23, is identical with **Netley Lucas,** alias Robert Clarke, C.R.O. No. 1927-

18, Case No. 14, 14-3-23, b. 1903, 5ft. 6in., c. fresh, h. brown, e. grey. A labourer ; native of Southampton. Pre. con. of fraud and minor offences on B and E.

Inf. to the C.C., Hastings.

FIGURE 3. Robert Clarke, arrested on the "worst street in the metropolis" in 1918. From "Portraits of Persons Wanted," *Police Gazette*, 21 March 1923. © The British Library Board.

In January 1918, however, the young sailor Robert Clarke and the unemployed Arthur Buckland were arrested for begging on Villiers Street. When Clarke's fingerprints were checked, he was identified as Netley Lucas (fig. 3).[32] Having breached the terms of his probation order, Lucas returned to prison on remand until he appeared again before Chapman at Westminster.

In February 1918 he was sentenced to twelve months on the training ship *Cornwall*. Anchored in the Thames at Purfleet, the *Cornwall* was an aging naval vessel now dedicated to preparing delinquent boys for a career at sea. Despite his voyage on the *Kenilworth Castle* and masquerade as a midshipman, Lucas, apparently, found this an unattractive prospect. Within a year he had escaped and resumed his criminal career.[33]

THE MAKING OF THE ENGLISH GENTLEMAN CROOK: ACT 1

COLOSSAL FRAUD ON COLONIAL OUTFITTERS.[34]

EXT. JOHN EDGINGTON AND COMPANY, COLONIAL OUTFITTERS, SARDINIA HOUSE, KINGSWAY, LONDON

13 May 1920. A saloon motorcar (a Daimler) stops outside an imposing red-brick building. The door opens; an immaculate young man springs out, walks briskly to door.[35]

INT. EDGINGTON AND COMPANY

Wood-paneled showroom: examples of everything that might be of use to a committed servant of empire displayed.[36] Close-up of series of documents:

An engraved calling card: The Honorable Netley Evelyn Lucas, 15 Alma Square, St John's Wood, London, and Hurst Park, Huntingdon.[37]

The register of the Rubber Planters' Association: Honorable N. Lucas is listed as seeking a position in Burmah.[38]

A letter of introduction from Messrs Steele, Colonial Outfitters, presenting Honorable N. Lucas as a valued customer.[39]

An inventory page: illustration of white canvas tent, etcetera, against background of palm trees, African servant attending fire in foreground. "As supplied to H.M. Government for East, West, and South Africa"; Recommended by Royal Geographical Society.[40]

A sheaf of credit notes on supplying factories and wholesalers: To Messrs
_____—Please supply to our customer, the Hon. N. Lucas, R.N., such goods
as he may choose from your stocks, and debit to our accounts. (Signed) John
Edgington and Co.[41]

INT. EVERITT PENN AND COMPANY, 16 PANTON STREET, LONDON

Five days later. A similar showroom. Guarantee displayed: One salesman with
expert knowledge of all tropical requirements will attend to your outfit. A young
gentleman talks with member of staff.[42]

SUBLIEUTENANT J. P. WHITTAKER: (Drawling—perhaps too mannered?)
. . . I have an appointment with Messrs Bright and Galbraith—do you know
    them? Their premises are in Martin's Lane in the City—on a rubber estate
    in Singapore. Well, I sail on the SS <u>Sardinia</u> next month and have been ad-
    vanced £150 towards my outfit. . . .[43]
FRANCIS PENHORWOOD: (Older, austere, cautious.)
    That is wonderful news. Please do excuse me, sir, but if I might ask about
    the delicate matter of references and payment. . . .
WHITTAKER: (Waves hand as though to dismiss a suggestion so trivial.)
    Oh, my guardian, Major General G. W. Rawlings, will see to that.[44]
PENHORWOOD: (Relaxes in expression.)
    Of course, sir . . .
WHITTAKER: (Boastful, swanking.)
Oh yes, the general is a generous old bird. . . .
PENHORWOOD: (Discreetly.)
Indeed, sir . . .
WHITTAKER: (Confiding.)
Between you and me . . . I'm supposed to be rather a bad hat, and my people
    have got me a job on an estate in Sarawak. They'd pay <u>anything</u>, so long as
    I clear out of England![45]
PENHORWOOD (Sees an opportunity.)
Now, Lieutenant Whittaker, what may I have the pleasure of showing you?
WHITTAKER: (Sits on counter, lights cigarette.)
I'm going to put myself in your hands. . . . You know what I shall want. I
    can't wear anything but silk next to my skin. I simply will not be bothered
    to stand and be messed about by a tailor's cutter who mumbles with his
    mouth full of pins. Fix me up with the best ready-made.[46]

INT. FURNISHED ROOM NEAR JERMYN STREET

Shabby, sparse; West End address that sounds better than it is.[47] Lucas/Whittaker sits among stores he has accumulated: a tropical helmet in its case, clocks and barometers, tailored suits for every occasion and climate, boots and shoes in scores, gold- and silver-fitted dressing cases, fitted portable writing cases, cigar and cigarette cases and boxes, hundreds of the finest cigars and cigarettes. Wines and spirits in profusion, soaps, haberdashery, sports requisites.[48]

LUCAS AKA WHITTAKER: (Smiles.)
Not bad for a morning's work![49]

INTERTITLE

NETLEY LUCAS'S frauds brought HIM property valued at £432. Today it would be worth OVER £15,000.[50]

THE MAKING OF THE ENGLISH
GENTLEMAN CROOK: ACT 2

Over the spring and summer of 1920, a young gentleman made a name for himself in London's West End, Brighton, and the leafy towns of Buckinghamshire. That is not quite right: he made several names for himself. He told stories of his wealth, education, and family, of his war record and work in the service of empire. Free spending and generous, he charmed women and cultivated men. Those who met this gentlemanly stranger did not realize he had lived by his wits since escaping from the training ship *Cornwall* in August 1919. Nor did they realize he had other names. Sometimes known as "Netley Lucas," he also called himself "Robert Clarke, Armstrong Mackenzie, Netley Evelyn Lucas, Robert Bernard Belfour Clarke, Robert Churchill, Bernard Churchill, Basil Vaughan, Bernard Carrington, Lord Lucas, Capt. Lucas, Lieut. Francis Deligny and Sub.-Lieut. J.P. Whittaker, R.N." Each was carefully chosen, carrying a patrician aura reflected in his personal style. Prefaced with a title or rank, names brought opportunities for leisure and pleasure.[51]

These names reflected Lucas's desires for advancement. His desires were irreducibly social, however, animated by ostensibly modern forms of mass culture that reinvigorated aristocrat Society after the Great War. The Honorable

Basil Vaughan embodied the psychological complex Patrick Balfour characterized as "Lordolatry." Here was an ironic symptom of the "snob disease" infecting public life. Lucas's grandiose claims echoed the aspirational snobbery of the suburban bourgeoisie and the familiar spectacle of Society gossip.[52] Lucas's "Lordolatry" coalesced in his efforts to be seen as a gentleman. In the 1920s the gentleman's position as an exemplar of national character was challenged by the demands of an industrial economy and new forms of professional expertise. His claims to social and political leadership were threatened by the expansion of the franchise, attacked by disenchanted ex-servicemen and leftist intellectuals, gently questioned by a growing association between Englishness and domesticity. The stories Lucas told reflected the gentlemanly ideal's enduring power, however. What did this ideal mean? The emphasis on a "good" family suggested the importance of genealogy and title; links to public-school and university education foregrounded connection, wealth, and social capital; when associated with ideas of disinterested amateurism, gentlemanliness became a matter of ethics and behavior. Increasingly it devolved into personal styles and emotional positions: self-control and coolness. Definitions of gentility were slippery.[53]

This meant "gentlemanly motifs" persisted as "a fluid and mobile cultural repertoire, which could be performed by different social groups as a means of distinguishing themselves from the common and the mundane" well into the 1950s.[54] Lucas quickly learned that among strangers, at least, title and education could be assumed rather than proved. If status was a matter of personal style, a debonair appearance was enough to rise in the world. "Gentlemanly motifs" were *not* open to everyone, however, and access to this "cultural repertoire" required social capital and money. While Lucas was not alone in pursuing this path to gentility, the privileges of class were accessible only to the few. The success of his stories depended upon the power to tell, to be heard, and to be plausible. Social advancement required more than chutzpah.

It was important that Lucas looked and sounded like a gentleman. His stories were plausible because they were delivered in the "drawling accent of the spoilt son of an aristocrat, [and with] a frank disarming smile," by someone who carried himself with the "dignity of a courtier."[55] In a society of strangers in which it was still widely assumed that character could be read from comportment and clothing, personal appearance was a powerful gambit in everyday social exchange. Lucas was slim, good-looking, and "dapper."[56] Maintaining the "impression of affluence" was a profitable investment when seeking to cultivate confidence. Smart clothes were a vital part of his "equipment" as a trickster.[57] Returning to London in 1920, "I dashed off to the world famous Moss Bros in Covent Garden. . . . Two hours later with . . . two lounge suits, evening clothes and all the usual 'trimmings' of a man-about-Town I was established in a flat in Jermyn Street." Clothing instantly secured a patrician address.[58]

Social distinction was both enabled and compromised by everyday forms of consumerism. In the 1920s mass production, the expansion of shops like Moss Brothers, and the introduction of ready-to-wear suits and hire purchase made fashionable menswear more affordable, while the impulse to read identity from sartorial details persisted. The broadcaster Rene Cutforth described the "paraphernalia" of cufflinks and tiepins as "counters in the class game."[59] That class was a "game," and accessories "counters," created opportunities for social mobility. Wallingford's of Oxford Street offered "West End suits" as a carefully packaged illusion of gentility for seven shillings sixpence a month.[60] Visible on screen and stage, in novels, newspapers, and advertising, the image of the gentleman captured the imagination of aspirational young men at the same time as innovations in menswear allowed those with enough money to buy their "trimmings." Lucas delighted in the cut and fit of "ready to wear" suits and modern mass tailoring.[61] Rather than vanishing into the crowd, he assumed the distinctive styles of the man-about-town: a "fashionably cut light-grey lounge suit," a shirt with "soft white silk collar," a black tie. Sometimes he wore a "grey cap" with a "large peak," but he soon exchanged this for a "light felt Trilby hat." His "striking" lemon gloves drew attention (fig. 4).[62]

Lucas's "genteel appearance" convinced many of those he met that he was "well connected, [and] of good education."[63] His stories were persuasive because of the privileges he could draw on. Despite Lucas's peripatetic childhood, his family was wealthy. He spent less time at Bedford than he admitted, but had been to public school and possessed social and cultural capital unavailable to ordinary criminals. When compared to a "less well-educated man," noted Eustace Jervis, the gentleman crook was more successful because he displayed the "polish which a Public School education gives."[64]

Polish was a word Lucas often used to describe himself, attributing it to both his background and his ability to learn the conventions of polite exchange. It was encapsulated in personal styles that, with luck and money, could be cultivated or mimicked. Just as fashionable menswear became more accessible, so the wireless meant the gentleman could be heard as well as seen. "Educated speech" was a potent marker of social distinction and a "valuable asset" in everyday life. In the 1920s, however, the rhythms and tones of received

FIGURE 4. The gentleman crook, in his "fashionably cut light-grey lounge suit." From "Supplement A: Expert and Travelling Criminals," *Police Gazette*, 18 July 1924, 1. © The British Library Board.

pronunciation were "taught [for] free" by the new British Broadcasting Corporation. Now the democratization of proper elocution meant "one could not always judge [class] by the voice."[65] It was the intimate tutelage Lucas received while having an affair with a wealthy woman that "gave me a polish which has enabled me to hold my own with the highest in the land . . . and assisted me tremendously in prosecuting my attentions to many beautiful and aristocratic ladies." This was the sine qua non of social and sexual success, and crimes of confidence. Burnished with careful effort and deliberate purpose, Lucas confronted the wealthy men and women he met with highly polished surfaces in which they saw only their own reflection.[66]

These personal styles coalesced in the figure of the charming gentleman crook. For the *World's Pictorial News*, "coolness, ingenuity, daring, and brazen audacity were among the numerous ingredients" that brought Lucas rich rewards. "Ingenuity" signaled his skillful deceptions; "brazen" suggested he intruded into worlds where did not belong. "Coolness" aligned Lucas with the self-control associated with the gentleman.[67] Criminal success and class identities were bound up with the personal styles coded as "charm." Deployed by skilled practitioners like Lucas, charm smoothed social exchange and cultivated the confidence of strangers. Interviewed by the *Empire News*, an acquaintance commented: "I had no idea that he was other than he pretended to be. . . . He had a fascinating way with other men and women. He would look you straight in the face and assure you that he was lord somebody or a hero of the war—and you believed him."[68] *Seduced*—that is the best word—by Lucas's "fascinating" personality, taken in by his assured performance of sincerity, comments like this underscored the qualities that made Lucas so plausible. Urbanity, charm, and a "disarming personality" were, he noted, lucrative sources of "capital."[69]

While charm was an essential currency of social exchange, this delicate economy had to be managed with care. Charm blurred boundaries between respectability and criminality. Was there any difference between the "confident, easy manner so typical of the British gentleman" and the "secret of obtaining something for nothing [through only a] smooth facility of tongue and charming personality"?[70] Charm became dangerous when carried to excess. In the *Daily Mail*, Nina Vane attacked an "unaccountable" quality that "wears many disguises," railing against herself when taken in by "some little trick of speech or turn of phrase." Charm could be a guileful insincere performance.[71] Linking charm to sexual seduction, Vane gestured toward the allure of the gentleman crook and placed him in a feminized realm of romance. Relying on personal charm for social and criminal success could be understood as a failure of masculinity, and crimes of confidence dismissed as trivial. "Is there anything clever in these petty crimes?" asked Eustace Jervis. The answer was no: "All it shows is how extremely easy it is to get board, lodging, pocket money and clothes for nothing . . . if only you have the stock-in-trade of a fashionable suit of clothes, unbounded cheek and a plausible tongue!"[72] Confronted by the public moralist's ridicule of his criminal accomplishments, Lucas was often defensive in his writing, stressing how his crimes required both skill and a gentleman's cool self-possession. Charm demanded a calculating mind as well as a ready smile.[73]

Lucas's stories were also enabled by the places where he told them. Even this most charming man could not hope to gain access to exclusive social circles interwoven through ties of family and friendship. Anonymity and flux were necessary preconditions for the gentleman crook. At times Lucas operated on the fringes of Mayfair. He was more often found within cosmopolitan social worlds where the movement of people frustrated personal knowledge and made questions of whom to trust particularly fraught. Tracking the characteristic settings of contemporary detective fiction, crimes of confidence were associated with transient sites of elite consumerism: transatlantic cruise liners, spa towns and seaside resorts, the French Riviera. These ever-changing societies of strangers afforded rich opportunities for personal reinvention and deception.[74] For men like Lucas, the modern metropolis was the most important of these sites. In London, he could exploit what Percy Smith described as the city's "variety and vastness" and a "floating population of colonial and foreign visitors."[75] Confidence tricksters from Australia or New Zealand preyed on unwary tourists visiting the British Museum or Buckingham Palace; the gentleman crook haunted the feverish postwar milieu described as the "Wild West End."[76]

It was the "swell hotels," upscale shops, and fashionable nightclubs and restaurants of central London, in particular, that provided Lucas with the anonymity his stories required. In the late nineteenth and early twentieth centuries, the luxurious opulence of grand hotels like the Ritz or Savoy became increasingly vital sites of elite sociability. These new public amenities threatened the importance of an older generation of gentlemen's clubs. Governed by strict rules of membership and the accumulated personal knowledge that bound both members and staff into a closed social world, clubland provided no space for the gentlemanly stranger. A well-appointed hotel lobby echoed the aesthetic of elite domesticity and created the illusion that friends were socializing. These were more open meeting places, however, inhabited by an ever-changing clientele and regulated by rituals of admission often no more demanding than looking the part. As metropolitan elites embraced the heterosocial pleasures of hotels and nightclubs, the democratization of hitherto exclusionary sites of elite culture created new opportunities for the aspirational social climber and gentleman crook. In the Imperial Hotel in Russell Square or Hatchett's Restaurant on Piccadilly, the man-about-town found a fitting environment and the opportunities for hedonism he sought so eagerly. Here the economy of elite consumerism allowed Lucas to turn a "genteel appearance" into financial reward.[77]

Like many others, Lucas quickly learned how "it 'pays' to have a title."[78] He began to present himself as the Honorable Netley Lucas or Lord Lucas around the start of 1920, even though he acknowledged that this was "a foolish pose which pandered to my innate vanity."[79] Names and stories brought material rewards upon which a debonair appearance depended. Looking like a gentleman was both style and substance of Lucas's deceptions. It allowed him to frequent fashionable restaurants, and generated the capital essential to his carefully crafted image.[80] In a declining economy of aristocratic rentiers, Lucas lacked estates and independent wealth. Telling stories of aristocratic lineage to hotel managers and shopkeepers, he turned charm into confidence, and class into credit. In a marketplace still governed by enduring notions of trust and deference, West End outfitters extended credit to well-mannered customers, whether they were personally known, credibly introduced, or simply insistent on their privilege. Matched with "topping clothes," Lucas found a title a "great help in getting credit from shopkeepers and hotel proprietors."[81]

Lucas's conversations with the men and women who worked in London's luxury service industries were echoed by those aristocrats who also relied on the nexus of deference and credit. In 1920 Lord Clancarty was convicted for obtaining credit without disclosing that he was an undischarged bankrupt. Privileges of class were available even to a displaced Anglo-Irish aristocrat whose financial problems were well publicized: at the Imperial Hotel the headwaiter, Auguste Sandigliano, trusted Clancarty enough to allow him to dine without paying "on account of his being a noble Earl."[82] Confidence allowed Clancarty to entertain lavishly at establishments like Oddenino's restaurant and to run up huge debts living at Belomo's Hotel in Jermyn Street. In the postwar decades, dissolute younger brothers, drunks, shell-shocked ex-subalterns, and impoverished bankrupts appeared in court for the same deceptions upon which Lucas relied.[83]

Informal cultures of deference and credit provided opportunities for the silken-tongued trickster and penurious aristocrat. Small shopkeepers were also defrauded in this way, but false pretenses were often understood as a problem of older forms of elite consumption. In *The Underworld of London* (1923), Sidney Felstead attributed the prevalence of such crimes to the "system of allowing well-known women to take away things bought on credit." It was understandable, he argued, that a "woman who has for years dealt at a certain place and run a valuable account can hardly be refused immediate delivery of anything she chooses to buy while on a shopping expedition." Caught "between the devil and the deep sea," shops had to "try to verify the bona fides of the purchaser . . . without going to the length of offending her."[84] In securing the confidence of the colonial outfitters John Edgington and Everitt Penn, Lucas drew attention to the points of tension between hierarchies of class, traditional forms of elite consumerism, and the logics of commercial capitalism. Addressed by apparently wealthy customers who claimed to have an account, hotel and shop staff rarely asked questions or sought confirmation of identity.

If charm was ephemeral, Lucas "proved" his "bona fides" through a material culture of confidence. Forged testimonials and letters of introduction were one gambit with the colonial outfitters; elaborate personal cards elicited trust at other times. Telegrams from his aristocratic "father" were Lucas's "stock in trade" when arriving at an upscale hotel.[85] He manipulated the proliferating documentation of individual identity to support his stories. Bureaucratic systems of identification expanded around the Great War to address the problems of a mobile population and "alien" migration through identity cards and photographic passports. Measures that ostensibly sought to enhance the power of the state created new opportunities for forgery.[86] Yet it was the simple check—stolen and endorsed with a forged signature—on which Lucas usually relied. This was ubiquitous in crimes of confidence. In the Buckinghamshire towns where his grandparents had lived, Lucas persuaded tradespeople to accept and cash his worthless checks. When arrested, he possessed a "cheque book issued by Messrs Henry King and Co., the counterfoils only remaining." The check offered material evidence of wealth and status, and the mechanism through which a plausible story was parsed into ready money.[87]

Worthless checks and credit scams had far-reaching consequences. Reporting a conference of the London Chamber of Commerce in 1923, the *News of the World* estimated that frauds and false pretenses had cost British businesses four million pounds. This was a pressing problem: "Confidence and credit are the two foundation stones upon which the great fabric of business is built. Both confidence and credit have had rude shocks in the last few years."[88] The plausible stranger mobilized suspicion rather than trust, polite interrogation rather than acquiescence, demand for proof of identity rather than unthinking confidence. He or she problematized the rituals of an older market governed by hierarchies of class and cultures of deference. Lucas was "flabbergasted at the idiocy of a system which permitted these vast purchases without security."[89] He berated those "ready to take plausible rogues at their own valuation" and, belatedly, advised staff to "make discreet inquiries before you get too intimate, or do credit business, with anyone whose position is not absolutely unimpeachable."[90]

Credit was a means to an end. In June 1920 Lucas embarked on a "whole hearted spree" characteristic of an "unconcerned young blood."[91] With good clothes and several hundred pounds after selling his colonial outfits, he exploited the giddy "reaction, violent and sudden" that characterized the "period which is vaguely known as 'just after the war.'"[92] At the fashionable Jermyn Court Hotel, Captain Lucas ran up huge debts: he "brought friends into the smoking room, drank the most expensive wines." Ostentatiously generous, he became "well-known in the West End," finding a stage upon which to perform in the sites of elite consumption. Drawing together a raffish circle of pleasure-seekers, Lucas "entertain[ed] on a large scale."

One evening he strolled into a fashionable restaurant and ordered dinner for six. . . . The fare was of the best, and there were drinks unlimited. Two of his guests were women well known in the district. After dinner Lucas burst into speech.

"I think life is just splendid," he said, "and that it is meant to be enjoyed. What do you say to a run out in taxi cabs?"

. . . He was out, he said, "to paint the town red."[93]

Lucas remembered enjoying the "life of the jeunnesse doree." He frequented cabarets and nightclubs, and charmed "indescribably beautiful and incredibly vulgar and mercenary 'actresses.'"[94] As he lived for the moment, his hedonism intensified. Existing in a state of "perpetual semi-inebriation," he recalled, "I grew more and more reckless and . . . dissipated."[95] From Jermyn Court he telephoned Harrods motor department. Colonel Lucas—the "rank of captain not being sufficiently exalted"—presented himself as the son of Lady Lucas, one of the firm's customers, and ordered a car and chauffeur.[96] Lucas was still only seventeen, and the rank he claimed was implausible—repudiated when the chauffeur arrived. Years later he berated himself for being "such a damned fool as to elevate myself to the peerage in a drunken moment of pure swank."[97] Over the next few days, he could be found "careering over the West End" and down to Brighton in a chauffeur-driven Daimler. On the first day he drove 91 miles, but "on subsequent days he was much more ambitious, doing well over 100."[98] The glorious summer of 1920 brought "lordly days . . . and wild joy rides."[99]

In this cosmopolitan world of fashionable hotels and restaurants, Lucas rubbed shoulders with "unobtrusive" house detectives, "duchesses and chorus girls, millionaires and bogus princesses, honest guests and shady adventurers, scoundrels and sirens." A genteel appearance concealed as much as it revealed.[100] If Lucas could pass unnoticed in the West End, he stood out among the working-class criminals with whom he sometimes associated. Lucas later described the "people of the underworld . . . to whom I, Netley Lucas, was the 'toff crook.'"[101] These "outcasts" recognized his superiority as a "toff crook," Lucas claimed, distancing himself from what he called "rough men." Elsewhere he identified "that mysterious something, that cachet, which birth and breeding alone can give," that made him accepted as a "freelance [criminal] on my own terms."[102]

To demonstrate his particular gifts, Lucas recounted his attempt to steal Gaby Deslys's pearls on behalf of a notorious gang. Born in Marseilles, Deslys was a renowned dancer, singer, and actor, who gathered plaudits for her role in

Suzette at the Globe Theatre in Shaftesbury Avenue. Her pearls were equally celebrated. They were a rumored gift from her lover, Manuel II of Portugal; journalists reported how she protected them while traveling and their sale for ninety-two thousand pounds after her death from influenza in 1920.[103] Stealing something so closely guarded was an ambitious coup. The story changed in the retelling, but it was always Lucas's "open face and charming manners" that made him the man for the job.[104] Waiting at the theater door each night, Basil Vaughan deluged Deslys with dinner invitations and flowers. She was reticent, but an intimate relationship developed over several weeks. The plot failed because of Lucas's weakness and Deslys's intelligence: he fell in love. "Overwrought" at the idea of robbing her, he confessed in tears. Deslys contemptuously dismissed Lucas, throwing her pearls at him: they were fakes worn for security.[105]

Stories like this secured Lucas's claim to be "something of a personality in the underworld."[106] Yet his own accounts suggest respect was tenuous. Those who identified him as the "toff crook" also "mimicked my cultured accents." In the West End gentility elicited deference. In a working-class milieu governed by different codes of masculinity, these were pretensions worth derision.[107] The gentlemanly trickster monitored the details of a suit's color and cut to cultivate confidence. While a faultless appearance was necessary to crimes of confidence, careful grooming was associated with the feminine world of fashion. Lucas's flamboyant sartorial choices—his light gray suits and lemon gloves—could be read as transgressions of gender. These tensions were compounded by his age. Lucas was too young to have fought in the war, and looked slight and boyish. The artists who illustrated his later journalism often compensated by drawing him as older and physically imposing. It was harder to compensate in London's streets and pubs. Among working-class men, the differences of class Lucas asserted could be read as a failure to meet the demands of masculine toughness. As Chief Inspector George Yandell investigated Josephine O'Dare's forgery ring in 1927, he visited William Cook in Brixton Prison. Cook knew both O'Dare and Lucas. He "recall[ed] the person you mentioned who does writing and has written a book I met. . . . He speaks more like a 'Queenie' or 'Nancy Boy.'" Refinement and poise elicited suspicion, not deference; a "cultured" accent marked Lucas as effete, not educated. The plausible gentleman was also a "Nancy Boy."[108]

Lucas's behavior increasingly attracted the attention of the hotels and shops he defrauded in 1920. The pleasures of crime proved finite, as Lucas left a trail of unpaid bills wherever he went. Lucas later described his growing anxiety at the prospect of arrest, but he pursued fast living until the dramatic moment when detectives caught up with him: he was arrested at the Imperial Hotel in Russell Square on 30 June.[109] Even then, he was self-possessed, observing "calmly" that "I have had a good run, and I expected you would get me sooner or later."[110] The *News of the World* reported a more insouciant response: "I have crowded a year of glorious life into a week, so now I don't mind what happens."[111] After appearing at Westminster Police Court, Lucas was remanded into custody before his trial at the County of London Sessions. He pleaded guilty to obtaining money by false pretenses from Harrods, John Edgington, and Everitt Penn, and was sentenced to three years in the Borstal institution in Rochester: the juvenile delinquent was again to be remade as a productive adult citizen. Dramatic newspaper reports like "Boy Posed as Peer" introduced readers to this remarkable young man, putting him in his place and confirming his image as an audacious gentleman crook.[112]

VAMPS AND OTHERS

The confidence trickster was always a man. That was not because women did not engage in crimes of confidence, but the association between duplicity and unruly sexuality made it difficult for observers to countenance that they had the necessary self-possession. Comparing Lucas to Josephine O'Dare is instructive. In the early 1920s, O'Dare was the lover and partner-in-crime of Guy Hart, who became Lucas's closest friend; later Lucas and O'Dare were friends and rumored lovers, and Lucas wrote about her for the *Sunday News*. Around 1926 the journalist Edward Waring Martyr recalled O'Dare talking about Lucas and Hart, observing how "from her remarks, she must have been in close contact" with them.[113] Personal ties and entwined lives means it makes sense to compare Lucas and O'Dare. Both pursued social advancement through storytelling; the similarities between what they did dramatize how differently they were understood (fig. 5).

O'Dare told contradictory stories about her life, but her origins were more humble than Lucas's. She was born around 1900: some said in Shanghai, others Dublin; most followed the official record and went for Hereford, where Trixie Skyrme grew up. From this starting point, social and geographical mobility collapsed in carefully staged dramas of an unlikely climb from "pig feeding on a Hereford farm to the glories of Mayfair."[114] Drawn into crime alongside Charles Hellier and Hart, O'Dare moved to London around 1922. Within two years she was at the heart of metropolitan Society. Her forgeries were now elaborate narratives of aristocratic origin through which she claimed the privileges of elite sociability and secured credit in fashionable costumiers. She

The Bystander, December 9, 1925

The
BYSTANDER

No. 1149.   Vol. LXXXVIII

MISS   JOSEPHINE   O'DARE

A well-known rider with the Quorn.   She is shortly going to train racehorses at Newmarket

FIGURE 5. Miss Josephine O'Dare, the "well-born Irish girl" and "leader of fashion." From "Miss Josephine O'Dare," *Bystander*, 9 December 1925. Published courtesy of The Bodleian Libraries, The University of Oxford, per. 2705 c. 64, vol. 88, 9 December 1925.

insinuated herself into networks of female patronage and cultivated profitable friendships with prominent men: Edwin Docker, an older Birmingham solicitor; Louis Millett, "ne'er do well son of a General Stores Contractor"; the Earl of March.[115] The names suggest the world in which O'Dare moved. So do her haunts: the Lyceum Club and Rumpelmeyers Tea Rooms.[116] In January 1926 she accompanied Docker to the exclusive dance celebrating the opening of the British Model House, a palatial Regent Street showroom for London's claims to rival Paris as a fashion center, backdrop for a glittering spectacle of Society at play that was filmed by the Gaumont company.[117]

Public events, intimate social gatherings, and her luxurious Park Street maisonette were an appropriate stage for O'Dare's storytelling. The maisonette was expensive, but she was plausible enough to incur substantial debts on its rent and furnishings. O'Dare created a raffish milieu in which, her butler recalled, aristocrats rubbed shoulders with "undesirable people who were continually changing their names."[118] If O'Dare's pathway followed that of Lucas, so did her fall: after she was declared bankrupt in July 1926, newspapers watched the impoverished "pretty Society girl" become caught up in London's biggest forgery ring alongside Hellier, her former lover. Rarely out of the news for twelve months, O'Dare was imprisoned for forging Docker's will in the summer of 1927.[119]

In understanding O'Dare's meteoric rise, contemporaries usually emphasized her personal qualities of charm and ambition. The *Daily Telegraph* noted her "liking for the atmosphere of wealth and social position," attributing her success to "inexhaustible impudence and force of 'personality.'"[120] O'Dare was a recognizable type, yet isolated from the conditions that made her stories possible. Like Lucas, she manipulated cultures of deference and credit; like Lucas, her appearance on the fringes of Mayfair went unnoticed because so many of its inhabitants were newcomers in the 1920s.

The way O'Dare exploited these opportunities took particular form. Despite her "undoubted charm," Hart remembered, her "queer Herefordshire twang required explaining away in the presence of fashionable people." The "soft rich huskiness of her voice" resonated with "Irish intonation," however, and O'Dare turned this to her advantage. The name she chose contained a "rich flavour" of nation and class. Here was a dual fiction that explained a distinctive accent and exploited the uncertain position of the Anglo-Irish elite. Around the Easter Rising of 1916 and the formation of the Irish Free State in 1922, the insecurities created by a war of independence and civil war, the sectarian violence of the Irish Republican Army, and the impositions of the 1923 Land Act forced many Protestant families from their estates. O'Dare's story was commonplace and plausible: "She was . . . a refugee from the ravages of the Sinn Feiners, and her family mansion in Ireland had been destroyed."[121] A "tale of Irish woe" allowed O'Dare to get "behind the social barriers which kept us from the smart set." An editor lent O'Dare money, introducing her to "influential friends" in London's "smart set."[122] In August 1924 a plausible story received official endorsement: O'Dare's British passport identified Dublin as her birthplace.[123]

Lucas told his stories in shops and Society. O'Dare's audience was larger. Establishing a productive relationship with the press, she aligned herself with the rhythms of patrician life through interviews and alluring studio portraits. The reinvigorated interest in Society made journalists and photographers complicit in O'Dare's storytelling. In Society magazines and popular newspapers, she could be found riding in Hyde Park, wintering on the Riviera, and hunting with the Quorn. Her appearance on the cover of the patrician *Bystander* in December 1925 and "various little gossip paragraphs which were circulated spread abroad the impression of Josephine as a well-born Irish girl . . . and a leader of fashion." The gambits of this imaginative self-publicist circulated through a modern mass media.[124]

The stories continued even when O'Dare was called before the Bankruptcy Courts. In interviews she talked of her racing horses and interest in dress design, and announced "she was to be presented at Court this summer." The *People*'s enchanted correspondent noted the "whimsical smile playing around her lips. She is dainty, yet curiously self-reliant, and one left with a feeling that she is undeniably clever."[125] After the interview, O'Dare invited the *Daily Express* to a Mannequin Parade in Park Street. Models appeared in outfits including "a dinner jacket suit with a short skirt and waistcoat." The journalist thought this "a little too obviously masculine." A "famous peer, known for his wit," visited. He "ambled out" after twenty minutes, remarking "that the mannequins were too thin." Temporarily, at least, O'Dare's judicious engagement with the press secured her status as a leader of fashionable Society.[126]

O'Dare's image was secured by the studio portraits circulating in newspapers and magazines. Echoing the spectacle of photographic modeling in *Tatler* and pictorial advertising, O'Dare presented herself through the visual conventions of fashionable femininity. One series of images showed O'Dare as horsewoman: photographed outside and shown mounted or standing with horse, the tailored riding habit made her the embodiment of the leisured Society girl on Rotten Row.[127] A second series, taken by the Society photographer Claude Harris, showed O'Dare as muse. Photographed kneeling in profile or portrait, an ethereal O'Dare appeared in white, a headdress covering her shingled hair and flowing over her exposed shoulders. "Striking and grace-ful," this echoed an image from the photographer Hugh Cecil's *Book of Beauty* (1926). Best known for his work for the *Bystander*, Cecil portrayed a glittering array of Society beauties, including Miss Nancy Kenyon, dressed and posed almost identically to O'Dare. O'Dare became a "Society girl" just by looking like one.[128]

The gentleman crook and social climber told similar stories but were un-derstood as different problems. O'Dare was rarely described as a confidence trickster. She was a "cunning adventurous" or "beautiful vampire."[129] Ubiqui-tous in cinema and popular music, the vamp was a ready trope through which to understand a young woman's transgressions.[130] O'Dare was of "prepossess-ing appearance, coy demeanour and invariably fashionably dressed"; she was also "immoral and unscrupulous."[131] Manipulating desire brought advance-ment and power: O'Dare cultivated "lucrative semi-liaisons" and succeeded "because she was countenanced by some wealthy and influential men whom her feminine wiles had . . . ensnared."[132] The *People* invited readers to:

> imagine a slim dark woman of rather petite figure, with a small round face and fine dark eyes possessing an almost Oriental lustre . . . and an enchanting little trick she has of seeming to lend her whole attention and interest to whomever she is conversing with. . . . [O'Dare's] social tact amounted to genius.[133]

Orientalized and eroticized, elusive and amorphous, consisting entirely in sur-faces and mirrors: these motifs coalesced in descriptions of O'Dare's "win-ning personality."[134] Treated as a metaphor rather than a criminal type, the vamp allowed journalists to explore women's growing personal freedom and position in public life. Novels and newspapers suggested that a bold sexual-ized front was a powerful weapon to entrance innocent men.[135] The duplici-tous female crook was also a cliché of 1920s criminology. Just as newspaper columnists characterized women as social chameleons, so the police officer Mary Allen observed: "A woman of no breeding can perfectly reproduce the accents, gestures, and manners of a society leader, and wear her clothes 'as to the manor born,' while men criminals not accustomed to the purple always find it so ill-fitting on their shoulders that it betrays them." This is why O'Dare was both successful and dangerous.[136]

The idea of the vamp's crimes as a kind of seduction echoed the charm of the gentleman crook. Most commentators nonetheless insisted that the confidence trick was a peculiarly masculine offense. Distinguishing the vamp from the trickster reflected physiological or psychological ideas of feminine

irrationality and hysteria, and presented women as incapable of rational planning.[137] When police officers discussed crimes of confidence, they rarely
mentioned women, defusing anxieties that they might become independent
economic actors able to outwit men. Frederick Wensley recognized O'Dare
as an "intelligent adventuress" and the "brains of a gang of forgers and swindlers," but insisted that women were "seldom master minds in crime." In print
and on patrol, police defined the confidence trick as a man's world.[138]

These assumptions were always challenged. Newspaper reports of jewel
thefts and frauds showed women engaged in elaborate tricks of confidence.[139]
At least some crime writers emphasized the female criminal's intelligence
and skill. Lucas praised his female counterpart: "There are certain branches
of lawlessness . . . for which women seem to possess special aptitude, and
in which their sex appeal can be a powerful weapon in their unscrupulous
hands. . . . As confidence tricksters, cheque-passers, and blackmailers they are
the equal of, and in some cases, the superior of many male criminals." Defining
"sex appeal" as a "weapon" emphasized the links between femininity and the
masquerade; Lucas retained a sense of female crooks' essential difference—
"those who utilise their sex and all its lure as an aid." Showing the female
crook's aptitude stretched the category of the vamp to the breaking point.[140]

AN EPIDEMIC OF BOGUS HONORABLES

The Honorable Netley Lucas's exploits were not unusual. In the years after the
Great War, newspapers regularly chronicled the swank of larger-than-life figures like the "artist in artifice" H. de Vere Clifton.[141] Through fraud and false
pretenses, it seemed, a remarkable string of bogus baronets, earls, and lairds
flourished in the West End, seaside resorts, and the playgrounds of the Riviera.[142] As early as July 1918, "H.H.R.-C." wrote to the *Daily Mail* to ask: "Is it
not full time that some effectual check should be placed on persons dropping
their names and assuming new ones and masquerading as members of well-
known families?"[143] Josephine O'Dare was the most notorious social climber
of the 1920s, but many other women claimed the rewards of a title. O'Dare,
the Baroness de Beck, and the Honorable Mrs. Margaret Robinson, daughter
of a Bootle stevedore, were, observed the Recorder of London in 1923, the
"type of woman who was getting very common indeed," throwing themselves
into philanthropic works and conspicuous consumption, storytelling and false
pretenses.[144]

While most relied on a plausible manner, others followed O'Dare in turning the turmoil of war and revolution and differences of nation or race to their

advantage. The displaced Russian aristocrat, his or her claim to title uncertain, was a familiar if mysterious figure across continental Europe and in Shanghai in the 1920s.[145] An unusual name or unfamiliar accent apparently served to disarm suspicion. Reincarnated as the Baron de Bouvret, the Belgian clerk William Menke, who arrived in Britain as a refugee from the Great War, lived luxuriously on credit.[146] More ambitious was the mysterious Emir of Kurdistan, whose imposture took him through France and the United States to the County of London Sessions charged with defrauding the Savoy Hotel in 1923. He appeared in the dock wearing "a fashionably cut morning suit, with fawn coloured spats," appropriate attire for a man who had presented himself as the owner of Kurdistan on a diplomatic mission to Britain. That claim was challenged through the structures of imperial governance: Mrs. Lindfield Soane, widow of the former governor of Kurdistan, testified that there was no Kurdish monarchy, since "the most notable people . . . are just heads of clans or tribes."[147] Dismissed as "an impudent and plausible swindler," the emir was imprisoned and deported.[148]

Cases like this prompted the *Empire News* to identify "an epidemic of bogus honourables."[149] It is difficult to tell if such crimes were increasing. Depending on the circumstances, Lucas's deceptions could be prosecuted as fraud, forgery, larceny by means of a trick, obtaining money by false pretenses, or wearing an unauthorized uniform. Evolving recording practices frustrate any sense of change over time: in London arrests for false pretenses rose sharply in 1933, when cases of larceny by means of a trick were consolidated under that heading. Yet the number of arrests and cases known to the Metropolitan Police suggests a marked increase in false pretenses from 1917 (when Lucas was first arrested) to a peak in 1923, falling back until they again began to rise around 1932. In 1917 there were 324 arrests; in 1923 there were 524. Police knew of 604 cases of false pretenses in 1918 and 1,373 in 1923.[150]

False pretenses was a portmanteau category, however: it included the bogus honorable's plausible stories but was also used against shady employment and marriage agencies, advertising scams, and duplicitous street beggars and spiritualists. The incidence of so inchoate a category tells us little about the proliferation (or not) of Lucas and his like. George Dilnot acknowledged, "You can't really define the 'con' man." "The 'con' man may merge into the plain thief, the blatant impostor, the practical joker, the blackmailer, the embezzler, the forger." Above all, the successful trickster was one who was never found out.[151] Commentators recognized these issues but nonetheless argued that crimes of confidence had become a serious postwar issue. In 1924 and 1928 the official *Judicial Statistics* noted an "increase of false pretenses."[152] Criminologists like

Henry Rhodes and Hermann Mannheim echoed this analysis, arguing that the "increase in false pretences" since the war was "no less characteristic [of the period] than the crimes connected with the coming of the Motor Age." Like car theft or speeding, this was a quintessentially modern problem.[153]

These figures were echoed in the stories of social mobility, deception, and individuals crossing boundaries of class, gender, race, and ethnicity in pursuit of adventure, romance, or prosperity that became ubiquitous in public life in the 1920s.[154] The trickster was a stock character in crime and detective fiction, providing rich material for serials like Edgar Wallace's "Kennedy, the Conman," published in the *Thriller* in 1929.[155] Newspapers reported on sensational trials.[156] Audacious scams of metropolitan tricksters shaded into those of notorious international crooks like Gerald Riviere or the "Prince of Swindlers," Michael Corrigan, who found fortune as a con man, gunrunner, financier, and general in the Mexican army before committing suicide in a British prison in 1946.[157]

Cases like these were common enough for newspaper editorials to regularly caution readers against the dangers of deception. Every spring, the *Daily Mail*'s "John Blunt" warned of the revival of the "confidence trick season" as visitors from Britain, the empire, and the United States returned to London. In the run-up to international events like the British Empire Exhibition in 1924 or the coronation of George VI in 1937, such warnings became more insistent.[158] They were often orchestrated by police. In 1933 the commissioner of police, Lord Trenchard, issued a widely reported statement advising public vigilance. Crimes of confidence looked like a pressing problem because the police identified them as such.[159] This raised a difficult question: were the deceptions of the trickster timeless or historically specific? The confidence trick was "London's perennial comedy-drama." "Age-old" and "childishly primitive," it was amazing it could still fool greedy victims.[160] Yet the gentleman crook was also part of a new breed of "modern criminals," and Lucas's deceptions echoed what one newspaper called a "crime fashion of the age."[161]

"Show me your crimes, and I will show you the nature of your society," promised Henry Rhodes. Lucas's lives were enabled by the social conditions of postwar London. His pursuit of gentility reflected the "Lordolatry" of middlebrow culture; his stories elicited confidence because he drew on the resources of a burgeoning consumer culture to manipulate systems of deference and credit; the frenzy of the postwar West End allowed him to pass unnoticed for a time.[162] In exploiting these opportunities, Lucas exposed the tensions that emerged through the legacies of the Great War and growing pace of change in peacetime. John Collier and Iain Laing's contemporary history

Just the Other Day (1932) noted how the war lived on through the enduring cachet of military rank. This prompted Lucas to present himself as an officer, and meant that veterans "continued to wear their British warms" and used their titles long after 1918.[163]

The consolations of the immediate past mattered because many Britons experienced the war as a moment of profound dislocation. Anxieties around women's changing position in public life were echoed in debates over the problem of the "temporary gentleman." High casualty rates eroded the exclusivity of the officer class. If war was an opportunity for thousands of clerical workers (and some working-class men) promoted from the ranks, demobilization was a crisis as they lost the status of rank and generous pay. Financial and psychological difficulties made the "perpetuation of a prefix—a worn out 'captain' or 'major' . . . a poor prop for self-esteem."[164] The journalist Louise Heilgers imagined the plight of Second Lieutenant Richard Smith without his uniform. The duke's daughter might have welcomed the junior officer, but not the "insurance clerk." Mrs. Smith might have enjoyed tea at the Ritz, but how would she deal with civilian pay and housework? Heilgers was sympathetic to these "minor tragedies," advising "Mrs Smith [to] love the man she married and forget all about that khaki tunic."[165] Others found rich material for satire. H. F. Maltby's play *A Temporary Gentleman* (1919) mocked the pretensions of ex-officer clerks, their aspirations unnaturally raised yet out of place in gentlemanly society.[166] The "temporary gentleman" focused unease over the upheaval of war. Just as postwar reconstruction attempted to recreate a more ordered world, Lucas and his like suggested social boundaries were more fragile than ever.[167]

The bogus honorable provided a focus for critical reflection on the legacies of war and the nature of peacetime society. Pleasure-seeking tricksters moved through fashionable restaurants and outfitters. Percy Smith linked the trickster's "boom years" to the postwar "reaction" that made London "a centre of gaiety and activity after the grim years of uncertainty."[168] This gave Lucas temptations and opportunities, as unwary men and women went looking for kicks without thinking about the silken-tongued strangers they met. The gentleman crook haunted the reinvigorated sites of elite consumption and display. Consider the *Empire News*'s discussion of "Ascot Sunday" in 1919: "Since the grim and ghastly ghost of war came the Thames carnival . . . has been a dead letter. With the early hours of today all the glories of the sun-draped stream will be revived." Satisfaction at the signs of national recovery was tempered by unease. Ascot's splendid "pageant" was also "a mask for devilry"—a "day for which the crooks and harpies, the parasites and the profligates have been waiting since the day armistice was signed." Lucas's parasitical and profligate pursuit of status crystallized fears about moral decline and national decadence, as the tenor of public life shifted from selfless duty to indulgent dissipation. The desire to enjoy the unearned pleasures of peace was defined against the sacrifices of national service. The gentleman crook was ill fitted for the demands of reconstruction.[169]

Lucas also exposed particular unease about the stability of social elites. Lord Lucas appeared at a moment of transition in the British aristocracy and Society. The war's effects went further than the loss of many young men. Rising interest payments on mortgages and new death duties and taxation exacerbated a long-term fall in rental incomes. The declining profitability of landed estates forced many to retrench, selling land and London houses. While the Representation of the People Act (1918) did not immediately transform the basis of political power, it signaled the hesitant emergence of a new mass democracy that threatened to make inherited power anachronistic. Social elites were remade. An increasingly open Society accommodated a new kind of American host like Lady Emerald Cunard and celebrities from entertainment or sport.[170] As political parties rewarded plutocrats for their work in war and support in peace, the peerage expanded. Between 1917 and 1921, the Prime Minister David Lloyd George created four new marquises, eight earls, twenty-two viscounts, and sixty-four barons.[171] Unease over this process came to a head in the explosive cash for honors affair after Lloyd George gave the disreputable South African diamond magnate Sir Joseph Robinson a peerage in return for party contributions. Fueled by shady touts like Maundy Gregory, the furore led to the 1922 Royal Commission on Honours and the 1925 Honours (Prevention of Abuses) Act. The "Trade in titles" revealed the corruption at the establishment's heart.[172]

The erosion of the aristocracy's economic and political position placed growing emphasis on consumption and display in defining social leadership. An ostensibly modern mass media sustained established elites. Gossip columns, novels, and magazines publicized the rituals of the fashionable season and Mayfair Society.[173] This change prompted Patrick Balfour's excoriating dissection of the *Society Racket* (1933). Balfour was sympathetic to the problems that made the 1920s a turbulent "age of transition" in which the "remaining dignity of an aristocratic order" coexisted with "a cosmopolitan machine-civilization."[174] Sympathy was finite, however, and Balfour launched a damning attack on the new social order: "Society today is a fiction."[175] No longer defined by birth or breeding, status was a game in which the rules could be learned, an illusion secured through good relations with journalists and editors. The debutante with an agent represented the "racket which London Society has become."[176]

Balfour was from an aristocratic family; as the *Daily Sketch*'s "Mr Gossip," he traded on his connections; if Society was a "racket," he was complicit in it. He was still scathing regarding the "scale of utterly false and dangerous values" governing social mobility.[177]

> In modern times true merit does not automatically rise to the surface; it must be assisted by the impetus of self-confidence and self-advertisement or it may drown unrecognized. Thus self-confidence and self-advertisement alone may often succeed in their imposture of merit. . . .
>
> If he has achieved his position by false pretences it is the more to his credit. Society judges only by results. . . . But she will always have a sneaking preference for the charlatan over the man who has "got there" by honest means.[178]

This "sneaking" admiration symptomized a moral malaise. Social success was a thin veneer created by the "imposture of merit." In the 1920s, Balfour implied, everyone achieved his or her position through false pretenses.

Lucas's disgrace suggests the limited respect a "charlatan" could expect. Social mobilities achieved through crime and plausible stories exposed the arbitrariness of elite status, however. Celebrated hosts like Cunard and Sybil Colefax were "mercurially self-made"; so were the social climbers who inhabited the fringes of fashionable Society.[179] Lucas had a respectable analogue in "male adventurers" like the photographer Cecil Beaton; O'Dare's rise tracked that of Doris Delavigne, who inspired the character of Iris Storm in Michael Arlen's *The Green Hat* (1924) and married Viscount Castlerosse in 1928.[180] The gentleman crook was different in degree rather than kind. Balfour identified the "modern" gentleman as "a person without culture, without personality . . . a person dependent on parrot conventions." The stories Lucas told revealed the power of artifice. A convincing social "parrot," he prompted a crisis of confidence that meant "nobody trusts anybody in the Mayfair racket any more than they do in the Chicago racket."[181] Lucas's movements inverted well-established forms of cross-class slumming. Rather than exploit the privileges of class to pursue pleasure or philanthropy down into the underworld, telling stories allowed him to move in the opposite direction. Passing through Society, he troubled the hierarchies of power on which slumming depended. This is why Lucas was often perceived as an impertinent interloper—a dangerous subaltern in a world where he did not belong.

The "temporary gentleman" suggested money and a commission were enough to become a gentleman; Lucas suggested money and front would do. His efforts to cultivate the image of a man-about-town betrayed the continued power of the gentlemanly ideal and the rewards it could bring. When exposed, however, his lives questioned that ideal, revealing the deceptive surfaces shaping everyday social exchange in a society of strangers. Charm concealed a cynical man on the make; his "mask of innocence" hid a "cunning brain."[182] The elusive gentleman crook suggested it was impossible to read character from appearance: neither the gentleman nor the criminal could be identified with any confidence. Observers still "*assumed* that the signs of class were readable from an individual's bearing, manner, and emotional reactions."[183] Yet it was precisely this assumption that Lucas questioned. It was the trickster's queer genius that he managed to convince gentlemen he was one of them—temporarily, at least. In 1925 Eustace Jervis described a trickster who was "a fairly good imitation of a gentleman, as 'gentlemen' go in these days of democracy." By then, perhaps, being a "fairly good imitation" was the best anyone could hope for.[184]

PROBLEMS OF CONFIDENCE IN A PLAUSIBLE WORLD

In the 1920s a growing body of guidebooks sought to expose the deceitful figures haunting modern urban life. The travel writer H. V. Morton's *Nights of London* (1926) observed:

> If you roam Piccadilly at night looking lonely and innocent you will meet various well worn characters; young men who overdo a careful Oxford accent, and eventually suggest a game of cards . . . the little vampire with the hard mouth and the big eyes and the cheap scent who slips an arm through yours.[185]

Positioning himself as defending the public interest, Morton warned visitors to be vigilant of the dangers lurking behind a "careful" accent and made-up face. Baedeker's *London and Its Environs* (1923) noted: "We need hardly caution newcomers against the artifices of pickpockets and the wiles of impostors," who were so numerous that it was "even prudent to avoid speaking to strangers in the street."[186] Writers sought to give unwary citizens the knowledge necessary to protect themselves. Echoing low-life writers of the nineteenth century, John Laurence's *Everyday Swindles and How to Avoid Them* (1921) listed an astonishing array of deceptions to "give the average man in the street a chance of learning some of the pitfalls about him."[187] He set out "rules which . . . would soon leave the swindler high and dry on the beach of unemployment." These included:

1. Never become friendly with strangers.
2. Be very cautious in accepting the help of strangers, especially if offered you in railway stations.[188]

This was a manual for modern life—instructions on how to negotiate a society of strangers. *Everyday Swindles* envisaged an uncertain, mistrustful world where danger lurked behind unsolicited advances.

Lucas's lives thus resonated beyond crime and Society. In May 1920 London hotel managers met to discuss how to deal with the "plague of moneyed swindlers which now infests the very best houses."[189] Percy Smith characterized the confidence man as a vulture hunting vulnerable "lambs" or preying on society's "carcass."[190] The metaphors were visceral and vivid. Notions of an epidemic or plague gestured toward the influenza pandemic that caused global devastation after the war. Contagious or carnivorous, hollowing out trust from within, crimes of confidence appeared as a disease inexorably weakening the body of the nation. Max Pemberton imagined a dystopian distrustful world: "If hostesses who ask barristers, lawyers, soldiers, doctors, and professional men to their houses, must look to discover a certain percentage of criminals among such guests, then indeed is the future of our hospitality to be difficult."[191]

Lucas's and O'Dare's stories were a limit case for a broader transformation of the meanings of selfhood. Rather than being defined by "character" or fixed in the body, social identities were increasingly understood as "personality." Personality consisted in external signs, personal styles, and charm. Advertising and consumer culture traded in these possibilities for personal transformation, selling cosmetics and clothing as ways to achieve the illusion of fashionability.[192] The image of the debutante advertising beauty products confronted "every suburban housewife and factory girl." Those who saw such photographs, Collier and Laing suggested, "were presumably uplifted by the belief that, for two pence in stamps, they could be as good as their betters, and the more critical certainly revised their opinion of the dignity and responsibility of the aristocracy. In either case a barrier crumbled."[193]

These changes suggested how shifting forms of mass culture troubled established social relations. Collier and Laing ironically noted how "democracy can go no further than the mass-production of exclusiveness."[194] Adverts encouraged aspiration and desire; mass production, artificial materials, and department stores made fashionable clothes more accessible. The crook who looked like a gentleman and the servant indistinguishable from her "mistress" meant it was increasingly difficult to have confidence in placing the strangers one met. Advertisers and retailers addressed a pressing problem: where was the line between the legitimate desire to be "well turned out" and dangerous tricks of confidence? The journalist Kathleen Rhodes evaded these awkward questions: "It is not a question of deceiving anybody, but one of presenting the best possible front."[195] It was not clear how "front" and "deception" differed. Bogus honorables deceived those they met; so did the plainclothes detectives wearing evening dress to enter London's nightclubs and the salesmen enticing customers to spend money on new consumer goods.[196] The principles of confidence underpinning modern consumerism and finance were indistinguishable from crimes of false pretense: "There is no difference between the mental make-up of this section of our modern world and the confidence trickster," argued Henry Rhodes.[197]

Concerns around the problem of identity in a society of strangers coalesced with particular force when the trickster was unmasked, but were embedded in everyday social exchange. Assessing a stranger's character was a dilemma for the ordinary citizen as much as for the shopkeeper. Confidence was the essential currency of social and commercial interaction, but remained precarious. After the war, a growing number of entrepreneurial boosters sought to profit from such uncertainties, styling themselves as experts in the demanding task of ascertaining identity. Organizations like the Pelman Institute interwove guidance on reading the details of self-presentation into ambitious courses of self-improvement.[198] The prominence of their advertising suggests this was a successful formula. In 1919 "Dr. Katherine M.H. Bradford" advertised a program on "How to Size People Up from Their Looks," teaching participants the "little signs that read character at a glance" but were hidden from the casual observer. Testimonials suggested these were essential skills in modern commerce, but they also equipped citizens for everyday life. A satisfied customer observed: "I can now tell almost the minute I lay eyes on people how to make them my friends . . . how to influence them to the best advantage. . . . I can tell at a glance whom I can trust and whom I can't."[199]

Newspapers and magazines provided opportunities to put such skills into practice. The *Sunday News* offered a prize of one hundred pounds "hidden in lines on man's face." Confronted with a series of photographs, readers were invited to "glance at the face . . . and see if you cannot read the secret of character hidden behind those eyes"—answering yes or no to whether a man was reliable, suave, or brilliant. Answers and explanations on how judgments could be made were published the following week. The assessment of character might have been "instinctive," yet now, it seemed, required practice.[200] In *Popular* magazine, the columnist Stylo invited readers who wanted him or her to "read their characters from lineaments of the face" to submit a "recent photograph." A single photograph rendered the problem of identity most stark, yet Stylo's careful responses provided guidance. "To watch the mouth," he or she advised, "is to form a sure judgment of the character." "Habitual compression of the lips signifies . . . secretiveness, decision, firmness, self-reliance, balance, and authority." A wide mouth and "full-formed" lips could signal "meanness and even a desire for illegitimate gain"—a telltale warning of the trickster. Popular cultures of psychology, desires for self-improvement, and a burgeoning consumer culture blurred together.[201]

Newspaper competitions that suggested that identity was self-evident appeared alongside adverts that cultivated the possibilities of personal transformation. The brash claims of Pelman's advertising echoed the storytelling trickster. Organizations sought the confidence of readers—playing on the anxieties of modern life yet offering a solution through self-help and hard work. The efficacy of their programs was nevertheless unproven, their scientific credentials and testimonials unverified. Courses like Blackford's "Judging Character" were compromised by other programs on offer. Presented under the title "Develop Your Personality," Blackford asked readers to consider "why some people are so popular . . . and get on so amazingly quickly." This played upon anxiety and envy, holding out the prospect of personal transformation and social mobility through eight books containing the "secrets of being able to hold people's interest and get on with anyone you may meet, and become a popular idol wherever you go."[202] How was it possible to ascertain the truth of identity when Blackford shared the secrets of social advancement and ABC Correspondence Schools taught "The Secret of Being a Convincing Talker"?[203]

Many of these contradictions were apparent to contemporaries. The Pelman Institute always presented personal improvement as self-realization—releasing powers contained within, rather than cultivating a mask to hide behind. The "slumbering unsuspecting Self" was the "man or woman you ought to be . . . the Self that will lift you from the masses of mediocrity to the heights of your dearest day-dreams; the Self that is calmly confident and self-possessed."[204] Opening up the demotic possibilities of unlocking talents contained within, regardless of differences of class, the "science of Self Realisation" was elided with dreamlike fantasies of social mobility usually associated with cinema fandom.[205]

Increasing *self*-confidence was integral to the techniques outlined in pamphlets like *The Efficient Mind*, achieved by addressing "defects and weaknesses" and cultivating "positive, vital qualities." Success, however, could only be measured by the responses of others. Cultivating self-confidence shaded into teaching individuals how to manage those they met. Pelmanism would allow you to "become a clever salesman . . . to acquire a strong personality . . . to talk and speak convincingly . . . to win the confidence of others"—precisely those qualities necessary for social advancement.[206] Self-realization shaded into the ordinary performances through which others could be manipulated; advice literature and advertising made petty deceptions and bold claims integral to everyday life.[207] Schemes like these addressed the crisis of confidence generated by the trickster, but reduced social life to precisely the game of storytelling, "poker-play technique and exercise of personality," that Lucas played so successfully.[208] Crooks, noted one detective, could "hazard an uncannily precise guess as to what the average man would do under any given set of circumstances. They could read the human expression, probe human motive . . . with an accuracy based upon their own minute observation and experience."[209]

CRIME IS ORDINARY

The confidence trickster was invariably described as the "aristocrat of crooks."[210] The label had three strands: first, the suave appearance essential to securing trust; second, the indulgent lifestyle crime made possible; and third, the skill that made the confidence trick both an "art" and "a subtle science demanding . . . nerve and brain."[211] The "aristocrat of crooks" suggested a hybrid of social and criminal status, pointing toward a gentlemanly demeanor and professional expertise. Since gentlemanliness was still associated with amateurism, this doubling was both paradoxical and potent. Mannered personal styles concealed a keen criminal intelligence. There were critical voices. Lucas found to his cost how privileges of class often carried penalties of gender. A cultivated accent could seem dangerously effete; turning charm to criminal gain aligned the trickster with the duplicitous vamp; unscrupulous lies compromised the gentleman's supposed integrity. While John Goodwin praised the safecracker's technical skill, he dismissed the confidence trickster as a "contemptible cad." The term suggested social vulgarity and dishonor in love, and presented untrustworthiness as a failure of masculinity and class. Worse than this: Goodwin compared the trickster to the blackmailer, defined as the lowest type of criminal through several notorious trials in the 1920s and 1930s. Blackmailers were venal and immoral. Inhabiting the fringes of an underworld of vice, adultery, and same-sex relations, they preyed upon secrets and shame.

That is why Lucas went to such lengths to distance himself from blackmail schemes.[212]

The idea of the "aristocrat of crooks" retained remarkable currency. The word *currency* matters: a criminal identity carried social and commercial value. Refracted through the court evidence of police officers and reproduced in their published reminiscences, ideas of elusive tricksters confirmed the image of the skilled professionals who brought them to justice. Sensational headlines sold the "amazing" exploits of Lucas and his like to readers. Despite his age, observed the *People*, Lucas had committed a "string of offences which few older criminals could equal" in the "most astonishing 'crook' career ever brought to light."[213] The clichés tell us as much about the conventions of popular journalism as they do about Lucas's criminality, but were terms in which he was deeply invested. You will see later how Lucas reinvented himself as a writer on crime under the patronage of the journalist Stanley Scott after being released from Borstal in October 1922. Reworking stories he had told as an itinerant confidence man, Lucas wrote himself into the role of the gentleman crook.

In the *World's Pictorial News*, Lucas reflected on his career: "The thing that astonished me . . . was the insignificance of the charges brought against me in comparison with the crimes I had committed."[214] The distance between the offenses for which Lucas was arrested and the grandiose exploits he claimed creates a sense of something not seen. The dissonance between petty charges of false pretenses and the "aristocrat of crooks" opened up a space that Lucas filled with dramatic accounts of his life in crime. An ex-crook's confessions accreted onto the stories told by the gentlemanly trickster. This is how Lucas summarized his career:

> I have met criminals of every description, have watched from the inside crimes which have baffled the police, have experienced the heights of luxury and the depths of poverty . . . and have run through in four years between £11,000 and £12,000 of other people's money.[215]

Court registers, newspaper reports, and published reminiscences echo fragments of this account. Contrast Robert Clarke's arrest for begging with Captain Lucas's hedonism and we see the movement between "poverty" and "luxury." These are only fragments, however, and the stories Lucas told in print often exceeded those in the archive. Where does truth end and falsehood begin?

As Lucas's writing developed, the stories he told diverged further from the offenses for which he was convicted. The articles that became *Crooks:*

Confessions (1925) presented the adventures of an international crook. Around 1922–23, Lucas claimed, he went rum-running on a tramp steamer between Nassau and the United States. Did he? I have no idea. It is plausible. Lucas might have enjoyed a romantic evening with Gertrude Lythgoe, the beautiful "queen of the bootleggers," in the Bahamas. Many years later Lythgoe described meeting Lucas, though she had strong commercial reasons for doing so. Lucas's account is a striking echo of H. de Winton Wigley's well-known *With the Whiskey Smugglers* (1923), however; what I know of his movements makes it hard to see when he might have sailed to the Caribbean. Lucas was a purposeful storyteller.[216] That is why he also concealed uncomfortable aspects of his career. Lucas never explained why he was taken back into Borstal in August 1922. As Sublieutenant J. P. Whittaker, he had visited an "employment agency . . . and asked the principal to supply him with a young lady to act as a secretary to his father and companion to his sister, in Madrid." Whatever his plan, it was frustrated when police officers intervened.[217] The scheme was unreported at the time, but newspapers later suggested Lucas was suspected of being involved in the white slave trade. Little wonder he did not mention it.[218]

Other than his spectacular frauds on the colonial outfitters, court reports suggest Lucas's crime was more ordinary than he would admit. The precariousness of his status as an "aristocrat of crooks" became most marked after February 1923. Within months of starting work for Stanley Scott, he betrayed the "very man who had befriended him."[219] While Scott was away, Lucas invited a former prison acquaintance, Cyril Collier, and two women into his flat, where "they had an orgy." Lucas was drunk, he claimed, when he stole and forged his employer's check and burgled his house. "Conscience-stricken," he confessed in writing, then decided to "make a run for it."[220] Lucas later called this the "dirtiest act of my crooked career," but his remorse was as strategic as it was deeply felt.[221] In one version of the story, Lucas simply ignored the morality of betraying a benefactor; each moved quickly to the more profitable task of describing his time as a "wanted man 'on the run.'"[222]

Here is the story Lucas told: he and Collier embarked on a whirlwind of crime that took them from the industrial midlands to the seaside resorts of the southern coast. In Devon he posed as Viscount Knebworth, deceiving a travel agency into providing a first-class rail ticket to Cairo on credit by claiming he was required there on urgent Foreign Office business.[223] Followed by detectives, Lucas and Collier became more desperate. They stowed away on a White Star liner bound for Canada, sneaking ashore at Halifax before traveling between Montreal, Toronto, New York, and Chicago. The *Autobiography* was dramatic. Relying on "nerve, initiative and resource," Lucas eluded detectives in the United States and Canada. "I had led my pursuers a noble chase," he claimed: "I had laid false trails, doubled, gone to earth and allowed the chase to pass me by," until finding his way onto a ship returning to Liverpool.[224] Yet he was defensive in justifying a brief and formulaic account of the American underworld. "This is emphatically a story of fact and not fiction," he asserted, and it "should require little explanation . . . why I must be reticent and rather vague about my exploits in America": he was afraid of being prosecuted.[225] The stories have little detail and no cor-roboration; it is difficult to track someone traveling under a different name, and with neither passport nor tickets. One newspaper reported that Lucas "got off to Canada without a passport," but Scott was skeptical, noting that his protégé "wrote decoy letters to his employers and to the Borstal Association purporting to come from Canada." How do we know whom to trust?[226]

Reconciling what Lucas called "crime de luxe" with the archival traces of his movements is frustrating.[227] The *Police Gazette* tracked Lucas and Collier between London, Hastings, Eastbourne, and Falmouth. In this episodic series of thefts and deceptions, there was no suggestion they might have left Britain, nor much time for an Atlantic crossing. Robert Clarke was linked to thefts in Hastings on 19 March 1923; two days later he was identified as "identical with Netley Lucas," and his mug shot circulated.[228] A description of Lucas's "gen-teel appearance" belied the mundane offenses he was wanted for: stealing from hotel rooms and trying to leave without paying.[229] In the suitcases Lucas stole, we see a snapshot of the holidaying bourgeoisie, a police officer's keen eye for detail, and a different version of Lucas's crimes:

> gent's new raincoat, shot silk lining, Cravenette on tab at top and square tab below with The Gold Medal Raincoat, Porous and Hygienic, Specially Made for the Irish Linen and Hosiery Association, Ltd. thereon; 8 new white linen collars, size 13 ½ by 2 in. The King thereon; gent's hair brush and comb; pair fawn spats, Abbot's Phit-eesi Gaiters thereon; pair gent's dress trousers; 2 dress waistcoats; 67 pairs fancy socks.[230]

Set against Lucas's acknowledgment that he was "frightened," the socks and spats he stole and sold betray desperation rather than drama. Here is the un-certain life of a petty thief on the run, not the calculating schemes of the aris-tocrat of crooks.[231] Cyril Collier strolled the promenade at Hastings wearing a pince-nez and carrying an ebony cane, but both items were stolen, and his overcoat was ripped and shoes slit across one toe.[232]

Lucas was not prosecuted for the grandiose exploits he wrote about. Denouement came when he was arrested in London in May. In one story he was chased down Piccadilly by detectives, who had seen him leaving the fashionable Hatchett's restaurant; in another he met Stanley Scott while waiting for a dinner date. Both gave the end of his time on the run an appropriate setting: the opulent Ritz Hotel.[233] Lucas was committed for trial at the Central Criminal Court. Three years earlier the County of London Sessions was captivated by the young man-about-town who had defrauded a colonial outfitters. In June 1923 he still "endeavoured to impress the gallery by extravagant gestures," but had "resorted to the meanest of crimes."[234] From Scott he stole a tiepin, topaz and black jade rings; at Paddington Station he stole a suitcase and "gents underclothing."[235]

Perhaps the greatest trick the gentleman trickster ever pulled was convincing the world that he existed. In the 1920s Lucas often appeared as a member of Britain's criminal aristocracy. Yet there were many people who gained by cultivating that image of him. Hyperbolic accounts of his notoriety were secured through the clichés of crime writing and the complicity of commercial and professional interest that bound him to police officers, journalists, and crime writers. When the writer Harold Castle later described Lucas as "one of the arch-criminals of our time," he did so to assert his own intimacy with London's underworld.[236] Percy Smith described Lucas as the "outstanding example of the gentlemanly trickster," but until 1931 he was considered only a "minor criminal and trickster."[237]

CONCLUSION

In *Con Man* (1938) Percy Smith described an incident that took place while he was in plainclothes in Bloomsbury's Russell Hotel: "Two men sauntered into the lounge—and I stiffened. Their type was unmistakeable; my training had made it possible for me to spot the average confidence trickster at a glance." Here we see how undercover policing demanded the masquerades necessary for detectives to pass unnoticed, and how Smith and his peers presented themselves as skilled observers of modern life. The deceptive surfaces behind which the trickster worked could not withstand a seasoned detective's penetrating "glance."[238] Smith's confidence was unusual. After the disruptions of war and as the pace of peacetime change quickened, many observers worried that it was increasingly difficult to "spot" who anyone was, let alone identify those who set out to deceive the unwary. The crisis of confidence that pervaded everyday social relations was rendered particularly acute by the chameleon-like trickster. How do you know when to trust someone? When can you have confidence in a stranger's stories? Can appearance tell you anything about who someone really is? Lucas ensured those questions acquired particular force in 1920s Britain.

Lucas's pursuit of social advancement was rooted in the everyday possibilities of new forms of mass culture. The lengths to which he went to cultivate a gentlemanly appearance were extraordinary; so was how he turned a plausible manner to criminal ends. Yet neither his aspirations nor his intuitive grasp of the power of self-presentation was unusual. Rather than fixed and stable, identity was increasingly presented as fashioned through self-perception and careful engagement with consumer culture. These shifts shaped how ordinary men and women engaged with the cinema or beauty industry. They coalesced with particular resonance in concerns over the "Society racket." At a moment of profound uncertainty, Lucas secured access to the cosmopolitan West End through charm, a plausible story, and the financial rewards they brought. He might have been desperate to be a gentleman, but when his deceptions were exposed, the authenticity of that role was threatened. By becoming someone, Lucas showed those he emulated how precarious their claims to status were. Demonstrating how the signifiers of class could be arbitrary and achievable, the "scandal of [Lucas's] existence was not simply that he had lied, but that he had effectively debased the very values which he had appeared to endorse."[239]

Lucas revealed the porousness of ostensibly discrete social worlds. He exchanged underworld for overworld, Mile End for Mayfair, Villiers Street for Jermyn Street; a pantryman became a gentleman officer; an unemployed down-and-out appeared in Society as an honorable gentleman; a public-school boy became a Borstal boy. These "changes from poverty to affluence, from the plebeian to the plutocrat in the space of an hour or so," were, Lucas recalled, "characteristic of my life of ups and downs." They made him both intriguing and an electric threat to an ordered society.[240] His "ups and downs" exposed the fault lines of 1920s social relations. In the short term, storytelling brought confidence and credit. In the long term, it undermined trust in the probity of the silken-tongued stranger. The bogus honorable's deceptions lived on as nagging suspicion, polite interrogation, and the erosion of older cultures of deference and credit.

In 1927 the cartoonist Victor Hicks explored these themes in the *Sunday News*. Hicks was prompted by a newspaper report that members of the aristocracy were holidaying in British seaside resorts rather than on the Riviera, itself a comment on the straitened conditions of the "new poor." Imagining the misunderstandings this might cause, Hicks presented the "awkward dilemma of a young aristocrat . . . who decided to take a democratic holiday." Three panels suggested how the gentlemanly trickster compromised the status of the true aristocrat. "But I am the Earl of Bilgewater," the well-dressed man protests as he is rebuffed by a beautiful woman on a seafront promenade; stopped by a policeman, he is charged with "giving false name and address"—his claims to title met with distrust. He seeks entry to a grand hotel but is kicked out by two commissaires: the earl appears in an undignified midair tangle, a foot poised beneath him. " 'Said 'e was the early of somethink. The young rip.' 'Confidence trickster, if you arsks me!' " they comment. Dazed and confused, failing in life and love, confronted by ingrained incredulity, the earl is "eventually driven to—This!"—watched by a crowd as he enters the sea in bathing costume and crown. Hicks was exaggerating for comic effect, but his cartoon captured the disruptive consequences of Lucas and his like.[241]

I might be wrong, but my guess is that Lucas did not realize the resonance of his deceptions. Their implications were far-reaching, however, and had political as well as social ramifications. Lucas's exploits were a self-serving echo of Patrick Balfour's witty social analysis: whether through their writing or their scams, both argued that gentlemanliness was a facade. In his 1932 essay "The Dangers of Being a Gentleman," the socialist political theorist Harold Laski translated these ideas into a forceful attack on the foundations of elite power. Redefining the gentleman as a cluster of personal styles and moral codes, Laski argued, shored up established social hierarchies. Like George Orwell and others on the Left, Laski saw his task as challenging those assumptions: the "potency" of ideas of gentlemanliness required "that one took as a given, indeed as 'natural' that society was divided" on lines of class.[242] The gentleman crook's deceptions did just as much to denaturalize those boundaries as pamphlets and polemics. The Honorable Basil Vaughan carried a radical critique of social hierarchies wrapped up in a Savile Row suit and ventriloquized in a cut-glass accent.

Lucas's unpredictable exploits paralleled the storm around the cash for honors scandal and the films and novels that, Christine Grandy argues, taught the "important lesson that neither businessmen nor politicians could be entirely trusted to their own devices." Popular culture encouraged skepticism toward authority; the trickster punctured deference and questioned hierarchy. Both pointed toward a "growing commitment to the idea that the ordinary man . . . could govern just as well," which underpinned the consolidation of social democracy after 1945.[243] The specter of the gentlemanly trickster did not mark the collapse of established elites; aristocratic power remained remarkably resilient well into the 1950s. Yet in nervous times Lucas and his like dramatized deep-rooted social anxieties. He could be a snobbish social climber, but his gentlemanly demeanor belied the ways in which he questioned the naturalness of social status and anticipated the more concerted attack on Britain's establishment after the Second World War.

CHAPTER 2

A Curious Kink in the Character

INTRODUCTION

In *The Human Side of Crook and Convict Life* (1924), the crime writer Stanley Scott reflected on the causes of juvenile delinquency. That most young offenders were from working-class families, he argued, suggested a correlation between crime and poverty. Yet he identified a "notable exception" to this rule: a "Borstal boy ... sentenced to three years before he was sixteen." Scott set out this young man's "amazing career" as a series of notes:

> Born of rich parents. Every luxury.
> Early death of parents. Taken to live with grandparents.
> Became ward of a Duke, fellow-officer of his grandfather.
> Admitted to a Public School at eight years old.
> . . .
> This boy, coming from a good home, and from educated, rich parents, had one of the most extraordinary records in juvenile crime.[1]

Netley Lucas is not named, but the fragments that comprise Scott's skeletal sketch highlight the difficulties of knowing his episodic lives. Each fragment is unreliable; they do not add up to a convincing whole. Lucas exists in pieces rather than as a coherent life story. Peripatetic movements and contradictory stories frustrate attempts to know where he was and what he did. The open-ended analysis suggests a nagging question: why did someone from a "good home" turn to crime?

For Scott this was a pressing personal question. We can read his depersonalized and inconclusive passage as a tentative attempt to understand why someone he had tried to help had betrayed his trust. *The Human Side* offered no immediate answer but, one hundred pages later, returned to something that resembled the problem raised in this "amazing career." Scott now focused upon a "peculiar" type: the "grandiose fraud" who "will go to the utmost limits . . . to satisfy his vanity, and pose, for his own gratification, as a person of high social station." Driven to crime through "sheer snobbery," a "longing for the lime-light . . . [is] a curious kink in the character of the educated type of criminal." An "educated type" passing as someone of "high social station"—here we might see how contemporaries began to make sense of the Honorable Netley Lucas.[2]

The question of why an ostensibly respectable young man had turned to crime was recurrent and freighted. Lucas's deceptions brought him into contact with police officers, magistrates, prison doctors, and chaplains; recounted in court, stories of his exploits were taken up by journalists and crime writers. When explored in court, the question shaped how Lucas was treated and the sentences he received: probation, Borstal, and successful reform only became possible if behavior was understood as contingent upon circumstances rather than innate. When explored in print, it reflected the importance of rendering the crook knowable—a task journalists engaged in with a mixture of amusement and anxiety. Always the question betrayed a powerful imperative to put Lucas in his place and to manage the threat he posed to boundaries of class and status. Rather than a matter of intellectual or criminological interest, the ways in which Scott's question was (and could be) answered carried important material and social consequences.

Lucas's arrests prompted a flurry of stories about his lives. The dramatic intervention of the law was presented as a moment when the "truth" was revealed and the unmasked trickster subjected to the searching light of public scrutiny. The stories Lucas claimed proliferated, however, and he eluded classification. Scott's hesitant analysis suggests both how understanding Lucas meant telling plausible stories about him and the difficulty of creating order out of his unpredictable exploits. The task of understanding Lucas absorbed diverse individuals and institutions. Drawing upon different forms of knowledge and resources, their narratives overlapped but were often contradictory. The sensations of popular journalism, the criminological case study, and forms of the Criminal Record Office addressed similar questions, but their answers could differ markedly. As Scott's comments suggest, storytelling was unsustained and episodic. Passing comments made by legal counsel during a trial contrasted with the case histories written by prison medical officers; journalists and crime writers subsumed explaining Lucas's exploits into the more compelling task of describing them.

Storytelling was an unfinished conversation.[3] Police investigations produced some details of Lucas's biography, but all observers relied on stories he had told to make sense of his life. How could they trust anything the plausible rogue told them? Contemporaries acknowledged this dilemma but still sought the "truth" of Lucas's criminality. We might resist this urge, emphasizing instead the contradictory stories told by and about Lucas, teasing out the resources through which his lives could be known, and the economic, social, and emotional imperatives that might have animated his crimes. Lucas's shifting memories of his childhood are instructive. Today the deaths of his mother and father seem like a powerful psychological trauma, but that idea remained only implicit in his writing. Lucas emphasized the privileges of his family life as often as its shortcomings, juxtaposing his gentlemanly birth and criminal life for dramatic effect. Lucas's stories, moreover, shifted because the circumstances in which he told them changed. In court Lucas was forced to justify his transgressions and mitigate the risks of a harsh prison sentence; prison elicited instrumental narratives of successful reform calculated to secure an early release. Voluntarily selling firsthand experience as newspaper life stories and published autobiographies after 1922, he operated within different constraints and generic conventions. Placing these stories in the contexts in which they were told, we see how criminal lives could be made meaningful.

In the early 1920s Lucas's crimes could simultaneously be understood as a failure of will amid the temptations of modern consumerism, the outcome of interiorized and pathological criminal "instincts," and the product of his troubled childhood. After the Great War, psychoanalytic notions of fantasy and pathological lying acquired increasing currency. While the case histories that defined these ideas echoed the deceptions of the gentlemanly trickster, Lucas was rarely understood in these terms. Turning down such paths not taken, we might understand the reach of psychoanalytic ideas and the social and cultural resonance of Lucas's lives.

Lucas frustrated all attempts to put him in his place. Between 1917 and 1924, he appeared in court and received institutional sentences five times: how can there be resolution with such repetition? This means the chronological frame of my analysis is complex. This chapter focuses on the period when Lucas was active as gentleman crook, picking up the threads of his lives to explore further how they exposed the precariousness of confidence in 1920s Britain. To understand the stories Lucas told (and that were told about him) in this period, however, I also reach forward, setting journalism and fiction written in the mid-1920s and early 1930s alongside courtroom exchanges and a prison chaplain's notes to tease out Lucas's investments in his storytelling. Writing with hindsight, Lucas worked to meet the demands of personal journalism and life-writing. The recurrent motif of gentlemanliness nonetheless suggests the enduring power of the status he had claimed as a crook.

The chapter follows Lucas and his newfound "pal and partner" Guy Hart from their meeting in the cells at Westminster Police Court in 1923 through their respective trials at the Central Criminal Court, incarceration in Wormwood Scrubs prison, and on to Toronto in the autumn of 1924. The New World offered a chance for a fresh start, Lucas claimed, but in Canada they were drawn back into crime. The agency they started suggests the privileges of Englishness in colonial Society. Yet the "racket" has left little archival trace, and telling plausible stories about it forces us to interweave different sources about similar schemes, and to approach the subject of inquiry sideways rather than directly. I conclude by reflecting on the curious unmaking of the gentlemanly trickster. Lucas was an exemplary postwar figure. By the 1930s, however, the refined gentleman was increasingly marginal in the ways in which crimes of confidence were understood. Ironically, as official and popular understandings of the confidence trick shifted, the man who had been the outstanding example of the gentlemanly trickster was written out of it.

PUNCTUM

In 1917, 1918, 1920, and 1923, Lucas was arrested and imprisoned on charges including false pretenses, theft, and begging. The charge for begging was different, of course, but every time he exchanged a well-cut suit for prison drab marked a point at which the gentlemanly trickster was put in his place. The bureaucratic process of the law and rituals of admission to Borstal or prison marked him as a convicted criminal. Grandiose names were redefined as duplicitous aliases.[4] When admitted to the Pentonville Remand Home in 1917, the "young midshipman" became prisoner number 9861.[5] While Lucas had passed through the West End as an honorable gentleman, court registers told different stories. They identified Lucas as of "no occupation" and "no fixed abode." Rather than of independent means, he was homeless, unemployed, and living off crime. This was an ostensibly transformative process that secured the integrity of established social boundaries.[6]

In some ways it was a very public process: Lucas's trials at the County of London Sessions in 1920 and Central Criminal Court in 1923 were reported widely in the press. The lives of the gentlemanly trickster provided rich material for sensation. While journalists savored the details of his masquerade, their reports were presented as an integral part of his unmasking. Headlines describing Lucas as a "Sham Peer and Colonel" made it explicit that the identities he claimed were fictive; so did the way that subeditors marked out "'Colonel'" and "'Lord'" in quotation marks.[7] In such accounts Lucas was simultaneously a daring adventurer and impertinent interloper. The pretensions of this "Swaggering Fool," who claimed privileges to which he was not entitled, could be mocked as well as enjoyed. In putting Lucas in his place, newspaper headlines reinstated an idea that the lines between classes and distinctions between "real" and "fake" were natural and impermeable—temporarily punctured rather than overwhelmed by the swank of the Honorable Basil Vaughan.[8]

Any sense of closure could only be temporary. Returning to crimes of confidence, Lucas exposed the limits of the law and modern penal institutions. Rather than being cowed by the imposing surroundings of London's courtrooms, he found a stage on which he reveled. Consider his trial at the London Sessions in 1920: he was seventeen and had been arrested after defrauding the colonial outfitters; he pleaded guilty, so there was no doubt he faced lengthy incarceration. Despite this, he appeared in the dock with the sangfroid with which he had charmed shopkeepers and socialites. As reported in the *World's Pictorial News*, this "diverting half hour" was closer to variety entertainment than a sober criminal trial. Lucas was "good-looking," his demeanor "gay and spruce"; all newspapers noted his fashionable suit and gloves.[9] The *Empire News* described how

> he stood in the dock self-possessed and dressed with perfect correctness. When he pleaded guilty his voice still retained the Oxford drawl that had stood him in good stead during his adventures. He bowed to the judge with the dignity of a courtier and carried himself through the trial with something approaching hauteur.[10]

Confident and mannered, the young dandy "listened with the air of a gratified music hall patron to romantic stories of life on his wits." He "joined heartily" in the laughter when the prosecuting counsel, J. D. Cassells, observed wryly that it "makes one's mouth water as a hardworking barrister . . . to see the number of pairs of trousers this youth obtained while we . . . are still wearing our prewar clothes." Even at this moment of "retribution," he was apparently unconcerned.[11] The *Aberdeen Journal* noted how Lucas "picked up his light felt hat and lemon-coloured gloves, and walked jauntily down the dock steps, smiling broadly."[12] In the same reports that described him as a "bogus peer," Lucas's drawling "hauteur" appeared convincing. The remarkable spectacle

Netley Lucas.

FIGURE 6. The gentleman crook on trial: Netley Lucas in the dock at the County of London Sessions, 1920. From "'Colonel' in the Car," *News of the World*, 1 August 1920, 3. © The British Library Board.

of an "unconcerned young blood" dramatized how social identities were all about front and defied attempts to place Lucas with a coherent regime of social classification.[13]

In some ways such reports were clichéd. This was how the trickster was supposed to behave in court, and Lucas's insouciance was a convenient fiction that sometimes belied his own accounts of being on trial. Years later he remembered his "terrifying" first appearance before the Westminster magistrate in 1917.[14] The idea that experience could "inure" against terror might point to the self-confidence Lucas showed in 1920, but he did not present the trial in those terms. Lucas often relished the chance to dramatize his nerve as a crook, but refused to claim those qualities in court. The *Autobiography* passed over the trial in a page, noting only the "cold truth" that punishment was certain. Rather than skip out of court, Lucas recalled, when sentenced to three years in Borstal "I bowed my head in silence. There did not seem to be anything worth saying just then."[15] The conventions of the crook life story perhaps demanded a retrospective remorse, but there was little trace of the jaunty self-possession newspapers described.

I think there is one image of Lucas in the dock in 1920 (fig. 6). It illustrated the *News of the World*'s trial report, taken during that brief period when technology allowed newspapers to mass-reproduce images but before the Criminal Justice Act (1925) prohibited courtroom photography. Its provenance is uncertain because it has been retouched. If the photograph was taken in the Session House, all traces of a packed courtroom have been removed. Lucas appears isolated in a screen of gray hatching, an effect enhanced by the harsh black lines demarcating his body and cut of his clothes. Photographed from the side and below, the image is cropped to show only his upper body and face. We see the smart suit (perhaps there is a handkerchief, too), a darker tie and pin, and his brilliantined hair. Lucas seems cowed rather than unconcerned: his arms are folded—perhaps resting on the dock rail. He is pensive rather than smiling: his head slightly bowed, he gazes intently up toward some unseen figure of authority.[16] How can we reconcile this image with newspaper reports of his trial? Here, perhaps, we see the uncertainty of social identities, and how courtroom audacity reflected both Lucas's own claims and the cultural power of ideas of the confident gentleman crook.

PIECES OF A CASE HISTORY

Putting tricksters in their place meant identifying who they "really" were and the causes of their offenses. The prominence of crimes of confidence in public life made this a pressing question in the 1920s. Understanding Basil Vaughan's storytelling was bound up with the broader process of understanding the conditions that made him a quintessential postwar figure. Reflecting on this "wave of impersonation" in the *Daily Chronicle*, Joan Sutherland observed the "curious" claims to title made by "young men and young girls" whose only rewards were a "career of poor deception and transient pleasure."

Sutherland was dismissive and pitying, but tried to understand what prompted such masquerades. In a capitalist economy, she suggested, the drudgery of working life created a "longing for colour, romance, a fair chance of happiness, the need to achieve something" among the clerks and shopgirls who, she assumed, were most often drawn into false pretenses. This was regrettable, but understandable.[17]

Criminologists interwove Sutherland's emphasis on the contradictions of labor and consumerism with a wide-ranging analysis of the Great War's legacies. As early as 1920, the *Report of the Prison Commissioners* identified the problems caused when the "normal restraints of conduct had been banished by the stress of war."[18] War's effects were psychological as much as social, economic, or political. John Goodwin's *Sidelights on Crime* (1923) identified a "state of mind" he characterized as "national neurasthenia." If war was a psychological disturbance, in its aftermath Britons were "swept along on the bosom of a mighty river of emotional instability"—something Goodwin saw expressed in "class consciousness, megalomania, and moral and social hysteria."[19] Amid this uncertainty, he argued, the "minds of the less virile turned . . . to anything that would furnish a palatable contrast" to the "dark background of reality. People began to dream dreams, to weave phantasies . . . to lose themselves and their identity in a city of unbeautiful nonsense." The masculine project of postwar reconstruction was compromised by a superficial mass culture.[20]

Lucas's lives resonate throughout these analyses, contributing to growing recognition of the prominence of crimes of confidence and the disconnect between "reality" and "fantasy." Ideas about the dangers of mass culture and the war's effects provided the deep context against which his career could be understood. These connections were rarely made explicit, however. While analyses of the conditions in which the confidence trick became a characteristic postwar crime sketched out the terrain on which Lucas's exploits might be situated, they did not address the particular contexts in which he turned to crime. As criminologists placed growing emphasis on the individualized causes of crime, Lucas was often isolated from the social worlds in which he moved.

Those who sought to understand the cause of Lucas's crimes thus emphasized his singular life story and character. Situated within pathological models of behavior, his deceptions could be attributed to what the *People* termed "a warped, if not criminal intelligence."[21] In court these ideas provided Lucas with a language through which to excuse his behavior. Invited to speak at the end of his 1920 trial at the London Sessions, Lucas said only: "They say there's a trace of insanity in my brain," seeking to lessen the threat of a long prison sentence.[22] Lucas and his solicitor, Martin O'Connor, offered contradictory but equally self-serving explanations of his behavior. Posing as Lord Lucas could appear simply as "foolishness"—a temporary failure of self-control prompted by the desire for adventure. Arrest and trial, O'Connor suggested, meant his client's "mind and conscience have been awakened, and he will try to do better in the future."[23] This was a plausible story that informed the judge's decision to sentence Lucas to Borstal to "pull you up" and "teach you to devote your undoubted abilities to right purposes."[24]

The imperative to understand Lucas's behavior in psychological terms was inconsistent. While the *Empire News* quoted the judgment of a "medical man" that the "young scapegrace" had "a kink in his brain," the logic of this analysis was immediately compromised: "It is not lunacy. It is badness, not madness," the doctor continued.[25] In *The Poor Man's Court of Justice* (1925), similarly, the magistrate Cecil Chapman reflected on dealing with Lucas in 1917 and 1918 in a chapter headed "Mental Deficiency." Other than this title, there was nothing to suggest Chapman understood Lucas's crimes in psychological terms. Quite the opposite: Chapman had placed him on probation and committed him to the West Drayton reformatory to "be trained during a stay of several months." Focusing on the possibilities of reformation reflected how the magistrate understood the causes of Lucas's offending: "What appeared to me was the chance of saving what looked like an innocent boy in naval uniform who had been drawn [into crime] by stress of circumstances." By 1925 Chapman could acknowledge how "I was . . . deceived in believing him to be the victim of misfortune"—taken in by Lucas's "plausible" performance in court; his argument that Lucas showed "there are some people who are not to be saved from disaster by any short term of probation or training" perhaps gestured toward an idea of "mental deficiency." Yet that analysis was implicit, and undercut by the difficulty of ascertaining the character of the man in the dock.[26]

In such accounts we see how the causes of Lucas's offenses were understood tangentially and fleetingly, crystallizing in the assumptions shaping a solicitor's defense and a judge's sentencing. When Lucas was arrested in 1920, he was examined by Doctor Griffiths, then medical officer at Brixton Prison; at the end of the trial, his case was referred to the prison commissioners for further analysis. If the conventions of a medical history suggest these reports would have addressed the problem of Lucas's offending in the context of an individual life story, neither of the documents survive. We know Griffiths denied Lucas's claimed "insanity" in court, but beyond that, their contents remain opaque.[27]

The evidence given in court and reported in newspapers presented Lucas's fraud on the colonial outfitters as the latest offense in a growing criminal record. Despite this, he invariably appeared out of time. That journalists were more preoccupied with the sensation of his deceptions than the details of his life story meant his crimes were located in the moment when they occurred rather than in a longer biography. There was an exception. The *Empire News* reported how "a detective . . . in his quiet methodical way, revealed the youngster's amazing past. Lucas, whose parents died while he was still a child, was placed at a good school in Bedford by his grandparents." His evidence might have been "methodical," but the details were unelaborated: the testimony hinted at the environmental factors that might have caused Lucas's behavior but did not explore the effects of losing both parents.[28]

There is something disconcerting here. The death of his parents was woven into stories about Lucas from at least 1920. Bracingly, it was rarely given much explanatory weight—a disconnect with our contemporary expectations that draws attention to the historically specific ways in which a life could be known. Details of Lucas's family background became increasingly central to newspaper reports around his appearance at the Central Criminal Court in 1923, but still confounded what we might expect. The *News of the World* set his crimes against the death of his parents and grandparents, and isolation in Bedford School. The argument was never explicit, but criminal behavior was presented as the result of a series of tragedies that compromised the privilege into which he had been born. The *World's Pictorial News* concluded: "He had the advantage of being born of respectable parents and a good education, but he had the misfortune to lose his father and mother at an early age." Without parental guidance and discipline, Lucas had developed "a warped moral character."[29] These arguments were undercut by alternative frameworks that emphasized psychological impulses—an inborn "criminal instinct" or the influence of heredity.[30] The *News of the World* concluded: "His capacity for spending was probably inherited from his father, who, after inheriting £20,000 married an actress and ran through his fortune in a little over three years."[31]

The most elaborate version of these ideas was provided by the Reverend Eustace Jervis, in his foreword to Lucas's *Autobiography of a Crook* (1924). Jervis had known Lucas since meeting him at Brixton Prison in 1917.[32] They met again before Lucas appeared at the County of London Sessions in 1920, when Jervis "prepare[d] a report on what he considered to be the basic reason for my criminal career" for the court.[33] That document might have informed the *Autobiography*'s foreword, which was organized as a medical case history. For Jervis, Lucas was an opportunity to revisit a problem posed in his *Twenty-Five Years in Six Prisons* (1925): "why people of refined birth and breeding take to criminal ways."[34] There Jervis scorned the deceptions of one gentleman crook as caused by "overweening vanity."[35] Now he was more sympathetic: "During the many conversations I have had with Lucas, I have gone deep down into his past, getting him to reach back to his earliest memories." Such comments established the depth of the chaplain's knowledge and aligned the ethical frameworks of Christian morality with the practices of Freudian psychoanalysis. Probing into Lucas's unconscious suggested how the criminal subject might be understood.[36]

Jervis attributed Lucas's lives to the effects of childhood trauma rather than misplaced vanity:

> Think what a terrible handicap it is to lose both parents when an infant. To be brought up by foster-parents, who, worthy as they may be, are not gentlefolk, is to lose more; and then, at the impressionable age of six, to be handed over to an elderly couple of grandparents who have practically lost all sympathy with childhood . . . [and] send him to a public school at that infantile age, is to be answerable for much that followed.[37]

Some of Jervis's details contradicted Lucas's stories; he emphasized a lack of domestic discipline and frustrated ambition—foster parents who were "not gentlefolk"—as much as the psychological formation of character. Jervis nonetheless isolated the loss of both parents as the defining event in the making of a gentleman crook. It was on this basis that he presented Lucas as deserving of compassion: "All along there seemed to be no sympathetic individual to whom he could attach himself, and whose influence over him would be a personal one. So with his high spirits and quick imagination, he became an Ishmael, with his hand against anyone and everyone." Partially excusing Lucas from personal responsibility, Jervis attributed Lucas's crimes to the absence or failings of parents, relations, and friends. As with the firstborn son of Abraham cast out into the wilderness, the youth's alienation from family life and personal intimacy was correlated with alienation from society.[38]

This marked a shift in the ways in which Lucas's crimes and character were understood. In part, this was because each time Lucas appeared in court, biographical knowledge accumulated through the files of the Criminal Record Office and the reports compiled by medical officers and chaplains. It also reflected Lucas's own capacity to shape his public lives. Jervis had talked to Lucas before writing his foreword but had also read the manuscript of *Autobiography*.

Storytelling was dialogic, the origins of different motifs never clear. Personal journalism and life-writing shaped how police officers and criminologists wrote about Lucas. In scrutinizing his childhood, in turn, Lucas drew upon the model of the case history to make himself publicly intelligible.

Lucas described the death of his parents and grandparents and his peripatetic upbringing in the first stories he sold to the *World's Pictorial News* and the *People* in 1922 and 1923. Being left "alone in the world" was presented not as a wrenching emotional trauma but as evidence of "ill luck." A privileged background and public-school education served to dramatize rather than explain an unlikely descent into crime.[39] In the *World's Pictorial News*, he described a childhood that was almost idyllic—playing with model boats with his grandfather, a strict but warm upbringing, being encouraged in self-reliance and a career at sea. Counterintuitively, Lucas concluded: "My childhood and its influences were conducive to an orthodox education, followed by a career in one of the recognised professions."[40] Even in 1923 the paper could note how he "had the advantage of being born of respectable parents, who provided him with the opportunity of a good education," without mentioning they were dead.[41]

From this perspective, masquerading as a midshipman or aristocrat reflected powerful yet frustrated "ambitions." Lucas's staged memory of the dazzling uniforms in his grandfather's mess meant that "from the earliest days I can remember, the idea of masquerade, high living by my own cleverness and trickery, have been in my mind." Captivated by the "glory of power," Lucas turned to crime because of his desire for social advancement.[42] This was what the *People* termed the "tragic history of a public schoolboy who, in spite of brilliant prospects . . . is now an outcast of society and a gaolbird." The publication never said whether the tragedy was losing both parents, unfulfilled prospects, or becoming an "outcast."[43]

The *Autobiography* distilled themes implicit in these earlier narratives into a traumatic account of Lucas's birth on the *Scorpion*: "My mother died in giving me birth. Had she been spared, this story might never have been written."[44] Lucas acknowledged his father's "ill-balanced temperament" and rejection, but focused on the maternal figure absent from his childhood. He confronted readers:

Ask yourself what *you* owe to *your* mother's, or your foster-mother's, love— and then spare a little pity for one who never knew his mother, who never felt the gentle influences which a mother radiates upon her son.[45]

Feelings of loss and isolation were compounded by the death of his grand-parents: "Sometimes I craved for sympathy, just someone with whom I could be absolutely natural, and in whose soothing presence I could lay aside the pose which . . . I wore as a garment."[46] The language betrayed a sense of the masquerade as defensive—addressing a nagging emotional absence and deflecting the anxieties of a lonely orphan. Even when Lucas was most self-conscious in identifying the loss of his mother as the defining influence upon his life, those ideas were interwoven with contradictory frameworks: the "world-old struggle between heredity and environment," a deep-rooted "perversity" of character, impulses that were "unmoral rather than immoral," and a fascination with fictional crooks like Raffles.[47] If causes were uncertain, consequences were clear: "That which was low appeared high, and right was transposed into—wrong. . . . I had to be in the limelight. Notoriety was food and drink to my overweening vanity." Within twenty pages Lucas had rejected the sympathy Jervis extended to him.[48]

It is tempting to impose a coherent biographical narrative on these disparate stories, isolating what now seems the overbearing trauma of Lucas's childhood as the cause of his criminality. A few contemporaries came close to that argument; it is a story he could, and sometimes did, tell about his life. If this was plausible in the 1920s, it was not the only version of Lucas's life, nor even the most compelling one. Other accounts emphasized the privilege rather than pathos of family life, and presented crime as a quest for adventure rather than an outcome of deep-rooted psychological instincts. Stories of childhood trauma developed fitfully and lacked the emotional power they acquired in hindsight. As much as Lucas tried to explain, he was often concerned with more proximate issues: defending himself in court or selling sensational stories. Above all, perhaps, he remained unknowable. Writing for the *Granta* in 1925, Lucas reflected on the crimes of one university-educated acquaintance: "How to account for this anomaly? I had many talks with him and tried to get him to tell me *why* he persisted in his life of crime. Strange to say he did not know himself, he just got an impulse suddenly to steal a car." Just as his interlocutor could not identify the causes of his criminality, so we should perhaps recognize the limits of Lucas's self-knowledge and the "strangeness" of the gentleman crook.[49]

The unknowable impulses that might prompt crime gestured toward another possible way of understanding Lucas's lives—a path not taken that still gives us useful ways of thinking about the resonance of crimes of confidence in the 1920s. A friend of Josephine O'Dare described how she "reached that stage in the art of lying when she herself believed the falsehoods she told."

Set against emerging cultures of popular psychology, O'Dare's "imagination" marked the point where daydreams became delusion. Unable to distinguish fiction from reality, deceiving herself and others, O'Dare was implicitly identified as a pathological liar.[50]

What was known as "pseudologia fantastica" drew growing interest from psychologists after Williamina Shaw Dunn's famous case history of a Canadian soldier in the Royal Edinburgh Asylum in the *British Journal of Psychiatry* (1916). The soldier told "wonderful tales" of his wealthy parents, heroism, and the "small ape he carried as a mascot of his regiment."[51] Subsequent case histories defined pathological lying as a discrete psychological condition. Telling stories was a "trait rather than an episode"; it was purposeful—the pathological liar sought to "enhance his own personality"—even if it was not instrumental. It was "pleasurable" in itself rather than for its potential rewards. Above all, telling stories reflected unresolved conflicts between "unconscious impulses" and social constraints, and the inability to distinguish between "fantasy" and "reality."[52] Unsuited to the demands of everyday life, driven to gratify uncontrollable desires, the pathological liar was marked as childlike and feminine, his condition aligned with "moral deficiency [and] chronic alcoholism."[53]

Lucas was never explicitly diagnosed as a pathological liar. He only twice gestured toward the possibility of this analysis. In the *World's Pictorial News*, he reflected on how, as a young midshipman, "I managed to hoodwink myself into the belief that I really was what I purported to be, and worked myself up into a fever of indignation at any breach of etiquette on the part of any person of lower rank."[54] Several years later, he described how he "lapsed subconsciously" into identifying himself as an honorable gentleman to a hotel manager and noted how this threw a "psychological sidelight" upon his character.[55] If the urge to classify was weak, the resonance between ideas of pathological lying and understandings of the gentlemanly trickster was striking. The connection between deception and alcoholism was echoed in Cecil Chapman's reflections on Lucas's crimes; it played out tragically before Lucas's death in 1940. Lucas's stories were sustained and repetitive: the claims of Lord Lucas were reiterated by Basil Vaughan. We can see Lucas's reflection in Dunn's case history:

> He was utterly unscrupulous in taking advantage of any indulgence or kindness shown him, but had a superficial suavity and politeness of manner which served him in good stead. . . . Systematically he was extremely selfish and inordinately vain.[56]

Just as the trickster's deceptions could be attributed to vanity, so the pathological liar was the "victim of an intense craving for notoriety" and sought to compensate for a painful awareness of "mental or social inferiority."[57]

Above all, the diagnostic category of the pathological liar was explicitly linked to the confidence trick and false pretenses. John Goodwin's *Insanity and the Criminal* identified "an over-weaning egotism . . . with its nauseating accompaniments of self-assertion and conceit" as a characteristic condition of modern life.[58] The pathological liar, the egotist, and the trickster were elided as Goodwin explored the conflicts between instinct and society. Lucas emerged in halftone shades as a psychological type defined by his "self-assertion complexes":

> He seeks to render others blind to his inferiority by dazzling them with the brilliance of an artificial side of his mental make-up which he assumes by way of compensating himself for his real shortcomings. The boastfulness, the self-praise, the plausibility, the outward show and glitter . . . are all parts of an intricate scheme to find favour and commendation in the sight of others; and if he can turn his posings and posturings to profitable account, and thus obtain both applause and hard cash, his Ego is satisfied and gratified. His love of display, of making a good impression, and of attracting others sometimes levers him into obtaining an easy living as a confidence trickster.[59]

Elaborate stories of aristocratic origin offered psychological compensation for a deep-rooted "inferiority complex"; "delusions of grandeur" were animated by anxiety, not confidence. "Plausible poseurs" should be pitied for their insecurities, not admired for their daring.[60]

Here we might begin to place Lucas back into 1920s society and culture and see how, implicitly, at least, he could be understood as a social being as well as an individualized biographical subject, and as an exemplary figure as well as a remarkable one. Goodwin sought to isolate the criminal as a particular modern problem, but reminded readers how "we are all liars."[61] In the United States, the purchase of ideas of pathological deception reflected scientific and popular interest in the "ordinary person's recourse to fantasy, deceit and lying," and the normality of the unconscious deceitful self.[62] For Goodwin, too, social exchange was governed by everyday deceptions and self-deceptions that made it difficult to distinguish between truth and falsehood, the pathological and the ordinary liar. While criminologists tried to isolate the deceptions of Lucas and his like, they acknowledged how such deceptions reflected common psychological states in modern consumer culture. Fantasy could fuel delusion, but was integral to the simple pleasures of reading or cinema going.[63] Left unchecked, however, the perils of excessive introspection were many. Associated with feminized forms of mass culture, what Goodwin characterized as "identification" and "delusion" offered a key to understanding the gentlemanly trickster.[64]

Observers could have presented Lucas as a pathological liar but did not do so. In his case, perhaps, the correlation between deceptions and financial reward suggested they were instrumental rather than impulsive; it was difficult to isolate unconscious impulses from what they might bring. If psychological ideas exercised growing influence on penal policy and criminology in the 1920s, the pathology of deception had limited reach in Britain compared to continental Europe and North America. British doctors were wary of this kind of analysis and the diagnostic possibilities of the lie detector, retaining a powerful emphasis on personal responsibility and self-control.[65]

GENTLEMANLINESS AS MASQUERADE

The proliferation of stories and Lucas's chutzpah in court made it difficult to put him in his place. These problems were compounded by his ability to tell his stories after prison and the ambiguities of his background. Unlike the aspirational clerks or shopgirls who were often the bogus honorables of the 1920s, Lucas had at least some claim to gentility. Stories of a "public schoolboy's amazing adventures" drew the attention of readers and made it harder to shut the case down. Throughout, Lucas insisted upon his own status. Colonial outfitters, courtrooms, and his published writing were all stages on which gentlemanliness was reiterated. The stakes were different, the performances tailored for discrete audiences; yet Lucas was preoccupied with asserting his status long after his deceptions were exposed.

The stories Lucas told in print after 1924 were ostensibly about earlier experiences of crime and prison. They remained always present centered in the social and psychological work they did. Reading them back against his exploits as a gentleman crook offers an alternative perspective from which to explore questions of agency and intention. In *My Selves* Lucas described how he felt when discharged from his voyage on the *Kenilworth Castle* in 1917: "My origin with its natural complement of a desire for refinement, craved for clean linen, [and] the cultivated conversation of the class to which I really belonged." The mundane details of everyday life—conversation and clean sheets—were entwined with telling convincing stories about who he was. While detectives exposed the bogus honorable, Lucas presented his "refinement" as "natural."

Only false pretenses could provide access to the Society to which he "really belonged."[66]

This meant the nature of Lucas's deceptions remained unclear. Stories he told to shopkeepers and socialites were reworked in print, creating uncertainties that would not go away. What happens if we shift focus, and think about what was at stake for Lucas in those later stories? I think they offer a way of understanding his criminal deceptions—as purposeful, for sure, but also as rooted in a sense of status that was deeply ingrained or, at least, deeply felt. In his burgeoning career as a writer, gentlemanliness brought status and profit. Its rewards were also emotional and psychological. Rather than the deceptions of a pathological liar, his claims to gentility perhaps addressed anxieties generated by a fractured family life, a sense of frustrated destiny, and a sense of absence in his writing. This seems plausible, doesn't it? Later accounts of Borstal and prison ostensibly described his institutional experiences, but also worked to distance him from men of the "hooligan class."[67] Consider his staged response to being sentenced at the Central Criminal Court in 1920: "A Borstal brat, *me*, the friend . . . of lovely ladies and high-bred gentlemen!" The exclamation mark is there for effect, but might betray an instinctive emotional reaction. It is in Borstal, not Mayfair, that the gentleman crook is truly out of place.[68]

> I found the confinement among the rough-and-tumble crew which constitutes the majority of boy criminals rather hard to bear. Among all the hundreds of boys who were my fellow prisoners there were only two or three educated ones besides myself, and the ideas, tales, and life there were of the crudest.

However benevolent the regime, Lucas found institutional life alienating. Here "an educated boy has . . . a rougher time than his less-cultured associates . . . and he is put to a severe test to knock all 'swank' out of him." Social difference might bring brutality and bullying.[69]

If other inmates tried to beat the "swank" from his body, Lucas reacted viscerally to the smells, sights, and sounds he associated with those of a "lower moral type."[70] In *My Selves* this coalesced in a charged account of an incident on the training ship *Cornwall* around 1918:

> I became lousy! This is not a pleasant subject but as it takes such an important part in the working out of my character I am forced to bring it in. I actually found myself one morning swarming with vermin, contracted goodness only knows how. It was not that I was uncleanly in my habits. My natural tastes and school training made personal cleanliness a fetish of my life and consequently

when I found my clothing, and particularly my hammock, to be verminous I very nearly went out of my mind.

At a moment when an older generation of privileged young men had found their bodies contaminated by lice and mud, Lucas echoed the characteristic motifs of war poems like Isaac Rosenberg's "Louse Hunting." Elsewhere he noted his revulsion to sharing washing water and exposing his body for public inspection. Despite the fetishistic regimes of "personal cleanliness" he had cultivated at school, his body was now permeable to the dirt of an outside world he always associated with poverty and class difference. Misery was compounded when he was isolated as a source of contagion: bathed in "nasty smelling disinfectant" and forced to eat alone in the middle of the mess deck. Physical discomfort and "cruel" taunts prompted an awful realization: "*I was a pariah*—an unclean thing." Emotional torment—remembered years later—came when his body could no longer sustain the privileges of class. The swarming lice that overwhelmed the "toff crook's" difference worked to confirm it. "Had I been used to slum life I might have stood things better," recalled Lucas. But he was not, and became so desperate that he threw his bedding and clothes overboard. The twelve lashes he received as punishment marked his back into the 1930s, just as the memory of being "lousy" marked his sense of being a gentleman.[71]

Lucas's stories resonate with Josephine O'Dare's account of her "mental suffering" in Walton Prison. Writing to Inspector Yandell in August 1928, O'Dare distanced herself from the women around her. After a year she was preoccupied with the prospect of an early release, and the return of her correspondence and squirrel fur coat. The letters were priceless, but she had paid two hundred guineas for the coat. Managing her personal affairs provided opportunities for O'Dare to insist on her status. Time passed slowly, but O'Dare found Walton comfortable, her duties "not very difficult," and the recreation "interesting." Like Lucas, however, O'Dare suggested that her status isolated her from the other prisoners:

I should find it very lonely excepting for one perfectly nice woman that came up from London with me. The other residents, well! It is somewhat painful to come in contact with them daily. I always try to be polite to everyone here but it is impossible to associate with them[;] the majority appear to be mentally deficient, one day you hear them talking in your magniloquent manner and the next you wonder if you are living in the most dreadful part of Billingsgate for the lewdness of their conversation with each other is fearfully disagreeable.

In asking Yandell if "there should be some classification in a place of this kind," O'Dare suggested her desire to be distanced from the rough milieu of a women's prison. Unable to find refined conversation and companionship, O'Dare sought escape in reading and reflection. Now her thoughts turned wistfully to the rhythms of the fashionable season: "I suppose London is rather quiet just at present and people are rushing away to Scotland & the Country." Dramatizing the emotional costs of prison was instrumental, of course—O'Dare appealed to Yandell's "good sympathetic side" and support for a reduced sentence. Yet her letter suggests the continued power of her desire for advancement, and how claims dismissed as fraudulent shaped her sense of self.[72]

Lucas's public stories about becoming lousy were thus more than a privileged young man's instinctive reaction to class difference and alien environments. Even when he was first arrested in 1917, Lucas was no ingenue. By 1920, on his own account, he had worked on a Union Castle liner, lived in lodging houses in the East End, slept rough on the Embankment and under the Adelphi Arches. *My Selves* stressed, "I was no longer the carefully nurtured public school boy," and so dramatized the horror of prison conditions.[73] No—these stories of isolation and revulsion allowed Lucas to secure the gentility he had claimed in London's West End. Consider the account of his fractious relationship with the matron of Rochester Borstal. Assured and patronizing, in "one of my flippant moods," Lucas asked if there was an Old Borstalian's tie. Hearing it was made of rope, he laughed: "Rather good! One to you, matron!" and "infuriated her more." Confronting the realities of institutional life, Lucas cultivated the "airs of a superior person."[74]

Claims like this allowed Lucas to reassert his strength of character, but were interwoven with different versions of his interactions with inmates:

> "Gaud!" exclaimed one of my fellow malefactors, sotte [*sic*] voce, "you didn't 'arf make the old trout look small. What are you in for? Swell crook, ain't you?"
> "No, I'm same as you mate," I said.
> "No fear you ain't," he said, almost with reverence.[75]

The idiomatic speech of his "fellow malefactor" allows Lucas to assert his superiority: *his* accent is unmarked, the Italian phrase revealing in its casual use. This is why the youth immediately acknowledges his status as a "swell crook." Lucas disavows this status, however: he insists—unconvincingly—that he is "same as you mate." Rather than cultivate "airs," here we see Lucas seeking the safety of sameness. In *My Selves* assertions of difference were undercut by attempts to present himself as an adept chameleon. On the Cornwall, rumors that he was a "young toff" meant "the age old antagonism of class began to assert itself."[76] Rather than the passive victim of earlier life stories, Lucas now appeared as hard-bitten and adaptable. "Disliked because of my educated voice," he nonetheless "managed to drop all outward indication of breeding and become as foul mouthed—if not fouler mouthed—than the majority of inmates." Erasing the signs of class difference, vanishing into the mass, and fighting back against tormenters "earned . . . the respect of most of my fellow inmates and the friendship of not a few."[77]

Renouncing gentlemanliness was temporary and instrumental. "In spite of all that he has been through, and the associates he has had in the reformatory and in prison," noted Eustace Jervis, he "has retained his gentlemanly manners and refined way of speaking." A foul mouth concealed his identity, but behind the mask "there was much that was good, much that was manly, much that was refined in him. The gentlemanly instincts were there."[78] The idea of gentlemanliness as instinctive gives us a way of understanding three stories— ostensibly fictional—that Lucas told as his freelance career developed. "The Boy Apache" and "The Borstal Boy" were serialized in the *Golden* and *Monster* story papers in 1926; both resembled Lucas's only novel, *The Red Stranger* (1927). Each story played with the idea of criminality as a mask. Lucas followed mysterious protagonists through the underworlds of Paris and London. In these working-class milieus, they were acknowledged leaders but distant from those around them. L'Etranger Rouge, for example, is the "King of Apaches." Although physically dominant and violent, he adheres to a code of honor whereby he only robs those who prey on others' misfortune. In the novel's closing scenes, L'Etranger is prosecuted for a murder he did not commit. He is visited in prison by Comte Francois Deligny, a shell-shocked ex-serviceman who has seen him at a masquerade ball.[79] When L'Etranger is later released and brought to the Chateau Deligny, there is a dramatic revelation: Francois greets him: "Raoul, my brother!"[80] For L'Etranger, the family portraits prompt a return of memory: on the Western Front an explosion had left him "a man with no past" who found himself in the underworld. His honor reflected the "old instincts that stayed with me."[81] However depraved his surroundings, fragments of the past reappeared: seeing the "well-dressed people in the Champ Elysees [*sic*]," L'Etranger "knew in some dim but certain fashion that I had not always been the associate of apaches."[82]

L'Etranger Rouge had analogues in Darky Kemp and Spider, whose aristocratic births were revealed in the closing scenes of "The Borstal Boy" and "The Boy Apache." Lucas repeats the plot device so often that it is hard not to read these stories against what I know of his background. After all, Lieutenant

Francis Deligny was an alias he used around 1920. In these accounts "old instincts" persist even when a privileged upbringing is forgotten; dreamlike reveries of a life of luxury resurface unexpectedly; recurring nightmares of a world now lost suggest the frustrated expectations that might have animated Lucas's insistent self-fashioning. That gentleman was exposed as fraudulent by the interventions of police and the drama of the courtroom. Rather than imprisonment and disgrace, here Lucas explored alternative stories in which the crook was unmasked as a gentleman—stories through which, he implied, revealing the "truth" of identity staved off prison and secured a life of luxury and the fulfillment of romantic love. Are these fantasies of what might have been? It is possible that *The Red Stranger* contained the happy ending the trickster imagined for himself.

Perhaps we get a sense of the power of these investments at the one moment when newspapers suggested Lucas's self-possession faltered. After stealing from Stanley Scott, he embarked upon a desperate series of thefts and forgeries, only to be arrested and tried at the Central Criminal Court in June 1923. Reports of his trial began as a familiar story of self-control. The illusion was temporary, undone not by the prospect of prison but by the "lash of [the] Judge's tongue." The recorder of London, Sir Ernest Wild, acknowledged Lucas's "intelligence" but concluded: "There was no excuse for his becoming a sneaking hotel and railway thief."[83] Such comments, noted the *Empire News*, meant Lucas "suffered greater pain through his wounded vanity than any physical punishment."[84] Confronted "with my lurid past," the trickster was crestfallen. Lucas was "staggered" at his lenient sentence, but recalled: "I stood there, saying not a word, feeling more utterly ashamed than I could find words to express." Even in hindsight, the memory of what he presented as a forced moment of self-realization was something to suppress: "I scarcely heard what was going on. . . . I do not wish to recall it." Self-possession was punctured at precisely that moment when the distance between Lucas's fantasies of gentility and the realities of his petty thefts became most visible.[85]

MY PAL AND PARTNER

In the summer of 1923, two young men meet in the cells at Westminster Police Court, and "an important event" takes place: they fall in love. There is no better word. Netley Lucas and the man he calls Dick are "instinctively attracted." Both face trial on charges of theft and false pretenses, but the life-changing recognition of their affinities goes deeper.

In future it will be necessary for our names to be coupled together, for ever since that time Dick has been by my side as my pal and partner, sharing all my ups and downs, my successes and failures, my happinesses and sadnesses.[86]

Like Netley, Dick is from a good family—his father runs a motorcar business in Hereford—and his careful manners betray his pretensions to gentility. Like Netley, his mother is long dead: I wonder if they ever talked about this shared tragedy.[87] Two lives now entwined, an enduring emotional bond sustains the men through all their "ups and downs." They are "inseparable," intimate, pals and partners; "coupled together" or simply a couple. Netley recalls "a bond which neither time nor hardship has since severed." This queer moment unfolds in the language of companionate marriage. Netley disavows this when he describes how their closeness ran "to the extent of marrying two sisters, so that we became brothers-in-law," but even then their "friendship" is "the one redeeming feature of both our lives."[88]

Pals become partners as Dick awaits trial for stealing a motorcar from Harrods. His path to a Westminster court is indistinct. Theft and forgery offer small consolation after his mother dies. He is led astray by William Davis or Charles Hellier, then beginning the career that makes him a forger "without equal."[89] He falls for the beautiful Josephine O'Dare: "The girl . . . has had a lot to do with his downfall," writes a police officer.[90] For Dick (and Hellier and O'Dare), Hereford proves too provincial. He is many things in the early 1920s: a deserter from the Royal Scots Regiment, a gentleman crook living by his wits, lover of an adventuress, and sidekick to a forger.[91] It takes what newspapers call the "drugged chauffeur case" to bring Dick into the light and under Netley's gaze. The case is the "kind of serial given in a penny novelette"—a confidence trick in which he is cast as valet to Captain St. Hellier and a chauffeur wakes up in a Cambridge garage with neither wealthy clients nor expensive car. It is not long before Dick and Hellier find themselves in police custody, the Central Criminal Court, and Wormwood Scrubs Prison.[92]

For over a decade after that freighted fateful day, Netley and Dick are pals and partners. Pals: inseparable friends, unswervingly loyal, confidants, sharing their problems and drunken nights out. Partners: roommates and traveling companions; living, loving, and working; participating jointly in crimes of confidence and a burgeoning literary career. Dick loves Netley; Netley loves Dick.

I want to believe him. Yet I cannot understand why Netley can only draw his partner in faint lines and halftones. This is one of the few significant relationships he acknowledges, but he still says very little about Dick. All we really learn *is that he is a "young public schoolboy" and ex-crook; Narcissus loses himself in his reflection.*[93] *It troubles me that Dick only acquires names and stories—substance—through police and court records, newspapers, and a prison chaplain's reminiscences rather than the pen of the man who loves him. Netley does not say that Dick is often identified as Guy Hart, and sometimes Albert Marriott or Richard Dent. If their bond is so powerful, why does he not say more?*[94] *Dick is everywhere yet nowhere in the pages that follow. I sense his presence near Netley in flashes in the archive or the names and signatures on headed notepaper. It frustrates me that I can say little more than that he is there in the stories I recount. Netley tells me that after the day they met, their entwined lives are filled with companionship and intimacy. He can only go so far, however. These long years are also "the time he played shadow to me." It troubles me, too, that Netley does more than anyone else to write the man he loves—the man he cannot name—into his shadow.*[95]

TO TORONTO (AND BACK)

Netley Lucas was released from Wormwood Scrubs on 7 March 1924.[96] Two months later a wealthy young Scotsman called George Armstrong Mackenzie caused a short-lived sensation when he intervened in one of the decade's most high-profile murder cases. At a beach house on the Sussex coast, the adulterous Patrick Mahon killed his pregnant lover Emily Kaye, dismembering her body, leaving parts in a trunk and a biscuit tin, and burning her head and limbs on the fire. On 5 May, three days after Mahon was arrested, Mackenzie wrote to him:

> In circumstances such as yours, practical sympathy and help are sometimes wanting. It is with this thought that I am going to offer you on behalf of a few friends and myself the assistance of the best legal advice obtainable.[97]

What Mackenzie described as a "genuine offer made from purely humanitarian principles" was misplaced: this was a gruesome murder, and there was little doubt of Mahon's guilt.[98] The nature of Kaye's death and the horrified fascination with which the case was reported meant that "sympathy and help" for Mahon were certain to draw attention. While the letter was received by local police, its contents were clearly shared with journalists. Mackenzie, observed Glasgow's *Weekly News*, "created quite a sensation by coming into the limelight" and "enjoyed the fuss that was made over his generosity." He told some journalists he had been at Bedford School with Mahon, and was offering help "for old time's sake . . . as he did not like to see a pal down and out."[99] He told others a different story: "I believe in the thing called British justice. I want Mahon to have fair play."[100]

This was an intriguing sideshow to a notorious trial. Mahon was convicted and executed at Wandsworth Prison in September, however; "nothing more was heard of the offer" once the trial began, though Mahon "expressed his gratitude" in writing.[101] What was Mackenzie doing? Perhaps he was motivated by fraternity and justice. Perhaps he wanted the "limelight": reports suggest he reveled in seeing his words and image in print. Perhaps Mackenzie was more cynical. The *Weekly News* noted his "attempt to make capital out of this, but, failing, he embarked for Toronto on another scheme."[102] That seems plausible: Mackenzie was living in a furnished room in Pimlico, but corresponded from the Westminster offices of the Society of Authors. When he and his roommate, Albert Marriott, boarded a Canadian Pacific liner at Liverpool on 8 August, they described themselves as journalists. Mackenzie looks to me like a cynical freelance writer trying to wring an exclusive out of Mahon.[103]

Mackenzie and Marriott arrived in Canada full of excitement as "two pioneers in search of a new world," their giddiness sharpened by Marriott's recent release from prison.[104] In Toronto they moved as English gentlemen. The palatial King Edward Hotel, downtown on King Street, provided an appropriate setting for their ambition. They were in good company: Mary Pickford and Douglas Fairbanks had stayed there a few months earlier; three years later the hotel would host a grand function for the Prince of Wales and Duke of York. Luxury was expensive, however, and the men soon took an apartment on Carlton Street, overlooking Allan Gardens.[105] Acting as "agent for several well-known British writers," Mackenzie sold articles like "Behind the Scenes with the Prince of Wales" to Canadian newspapers and magazines.[106] The agency was later described as "bogus," but the men approached their "business" meticulously, creating a burgeoning corporate archive that included correspondence with "numerous titled Englishwomen and men" about "having their memoirs written and sold."[107]

This was impressive, but did not bring the rewards the men anticipated. Their response was the Marriott and Mackenzie Employment Agency. An ostensibly respectable literary agency contained little to which police could take exception, but the men's activities now blurred the line between sharp practice and criminal deception. Mackenzie later described the agency as a "racket."[108] What did he mean? His account is frustratingly short; the agency's activities left no trace in police or court records; as far as I can tell, Mackenzie and Marriott's encounters with immigration officers have not survived in the historical record. How do you make sense of something you know little about?[109]

One possibility is to set the racket's fragmentary traces against published accounts and archival traces of similar schemes. I know, for example, that Albert Marriott had previous experience: in London in 1923 he ran an employment agency that drew complaints and the attention of detectives. I know that Netley Lucas described something similar: a firsthand account of how "advertisement columns" were a "great medium for the confidence trickster" appeared in the *Detective* in October 1924, just when Mackenzie and Marriott were in Toronto. You might guess why that is a useful connection to make.[110] Approaching the agency sideways gives it the illusion of substance, and a story that is speculative yet plausible. The gentlemanly trickster exemplified broader cultures of aspirational dreaming that adventurers like Mackenzie and Marriott could exploit. The racket, observed Toronto's *Evening Telegram*, "brought to light the fact that there are hundreds of young women who are anxious to step into moving pictures or become connected with the English nobility."[111]

The Mackenzie and Marriott agency is a story of two adverts. Placed in Toronto newspapers in August 1924, the first invited young women to apply for the position of "secretary-companion" to the Countess of Clancarty, a member of the Anglo-Irish aristocracy with estates in Ballinasloe in Galway. In later correspondence, Mackenzie claimed to be "a close friend of [the] Irish peeress," whose companion "would . . . be introduced to the most exclusive circles in London."[112] The advert echoed something printed in the *Daily Telegraph* and *Daily Mail* in Britain fifteen months earlier. Placed by Marriott and Captain R. W. Dammers, later identified as the forger Charles Hellier, it was the gambit in a case of suspected employment fraud:

> A VACANCY occurs for a YOUNG GENTLEMAN as private secretary, educated, well groomed, possessing private means preferred. Prepared to travel. Not considered an employee. Salary £500.[113]

Applicants were invited to write to an address in Hertford Street, London. Dammers's rank, the emphasis on education, appearance, and means, and the disclaimer that this was not the position of an "employee" were perfectly judged to cultivate the illusion of gentility and the ambitions of young men wanting to rise in the world. So was the address in aristocratic Mayfair.[114] Letters came from across Britain: in reply Dammers offered each man the appointment. The Glamorgan clerk Henry Wayne was offered the post pending "confirmation as to the authenticity of your remarks," and asked for five pounds as "a guarantee of good faith." A second letter hurried him into action, asking for a passport photograph, since "I am leaving London for the continent shortly." When the photograph and money arrived, Dammers and Marriott disappeared.[115]

The men were already under suspicion. Then living in Bristol, Arthur Taylor was typical of those who applied for the post. If not wealthy, his family was respectable: he had seen the advert in the *Daily Mail*; his father worked for the Law Union and Rock Insurance Company; Arthur was educated at public school. Despite this, he had "had no permanent situation since he left the Army." The prospect of a position as a private secretary exploited the lack of secure professional employment after the Great War as much as the aspirations of the upwardly mobile. Arthur's desperation explains his father's concerns. In several touching letters, C. F. Taylor outlined his sense that something was not right. Dammers's haste worried him; so did a "peculiarity" of his letter: the "date is apparently written at a different time from the address and the sender of the letter. The ink certainly is not of the same tint." Here, perhaps, we see Dammers and Marriott's methodical approach—writing standard letters to be addressed and dated later. Taylor was anxious enough to forward the correspondence to his brother in London, asking him to check the street directory and Army List.[116] Signing himself "Yours affectionately, Dad," Taylor explained to Arthur his concerns that the "whole thing is a plant, [and] it seems to me cruel in the extreme."[117] He contemplated exposing Dammers in the press, but eventually went to the police: "It might be the means of saving money to many scores of young fellows who would otherwise fall in the trap laid by this man."[118]

Despite these complaints, Marriott and Dammers were never charged. Their carefully worded letters provided insufficient evidence; they had been imprisoned over the drugged chauffeur affair. Yet Dammers's role in Josephine O'Dare's forgery ring ensured that their scam left rich traces in Metropolitan Police files. Their handwritten letters and the typed police reports might fill in the silences around the advert for the Countess of Clancarty's secretary-companion, allowing us to understand the correspondence it prompted. Those silences might also be filled by Lucas's description of a similar advert in the *Detective*. This appeared in a New York newspaper: "Old English titled Family will receive young American debutante in their country and town residences for the London Season." The "visions of presentation at Court, and of all the whirl of gaiety and glitter," Lucas explained, inspired the aspirations of upwardly mobile American plutocrats.[119]

Reading Lucas's article and the file on Dammers and Marriott alongside newspaper reports gives us a way of understanding Marriott and Mackenzie's racket. Predicated upon what Patrick Balfour characterized as "Lordolatry," advertising for the Countess of Clancarty's "secretary-companion" suggests an intuitive grasp of how the gossip column had reinvigorated traditional social elites. Marriott and Mackenzie reworked old scams in the New World at the same time that *John Bull* described how the "craze to get into English Society has called into being an entirely new profession for impoverished aristocrats— that of Society chaperon." Adverts offering to introduce "wealthy 'outsiders'" into Society reflected the "despair and humiliation" into which "pauperised bearers of great names" had fallen. Desperate attempts to maintain appearances shaded into "all sorts of subterfuge and deceit," selling invitations to functions or staging exclusive parties for "hoodwinked strangers." In this "game of sham and deception," boundaries between crime and necessity were unclear.[120]

The second advert associated with the Marriott and Mackenzie agency appeared in Toronto's *Daily Star* in August 1924: "English film producer requires Canadian girls for films to be produced shortly in Canada, some film experience a recommendation but not essential." A longer version invited women to apply for a starring role in the "Oriental Film," then being produced in Vancouver.[121] Like the advert for a "secretary-companion," this reiterated an established formula and played upon fantasies of social mobility. By 1924 the bogus cinema school had become a pressing problem of modern culture. "The romance and gaiety associated with the film world," observed one journalist, "has always presented a lure to countless unsophisticated girls to whom the false glamour suggests a pleasant path to fame and fortune."[122] The dangers of cinema fandom were many, but here coalesced in concerns that the desire for fame left young women, in particular, vulnerable to financial and sexual exploitation. From the late nineteenth century, such concerns focused upon the bogus theatrical manager who advertised for girls to join the chorus of traveling shows. Newspapers continued to expose such sharks, castigating those who, they suggested, preyed on the unwary and worked on the fringes of the white slave trade, and orchestrating the campaign that culminated with the Theatrical Employer's Registration Act (1925). As screen supplanted stage as the site of leisure and aspiration, however, the terrain took shape on which Marriott and Mackenzie sought a star for the Oriental film.[123] By 1929, after a series of high-profile scandals, Basil Tozer could comment of "schools of acting [and] 'talkie' voice production": "Without venturing to say that all such schools are run by gentlemen of the confidence trickster type, I would state emphatically that some of them are, for which reason persons who may contemplate joining any one of them would be well advised to exercise caution."[124] The endless spectacle of companies whose only assets were an imposing name and premises within walking distance of Britain's film industry in Wardour Street "fleecing film fans" forced the London County Council to introduce a new system of control: after 1920 film schools were required to obtain an employment agency license and register the work they found for pupils.[125]

Unlike the perpetrators of other cinema rackets, Marriott and Mackenzie never tried to teach acting nor film wannabes in fictional scenarios. An advert and audacity were enough to sustain the promise of celebrity. Gesturing toward the rackets that absorbed newspapers in the early 1920s, they improvised from the established scripts of the gentleman crook. The Oriental film scam was deeply embedded in cultures of celebrity and aspiration characteristic of the 1920s. Popular newspapers and magazines like *Picturegoer* cultivated the stardom of Clara Bow or Douglas Fairbanks.[126] Columnists offered advice on how to get into the movies; competitions invited women to put themselves forward for roles in big-budget films by submitting a photograph and self-addressed stamped envelope. Widely publicized, their rags-to-riches stories held out the tantalizing prospect of being transported from the mundanities of everyday life to the glamour of Hollywood. On the borders between the ordinary and extraordinary, and between Britain and its empire, two entrepreneurial men found a gray area in which to seek their fortune.[127]

Adverts could pique curiosity, but to turn this into profit, Marriott and Mackenzie needed the confidence of potential respondents. In a period when journalists and detectives regularly exposed bogus cinema schools, and consumers were warned of the dangers of the classified ads, this was not easy. Seeking the elusive effects of authenticity, Marriott and Mackenzie addressed themselves to the demands of an Anglophile colonial world. Exploring Toronto as English gentlemen abroad, they introduced themselves as "authors and journalists," and talked nonchalantly of their wealth and education.[128] These "young gentlemen," one journalist observed, "played the role of intermediaries with éclat."[129]

Performance required a stage. The *World's Pictorial News* noted how the agency "took imposing offices in the heart of Toronto"; other newspapers described it as a "small affair . . . furnished with a secondhand typewriter, [and] a desk that had seen better days."[130] Carlton Street was not quite at Toronto's heart, but it was close, a row of well-appointed apartment houses where wealthy Anglo-Canadian bachelors could find suitable accommodation. Though its character was changing, Allan Gardens retained much of its cachet as a fashionable public space. This might have been the perfect location for men seeking to project the impression of wealth, respectability, and Englishness—even if they could only afford secondhand furniture.[131] The office's decor furthered this impression: photographs of film stars adorned the walls and "a British 'Who's Who' [was] marked very prominently opposite the titled lady's name."[132] The shelves displayed a "conglomeration of correspondence," including letters from "various noted British cinema and stage stars," "Lloyd George and other aristocratic and plebeian Britishers."[133] One of the men possessed a letter from Patrick Mahon, who wrote from Maidstone Prison to say that "he would like to receive some good novels to read."[134] Marriott and Mackenzie "set the scene of their bogus agency very neatly."[135]

The literary agency was abortive, but at least to begin with, the employment agency had more success: over seventy women wrote from across Canada. Most wanted to be in the movies; some enclosed photographs "taken in various dancing competitions." Other "refined young women" wanted "to bask in the sunlight of the countenance of a Countess."[136] Here we might return to the "Odd Tricks" Lucas described in the *Detective*, particularly C. Gifford Ambler's accompanying illustration (fig. 7). It depicted a small yet smart office—similar, perhaps, to the premises in Carlton Street—behind a glass door marked "private." There is an imposing desk and neat pile of papers, a telephone on a sideboard, an overflowing wastebasket. We see "two immaculately dressed young men." One is at the desk: dressed in a lounge suit, he smokes a cigarette in a holder. The other stands in evening dress and spats: he reads out the letter in his hand, and the men are "grinning at the guilelessness of the American Society woman." Here we might see traces of the facade Mackenzie and Marriott cultivated in Toronto, and hear their delight as applications began to arrive. Perhaps—it seems plausible—they followed the system Lucas described, replying "on expensive paper heavily embossed, and bearing a coronet." How better to secure confidence before seeking a financial guarantee?[137]

Marriott and Mackenzie's agency suggests a tension between competing aspirations. The cosmopolitan modernity of an "Oriental Film" produced in Vancouver and released in Hollywood contrasts with older and local visions of aristocratic status associated with Mayfair and Irish estates. Both adverts evoke fantasies of social mobility, but is stardom the same as being secretary-companion to an aging countess? While we have often assumed that the Hollywood starlet supplanted the debutante as an icon of fashionable femininity in the 1920s, that does not quite work here. Mackenzie and Marriott were on the make. They were also astute observers of the world they inhabited. Moving between London, Toronto, Los Angeles, and Galway (at least in the realm of the imagination), mediating between everyday life and commercial cultural production, they exploited the distance and complexity of modern mass culture. Gossip columns and fan magazines made the Hollywood starlet and

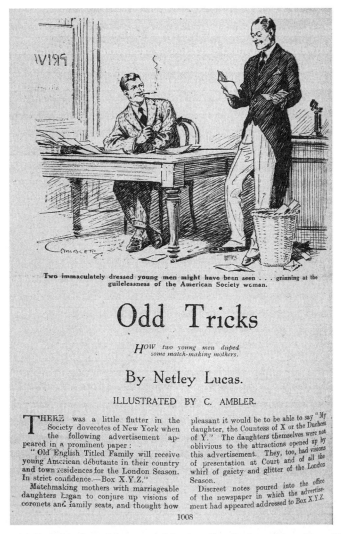

Two immaculately dressed young men might have been seen . . . grinning at the guilelessness of the American Society woman.

Odd Tricks

*H*OW *two young men duped some match-making mothers.*

By Netley Lucas.

ILLUSTRATED BY C. AMBLER.

THERE was a little flutter in the Society dovecotes of New York when the following advertisement appeared in a prominent paper :
" Old English Titled Family will receive young American débutante in their country and town residences for the London Season. In strict confidence.—Box X.Y.Z."
Matchmaking mothers with marriageable daughters began to conjure up visions of coronets and family seats, and thought how pleasant it would be to be able to say "My daughter, the Countess of X or the Duchess of Y." The daughters themselves were not oblivious to the attractions opened up by this advertisement. They, too, had visions of presentation at Court and of all the whirl of gaiety and glitter of the London Season.
Discreet notes poured into the office of the newspaper in which the advertisement had appeared addressed to Box X.Y.Z.

1008

FIGURE 7. Grinning at the guilelessness of the American Society woman. From Netley Lucas, "Odd Tricks," *Detective*, 10 October 1924, 1008. © Time Inc. (UK) Ltd. Published courtesy of Time Inc. (UK) Ltd. and The Bodleian Libraries, The University of Oxford, per. 25612 d. 15, vol. 5, 10 October 1924, 1008.

Society host familiar yet enchanting subjects of aspiration. Marriott and Mackenzie promised guidance and sustenance for those seeking social advancement. They relied on front to secure the confidence of applicants. So did the international film studios that created "stars" like Theda Bara and women like Lady Diana Cooper, daughter of the Duke of Rutland, whose public profile was sustained by the gossip columnist and Society photographer. Marriott and Mackenzie's agency took shape around the point where celebrity cultures and older ideas of aristocratic status converged.[138]

These were the contexts in which Marriott and Mackenzie sought to defraud unwary "seekers of fame and fortune."[139] They took a guarantee of five dollars for forwarding letters to the Countess of Clancarty; from aspiring actors they took twenty-five dollars for "recommending you to film producers."[140] As the fees flowed in, the agency came under scrutiny from immigration officials, who visited the office to inquire how the agency proposed to overcome labor quotas in the United States.[141] Worse followed. When the promises of employment melted away, many correspondents turned to the police. Mackenzie and Marriott were arrested. Questioned at the Sixth Precinct Police Station, they "strenuously objected to being taken into custody," threatening to "report the matter to the British authorities" if they were not released.[142] Bluster did not work, and after a night in cells the men were charged with false pretenses in a police court in Toronto's imposing City Hall.[143] After a week on remand, there was a dramatic revelation when they returned to court: information received from London's Criminal Records Office suggested that Marriott was the convicted criminal Guy Hart; Mackenzie was "known to Scotland Yard by a variety of names, including those of Netley Lucas [and] Robert Clarke."[144] "As a result of the revelation of their characters," observed the *News of the World*, "the men . . . wilted, and confessed to their misdeeds."[145]

The racket's denouement was hurried and unspectacular. The men were offered a thirty-day sentence and deportation in return for pleading guilty; the *Evening Telegram* wryly noted: "If there is anything quicker than Counsel W.B. Horkin's pleas of 'Guilty,' scientists should be given particulars." On leaving the dock, the men "tripped down with evident glee," excited at a lenient sentence and the prospect of returning home.[146] Any pleasure was mutual: their "translation to other shores," remarked the magistrate, "would permanently release a couple of seats in the patrol wagon."[147] Canadian journalists reporting the trial mocked the morality of "Old Land citizens."[148] In Britain, by contrast, this was another chance to rehearse the "amazing career" of "Netley Lucas, the youthful adventurer," and Hart's role in the drugged chauffeur case.[149] For some readers, there was one more revelation: Netley Lucas, George Mackenzie, and "Armstrong Mackenzie . . . the man who was prepared to pay for the defence of Mahon," were the same person.[150] The *World's Pictorial News* elaborated:

Lucas, posing as a wealthy man interested in criminology, approached the editors of various papers and offered to sell the life-story of a certain man then being tried for murder, pretending that he had access to the man in question through the medium of his legal adviser.[151]

All of this was still to come when the trial ended; as far as I can tell, it went unreported in Canada. After a month in the fresh air at Langstaff Jail Farm—the "most marvellous jail I had ever entered"—the men were escorted to Montreal.[152] Mackenzie and Marriott had left for Canada in August, but it was Netley Lucas who disembarked with Marriott at Southampton on 7 November. There was little in the record of their arrival to suggest the circumstances in which they left Canada. That the men still described themselves as journalists suggested they had prospered. Having left the cheap rooming district of Pimlico, they returned to the opulence of the Savoy Hotel.[153]

THE UNMAKING OF THE ENGLISH GENTLEMAN CROOK

Netley Lucas's criminal standing was confirmed in July 1924, when he appeared as case 260 in Supplement A of the *Police Gazette*. Published fortnightly from the 1890s, the supplement contained the records of "Expert and Travelling Criminals." To address the challenges posed by the "aristocrat of crooks," it accumulated and circulated knowledge among police across Britain. That Lucas's lives were abstracted into a numbered case history suggested he had made it as an "expert criminal" and drew attention to the bureaucratic processes through which criminal identities were created. Supplement A called into being the category of criminality it ostensibly sought to suppress.[154]

Case 260 codified Lucas's storytelling into a standardized format. What had bewildered detectives and shopkeepers appeared as numbered paragraphs and ordered blocks of text. Proliferating names were now the aliases of a known criminal, translated as a short description and list of previous convictions. The unruly gentleman crook was contained and categorized. While an anonymous records clerk mistook Lucas's date of birth, the comments entered under "Personal Weaknesses, Peculiarities, etc.," reflected hard-won knowledge: "Smart appearance, cunning, well educated," he was a "clever and troublesome criminal who travels extensively." Rather than a systematic analysis, the section on Lucas's "Method" summarized his different crimes. Details of the colonial outfitters fraud or stealing from Stanley Scott appeared out of sequence, frustrating any coherent sense of chronology. Several offenses were not included. The order of case 260 was precarious—its provisional nature betrayed by frayed edges and contradictions. Reflecting the procedures that emerged with the development of criminalistic science in the late nineteenth century, it included Lucas's fingerprints and photograph, and noted the handwriting specimen held on file. These technologies sought to fix the "truth" of Lucas's identity, but their capacity to do so was limited. In Lucas's mug shot (probably taken in July 1920), he seems insouciant, almost patrician, holding the camera's gaze and immaculate in his fashionable suit. Rather than reliable documentary evidence, the photograph's veracity had to be confirmed by an annotated credential: "The portrait is a good likeness."[155] Above all, case 260 contained the basis of its own unmaking. A final heading "Subsequent history" marked a blank space on the page. The document was incomplete and open-ended, to be elaborated and revised in unanticipated ways by another anonymous clerk at an unknown future date.[156]

Lucas's inclusion in the *Police Gazette* reflected how changing patterns of policing and the elaboration of official knowledge contributed to the confidence trickster's emergence as an archetypal postwar figure. His encounters with the law contributed to the process through which the "aristocrat of crooks" was isolated as an urgent problem. The preoccupations of beat constables, divisional officers, and (after 1920) a specialist unit at Scotland Yard were codified in the pages of Supplement A. Gentlemen crooks were here understood as part of the broader problem of criminal expertise and mobility. In the early 1930s, however, they were increasingly identified as a distinct public threat. Percy Smith had first pitted himself against the "con men" as a young detective after the Great War. When he took charge of what he called the "Confidence Squad" in 1929, he and his colleagues turned their experience into the *Illustrated Circular of Confidence Tricksters and Expert Criminals*.[157] Working with the Criminal Records Office, Smith drew together the "photographs, descriptions, histories and details of the methods of operation of the many hundreds of confidence tricksters known to me personally," compiling "an official Who's Who of that aristocrat of all crooks."[158]

A foreword set out the *Illustrated Circular*'s aim "to furnish police officers with useful information about these criminals and their methods. Its publication, it is hoped, will result in the hindrance of their activities."[159] Like Supplement A, the *Illustrated Circular* sought to suppress a crime by identifying its practitioners, understanding its "methods," and sharing "useful information." In so doing, it redefined how criminal categories were understood and policed. Rather than a subset of "Expert and Travelling Criminals," the confidence trickster was now a discrete problem. When these changes in reporting practices were set against the gentleman crook's deceptions, we can see how understandings of the trick itself were narrowing. The "methods" described included the disbursement of fortune and the "pay off" and other stock exchange frauds. Such elaborate set-piece scams and commercial frauds relied upon "specially prepared documents and printed forms" to secure the confidence of victims. The *Illustrated Circular* included photographs of them: letters of credit and adapted newspaper "stop press" columns. Lucas had stolen checks and corresponded on imposing headed notepaper, but these material cultures of confidence represented a different kind of crime.[160]

The substantive body of the *Illustrated Circular* was an alphabetical index of confidence men (they were all men), including details of their appearance and convictions, and mug shots. Lucas had relied upon his youthful good looks and plausible English gentility. These men were usually older; their appearance suggested a bluff colonial masculinity rather than suave public-school manners; their "charm" was refracted through different codes of class and gender. Men from Australia, New Zealand, Canada, and South Africa were the confidence trick's leading practitioners, observed the foreword. By the mid-1930s the "old type of English trickster has been practically superseded by his Colonial brother, who made his debut here after the war."[161]

To address a crime defined by mobility and distance, the *Illustrated Circular* disseminated information between police in Britain and the empire, Europe, and the United States. It had to be an organic document, revised as the demands of crime changed. A new version, including an updated foreword and list of tricks, was issued in 1935 as officers prepared for the celebration of George V's jubilee.[162] It was reviewed again before George VI's coronation in 1937, when members of the "confidence squad" worked with a "knowledgeable informant" to further their knowledge, and asked foreign and colonial forces to share details of tricksters likely to visit Britain during the celebrations. Reports and mug shots came in from across the world.[163] Overwhelmed by this material, officers gave up and reissued the *Jubilee Circular of International Confidence Tricksters* instead.[164]

Lucas did not appear in any version of the *Illustrated Circular* I have seen. By the 1930s he went under different names, and his energies no longer focused around straightforward crimes of false pretenses. Neither were there any men *like* him in the dossier: the gentleman crook and ersatz aristocrat who were so prominent after the Great War were notable only in their absence from the pages of descriptions. Just as Lucas's later offenses made case 260 anachronistic, so the *Illustrated Circular* displaced the *Police Gazette* supplement. The flamboyant storytelling of Lucas and his like had been integral to the postwar crisis of confidence within which crimes of deception were identified as a pressing operational problem. While the dossier built on that process, it paradoxically excluded those like Lucas from working notions of the confidence man. Rather than document a class of crime, the *Illustrated Circular* redefined it. Lucas was rendered out of time and place. He had become a marginal criminal type, now aligned with the adventuress, his behavior no longer considered that of the genuine confidence man. From the mid-1930s the *Illustrated Circular*'s definition of the trickster continued to narrow. The creation of the Sharepushing and Confidence Trickster Investigation Group in 1935 marked *both* the institutional demarcation of a discrete operational problem *and* the gradual shift of its center of gravity toward commercial fraud and white-collar crime. This process culminated in 1946, when the group was replaced by the Metropolitan and City Police Company Fraud Department. In 1951 Scotland Yard decided to cease updating the *Illustrated Circular*.[165]

To be clear: people did not stop masquerading as gentlemen or Society women. Their exploits drew less attention in the press than they had in the early 1920s, but we can find figures comparable to Lucas and O'Dare throughout the 1930s and beyond. I think two things happened. First, the Met became increasingly confident that intensified surveillance and the effects of economic depression were working to reduce the confidence trick. The 1937 *Report of the Commissioner of Police* noted a "decided falling off in the number of [confidence tricksters] reported," attributing this to the "special provisions made . . . to protect visitors who came to London for the Coronation." While twenty-three cases were reported in 1936, that figure fell to fourteen in 1937, when officers made only two arrests.[166]

That these figures seem so low reflects the second process that took place in the 1930s: Lucas and his like were written out of formal and informal definitions of crimes of confidence. The trajectory of the *Illustrated Circular* was tracked by the reminiscences of police officers. Percy Smith made his name through his work combating the confidence trickster. In retirement he sought to secure that reputation and profit from it. His first memoirs, *Con Man*, appeared in 1938. Returning to the subject, he worked with a ghostwriter on what became *Plutocrats of Crime* (1960). Smith traded on the experience only a long police career could bring: "During the 'twenties' and the 'thirties' . . . I knew every international confidence trickster of any stature, either through personal contact or a Yard dossier."[167] Smith certainly knew Lucas: he arrested him for false pretenses in July 1931, then appeared at the Central Criminal Court two months later to describe his life story. Despite this, Lucas did not appear in *Con Man*. Perhaps this was because he was still alive and Smith was wary of causing offense or inciting a lawsuit. Yet Smith was happy to share details about other tricksters, and it is more plausible that he ignored Lucas because the suave gentleman did not fit the image of the confidence man that was coalescing in the 1930s.

This was an image in which police officers had a great deal invested. Presenting the trickster as a skilled adversary allowed them to affirm their own professional expertise and the image of the skilled modern detective. When Smith described "my fascinating, exciting battle of wits against the 'con men,'" he established the terrain on which ideas of police and policed were defined against each other.[168] Rather than simply being adversaries, the trickster and detective had much in common. Smith understood the organization of crime as part of the reconfiguration of capitalist modes of production: "We live in an age of specialization. That word is one of the most important in the modern business world, and it loses none of its significance in the world of crime." In this Fordist regime, the trickster was "the specialist par excellence." The only response to this "paramount operator" was what Smith called his "life of anti-crime specialization." Smith's career shadowed the development of the "confidence squad" and *Illustrated Circular* in the 1920s and 1930s.[169]

In their memoirs, other retired detectives, like James Berrett and Percy Savage, emphasized the trickster's intelligence and skill, focus on set-piece commercial scams, and the importance of craft rather than charm.[170] Such schemes required specialist knowledge, careful planning, and nerve. So did their detection. "Audacious, ingenious, tenacious—those adjectives exactly describe the successful con man," Smith observed. In doing so, he identified the qualities that characterized a successful detective.[171] This made it difficult to acknowledge, let alone accommodate, the debonair gentleman crook. In London's underworld, Lucas found he was often perceived as effete. Among police officers, too, those who relied on charm to secure credit could seem unworthy adversaries. The status they claimed was emasculating; their offenses seemed petty and their stock-in-trade of good looks and a plausible story dangerously effeminate. In his *Forty Years of Scotland Yard* (1930), Frederick Wensley, who had always presented himself as a tough East End beat copper, relegated the discussion of crimes of confidence to a chapter on female crime. By the 1930s the "aristocrat of criminals" did not masquerade as an aristocrat but secured that status through his aptitude as a crook.[172]

There is one exception. In 1960 Percy Smith revisited his police career in *Plutocrats of Crime*. Excluded from *Con Man*, Lucas reappeared as the central character in chapter 8, "The 'Gentlemen' Tricksters." Over twelve pages Smith set out a detailed account of Lucas's life story. Smith focused on the moment when he met Lucas in 1931, but he ranged more widely, elaborating the account presented to the Central Criminal Court and interweaving Lucas's writing, criminal record, and newspaper reports. Smith could still not accommodate Lucas within the broader structures of *Plutocrats of Crime*. Anomalous and marginal to Smith's definition of the confidence trick, he was isolated within a discrete chapter. Smith was at pains to argue that the "smooth gentleman crook played a smaller part in the 'con' game . . . than many would imagine." Echoing the *Illustrated Circular*, he noted how the "rugged, honest-looking types"—particularly Australians—were the most "skilled operators" in the field. The "plain-talking, open-faced man" could most easily secure the confidence of "strangers." By 1960 the "outward appearance of 'gentlemen'" could be viewed with suspicion rather than deference. If this reflected shifting ideas of class and status, it also reiterated Smith's investment in presenting crimes of confidence as a tough masculine domain. Reflecting on the "surprising" absence of the "smooth gentleman crook," he observed:

> Women are often disappointed when I tell them this. They imagine that "con men" are usually urbane, public school "cards," whose victims are deluded by their social background and impeccable manners. Women forget that many people are put off by excessive smoothness and charm.[173]

Charm and manners were now perceived as a deceptive front, to be approached with suspicion rather than taken at face value.

We might understand this cynicism against the prominence of the gentleman crook after the Great War. When revealed, Lucas's deceptions undermined confidence in the gentlemanly stranger and drew attention to the performative nature of social identities. We might also set it against growing awareness of the "Society racket"—the unease around the permeability of social elites generated by the cash for honors affair and Lucas's and O'Dare's effortful mobilities. We might, finally, see this cynicism as reflecting growing distrust in the establishment after the humiliations of appeasement, the consolidation of British social democracy after the Second World War, and the sense that the gentleman was being displaced from the imaginative center of national life in the New Jerusalem. The redefinition of the confidence trick perhaps anticipated the scandals of the Profumo affair and the barbs of British satirists. When Smith introduced Lucas, he appeared as an anachronism. He was an "impudent young playboy from a good home"—his "confessed" status as a con man was unconvincing; his career "brief" rather than enduring; his impudence out of time rather than of this moment; his deceptions "bizarre" rather than representative. Once the "outstanding example" of the gentleman crook, Lucas was written out of history by someone who had secured his part in it.[174]

Lucas could be complicit in this process. His most sustained reflection on "The Gentleman Crook," published in Cambridge University's literary magazine *Granta* in 1925, was a remarkable exercise in disavowal. Cognizant of his audience, he was in a reassuring mood:

> It is very rare that one meets with what fiction writers are so fond of calling the "Gentleman Crook," because the two characteristics do not harmonise. . . . Immediately a man of good upbringing takes to a life of crime he loses his "caste," and although he may retain all the outward mannerisms and speech of education, he is beyond the pale of the class to which he belongs by birth.

Lucas's lives belied the idea that the gentleman crook only inhabited the realm of fiction: it was a status he often strove to achieve and on which he continued to insist despite his transgressions. While a criminal record might mark the public-school boy as dangerous, neither was it quite the case that Lucas remained "beyond the pale" of the class into which he was born. For long periods of time, he maintained his "caste" through "outward mannerisms and speech"—substantial in effects if superficial in nature. "I am a strong believer in what is called 'nature's gentlemen,'" Lucas claimed, "and a despiser of that class which is called by the innate snobbery of the world 'gentle-folk.'" His attempts to enter Society suggested his snobbery; his revulsion toward fellow Borstal boys sat uneasily against the idea of "nature's gentlemen." In an ostensibly detached analysis of crime, Lucas rewrote his life stories. In this sense, perhaps, the article's final sentence was an implicit statement of intent:

> A man of education who has the brains and enough resourcefulness to be a successful criminal can put these qualities to a more legitimate use, and make quite as good a living as by dishonesty. . . . At least that is the conclusion I have come to.[175]

Regrets about his past? Or the realization that a better future—a good one—might lie ahead?

* 2 *

Selling Selves:
Ghosts and Life Stories

CHAPTER 3

The Ex-crook Who Has
Now Taken Up the Pen

On 11 June 1925, two sisters marry two friends at St. Matthew's Church, a short walk from Westminster Abbey and the Houses of Parliament. The grandeur of central London is very different from the shabby streets of Bethnal Green, where Florence and Elsie Liggins grew up. They no longer live in the East End, having moved with their family to a larger house in the quiet suburbs around Epping Forest. Yet they still work there, helping their parents run a small chain of coffee rooms, including one on Commercial Road, a bustling neighborhood dominated by Jewish shops, warehouses, and manufacturers. At a dance somewhere in London, Florence meets a young man called Richard Dent. A few days later he invites her for tea at the rooms in Westminster Mansions he shares with his friend Leslie Graham, a journalist from a wealthy family, though his father is now dead. Florence brings her sister along for company. That afternoon Leslie falls "head over heels in love," captivated by Elsie's "physical beauty" and "lightning-quick" mind. A week later they meet near her home and he proposes; we do not know what Elsie thinks of Leslie, but she says yes. The wedding of Florence and Dick, and Elsie and Leslie takes place in the church near the men's rooms. Leslie calls it a "red letter day in my life." Their marriage certificate is the public record of an intimate moment of joy, but also a strangely uncertain document. Elsie was born in 1901, but, like Leslie, she gives her age as twenty-one. The following April the couple return to see the parish curate. When they leave, he adds a marginal annotation to the certificate: "For 'Leslie Evelyn Graham' read 'Netley Lucas' otherwise 'Leslie Evelyn Graham.'... For 'Hubert Evelyn Graham' read 'Hubert Evelyn Bernard Lucas' otherwise 'Hubert Evelyn.'"[1]

FIGURE 8. Mr. Netley Lucas, the respectable man of letters. From Netley Lucas, *Criminal Paris* (London: Hurst and Blackett, 1926), frontispiece. Published courtesy of The Random House Group.

INTRODUCTION

Netley Lucas began his 1926 book *Criminal Paris* with a simple thanks. It was "Dedicated to My Wife: Guide, philosopher and friend on the Highway of Honesty."[2] The book marked another step into his burgeoning career as a freelance journalist and writer on crime that had begun with the success of *The Autobiography of a Crook* just over a year earlier. Lucas's wedding to Elsie

Liggins became the redemptive moment at which the emotional rewards of companionate marriage led him away from a disreputable past. Elsie's guidance was timely: by the mid-1920s Lucas had been convicted five times, and served sentences in the West Drayton Remand Home, the training ship *Cornwall*, Rochester Borstal, Wormwood Scrubs and Brixton prisons, and the Langstaff Jail Farm in Ontario. Deported from Canada in the autumn of 1924, he underwent "metamorphosis": the gentlemanly trickster remade himself as one of Britain's best-known "ex-crooks."[3] Turning his disreputable past into a salable commodity, Lucas wrote about crime prolifically. Stories of his life appeared in the *World's Pictorial News*, the *People*, and *Detective* magazine. Firsthand accounts of the underworld sold well in Britain and beyond: the *Autobiography* was followed by *Crooks: Confessions* (1925), *Criminal Paris, London and Its Criminals* (1926), and *Crook Janes* (1926). His "confessions" were serialized in magazines like *Mystery Story*. Periodicals including *Railway Review* published his work; the *Golden* and *Monster* penny comics serialized his dramatic tales of crooks and detectives. Later he wrote a melodramatic novel, *The Red Stranger* (1927), and the *Sunday News* employed him as a "special correspondent" on crime. Lucas had been a "distinguished ornament of the criminal world," but by 1930 the German writer Hans Rudolf Berndorff could note how writing "paved the way to a life of tranquil respectability."[4]

With the metaphor of the highway of honesty, Lucas presented this period of remarkable productivity as a purposeful movement from crime to citizenship. Personal reform took place under the gaze of readers and was staged for their benefit. Ambition and the frontispiece to *Criminal Paris* took Lucas to the Mayfair studio of the well-known photographer Frank Swaine (fig. 8). Having exhibited at the Royal Photographic Society, Swaine photographed aristocrats and army officers as well as public figures like the explorer Ernest Shackleton.[5] Turning his camera on "Mr Netley Lucas," Swaine created a portrait that shows a debonair seated figure who looks reassuringly at the viewer. A tailored suit and neat handkerchief meet the sartorial conventions of gentlemanliness. Here is the handsome man of letters. Reproduced in *Criminal Paris*, the photograph claimed a respectability that was always precarious. Interweaving travelogue and memoir, Lucas recounts the journey undertaken at the invitation of Etienne Gaspard, "one of Europe's cleverest international crooks":

Etienne . . . agreed to act as my cicerone through the human jungle of Paris's underworld. In his company I was able to re-visit haunts which I knew, and visit strange places and meet criminals where a journalist or an ordinary author would have failed utterly. As one of the "profession," but from another country, I was on many occasions an honoured guest.

Lucas switches positions with disorienting speed. Having "given up crime," he is still welcomed by "Paris's cleverest crooks." He conjures up an idea of the "underworld" that exists at the city's heart yet can only be found with an expert guide—a bounded realm of strange places and stranger people. Extricating himself from a world of his making, he remains an insider with privileged access to this "human jungle." No "ordinary author," his "profession" is crime. As Lucas shuttles backward and forward along the highway of honesty, the road speeds his journey but is also a lawless place, the allusion to the highwayman perhaps deliberate. Repudiating and embracing a notorious past, *Criminal Paris* was authenticated by Lucas's status as an ex-crook. Treating Swaine's portrait as documentary evidence of an unlikely journey from Wormwood Scrubs to Bond Street belies how it struggles to contain a disreputable past and respectable present within the same frame.[6]

Placing Lucas's published work against what I know of his personal circumstances and interactions with cultural power brokers, the next three chapters trace how Lucas managed to transform himself into a writer on crime, and suggest the aspirations and anxieties that might have fueled his pursuit of literary success. What did it mean to write as an ex-crook in 1920s Britain? This public identity was both central to Lucas's attempts to rebuild his life and an increasingly common position, freighted with social, cultural, and political significance. Lucas's success was unusual, but exemplified a process through which the transformation of journalism and popular publishing sustained growing demand for inside stories from the underworld. Daniel Defoe's *History of the Remarkable Life of John Sheppard* (1724) and the Newgate novels of the early nineteenth century suggest how such narratives were well established in popular culture. In the 1920s this unruly genre was reinvigorated by the rapid growth of newspapers and specialist periodicals. Personal journalism and competition for readers meant newspapers displayed insatiable appetite for firsthand accounts of crime. As experience became a valued commodity, entrepreneurial ex-crooks found more ways to turn criminality into celebrity, prison into opportunity, and engaged in the apparently necessary work of making sense of a life in crime. In published autobiographies and the pages of the *News of the World*, Netley Lucas, Josephine O'Dare, and others challenged pejorative images of their character, settled scores, and forged a precarious living.

The "true" life story was embedded in an expanding commercial mass culture, new modes of selfhood, and heated debates about the management of crime. For Lucas, the convergence between established traditions of writing about a life in crime and modern consumer markets opened up different possibilities for profit and social mobility, and provided ways of seeing through which to represent his past. The stories Lucas told were shaped by the conventions of popular crime writing and the politics of penal reform. He later presented his "metamorphosis" as a conscious decision to leave the past behind, having realized "that I possessed the real journalistic sense, and . . . was capable of developing it into a valuable asset if only I had the chance."[7] The device of the highway of honesty allowed Lucas to negotiate the tensions between demand for firsthand "revelations" and a growing emphasis on prison as an instrument of reform. His writing had to thrill readers and convince them of its authenticity, alleviate fears he was profiting from notoriety and debasing public morality, and secure his newfound professional status; it had to manage the contradictions between cashing in on his past and convincing readers of his successful reform. Lucas's stories were rooted in firsthand experiences of crime and prison, and, at times, evoked an intimate sense of their psychological and emotional costs. They were also marked by the demands of a commercial market and disciplinary state. Writing as an ex-crook allowed Lucas to rebuild his life after prison: it validated his claims to knowledge and brought the material rewards that allowed him to have his portrait taken by a noted photographer. The highway of honesty was a personal journey, a legitimating device, and a story that gave an ex-crook's writing social and political value.

The ephemeral world of popular life-writing has rarely been taken seriously. Modern scholars and contemporaries have treated such stories as fantasy or formula. Lucas's work has been mined for information but never treated as exemplary of a vibrant genre with its own codes and conventions.[8] Yet his writing allows us to trace the conflicted relationship between the logics of the market and the problems and possibilities of writing as an ex-crook. Following the stories Lucas and others told about their lives, and their interactions with journalists, editors, and publishers, suggests the ways in which ex-crook lives were repackaged, and authenticity effects constructed for public consumption. Just as "press reporting of sensational crime . . . self-consciously adopted hybrid and partially fictionalized representations and market strategies," so writers like Lucas sought to render the sensational life story a "genuine" "human document."[9] His work invites us to explore the commercial practices, social encounters, and narratives through which the crook's interior world was repackaged for public consumption. Uniquely, perhaps, the material around his lives allows us to map how lives became stories, and the volatile politics of 1920s and 1930s life-writing.

If our understanding of these rich sources has been impoverished, then how we think about the relationship between life-writing and understandings of selfhood has been overdetermined by particular elite sources. The literary critic Sharon Marcus notes how "in the 1930s a new form of life-writing, the modernist memoir, began to emphasize inimitable personal details, subjective internal processes, and self-reflexive accounts of the development of perception and expression." This sense of the 1920s and 1930s as a key moment in the interiorization of the modern self is widely shared by historians, sociologists, and philosophers.[10] Crook life stories *were* partly reshaped by and contributed to this reconfiguration of the meanings of selfhood. Like later writers, Lucas sometimes engaged in a process of reflection "in which the outer, the public, the visible, the surface is to be interrogated to see how it expresses, is shaped by or disguises an inner personal truth."[11] Yet his work disrupts this chronological arc—in part, by demonstrating how the task of introspection could animate different literary forms and cultural and commercial goals; in part, by being just as preoccupied with penetrating the social realms of the underworld or prison as with the inner self. Considering the crook life story alongside the introspective memoir suggests the capacious nature of contemporary life-writing and blurs distinctions between elite and popular culture. The contradictions of popular psychology resist easy assumptions about the rise of the psychoanalytic subject.[12]

THE AUTOBIOGRAPHIES OF A CROOK

In 1927 the criminologist John Goodwin argued that Britons had become dangerously obsessed with crime: "We often offer hero worship to some prominent criminal during his trial; and, on his release from prison, we eagerly devour his reminiscences in the Sunday newspapers."[13] Twenty years later, Goodwin's sense of moral topsy-turvydom was echoed when the starstruck Mark Benney tried to explain why he had turned to burglary: "In my boyhood there were a handful of names that meant more to me than the most highly glamorized film-stars and sportsmen. . . . Fred Ford, Cammi Grizzard, Derby Sabine, May Sinclair, Eddie Guerin, Josephine O'Dare—these were underworld characters of picturesque histories and achievements."[14] The "picturesque" criminal was never just a passive subject of a sensational media. Goodwin acknowledged how O'Dare, Guerin, and Sinclair (also known as "Chicago May" Churchill) actively shaped their colorful public identities, selling their stories to newspapers and publishers. Serialized lives of people like the pickpocket George Richards were a staple of periodicals like the *News of the World*; figures like the burglar George Smithson published autobiographies. Empowered as actors in a popular literary marketplace, confessing ex-crooks found opportunities for financial reward as they rebuilt their lives after prison.[15]

To begin with, at least, Lucas followed a well-trodden path when he first sold his story to the *World's Pictorial News*. The crook life stories of the 1920s were the latest iterations of longer traditions of writing about crime and urban lowlife. Criminal (auto)biographies had been ubiquitous since at least the seventeenth century. Trial reports, broadsheets, and gallows speeches enjoyed huge success, titillating and tutoring, reflecting on social and political change, seeking the origins of criminal transgression in their "soul" and circumstances. The authenticity and morality of commodifying criminal lives were recurrent issues, anticipating debates that flared up in the 1920s and 1930s. In the nineteenth century, these unruly traditions existed alongside more explicitly moralizing autobiographical forms, embodying the redemptive power of faith and new penal practices.[16]

While the crook life story was familiar in some ways, Goodwin's comments suggest how it was understood as a cultural form and social problem that was particularly pressing after the Great War. Commentators often rehashed earlier debates, but we should take seriously their sense of dealing with something of its time. Older styles of criminal confession were reworked through new forms of personal journalism and psychological languages of selfhood. Explosive debates over prison reform and the management of crime shaped the stories Lucas told and gave them particular social and political resonance. The crucial difference was scale: Lucas's productivity was sustained by a commercialized print culture that was growing in size, complexity, and ubiquity, and that disrupted the political imperatives of Victorian life-writing. The criminal celebrity of O'Dare or Sinclair echoed but exceeded that of earlier figures like the burglar Charles Peace.[17]

Think about the importance of the term *crook* to Lucas's public persona. He published as the "Ex-Crook who has now taken up the pen"; his first books were the *Autobiography of a Crook* and *Crooks: Confessions*.[18] Originating as a label for the professional criminal in the United States around the 1870s, and carrying older associations with deceit and artifice, *crook* acquired huge currency as a way of thinking about crime in the 1920s.[19] Rather than particular behaviors, it signaled a mediated social identity defined by the intersection between law and consumerism. We might understand the place of the crook in the lexicon of crime against a significant statistical decline in crime around the turn of the twentieth century and a reappraisal of the criminal as a social problem to be managed rather than an apocalyptic threat to state and society.[20]

Bringing the ludic and the disorderly into uneasy relation, *crook* defined the exploits of the gentleman trickster as more entertaining than threatening. It suggested a "pleasure culture of crime" that persisted over the course of the nineteenth century but gained vigor through the burgeoning mass culture of the 1920s and 1930s. The crook play, crook mystery, and crook life story were symptomatic of this process.[21]

The entrepreneurial ex-crook thus found unprecedented opportunities through the changing character of the press and the growing number of specialist periodicals. The development of reading as a leisure pursuit and an expanding literary marketplace created growing demand for inside stories from the criminal underworld. There are no figures for the 1920s, but surveys in the 1930s identified a dramatic growth in newspaper and magazine readership. By 1936 newspaper sales equated to 95 morning papers, 57.5 evening papers, and 130 Sunday papers for every hundred families; leading Sundays like the *News of World* sold over three million copies.[22] The same surveys identified the popularity of crime news among readers. In a Sunday paper "of the more sensational kind," one survey found that "crime and divorce occupied twenty-five columns and sport thirty-five" compared to four columns on "affairs of the nation." Critics often associated crime reporting with sensational titles and working-class readers, but its appeal crossed class boundaries.[23]

This made crime a key battleground in the newspaper circulation wars of the period. "We cannot afford to be beaten on crime news," Lord Northcliffe told the editor of his *Daily Mail*: "We must have more and more exclusives, and every time we get an exclusive we must tell the public so in the story—and tell them again the next day, and the next day after that, too. Crime exclusives are noticed by the public more than any other sort of news."[24] These imperatives were reflected in the prominence given to dramatic accounts of trials and investigations, and the testimonies of participants. Competing ferociously for a scoop, newspapers made first-person revelations increasingly valuable. Acquitted of poisoning her husband in 1928, Beatrice Pace sold her story to the *Sunday Express* for three thousand pounds and fielded offers to write a play about her life.[25]

The editor of *John Bull*, Charles Pilley, thus described crime and mystery as the "very stuff of journalism." The subject's importance demanded that journalists improve their grasp of "elementary legal principles" so they could turn "crude amateurish reporting" into the "finished descriptive sketch, correct to the last detail." If this was an argument for professional specialism, it also enhanced the value of the ex-crook's knowledge.[26] Like retired police officers, they became "entrepreneurs of experience," making money in return for "authentic" stories of a life in crime.[27] *Sovereign* magazine introduced readers to "Netley Lucas, until recently one of the most notorious criminals in the underworld," who had now "taken to the pen as a means of livelihood." While Lucas's story "Vanity's Consequence" suggested "a writer of no mean merit," success required more than literary "merit."[28] Countless others profited from their notoriety in the 1920s. Most never achieved more than fleeting celebrity, however, while Lucas lived off the pen for much of his adult life. What made him different? You might have some sense of his ambition and energy. His background and education provided access to elite social networks and cultural power brokers from which most offenders—typically unskilled and uneducated—were excluded. Often trading on his unusual biography, he wrote about a world of petty crime and violence but distanced himself from it. The gentleman crook was both less threatening and more glamorous.

Lucas's metamorphosis began through more prosaic social connections. Released from Borstal in 1922, he was mentored by Stanley Scott, an "old friend of my family, a well-known Fleet Street journalist who had taken an interest in me."[29] Scott devoted much of his career to writing about crime. His interest in Lucas might have been philanthropic and paternal, but also suggested he knew the opportunities their relationship could bring. As Scott's secretary, Lucas "prov[ed] himself a hard, capable worker."[30] He gathered material for Scott's reports on criminal cases: covering Edith Thompson and Freddy Bywaters's trial for the *People* in 1922–23, Lucas interviewed Thompson's parents.[31] Through an acquaintance, he secured "rights in some amazing prison stuff from an ex-convict" that was published under Scott's name as *The Human Side of Crook and Convict Life* (1924).[32] Encouraged by Scott, Lucas began to write for publication: the anonymous "Confessions of a Motor Car Bandit" was published in the *People*; an account of "my own amazing experiences" appeared under his byline in the *World's Pictorial News* in 1922 (fig. 9).[33]

Lucas's first steps down the highway of honesty were abortive, but this gave him a chance to leave crime behind. Working with Scott "taught me the rudiments of journalism."[34] Building personal connections with editors, journalists, and publishers, he "made many friends in the literary world."[35] He worked with the publishers Hurst and Blackett, and staff at the *People* and *Pearson's*. All later published his work or, in the case of the *Sunday News*, employed him as a correspondent. When Lucas returned to journalism in 1924, "I had not forgotten the coaching I had received from Stanley Scott, so I went along to the Amalgamated Press and saw the Editor of the *Detective Magazine*."[36] Edited by the "crime aficionado" George Dilnot, the *Detective* was Britain's first specialist crime magazine, offering a mix of fiction, criminology, and "reminiscences

SUNDAY.   **The People.**   JULY 1, 1923.

PUBLIC SCHOOLBOY'S OWN STORY OF EXPLOITS AS A CROOK.

POSED AS PEER IN AMAZING FRAUDS.

An innocent boyish face, fair hair brushed back from his forehead, the drawling accent of the spoilt son of an aristocrat, a frank disarming smile—these were the distinguishing characteristics of Netley Evelyn Lucas, aged 20, who was sentenced to 12 months in the second division at the Old Bailey by the Recorder (Sir E. Wild) on charges of forgery and house-breaking.

Smartly dressed and dapper, he looked singularly out of place in the dock. Yet he admitted his guilt of a string of offences which few older criminals could equal either in number, ingenuity, or in sheer audacity.

NETLEY EVELYN LUCAS.

Lucas, a former public schoolboy, whom Borstal treatment failed to cure of his mania for crime, pleaded guilty to thefts of articles worth some £300, and asked that other charges outstanding should be taken into consideration. He put forward the plea that he had been influenced by a man he had met in prison.

Such, in brief, is the story of Lucas's first appearance at the Old Bailey, but behind it is perhaps the most astonishing "crook" career ever brought to light.

Since his detention by the police this remarkable youth whiled away the monotony of awaiting his trial by writing the full details of his amazing escapades.

I had a pony of my own and used to ride about quite a lot, attended by a groom.

It was just after I had sat at Westminster Hall for the examination for the R.N. College, Osborne, that I ran away to see " life."

Although I had failed at the examination, I had had a glorious holiday in London, staying with a distant relation, a society widow.

I did not relish returning to school at all, so when I was put into the train at St. Pancras for Bedford I got out at Kentish Town.

I floated round London in and out of various jobs, and then decided to don the uniform of a naval midshipman and to masquerade. Life then became one long round of pleasure for me.

A Gay Life.

dozens of silk shirts and other underwear.

The value of my outfit exceeded £500. Not bad for a morning's work !

FIGURE 9. The autobiographies of a crook. From "Public Schoolboy's Own Story of Exploits as a Crook," *People*, 1 July 1923, 7. © Mirrorpix.com. Published courtesy of Mirrorpix.com and The British Library Board.

by leading detectives and specialists" for sevenpence.[37] Knowing Dilnot and the magazine brought Lucas a contract for a long series of articles on crime and prison. "Sidelights on Crime," for example, thrilled readers with "firsthand information on 'smashers,' 'drummers,' 'whizzers,' and other things."[38] Working with Scott, Lucas recalled, "I was gradually being turned into a trained journalist." He betrayed Scott's trust, but was always grateful to the man he called "my benefactor."[39]

Contrast this to the difficulties facing other ex-crooks trying to sell their stories. The uncertainties of a trial and leaving prison meant many were overwhelmed by predatory journalists after a scoop. Even the more savvy struggled if they did not understand how newspapers worked. Charles Hellier, O'Dare's lover, first sent a manuscript to *John Bull*. It was rejected—editors were unconvinced of its veracity—so Hellier turned to Glasgow's *Weekly Record* and added "a synopsis of the fraudulent career of Josephine."[40] O'Dare drew on connections she had established as a Society beauty. In 1926 she addressed her rumored bankruptcy in an interview with *Reynolds's*; on remand a year later, she again approached W. R. Davidson and T. H. Carter, the paper's news editor and manager, offering her life story and letters. In prison and relying on her brother as an intermediary, she struggled to negotiate on her own behalf and received little of the money *Reynolds's* paid for her reminiscences. The ex-crook was usually a vulnerable party in an unequal and exploitative relationship, whose ability to secure anything more than short-term profit was limited.[41]

Lucas first sketched his life story in the *World's Pictorial News* in 1922, returning to it throughout his career so that the stories accreted in layers.[42] An expanded version was published by T. Fisher Unwin as *The Autobiography of a Crook* (1924). Lucas had worked sporadically as a journalist for two years, but the book marked the beginning of his greatest success as a writer. Advertised and reviewed widely in Britain, the empire, and the United States, the *Autobiography* was hailed by the *Daily Mail* as "a study in the real psychology of the criminal of the upper classes."[43] Such comments highlight the proposition around which Lucas's writing took shape: firsthand experience gave him privileged knowledge of Britain's criminal underworld and justice system.

> I was still Netley Lucas—but demobilised from the army of crime—and in consequence privileged to put the prefix "ex" before the word "crook." . . . As a writer I was established in Fleet Street and crime was forgotten as an active part of my life. My knowledge of the underworld . . . [was] becoming a gold mine for journalistic purposes.[44]

Rather than social stigma, a criminal past was now a commercial asset. Seizing this opportunity and "trading" on his notoriety, Lucas went into overdrive. He wrote six books in three years, all published with reputable firms like Hurst and Blackett, Stanley Paul, and Williams and Norgate. Firsthand knowledge was an exciting prospect for publishers; its prominence in adverts suggests it was also attractive to readers. Hurst and Blackett included *Crooks: Confessions* among the "important new books" in its autumn list, heralding the work of a "self-confessed criminal" who was "narrating his personal experiences in burglary, forgery, rum-running [and] dope dealing."[45] I cannot tell how many copies sold, but the ease with which Lucas found publishers, the speed with which his books went into second editions, and their cheapness provide evidence of their popularity. The *Autobiography* cost only five shillings in Britain.[46]

This success indicates Lucas's intuitive grasp of the demands of commercial publishing. He initially benefited from Scott's tutelage but had destroyed their relationship well before the *Autobiography* appeared. Lucas often dealt with editors and publishers himself. Sometimes he worked with the literary agent Robert Somerville. Lucas used Somerville's offices as a correspondence address.[47] The agent had the idea for *Criminal Paris* and advanced Lucas fifty pounds to visit the city. It might have been Somerville who ensured that Lucas's work was reprinted in the United States: *Criminal Paris* was serialized in Hearst newspapers like the *Oakland Tribune*.[48] The *Autobiography* was published by the Dial Press in 1925; George H. Doran published editions of *Crooks: Confessions* (1925) and *Criminal Paris* (1926); J. H. Sears reprinted *Crook Janes* as *Ladies of the Underworld* (1927).[49] Perhaps this is why Somerville would "always have my gratitude as being the man who assisted me in the very early days of my writing career."[50]

Lucas might also have used the mediating structures that developed to support aspiring writers in the 1920s. Looking for an experienced collaborator for the *Autobiography*, he sought advice from Max Pemberton's School of Journalism. He did not participate in the popular writers' circles, but sometimes echoed their emphasis on sincerity of style and subject.[51] In placing his work, he might have consulted the annual *What Editors and Publishers Want*, which described the demands of newspapers, periodicals, and publishers, and advised writers how to manage their work. The 1924 volume included twenty-five of the titles in which Lucas published: the *Detective* had "fair scope for O[outside] C[ontributor] who can write good matter"; *Union Jack* looked for "long complete detective stories dealing with one central character." Such knowledge was commonplace to experienced agents, but the manual allowed budding writers to bypass the literary market's established gatekeepers.[52]

Lucas also exploited the voracious demand created by the vibrant and expanding periodical sector. Commentators like Philip Harrison, editor of the *Writer*, were confident that the ambitious writer "has a score of markets open to him for any single article he writes. If one editor rejects his article, our freelance simply fires it at another." Lucas found to his benefit that the "duplication of markets" meant it was "possible to write half a dozen articles based on the same idea, but treated . . . in widely different ways."[53] New titles like the *Detective* reflected the "genre-fication of mass market fiction" and provided a ready market. Hutchinson's *Mystery Story* was the most popular fiction magazine in Britain until it folded in 1927. For a shilling, readers were offered stories of crime and mystery, including the serialized "Criminal Paris."[54] Yet crime's value went beyond specialist periodicals. In *Cycling* Lucas described how bicycles were stolen and encouraged readers to "invent your own secret device—an invisible one if possible, as standard 'thief-proof' locks soon become known to crooks."[55] A piece on "Prison Libraries" in *Library World* challenged the "popular fallacy" that all the books were "goody-goody." Reading was vital to the everyday life of prisoners, Lucas argued, and their preferences "make an interesting study, both to the psychologist and the bibliophile." E. Philips Oppenheim's popularity reflected desires for escape: "It is possible to merge oneself into a book so much as to forget even the uncongenial atmosphere of a prison cell, for I have done it myself."[56]

Lucas's savvy approach to freelancing crystallized in his entry in *Who's Who in Literature* (1927):

> *Dy Mail, New York, Ideas, People, Star, World, New York American, Star, People, Sun. Chron., World's Pictorial News, Pearson's Mag., Sovereign Mag., Detective Mag., Mystery Story Mag., Popular Mag., Action Stories Mag., Glas. Wkly Rec., Birmingham Mail, Yorkshire Even. Post, South Wales Echo, Bristol Times and Mirror, Ideas, Union Jack, Competitors Jl., Everybody's Weekly, Humanist, Police Rev., Popular Science Siftings, Library World, Railway Review, Hotel Review, Motor Cycle, Motor Boat, Cycling, Motor Transport, Granta, Writer, Wireless, Car Topics.*[57]

We might read this as an index of the growth and specialization of commercial publishing, and Lucas's remarkable success. His life stories appeared in national and local newspapers; he wrote for genre periodicals, but found a lucrative niche analyzing crime for specialist magazines like *Cycling* and general-interest periodicals like *Ideas*. Reworking the "same idea," he turned firsthand knowledge into entertainment and education, and blurred putative boundaries between popular and middlebrow publishing. How many writers—let alone ex-crooks—confessed for the *World's Pictorial News* while writing for *Granta* or the *Humanist*?[58] This was a competitive market: very few freelancers published in a national daily; while writing was "a well-trodden career path for energetic people without elite backgrounds," even in the 1920s most authors were men "from a professional or merchant family who had been educated at a public school and then Oxford or Cambridge." Lucas was energetic and educated, but his chaotic past made him an unusual candidate for literary success, just as his background made him an unusual ex-crook. A criminal record provided the marginality that created the valued effects of authenticity, but it was social privilege that meant he could exploit that demand.[59]

Journalistic success was hard-won, but increasingly remunerative. It is hard to know how much Lucas earned in the mid-1920s: few newspaper archives survive, and he was strangely reticent about money. There are hints: £30 from the *People* for reporting on the Thompson-Bywaters case; £50 for the first six

Detective articles; £300 for book and serial rights to *Criminal Paris*.[60] I do not think Lucas was as alluring as O'Dare, but his life stories might have been worth something approaching the £150 and £800 *Reynolds's* and the *People* paid her. Having established their reputation and contacts, even ordinary writers who do "regular work for a number of newspapers" could earn up to £20 a week. The speed at which Lucas wrote suggests he was in that position by 1926.[61]

Lucas later parlayed financial success into geographical mobility. Over the winter of 1924–25, Lucas and Guy Hart struggled to find work: "gloriously broke," they lived in a "meagerly furnished room in a Chelsea slum." The *Autobiography* heralded a new phase: "As our fortunes improved, so did our mode of living and we . . . moved camp . . . to Westminster Mansions."[62] Writing brought money, a prestigious address, and something approaching status. In the 1920s *Pearson's* remained a benchmark for quality middlebrow publishing. In September 1925 it included Lucas's short story "The Convict's Prayer" alongside a story by Sapper and E. M. Hull's best-selling "The Sons of the Sheik." The literary company suggests the upward social mobility visualized in the photograph of "Mr Netley Lucas."[63] Yet the ex-crook's position within the structures of class and professional identity shaping authorship was uncertain. An entry in *Who's Who in Literature* was a measure of success, but perhaps also reflected Lucas's desire for acceptance and respectability.

Renown could cause problems as well. By 1926 Lucas was prominent enough that Victor Carasov gave "false names including that of a writer of books and articles relating to criminology" when he was arrested for armed robbery.[64] Newspapers reported the moment he confronted a detective in a stockbroker's office like a scene from a Hollywood gangster film: "Netley produced a revolver . . . shouting 'Hands up. The game is up.'"[65] The sensation threatened Lucas's newfound success: he wrote to police in Harrogate to distance himself from the offense.[66] Fifty years later, Carasov described this as a case of mistaken identity: he was "puzzled" when officers confused him with the man he anonymized as "Mr Thomas X," but realized it "could serve my purpose."[67] Carasov claimed he eventually admitted his name, but in court, detectives stated that "inquiries showed that Netley Lucas . . . was not his name, Mr Lucas being in France."[68] Mindful of the "considerable publicity" given to "Lucas's" arrest, they "asked that, in fairness, equal publicity be given to the fact that the prisoner was not Netley Lucas" and "that what appeared in the papers regarding the man's career was not furnished by the police."[69] Lucas also wrote to Carasov while he was on remand: "Thanks for disassociating yourself from my name . . . [and] for a kind of honesty very unusual in cases like yours." Carasov declined the offer of help, and "from that day to this, I've never heard of or from Mr X."[70] That he could be impersonated by a petty criminal was ironic confirmation of Lucas's prominence in the mid-1920s. His reputation secured, Lucas found a chance for self-promotion: he told journalists he was in Paris "at work on a novel which is to be called 'Madame Murder of Monte Carlo.'"[71]

VERISIMILITUDE

Lucas's writing had long prehistories in the low-life literatures of the eighteenth and nineteenth centuries. In the 1920s, however, the expansion of commercial publishing and journalism made many observers concerned that the number and nature of crook life stories were spiraling out of control. By 1935 the seasoned journalist Sydney Moseley could reflect: "Crime may be less profitable, but confession is a positive gold mine." Confession was a "talismanic word. . . . It pairs with 'revelations.' It lures the reader with the hope of 'true facts' and 'inside stories.' He is still greedily capable of believing that these 'confessions' will be 'sensational'" instead of cautious, inadequate, and hypocritical."[72] Cynical and antagonistic, Moseley nonetheless recognized the recurrent motifs of revelation and truth that framed the work of Lucas and his like. Just as personal journalism became increasingly preoccupied with "the emotions of private life," so life stories took shape around the confessional movements between inside and outside.[73] Exercised by the apparent obsession with revealing hidden worlds for "monetary gain," the *Saturday Review* commented: "The whole of the 'stunt' Press . . . has . . . become one vast whispering gallery. Secret Histories of the Week, Society from the Inside, What the Butler Overheard, Prison Revelations—this is the kind of stuff with which the public has been fed."[74] Writers like Lucas collapsed descriptions of crime or prison "from the inside" into accounts of private lives that emphasized interior realms of emotion and thought. In the United States the development of journalistic practices "geared toward the exposure of the 'real selves'" behind what were understood as deceptive public masks reflected the growing influence of psychoanalytic understandings of the self-within.[75] In Britain the interview or life story was just as likely to focus on the social realm. Writing as an ex-crook promised a tantalizing "encounter with biographical reality" that was simultaneously social and subjective.[76]

Moseley's criticisms suggest the demands of this process. For Lucas, the most pressing challenge was to tell stories that were both exciting and credible. As the life story grew in value, writers, editors, and publishers sought to secure the effects of authenticity for firsthand accounts of crime. "Truth" was a "marketing ploy"—"a label, an adjective to mark . . . stories as popular constructions free of the deceits of artifice." It could never just be a label, however: the illusion of "truth" had to be meticulously constructed. Transforming the sensational life story into a factual "human document" required care, and was not always easy for writers of limited education and dubious honesty.[77] Ironically, that process often meant reworking devices that had been clichéd in the work of low-life writers since the eighteenth century. One starting point was to define "truth" against public ignorance. *Crooks: Confessions* confronted readers with their inability to know those who "live their lives apart, in a world which you could never penetrate, in a world the language of which you would not understand." Imagining the underworld as alien and bounded made Lucas a privileged and necessary interpreter.[78]

Recounting the "truth" also allowed writers to protect their reputation. This was less pressing for Lucas: newspapers damned his honesty but never systematically dismantled his character. Josephine O'Dare, by contrast, was widely portrayed as an immoral adventuress. In the spring of 1926, she was exposed as a criminal vamp in Hellier's *Weekly Record* articles.[79] A year later, acquaintances cashed in at her moment of notoriety: "My Partnership with Josephine O'Dare" by Guy Hart in the *World's Pictorial News*; Maisie Chilton, O'Dare's maid, sold her story to Glasgow's *Weekly News*; George Poole, her butler, was interviewed by the *Evening News*; Lucas described "The Country Girl Who Duped Mayfair" in the *Sunday News*; "My Life and My Lovers" appeared under O'Dare's name in *Reynolds's*.[80]

When O'Dare sold her "exclusive" to the *People* after leaving prison in 1930, it was partly to reassert control over her reputation: "I shall refute the lying vicious stories which those who could profit from it . . . chose to circulate about me after I had been sent to prison."[81] "Frank and truthful," O'Dare admitted her ambition and the deceptions to which this had led. Yet she refuted allegations of immorality and blackmail that dominated earlier versions of her life. Reasserting her own morality gave O'Dare the basis for a damning attack on Society's hypocrisy: "I have been very unconventional . . . but no more unconventional than the 'Bright Young Things' of today," she claimed, and there was "more harm going on behind the screen of convention and respectability . . . than I was ever guilty of in my wildest flights of unconventionality."[82] Echoing the satirical barbs of Evelyn Waugh's *Vile Bodies* (1930), this aligned O'Dare with the respectable reader, embracing yet repudiating Society and its excesses. She countered newspaper descriptions of her as a heartless schemer: "I know dozens of Society women who have spent their whole lives scheming without any results beyond eking out the barest existence, scarcely keeping their heads above water." Sympathetic to the new poor's "desperate straits," she was, nonetheless, damning of their immorality, corruption, and abuse of privilege.[83]

The authentic "human document" was underpinned by the mediating processes through which lives became stories. Lucas's negotiations with publishers and editors have left no archival trace, but it is plausible that they resembled O'Dare's dealings with *Reynolds's*. Their signed contract promised exclusive rights to her life story and guaranteed its veracity—important for newspapers negotiating with unknown writers of dubious honesty.[84] As part of his "arrangements" with the *Weekly Record*, Hellier "produced a document shewing he was a convict on licence." A ticket-of-leave was material evidence of Hellier's criminality. Confirming the "truth" of his writing, it now carried pecuniary reward rather than stigma.[85]

These original documents convinced editors of the value of a manuscript and indemnified them against the risk of financial loss. Reproduced in print, they became part of the paratextual apparatus that sought to mobilize the confidence of readers. Lucas's reminiscences in the *People* were published above a facsimile of his signature, authorizing and individuating a story that was in many respects generic.[86] Echoing the ways in which earlier marginal writers had established their bona fides, T. Fisher Unwin solicited an endorsement for the *Autobiography* from the prison chaplain, Eustace Jervis. "I have been asked to write a foreword to the life-story of Netley Lucas," Jervis noted, "as it contains statements so strange that people may doubt . . . whether such a person exists." The moral rectitude associated with Jervis's religious faith and the firsthand knowledge he possessed from having known Lucas since 1917 defused potential unease about the book's veracity.[87] Lucas's "extraordinary life-story," noted the *Daily Mail*, "could never have been taken for anything but the wildest of fiction had not the real existence of the author been vouched for."[88]

O'Dare's "intimate revelations" were also comprehensive in the "devices of authentication" that gave them the status of truth.[89] Alongside photographs from her personal album, *Reynolds's* reproduced O'Dare's scrapbook ephemera, including invitations to her infamous Mannequin Parade and extracts from "love-letters written to her by suitors in all grades of society."[90] In the *People*, O'Dare appealed to "documentary evidence which cannot be gainsaid" to support her claims; printed asides affirmed the "originals are in the possession of the editor." Experience became truth through the elaborate material practices in which authenticity was located.[91]

Moseley's withering comments on "confession" and "revelation" suggest how Lucas's writing was also shaped by a countervailing emphasis on the pleasures of crime. To read his work is often to meet someone at the center of a transnational criminal underworld, who knew the most notorious blackmailers and forgers. The rewards of commercial publishing pushed storytellers toward sensation and, perhaps, exaggeration. In the *World's Pictorial News*, Lucas was complicit in the paper's attempts to present him as a "human document unique and outstanding." The story of a public-school boy turned crook was "unequalled for sheer audacity"; the heartbreak of a broken family was tempered by the excitement of daring exploits and close shaves with the law.[92] Lucas delighted in his "most audacious fraud" on the colonial outfitters in 1920. Despite "pangs of remorse," he concluded, "I do feel rather proud of this—my supreme fraud . . . of my own conception, and probably without precedent in the annals of fraud." In this guise, confession offered a pathway toward financial reward rather than religious redemption.[93]

It is easy to be skeptical about Lucas's claims. Paradoxically, what we might see as the life story's excesses worked to confirm its authenticity. The furore around the cocaine-related deaths of Billie Carleton and Freda Kempton made the Chinese playboy Brilliant Chang an ever-present figure in confessional journalism in the 1920s. Lucas identified him as the "King of the Drug Traffickers" and "one of the few men whom I feared."[94] Lucas might have known Chang, of course, but that is not really the point: the conventions of popular crime writing meant readers *expected* to meet such notorious figures. Chang's appearance implicitly endorsed the ex-crook's veracity. Lucas's *London and Its Criminals* (1926) took as its starting point "the seven years in which I lived entirely by my wits [when] I visited practically every haunt of any special interest."[95] On this basis he promised to share "inside knowledge—not only of the criminal himself, but of his secret haunts, his manner of living and the means of that livelihood he derives from preying upon his fellow creatures."[96]

Such claims to originality were offset by an account many readers would have recognized. In Limehouse, Lucas witnessed a meeting of a Chinese tong. In prison he spent time with the Emir of Kurdistan. An enigmatic dedication offered the book "to Chief-Constable Wensley of Scotland Yard, in memory of an incident which he perhaps forgets but which I shall always remember."[97] I cannot tell what Lucas is talking about from official records or his writing. He does not obviously appear in Wensley's memoirs; John Long's *Crime from the Inside* (1933) suggested Wensley was "directing a special campaign against confidence tricksters, blackmailers, jewel thieves and others" around the time Lucas was arrested in 1923, so they might have met.[98] Yet the detective was annoyed by the "effrontery" of a dedication made "without [his] consent, or even . . . knowledge." Objecting "to the association of his name with that of a man like Netley Lucas," Wensley distanced himself from the book in an interview with the *Daily Sketch*, then pasted the article into his scrapbook of cuttings.[99] The paratextual appearance of Wensley, one of Scotland Yard's renowned "Big Four," nonetheless confirmed the "truth" of *London and Its Criminals*. The stylizations of the crook life story remind us that authenticity was an illusion rooted in convention.[100]

Lucas's writing was braced by the tensions between revelation and realism. Adverts describing *Crooks: Confessions* as an "authentic picture" were unsettled by praise for its "highly dramatic chapters."[101] Retelling the theft of Gaby Deslys's pearls, the *Aberdeen Journal* welcomed "true life stories" with the "merit of having a 'kick' in them." At best, such reviews tacitly acknowledged the "truth" of his writing; at worst, they were complicit in the devices through which authenticity effects were secured and confidence engaged.[102] There was always knowingness around the generic clichés of crime writing. Having read Hellier's life story, Inspector Yandell noted that his claim to have met O'Dare on a transatlantic liner "cannot be taken seriously," as she did not leave Hereford until 1921. O'Dare and Hart's visit to Canada was a "tonic to the imagination," and Hellier "lost no time in embellishing in his most entertaining style, the undoubtedly interesting reminiscences of his two former confederates."[103] At least some reviewers questioned the "truth" of Lucas's lives, but he usually managed to sustain the illusion of authenticity. The "startling revelations" of *Criminal Paris*, thought the *Bookman*, "breathe the stark, naked reality of truth," making it a "valuable fact document for the sociologist, criminologist and physician."[104]

As Lucas piled on the detail, claimed acquaintance with the famous and infamous, and set out an elaborate paratextual apparatus, he looked outward. To secure the status of "truth," his writing reworked older literary devices and interwove them with contemporary social worlds and cultural forms. This process was furthered by his tentative engagement with a growing emphasis on exploring the self-within. At the same time as Lucas subjected the underworld to public scrutiny, he also registered the emotional and affective experience of crime and prison. In the *Humanist* he reflected on the anguish prompted by being alone in the "cells in the silent watches of the night." It was then he had witnessed the "haunted look of acute mental suffering and shame" in the eyes of men in prison for the first time.[105] Elsewhere, Lucas turned the psychological gaze onto himself. Painful personal reflections gestured toward that "interiorised subjectivity, [that] sense of the self-within," which was "formalised" by 1920.[106] The *Autobiography* found the origins of his criminality in the youthful "struggle between heredity and environment" that shaped his "personality." Lucas was hesitant—"dimly groping in my ignorance of my own psychology"—but his work exemplified forms of popular life-writing in which revealing hidden social worlds and the unconscious bled together.[107]

When compared to writing in the United States, Lucas's writing underscores the limited resonance of psychoanalytic ideas in British popular psychology. The "psychoanalytic craze" and Pelmanism's guidance on harnessing the power of the unconscious featured regularly in the newspapers he wrote for. Unease about the perils of excessive introspection and the sexualized nature of Freudian thought meant psychological techniques were more often linked to self-improvement than sustained critical analysis. Criminologists could be proselytizing in their Freudianism, but the ex-crook's reflexiveness was more complex.[108] Lucas's *Autobiography* echoed Cyril Burt's "modified environmental approach," emphasizing the "psychological conditions obtaining in the home and family" and envisaging the mind "in constant dynamic interaction with its environment."[109] Above all, the process of reflecting upon the self-within was unsustained. Lucas could simply deny the possibility of psychological self-understanding: "I have given up speculating on why I was thus mentally constituted. Criminologists, disciples of Freud, dabblers in the latest fashionable 'isms' and 'ologies,' may be able to supply an answer. For my part, I can only say, like poor ignorant Topsy in *Uncle Tom's Cabin*: 'I 'spect I growed that way.'"[110]

THE HIGHWAY OF HONESTY

In July 1922 Lucas began "Four Years of My Life" in the *World's Pictorial News* with a disclaimer: "I am not now proud of these exploits, and perhaps their publication will prevent other young men taking a course which was so disastrous to me."[111] The ersatz morality of the crook life story was grounded in the politics of mass culture. It was never enough for writers like Lucas to disavow the pleasures of crime or wrap their accounts of stealing cars in the hope that they would serve as a public good. Perfunctory framing devices like this addressed growing disquiet over the effects of glamorizing crime and the morality of providing for the continued wages of sin while allowing editors to justify scandal and sensation.

Writing as an ex-crook was a lucrative exercise, but it also had huge social and political significance after the Great War. Although his literary efforts were called into being by the imperatives of the market, Lucas was still required to engage with the disciplinary apparatus of the state and, in particular, the reformist project of contemporary penal policy. From the late nineteenth century, crime became the focus of systematic surveillance and social management. No longer an apocalyptic threat to national stability, the criminal was now a societal failing to be redressed. Decarceration and the development of alternative institutional mechanisms—shorter sentences, probation, separation of the juvenile offender, and new programs of education and training—isolated the criminal as the subject of regimes of discipline and reform. The result was a new emphasis on restoring offenders to the full responsibilities of adult citizenship.[112] Lucas was drawn into the modernizing agencies of prison, the Probation Service, Borstal, and the Central Aftercare Association: through hard work, education, and moral guidance, the offender was to be remade as a productive citizen who could return to the community. When Lucas was released from prison, this personal experience made him well placed to engage in debates prompted by the accelerating pace of prison reform.[113]

This meant Lucas never wrote in isolation. In the nineteenth century, prison autobiographies were often narratives of spiritual awakening and repentance elicited by visitors and chaplains and providing vital evidence of the effectiveness of prison.[114] There were residual traces of these imperatives in Lucas's writing, but by the 1920s they were complicated by the need to address generic expectations associated with reinvigorated pleasure cultures of crime.[115] As Lucas negotiated his criminal past, he addressed demands for retelling and reform that could be irreconcilable. *Criminal Paris* underscores how his writing oscillated between distance and closeness, emphasizing the success with which he had been reformed while celebrating his transgressions. Simultaneously, he sought to give his writing moral legitimacy while falling back on the experiential knowledge only his criminal past could provide. This precarious balancing act provided authority to talk about crime and to voice a critical inside perspective on Britain's penal system.

The highway of honesty thus reflected renewed emphasis on reform and rehabilitation within the criminal justice system, addressed concerns that notoriety could be rewarded, and, perhaps, crystallized Lucas's wish to remake his life. Victorian evangelicals had imagined writing as a process of painful contemplation through which the criminal might achieve "metamorphosis." That was not how Lucas understood the relationship between writing and reform. Instead, he emphasized the material rewards writing might bring. When Lucas submitted articles to newspapers, his agent included a "covering letter requesting sympathetic consideration . . . [as] the effort of a man 'trying to make good.'"[116] Just as Somerville's gloss presented writing as a personal and public good, so the *Autobiography* was "dedicated to those who buy this book, thereby giving the author a chance to start afresh." Having served his sentence, Lucas had atoned for his crimes and deserved public trust. Once he had done just enough to show that his crimes were in the past—identifying himself as an ex-crook rather than demonstrating his personal reinvention—the success of Lucas's efforts to "make good" was devolved upon those who might buy his work. In this benevolent economy of virtuous consumerism, readers were encouraged to take responsibility for reform of the criminal. In return, their interest in sensational crime stories was justified.[117]

At times Lucas wove these themes into a progressive narrative of reform. The *Autobiography* presented his 1923 conviction at the Old Bailey as a shocking moment of realization. "More utterly ashamed than I could find words to express," the penitent narrator asked: "Where was the glamour of a crook life; the false gods which I had so long worshipped?" Reworking conversion narratives of the nineteenth century, Lucas presented prison as a period of psychological and physical transformation that "strengthens my resolution to make a clean start in a new country." Here Lucas attributed his decision to begin afresh to the painful self-scrutiny that confinement made necessary.[118] He offered different explanations of that decision, however. Making a clean start could be a reaction to the inevitability of punishment. Gesturing toward ideas of shell shock that emerged during the Great War, he described the "strain . . . on the nerves" caused by a "life of perpetual suspense." Bitter experience meant he knew that the "fear of arrest is always there, hanging over one like a dark cloud . . . taking the essence even from those pleasures which the spoils might buy." In contrast to the suffering of victims of modern war, self-inflicted suffering could be remedied: both prison and legitimate employment might bring "peace."[119] Above all, metamorphosis was sustained by personal relationships: a kindly prison chaplain or Elsie's sustenance.[120] The success that followed Lucas and Hart's return from Canada came after they decided to "have a good shot at going straight." In the following months they were poor, but "we both kept our words, principally because we hated to show any weakness to each other."[121]

The question of reform was both personal and political. By 1932 Lieutenant Colonel C. E. F. Rich's *Recollections of a Prison Governor* could observe: "This is a time when questions of the organisation and government of prisons have a special appeal, and when the public mind is more than usually alive to the pressing importance of deciding how best to deal with crime and criminals."[122] An assertive penal reform lobby and a new generation of officials in the Home Office and Prison Commission placed renewed emphasis on therapeutic rather than deterrent responses to crime. Emblematized by the progressive agenda initiated by Alexander Paterson as commissioner of prisons, reform-ist ideas were increasingly enshrined within the penal system.[123] At the same time, a protracted scandal around the Borstal system of dealing with juvenile delinquency focused attention on the management of crime. After escapes and a suicide at the Portland institution in 1921, newspapers like the *Evening Standard* mounted a vitriolic attack on a dehumanizing system that was taken up by progressive organizations like the Howard League.[124] The beleaguered Borstal Association monitored this criticism, noting "nine delirious articles denouncing the brutality and failure of the Institutions and the unsympathetic treatment meted out by the Borstal Association" in the "gutter press," and considering the possibility of legal action.[125]

My Selves encapsulated how Lucas deliberately positioned himself in these debates around the management of crime:

> The care and treatment of the young offender is a subject upon which I can write with some authority. For I know, and have experienced, both sides of the question. Not only have I spent time in reformatories, at Borstal, and in a boys' prison, but during my journalistic life I have dealt with the subject both in books and newspaper articles. . . . I know the treatment which is meted out to the young crook in the many institutions which exist in this country with the object of reforming the young offender under the "fatherly" jurisdiction of the Home Office. I know, too, how the majority of these places fail in their object—and what is more to the point—WHY.[126]

Prison and penal reform became stock themes for a freelance journalist seek-ing to exploit a hot political issue. Lucas praised Toronto's Langstaff Jail Farm in Auckland's *Advertiser*.[127] In the *Detective* he provided "an intimate descrip-tion" of the training ship *Cornwall* and "impressions . . . of prison life today" in Wormwood Scrubs. Taking readers through the prison gates, he mapped an unfamiliar institution's rhythms and rituals.[128] Elsewhere he reflected on confinement's psychological costs. The *Cornwall* was a "phase of horror in my subconscious life" that "took the happiness out of my nature like a bee robbing a flower of its pollen."[129]

Personal reflections were woven into a more wide-ranging consideration of prison's successes and failures; the life story became both part of the politics of penal reform and popular entertainment. Lucas was not alone in making this move. In the 1930s "grim experience" was central to the politics of unem-ployment and economic decline, the prominence of novels like Walter Green-wood's *Love on the Dole* (1933) leading the *Bookseller* to argue that "fact is now the fashion in publishing."[130] Public debate about prison similarly often hinged on attempts to secure a position from which to speak authoritatively about an institution of which most Britons remained ignorant. Sydney Moseley challenged the "embroidery and sensationalism" that characterized popular accounts of Britain's penal system.[131] Prompted by the Borstal scandals, Moseley began the "independent investigation" that was published as *The Truth about Borstal* (1926). Challenging its public demonization, Moseley emphasized the "new Borstal" created by the "excellent innovations" of Sir Wemyss Grant-Wilson. New forms of training and work, the rejection of military discipline, and modern psychological knowledge had created "humane and scientific means of reforming our young delinquents into estimable citizens."[132] Such conclusions drew heavily on the "documentary testimony of ex-Borstal boys." Aware of the political power of these "moving human documents," Moseley stressed how "their stories, frank and open, did much to help me."[133]

Such interventions followed a broader tradition of writing about crime. The "penal crisis of the 1890s" was prompted by first-person memoirs criticizing the prison system.[134] In the 1920s personal testimony again acquired huge significance within the debate over prison reform. The damning investigation published by Stephen Hobhouse and Fenner Brockway as *English Prisons Today* (1922) interwove questionnaires from prison officials with interviews with ex-prisoners, primarily conscientious objectors. Their attack on "a huge machine which is felt to be repressive at every point"—destroying character and making men more likely to reoffend—drew emotive force from this "searing personal testimony."[135] The Borstal Association, by contrast, publicized appreciative letters from reformed boys and their parents. Life stories of recently released boys appeared in the monthly *Borstal Association Review* to "point out to present inmates . . . conspicuous successes or failures as examples or warnings."[136]

When Lucas began writing about prison, he was working with an established genre and political grammar. While *English Prisons Today* was driven by an ideological commitment to penal reform, we might be more cynical about Lucas's engagement with these debates. The demand for authenticity enshrined in the elevation of the ex-prisoner's testimony collapsed boundaries between the politics and pleasures of crime, bringing together the high-minded motives of reformers and the freelancer's desire to make a living. Discussions of prison reform circulated across elite and popular journals, and drew together sensationalism, entertainment, education, and polemic.[137] Lucas explored similar issues in periodicals like the *Detective* and newspapers like the *World's Pictorial News*. Always writing for a specific audience, Lucas took a contradictory position. His most sustained exploration of the penal system was "The Only Way to Reform Criminals" in the *Humanist*, a journal at the vanguard of calls for prison reform. He argued strongly for reform of the criminal:

> There is a saying current in police circles that "once a crook always a crook." This is a fallacy and has been proved so on innumerable occasions. Crooks, unlike poets, are not born, they become so either through the force of circumstances . . . or by their own inclinations, or through environment.[138]

Emphasizing the environmental and psychological origins of crime and the possibilities of social management reflected contemporary progressive opinion. Yet Lucas quickly went off-script. Introducing a critical perspective on prison reform, he ventriloquized conservative voices like the former prison governor Rich. Rich had attacked Paterson's reforms as "soft sloppy 'sob stuff'" that contributed to the escalating problem of crime and delinquency.[139] Like Rich, Lucas suggested that "coddling prisoners" compromised the deterrent effect of punishment. Lucas was not a straightforward disciplinarian, though. In the *Humanist* he argued that "reformation stops where it should begin: at the prison gate where prisoners are released," and called for investment in organizations like the Central Aftercare Association to help the ex-crook forge a new life. More bracingly, he demanded society change its attitudes: American sympathy contrasted with British hostility and "employers [who] do not want to employ a jail-bird." Lucas concluded:

> The only way to reform is to trust [and] to give the criminal a sporting chance to make good. . . . Punish [the criminal] rigourously for his wrongdoing, but when he has expiated his crime allow him and help him to forget the past. Stimulate new hopes and ambitions and give him a chance in the form of a *congenial* job.[140]

Lucas's take on prison reform was inconsistent. In the *Autobiography* he spoke approvingly of how "Borstal is now run on semi-military lines."[141] Such interventions elaborated critical perspectives on the prison system that undermined his claims to respectability: if the institutions in which Lucas had been confined were fallible, then what was the likelihood of his successful reform? He had "mixed feelings" about the training ship *Cornwall*: while the "theory" of a training ship run along naval lines was good, Lucas drew attention to the "abuses, vices [and] consequences" that resulted from "herding together . . .

so much human scum." Concerns about the lack of useful employment and training coalesced in his depiction of the *Cornwall* as an ineffective instrument of reform. It was "a school for crime." However critical this analysis, Lucas evaded the sustained political engagement that might have allowed him to envisage an alternative.[142] In the *Detective* he commented: "I have been asked on innumerable occasions, does Borstal do any good? The only answer to this question is that it depends entirely on the boy." For those determined to "chuck crime," it "gives every encouragement and help." For others—Lucas reflected:

> I spent twenty months in a Borstal Institution and I do not look on the time as wasted as I learnt many useful things and I had ample opportunity to study. The question "Did Borstal reform me?" is on the tip of your tongue, I know. All I can say is that when I left Borstal I intended to go straight, but attracted by the false glitter and attraction of the "fleshpots of Egypt" I fell and I paid again.[143]

Lucas's success reflected the value of personal testimony in 1920s culture and politics. Writing as an ex-crook meant finding ways to reconcile demand for sensational "revelations" with growing emphasis on prison as an instrument of reform. Lucas was often able to manage these contradictions. Yet the impetus toward reform was always compromised by the need to entertain readers. However much Lucas emphasized his hard-won authority, he also celebrated the pleasures of crime. While demonstrating progress down the highway of honesty brought moral legitimacy, the ex-crook always had to fall back on lucrative firsthand experience. This balancing act secured the authenticity effects that gave his writing political and commercial value, but meant reform was always uncertain.

AT THE LIMITS OF REFORM

In 1925 the editor of *Truth* received a manuscript from Lucas. He rejected it as "nothing more than a brazen attempt of a gaolbird to capitalise his shady past." From this perspective, reform looked like a cynical deception meant to turn notoriety into profit. Showing "little regard for the truth," it revealed the expediencies on which the highway of honesty rested.[144] In Lucas's hands this convenient fiction effaced the contradictions of his lives. His repeated failure to fulfill his grandiose promises made the uncertainty of reform most obvious. Trapped in a cycle of reform and imprisonment, he protested his newfound respectability in print only to be drawn back into crime. Personal failures always unfolded in public; readers who had bought his books and invested in his reform might have thought themselves shortchanged. "The Resolve of Netley Lucas" was the final installment of his *World's Pictorial News* life story. Despite describing his "life of excitement," Lucas reassured readers that "I doubt if it is really worth while" and anticipated a fresh start in "a better land."[145] Eleven months later, reporting his conviction at the Central Criminal Court, subeditors mocked his "resolve" in a cruel headline: "The Craving Weakness of Netley Lucas."[146]

It was not just Lucas's criticism of the prison system that belied the possibilities of reform. As often as he engaged with debates around penal policy, he also ignored his encounters with the law. Serialized life stories like "Public Schoolboy's Own Story of Exploits as a Crook," published in the *People* in 1923, passed quickly over his time in prison, almost as if crime went unpunished. Lucas began defensively—"I do not write this story of my life in bravado"—but the "absorbing narrative of reckless adventure" left very little space for moving along the highway of honesty.[147] Stories of personal reform were unsettled by accounts of the pleasures of crime and social mobility.

Consider the serials Lucas wrote for young readers of the *Monster* and *Golden* penny comics. "The Borstal Boy" began in the *Monster* in April 1926. Lucas was "the now reformed crook" who "knows what he is writing about." The editor framed this as a cautionary moral tale. Lucas "has now realised the error of his ways, and so I am going to give him a helping hand back to the straight path by accepting this thrilling human document."[148] Presented as a way to restore Lucas to "his position as an honest citizen" and encourage readers to "keep on the straight path," the serial nonetheless emphasized the pleasures of crime. Lucas had praised Borstal as "kind, if strict," waxing lyrical about the education, and singling out the "system of supervision after release" as "specially praiseworthy."[149] Now this praise disappeared. "Darky Kemp," the "Borstal Boy," was a heroic figure, his exploits celebrated rather than condemned. Effacing the humanizing reforms introduced in the mid-1920s, Lucas returned to *John Bull's* earlier criticisms of a brutal regime. Darky's challenges to institutional discipline were commendable rather than threatening. He tries to escape and succeeds; he rejects the chaplain's pathetic attempts to moralize him; he orchestrates a riot that culminates in a violent struggle with warders and police. "The Borstal Boy" is an exemplary text in the pleasures of crime. In the final episode Darky chooses to serve his sentence and go straight. Yet reform comes not through the effectiveness of the state but through his love for his bête noire, the girl detective Julia Six. Only then did he exchange prison drab for marriage and the professional rewards of the Kemp International

Detective Bureau, a metamorphosis that shadowed Netley and Elsie Lucas's relationship.[150]

Tensions between citizenship and criminality were played out through the images of Lucas circulating in the 1920s. Advances like the handheld camera and new technologies for reproducing illustrations in print created an everyday culture saturated with images.[151] Photographs, particularly those conforming to the naturalistic conventions of the snapshot, became central to the authenticity effects of newspaper lives. Constructed as a window onto hidden social worlds, the camera captured Lucas in his earlier guises as a gentleman crook. The *World's Pictorial News* showed the man-about-town in an unguarded moment relaxing with a cigarette. Accompanying articles in magazines and periodicals, studio portraits staged the act of "taking up the pen" for readers and claimed a newfound professional identity.[152]

Such photographs coexisted with very different images created by police photographers and commercial artists, particularly the mug shots circulated in the *Police Gazette* in March 1923 and July 1924 (figs. 4 and 5). Arrested, fingerprinted, and photographed, Lucas looks into the eye of power.[153] The images were part of the process through which he was rendered knowable and controllable. Shot from the front and in profile in a tightly bounded frame, mug shots conformed to wider conventions for depicting criminals and ostensibly documented the "truth" of their criminality.[154]

Contrast these mug shots to the studio portraits of Lucas and Guy Hart that accompanied "Two Crooks Confess" in *Cassell's Popular Magazine*. While they were part of the process through which Lucas fashioned a new identity, the mug shot and publicity photograph looked very similar. The softer oval frame still isolated its subject. Half turning from the camera, Hart refused the enforced geometric pose of the mug shot. Lucas was again captured face-on. Ironically, it was here that his gaze guiltily evaded the camera. Captions refused to let the men leave the past behind. They were "notorious criminals" rather than the "ex-crooks" they claimed to be. Lucas looked just as he did when arrested in 1920: the duplicitous trickster was identical to the man of letters. Reform went no deeper than a smart suit.[155]

Lucas's awkward relationship to his criminal past was worked out in the dramatic cover illustration for *Cassell's* first installment of "Two Crooks Confess." Influenced by the visual conventions of the woodcut, the heavy blocks of black and gray created an ominous mood. A faceless, threatening figure—a more masculine version of Lucas—was partially framed by the vertical and horizontal lines scored across the page. Was this crook contained behind the bars of a cell or gazing through the windows of a wealthy home? Did the tilted head represent remorse or an attempt to see what was within? Such ambiguities suggested that Lucas's claims to respectability might ring hollow.[156] They were reinforced in *Mystery Story*'s serialized version of *Criminal Paris*. Framed as firsthand testimony from "a reformed denizen of the underworld," the series opened with a thick description of streets and crowds that became a direct address to the reader: "Come with me now for a moment, and let us look into the shadows of Paris." Moving down into the underworld, Lucas deployed personal knowledge to open locked doors and enter the crook's den.[157] His relationship to the underworld remained opaque. Edward Potts's pencil illustration of a figure in evening dress leaving a shady club arm in arm with a young woman confirmed Lucas's claims to reform: here he was respectable yet vulnerable, charmed by a seductive vamp and about to be attacked in a story that "illustrate[d] the truth of statements concerning the victimisation of tourists."[158] Elsewhere Potts played with the tropes through which Lucas led readers underground. The reader was invited to sit with Lucas at his table in a Parisian dive, enjoying a glass of wine and gazing at the attractive "cocotte" dancing above him. Distance from the underworld was nominal. Like Lucas, the viewer was immersed in events that, despite his protestations of horror, were exciting and intriguing (fig. 10).[159]

These images unsettled narratives of the highway of honesty and the authenticity of Lucas's writing. Personal photographs often belied the documentary status attributed to them. A photograph of "Lucas in a car he 'commandeered'" in the *World's Pictorial News* ostensibly depicted his crimes. It was an ambiguous image, however: a young man in an expensive motorcar suggested the pleasures of crime; the photograph's posed qualities and the inscrutable figure behind the wheel made it unclear whether this was Lucas, let alone that the car was stolen.[160] The pencil sketches accompanying Lucas's writing blurred fact and fiction, reworking personal experience through generic conventions of romance and adventure. Illustrators drew Lucas as both an archetypal gentleman crook and someone we might recognize from his contemporary photographs, and placed him in scenes described in his life-writing and short stories. L. Penn Bird's illustration for "Vanity's Consequence," published in *Sovereign* in 1925, depicted Lucas as the war hero and secret burglar "Joe," sharing a cozy suburban home with his unsuspecting wife, Lucy. When Joe hears a knock at the door, Lucy "felt him start and stiffen" as "some instinct warned him" that the police had arrived. Lucas never described this scene in his life-writing, but Bird turned him into a character from fiction.[161]

FIGURE 10. Savoring the delights of the Parisian underworld. From Netley Lucas, "Criminal Paris," *Hutchinson's Mystery Story Magazine*, published by Hutchinson, October 1925, 27. Reproduced by permission of The Random House Group Ltd. and courtesy of The Bodleian Libraries, The University of Oxford, per. 25612 d. 22, vol. 6, October 1925, 27.

LOVE WILL TEAR US APART

In the *Autobiography* Lucas looked forward to the possibilities marriage might bring. Desperate to leave his past behind, he was fortified with a new self-awareness that meant "I cling to that other priceless treasure which I have found—the love of a good woman, unselfish and purifying."[162] In 1924 he was probably not talking about Elsie, but the idea that love could "purify" informed the dedication of *Criminal Paris* and his later account of their marriage. *My Selves* depicted a moment of rare bliss. For six months after June 1925, he was absorbed in domestic respectability. Leaving the temptations of the West End behind, the couple took a "pretty little bungalow" in Westenhanger, overlooking Folkestone racecourse, where they lived with Guy Hart and Florence. Despite their precarious finances, they were "supremely happy." Lucas wrote; Hart and his wife "looked after the secretarial side of my work"; Elsie was "as good a housekeeper as could be desired."

> We had a large garden, two bicycles and a pet donkey we called "Archie." As it was summertime and the weather idyllic our happiness was complete, and such as I have never known since. . . . For the first time in my life I was experiencing the peculiar joys of a respectable and ordered existence.[163]

Lucas interwove emotional fulfillment with professional endeavor, personal reform with the security of an "ordered" life. His account was echoed in the criminologist John Goodwin's *Crook Pie*, the only other depiction of this marriage I have found. Goodwin tried to understand why women would "marry a reformed criminal."

> They . . . want to mother him, and to show him that by substituting an honest existence for his former crooked ways he will be happier and more useful to the community on which he formerly preyed. I know an ex-crook whose wife is thus loyally fulfilling her mission. She looks after their flat, cleans, cooks and mends; and types all his books and articles—for he is now an author. She is of enormous practical and moral help to him. Good luck to her![164]

Like Lucas, Goodwin presented Elsie as loyal and dutiful, her maternal qualities providing the sustenance necessary to render her husband happy and "useful." Her "mission" was subordinate to his career.

Elsie would need more than luck. When her sister Florence became pregnant, the "joys" of domesticity ended. Hart took a job as a valet; Elsie and

Lucas returned to London. Respectability lasted only six months.[165] In any case, Lucas's commitment to this path was inconsistent. The preoccupations of his writing questioned the redemptive power of marriage and the truth of love itself. These ideas offered a way of making sense of his lives, but the stories they allowed sat uneasily against other narratives of deceptive criminality. Despite the frontispiece of *Criminal Paris*, Elsie was quickly forgotten in the rest of the book. The preface noted: "I had the pleasure . . . of meeting many of Paris's cleverest women crooks, and very charming many of them were. Willingly and unwillingly, I even participated in several little 'affairs.'"[166] The quotation marks left the word ambiguous, but Lucas appeared as an inveterate cruiser, a "pleasure-seeker" enjoying undefined yet illicit meetings.[167] Strolling at night through the Bois de Boulogne, he was picked up by an enchanting woman in an expensive car: "It was not the first time I had mounted an unknown lady's chariot in Paris," he observed knowingly. As they drove, the pair moved closer: "Slowly I bent my head, my lips sought hers and had almost met them." Caught in print and Potts's *Mystery Story* illustration, this moment of intimacy was unconsummated. The car stopped with an "unkind jerk." Lucas was knocked unconscious and robbed: he had been trapped by "one of the prettiest and most alluring decoys."[168]

None of this necessarily means Lucas was unfaithful. Filmmakers and novelists invariably presented Paris as exotic and erotic. *Criminal Paris* was sexualized through its subject and its generic conventions; a firsthand account of the underworld required a knowing man-about-town as guide; Potts's illustration typified those accompanying serialized romantic fiction. The demands of fidelity were unsettled by the forms within which Lucas wrote. By 1926 he had fashioned himself as a gentlemanly trickster, profiting from the sexualized qualities of plausibility and charm. In *Criminal Paris*, Lucas had no choice other than to talk about his "affairs." We cannot collapse genre and form into personal relationships, but their prominence in his writing cast doubt upon his stories of reform.

Those stories were unsettled by other aspects of his writing. *London and Its Criminals* (1926) considered women's "odd fascination" with criminals. Lucas acknowledged the idea of love as "purifying," but now presented this as an impossible fantasy:

[Women] will sacrifice themselves in the hope of reforming the object of their affections. Here and now I may say that this sacrifice is usually in vain. A woman's love may sometimes perform the miracle she desires, but more often it is she herself who is degraded rather than the man uplifted, and her heart may be broken, her life ruined and the criminal's nature remain untouched.[169]

In a period when marriage manuals and romantic fiction placed increasing emphasis on the mutuality essential to modern love, Lucas suggested that any relationship with an ex-crook could only be asymmetrical. Narcissistic and self-absorbed, men like that were incapable of reciprocating love and personal reform—"oblivious and wholly indifferent to the degradation, shame and misery they have brought on those who love them."[170] However strong a woman's "maternal instinct," her sacrifice was inevitably "in vain." Lucas wrote as a criminologist, distanced from his arguments and examples, but it is hard not to think about Elsie. The time and place he invokes—the "here and now" rooting his pessimism—points toward his own marriage. Was he an "unprincipled scoundrel"? Was Elsie wasting her time? Whatever he said elsewhere, Lucas implied no woman could guide him to honesty.[171]

My Selves returned to these themes, turning allusion into an explicit acknowledgment of marital infidelities. Elsie accompanied Lucas to Paris, yet "[I] was able to enjoy to the full all those things for which the Gay City is so notorious." He was unrepentant, admitting his adultery but excusing it as "collecting material for my book." Distinguishing between erotic and emotional intimacy, Lucas portrayed these episodes as "essentially *amours passant*," which "did not make me love my wife any the less."[172] Elsie might have disagreed. With *Criminal Paris*'s dedication revealed as a lie, the ex-crook seemed untrustworthy, the idyll of Westenhanger misleading. I think this was deliberate—a way of playing with readers and creating an aberrant counterpoint against which Lucas defined a life characterized by promiscuity and excess. His memories were moving, but brought to a knowing halt: "To end a chapter with marriage savours of a completeness which unfortunately does not synchronise with what took place in my own life as a husband, but it will be obvious to anyone that I was not cut out for marital happiness."[173] Few would have doubted that: Lucas dwelled upon the relationships that characterized his adult life. Priapic and predatory, he presented desire as a "wild and utterly ungovernable impulse," disrupting all attempts to find emotional fulfillment and respectability.[174]

Lucas's earlier work anticipated some of this. The *Autobiography* interwove stories of crime with the flirtations that brought entry to Society and opportunities to rob wealthy women. The pleasures of crime often consisted in the sexual opportunities it created. Masquerading as an officer at the Cosmopolitan

Club around 1917, Lucas "picked up a 'fairy,' who seemed anxious to teach me to fox-trot. I do not remember much about her except that she had very bold eyes, and that she bent very easily in the middle."[175] *My Selves* went further. Lucas now understood desire as a source of pleasure and cause of his transgressions. At times he tried to distinguish "pure lust" from his "definite worship of [women's] beauty and their femininity," but the book was often explicitly corporeal. "To hold a beautiful woman in my arms, to feel her soft breasts against me, to inhale her fragrant breath and the sweet scent of her skin, to look into her eyes and kiss all her little kinks," Lucas explained, "is to me the supreme gift of the Gods."[176]

Much of *My Selves* tried to explain the social and sexual excesses Lucas's desires drove him to. He dwelled on his discovery of the "innate sensualism of [women's] natures and the perversion of their vices" from the married Society woman who provided his "first grounding in the etiquette of the bedroom" in 1917.[177] Insatiable and boastful, he had "made love by telephone, by cable and wireless." Reflecting on a secretive "violent 'affair'" in Borstal, he commented: "I have made love in many queer places during my lifetime, including an Imperial Airways air liner 2000 feet up flying from Brussels to Cologne, but I think that this chicken house was by far the most uncomfortable."[178] The "only time I slept alone was during my periods in prison." Disavowing the rich sexual opportunities of this all-male world, Lucas implicitly established the limits of his otherwise rapacious desires: sleeping alone was as much a story of what he did not do in prison.[179]

Perhaps. Lucas tacitly acknowledged the growing reach of ideas of companionate marriage in the 1920s, but moments of redemption were overwhelmed by his compulsive infidelities or betrayal by the women he loved. This unceasing spiral confounded boundaries between respectable domesticity and adulterous promiscuity. Longing for intimacy yet trapped by insatiable desires, Lucas elsewhere suggested the uncertain boundaries between sexual transgression and normality. On two occasions a decade apart, he described something that happened when he was around fourteen and working as a pantryman on the *Kenilworth Castle*. He wove the voyage to Cape Town into a story of adventurous mobility, but was troubled by an enigmatic incident en route. The *Autobiography* observed, "upon mature consideration, that the 'glory hole' of a large liner is about the most vicious and immoral place I have ever had to live in, and that is saying a great deal." By 1924 Lucas had spent time in prison and Borstal; he had lived in dockside lodging houses, slept rough under the Adelphi Arches, and stayed at the Union Jack Club, a military leave hostel on Waterloo Road. Set against these sites of rough masculinity and illicit sex, the viciousness of the oceangoing liner was stark. Lucas was brash when describing his dalliances with beautiful women; his hesitancy here made the *Kenilworth Castle*'s immorality more acute.[180]

My Selves revisited the "glory hole." This account was more detailed—perhaps Lucas wanted to shock readers—but still did not explain what had happened. Charm and good looks allowed the gentleman crook to cultivate the desire of those he seduced. Desire had to be managed carefully, however. In the confines of a ship, the young man found that task impossible; the predatory rake was himself vulnerable:

> The Chief Pantryman was a swine, for realising my callow youth, innocent appearance, and clean boyishness, he made a suggestion to me upon the second day out at sea which caused me in fury to flash my fist quickly toward his face.[181]

An unnamed "suggestion" warranted a furious response. Resistance brought only more attention. As the voyage continued, the man "did his best to make my life a real hell." Senior and physically stronger, the pantryman was in a "position to achieve his object with ease, and the more I resisted his foul intentions the more he bullied me."[182] The "ease" with which he enforced those "foul intentions" belied Lucas's claims to resistance. Now he could only rely on his "equanimity of mind" to survive. Honed at sea and in prison, this meant that "no matter what I am called upon to endure a queer fatalistic and stoic streak in me has always made it possible for me to keep my chin up." While this might have allowed Lucas to present himself as an innocent victim, *My Selves* suggested he could derive pleasure from experiences others might "endure"— finding a "perverted enjoyment of the very sordidness of the situation."[183] Voyaging to the Cape, Lucas "passed" his "first test into the realm of sophisticated manner":

> [This] in the greasy sordidness of the third class pantry, the object of perverted attentions from most of my shipmates, was the most enjoyable trip I have made. This may sound very strange, but in those early days life was very new and rather exciting and I welcomed each new experience, each new sensation, with the eagerness of youth.[184]

"Perverted attentions" brought exciting and pleasurable sensations, analogous to the pleasures of crime and beautiful women. In his lives and life-writing, Lucas resisted any attempt to fix the "truth" of his sexual practices and character.

All of this made it obvious that Lucas was unsuited for companionate marriage. Although he often seemed to enjoy describing his "affairs," they could also prompt reflection. He envied those men who "achieve greatness and happiness in the love of a good woman . . . [since] the contentment of family life is one of the things for which I have craved, and yet been unable to obtain."[185] There is an emptiness here—an unfulfilled "craving" for family life. As a child, Lucas was denied this by the death of his parents; as an adult, his instincts made it impossible. *Crooks: Confessions* described how "when I am with men who do not know me for what I am, I like them to tell me all they can about themselves, but principally about their homes, for I have never had a home and it has become my pet subject." Noting his jealousy of their "comfortable fireside, and a front-door bell which rings but does not alarm," Lucas hinted at an unstated personal tragedy.[186] Picking up that story in *My Selves*, Lucas could be somber and self-pitying. Despite his efforts to "get down to living an ordinary respectable sort of existence," compulsive desires always meant "I have thrown respectability and decency to the winds." Justifying this as a response to prison was self-serving: being "tied to one woman for any length of time" seemed like "only another form of captivity," and meant "I feel an urge to throw off the restraint, fancied or real, and to go out into the streets and get away by myself—to be myself, alone, free to go wherever I want to go." Here he came close to a Freudian understanding of the conflict between self and society.[187]

Now, finally, Lucas returned to Elsie:

> She made the greatest mistake in her life by becoming my wife, and today she realises it, but at the time we were both young and in love. . . . My marriage was a failure solely because I was, and am, a failure—a failure as a man, a human being, an individual, a citizen and finally as a husband. There is no woman in the world bad enough to be my wife, because my inverted character is so soaked in selfishness and deceit, that I have no right to have the happiness of any woman placed in my hands.[188]

Lucas's "inverted character" signaled both his refusal of conventional moral codes and the narcissism that frustrated his personal relationships. This is the pessimism of *London and Its Criminals* rendered as powerful personal reflection; here are the haunting traces of *Criminal Paris*'s dedication. If companionate marriage allowed Lucas to navigate the highway of honesty, failure as a spouse acquired greater import as a sign of a more comprehensive failure as "an individual, [and] a citizen." Lucas was ill suited to the demands of marriage and citizenship. The stories he told about his successful reform often depended on the redemptive power of personal relationships. If those relationships were not as they seemed, then the threads interwoven in the ex-crook writer threatened to untangle.

CONCLUSION

Ex-crooks like Lucas and O'Dare wrote at the leading edge of the "first modern age of confession." Unabashed and explicit, retelling intimate stories of criminal exploits and sexual dalliances, they anticipated the agony aunts and "I confess" competitions prominent in newspapers like the *Daily Mirror* from the 1930s.[189] By midcentury the compulsion to render inner lives visible had become ubiquitous and ordinary. The market and the state sustained elaborate mechanisms to elicit the "truth" of the self-within; psychologists identified secrecy as emotionally damaging and socially corrosive. Yet the "desire many people felt—very evident first in the 1930s, today a cultural mainstay— both to talk out loud about shameful subjects and to stake a claim to their inviolable privacy" was driven by those who had nothing more to lose, and underpinned by financial gain more than psychological well-being and moral redemption. Lucas and O'Dare found their "secrets" divulged when they were arrested, and again as they came under scrutiny from an intrusive press.[190] Forced into the public gaze, they waived further right to privacy to entertain readers and for pecuniary gain. Just as emerging forms of personal journalism meant the boundaries between public and private life were "undergoing wrenching reconfiguration," so Lucas and his like became complicit in and exploitative of that process.[191] The storytelling ex-crook deliberately violated boundaries between inside and outside to sell a carefully packaged version of individuality and the underworld. Never straightforwardly reflective, Lucas was just as concerned with dissecting the worlds he had inhabited. While the crook life story was reshaped by (and contributed to) a process of interiorization, the task of introspection could be harnessed to different ends.

Even at the height of his success, many observers were unconvinced by Lucas's claims to respectability. The Westminster magistrate Cecil Chapman first met Lucas when sending him to the West Drayton Probation Home for false pretenses in December 1917. They met again a month later after Lucas was arrested for begging and breaching the terms of his probation order and in July 1920, when Lucas was prosecuted for defrauding the colonial outfitters. *My Selves* wryly observed: "I don't think he was *very* surprised to see me!"[192] In the *Poor Man's Court of Justice* (1925), Chapman reflected on the tensions between crime and literary aspiration. Lucas's *Autobiography* had expressed contrition and a desire to start a new life overseas. Chapman was skeptical:

> I am much afraid that his success as an author may have led him to change his mind. The autobiography is a brightly-written, clever book, but it has an atmosphere of jaunty self-satisfaction which makes it painful and demoralising. It has been my habit when a "reformed character" says he is going somewhere, to buy his ticket and get somebody to see him off, and even then he sometimes gets out half-way and is found again in his old haunts the next week. I wish Netley Lucas's intention to go to the Colonies had been made before a judge and treated in this way. I should have felt more confident about his future.[193]

The "self-satisfaction" that disconcerted Chapman was partly a world-weary magistrate's assessment of Lucas's character and insouciance in court. Quotation marks suggested his pessimism that Lucas was a "reformed character." We might also see "self-satisfaction" as a sensibility animated by the demands of writing about crime. The "atmosphere" Chapman found "demoralising" reflected the nature of popular publishing and journalism. It crystallized at a point at which the personal and the political converged. Chapman glossed over the structural contexts shaping the ex-crook's writing, preferring to emphasize Lucas's responsibility for his behavior. Yet his comments were prescient. In the summer of 1924, Lucas *did* go to "the Colonies," but his destination was Canada rather than Australia, and it was not long before he was arrested again.

Although the idea of the highway of honesty suggested a chronological and geographical distance between crime and writing, they were never as discrete as Lucas and his sponsors sometimes implied. For at least eighteen months, he moved between the two. He worked with Stanley Scott, then stole from him; in Toronto, Mackenzie and Marriott combined journalism and a fraudulent employment agency; *Who's Who in Literature* (1926) listed the books *Crooked Ways* and *Criminal New York* under Lucas's name: neither appeared in print.[194] The *Autobiography*'s success went some way toward effacing this, but Lucas's path was hesitant and circuitous. Personal transformation also depended on expediencies analogous to the confidence trick. Never just something achieved by hard work, professional respectability was a mask to assume and discard. In O'Dare's raffish circle, Hart masqueraded as Sir Burton Pomeroy, editor of the *Times*. As single-mindedly as Lucas could work in pursuit of literary success, a contradiction of his lives was that he often just assumed a status he was not entitled to.[195]

Lucas *did* work hard. Creative energies, personal connections, and social capital brought success. Taking up the pen allowed him to remake his public identity as he rebuilt his life. Yet the same markets and cultural forms that brought opportunities also forced him to return to what had come before. As the project of personal reform and his apparent desire for respectability pushed Lucas to reject his criminality, the value of firsthand testimony and reinvigorated pleasure cultures of crime pulled him to revel in it. There was no worth in the ex-crook who had left his or her past too far behind. Literary success accreted onto enduring awareness of Lucas's crimes of confidence. Traces of crime and prison lingered, leaving his integrity suspect, troubling his relationships with editors and publishers, and frustrating his attempts to put his past behind him. The ex-crook would always be a man or woman with a past. Lucas's striking mobilities belied how he was caught in a trap not wholly of his own making. Frustrating and irreconcilable, these contradictions would lead to his dramatic fall from grace. That story comes later, though.

CHAPTER 4

The Comic Book Criminologist

WE'LL ALWAYS HAVE PARIS

Netley Lucas wrote a lot about Paris. After two well-publicized visits "to obtain material for a book on Parisian crime and criminals," he began to produce work at a prolific rate.[1] From November 1925 a series of essays on "Criminal Paris" appeared in Hutchinson's *Mystery Story* in Britain and the syndicated *American Weekly* before they were published as *Criminal Paris* (1926).[2] Later Lucas turned his hand to fiction. Over three months from August 1926, "The Boy Apache" was serialized in the penny comic the *Golden*.[3] In 1927, finally, Stanley Paul published Lucas's melodramatic novel *The Red Stranger*. He made the most of his visits to the city.

Lucas was an astute freelance writer. He capitalized on, and contributed to, the fascination with Parisian lowlife and highlife in the 1920s. Paris was already associated with cosmopolitan glamour, but its charms became more compelling after the Great War.[4] The armistice brought renewed opportunities to travel for British and American tourists; the weakness of the franc and the agencies of mass tourism made it easier for many to visit France. A burgeoning consumer culture rekindled interest in the city. Paris drew attention from travel writers and fashion pages; gossip columns like the *World's Pictorial News*'s "On the Boulevards" gave readers intimate glimpses of metropolitan life. The city's status was reinforced by its hold over a remarkable group of expatriate novelists and artists. As much as Ernest Hemingway or F. Scott Fitzgerald distanced themselves from the excesses of mass culture—railing against the ingenue tourist and emphasizing their own grasp of the city's language, history, and culture—their visions of Paris had much in common. Paris was cosmopolitan and sexualized, offering opportunities for personal remaking that Hemingway and others reveled in. These themes played out differently in the hands of commercial writers and a self-conscious literary elite, but they appeared across guidebooks and gossip columns, novels like *The Sun Also Rises*, and melodramatic fiction like Lucas's *Red Stranger*.[5]

The bars and boulevards of nighttime Paris provided fertile terrain on which to explore these themes. The spectacle of beautiful cocottes and working-class gangs known as the "Apaches" was threatening yet alluring. Guidebooks warned tourists to beware, but Lucas and his like turned this seamy world into a commodity for fascinated readers to consume.[6] The Parisian underworld captivated filmmakers. Introducing Lucas's "The Boy Apache," the *Golden*'s editor confidently assumed that "you have, of course, seen the Apache of the pictures." Lucas presented himself as an authoritative guide who could take readers beyond film clichés and Baedeker conventions. There was some truth to these claims, but they were a common rhetorical device. *Criminal Paris* and *The Red Stranger* confirmed rather than challenged dominant images of the city.[7]

The stylized sex and violence of the "Apache dance" became something of a craze in the 1920s. Ubiquitous in films like Ivor Novello's *The Rat* (1925), it was inevitable Lucas would offer his own version.[8] In *Criminal Paris* he described meeting Yvonne, the "real, full-blooded apache girl, a dashing brunette with full red lips, and sinuous body," in a cabaret near the Boulevard Saint-Germain.[9] Her "primitive wildness" plays out in a "fantastic kind of valse," characterized by "unrestrained love-making" and the "murmur of love passages which take the form of epithets, reserved by most men for their irate moments."[10] "The Boy Apache" described a "villainous looking ruffian . . . swinging his girl-partner round and round by the red kerchief she wore about her throat—and, most curious of all, *she seemed to like it!*"[11] Such accounts made the "Apache dance" ripe for parody: in *Queen of Hearts* (1934), Gracie Fields fought back, throwing her assailant out of a window.[12] Lucas was neither ironic nor knowing, however: he was a commercial writer giving readers what they expected. His work echoed the charabancs that took slumming tourists through "Paris by Night," allowing them to gaze safely upon nightclubs and streetwalkers—choreographed scenes that, weary observers suggested, were staged by actors.[13]

To write authentically about Paris, Lucas ventriloquized images of a cosmopolitan metropolis. The illusion of veracity was partly achieved by meeting generic conventions. His ostensibly "fictional" stories might also have been familiar to readers. *The Red Stranger* and "The Boy Apache" echoed *The Rat*: love that overcame class boundaries and the distance between underworld and overworld.[14] *The Red Stranger* follows the misadventures of the beautiful socialite Cornelia Wild. Captivated by nighttime Paris, Cornelia ignores her father and goes in search of the underworld.[15] She finds it in La Maison Diable, where she falls in love with "L'Etranger Rouge"—"King of the Apaches." The natural freedom of L'Etranger's world is compelling. The spectacle of unrestrained working-class couples dancing "held the attraction of stark sincerity."[16] L'Etranger is a "fascinating figure, a virile, forceful adventurer."[17] Cornelia is caught up in the rivalry between Apache gangs; the blackmailing schemes of Debu, her father's business partner; and the jealousy of her rival for L'Etranger's affections. She falls prey to Debu's predatory advances—an unnerving scene that culminates with Debu dead and L'Etranger sentenced to the guillotine.[18] "The Boy Apache" guided the *Golden*'s young audience over similar terrain, following seventeen-year-old Spider's romance with Jacqueline Petin. *The Red Stranger* and "The Boy Apache" were the same story. Their final chapters followed the "drama of life and death" as Cornelia and Jacqueline desperately sought to identify those responsible for the murders for which their lovers were to be executed.[19]

Criminal Paris, *The Red Stranger*, and "The Boy Apache" exchanged plots, characters, and scenes. Lucas plagiarized and pillaged his own writing, reworking material for different markets and audiences. Perhaps the rate at which he wrote made this inevitable. Just as travel writers challenged the inauthentic experience of the tourists unthinkingly following guidebook itineraries, so Lucas offered authoritative firsthand visions of the underworld. Translating scenes from *Criminal Paris* into *The Red Stranger*, however, unsettled the distinctions between firsthand reminiscences, investigative journalism, and melodrama, and blurred fact and fiction.[20] *Criminal Paris* described "How Tourists Are Victimized" and cautioned the unwary to beware the "pitfalls for the stranger" and "mistrust all suave, helpful, tactful strangers!"[21] "The Boy Apache" was aligned with a Baedeker guidebook. Readers were warned: "If you hope to go to Paris one day, then read these fearless exposures of the night life—they will save you your money and perhaps your very life."[22]

The results were ironic: *Criminal Paris* was criticized as overblown, while Lucas's "melodrama of the Parisian underworld" was lauded for its veracity.[23] Critics acknowledged *The Red Stranger*'s clichés but still treated it as a remarkable work of social realism. Lucas's vivid writing and knowledge of his previous work secured the effects of authenticity. The *Dundee Courier* noted:

Netley Lucas, who showed remarkable intimacy with crime and criminals in his "Criminal Paris," welds fact and fiction together in a first novel . . . so creditably that he must be regarded as no mean story teller. . . . Many have written round the same subjects, plot and counterplot, and made use of the same types, but they lacked the personal touch. One feels that the types drawn by Netley Lucas are real flesh and blood and that they have figured in his own life.[24]

"Fact and fiction" were "welded" together; the literary talents needed for a "thrilling plot" shaded into the "personal touch" that sustained Lucas's "realism." Here was a paradox: an original narrative that echoed other films and novels.[25]

In writing about Paris, Lucas moved between genres and audiences in a way that underscored the energies and expediencies that secured his reputation as a writer on crime. Those energies often fixated on the pursuit of financial reward. This body of writing also suggests the slipperiness of the ways in which crime could be understood in the 1920s. It emblematized conflicted cultures of criminality that shaped both public understandings of crime and how Lucas could make sense of his lives. The confessing ex-crook found new opportunities for storytelling by moving between authorial identities and markets. *Criminal Paris* and *The Red Stranger* draw attention to the uncertain boundaries between what now seem very different genres.

Lucas first wrote for the *Monster* as a "Borstal Boy" recounting his personal experiences. In April 1927, however, the editor introduced him in a new guise: "I have decided to reincarnate the Kemp International Detective Bureau, and Mr NETLEY LUCAS, the WORLD'S GREATEST CRIMINOLOGIST, will resume this wonderfully absorbing and thrilling Detective Series."[26] A grandiose description in a children's story paper echoed the effortful ways in which "Mr Netley Lucas" refashioned his public identity. While most ex-crooks achieved only fleeting notoriety, Lucas renegotiated his relationship to his criminal past. Dexterous and imaginative, he continued to cultivate the confidence of editors and readers. By 1927, however, he was rarely identified as an ex-crook in print. As "special correspondent" at the *Sunday News*, he reported on notorious cases and approached crime as a social and political problem. Meticulous research allowed him to dissect patterns of crime and policing in periodicals like *Pictorial Weekly*. Writing for popular newspapers and specialist periodicals, Lucas sought the professional rewards available to a crime reporter and criminologist. He still found rich material in older networks of acquaintance, but reworked it through the practices of investigative journalism. His claims to "truth" were now underpinned by the analytic tools of a dispassionate expert rather than personal experience.

Placing Lucas's journalism, criminology, and fiction against the stories he told as a gentleman crook suggests the personal circumstances and anxieties that could have animated his ambition. The transformation of modern journalism and emergence of the crime reporter as a distinct professional type gave him new opportunities. Lucas's remaking as a correspondent and criminologist reflected both his own insecurities and the growing authority of criminal science in society, culture, and politics. The comic book criminologist prompts us to think critically about the extent to which criminology was the modernizing project it claimed to be. In the hands of writers like Lucas, different ways of writing about crime merged together. Older forms of criminal confession coexisted with and informed "modern" criminological knowledge. Despite efforts to isolate a discrete academic field, the borders between popular and scientific cultures of criminality were porous. Popular criminology was an emerging and conflicted discipline that encompassed psychoanalytic studies of criminality, large-scale sociological surveys, and dramatic first-person confessions and cut across boundaries between sensation and instruction, pleasure and rational investigation. Lucas's work on Paris exemplified an emerging realm of crime writing that sat between sensationalism and scientific criminology, and bridged older narratives of low-life slumming and the investigative reporting of the 1950s.

OUR SPECIAL CORRESPONDENT

In the spring of 1926, Lucas began work for the *Sunday News*. This marked an important shift in his career. The gentleman crook reported on high-profile cases, identified social problems, and conducted systematic investigations that developed into books like *London and Its Criminals* (1926). Lucas had described himself as a journalist since 1922. Now he resumed the work of reporting he had undertaken with Stanley Scott. Writing as an ex-crook secured his reputation as an authoritative observer of crime: it made him an attractive proposition to the editors of the *Sunday News*. Yet Lucas increasingly removed himself from his writing, eliding any sense that his knowledge was other than that of a skilled journalist. Foregrounding investigative research instead of (or alongside) firsthand observation, he sought readers' confidence on a different basis. As Lucas's reputation as a writer grew, it was often decoupled from his criminal past.

I think this shift reflected Lucas's ambition and discomfort at the tensions of writing as an ex-crook. It was made possible by the transformation of modern journalism. The special correspondent's pathway was shaped by growing emphasis on the journalist's name as a sign of authority. In the 1920s earlier traditions of anonymity were effaced by the prominence of signed articles by public figures and "experts." Journalists were advised of the "value" of their byline—what Sydney Moseley described as a "kind of 'reminder advertisement'" that would "compel [readers] to read his work."[27] The resonance of "Netley Lucas," already a familiar name, was subtly reworked—he ditched the "ex-crook" prefix—but his work for the *Sunday News* attested to its continued value.

Lucas's employment as a special correspondent reflected the specialization of modern journalism. Competition to be first with the news made reporting fast-paced and demanding. The *Autobiography of a Journalist* (1929), edited by Michael Joseph, described a "helter-skelter business" in which "the amount of material to be absorbed is so great, that only the man who devotes all or most of his time to one subject can hope thoroughly to master its intricacies."[28] For progressive critics, this was a means to improve professional standards and, in particular, journalistic truth and accuracy.[29] Specialization was usually seen as a way to exploit a commercial market, however. Knowledge, whether of films or foreign affairs, "gives the writer a certain status, helps him to become known and . . . supplies him with a . . . regular market." Specialism was lucrative and convenient. Linked to a familiar byline, it secured the effects of authenticity, even if it could not guarantee them.[30]

Lucas's unusual career path thus exemplified the emergence of a distinct professional type. In 1935 Sydney Moseley noted:

> Many reporters . . . have become absolutely labelled as "crime reporters." A good one need never be out of a job. On each daily newspaper is at least one such expert who knows all the Scotland Yard men as well as the principal crooks.[31]

Specialist crime journalism is usually associated with the period after 1945, but Moseley's comments underscore its development through the competitive news market of the 1920s and 1930s. The practices of investigative journalism had crystallized in late-Victorian Britain through the work of campaigning figures like W. T. Stead. Motivated by politics and profit, writers and reformers explored London's poorest neighborhoods and exposed pressing social problems. Slumming narratives continued to be reworked after the Great War as writers like Sidney Felstead descended into *The Underworld of London* (1923) to scandalize readers. These trajectories intersected in the 1920s: reporters forged new styles of writing about crime by interweaving investigative journalism and older narratives of low-life sensation.[32] Being first with the news made journalists more proactive, going beyond the older roles of the court reporter to conduct systematic inquiries that paralleled police investigations.[33] Scotland Yard's Press Bureau began issuing bulletins in the mid-1920s, when the relationship between press and police was in its infancy. Cultivating relationships with "principal crooks" and police, reporters sought to build trust and knowledge in pursuit of exclusives.[34] Correspondents like Bernard O'Donnell at the *Empire News* and Norman Rae at the *News of the World* embodied the "recent tendency . . . towards an ever-increasing emphasis on news-getting, in some cases almost regardless of expense," and anticipated the work of the better-known reporters of the 1950s.[35]

In *My Selves* (1934) Lucas explained the qualities he brought to the *Sunday News*:

> I not only knew . . . more about crooks and the underworld than any man in Fleet Street, but I could go to secret places and secure exclusive news from the crooks themselves because they knew me.[36]

Experience and talent made Lucas an effective reporter. This account gestured back to the firsthand knowledge that brought access to "secret places" from which others were barred, but quickly effaced the traces of personal notoriety. Association with crooks was overlaid by facility with the practices of investigative journalism: the editors, J. E. Williams and E. J. Minney, "recognised the special aptitude I had for gathering crime news."[37] Distance between criminal past and respectable present was unsettled by an earlier passage in which Lucas reflected on working with Stanley Scott:

> Journalism is the only honest profession for which a criminal life is a good training. This statement may sound strange, but as a crook one has to be continually on the *qui vive*, to be watchful always of what is going around one, and to be susceptible to small incidents and influences which are often missed by the man-in-the-street. In . . . news reporting there is all the thrill of fighting to get there first, and the excitement of pitting one's wits against other journalists.[38]

The demands of an "honest profession" were aligned with the resourcefulness and watchfulness essential to a "criminal life." Lucas did not quite link journalism to the deceptions of the trickster, but still suggested the uncertain boundaries between the roles. A disreputable past was both repudiated and singled out as the sine qua non of journalistic success.

Perhaps Lucas's nagging awareness of his ambiguous position made him grateful for Williams and Minney's trust. They "generously took me to their hearts [and gave] me the first real chance to show what I could do." *My Selves* dramatized his skills through two examples of his role as "accredited representative of the paper on many big crime stories."[39] First was the "Stella Maris" case, on which Lucas claimed to report between August and December 1926. Named after the villa in Herne Bay where Frank Smith allegedly murdered John Derham over the latter's affair with Smith's wife, Kathleen, this was a captivating narrative of a Society love triangle gone wrong. Smith and Derham were prominent public figures—Smith the dissolute grandson of Canadian business magnates, Derham a former international hockey player. The *Sunday News* correspondent covered the case from the discovery of a "tragic death" until the "crowds cheer[ed] Smith's acquittal" outside Maidstone Assizes.[40] Second was the Nurse Daniels case, which Lucas was apparently sent to France to cover in the spring of 1927. May Daniels had disappeared while visiting Boulogne. Despite the best efforts of French and British authorities, it was five months before her body was found in woods north of the city. Even then the case remained unsolved and drew the attention of "many London and Paris newspapers [that] have sent correspondents to Boulogne."[41] At the Hôtel Christol et Bristol, Lucas "joined a happy band of newspaper men who were trying to unravel the mystery."[42] The murder of an attractive young nurse was both tragedy and opportunity. Relishing the raffish camaraderie at his hotel, Lucas aligned his role with the unfolding police investigation. Filing weekly articles from Boulogne, the *Sunday News* correspondent tracked the meticulous inquiries of detectives and Daniels's tragic life story.[43]

Lucas had placed himself at the center of two of the most notorious cases of the 1920s. The reports were attributed to an anonymous "special correspondent" and contained nothing that confirmed his authorship. *My Selves* might say more about Lucas's self-importance than his activities as a journalist. I think he did write the stories, though: between January and July 1927, the *Sunday News* published regular articles under his byline. None of these appeared when the special correspondent was in Boulogne, nor in weeks when Lucas claimed to have covered other stories. Reading *My Selves* against his journalism, we might see a skilled correspondent plying his trade. Lucas's work on the Daniels and Stella Maris stories suggests he was highly regarded at the *Sunday News*.[44]

If *My Selves* worked hard to confirm this impression, Lucas apparently relished the challenges of chasing a story. Describing himself as a "born news gatherer," he claimed:

> No better outlet for my easy going manner and my impetuous enthusiasm could have been found. . . . I loved the game with all my heart and soul, reveling in its difficulties, its disappointments, and the supreme joy of getting a good story and seeing it in print.[45]

In Metropolitan Police files, we see Lucas cultivating relationships with detectives and civil servants and using personal ties to the underworld to secure "exclusives."[46] His published work often concealed its dubious origins, but *My Selves* suggests the lengths Lucas would go to. Covering the release of Horatio Bottomley, disgraced editor of *John Bull*, former MP, and fraudster, from prison was "rather difficult," as Bottomley's reminiscences were contracted to the *Sunday Dispatch*. Competition demanded a cynical trick. Lucas and Elsie visited Bottomley's house. Claiming friendship with the financier Gerald Lee Bevan, then also in prison, Elsie secured an audience by asking after Bevan's health. Lucas was amused but delighted with his "exclusive interview."[47] In the Stella Maris case, he crossed boundaries between observing and participating in events. Interviewing Kathleen Smith, Lucas took her for lunch at a Maidstone hotel. At the trial's conclusion, he drove her to prison to be reunited with her husband. The resulting account was published as the "Truth about My Husband and Myself." By 1934, unabashed at revealing the sharp practices of modern journalism, Lucas implied that the end justified the means.[48]

Journalistic investigations like this focused concerns around the deleterious effects of mass culture on press standards, public taste, and legal institutions.[49] In 1924 Sir Patrick Hastings, the attorney general, successfully prosecuted the *Evening Standard*, *Guardian*, and *Daily Express* for contempt of court over their handling of Patrick Mahon's murder trial. Ostensibly an attempt to ensure a fair trial, the case prompted extended reflection on new forms of reporting. The *Evening Standard* had bought rights to Ethel Duncan's account of Mahon's marriage. Ignoring the police, the paper took this vital witness to stay with one of its employees, arguing in court that this was in the public interest. The lord chief justice acknowledged the differences between papers devoted to sensational crime reporting and those whose approach was more sober, but concluded that at least some "entered deliberately and systematically upon a task described by some of them as criminal investigation." Their "independent staff of amateur detectives" combined "an ignorance of the law of evidence" with "complete disregard of the interests whether of the prosecution or the defence." From this perspective, what papers cynically presented as their "duty" to "elucidate the facts" was driven by profit and the "public appetite for sensational matter." The *Evening Standard* was fined one thousand pounds; the *Guardian* and *Daily Express*, three hundred pounds each—a warning that this "perilous enterprise" should be brought under control. Proprietors and editors had to assume "central responsibility" for journalism's excesses lest a prison sentence be required to address concerns about the market's effects on modern journalism.[50]

Lucas also wrote under his byline for the *Sunday News*. He was introduced to readers in January 1927 as "a one time member of the underworld of crime." That designation quickly disappeared. Lucas never mentioned it and did not describe his criminal exploits.[51] Intimate portraits of figures like Josephine O'Dare echoed earlier work, but this was crime writing in a different register.[52] Lucas analyzed the pressing issues facing police and Home Office: forged passports and the "influx of alien undesirables" threatened social stability and public order.[53] Rather than personal experience, Lucas rooted his authority in statistics, examples, and a close working relationship with state institutions. Apparently familiar with the Met's internal operations, Lucas alerted readers before "an intensive campaign to cleanse one of the most pernicious spots in London."[54] Connections to officialdom were interwoven with shadowy personal ties. He exposed the "Hawks of Hyde Park" after "I was told on good authority" about touts blackmailing unwary citizens. Reputable and disreputable "informants" reflected the affinities between Lucas's reporting and crime writing.[55]

Lucas's claimed knowledge of crime and policing allowed him to identify problems, suggest solutions, and challenge official mistakes. Entering a heated debate over the regulation of London's commercial nightlife, he criticized the raids on registered clubs "whose worst crime is the selling of intoxicants during prohibited hours." The home secretary should address the greater threat of the "secret clubs, dance cafes, and houses of ill-repute," he argued. Detailed and strident, his analysis looked like an official report, citing a "police census of the most criminal square mile in London" as evidence of "the following undesirable haunts":

27 unregistered nightclubs frequented by crooks and women of a certain class

58 cafes of known ill-repute

23 receivers of stolen property with business premises

5 registered clubs with ex-convict proprietors, where drug-trafficking and
    worse offences take place . . .

secret and exclusive houses where gambling and the exhibition of immoral
films take place.

These were more pressing targets for Scotland Yard than clubs that sold alcohol after hours.[56]

In Lucas's *Sunday News* articles, scientific rigor and sober analysis were interwoven with (and disrupted by) sensation and scandal. Reflecting on modern forms of scientific detection, Lucas argued that the possibility of surgical alteration rendered fingerprinting fallible.[57] A few weeks later, he described the "perfect orgy of brutal and sordid robberies of Servicemen" in the "mean streets" around Waterloo Station. Setting sobriety aside, he attributed the crimes to a "systematic traffic conducted by gangs who know the psychology of the sailor."[58] In this guise Lucas worked through the dramatic clichés against which academic criminologists railed: Waterloo Road had to be "cleansed"; Hyde Park was haunted by "an army of undesirables of both sexes." Melodrama was never Lucas's exclusive stock-in-trade, but he was adept with it.[59]

Following Lucas suggests how crime reporting was transformed by broader shifts in 1920s journalism. Crime writing's position in this process was paradoxical. When the status of journalism remained insecure, working on crime might further compromise a reporter's claims to respectability. Commentators deemed "special knowledge of the haunts of criminals . . . no part of the sensible journalist's equipment."[60] Seeking to isolate crime writing as a discrete field, they described it as "sordid and wearisome," unsavory and intrusive, to protect the integrity of the modern press.[61] Here was a convenient scapegoat for the accusations of sensationalism leveled at all papers. The anonymous author of the *Autobiography of a Journalist* (1929) had written on crime for *Lloyd's Weekly* but railed against this earlier work. For the freelance journalist, specializing in crime was "easy and profitable" but a mistake for the aspiring "responsible journalist." Writing about crime "ties one down to a melodramatic and 'cheap' vein that will in time . . . affect one's style as a whole." Crime writing was more susceptible to the effects of the market and more degrading to style and status.[62]

Lucas clearly found writing about crime "easy and profitable": the *Autobiography*'s success created momentum that made it difficult, if not impossible, to diversify. Disinterested in the rarefied task of improving his style, he challenged pejorative images of the duplicitous sensation-monger and presented himself as a "responsible" journalist. There is no sense that he agonized over the status of the crime reporter: this was a label he relished rather than resisted. Respectability was relative for an ex-crook. His idiosyncratic career rendered the crisis of contemporary journalism particularly acute, however. He had a criminal record; his subject and style were often seen as disreputable at best. Exploiting opportunities created by the transformation of professional identities, Lucas drew attention to crucial points of antagonism in a changing industry.

The crime reporter was one of several journalistic types to appear or proliferate in the 1920s. A growing number of correspondents joined newspapers after university or the career from which specialist expertise derived. When most journalists still learned their craft through an apprenticeship in the provincial press, this caused resentment as a threat to journalism's democratic nature and was resisted by the National Union of Journalists.[63] Political and Economic Planning noted "two quite separate elements" in newspaper offices: the "small group of leader-writers and specialists, usually with a university education," and the "great mass of working journalists." "Working journalists" often considered figures like the aristocratic gossip columnist to be interlopers; lacking experience and skill, their only qualifications were privilege and connection. These tensions were reinforced by the hierarchical structures that rewarded specialism. Graduates were promoted to "handle the more important stories and provide the interpretation of the news." Union pressure meant daily newspapers established a minimum wage of nine guineas a week after 1920; by the 1930s a foreign correspondent could earn one thousand pounds a year.[64]

Professional and class antagonisms played out through differences of personal style. Political and Economic Planning snidely argued that the provincial background and limited education of many journalists was a "considerable obstacle to the raising of the cultural standards of the press," but saw no irony in bewailing the hostility facing graduate journalists.[65] Learning to produce news required guidance from experienced colleagues. If "other reporters take a dislike to [the graduate journalist's] accent or mannerisms, he may not get enough to enable him to struggle through. There is a definite prejudice against university men."[66] Lucas did not go to university. His gentlemanliness was meticulously cultivated, however, and his "accent" and "mannerisms" could have drawn the ire of other reporters in offices that remained "bastions of an aggressive, rough-and-tumble masculinity."[67] His career path sat somewhere between older ideas of journalism as a craft to acquire and appointing experts to remunerative high-status roles. Lucas was "very happy" at the *Sunday News*, but his professional relationships could be fraught:

> There was . . . a good deal of jealousy of me on Fleet Street, because I had a definite flair for the job. Fleet Street men and reporters . . . openly said that it was unfair that an ex-crook like myself should be given work reporting big crimes. . . . My reply to this is that in Fleet Street, more than anywhere else, it is a case of the survival of the fittest, and a man who can deliver the goods is welcomed no matter what may be his past or his antecedents.[68]

The "jealousy" Lucas experienced reflected resentment of his success and unease over the ethics of employing an ex-crook. Drawing attention to his "flair" for reporting, he reworked powerful narratives of journalism as a fluid, open profession.[69]

Prioritizing openness allowed Lucas to justify his employment and confront the hostility of colleagues. In this guise, the story he told about his career paralleled the *Autobiography of a Journalist* (1929), edited by Michael Joseph, which attributed success to a "fundamental honesty of purpose and an unflagging industry" in a "hard school." The anonymous autobiographer remained confident that journalism was a "most democratic profession. There are no social barriers, and 'influence' . . . counts for little. It may help some but the lack of it will not hinder others."[70] Journalism's opportunities were unfettered by class or connection, and criminal "antecedents" were not a barrier to success. This is why Lucas emphasized the "vicissitudes" of his career. Struggling "in a great profession in which it is particularly difficult to make headway," he faced rejection and criticism that meant "I learned the inside ropes of Fleet Street." What Lucas called "survival of the fittest" was a more self-serving version of the *Autobiography of a Journalist*'s democratic ideal. Emphasizing hard work above background, however, invoked dominant visions of contemporary journalism.[71]

The "golden age of crime reporting" in the 1950s was anticipated by an earlier generation of journalists. We might compare Lucas to later correspondents like Duncan Webb, who fashioned a distinctive identity as a crime reporter and cultivated the celebrity reserved for detectives and ex-crooks in the 1920s and 1930s. Webb's *Deadline for Crime* (1955) began:

> I am a newspaperman. My job is to obtain facts about events and write them into readable articles for public consumption. My speciality is crime. It is not easy to obtain facts relating to crime. There is competition in being the first to

obtain them. The police want them first. Rival newspapermen want them first. The criminal world does not want anyone to have facts about crime.[72]

Like Lucas, Webb portrayed the "criminal world" as a secretive domain accessible only through painstaking research and connections. Informers and police shared information; experienced reporters decoded signs unintelligible to others. Lacking the detective's resources, reporters relied on their wits, "hav[ing] to smell out the facts, check them many times, and find their information from other sources."[73]

There is much of Lucas's journalism in Webb's account, but they differed in important ways. Both presented themselves as privileged observers of crime, but there were few similarities between the urbane gentleman and hard-bitten newspaperman. Webb deliberately showed himself working on the edges of the law, picking up a West End prostitute to investigate the Messina vice networks. Blurring boundaries between crime and crime journalism generated moral ambiguities central to his public image. Lucas also moved between underworld and overworld, but found the demands of respectability both more compelling and elusive.[74] Lucas tried to cultivate a relationship with the police, but it was never central to his image. Suspicion rather than cooperation marked his interactions with Scotland Yard. Investigating Josephine O'Dare's forgery ring in 1927, Inspector Yandell noted how Lucas and Hart were "devoting their time to journalistic work and the case . . . has given them excellent material." While they exploited their "intimate knowledge of various members of the O'Dare gang," the men's reporting was limited by the hostility of officials.[75] Lucas and Hart, Yandell observed, have "frequently attended Westminster Police Court and displayed a lively interest in 'O'Dare's' welfare, so much so, that it has been deemed prudent to refuse them admission to the Court."[76] Not only was he denied access to the legal process, but suspicion threatened to draw Lucas himself into court: annotated notes on the expanding file suggest officers contemplated arresting him. On 19 February, A1 scribbled: "Shall we get Netley Lucas into the box in this case. Also what for." Three days later, ACC replied: "He is interested, but we have no <u>evidence</u> that he is implicated in this case." Two years after his last conviction, the crime reporter was still suspected of being a criminal.[77]

THE CRIME CLUB

The suspicions of detectives highlight Lucas's unsure progress along the highway to honesty. The idea of a seamless movement toward respectability belied his shifts between forms and genres of writing. At the same time as he reported on crimes and wrote a novel, Lucas contributed melodramatic stories to the *Monster* and *Golden* penny comics. Owned by the United Press then the Amalgamated Press, the publications were indistinguishable in appearance and content, and cross-promoted through adverts and editorial comments. A penny bought boys and girls a lively mix of competitions, cartoons, features, and illustrated stories of cowboys or detectives by leading writers like Gwynne Evans. Lucas was a prolific contributor. Between April 1926 and February 1928, an episode of one of his stories appeared almost every week. Lucas dissected scientific handwriting analysis but also thrilled readers with "The Trapping of the Black Vampire" and "The Case of the Kidnapped King."[78]

Writing for the *Monster* and *Golden*, Lucas recycled incidents and characters that appeared elsewhere as autobiography, reportage, or criminology. Readers might not have realized, but Lucas blurred life-writing and fiction, collapsing his lives into those retold in print. O'Dare became the protagonist of "The £10,000 Cheque Fraud," published in the *Monster* during her trial. Lucas wrote about O'Dare in the *Sunday News*; she was partially disguised as Hart's accomplice in *Crooks: Confessions*.[79] Now she was reincarnated as Theresa or Trixie, passing forged checks and working with a "notorious gang." O'Dare's traces were explicit in a lingering description of a "luxuriously furnished flat" in which a beautiful woman was "smoking a cigarette in a long amber holder." Her "beautifully coiffured" shingled hair, "black lace frock," and pearls meant "she looked anything but what she was—a daring and clever crook and forger." Trixie's sexualized glamour could have come straight from descriptions of O'Dare and her Park Street apartment. Yet the denouement of "The £10,000 Cheque Fraud" was different. It was not painstaking police work that brought Trixie and the gang to court, but Darky Kemp's mastery of disguise. Lucas might have been settling scores with Hellier—we know from *My Selves* that he "took an instinctive dislike to him"—since he was at pains to present the forgers as dull and ignorant. Posing as a messenger boy, Darky met Trixie in a West End hotel, snapping handcuffs upon her wrists when she reached out to take the money he was delivering.[80]

Critics often treated this kind of juvenile fiction as a discrete field appealing to a discrete audience. O'Dare's appearance in the *Monster*, however, suggests how crime writing confounded such distinctions. Crime and detection were staples of children's story papers, and were equally popular with adult readers; writers traded in stock characters and plots whether they published in the *Monster* or *Mystery Story*. Lucas's shifting authorial identities informed all his work. Editorial comments suggested it mattered to young readers that stories were written by a former "borstal boy" or "criminologist."[81] Compared to other work, Lucas could range more widely in writing for the *Golden* and *Monster*. Published in the *Golden*, "Sea Dogs: Or, the Boys of the Training Ship *Pelican*," was a "rollicking yarn" of "adventure on the high seas."[82] The *Autobiography* described Lucas's early interest in the sea. Read alongside his voyage on the *Kenilworth Castle* and his masquerade as a midshipman, we might read the "Sea Dogs" as an imaginative exploration of his own youthful fantasies. It might equally have been an attempt to exploit the popularity of maritime adventure stories. Lucas never claimed to have served in the French Foreign Legion in the Sahara. That was the setting for his story "The Desert Watchers," however, also published in the *Golden*. Personal experience usually shaped Lucas's stories but did not always constrain them.[83]

"The Borstal Boy's" first iteration suggested the enduring pleasures of crime. Darky Kemp did go straight at the end of the series, however, and Lucas's later *Monster* and *Golden* stories shadowed his progress along the highway to honesty. Reinvented as a criminologist, Lucas now wrote about those who tried to prevent crime rather than commit it, folding an implicit story of personal reform into the popularity of detective stories.[84] "The Borstal Boy" became the "Darky Kemp International Detective Bureau." Is this a fictional echo of the process through which the *Autobiography* became *Crook Janes*? Perhaps. The first stories were published anonymously between July 1926 and February 1927. I don't know if Lucas wrote them; the collaborative writing through which story papers sustained popular characters and "authors" makes him elusive.[85] By the spring of 1927, Lucas *was* recounting the exploits of "Anthony Grex—the human bloodhound," named because of "his uncanny 'scent' in tracking down criminals." Any traces of unruly resistance disappeared.[86]

Taking Lucas's *Monster* and *Golden* stories seriously allows us to understand how he remade his public identities in the mid-1920s. Exploring how readers were encouraged to engage with them allows us to see the contradictions of popular cultures of criminality. In the *Sunday News*, Lucas often presented crime as a puzzle to solve. Stories like "Anthony Grex" extended that challenge to younger readers. Grex was assisted by the paperboy "Breezer." Like the "boy" and "girl" detectives Darky and Julia Kemp, Breezer was a familiar figure from the everyday lives of working- and middle-class boys and girls. He offered a point of identification through which readers could imagine themselves into his extraordinary adventures.[87]

While reading was often regarded as a solitary pursuit, magazines encouraged readers to think of it as a social activity. The *Monster* and *Golden* were collaborative projects—sustained by an ongoing conversation organized around the weekly "Editor's Secrets." Gregarious and confiding, the editor invited "my old shipmates" to share in his work behind the scenes, prompting them to understand themselves as part of a vibrant community that crossed boundaries of class, gender, race, place, and nation.[88] Crime was a productive subject upon which to mobilize such camaraderie. Readers were invited to join "The Golden League Detective Bureau," collecting coupons in return for a membership certificate, badge, and a "Secret Cypher Alphabet," which would allow them to recognize and communicate with other members. They were set demanding challenges: printing photographs of readers' fingerprints, the editor offered prizes to those who could recognize their own and tested the observation "skills" necessary for an effective "amateur detective."[89]

This challenge was most elaborate in Lucas's most successful *Monster* story. In May 1927 readers were invited to join "The Crime Club." As part of the "Kemp International Detective Bureau," they would

accompany . . . Darky Kemp and Julia and will ACTUALLY ASSIST IN THE INVESTIGATION OF CRIME in each of our Big Towns every week.

My! Won't your pals be green with envy when they read how YOU have helped the GREATEST MODERN DETECTIVE to unravel one of his baffling crime mysteries.[90]

This was an original and imaginative promotional scheme: to join the bureau, readers had to collect six coupons from the magazine and send them with two stamps to cover the postage for their membership badge and code.[91] They were warned to subscribe to avoid missing out:

The scheme has never before been worked by any periodical newspaper, so you can betcher sweet young lives it will be enthralling. Everybody will be positively EATING the "MONSTER" next week, so tell your chums to order it in advance from their Newsagent.[92]

Lucas wrote adventurers, identified by their membership number, into his stories, encouraging them to watch for their appearance as protagonists in criminal investigations.[93] The "Newcastle Necklace Theft" staged the bureau's origins: a letter from the *Monster*'s editor offers Julia and Darky the services of his readers. Describing them as "red-hot keen to do some crime investigation," Julia notes how "they should be very useful indeed." The detectives receive a "large black leather-covered book" from which they choose their operatives each week. Hunting a jewel thief, Darky summons six local boys to the Central Station Hotel and briefs them on the neighborhoods they are to patrol.[94] Over the course of the series, Darky and Julia visited towns across Britain, the sense of place encouraging personal identification. Adventurers outwitted Manchester counterfeiters, foiled Glasgow gunmen, and kept the cosmopolitan Cardiff "Tigers" at bay.[95] They exhibited the bravery and intelligence necessary to fight crime and were flattered for these fictional qualities. Adventurer 30,003 had "an intelligent face and a look of determination and trustworthiness about him." Darky admiringly called him "a born detective." Julia preferred 7,032: "by far the handsomest, although they were all good-looking lads."[96]

The accompanying illustrations allowed lucky readers to see themselves engaged in feats of daring. An amazing act of agility secured the arrest of the Glasgow gang who had murdered a police officer. Two cars traveled side by side—the disorienting lines suggesting a blur of speed—as, "With a death defying leap, Adventurer No. 4,003 boarded the crook's car." The illustrator showed him poised between the vehicles "like an acrobat" before he drew a revolver and shouted, "Hands up!"[97] Bravery was often interwoven with patrician glamour, echoing Lucas's own past as a gentleman crook. In June 1927 adventurers went undercover after an undergraduate was cheated in a West End gambling den. While the boys donned dinner jackets, "Miss 45,017" wore "an evening frock." The sexualized interactions that followed sat uneasily with the age of the *Monster*'s readers: Lucas showed the girl drinking in the Savoy Hotel, where a gentleman picked her up. In the gaming salon she discovered rigged roulette tables. The illustration captured this moment: the undaunted fashionably dressed girl faced down the dark-haired vamp who threatened her with a revolver (fig. 11).[98]

Assisting Darky and Julia brought readers material rewards and considerable status. Those who identified themselves received a handsome "watch for watching."[99] Promising to publish photographs of those who appeared in print, the editor noted: "Wouldn't this make your pals envious? I can see them turning red, white and blue when they read of your doings."[100] Reading and collecting coupons held the tantalizing prospect of participating in "vivid and fast-moving Detective Stories."[101] Here were "thrills galore, training as a Detective, and a real insight into the mysterious and amazing working of Scotland Yard's famous Sleuth-Hounds."[102] Melodramatic stories were aligned with the stereotype of the armchair detective "assist[ing] the World's Greatest Fiction Detective in unravelling a crime without stirring from your sofa."[103] Just as newspaper reports of sensational crimes prompted readers to weigh up clues

The Adventures of Darky and Julia Kemp who direct the Kemp International Detective Bureau.

DARKY AND JULIA WITH SIX ADVENTURERS RAID A LONDON GAMBLING HELL

By

NETLEY LUCAS

⊚⊚⊚⊚⊚⊚⊚⊚

FOREWORD

Every detective has a watch! Have you got one? If not, then :—
JOIN THE MONSTER ADVENTURE CLUB
and help Darky Kemp to unravel baffling mysteries. If your Registered Number is mentioned in one of these amazing stories you should write to the President of the ADVENTURE CLUB and claim a beautiful watch. If you do, you will

The dark-haired woman levelled a revolver at the girl Adventuress, No. 45,017.

FIGURE 11. The Monster Adventure Club and the pleasures of crime. From Netley Lucas, "Darky and Julia with Six Adventurers Raid a London Gambling Hell," *Monster*, 3 September 1927, 6. © Time Inc. (UK) Ltd. Published courtesy of Time Inc. (UK) Ltd. and The Bodleian Libraries, The University of Oxford and Time Inc. (UK) Ltd., N.2706 b. 12, 3 September 1927, 6.

and ascertain guilt, so following Darky and Julia gave younger readers the chance to scrutinize the "most meagre and fragile evidence."[104]

The lack of sources makes it difficult to know how boys and girls read Lucas's stories. The series' long run suggests that the opportunity to join the Detective Bureau was enormously popular, however; so does Lucas's attempt to work the same trick with his "Anthony Grex" stories in September 1927.[105] Each week the printed list of names showed how many readers identified themselves in print. In July the editor was "bucked" to "find a GIRL ADVENTURER—Miss Dorothy McGlashan, . . . claiming her watch."[106] Nor were adventurers passive readers. Several wrote with questions about the bureau. Others sought to create their own networks around its activities. "Master Lawrence Taylor" expressed his "wish to form a Birkenhead Branch," and invited "interested Members . . . to communicate with him."[107] For a year, such conversations made Lucas's writing dynamic and playful. His characters exchanged letters with the editors whose readers they enlisted; in a *Golden* story, an assistant read the *Monster* at his desk in Grex's "Secrecy House"; Darky and Julia intervened in Grex and Breezer's investigations. Identities multiplied, boundaries collapsed, and Lucas often seemed in his element. When the "Crime Club" ended in February 1928, however, it had quickly become tired and repetitive. The stories were clichéd, the writing flat. Adventurers still appeared in print, but any sense of interaction had gone.[108]

A CERTAIN EX-CROOK OF MY ACQUAINTANCE

Running for nine months, "The Crime Club" lasted longer than any of Lucas's other serialized work. He never publicly acknowledged writing for the *Monster* and *Golden*, however, seeing it, perhaps, as compromising his cultivated image as a journalist. The archival traces suggest the strength of his investment in this new profession: Lucas identified himself as a journalist on business cards, headed notepaper, and his marriage certificate. Repudiating his criminal past, he redefined the basis on which he wrote. Crime reporting remained associated with sensation and duplicity, but brought the ex-crook at least some respectability. Still, apparently, restless and dissatisfied, Lucas again tried something new. The special correspondent became a criminologist.

For Lucas, I think, this move reflected the allure of professional respectability. It also suggested growing emphasis on the capacity of expert knowledge to isolate and address social problems in the early twentieth century.[109] Studies like Cyril Burt's *The Young Delinquent* (1925) and William Norwood East and W. H. de B. Hubert's *Report on the Psychological Treatment of Crime*

(1939) emblematized a broader project that sought to delineate scientific understandings of criminal behavior after the Great War. Such approaches gained
considerable currency among officials at the Home Office and Prison Commission, and institutional impetus through Norwood East's appointment as
lecturer on criminology and psychiatry at the Maudsley Hospital Medical
School, and the formation of the Institute for the Scientific Treatment of Delinquency. The *British Journal of Criminology* only appeared after the Second
World War, but the consolidation of criminology as an applied academic field
set out a realm of knowledge in which the scientific expert acquired increasing authority in managing crime. Criminology, in this guise, was a consciously
modernizing project defined against the excesses of sensationalism and
moralism.[110]

Lucas's professional credentials were tendentious. In assuming the mantle
of criminologist, he still managed to shift the basis on which to write authoritatively about crime. His moves underscore the contradictions of contemporary
criminology. Middlebrow periodicals and publishers like Hurst and Blackett
sustained hybrid forms of crime writing that blended science and sensationalism. Lucas first engaged with criminology by soliciting endorsements for
his life-writing. *Criminal Paris* included a foreword by Dr. Edmond Locard,
"scientific detective" and director of the Technical Police Laboratory at Lyons.
Locard sought to isolate the domain of knowledge (criminology) and object of
study ("the Apache race") to which Lucas contributed. The "Apaches" were
rendered anthropologically Other through their distinctive "code of morals,"
behavior, and physiology. *Criminal Paris* was a "specialised ethnography . . .
of overwhelming interest for the sociologist, the moralist, the criminologist
and the doctor." For Locard, careful research subjected the distortions of
popular culture to the scrutiny of rational scientific method. In challenging
the distortions of the "poet or the music hall," he concluded: "I congratulate
Mr Netley Lucas on having undertaken a monograph dealing with this race."[111]

Locard and Lucas's paratextual dialogue underscores how the boundaries
between scientific and popular discussions of crime were more slippery than
we have often recognized. What Locard saw as an ethnographic monograph
was, for the *Times Literary Supplement*, an "exceedingly 'colourful' and highly
flavoured account," closer to fiction than scientific truth.[112] Yet Locard saw his
work and that of writers like Lucas as part of a common project to address the
problem of crime. Reviewers often expressed doubts over the authenticity of
Lucas's writing. They were still willing to treat it as a source through which
to engage in political debate. Sir Basil Thomson, former assistant commissioner of the Criminal Investigation Department and Home Office director of

intelligence, questioned the *Autobiography*'s "truth," but found Lucas compelling evidence for his attack on the Penal Reform League: "In his case, the practical certainty of punishment would have been a more efficient protection for society than all the well-meant expenditure in Borstal Institutions for changing the hearts of the inmates."[113]

At a moment when disciplinary conventions and research practices were up for grabs, writing as an ex-crook meant Lucas turned himself into a subject of criminological knowledge. We can understand this process by teasing out the conversations between his output and that of John Goodwin. Working with commercial publishers like Hutchinson, Goodwin was a prolific, proselytizing, and popular scientific criminologist in the 1920s.[114] *Insanity and the Criminal* (1923) and *The Soul of a Criminal* (1924) "turned to the psychology of crime, and endeavoured to dissect the mind of the abnormal and apparently normal criminal . . . treating both subjects from the standpoint of Freud, with whose views I wholeheartedly concur."[115] A novel, *The Zig-Zag Man* (1925), turned a psychoanalytic case study into fiction, showing how the "individual's conduct is the inevitable . . . result of the clash between his inherited propensities and his environment."[116]

For Lucas, Goodwin was the kind of figure necessary to lend credibility to his sensational life stories; conveniently they shared a publisher. Goodwin wrote a supportive foreword for *Crooks: Confessions* (1926). Describing it as "too interesting to need assistance from me," he instead placed the book within the development of criminological ideas. It prompted him to explore definitions of the criminal. The uncertainty he found was "evidence that views concerning crime are in a fluid state and . . . offer hope to reformers with something to say and the energy to say it." This was, he implied, a project to which Lucas contributed.[117] Their relationship was mutually productive. Lacking the expansive sociological and psychological surveys of offenders that characterized Norwood East's work (as well as his institutional affiliations and funding), Goodwin used Lucas as evidence in which to ground his arguments. The ex-crook was a human document, his writing a fertile testing ground in which to theorize about crime as a social and psychological phenomenon. In *Crook Pie* (1927) Goodwin considered how drug dealers intimidated smaller crooks. A firsthand account of an encounter with Brilliant Chang was attributed to "a certain ex-crook of my acquaintance, who has reformed and is now earning an honourable living with his pen."[118] Goodwin's scientific credentials made Lucas's confessions credible; Lucas's testimony authorized Goodwin's interpretations. Criminologist and ex-crook existed in productive interdependency. The *Scotsman* noted that *Crooks: Confessions* "support[s] the plea of

Mr Goodwin for a broad view of the relativity of crime and the commercial encouragement of a writer so skillful" as Lucas.[119]

Lucas needed little encouragement. Building on his interactions with Goodwin and Locard, he turned himself from a subject of criminological knowledge to a participant in its production. The anonymous author of the *Autobiography of a Journalist* criticized the excesses of crime reporting, but acknowledged legitimate ways to handle the topic, particularly the "expert criminologist, who studies his subject and writes illuminatingly upon the influence of crime." Would he have considered Lucas an "expert"? Maybe. Lucas's journalism analyzed crime as a social problem as much as a source of sensation. Unconsciously, perhaps, he took up the advice that journalists should not write about crime "until they have mastered their subject sufficiently to publish a book." By reporting and researching, Lucas improved his "mastery" of his subject and wrote popular criminology for the mass market.[120]

Consider the series "Crime and Criminals in Britain To-day," published in the glossy general-interest magazine *Pictorial Weekly* between April and July 1927. Introduced as a "famous criminologist," Lucas "revealed startling facts and figures about crime and criminals in some of our greatest British cities."[121] This echoed Lucas's work for the *Sunday News* but was more ambitious: a wide-ranging argument that crime "is subject to climactic, racial and local conditions." Tracing the "effect of topography on crime," Lucas showed how Bradford's "criminal fraternity [was] naturally a product of industry," their offenses mundane and petty.[122] Burglary was uncommon in the City of London—no one lived there—but fraud proliferated in the "richest business area in the world." These particularities demanded local forms of policing: white-collar "business bandits" tussled with "detectives who understand all the principles of company law and the inner workings of the great business machine."[123]

While this was criminology with a broad brush, Lucas's analysis was more finely calibrated, attuned to the differences between cities with similar economic structures. Ports like Liverpool, Cardiff, and Hull had transient populations that created problems of public order and vice, but differed in important ways. The size of Liverpool's dockland and status as "one of the main gateways of the country" made it the "hunting ground of both a vicious and varied criminal fraternity."[124] Races and nationalities mixed around Liverpool's docks, but it was in Cardiff that the "colour question has long been a daily problem." Echoing the rhetoric of populist politicians, Lucas suggested that allowing "free entry to men of the coloured races" should end, since their presence made crime more prevalent and "baser and more despicable."[125] Lucas challenged the "well known cleric and sociologist" who described Hull's docklands as the "most vicious and scandalous in the whole country." This claim was ill informed. Having "investigated the conditions of the various docklands of the country," Lucas argued that Cardiff and Swansea were more "vicious and scandalous." That Hull's "mercantile population is not so cosmopolitan" meant drunkenness was more pronounced, but this was "preferred by the police to the secret iniquities of Asiatic and African sailors with their opium and gambling."[126]

Rather than recounting crook lives, Lucas now focused on the "inner story of the police work of our big cities."[127] Aligning himself with the state, he emphasized the testimony of detectives and their efforts to defend citizens. He applauded the "energy and resourcefulness" that Chief Constable Percy Sillitoe brought to the "pitched battle" against Sheffield's gangs.[128] Photographs showed officers on parade or in action, and imposing prisons like Strangeways. Here we come to a recurrent theme in the series: praise for the provincial forces driving the development of modern policing. A photograph of officers on motorcycles illustrated how Bradford had one of the most up-to-date flying squads in Britain.[129] Following the example of the United States, provincial forces engaged in "pioneer work" to modernize policing. In a period when police drew intense public criticism, Lucas was one of their most strident defenders.[130]

Above all, Lucas's arguments were marked by precision and scientific method:

> I have compiled what I have called a "Burglary Chart," which shows the percentage of burglars per population. Thus in London there is probably one burglar to every 15,000 persons; in Liverpool the percentage is smaller, being about one to every 21,000 persons; and in Manchester even less, there being about one burglar to every 50,000 of the population.

Animated by the practices of criminological research rather than sensation-mongering, Lucas came close to the writing of better-known academic criminologists. He did not state the methodology that underpinned the "Burglary Chart"; he did not explain how he calculated the number of burglars in a city; his figures were ratios rather than percentages. There is still something striking about this analysis. Set against the greater ratio of police officers to population, he drew a comforting conclusion: "Manchester readers of the PICTORIAL WEEKLY may feel fairly secure in their 'Englishmen's castles.'"[131]

As surprising as it is to come across something like the "Burglary Chart," reading Lucas's work in this period, I often get the sense that he is losing energy or focus: so many projects fizzle out or end abruptly. The final articles in *Pictorial Weekly* were shorter and more formulaic than the initial ones. Perhaps the range of Lucas's activities made this inevitable. What I have characterized as his creativity was accompanied by a sense of restlessness.[132] In 1927 he wrote for the *Sunday News, Monster, Golden,* and *Pictorial Weekly*. Perhaps there was another project. A letter written on headed notepaper in July identified Lucas as the author of *Everyday Frauds*.[133] Goodwin's *Crook Pie*, in which Lucas appeared, mentioned the same title: a film then "being prepared . . . under the direction of Mr F.W. Engholm . . . in which confidence tricksters, backdoor crooks, [and] cardsharpers . . . are to be pictorially depicted actually at work."[134] *Everyday Frauds* went on general release in March 1927. Lucas does not appear in any publicity material or reviews; no copy of the film survives, so I cannot know whether he is listed in the credits; he did not mention it in *My Selves*—though that is true of much of his work. All I have is two typed words on one sheet of notepaper. What can I write about a trickster's uncertain role in films that no longer exist? Taking Lucas's claims seriously might mean the *Everyday Frauds* would be on me.

Frederick Engholm gives few clues. Engholm had served in the Royal Navy before becoming a cinematographer for the Topical Budget company around 1911. His work documenting the conditions of modern war was groundbreaking—first the conflicts in the Balkans and then amid the German invasion of Belgium. In that fleeting moment before the War Office prohibited filming on the front line, Engholm secured remarkable footage used in films like *With a Skirmishing Party in Flanders* (1915).[135] Later he was drawn into official efforts to control the public presentation of the war as "Official Kinematographer" to Royal Naval Intelligence.[136] Having secured his reputation, Engholm continued to work as a commercial filmmaker after the war. The subject of *Everyday Frauds* was a new departure, however. Goodwin saw it as evidence of crime's profitability and "grip . . . on the public imagination." It might also suggest the influence of a collaborator—one sensitive to the new markets and opportunities created by the rising popularity of cinema-going in the 1920s.[137]

Reviews and advertising give some sense of the film's content. *Everyday Frauds* comprised eight episodes—"little pictures" shot on single reels of film—that lasted around fifteen minutes and were screened in a longer cinema program.[138] Actors and intertitles recreated "well-known devices for coming by money dishonestly."[139] There is no definitive list of episodes, but titles included "Miscreants of the Motor World" and "Dud Cheque Chicanery."[140] *Kinematograph Weekly* described how the "confidence trick is elaborately detailed and relates how an American man of wealth is robbed of his pocket book."[141] The "working methods of the clever gentry" were exposed to public scrutiny. Echoing themes Lucas explored and titles he used, *Everyday Frauds* displayed striking affinities with his writing about crime.[142]

The elaborate publicity for *Everyday Frauds* suggests someone with a keen grasp of self-promotion. Trade advertising introduced this "unique series" to cinema halls, quoting positive reviews to demonstrate the commercial potential of the films.[143] An article in the *Nottingham Evening Post* emphasized the "ironic touch of realism" audiences could expect. *Everyday Frauds* "will 'feature' among its stars several reformed criminals, well-known to the police as experts in their own particular lives," and "a retired Scotland Yard detective is helping to lay bare these secrets of the 'profession.'"[144] Privileged access to the underworld was brought to the screen: "reformed criminals" reenacted their deceptions; retired detectives orchestrated scenes. Engholm was presented as a diligent researcher. The mock auctioneer's "patter" had a "ring of reality" because the producer "tracked down one of the fraternity to his hunting-ground in a small market town" and recorded his speech.[145] In the *Evening News*, A. Sympson Harman described Engholm's conversations with an East End "fence." When Engholm outlined his plans, the fence "listened as long as he could restrain himself, and then exclaimed: 'Frauds, guv'nor! They ain't frauds; they're tricks we teach our rabbits.' Thereupon he proceeded to tell Mr Engholm about some real frauds!" Here, Harmon argued, was ironic confirmation that "everybody wants to act in films or help in their production."[146] There are also hints that the producers cultivated controversy. Describing the "Banned Film," the *Singapore Free Press* noted: "One fraud we should all have enjoyed watching in slow-motion—the three-card trick—is to be denied us. The authorities have banned it saying it would teach people how to do it!"[147]

Everyday Frauds was well received in trade publications, including *Impartial Film Review* and *Film Renter*, and newspapers like the *Star*. Only the *Daily Mail* sounded a dissenting note, remarking on "that pathetically amateurish air which mars too many British film efforts."[148] Entertainment and education blurred together. *Faulkner's Film Review* praised the "human touch" that made the films "true to life." Alerting audiences to the dangers of a society of strangers, they would "do a lot of good, even to the wisest."[149] It seems cinema proprietors and audiences also welcomed *Everyday Frauds*. Released at fortnightly intervals, the films appeared on programs at cinemas that included the Princess in Dundee and Cosy in Derby.[150] Audience reactions are harder to trace, but a young cinemagoer questioned by the Birmingham Cinema Enquiry of 1930–31 had apparently seen one episode. Concerned about the cinema's "baleful effects on children and adolescents," the inquiry surveyed fourteen hundred younger Britons. Adventure and detectives were among their favorite subjects. One boy recalled: "Not long ago the _____ Picture House showed an item every week about confident tricksers, which learned me dodges used by people who make their living by frauding innocence people." His comments might have troubled the inquiry, but they give a sense of the popularity of films like *Everyday Frauds*.[151]

That Lucas remained invisible in *Everyday Frauds* was an appropriate end for the process through which he effaced personal exploits from his writing. *Criminal Paris* exemplified the contradictions of his authorial identities. In *Crook Janes* (1926), by contrast, Lucas appeared only opaquely as a narrator connected to the underworld, reflecting that "my varied—and unhappy— experiences have brought me into touch with women crooks in many parts of the world." Where his knowledge of these women was attributed, it was more professional than personal. Lucas recounted exchanges overheard in restaurants and cited a conversation with "the Matron of one of the largest female prisons in England."[152] The transition from ex-crook to crime writer crystallized in the book's geographical and chronological range. Lucas ventured to London, Paris, and New York and described "appalling scenes I have witnessed in the Halb-Welt of Berlin."[153] These were ostensibly familiar territories, but excursions to the "frozen north" and "near and far east" were the point at which any claim to firsthand knowledge collapsed. *Crook Janes* became the kind of breathless survey of notorious crimes Lucas criticized in his earlier work. His subjects were unsurprising; the personal touch that enlivened previous books, sporadic and unconvincing. *Crook Janes* reflected how far away from the *Autobiography of a Crook* Lucas had written himself.[154]

WE ARE ALL CRIMINOLOGISTS

That Lucas's work was already incorporated into debates over crime meant it was relatively easy for him to be taken seriously as a *popular* criminologist in the mid-1920s. Later books resembled his work as a special correspondent more than the first-person confessions that brought him to prominence. Investigative journalism and research allowed Lucas to isolate patterns of criminal behavior from which he remained distant. Reviewing *London and Its Criminals*, the *Dundee Courier* noted how the "well-known writer on criminology . . . opens new fields of research in the lives of crook and super-crook." Lucas could now be treated as an authority, setting research agendas and opening "new fields" rather than entertaining or scandalizing.[155]

My guess is that writing for popular newspapers and story papers still provided most of Lucas's income, but redefining himself as a criminologist impressed provincial journalists and brought a growing audience of "experts" seeking to enhance their knowledge.[156] The criminal pathologist Dr. Francis Camps bought a copy of *London and Its Criminals*, pasting a plate giving his name and affiliation to the London Hospital's Department of Forensic Medicine inside the cover.[157] Others engaged seriously with Lucas's ideas as they argued about how to manage crime. In the United States, Dr. Frank Crane challenged Lucas's argument that the "best way to cure the crime wave . . . is to resort to corporal punishment." This was, Crane suggested, a "restatement of an old point of view that happily is dying out." Drawing on modern scientific knowledge, he argued that the "criminal should be segregated and treated by those experts who understand the psychology of human nature." Crane disagreed with Lucas but accepted him as part of the same field.[158]

It is in this context that we should understand Lucas's most audacious public reinvention. Unsatisfied with his prolific journalism and books, he launched a journal: the *Criminologist*, published in May 1927. When magazine ownership was increasingly concentrated in corporations like the Amalgamated Press, the *Criminologist* was an independent venture. Printed by the obscure John Missenden, the journal had its editorial offices at the Clifton Works in Harlesden, an unfashionable north London suburb. Lucas was not identified as editor in the journal itself, but appeared in that role on the headed notepaper he used during 1927; signing over the initials "RD / NL" suggested he was still working with his "pal and partner" Richard Dent, or Guy Hart. Only one issue appeared, but the *Criminologist* was envisaged as a long-term project. It was numbered "Vol. 1 No. 1"; a single issue cost one shilling, but readers could subscribe by paying "4s for four consecutive numbers."[159]

None of this was particularly remarkable. In a period when magazine aesthetics were increasingly sophisticated, the *Criminologist* even looked ordinary. Though it cost as much as glossy monthlies like *Pearson's*, its twenty pages made it considerably shorter than those publications and included no photographs or illustrations. The *Criminologist* did not meet the conventions of popular magazine publishing. Nor did its content suggest it was meant as a straightforwardly academic title. Understood as the intellectual and commercial labor of an ex-crook, however, the *Criminologist*'s existence was remarkable. Its content and contributors were more striking still. Psychoana-lytic interpretations of criminality sat alongside tabloid gossip and sensation; analysis of notorious cases coexisted with wry snippets about the quirks of police and criminals. Above all, Lucas secured contributions from well-known public figures, including the psychiatrist and phrenologist Dr. Bernard Hollander, the Professor of Chemistry C. J. S. Thompson, the radical MP J. M. Kenworthy, and the crime writer H. Ashton-Wolfe. This remarkable network of progressive politicians, forensic pathologists, and popular writ-ers embodied how Lucas positioned the journal as an authoritative source of knowledge about crime.

The contributors' short essays encapsulated the polyvalent nature of crimi-nology. Hollander drew on "several hundred" case studies to show how brain injuries or diseases could cause lapses in control of the "emotions or instincts" that led to particular criminal behaviors.[160] Others focused on the processes of observation and scientific detection then being pioneered by police forces and pathologists in Europe and North America.[161] Exploring the "Secrets of Poisoning," Thompson described the chemical components and effects of dif-ferent toxins and how they could be identified.[162] Ashton-Wolfe's essay on "Languages and the Criminal" treated underworld slang in France, Germany, and Spain as exemplary of differences of national character. In books like *The Invisible Web* (1928), Ashton-Wolfe showed the "extraordinary precision of modern scientific investigation," including the use of the Bertillion identifica-tion process and ballistics analysis.[163] This was interwoven with flamboyant accounts of using disguise to penetrate the Parisian underworld. The fron-tispiece to *Warped in the Making* (1928) showed a costumed "Ashton-Wolfe in the *role* of Apache. . . . One eye is made up to look like an inflamed hollow, with an ugly scar running up the right cheek." Norwood East was never pho-tographed like this.[164]

The *Criminologist* also engaged in contemporary debates over the man-agement of crime. Lieutenant Colonel Edwin Richardson, author of *Brit-ish War Dogs: Their Training and Psychology* (1920), considered the use of "Bloodhounds as Man-Trackers."[165] Kenworthy addressed the contentious politics of penal reform. As MPs debated the private member's bill to abol-ish the death penalty that he proposed to Parliament, Kenworthy used the *Criminologist* to make the "commonsense" and statistical case against capi-tal punishment.[166] The *Criminologist* ranged across scientific detection, psy-choanalytic etiologies of behavior, and human-interest stories of crime. That the contributors published with firms as diverse as the Scientific Press and Hurst and Blackett suggests the breadth of Lucas's connections and how criminology could collapse boundaries between ostensibly discrete modes of knowledge.

The editor thus introduced the *Criminologist* to diverse reading publics:

> Few can say that they are not interested in crime. One can picture the school-boy, walking along the street, being thrilled by his penny shocker; the youth, interested in the spectacular and sordid aspects of the real thing; and the man and woman of maturer years reading it idly, or studying it intently, bent upon interesting themselves in "the extraordinary things people will do."

It is easy to imagine all these readers engaging with Lucas's disparate body of writing after 1922. Attuned to their diverse needs, the editor attributed interest in crime to the thrill of the spectacular, the demanding task of interpreting clues, and "dramas" of human character. If readers' interest in the subject varied, then the institutions that dealt with crime also isolated it as a different kind of problem. An operational challenge for the police was a "psychological study for the doctor, a spiritual one for the cleric, a problem for the bench and the jury, and a human 'document' for the journalist"; for the politician, crime had pressing "community import." This was an expansive version of criminology. The *Criminologist* promised to entertain, inform, and demonstrate crime's "vast complexities" to those with "rudimentary" knowledge.[167] The "Potpourri of Crime" on the next page was a miscellany including the likelihood of identical fingerprints and the costs of London's "motor bandits." This single page encapsulated the *Criminologist*'s diffuse content. Its author was identified only as "Cerberus." The mythological three-headed hellhound who guarded the entrance to the underworld was an appropriate avatar for a journal that presented itself as a gatekeeper to knowledge of crime, and the many voices of contemporary criminology.[168]

Criminology was thus an emerging field, its disciplinary and scientific status still uncertain. Criminologist applied equally to psychoanalytic studies of crime, panoramic social surveys, firsthand revelations, and the rational amateur detective. Criminologist dignified the reader who devoured newspaper reports (and the journalist who wrote them) through "morbid fascination" with the "cult of the crook."[169] In particular contexts, these realms of knowledge bled into one another, trading in stock tropes and a common emphasis on authenticity.[170] By 1927 Basil Thomson could comment of this baggy demotic field: "We are all criminologists now."[171] Experts like Norwood East might have disagreed, seeing no common ground between rigorous academic work and the popular writing from which it sought intellectual distance, but such comments underscored the fractured nature of the criminological project. Lucas's adventure in magazine publishing nuances linear narratives of the expansion of professional expertise and scientific rationality, and suggests how market, science, and state were deeply imbricated ways of making sense of crime.

The *Criminologist* was embedded in the characteristic social, cultural, and intellectual conditions of 1920s Britain. It was also, I think, a very personal project. It is difficult to know whether Lucas wanted to make a lasting contribution to criminological knowledge or profit from public interest in crime. Either way, the journal was integral to the process through which he reinvented himself. It was shaped by the tensions between his shifting public identities and personal dilemmas. Content and contributors reflected the legacies of his earlier work—essays on Paris by Edmond Locard and Emile Laurent.[172] Under his byline Lucas contributed a piece on "Innocent Murderers" that included the cases of Patrick Mahon and Edith Thompson on which he had reported.[173] Beyond these discernible influences, Lucas's presence haunted the journal. Unless they knew who the editor was, it might not have been obvious to readers, but at times the *Criminologist* became bound up with the process of promoting the work of Netley Lucas. "The Underworld of Books" contained a short review of *London and Its Criminals*: "Although sensationally Mr Lucas succeeds in inspiring the interest of his readers, leaving them with an intriguing sense of insecurity." Readers might have become more insecure to learn Lucas was selling them his own book.[174]

These two lines were nothing compared to the half-page feature on "Crook Life on the Screen." The anonymous "Holepicker" reviewed the "remarkable series of films entitled 'Everyday Frauds.'" Inevitably, perhaps, Holepicker's praise was unstinting. Lucas had presented his contributions to *Motor Boat* as a necessary preventive measure, instilling vigilance in readers and offering practical advice on protecting property.[175] *Everyday Frauds* was also characterized as a public good:

> The Prefect of the Paris Police said to me not long ago, "The only way to reduce the number of frauds is to make the public less gullible. . . . If the police could broadcast satisfactorily a circular revealing the methods of swindlers of all kinds, the activities of thousands of criminals would be curtailed." . . . Now it gives me great pleasure to be able to write to my police friend in Paris and tell him an even more effective way of forewarning the public has been produced.

Echoing Lucas's characteristic appeals to authority, Holepicker described how the series of short films succeeded as entertainment and education. Having congratulated Engholm, "I asked him where he obtained all the detail. He was discreet!" We might hear Engholm's ostentatious silence as the point where Lucas wrote himself into the production of *Everyday Frauds*: discretion concealed and revealed the firsthand knowledge essential to the films' success. Rendered accessible to a mass audience, *Everyday Frauds* "will forewarn the public against the ever-growing army of swindlers." Holepicker recommended that "everyone interested in crook life should see them."[176]

As brazen as this was, the *Criminologist* was more than elaborate self-promotion. Short and short-lived, it nonetheless gave form to Lucas's efforts to remake himself as a writer. It is a material trace of stories he told about his newfound professional status and the entrepreneurial energies he brought to redefining this realm of popular publishing. Read against his work for the *Sunday News*, it betrayed his continued ambition. Setting up a journal suggests imagination, creative flair, and the contacts and charm necessary to secure contributions from notable writers; the archival fragments suggest his powerful investments in the journal. It was as editor of the *Criminologist* that he wrote to the secretary of the London P.E.N. Club in March 1927, asking for particulars, "as I feel I should consider it an honour to be a member."[177] Seeking entry to this progressive international community of writers was unlikely. Lucas made his name writing about crime for the mass market; his politics were ephemeral at best. When the writer John Gray attended P.E.N. meetings in the 1930s, he found a Bloomsbury basement packed with "serious" and "intense-looking young men and young women, all very artily dressed," reading their poetry. It is hard to reconcile Lucas's oeuvre and personal style with this rarefied atmosphere, but even contemplating membership reflected the effortful ways in which he sought credibility. Joining P.E.N. offered the prospect of social cachet and literary accreditation. These must have seemed priceless assets for an ex-crook who had begun confessing in the *World's Pictorial News*. For all these reasons, I cannot understand why Lucas did not mention the *Criminologist* in his final autobiography.[178]

By July 1927 Lucas had moved to an office in Shaftesbury Avenue. Its location signaled his growing confidence; new headed notepaper proudly identified him as author of five books and editor of "THE CRIMINOLOGIST," even as the initials "M.S.P." and "F.P.E." affixed to his name suggested a preference for style over substance. I have no idea what the initials are supposed to stand for, but the allusion to (and illusion of) professional qualification is clear

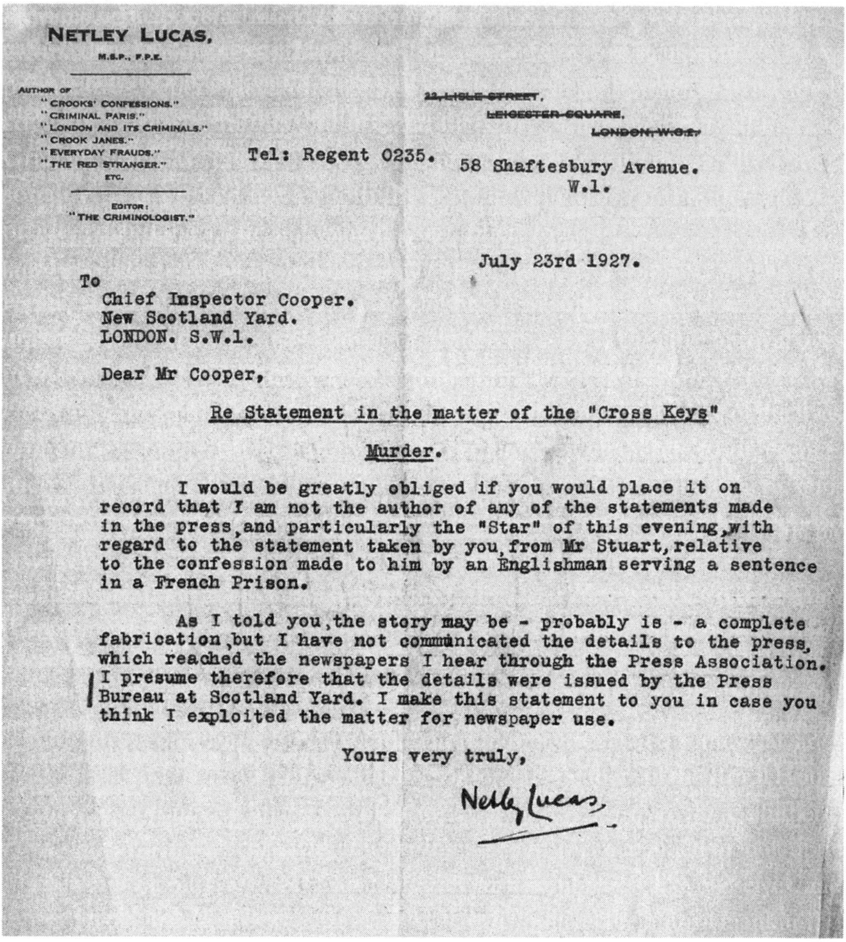

NETLEY LUCAS,
M.S.P., F.P.E.

AUTHOR OF
" CROOKS' CONFESSIONS."
" CRIMINAL PARIS."
" LONDON AND ITS CRIMINALS."
" CROOK JANES."
" EVERYDAY FRAUDS."
" THE RED STRANGER."
ETC.

EDITOR:
" THE CRIMINOLOGIST."

22, LISLE STREET,
LEICESTER SQUARE,
LONDON, W.C.2.

Tel: Regent 0235.   58 Shaftesbury Avenue.
W.1.

July 23rd 1927.

To
Chief Inspector Cooper.
New Scotland Yard.
LONDON. S.W.1.

Dear Mr Cooper,

    Re Statement in the matter of the "Cross Keys"

    Murder.

    I would be greatly obliged if you would place it on
record that I am not the author of any of the statements made
in the press and particularly the "Star" of this evening, with
regard to the statement taken by you from Mr Stuart, relative
to the confession made to him by an Englishman serving a sentence
in a French Prison.

    As I told you, the story may be - probably is - a complete
fabrication but I have not communicated the details to the press,
which reached the newspapers I hear through the Press Association.
I presume therefore that the details were issued by the Press
Bureau at Scotland Yard. I make this statement to you in case you
think I exploited the matter for newspaper use.

            Yours very truly,

            Netley Lucas,

FIGURE 12. Netley Lucas, M.S.P., F.P.E. From TNA, MEPO/3/268B: Netley Lucas to C.I. Cooper (23 July 1927). Published courtesy of the National Archives of the United Kingdom.

(fig. 12).[179] While the *Criminologist* can, and should, be understood as part of Lucas's navigation of the highway to honesty, his application to P.E.N., his insistent status claims, and his restlessness perhaps also betrayed persistent insecurities. Although Lucas was desperate to distance a notorious past from his ostensibly respectable present, his criminal lives remained problematic. In the *Criminologist* a short paragraph praising the Prince of Wales's "humanitarian views" on crime included this quote: "Punishment is a cleansing fire and a criminal who has served his sentence ceases to be a social outcast. He is an honest man again . . . and is, therefore, deserving of a helping hand." Lucas had been through the "cleansing fire" of prison several times. Am I pushing the argument too far in suggesting that here we see an ex-crook's powerful emotional and material investments in his own reform? Is there a desperate cry for help here—a plea for support and another chance? This might, after all, be what the *Criminologist* represented.[180]

CONCLUSION

The anonymous author of the *Autobiography of a Journalist* warned budding journalists against writing exclusively about crime. He or she made one exception: "If the freelance believes he will develop into an Edgar Wallace, a Charles Kingston or a George Dilnot then by all means let him confine himself to crime." Gaining this exalted status required an "exacting course of study and research" and became harder each year as the field "becomes more crowded." Lucas was never as well-known as Wallace, but for a time his reputation approached that of Dilnot. Focused and prolific, he was either confident in his abilities or willing to accept the risks of specializing as he chased its rewards. Whether reporting on sensational trials or exposing the white slave trade, his writing foregrounded the effects of diligent research.[181]

Lucas ranged across genres, markets, and readerships. Between 1926 and the start of 1928, however, he slowly redefined the terms on which he engaged with his criminal notoriety. While he still wrote extensively about crime, authority no longer rested in personal experience, but the analytic tools of a dispassionate expert. In part, this reflects Lucas's apparent desire for professional respectability. In part, it underscores the growing authority of criminal science. It also provides an opportunity to think critically about the extent to which criminology was the modernizing project it claimed in the 1920s and 1930s. In the hands of writers like Lucas, different modes of writing about crime became entwined. Despite assertive efforts to isolate criminology as an academic domain of knowledge, the borders between popular and scientific cultures of criminality remained porous. The comic book criminologist embodied a hybrid cultural form that was neither unequivocally sensationalist nor rigorously academic.

The *Criminologist* was only one visible part of Lucas's personal metamorphosis. Perhaps taking another step along the highway to honesty, the reformed crook repudiated his criminal past and made the decisive move into respectability. Yet this doesn't quite work. For a start, while the burglar-turned-sociologist Mark Benney would follow a similar path a decade later—ending eventually in a teaching post at the University of Chicago—such success remained exceptional.[182] This analysis also effaces the contradictions of contemporary criminology, imposing rigid and impermeable boundaries between popular and scientific modes of knowledge. The sensational firsthand revelations that dominated popular publishing always informed (and were informed by) emerging psychoanalytic and sociological studies of crime and criminality, even as the institutional apparatus of academic criminology sought to repudiate this unruly demotic realm. Lucas's interactions with John Goodwin and Edmond Locard underscore how older forms of confession could coexist with "modern" criminological knowledge. Treating the *Criminologist* as part of a linear narrative of reform—a story that Lucas could both deploy and deny—flattens out the tensions that braced his writing and the unpredictable turns his career took.

The *Criminologist* also encapsulated the transformation of popular publishing after the Great War. Lucas sought to take advantage of the technological and cultural changes that made the 1920s the golden age of magazine publishing. His initiative was shaped by and contributed to a marked growth in the number of titles and their fragmentation into discrete genres. It was probably the challenges of this competitive marketplace that accounted for the fact that only one issue of the *Criminologist* appeared. I cannot tell how Lucas funded his venture, but he could never hope to draw on the resources available to the corporations then coming to dominate magazine publishing. Neither could he produce something of the same quality as titles like *Britannia and Eve*. Despite the public obsession with crime and its remarkable contributors, the *Criminologist* was also, perhaps, misjudged. It was overpriced. More important, Lucas created a specialist periodical at precisely the moment at which the sector's decline was imminent. Around 1930 the number and popularity of magazines was challenged by competition for leisure time from the cinema, radio, and new cheap novels; the growing pressures of economic depression; and the inexorable rationalization of the publishing industry. When Hutchinson closed its magazine empire in favor of mass-producing books in 1929, the future was clear. The *Criminologist* appeared just as dozens of similar publications folded: 1927 was also the year in which the *Golden* and *Detective*, in which Lucas had published, disappeared.[183]

The tensions that braced Lucas's writing went well beyond his idiosyncratic lives. The position from which Lucas wrote was pulled in different directions by the insistent demands of the individual project of reform in which he notionally engaged after prison, the institutional imperatives of a modernizing penal system, and the emergence of elaborate commercial mechanisms for generating human-interest stories about crime. Popular criminology was an emerging conflicted discipline that encompassed psychoanalytic studies of criminality, large-scale sociological surveys, and the first-person confession, and that interwove sensation and instruction, pleasure and rational investigation. Whether Lucas wrote as an ex-crook, special correspondent, or criminologist, his work allows us to explore these conflicted cultures of criminality. The ideas of reform around which his work often turned were the point at which the disciplinary state and market demands for entertainment and instruction became entwined.

CHAPTER 5

Ghosts and Their Doings

WHEN NETLEY MET BASIL

Two months after the editor of the *Monster* introduced the "world's greatest criminologist," he announced a new serial with similar fanfare:

> I've a further surprise tit-bit, too, Young Sirs! . . .
>
> I have been fortunate in prevailing on one of our greatest writers of Sea Stories, Mr Basil Vaughan . . . to work a bit of overtime on a very fine yarn of the Sea.[1]

From June 1927 Vaughan's "Sons of the Sea" followed the adventures of two young apprentices on a tramp steamer. Its first installment appeared the week after Netley Lucas's "The Desert Watchers" had ended, and for several months the men shared the *Monster*'s pages.[2] Then, in August, Netley met Basil. The editor confided in readers: "Two of your favorite authors, Mr Netley Lucas and Mr Basil Vaughan, came into my office the other day unexpectedly, and seeing each other, made the atmosphere so cold I had to put on a fur coat!" Navigating the professional rivalries between men who "have for years been at friendly enmity" required delicacy and tact. Now, however, the editor "had a wheeze to bring together these two great wielders of the pen to write a story between them."[3] The serialized "collaboration" "East at War with the West" brought together characters from Lucas's "Sea Dogs" and Vaughan's "Sons of the Sea" in "a battle between the White and the Coloured Races—the greatest wartime sea-story ever written."[4]

Vaughan might have been known for his storytelling, but his career was more checkered. Presenting himself as a member of the Junior Civil Service

Club, in 1920 he cashed a dud check in a West End bank; in 1924 the *Police Gazette* included Vaughan among the "aliases" used by Netley Lucas; Lucas's *Crooks: Confessions* (1925) described how "I was known as the 'Honourable Basil Vaughan'" in London's underworld.[5] Having eluded the historical record for several years, Vaughan reappeared in the same story paper to which Lucas was a prolific contributor. Their staged meeting in an editor's office was unlikely, if not impossible. Switching between names and stories, claiming inside knowledge of crime and the sea—this seems like a literary confidence trick.

Lucas and Vaughan's encounter evoked debates over the market's effects on the nature of authorship in the 1920s and 1930s. A writer's name acquired growing importance as a sign of authority and knowledge. The power of the authorial brand both meant that journalists increasingly published under their byline and underpinned an extensive apparatus of collaborative cultural production that sustained the illusion of authorial singularity. Jobbing freelancers wrote articles on current affairs by leading public figures; teams of reporters compiled signed gossip columns; ex-crooks worked with ghostwriters to "confess." All this prompted concerns that truth had become a performance, and the author a facade. Lucas's transformation into a writer was animated by these processes, but the proliferation of names around his work made its authorship and provenance uncertain. One article in a series of first-person "confessions" appeared under a different name; the name on a title page changed between editions; reviewers probed the limits of his knowledge. For at least three years, Lucas managed to conceal these frayed edges. Others were less fortunate. Josephine O'Dare's autobiographical reminiscences had been a hot commodity for newspaper editors, but in 1933 she sued *Reynolds's Illustrated News* for libel and exposed the mediating networks of personal journalism to public scrutiny. Court reports suggested O'Dare had not written her own autobiography.

If "Basil Vaughan" was an illusion, then was that also true of "Netley Lucas"? If O'Dare or Lucas did not write their life stories, then could their veracity be taken for granted? Lucas's success as a writer on crime depended on securing the effects of authenticity for his work. The elasticity of popular criminology and Lucas's movements across genres of print culture, however, created a space in which the truth of his work came under critical discussion. Sensational crime narratives characteristic of popular magazines registered differently when reprinted by reputable publishers and reviewed in middlebrow periodicals. Lucas's work could be treated as emblematic of the excesses of commercial publishing: reviewers usually criticized it for what it represented rather than as a particular problem. In the summer of 1927, however, uncertainties coalesced to discredit Lucas and destroy his career. After careful investigations, reporters at *John Bull* now suggested that Lucas had moved beyond the conventions of modern journalism into deceptions that resembled the criminal offense of obtaining money by false pretenses. Placing profit over accuracy, prioritizing the end above the means, and, perhaps, deceiving readers and publishers, the moment when Netley met Basil underscored how the criminologist was remade as the confidence trickster.

HAUNTED BY YOU

In the mid-1920s Lucas was famous, and his crime writing ubiquitous in Britain, the empire, and the United States. Accepting it as an authentic "human document" often required tacit awareness of the genre's clichés, but Lucas managed to secure the confidence of editors, publishers, agents, and readers. At the same time, a growing number of names began to be attached to his work. Appearing as flashes in the historical record, they betrayed nagging uncertainty over its authorship and authenticity. The contradictions within and between Lucas's work, and the pointed comments of reviewers, hinted that not all was what it seemed.

When Lucas was a young journalist, his notoriety made changing names a necessary expedient. In 1922 he introduced himself to editors as " 'Paul Evelyn,' Journalist." In 1924, to alleviate suspicion about his honesty and dissociate himself from his criminal past, Lucas took a "nom de plume" and wrote for the women's pages as George Armstrong Mackenzie.[6] This "high sounding Scottish name" suggested the uncertain boundaries between necessity and cynical deception. In his burgeoning career as a writer, the names Lucas claimed were not always as innocent as he later suggested, carrying social and material possibilities through which journalism blurred into crime. It was as Mackenzie that he was convicted in Canada.[7]

I am not sure why Lucas continued to claim different names in this period. *My Selves* described the journalistic agency he and Guy Hart set up in the mid-1920s. There is no trace of any organization under their names, but Mackenzie and Albert Marriott worked together as "literary agents" in Toronto.[8] Journalists and police presented this as a scam, but the later venture was apparently more respectable even if its directors' identities were uncertain. In 1925 "Graham & Dent: International Press Agents" began work from an office in the Adelphi in London. Also claiming offices in New York and Montreal, they promised "everything newspapers need." In February, Richard Dent wrote to the James B. Pinker literary agency. Soliciting fifteen thousand words on the "Land Question" from Pinker's client John Galsworthy, he promised "a very attractive figure" in payment. Several years later Graham and Dent (and Pinker) would be implicated in the bogus biography factory scandals. In 1925 they remained elusive.[9]

After publication of *The Autobiography of a Crook* (1924) secured Lucas's celebrity, he built a reputation writing under his own byline. These shifting names were usually hidden from publishers, editors, and readers. They nonetheless left their impress upon his work. In 1924–25 Lucas described "my own experiences" of crime, prison, and Borstal in a series of articles in the *Detective*. Yet the promised "firsthand information" was unsustained.[10] Lucas only appeared in the abstract account of being "On Trial," refusing to describe his experience—"I don't want to go into all the details of my trial again"—and disclaiming any inside knowledge of London's courts.[11] An editorial slip inadvertently exposed the illusions of authenticity. "Pearls and the Woman," published in August 1924, retold the theft of Gaby Deslys's pearls. Still ostensibly a firsthand account, changing the names of protagonists made it more like fiction than personal testimony: the story was prompted by the "death of Sidonie Desprit" and narrated by the gentleman crook "Christopher Tallentire." Attributed to "Netley Lucas" on the contents page, the story appeared twenty-six pages later under the byline of "R. L. Dearden." An attentive reader might have wondered whether Lucas really was writing of his "own experiences" (fig. 13).[12]

We can understand these tensions by setting the *Detective* against Lucas's later reflections on the *Autobiography*'s origins. In 1924 he approached "a retired naval officer, a Commander Dearden . . . who agreed to take my material and facts and collaborate with me in the writing of a book," sharing the advance royalties equally.[13] Best known for his stories of the Royal Navy, Dearden now collaborated in a different literary endeavor. After Lucas left for Toronto in the autumn of 1924, Dearden worked on the manuscript and negotiated its sale to the publisher T. Fisher Unwin.[14] Lucas claimed the *Autobiography* was published without his knowledge: in London in January 1925, he was "mystified" when congratulated by an acquaintance on a "flattering" *Daily Mail* review.[15]

Neither Lucas nor Dearden acknowledged that their collaboration extended to the *Detective* series, though "Pearls and the Woman" implied it did. Identifying Dearden's authorship called Lucas's contribution to the series into question and unsettled the illusion of his involvement with his *Autobiography*. The book's first edition was attributed to Lucas. In the second edition, published in February 1925, the title page had changed: it was written "by R.L. Dearden, from material supplied by Netley Lucas," even though the final page

"For Heaven's sake, stop!" I cried, in an agony of bitter remorse. "You do not know what you are saying!"

Pearls and the Woman

A ROMANCE, founded on fact, of a king's gift and—a woman's.

By R. L. Dearden.

ILLUSTRATED BY C. AMBLER.

THE death of Sidonie Desprit, La Belle Sidonie, once the petite amie of a king, and the idol of theatrical Paris and London, impels me to relate, as a tribute to her memory, the story of my own affaire with her.

She died as she had lived, with a smile in her childish eyes and a £20,000 rope of pearls about her slender throat. Those pearls, given to Sidonie by King Maritz of Portonia, purchased, it is said, out of the state coffers, caused a revolution in Portonia,

and also marked a crisis, the crisis, of my life.

Of the other characters in my drama, Anderton Shairp, like Sidonie, is dead. Henley and Marks are in penal servitude for life, for a crime unconnected with the present story. Thanks to Sidonie, I am still an honest man.

I first met Anderton Shairp in the long bar of the Galleon Tavern, situated just west of Aldgate. I was down and out, literally —sent down from the 'Varsity, kicked out

FIGURE 13. Ghosts and their doings are often perplexing. From Netley Lucas, "Pearls and the Woman," *Detective*, 15 August 1924, 601, 637. © Time Inc. (UK) Ltd. Published courtesy of Time Inc. (UK) Ltd. and The Bodleian Libraries, The University of Oxford, per. 25612, vol. 4, 15 August 1924, 637.

was still signed "Netley Lucas, London, 30 July 1924." It was with this double attribution that the book appeared in the United States. Its ambiguous authorship and uncertain "truth" were embedded in the *Autobiography*'s frame.[16]

As far as I can tell, no British reviewers noticed the appearance of Dearden's name in the *Autobiography*. I think they were sent the first edition, and accepted Lucas's claims to authorship even when they criticized his style and veracity. In the United States, by contrast, it was Dearden rather than Lucas who drew criticism. A withering essay in the *New York Times* assumed "Netley Lucas" was an alias:

> Although what must be termed the "Lucas" narrative is labelled "The Autobiography of a Crook," the reader will be glad to let whatever scapegrace chose the alias stand acquitted of the crime of indicting the tale. The man who appears to have committed this truly atrocious assault on the body literary appears from the title page to have been one R.L. Dearden.

Even Eustace Jervis's foreword could not convince the reviewer this was "not a piece of fiction"; quotation marks around "Lucas" signaled his dubious authenticity. Here was vivid evidence of the indiscretions to which the market's perverse incentives might drive a writer addressing "the lower classes of British readers."[17]

These criticisms were echoed in the *Saturday Review*. Noting the "pathetic glimpses of Lucas's better nature" and remorse, the reviewer observed:

> How far this is genuine, and how far it is the creation of Mr Dearden, it is impossible to say. One has a feeling that it is Mr Dearden's moralizing, Mr Dearden's acquaintance with literature, and Mr Dearden's adeptness with storytelling that are being revealed, rather than those of the young crook.[18]

The dispersal of authorship meant Lucas's "nature" was refracted through Dearden's attitudes. It was the ghostwriter who brought Lucas into contact with the demands of the market and the logics of contemporary life-writing. It was the ghostwriter who ventriloquized Lucas's lives and prompted him to work within particular cultural forms and languages of selfhood. The storytelling ex-crook disappeared behind the impress of his ghost. Where did the "genuine" end and the creation begin?

Despite the embarrassing reviews, Dearden always insisted on his involvement in the *Autobiography*. I think the changing title pages probably reflect pressure that he or the Society of Authors placed on T. Fisher Unwin to acknowledge his intellectual labor. Six years later, as the furore around the biography factory gathered pace in December 1930, Dearden wrote to correct the suggestion that Evelyn Graham (writing as Lucas) had published the *Autobiography*. The book "was written by me, under a complete misunderstanding." Younger and naive, he "was merely another of the dupes of this young man" who presented himself as "a well-to-do journalist in search of a collaborator." Dearden himself was a victim: credit for his literary work had been taken by an unscrupulous trickster.[19]

In 1933 Dearden again insisted on his involvement with the book, writing to the *Daily Express* in response to the announcement of the forthcoming *My Selves*. The *Autobiography*

> was written by me as fiction. Its main theme was supplied by a person I then knew as Mr Armstrong Mackenzie and with whom I had been put in touch, by post only, by reputable people. This person turned out to be none other than Netley Lucas, from whose sordid and commonplace exploits I had evolved what some describe as a "best seller." . . . Though many of the episodes and characters in that book and all the actual writing were my own invention and labour, I received no kudos and very little money from it.

Challenging Lucas's claimed ignorance of the book's publication, Dearden argued that he did not know his collaborator's identity "until [Lucas] published the book as his own story." The *Autobiography* was "fiction," not first-person testimony. Lucas was a dishonest parasite rather than a repentant ex-crook, passing off Dearden's work as his own. While the book had "evolved" from Lucas's career, its protagonists were "characters" and episodes "invented" rather than "his own story." The affinities between Dearden's work and Lucas's writing for the *People* and *World's Pictorial News* cast doubt upon some of this account. Whatever their collaboration, Dearden found himself in the unusual position of admitting his role in a "curious literary hoax."[20]

The *Autobiography* was not the only book marked by such uncertainties. *Crooks: Confessions* (1925) was attributed to "an author who professes to be narrating his personal experiences," but the plural "crooks" of the title revealed more than was intended.[21] The project began under the "guidance" of the agent, Robert Somerville.[22] Two other names associated with the book remained unspoken. In the 1950s the writer Harold Castle recalled meeting Lucas in the mid-1920s, "when I helped in the preparation of some of his reminiscences." In a publisher's office Lucas demonstrated his criminal accomplishments by picking their pockets. Castle did not identify the book, but his account fits *Crooks: Confessions* most closely.[23] More than this: the experiences Lucas "confessed" were not entirely his. Introducing his "true life stories," he acknowledged that "my assistant in this series is Mr Guy Hart. What I don't know about crime and criminals, he does."[24] Their experiences as pals and partners were interwoven in a jarring narrative written in a singular authorial voice. The contents page promised "my experiences in English and Canadian prisons and strange people I have met, including Bottomley, Brilliant Chang, Frederick Bywaters." It was "our prison experiences" in Toronto that Lucas described, however, and Hart who had been in prison with Bywaters.[25]

Even these slips did not fully accommodate Hart's role in the book. It first appeared in *Cassell's Popular Magazine* as "Two Crooks Confess; by Netley Lucas and Guy Hart." Illustrated with portraits of both men, the series was nonetheless introduced as something written by "I, Netley Lucas," with Hart as "my collaborator."[26] As the putative author of each installment shifted, the narrator's voice was unchanged. On 16 May "Guy Hart takes up the story and narrates some adventures with grasping moneylenders"; the following week Lucas returned to describe their exploits rum-running in the Caribbean. Such shifts called the series' authorship and veracity into question.[27]

Lucas's later autobiography did not acknowledge these uncertainties. In *My Selves*, Lucas was remarkably generous in admitting Dearden's contribution to his success—cognizant, perhaps, of the fury that prompted Dearden's letters to the press in 1930 and 1933. The *Autobiography* "was not actually written by myself, but by Commander Dearden," working from "rough facts which I had supplied." By 1934 he could comment: "I have no wish to take credit for the brilliant success of the book." This was disingenuous because for eight years he had done exactly that. As early as 1925, Lucas thanked readers for their "patient sympathy" for "my screed, 'The Autobiography of a Crook.'"[28] Value rested in Lucas's byline, not Dearden's writing: "As an unknown freelance journalist I had found it very difficult to sell articles, but now with the success of the book Commander Dearden had written about me, came the opportunity to capitalise the fact that I was an ex-crook." The name he could capitalize was invested with value by the work of a ghostwriter.[29] The flurry of publishing that followed concealed Dearden's interventions; the generosity of *My Selves* was compromised by Lucas's efforts to reestablish the illusion of his own creative endeavor. Describing "the publication of my first two books" and "my growing success as an ex-crook-cum-author," Lucas wrote Hart, Castle, Dearden, and (perhaps) others out of the public history of his literary success.[30]

I do not know how much of this was apparent in the mid-1920s. The slip-pages I have noted are the public traces of collaborative forms of cultural production, but it would have taken a reader of considerable acuity and devotion to Lucas's oeuvre to piece these fragments together. The criticism of Dearden in the United States suggested some awareness of his complicity in Lucas's career. When British critics questioned his books' authenticity, their concerns focused upon their internal contradictions and impossibilities. This was particularly marked in literary periodicals and middlebrow newspapers. In the *Times Literary Supplement*, Sir Basil Thomson noted that without Eustace Jervis's "certificate of accuracy," he "should have been inclined to ask Mr Netley Lucas a few searching questions" about the *Autobiography*'s claims.[31] Lucas's tales were "extraordinary," but many of them left public archival traces. The *Daily Mail* noted that the "variety and number of his various swindles" and masquerades "almost passes belief," but still accepted the book's truth.[32]

It was in this context that Lucas's veracity came under scrutiny. Of *Criminal Paris* the *Scotsman* observed: "It is perhaps an invidious sort of compliment to say that Mr Lucas knows what he is writing about," praising a "lively and interesting volume."[33] Yet the drama that drew readers compromised its claims to authenticity for some critics and was considered inappropriate in an "authoritative" survey of crime. Elsewhere Lucas's public persona prompted unease. The *Queenslander* observed pointedly: "It is rather a pity that he published his own boyish photograph as a frontispiece. Youth and a profound firsthand knowledge of the 'underworld' of Paris hardly go together."[34] His errors drew vicious sniping. The *Times Literary Supplement* itemized the mistakes puncturing Lucas's claimed expertise in *Crook Janes* (1926). Could he really have visited the "Frozen North" when he described Iceland's inhabitants as "Eskimo"?[35] At best, mistakes might be attributed to "hasty writing or a faulty memory"; at worst, they cast doubt on his truthfulness.[36]

The authenticity and accuracy of Lucas's books were central questions for reviewers. Their comments often policed the boundaries between genres of writing and, in particular, between popular and middlebrow culture. Reviewers returned to the idea that his books' content and style were somehow out of place. They included "beautiful women apaches who might have stepped right out of the movies" and were written "for people who like the tabloid newspapers between book-covers."[37] That Lucas's writing moved across genres compromised its authenticity. The *Dundee Courier*'s description of *Crook Janes* as "astonishingly informed" was tempered by the suggestion that "sensational serialists and scenario writers should find it a gold mine"—identifying a "powerful plot ready in the case of two well educated sisters, one of whom acted as a decoy, while the other mesmerised wealthy victims."[38] In the feminist periodical *Time and Tide*, Algernon Blackwood dismissed *Criminal Paris* as "impressionist and somehow unconvincing." Lucas drew the reader underground, but when returning, "you feel you might have seen little more than a clever, well-informed journalist might have shown you from a mixture of hearsay and observation." Lucas was clever; he had visited Paris; such criticism still exposed the conflicts his ambition created.[39]

GHOSTS AND GHOULS

Despite some critical reviews, for most of the mid-1920s, Lucas managed to efface the collaborations that underpinned his work and secure his growing reputation as a crime writer. His name signaled knowledge and authority. "Netley Lucas" was a precarious fiction—at least one magazine thought it "a pseudonym which conceals the identity of the [*Autobiography*'s] author"—but maintained judiciously enough that it brought literary success and financial reward.[40] Lucas was unusual among ex-crooks in both managing to shift the position from which he wrote about crime and preserving the integrity of his authorship. The "truth" of sensational "inside stories" drew increasing suspicion after the Great War. In 1936 Robert Thurston Hopkins reflected: "Many sketches of the early life of Josephine O'Dare appeared in the newspapers at the time of her trial, but much of the 'information' used in them was invented by attic scribes in Fleet Street. . . . In the press biographies of her, traces of the scandalmonger and the literary ghoul are met at every turn."[41]

Hopkins linked O'Dare's lives to a broader crisis of cultural production and the mediating practices through which lives became stories. The insatiable demand for "confessions" meant shadowy journalistic practices like ghostwriting proliferated in the 1920s. This was Lucas's way into journalism: he wrote material attributed to Stanley Scott; he was introduced to "a titled Lady ——," under whose name "I wrote numerous articles" and found a "fairly comfortable subsistence."[42] Working with Dearden and Castle drew him into such practices from the other direction. It was in this context that Hopkins isolated the "literary ghoul" as a pressing problem of modern publishing. Privileging the illusion above the reality, ghostwriting rendered authenticity a matter of style and the first-person voice something that could be ventriloquized by grafting freelancers. In this "culture of the factitious," readers and critics struggled to distinguish legitimate from illegitimate writing; it was no longer easy to establish where necessity ended and deceit began.[43]

Such dilemmas had shaped discussions of criminal life stories since the eighteenth century, but the expanding literary marketplace gave them particular force in the 1920s and 1930s. By 1928 H. M. Paull's *Literary Ethics* could observe: "The employment of ghosts is more or less recognised as inevitable and justifiable; though sometimes it is abused." Partially acknowledging its legitimacy, Paull remained uneasy about something he associated with the confidence trick:

> Readers . . . have accepted as genuine works with which their supposed author have had nothing to do. The practice is the more reprehensible because of the difficulty of detection. . . . A writer has no right to owe his reputation to the work of another and thus deprive him of credit; and to deceive the public is as much a crime in literary matters as in anything else.[44]

Sydney Moseley's *Short Story Writing and Freelance Journalism* (1926) instructed budding freelancers how to produce "signed interviews" with huge "commercial value."[45] In 1935, however, he launched a stinging attack on journalism's "growing evils." Exercised by recent cases like Elvira Barney and Montague Noel-Newton, Moseley singled out "the confessions and 'life stories' of the crooks, the near crooks and the innocently notorious." Paradoxically, his critique encompassed the economy of excess around this "disgraceful exploitation of notoriety," and the "worthless and largely 'faked' life stories" that were produced "upon a colossal scale" by "some capable write-up man."[46] "Immoral . . . degrading . . . and bad business," the ghost's "imaginative work" compromised the prestige of the press and the confidence of readers. If the Newspaper Proprietors Association did not "set its house in order," Moseley argued, "journalism itself will be debased and the public will begin to think here, as it already does in America, that half the 'stories' it reads are 'fakes' and that the entire 'newspaper game' is only another 'racket.'"[47]

Such comments linked the ghosted life story to concerns about the pernicious influence of American mass culture. Moseley elided modern crime with modern crime writing, both alien threats to ideas of Britishness. In this view, the United States was more violent in criminality, more sensational in reporting, more reliant on the deceptions that threatened the integrity of British journalism. Never simply resisting American influences, commentators tried to reconcile new forms of personal journalism with what they presented as enduring British characteristics.[48] "Our popular journalism is essentially a native product," noted Harold Herd. Challenging "those who believe that it is merely an adaption of American journalism," he highlighted crucial differences of scale, the centrality of truth, and the boundaries between public and private life. Acknowledging the influence of the United States in "exploiting of the human interest in the news," Herd was still convinced "the limits of good taste are . . . more rigidly drawn" in Britain. Others were less sanguine, but such arguments underscored how the crook life story fueled a fraught national cultural politics.[49]

Although these concerns shadowed Lucas's writing, he evaded sustained scrutiny for at least three years. In 1933, by contrast, the authenticity of O'Dare's life stories exploded into public debate when she sued John Dicks Press for libel over the "My Life and My Lovers" series published in *Reynolds's* in 1927.[50] O'Dare's suit went to the heart of debates over journalistic ethics because it turned on the disputed question of authorship. Representing O'Dare at the High Courts of Justice, the Irish barrister Serjeant Sullivan set out her case: the serial "purported to be a publication of the history of her life written by herself. If there was one thing which he could state, with confidence . . . it was that Miss O'Dare did not write one word of it."[51] *Reynolds's* admitted publishing the articles, but pleaded that they appeared with O'Dare's "knowledge and consent . . . and for good consideration paid to her."[52] The statement of claim filed by O'Dare's solicitors set out the words through which she had "suffered damage in her character and reputation" by transcribing the whole series.[53] Sullivan identified the most injurious passages: first-person accounts of "passionate lovers made to pay" and consolation "in the mad excitement of 'white snow.' "[54]

Reynolds's distasteful invented life, Sullivan told the jury, should be suppressed. Faced with "cleverly written stuff of a highly flamboyant nature," it was "in your hands to teach newspapers that they cannot print this sort of stuff with impunity."[55] Sullivan's address was a powerful attack on cultural forms from which O'Dare and Lucas profited: the "system of the glorification of crime and criminals" through which newspapers "competed with one another in publishing what purported to be a history of the criminal."[56] Such comments reflected concerns over the transformation of the press—attacked in increasingly strident terms for debasing public taste, glamorizing crime and profiting from sin, eroding boundaries between truth and fiction, and threatening the sanctity of private life in what the *Saturday Review* called "our sensation-sodden democracy."[57]

Sullivan aligned O'Dare's personal reform with the changing imperatives of the state—both derailed by depicting her as a drug-taking sexual predator. The modern penal system sought to provide criminals with "a real opportunity of becoming decent citizens in the future. If there was any person to whom that consideration most applied it was to one who was merely a girl at the time she got into association with criminals."[58] O'Dare had served her sentence, but in revisiting the past, such stories ruined any chance of reform. Sullivan asked:

"Who will accept this girl when it is publicly stated . . . in a so-called 'signed article' that she boasted that she cultivated the friendship of decent people with the sole aim and object of plundering and blackmailing and betraying them?"[59] An ex-crook's libel suit became an intervention in the politics of mass culture. Suing the *Daily Express* in 1929, Hayley Morriss argued: "Newspapers are obtaining money from the public by false pretences [and] publishing a lot of rot . . . at the expense of individuals." It was "everybody's duty to stop this orgy of libel."[60]

These debates focused attention on the mediating practices through which O'Dare's life was retold for public consumption. Following Lucas, we see these opaquely, but with O'Dare the demands of legal process spotlight the shadowy methods through which lives became stories and suggest plausible accounts of Lucas's interactions with newspapers and publishers. In O'Dare's case, the first figure under scrutiny in court was her brother, George Skyrme.[61] Skyrme described how he was approached by *Reynolds's* news editor and asked for details of her life story, photographs, and letters as the trial ended. Receiving this material from her butler, Skyrme gave it to the newspaper but "insisted that anything written must be submitted . . . for her approval." *Reynolds's* claimed otherwise, but Skyrme denied writing the serial or providing the material on which it drew.[62]

O'Dare's "literary ghoul" was the enigmatic Vincent Wray. A jobbing journalist and editor, Wray was in his sixties when engaged to ventriloquize "My Life Story." While his presence haunted the libel trial, his role remained unclear—not least because he died before the case reached court. By the mid-1920s he had established a reputation as a writer under his own byline. "Vincent Wray, the well-known criminologist," reported on the Stella Maris case and published "startling revelations" of London vice in 1926.[63] Due to Wray's experience, he was approached to work with O'Dare. He visited O'Dare in the hospital at Holloway, where, she admitted, he "started to discuss her life-story" until stopped by a nurse. O'Dare and her brother denied *Reynolds's* claim that Skyrme "had many interviews with Mr Vincent Wray." Yet Wray had clearly seen O'Dare's "bundle of letters"—still in the paper's possession in 1933.[64] Wray was both "capable write-up man" and "carrion 'ghost,'" the indeterminacies of his role encapsulating the problem of contemporary ghostwriting.[65]

In addressing these uncertainties, *Reynolds's* sought to document its negotiations with O'Dare and Skyrme. In pretrial exchanges and in court, it produced a signed letter "authoriz[ing] G.W. Skyrme to dispose of all rights to my photographs, letters and the history of my life."[66] It presented receipts including "full settlement for a series of articles signed by Josephine O'Dare written on information supplied by her."[67] It produced a publication agreement signed on 12 May 1927. For £115 Skyrme agreed to "hand over to J. Dicks Press Ltd. for publication as they may decide . . . all letters received by Josephine O'Dare from her intimate friends and acquaintances together with full particulars of her life-story and photographs." Confirming that he held exclusive rights to this material, he "declare[d] that I hold the full authority of Josephine O'Dare to publish her life-story and letters."[68] In court, Philip Vos cross-examined Skyrme over his contractual obligations: the agreement included nothing about the right to prepublication approval; he had not "raise[d] any objections" when the articles appeared; he read proofs on five occasions in the presence of a subeditor. Skyrme denied much of this but admitted he received money for the "signed story."[69]

While Skyrme's role remained unclear, O'Dare was more definite: "She supplied none of the material for the articles."[70] She had not given "Skyrme permission to sell my life-story or my letters," nor had she even seen the publications until she was released from prison. Such claims were undermined by letters produced in court. Writing to Skyrme in May 1927 "regarding my story over which you have taken so much trouble," O'Dare "consent[ed] to all moneys in this connexion being paid to you," but noted how "it is understood that you will help in my defence."[71] Facing such evidence, she pleaded diminished agency: "My mind was in such a state in prison that I did not know what I was signing."[72] *Reynolds's* disputed this version of events, but it was plausible given hints that Skyrme was seeking to exploit her misfortune.

Vos attempted to demonstrate that O'Dare had authorized *Reynolds's* life story by drawing attention to her autobiography in the *People*:

> Mr Vos—Were you anxious that your true lifestory should be published to the world?—I published my life-story myself.
> . . . I was quite anxious . . . that the true story of my life should be made known to the world.[73]

Such exchanges revealed the shadowy underpinnings of modern mass culture. The "illusion of self-determination" characteristic of autobiography quickly evaporated.[74] Just as one reviewer was uncertain whether Lucas was involved "in writing or dictating" the *Autobiography*, so O'Dare's reply was reported variously as "I published my lifestory myself" and "I had to dictate that myself."[75] Later she "agreed that she read the proofs for an article about her," asking that she not be called an "adventuress."[76] Writing, dictating, approving—O'Dare's relationship to her autobiographies shifted. Author, narrator, and protagonist were identical yet different. The autobiographical pact—the author's commitment "to the sincere effort to come to terms with and to understand his or her own life"—was exploited and exploded. Exposing the fragmentation of authorship in commercial publishing, the libel trial compromised the possibility of autobiographical truth and disrupted the foundational premises of personal journalism.[77] Little wonder Lord Riddell, owner of the *News of the World*, observed how "ghosts and their doings are always perplexing."[78]

THE LIBEL RACKET

O'Dare's suit against *Reynolds's* was not the only case that questioned the authenticity of personal journalism and publishing. In court Philip Vos presented her as a parasitic and deceitful social climber. As the trial continued, he focused on her pursuit of reform through the pages of the *People* and London's courts. O'Dare's desire to "start afresh" was "humbug" since "directly she came out of prison, the first thing she did was to make a bargain with 'The People' that, for . . . £800 they should have her lifestory and blazon it all over the country in large type."[79] Pushed to acknowledge the patrician names and addresses she had taken since prison, O'Dare denied having large unpaid bills, but the inferences were clear: she had fallen into a downward spiral of debt and fraud.[80]

Throughout the 1920s observers worried that ex-crooks like Lucas and O'Dare were profiting from notoriety. Selling sensational life stories to the highest bidder revealed the excesses of commercial mass culture. In highlighting O'Dare's straitened present and publicity-seeking past, Vos went further, insinuating that her case against *Reynolds's* was mercenary rather than redemptive. It was, he argued, part of a systematic assault on the press undertaken for profit rather than to restore her good name. When cross-examined, O'Dare admitted bringing libel cases against "nearly all the newspapers" and receiving "substantial" damages totaling twenty-five hundred pounds.[81]

In so doing, O'Dare gestured toward a heated debate around the abuse of the libel laws, animated by a series of cases in which ex-crooks took legal action over their published life stories. William Hobbs—imprisoned for blackmailing Sir Hari Singh—sued the *Liverpool Evening Express* and *Nottingham Evening Journal* in 1928.[82] Acquitted of murdering his rival in the Stella Maris bizarre love triangle, Alfonso Smith won five hundred pounds' damages from *Good Housekeeping* in 1928 and one thousand pounds from *Everybody's Weekly* in 1937.[83] The stockbroker Hayley Morriss, imprisoned for sexual assault and procuring underage girls, unleashed actions against newspapers that included the *Daily Express, Leeds Mercury*, and *Daily Chronicle*.[84] By the time O'Dare's case reached court, Mr. Justice Branson could comment: "The spectacle of newspapers publishing sensational articles about people whose only claim to notice is that they have been convicted of some crime, and . . . these people . . . bringing actions in these courts to recover damages from these newspapers for things said about them, is one of which we have recently had quite enough."[85]

Branson's comments echoed Sydney Moseley's suggestion that Britain's "antiquated libel laws" made such suits "part of the running costs of modern journalism!"[86] In 1939 the *Evening Standard*'s solicitor, Arnold Maplesden, estimated the paper paid five thousand pounds each year in damages, settling out of court because it was inviable to fight cases in which plaintiffs could often not pay costs. Maplesden and others considered such suits part of an organized scheme orchestrated by "the well-known type of speculative solicitor," identifying "a certain firm which has now ceased to practise."[87] That was probably Edmond and Martin O'Connor of Chancery Lane. In 1920 Martin O'Connor defended Lucas at the London Sessions.[88] By 1933 his brother had acquired a reputation for his work in the libel courts, acting for O'Dare, Hobbs, and Smith. Declared bankrupt in 1936, Edmond O'Connor was in prison two years later, convicted alongside Hobbs for forging the theatrical costumier Willie Clarkson's will.[89]

O'Dare's links to the "libel racket" were plausible. When Charles Hellier first submitted his account of her exploits to *John Bull* in 1924, Superintendent Yandell noted, it "became known that Hellier and O'Dare were associated in the West End and apparently on good terms of friendship." On this basis, "the articles were rejected as it was thought—and perhaps rightly—that these two persons were in all probability, out for damages for libel."[90] Yandell's speculations sat uneasily with Hellier's violent relationship with O'Dare, but were thinkable because they gestured toward criminal networks in which she was implicated.[91]

By the mid-1930s Moseley's unease had become generalized and politicized. It was taken up by professional organizations like the Institute of Journalists and Newspaper Proprietors Association, which campaigned against the effects of fear of "blackmailing actions" in stifling press freedom.[92] Handbooks for "everyday use to the practical newspaper man," like Edward Wooll's *Guide to the Law of Libel and Slander* (1939), provided advice.[93] Professional bodies cooperated with Members of Parliament A. P. Herbert and Sir Stanley Reed to introduce reforming private member's bills to protect authors and newspapers.[94]

These pressures culminated in the creation of a Committee on the Law of Defamation.[95] Although the committee was quickly mothballed at the start of the Second World War, it provided a focus for the debates of the previous decade. The committee allowed professional bodies to pursue their demands for reform and enabled a critical perspective on modern journalism. Informed by debates implicit in O'Dare's case, hostility focused on the boundaries between public and private life, the mediating practices of cultural production, and the importance of journalistic responsibility. Concerns over the power of the press coalesced around both the erosion of privacy and the dangers of what Wooll called a "press-controlled country." The wealth and circulation of newspapers made Wooll skeptical about their claims to be "oppressed" by the libel laws. By contrast, he argued, if a newspaper "successfully invades daily some millions of happy homes, and should on some occasion convey to each of their occupants the permanent depreciation of an innocent member of the community, there seems every reason why the damages should be on a genuinely expansive scale."[96]

Wooll's comments reflected growing concerns over new forms of personal journalism, partly fueled by the controversies around the crook life story. The most wide-ranging version of this position was submitted to the Committee on the Law of Defamation by the barrister Richard Willies as a structural analysis of the press's "modern activities." Willies focused on those popular newspapers

> in which . . . exaggerated importance and wide publicity are given to comparatively trivial events of little or no public interest; newspapers which cultivate and rely upon public curiosity in the private affairs of quite unimportant people; newspapers which cultivate and pander to a morbid interest in crime and outrage; newspapers which rely for their extensive circulation on the interest in scandal which they cultivate and create by publishing defamation in sensational form.

While recognizing the risk of speculative libels, Willies emphasized the human costs of this rapacious drive for profit. The threat of publicity and "prohibitive expense" prevented ordinary citizens from using the law to protect their reputation. Newspapers' "relentless search for sensational material" and "disregard" of the truth "results in the publication of that which causes unnecessary and unwarranted interference, injury and mental suffering." He reserved particular scorn for the bullying freelancers and ghosts "whose livelihood depends upon their capacity to invade privacy; to ignore tragedy; and to market horror."[97]

As such concerns intensified, they prompted abortive proposals for new forms of press regulation. "Press intrusion" into private life concerned both the market research organization Political and Economic Planning's *Report on the British Press* (1938) and the *Report of the Royal Commission on the Press* (1948). Wary of the dangers of restricting newspaper freedom, both reports sought to improve journalistic standards by advocating new professional structures, forms of self-governance, and minimum standards of education and training. The Royal Commission proposed a General Council of the Press to deal with public grievances and "build up a code of conduct" to govern modern journalism. If self-regulation was unsuccessful, legislation would be necessary. While debates over the relationship between privacy and the press coalesced around the intimate lives of politicians and celebrities from the 1970s, it was the crook life story that drove such questions in the 1920s and 1930s.[98]

Dramatized through the legal process, the conflicts around O'Dare's newspaper lives culminated with the 1933 libel trial. Edward Wooll noted that, except for murder, "no type of litigation elicits such popular interest as is evoked by the perusal of Press accounts of causes celebrés in the form of sensational libel actions." Wooll's *Law of Libel and Slander* sought to "promote a more intelligent appreciation" of proceedings that could be "bewildering."[99] While the libel trial notionally sought to ascertain "reputation," it produced mannered performances that confounded rather than confirmed the "truth." The exchanges between plaintiff and defense created a maelstrom of claims in which identity was to be challenged, not accepted; life stories to be discredited, not endorsed. This was reinforced by necessary standards of proof. The barrister Charles Pilley's suggestion that "libel is not a question of truth and falsehood" was neither flippant nor inflammatory: identity was "entirely a question of evidence."[100]

O'Dare's case against John Dicks Press thus failed to fix the "truth" of her identity and interactions with the press. A *Daily Express* headline trumpeted "Libel Verdict against Publishers" but was undercut by details of the "Scathing Comments" on O'Dare's character.[101] The jury agreed that "My Life and My Lovers" was libelous but awarded O'Dare only a farthing's damages. The verdict threw into relief the shady practices through which lives became stories, questioning the truth of the crook life story and the integrity of popular journalism. Despite extensive evidence, the jury was unconvinced that O'Dare had authorized, let alone written, her "autobiography." Authenticity was compromised and credibility undermined. At the same time, the papers struggled to understand what the *Straits Times* called "Miss O'Dare's Farthing."[102] Damages were assessed against the jury's consideration of the "presence of malice or negligence on the defendant's part, the extent of the defendant's circulation, the rank and character of the plaintiff, whether an apology has been published, or provocation on the part of the plaintiff" and could be "contemptuous, nominal, substantial or vindictive."[103] O'Dare's farthing was contemptuous because it signaled that despite being libeled, she "was not free from blame, or [her] character was disreputable and not likely to suffer much injury."[104] O'Dare's story sold for £150 in 1927 and £800 in 1930; now she "had to accept a farthing as the jury's considered valuation of [her] good name."[105]

THE DEATH OF NETLEY LUCAS

O'Dare's libel suit drew unwanted attention to the mediating forms of cultural production that simultaneously sustained and disrupted her life stories' authenticity. It raised questions about the "truth" of sensational crime writing and threatened readers' confidence in the stories they consumed. As far as I can tell, Netley Lucas was not drawn into this furore. In 1933 he had recently left prison and was struggling to rebuild his life. Setting his earlier writing in this context still suggests ways of understanding his career and the freighted politics of 1920s and 1930s mass culture.

Questions of truth and confidence haunted Lucas's career and ensured that the delicate balancing act through which he turned himself from ex-crook into criminologist was unsustainable. Over six months in 1927, the tensions between his disreputable past and respectable present became irresolvable. Then working for the *Sunday News*, Lucas later described a visit from a convicted criminal offering "exclusive information" about Lieutenant Colonel Norman Cecil Rutherford's imminent release from Broadmoor Criminal Lunatic Asylum. Rutherford was notorious—a decorated war hero who had shot another officer in a jealous rage over his wife's affair. "Scenting a story" yet concerned to confirm its truth, Lucas questioned the man and telephoned officials at the Home Office and Broadmoor. While neither institution would make a statement, the editor ran the story.[106] The "Broadmoor Sensation" was front-page news on 10 July. Despite the "great secrecy" maintained by authorities, it was nonetheless "stated that Rutherford . . . will leave England to take up a position on a farm owned by relatives."[107]

Lucas's connections quickly brought another scoop. A man recently released from prison in Lille claimed a fellow inmate had confessed to the unsolved murder of Frances Buxton, landlady of a Chelsea pub, in 1920. "Having heard that Lucas was writing a book on Prison life in France," he approached the journalist.[108] Lucas was excited but wary: "I rang up Chief-Detective-Inspector Cooper at Scotland Yard and told him what I had learned." After taking the man to the "police fortress," he realized "I now had the makings of a fine little 'scoop.' . . . Within an hour my story was written and delivered."[109] The "New Chelsea Murder Hunt" was front-page news on 24 July: a "dramatic statement" to the police now promised resolution to Buxton's mysterious death.[110]

These stories instantiated the preoccupations of contemporary journalism: the demand for a "scoop," the emphasis on professional craft, enduring interest in notorious crimes. Lucas meticulously reworked the conventions of modern journalism to secure the "truth" of his exclusives. Yet the *Sunday News* went to press without official corroboration. As journalists competed for news, veracity was often sacrificed for speed. G. W. Mitchell, president of the National Union of Journalists, noted how the modern newspaper "call[ed] for even swifter movement, ceaseless vigilance, and greater concentration" from editors and journalists. In this case, perhaps, the concentration of Lucas and his editor lapsed.[111]

There was something mysterious about the *Sunday News* exclusives. Lucas later claimed to have guarded his Chelsea scoop jealously. Even before the story was published, however, he tried to share it. He visited Bernard O'Donnell, crime reporter at the *Empire News*; O'Donnell telephoned Cooper, "asking if I could verify [the story]"; the detective would not answer.[112] What was supposed to be a *Sunday News* exclusive first appeared in the *Star* on 23 July. Lucas approached O'Donnell; he wrote the *Sunday News* piece. Now he wrote to Cooper to disclaim the story:

> I would be greatly obliged if you could place it on record that I am not the author of any of the statements made in the press . . . with regard to the statement taken by you from Mr Stuart. . . . As I told you, the story may be—probably is—a complete fabrication, but I have not communicated the details to the press, which reached the newspapers I hear through the Press Association. I presume therefore that the details were issued by the Press Bureau at Scotland Yard. I make this statement to you in case you think I exploited the matter for newspaper use.[113]

Lucas's behavior and the attentions of journalists and police meant the *Sunday News* exclusives had dramatic fallout. The Home Office denied reports of

Rutherford's release. Two weeks later, the *People* linked news of the reopened Chelsea investigations to an elaborate attempt to "bluff the Yard."[114] Lucas went unnamed, but in August *John Bull* linked him to a "partly successful attempt to hoax the two most wide-awake communities in the country." This "well known . . . writer of books of crime" had tried to sell "hot piece[s] of 'copy'" to several newspapers. Rather than exclusive scoops, his stories were fictitious.[115] Rather than a diligent investigator, he was peremptory and arrogant, a telephone caller "whose business was far too important to be dealt with by minor officials" at Scotland Yard. Rather than authoritative, he was untrustworthy: police found that a "few enquiries . . . confirmed their first suspicions that he was a gentleman on whose word no credence could be placed." Mercenary and unscrupulous, the author of the *Autobiography of a Crook* had cooperated with a convicted criminal to "spoof" journalists and police for financial reward. The men were left with a "broad hint as to caution in concocting sensational crime stories. Neither Fleet Street nor Scotland Yard likes practical jokes of this kind" (fig. 14).[116]

The "interesting lad from Lille," Lucas's mysterious informant, was perhaps more interesting than *John Bull* realized.[117] John O'Connor or Stewart had a long criminal record. He "associated with the notorious adventuress Josephine O'Dare," and was convicted for his role in her forgery ring in 1927.[118] He was implicated in the "libel racket": at the same time as it reported his conviction for forgery, the *Daily Mirror* noted an "audacious trick" on British newspapers. Then living in Calais, in August 1927 an interpreter calling himself Frank Stewart had arranged a meeting with the editor of the *Kent Evening Echo*. While the details of their discussion went unrecorded, Stewart agreed "to send him news items from France." Soon after, the editor received a report: "John Francis Kingsley O'Connor . . . had been arrested in Lille for the alleged murder of Nurse Daniels." It was over a year since May Daniels mysteriously disappeared in Boulogne.[119] As journalists (including Lucas) scrambled to be first with the news, Stewart's revelation seemed a profitable scoop. Events took a surprising turn: O'Connor and Stewart were the same person, and this was a "bogus news item." When the *Evening News* reported O'Connor's arrest, the interpreter "sued for libel he wrote of himself," claiming £750 in damages. Showing remarkable nerve, he approached the London correspondent of the *Liverpool Echo*, describing the "distressing sequel" to a "simple holiday adventure." Apparently oblivious to the unfolding furore until returning home, O'Connor claimed he could not explain stories of his arrest.[120] Even when O'Connor was arrested for his earlier thefts, he convinced the Liverpool mag-

MURDER MYSTERY : Amazing Hoax
AN AUTHOR'S STRANGE BEHAVIOUR
The Crook and the Detectives

A PARTLY successful attempt to hoax the two most wide-awake communities in the country, Scotland Yard and Fleet Street, has recently been perpetrated.

The attempt being as ingenious as it was audacious, Fleet Street fell, though Scotland Yard has retained unsullied its reputation for being 100 per cent. fool-proof.

Chapter I. of the story opens with the receipt of a telephone call at Scotland Yard itself. The caller, whose business was far too important to be dealt with by minor officials, asked to be put in touch with Chief Detective-Inspector Cooper. He gave his name as Mr. Netley Lucas.

Now Mr. Netley Lucas is well known as a writer of books of crime. He is the author of, to name only two of his works which have had a wide circulation, " A Crook's Confessions " and " The Autobiography of a Crook." Naturally Scotland Yard had heard all about him. It was all agog.

Hot "copy"

Mr. Lucas announced that he had at that moment in his office a man who had just been released from prison in Lille, and who while there had received a confession from another Englishman who had been incarcerated by the French authorities.

This confession was to the effect that he had been guilty of the murder of the landlady of the Cross Keys Inn, Chelsea, one of the great unsolved mysteries of London crime.

An appointment was made with this interesting lad from Lille, whose name transpired to be Stewart or O'Connor, and he was duly inter-viewed the next day by two Scotland Yard officials.

Meanwhile Mr. Netley Lucas, who, we had better explain, apart from being a successful author has also established a journalistic connection with Fleet Street, got in touch with various editors for the purpose of selling to them the very hot piece of " copy."

Fleet Street was no less interested than the Yard.

Confirmed suspicion

Some of the editors were satisfied that Scotland Yard was investigating the statements made by Mr. O'Connor, otherwise Stewart, and the sensational story appeared in an evening paper two Saturdays ago. Next day certain Sunday newspapers also published it.

Only after the newspapers were in circulation was it possible for them to learn that neither Chief Inspector Cooper nor any of his colleagues at the Yard intended to move one step in the matter.

A few enquiries into the ante-cedents of Mr. Netley Lucas' infor-mant confirmed their first suspicions that he was a gentleman on whose word no credence could be placed. And so the Chelsea murder mystery remains unsolved.

The mystery of why the two of them should have gone to such elaborate pains to " spoof " Scotland Yard and Fleet Street is not very difficult to explain.

Newspapers have a habit of paying for interesting contributions, and presumably neither O'Connor nor Mr. Lucas had any intention of parting with the information for the mere vanity of seeing their names in print.

Although the newspapers cannot very well be blamed for publishing the story in good faith, we can hardly say the same of Mr. Lucas.

Assuming that he really believed O'Connor's story, he has proved to be surprisingly credulous for one who has been long enough in touch with the underworld to know that such gentlemen would " spoof " their own grandmothers for 5s.

The Chelsea murder story is not the first by any means that Netley has passed on to Fleet Street. It was only a fortnight before that a Sunday newspaper was induced to publish a no less sensational story, and one which it had every reason to believe was absolutely authentic.

This time the central figure was Colonel Rutherford, D.S.O., who was found guilty of murder eight years ago, but was admitted to be insane and was put away for life in Broad-moor Criminal Lunatic Asylum.

Cause of secrecy

Mr. Lucas introduced a person who claimed to have been newly released from Broadmoor, and made the sen-sational announcement that Colonel Rutherford himself would be at liberty a few days later.

" Great secrecy," we were told, was being maintained by the Home Office authorities and the medical superintendent of Broadmoor, a fact which does not astonish us, for they had never heard of the intended release until Mr. Lucas's Broadmoor friend made the announcement.

There is also the entertaining little story of the " Gathering of the Chinese Clans " or Tongs in London.

The gathering, we were told, was " timed to commemorate the Festival of Yang-Vee-Li," with the accent on the last syllable, who, we were in-formed, is the Chinese God of Marriage.

Part of the gathering would be the holding of judiciary courts to try under Chinese law any offenders against the well-being of Chinese in the West. Sentences would be passed just as if Mr. J. A. R. Cairns of Thames Police Court himself had presided.

We will say no more than to give Mr. Netley Lucas and Mr. O'Connor a broad hint as to caution in con-cocting sensational crime stories.

Neither Fleet Street nor Scotland Yard likes practical jokes of this kind, and the latter, of course, can always hit back.

Mr. Netley Lucas

FIGURE 14. The business of faked newspaper sensations. From "Murder Mystery Hoax," *John Bull*, 6 August 1927, 13. © The Advertising Archives. Published courtesy of The Adver-tising Archives and The Bodleian Libraries, The University of Oxford, N.22891 c. 2, vol. 42, 6 August 1927, 13.

istrate that he was about to receive compensation as a victim of libel and was bound over rather than imprisoned after promising to reimburse his victims.[121]

Lucas knew O'Dare and her circle; he was probably in Boulogne at the same time as O'Connor; the "Murder Mystery Hoax" coincided with the "au-dacious trick" on the *Evening News*. Another thing: Lucas and O'Connor had served sentences in the same Borstal in 1921.[122] A tangle of personal connec-tions drew the special correspondent towards the "libel racket," collapsing the distance from a past marked by crimes of confidence. Dramatic newspa-per revelations and discreet police investigations aligned the *Sunday News* exclusives with speculative libel actions. The *People* noted how "unscrupu-lous persons have latterly made a business of faked crime sensations" to "sell their fabricated stories" to newspapers.[123] This confidence trick on editors and readers exposed the fault lines of contemporary mass culture: the soaring value of exclusive news made authenticity and revelation irreconcilable. For three years the innuendos of critics and the accumulation of names around Lucas's writing betrayed some unease over its "truth." This was not unusual: the crook life story, celebrity interview, and gossip column all demanded knowing complicity from readers. In the summer of 1927, however, rumor threatened to materialize as a specific allegation: accepted journalistic practices had shaded into fraud; a crime writer had "fabricated" stories for profit.

What did Lucas have to do with the "business of faked crime sensations"? The sources are uncertain. Fraud and forgery allowed Lucas to claim the privileges of a man-about-town after the Great War. Perhaps his pursuit of social advancement now animated a different order of deceptions. His connections to O'Connor make it plausible that they worked together to deceive the *Sunday News*. Cooper was "convinced" that Lucas "engineered [stories of the Chelsea investigation] for his own personal benefit." Cooper did not identify his source, but in July he reported being "told that Lucas and a friend of his named Lake (both of whom are down and out) intend engineering stunts of this kind at frequent intervals."[124] He later elaborated this theory: working at a hotel in York Road, a notorious red-light district next to Waterloo Station, O'Connor had met Albert Adams, another Borstal friend. He confided his renewed acquaintance with Lucas—"Editor of the 'Criminologist' and 'Smart Life'"—and how they were "making money by writing articles for the newspapers." The men visited Lucas in his office in Shaftesbury Avenue.

> Adams remembers O'Connor saying to Lucas "What about getting an article up about the Chelsea Murder. We can ring up Scotland Yard, and say that we have a man in the office who has just come back from France . . . and while in the French prison say he got into conversation with another Englishman and bluff the 'Yard' that this Englishman admitted having committed the Chelsea Murder."[125]

Although Adams refused to join the scheme, when he returned the next day, Lucas told him the article was accepted but "they looked like getting into trouble" over the Rutherford article. There is something suspicious about Adams's account: I cannot tell who he is or how Cooper found him. Still, it makes Lucas central to attempts to exploit the perverse incentives of contemporary journalism through "bogus information."[126]

There were other versions of Lucas's behavior, however. By 1927 he had expended time and energy remaking himself as a criminologist and journalist. His West End office and headed notepaper betrayed a desire for professional respectability. Rather than an untrustworthy fraudster, we might equally foreground his desperation to leave his past behind.[127] In 1927 he was publishing more than ever; *My Selves* suggests no financial problems; it is difficult to understand Cooper's conclusion that Lucas was "down and out." Even *John Bull* was circumspect about his relationship with O'Connor, noting only that Lucas was "surprisingly credulous" for a man of his experience.[128]

Lucas inevitably denied any involvement in this racket, describing his shock at the *Star*'s placard announcing its exclusive Chelsea story and realizing he had been "double crossed" by O'Connor. Presenting himself as "perfectly innocent," Lucas suggested that O'Connor "had gone along to *John Bull* and told a yarn as to how he had pulled my leg."[129] Is this so far-fetched? Adams told Cooper how "the substance of this article . . . was given to 'John Bull' by O'Connor because he and Netley Lucas had fallen out owing to a dispute they had over money." Cooper was wrong to suggest Lucas "might very well have turned the tables on O'Connor by giving his name to the Press in connection with the Nurse Daniels case" to settle scores.[130] Yet the furore around the *Sunday News* exclusives could be the public ripples of the tensions between these cynical journalists and ex-crooks. Lucas was perhaps an easy target as much as a criminal accomplice. The weekend before the Chelsea exclusive, a visitor to the *People* "warned us to be on our guard against a sensational story that was likely to be 'released.'" Here, perhaps, we see O'Connor setting Lucas up.[131] These entwined stories make it hard to understand the personal stakes behind the *Sunday News* scandals. Lucas's later protestations of innocence sat uneasily against his behavior in 1927; journalists implied a criminal offense but stopped short of any concrete allegation; Lucas appears in police reports as victim and suspect; no prosecution was brought. Whom do we trust? Lucas was a convicted trickster; so were O'Connor and Adams, and Cooper relied heavily on their claims.

In many ways, none of this matters: the affair's political stakes and public effects were immediate and certain. Like the "literary ghoul," the "faked newspaper sensations" provided a focus for concerns about the precariousness of authenticity in contemporary journalism. Editors and journalists insisted on truth's importance to the modern newspaper—cautioning their colleagues to adhere to the highest professional standards—and were confident that outright deceptions were rare.[132] There remained considerable unease that the influence of the market and new journalistic styles were eroding the lines between "truth" and "fiction." These concerns were underpinned by a critical analysis of the conditions in which journalists and editors worked. The conventions of human-interest reporting meant events were repackaged for public consumption in particular ways; how a story was reported might "create a false impression"; pressure to be first with news left little time to verify sources and led to speculation, simplification, and mistakes.[133] The *Report on the British Press* (1938) noted how reporters and editors were pulled in different directions:

> In principle news should always be true, but even in principle truth is not always news. The marriage between truth and news is . . . a difficult and exacting one. Very often it is impossible for various reasons to ascertain the whole truth or to express it with completeness and accuracy until it has almost ceased to be news. The press, therefore, is constantly working against time to produce the best practicable synthesis of these two elusive elements.[134]

Others were less understanding of the "deliberate perversions of fact" that characterized the modern "newspaper racket."[135]

The *Sunday News* "exclusives" brought these tensions to a head. By 1927 Lucas had stopped writing as an ex-crook and recast himself as an investigative journalist and criminologist. These were different forms of writing, but *John Bull* and *People* questioned the authenticity on which their value rested. Once Lucas was no longer able to maintain the distance between past and present, his ability to write about crime collapsed. Rather than representing a gold mine of stories from the underworld, his name became a liability for periodicals and publishers trading in readers' confidence. "Give a dog a bad name and hang him," Lucas later suggested bitterly. Viewed from August 1927, his success looked like an elaborate confidence trick.[136] Boundaries between con man, ex-crook, and criminologist dissolved, leaving Lucas "discredited in Fleet Street" and his reputation in tatters.[137] No articles appeared under his byline in the *Sunday News* after July; the *Pictorial Weekly* series finished abruptly; "Netley Lucas journalist was as dead as Netley Lucas crook."[138]

NEWSFLASH

Among the first-class passengers disembarking from the SS Aurania today was the young English journalist Leslie E. Graham. I understand that Mr. Graham is pursuing further literary endeavors with Messrs. Doubleday, Doran, and Company, the well-known publishers. He is accompanied by his secretary, Richard Dent. New York, 22 December 1927.[139]

C.O.   STREET EFFECTS IN BACKGROUND

NEWSBOY: (FADING IN AND OUT) Read all about it—young English author and Chicago May get together! Read all about it!

C.O.   FLASH OF "HURRY" MUSIC

NARRATOR: And from the crystal sets and old-fashioned radio loudspeakers—

C.O.   STATIC CRACKLE

NARRATOR: Flash! Who is the debonaire young Englishman who's just swept Chicago May Churchill off her feet? He's an author of crime books, we know that, but who knows anything else about him? Last reports state Chicago May has been seen out and about at the top spots dancing with her handsome young man. May looks as fluttery as a school girl on her first date—(FADING)—and that's something to be seen![140]

RESURRECTION

Netley Lucas was not long dead. Passing unrecorded in the files of immigration officials and the manifests of cruise liners, his arrival in New York in December 1927 was marked by a media sensation. Later Lucas would rhapsodize over the "spires of the cathedrals of commerce," seeing an alluring cosmopolitan modernity that signaled "the possibility of making my name as a writer in a land where genius and ability always gets its fitting reward . . . the only country where what one can do counts before what one is, or what one has been." Unable to escape his past in Britain, the ex-crook used his personal connections and the well-worn itineraries of transatlantic travel to pursue a new start and the American dream.[141] Lucas's *Ladies of the Underworld* had been published in New York by Doubleday, Doran, and Company. Visiting its offices with his "secretary," Richard Dent—perhaps his "partner," Guy Hart—Lucas was gratified when greeted "as if I were an old friend, instead of an ex-crook who had written a couple of extraordinarily bad and unprofitable books."[142]

For Doubleday this was also an opportunity. On 4 January 1928 the *New York Herald Tribune* announced "the engagement of an internationally known woman criminal to marry the internationally known criminologist whose inspiration she was in the preparation of a book on the famous woman criminals of all time."[143] Despite his marriage to Elsie, Lucas was to marry "Chicago May" Churchill. Thirty years his senior, Churchill was born in Ireland but moved to the United States as a young woman, one of tens of thousands of emigrants seeking a new life. In the expanding cities of the Midwest, the resourceful and attractive Churchill found alternative opportunities for advancement. Her exploits included prostitution, blackmail, and theft; she was imprisoned in the United States, France, and Britain. Together with Eddie Guerin, her onetime lover and the only man to escape from the French penal colony on Devil's Island, she robbed the American Express offices in Paris in 1902. After her relationship with Guerin soured, Churchill and her new lover, Charles Smith or Considine, served long sentences for their attempted murder of Guerin in London. By the mid-1920s her notoriety was in the distant past. Now in her fifties and struggling with ill health, she lived a peripatetic existence through petty crime in Detroit.

In 1927 Churchill came under the patronage of August Vollmer, former head of the Berkeley Police Department and a pioneer of modern criminal investigation. Vollmer encouraged Churchill to write her memoirs and leave her past behind. Moving to Philadelphia, she became a regular correspondent, seeking Vollmer's support as she struggled with the manuscript that became *Chicago May: Her Story* (1928).[144] She described her difficulties finding a "rewrite man," before approaching Ruth Holland, a reporter for the *New York World*.[145] Charles Smith was then in prison in California: Vollmer was also a conduit through which to ask after his welfare and communicate her love.[146] Churchill's letters and Lucas's autobiography make it clear this was an engagement of convenience. Writing to Vollmer in January, she noted "that publicity stunt they framed it over in NY." She ended this letter abruptly, since "I am sick and weary of life."[147] Recalling their first meeting in Philadelphia, Lucas thus described his shock: exhausted and dying of cancer, this "once beautiful adventuress" lived in a chaotic hotel room surrounded by cigarette butts, bootleg liquor, and "lurid magazines." Far from exciting, it was "tragic" to listen to her "soliloquizing in maudlin fashion over the past." Temporarily, however, a publisher's stunt gave Churchill renewed energy and brought her back into the headlines.[148]

Central to Doubleday's publicity was the claim that Churchill had inspired Lucas's recent study of female criminals. The stunt shored up the couple's claims to knowledge and brought their work to public attention. Marriage became an unexpected outcome of Lucas's research; Churchill, a "human document" for his investigations into the "underworld."[149] They met, the story went, in Toronto's King Edward Hotel, when Churchill halted her attempt to trick Lucas because his "familiarity with underworld lingo" and "obvious knowledge of criminal affairs convinced her that he was either a detective or a crook."[150] He was neither, he claimed, but as love blossomed, the criminologist found a wealth of material. The *American Weekly* noted how just as "artists often marry favorite models for inspiration," the "greatest living woman thief"

had become muse to the "student of crime." Lucas had secured "a living ency-
clopedia of criminal wisdom and experience which can scarcely be matched
in the files of Scotland Yard."[151]

It is not easy to reconcile these claims with Lucas's writing. He described
Churchill as a "woman whom I had long wished to meet," but never claimed
to have done so before 1928.[152] Nor was Churchill an obvious presence in his
Ladies of the Underworld.[153] In *London and Its Criminals* (1926), Churchill
appeared only as a point of comparison: Lucas knew a blackmailer "whose
reputation . . . was second only to that of May Churchill."[154] He was rarely
reluctant to claim association with notorious criminals. Churchill's absence
from his writing was unlikely and obvious to any reporter minded to check.[155]

Lucas later characterized his arrival in New York as that of a provincial ingenue, relishing the delights symbolized by Broadway's "flashing sky-signs."[156]
After his engagement was announced, however, he was overwhelmed by an
intrusive media that often seemed beyond his comprehension. The differences between American and British journalism shifted the boundaries between public and private life, prompting a disorienting loss of control over
processes of self-fashioning on which he had relied. "I little realised the power
of the American press or the extent to which May Churchill and I would be
placarded all over the world," he recalled.[157] Circulating through teleprinter
networks and newspaper syndicates, a press statement triggered a media
storm. News of the couple's engagement and photographs appeared across
the United States, Ireland, Britain, and the empire.[158]

> Neither my time nor my soul was my own. Dogged by reporters and news
> reel cameramen night and day, questioned by feature writers from every news
> agency in the whole of America, my hotel bedroom always being invaded by
> someone who wanted to hear my views on something or other . . . it was posi-
> tively embarrassing.[159]

Optimism became a "New York nightmare."[160]

At least to begin with, Lucas apparently relished the attention. His playful interviews belie later claims to embarrassment. Sensation created a stage.
To the *New York Evening Post*, he described his "fascination" with Churchill,
and the opportunities marriage provided. It would be like a "laboratory ex-
periment, perhaps the greatest one of his crime-studying life," allowing him
to further his criminological investigations, and "put it all in the movies." Interviews also allowed Lucas to respond to how he was described in the press.
"I am just as hardboiled as 'Chicago May,'" he claimed, then "leaned back in

his chair at the Hotel Chelsea, where he is living with a friend and country-man, Dick Dent . . . and tried to make his good-looking young face as stern and hard as possible. He succeeded only in looking like a boyish university undergraduate."[161]

Mimicking American detective fiction and gangster films, Lucas presented himself as masculine and tough. The reporter's sardonic comments suggest how the interview was a dialogic process, in which claims were probed through critical asides then unusual in British journalism. The *New York Times* ridiculed his appearance "in a cinnamon-coloured suit with a citron-colored necktie and handkerchief bordered to match." He was an unconvincingly effete criminologist.[162] In other interviews, Lucas challenged such comments and presented dress and demeanor as peculiarly English signs of class. The *Evening Post* noted "his well-modulated English voice, with his clipped words and soft tones." He resisted the implicit criticism: " 'Every one so far has described me as a coy, embarrassed youth,' he said, a trifle peevishly. 'I'm not. I'm really hard boiled. Perhaps folks mistake the English manner.' " Rather than being "afraid" of marrying someone who had tried to kill an ex-lover, he concluded: "I've a will of my own." As if to corroborate this claim, he "flicked the ashes off his cigarette with a quick gesture of his arm, like the click of a steel machine."[163]

Lucas also elaborated his credentials as an expert on crime: ten years of freelance journalism, work for the *Sunday News*, and "four books on crime" made him "well acquainted with the gentle art of 'knowing crooks.' "[164] Lucas now attributed his career to tragic personal circumstances. Learning of his father's murder when twelve, he became "impressed with the importance of criminology at an unusually early age." In this account the professional tools of modern criminology served an intimate quest for closure. After painstaking investigations, he "was able to track down the slayer" in 1925, only to find "the murderer was dead."[165] The details were not reported widely in the United States, and not at all in Britain, but Lucas initially succeeded in shaping his public image: newspapers described him as an "internationally noted criminologist."[166]

What made Lucas and Churchill's engagement newsworthy? Speaking to reporters from the *New York World*, Lucas described a "real romance that might be called stranger than fiction."[167] The strangeness of a relationship across occupation and generation was a recurrent motif. Churchill's notoriety endured: compared to Lucas, she rarely spoke to journalists, yet newspapers usually focused on her exploits. Her life was always contrasted to his profession, however, dramatizing the distance between criminal and criminologist.[168] Journalists were equally obsessed by the difference between their ages, exaggerating

Lucas's youth and presenting Churchill as a woman out of time. Their unlikely engagement provided opportunities for cruel humor, particularly around the couple's staged publicity photographs: "May to December," mocked one caption.[169] Awkward—almost excruciating—Lucas and Churchill were portrayed through the visual conventions of modern love. In one series they sat together on a sofa. Wearing a light suit and glasses that enhanced his gaucherie, Lucas read the copy of *Ladies of the Underworld* on his lap; Churchill, her face made pale and drawn by an overexposed image, leaned her head into his shoulder, a proprietorial hand on his arm.[170] A second series presented the "youthful criminologist" as vigorous and attractive, and Churchill as older by comparison. Lucas lounged in an armchair. The debonair man-about-town wore a dark suit and patterned tie, his crossed legs emphasizing the white spats on his shoes. Standing behind him, Churchill rested her hand on the back of the chair. Such photographs underscored the idea that this relationship really was stranger than fiction.[171]

While the "Chicago May" affair began in the United States, news of the "underworld romance" quickly crossed the Atlantic, then reverberated again with unexpected force in New York. International news agencies ensured that newspapers in Britain and the empire picked up the story within a day. Even papers that had reported Lucas's crimes or published his work were more interested in Churchill: here was chance to rehearse the biography of "one of the most remarkable figures in modern criminal history."[172] The *People* mischievously announced the engagement on the same page as Eddie Guerin's serialized memoirs.[173] Sketches of Churchill followed the outline established in the United States, but British journalists treated Lucas differently. Ignoring the furore around the Rutherford and Chelsea "exclusives," the *Sunday News* described "a prolific writer on crime and the underworld whose books on the ways and wiles of the crook are regarded as authoritative." It was only six months since Lucas had been discredited, but time and the distance between London and New York created a convenient not-knowing about the earlier scandals.[174] British newspapers were more likely to focus on Lucas's past as a gentleman crook rather than his work as a writer, however. The *Empire News* described him as a "reformed English criminal," whose engagement illustrated love's redemptive power.[175]

This was the high point of Lucas's celebrity. A publisher's publicity stunt put his name and image in newspapers across the world for several days in January 1928. He was not the main focus of media scrutiny, and it was for Churchill that the effects were most pronounced. The announcement "brought her back to the news columns, where she once figured so prominently" and helped sell her manuscript.[176] Lucas later suggested Churchill enjoyed being back in the public gaze. That is not obvious from her letters to Vollmer, but any unease was personal rather than public. Apologizing for not replying sooner on 4 January, she explained, "I was busy with my fiancee I suppose you have read it by now it is in all the papers." Writing in confidence, and including the postscripts "PS I know I can trust you" and "two more know the truth," Churchill continued: "I am only worried about Considine he may believe it is on the level and I got to be careful what I write to him. I shure hope you will talk with him and of course can put him wise."[177] Having reassured Charles Smith that the engagement was a sham, Churchill could look forward. By the end of January, the manuscript was finished and she was confident about finding a publisher. While *Chicago May: Her Story* appeared in print that spring, Churchill died in Detroit the following year, aged fifty-nine.[178]

For Lucas, the publicity was disastrous. He was unmade by the modern media through which he had remade his life. During the *Sunday News* furore, he lost control over the stories around him. In January 1928 that happened again as his past came under renewed scrutiny. Although the circulation of information and people between Britain and the United States had created exciting opportunities for a gentleman crook and crime writer, now it meant that Lucas could not separate out stories told in London and New York. Inveterate claims to notoriety returned to haunt him. Stories of his crimes played out in dangerous ways after the *New York Times* "discovered" his criminal record. When announcing the engagement, its reporters in the United States uniquely—albeit inaccurately—noted that Lucas's "score is two terms in British reform schools for thefts." Rather than rehearse Churchill's life, they dissected the excesses of tabloid journalism and the contradictions of Lucas's claims. This was investigative journalism with an edge.[179]

At the center of the *New York Times*'s investigations was the dubious status of the "cherubic villain's" criminal record and "semi-autobiographical works." Lucas was "one of the most copious and indefatigable confessors in that crowded field," but his bombastic claims made it impossible to know where truth ended and deception began. In his room at the Hotel Chelsea, "he was engaged daily in the work of self-revelation." Despite his prolific writing, he had "reserved a number of staggering enormities which will totally overshadow the chambers of horrors which he has unveiled up to the present."[180] Irony and exaggeration exposed the clichés of crime writing. Lucas's work should be read cautiously, and its authenticity and his trustworthiness approached with skepticism. The lucrative "work of self-revelation" now carried real dangers: immigration controls barred anyone with a criminal record from entering the United States. Pursued by journalists, Lucas found that the boundaries between being a respectable citizen and a dangerous outsider were porous; the American dream was not open to all.

The day after the story broke, Lucas was forced to give another anxious interview to the *New York Times*—"arranged over the telephone with his secretary, who has a voice astonishingly like that of his employer."[181]

> Lucas confessed yesterday that his confessions were false, that he is not the Raffles or beguiler of Duchesses that he has painted himself, that he has never served two terms in British reformatories, that he has not so much as been up for juvenile delinquency and that he has written his five volumes of confessions . . . altogether out of a conscience void of offense.

Rather than firsthand knowledge, his "reminiscences" drew on journalism and "reading up on the subject." There was some truth to this, but Lucas glossed over how he had begun as a confessing ex-crook. Once Lucas had started to write what he called "third-person fiction," his "publishers hounded me into putting it out in the first person and under my own name." After its "tremendous sale," he could not resist the pressures to continue writing: "I confessed enough for two or three lifetimes in that first book, but it went so well that I have just had to confess, confess and confess ever since to everything I could find that was interesting." Mercenary and duplicitous, the "confession kid" was trapped by an insatiable market.[182]

When questioned, Lucas responded with lies and half-truths. The masks he had worn as a writer were concealed behind new names and stories. It was impossible to know who he was and what he had written, let alone understand the relationship between lives and stories.[183] Temporarily, however, these uncertainties coalesced into the necessary yet duplicitous "admission" that his writing was fictitious. On 6 January the *New York Times* printed a statement from an Ellis Island immigration commissioner: "If [Lucas] actually has a criminal record . . . he would be deported. But I understand that his confessions are fiction." Uninterested in "the kind of a literature a man puts forth," he concluded, "Immigration authorities have too much to do to bother with matters of that kind." Journalistic scrutiny and a dismissive government official left Lucas publicly humiliated.[184]

"I don't know just how my public is going to take the acknowledgement that I have never actually done any of the things that I have confessed," Lucas fretted.[185] He was right to worry. The success of his writing often depended on its status as firsthand testimony from the underworld. It was misleading for him to attribute it to secondhand knowledge, but that admission ironically reinforced *John Bull*'s revelations. The confessing ex-crook was a facade, a cynical pose to deceive publishers and readers, a crime of confidence. How could his work have any value if this was the case? Despite his desperate "admission," Lucas was still paranoid about being arrested. On 13 January 1928, the author Leslie Graham arrived in Southampton on the SS *Aquitania*: he had only been in New York for five weeks.[186]

CONCLUSION

He never acknowledged it, but Lucas continued to write for boys' story papers in the months between the *Sunday News* "hoax" and his hurried departure from New York. Although Lucas himself was discredited among editors and publishers, his names lived on in the *Monster* and *Golden*. For a time, Lucas could earn his living by writing for an audience insulated from the headlines that made his name synonymous with deception. "Anthony Grex—The Human Bloodhound" ran for thirty-nine weeks in the *Golden*, ending only when the publication folded in January 1928.[187] The *Monster*'s Darky and Julia Kemp adventures ran throughout the period.[188] Either ghosted or written before his departure, stories appeared under Lucas's name while he was in New York.[189] An unattributed story was published on 28 January, before Lucas returned with "Julia in Prison" and "The Secret Society" on 4 and 11 February, just after Leslie Graham landed in Southampton. That was the final appearance of the comic book criminologist. Perhaps the damage to his reputation caused by the "Chicago May" affair was enough to ruin his credibility among the staff and young readers of the *Golden* and *Monster*. Perhaps he still wrote but was now anonymous or using a different pseudonym. Perhaps this reflected nothing more than an editorial change to the papers' style: few stories were attributed to named writers after February 1928, and none immediately after Lucas ceased to publish. Whatever the cause, Netley Lucas vanished. It was December 1930 before that name again appeared in print.[190]

Tracing Lucas and O'Dare's difficult engagements with popular journalism and publishing generates deeply personal stories of how two ex-crooks sought to remake their lives by retelling them. We see how new forms of commercial mass culture provided the resources through which they could seek material reward and a new life. Access to these lucrative opportunities also provided a framework within which to make sense of a life of crime, prompting Lucas, O'Dare, and—perhaps—their ghosts to reflect on their lives in the context of broader debates around crime and culture, and changing understandings of selfhood. We might celebrate their successes, drawing attention to the imaginative ways in which Lucas, in particular, refashioned himself as a writer on crime. O'Dare's tortuous relationship with the press, however, is an important reminder of the exigencies that forced them to transform notoriety into a fetishized commodity. Lucas and O'Dare were simultaneously agents and objects of cultural production, their capacity to control their public lives restricted by the conventions of form and genre through which a criminal life might be narrated. It was constrained by the need to engage with "official" biographies articulated in court and their depiction in print. The storytelling ex-crook entered into conversation with other voices elicited at the conclusion of their trial—ex-lovers, family, and victims tapped for the inside story by journalists seeking an exclusive. Comparing O'Dare's life in the *People* with that in *Reynolds's* underscores how any narrative could not depart too far from these scripts if it were to remain credible.

Lucas and O'Dare were also often limited by their own marginal social position. Lucas could draw upon his public school education, at least some social capital, and personal connections in moving into freelance writing. He was still a convicted criminal, however, and was haunted by his past throughout this phase of his career. O'Dare was in prison and struggled to negotiate on her own behalf when she sold her story. Reliant on friends and family, she received little of the money *Reynolds's* paid for her life story. It is tempting to see her as a self-possessed young woman: managing her reputation after prison with the care that underpinned her meteoric Society rise, she refuted pejorative versions of her life in print and in the courts. Allusive and suggestive, her lives anticipated the kiss-and-tell stories that became more current in the 1950s and Christine Keeler's assertive approach to "cheque book journalism."[191] Yet to revel in O'Dare's agency is to ignore her circumstances—unemployed, removed from the patronage that had sustained her, and tainted by one of the most notorious trials of the 1920s. Above all, in a news market that emphasized speed, criminal celebrity was ephemeral. For every ex-crook like Lucas who negotiated the transition from criminality to respectability, countless others remained trapped in a shadowy hinterland between mass culture and criminal underworld.

The constraints on the stories Lucas and O'Dare could tell reflected the mediating practices through which their lives were commodified. Storytelling enmeshed the ex-crook within competing and often irreconcilable imperatives. Following Lucas and O'Dare allows us to understand how their lives were embedded in the characteristic social relations and cultural forms of the 1920s and 1930s. They found opportunities within a burgeoning market but also unsettled emerging forms of personal journalism and publishing. In 1924 *John Bull*'s editor Charles Pilley issued a call to arms. The much-vaunted "Freedom of the Press" depended upon "a due sense of responsibility by the profession of journalism." The "restraint" of the law was always light, and the "honest journalist need not shrink from his public duty, fearlessly to proclaim the truth, to denounce fraud and imposture."[192] Pilley's bombastic vision of the fourth estate as the guarantor of truth was abraded by the transformation of newspapers in the 1920s, and by the scandals around O'Dare and Lucas. Rather than proclaiming "truth," they suggested that popular journalism compromised it. Rather than denouncing "imposture," journalists deceived readers. Rather than being "honest" public servants, they manipulated readers.

Lucas and O'Dare's lives thus mattered because this was a period of transition in journalism and publishing. Coupled with intensifying debates about mass culture's pernicious effects, this uncertainty generated opportunities on which Lucas and O'Dare drew and gave public revelation of their deceptions explosive resonance. That the ghosted life story shaped ferocious debates over the laws of libel underscores the political stakes and commercial interests entwined with Lucas and O'Dare's lives. The criminal underworld haunted Fleet Street and the Houses of Parliament.

Just as the crook life story focused concerns over the nature of modern journalism, so these debates also transformed it. In many ways O'Dare's case against *Reynolds's* was the faint echo of old news. While the trial was widely reported, it never attracted the furore that engulfed her in the mid-1920s. *Reynolds's* itself remained silent: after it was bought by the National Cooperative Press in 1929, the paper's character shifted. Increasingly preoccupied by the economic slump, the failings of the National Government, and the troubling international situation, and articulating a radical critique of the vacuity of Society and mass culture that took it closer to its nineteenth-century heyday, the paper repudiated the sensationalized crime coverage of the 1920s.[193]

The transformation of *Reynolds's* reflected a more general consolidation of how the press handled personal narratives and crime reporting. After 1930 journalistic styles were transformed by what Political and Economic Planning called the "*Time* technique." Economy of style, a focus on news gathering and "fact," and emphasis on accuracy and precision displaced the sensation and irrelevant details that characterized 1920s popular journalism.[194] By 1937, defending Victor Gollancz against Hayley Morriss's libel charge, one barrister could comment: "At one time a certain type of newspaper used to publish an account of the life and doings of a man who had been the central figure of a sensational trial. Frequently those accounts were quite mythical and the persons concerned successfully brought libel actions."[195] Respectable present was set against disreputable past in ways that suggested that the boundaries between good practice and dangerous fakery had been redrawn under the strident criticisms that coalesced around Netley Lucas's *Sunday News* "exclusives." Crime remained a staple of popular newspapers; confessing remained a source of profit for entrepreneurial ex-crooks; still, the worst excesses of the "literary ghoul" had, at least temporarily, been circumscribed.

* 3 *

Bogus Biographies: Literary Scandal and the Politics of Culture

CHAPTER 6

Writing Royal Lives

INTRODUCTION

Evelyn Graham's "bogus biography factory" collapsed in the summer of 1931 in what the *News of the World* described as "the most impudent literary scandal of the century."[1] In just three years Graham had published over a dozen biographies of British and European royalty. From nowhere he had come to dominate publishing lists and magazines across the Atlantic, establishing himself as what the *New York Times* termed "biographer-in-chief to the courts of Europe."[2] All was not as it seemed. Mysterious and entrepreneurial, Graham's work drew him into an increasingly antagonistic relationship with the royal household, newspapers, and publishers, and triggered a series of furious public scandals—a spurious *War Diary of the Prince of Wales* and tasteless revelations of the private life of George V. Over the winter of 1930, Graham was unmade by the newspaper that had launched him to literary celebrity. Working the conventions of stunt journalism, the *Daily Mail* exposed the shady past of a confidence trickster and discredited crime writer. Evelyn Graham was the ex-crook Netley Lucas. Graham was the publisher Albert E. Marriott, who had amazed the book trade with his innovative business practices. Graham was the Buckingham Palace press officer, Richard Dent, and the courtier Charlotte Cavendish, writing royal lives from a position of privileged intimacy. Graham's success rested on fakes, forgeries, and ghosts. Arrested in July 1931 for obtaining money by false pretenses from James Pinker and Sons, one of the most prestigious Anglo-American literary agencies, and the editor of *Weldon's Ladies Journal*—selling a manuscript life of Queen Alexandra written by the Lady-in-Waiting "Lady Angela Stanley"—Graham was imprisoned for eighteen months.

The three chapters that follow trace the rise and fall of the bogus biography factory. Graham's success reflected his ability to exploit the remaking of the royal family as modern celebrities, increasing demand for the "inside story" in biography and journalism, and new opportunities created by the expansion of book and periodical publishing. Royal biography sold. In his brief career Graham claimed to have made over twenty thousand pounds—all "squandered on wine, women and vice."[3] Setting Graham's published work against what I know of his interactions with publishers, editors, agents, and courtiers allows us to track both how emerging forms of mass culture transformed monarchy's public image and what it meant to write an "authentic" royal life. Like all biographers, Graham quickly learned that authenticity was neither immanent nor self-evident. Instead, it was an effect to be achieved by conforming to the conventions of the genre or a label secured through processes of artistic and social accreditation. Authenticity was a fetishized commodity in publishing, but constantly imperiled through the mercenary behavior of writers like Graham.

The furore over Graham's work provides a starting point for rethinking the historical significance of literary scandal. Within literary studies and art history, scandal has usually been understood as a moment of crisis in processes of cultural production. Exposing a painting or book as fake challenges ideas of expertise and connoisseurship, and the integrity of gatekeepers like the dealer, reviewer, editor, or agent.[4] Approached from this perspective, scandals can enrich our understanding of the politics and practice of culture. While the scandals around the bogus biography factory can be read against specific crises of literary production and accreditation, they resonated more widely, raising questions around the transformation of British social and political life and how it was to be represented. Not just concerned with the legitimate ways in which monarchy could be depicted, the debates prompted by Graham's work addressed the position of social elites in a period when established structures of class were being questioned. Following Graham suggests the freighted relationship between the politics of monarchical authority, the ethics and practice of life-writing, and commercial mass culture.[5]

Graham's "impudence" exposed a pervasive mood of crisis in Britain's royal household in the period around the Great War. Domestically, the monarchy was increasingly beleaguered through the quickening pace of political and social reform, the erosion of prerogative powers, the decline of the aristocracy, and the rise of organized labor and the industrial conflict that coalesced in the General Strike of 1926. Internationally, the risks posed by these changes were dramatized by the collapse of the European monarchies and the specter of revolution. In *After the War* (1918), Lord Esher, Liberal politician and lieutenant governor of Windsor Castle, observed how war "has loosed new and volcanic forces." Amid this destructive maelstrom, "Old names survive, but they have lost their meaning. An avalanche of women has been hurled into the political chaos. Institutions as well as ideas will have to be re-sorted."[6] Esher reiterated his concern in a letter to Lord Stamfordham, George V's private secretary. Writing in November 1918, a month before the first election held under the new Representation of the People Act, he commented: "We stand at the parting of the ways. . . . The Monarchy and its cost will have to be justified in the eyes of a war-worn and hungry proletariat, endowed with a huge preponderance of voting power."[7] Concerns over the fit between an anachronistic institution and modern mass democracy underpinned a growing sense that the "crown needed a strategy for survival more urgently than at any time since 1848."[8]

While courtiers often worked to maintain constitutional powers against the encroachments of party politics, monarchical power was increasingly displaced into social and cultural life and, in particular, the royal family's public image. The spectacular reinvigoration of monarchical ceremony after the late nineteenth century has drawn most attention, but the modernization undertaken by the royal household in the 1920s and 1930s was more everyday and rooted in attempts to cultivate "emotional bonds" with subjects. Realigned with the demands of mass democracy, royal lives were repackaged around ideas of domesticity, ordinariness, and philanthropic national service.[9] Monarchy, Harold Laski commented in 1938, "has been sold to the democracy as the symbol of itself; and so nearly universal has been the chorus of eulogy which has accompanied the process of sale that the rare voices of dissent have hardly been heard."[10]

Like other leftist commentators—including Kingsley Martin, editor of the *New Statesman*; Ernest Jones, the pioneering Freudian psychoanalyst; and the social research group Mass Observation—Laski became preoccupied with the monarchy's continued public influence around the silver jubilee of George V, the abdication of Edward VIII, and the coronation of George VI in the mid-1930s. Treating this popularity as a social and psychological problem, several studies scrutinized the affective ties between monarch and subject and the "intense propaganda by public men, in the Press, and in the cinema" that, Martin argued, fostered "an irrational feeling about the whole Royal Family."[11]

Historians have followed such studies and traced the emergence of "monarchy for the mass market," but rarely tried to unpack what Laski called the "process" through which the royal family was commodified and sold.[12] This is where my interest lies. The comparison with industrial production suggests the scale of Graham's factory. Working in Britain, the empire, and the United

States, he churned out best-selling biographies and countless newspaper and magazine articles. Ambition and the authorized life's commercial value drew him into prolific correspondence with courtiers and editors, and prompted a flurry of letters and phone calls among those who tried to deal with him. Files in the Royal Archives invite us to explore the material and social networks within which royal life-writing took shape. Following Graham's path through the mediating practices governing cultural production and consumption, we see the points of connection among culture, politics, and power. Through on-going conversations with key cultural power brokers, courtiers managed the monarchy's representation and suppressed Graham's work.

The biography factory thus marked a broader crisis in alignment between changing social relations and what the historian Dan LeMahieu calls a "culture for democracy." At this formative moment, Britain's hesitant movements toward democracy intersected with new forms of mass consumerism. After the franchise was extended in 1918 and 1928, "what culture was appropriate for that democracy became a question pitting the forces of the market place against the influence of an articulate minority." For many commentators the mantra of "giving the public what it wants" provided the economic rationale for a "more egalitarian culture."[13] Set against debates about the ethics of life-writing and journalism, the scandals over Graham's work crystallized anxieties regarding the challenges of a commercialized mass media. Such concerns linked the monarchy's authority to the imperiled condition of deference and privacy. Graham's unpredictable private conduct and published work exposed the fragility of monarchy after the Great War.[14]

While mass culture was widely perceived as a threat to deference, its "egalitarian" nature was as compromised as Britain's democracy. Just as the royal household was able to use newspapers, periodicals, and publishing to shore up the monarchy's authority, so Graham exploited the opportunities this provided. The resilience of older notions of social hierarchy, and the connections between culture and politics, ensured that patrician power was transformed rather than undermined in the 1920s and 1930s.[15] Communicating with editors and publishers, courtiers like Sir Clive Wigram insinuated established networks of power and patronage into ostensibly modern forms of cultural production. Rather than spectacular, their political influence was ordinary, a ubiquitous combination of off-the-record briefings, polite suggestion, and veiled threat.

Courtiers could work like this because of the commonalities of class, education, military service, and club they invoked to bind themselves to an emerging elite of cultural power brokers. There was more to it than the old school tie, however. The willingness of publishers or editors to respond to official pressure was neither innate nor wholly a function of sentiment. The biographer David Sinclair rightly notes how "by [1931] the well-established national press was more than alive to its responsibilities and their rewards in terms of circulation" in reporting monarchical affairs. What this misses are the written and oral communications that *made* press and publishers aware of those responsibilities and rewards. The monarchy's stability was increasingly founded on the complicity of interest between a commercialized media and traditional social hierarchies.[16]

The proactive public relations in which courtiers engaged after the Great War ensured that patrician society and mass culture were (temporarily, at least) deeply invested in each other rather than antagonistic. When set alongside their hesitant engagement with emerging technologies of newsreel and radio, most famously through the introduction of the annual Christmas broadcast in 1932, the patterns refined through the household's interactions with Graham prefigured its ability to address the crisis of Edward VIII's abdication.[17] As the boundaries between politics, society, and culture shifted, Esher's concerns about the demands of the "proletariat" underscored how the royal household followed political parties, charities, and advertisers in defining the "people" as a social formation to be engaged through a modern mass media in the 1920s and 1930s.[18]

This means we might think critically about the *News of the World*'s description of a royal biographer's trial as an "impudent literary scandal." At the same time as modernist writers tried to define an exclusive domain of intellectual life—consciously distanced from the debasing influences of public taste and the market—the idea of the literary continued to serve as a capacious everyday shorthand for very different forms of writing and reading. Graham always placed himself and his work within the "literary world," claiming the status the term carried, even though the pace of his writing and desire for material reward might have appeared its antithesis to some observers. Most newspapers followed the *News of the World* and characterized his work as literary. In so doing, they collapsed distinctions between mass-market biography, the best-selling novels of Arnold Bennett, and the work of "difficult" writers like Virginia Woolf. Like countless other writers, Graham confounded putative boundaries between popular, middlebrow, and highbrow culture. That could be seen in the periodicals where his work was serialized, the agents he worked with, and the publishers who bought his manuscripts. However indignantly highbrow critics insisted otherwise, the realm of the literary was still not their exclusive preserve. Claimed by entrepreneurial writers like Graham, and drawn through the interventions of newspapers and magazines, the shape of the "literary world" was up for grabs.

If the *News of the World* glossed over the question of what counted as "literary," it also suggested a distinction between cultural and political life. Defining Graham's deceptions as literary highlighted yet contained their capacity to question new forms of life-writing and journalism. In seeking to restore an impermeable line between authentic and fake, newspapers reasserted the integrity of processes of artistic accreditation—temporarily punctured but not irrevocably damaged. Presenting this as a *literary* scandal secured the convenient fiction of a nonpartisan monarchy, above the sectional conflicts of democratic politics, and a site of social cohesion and shared national values. Yet isolating the effects of Graham's activities within these bounds worked to conceal elaborate networks of patrician power and his problematic relationship with emerging structures of monarchical authority. The royal household's engagement with mass culture was predicated upon both performing monarchical virtue and deliberately manufacturing silence. The historian Priya Satia calls this agnotology: addressing the "insistent demand for openness" by systematically cultivating ignorance. Graham found to his cost that writing royal lives could bleed together notionally distinct realms of culture, market, and state.[19]

A NEW STAR

Evelyn Graham was a publishing sensation. In 1928, the *Empire News* observed, a "new star seemed to appear in the literary firmament. . . . With as busy a pen as even Mr Edgar Wallace's . . . he was precipitately furnishing the publishers' lists with intriguing titles."[20] Wallace made his reputation writing crime mysteries; Graham's specialty was the mass-market royal biography. Despite the "slump" of monarchical governments, noted the *New York Times* in August 1929, the "announcements of Fall biographies" indicated that there was "still a keen interest in the personnel of royal families." The list prompting this comment included Graham's *Princess Mary* (1929), *The Queen of Spain* (1929), and *Albert, King of the Belgians* (1929)—all published by the reputable Hutchinson—and *His Royal Highness the Duke of Connaught and Strathearn* (1929), written with Major General Sir George Aston.[21] Biographies of the Prince of Wales, king of Spain, and Lord Chief Justice Darling, and *Fifty Years of Famous Judges* (1930) would follow, along with an astonishing number of newspaper and magazine articles in Britain, the empire, and the United States.[22] Later Graham worked behind the scenes, collaborating on Aston's

Secret Service (1930) and Margaret Prothero's *History of the Criminal Investigation Department* (1931).[23] An inveterate self-publicist, Graham remembered how he would "take the literary world of London by storm," becoming "not only . . . the most curiosity provoking writer of those few years but also a name which was to reverberate in every royal court of Europe."[24]

Like many writers in the 1920s and 1930s, Graham found new opportunities as the effects of state educational provision and the increasing affluence and leisure enjoyed by many Britons transformed publishing and made reading a genuinely demotic pursuit. The growth and increasing complexity of book and magazine publishing were evident through the number of titles issued and the proliferation of cheap editions and lending libraries. Opportunities created by new readerships were enhanced by the growing field of royal biography.[25] The *Empire News* commented: "People love to read of the intimate lives of Royalty, detailed by somebody behind the scenes who lifts the curtain and reveals noble lives in their gentle, homely moods."[26] The genre was already well established, although its ebb and flow tended to follow royal deaths, coronations, and jubilees. That remained the case, but the imperatives of commercial publishing made the royal family ubiquitous biographical subjects. Companies like Hutchinson attracted considerable attention with their series of authorized biographies after the Great War. Graham's work typified a list that included Lady Cynthia Asquith's *The Duchess of York* (1927) and Kathleen Woodward's *Queen Mary of England* (1927).[27]

Graham attributed his new career to the prominence of such books and a "few chance remarks" overheard while traveling on the SS *Aquitania* from New York in January 1928: a smoking room conversation between an American publisher, magazine editor, and Lord Beaverbrook, owner of the *Express* newspapers, about their interest in "biographies of royalty."[28] His attention piqued, Graham sensed opportunities for financial reward. Having learned "from a certain source" that Hutchinson would find Princess Mary a "very acceptable subject of a biography," he "wrote a tactful letter to Her Royal Highness asking for permission to write the story of her life."[29]

Graham's opportunism reflected and contributed to the growth of royal life-writing. Nonchalantly admitting his mercenary motives crystallized fraught debates about the relationship between literature and the market. Despite acknowledging the "artistic" and "monetary" value of books, commentators like H. M. Paull still warned the writer to "beware of the temptation to let the pecuniary aspect of his endeavour have undue weight." At the same time, Paull suggested, the good writer should also be a "good man of business."[30] Graham was certainly that, relentlessly exploiting public demand and writing at a pace that amazed contemporaries. Attuned to domestic and international affairs, he chose newsworthy subjects. Princess Mary attracted attention because of her romance with Lord Lascelles and the growth of her young family. Later biographies of the king and queen of Spain tracked the escalating tensions in Spanish politics, which gave them what the *Sunday Times* called "strong topical interest."[31]

Both Graham's success and the phenomenon of mass-market monarchism were further sustained by the possibilities of popular and middlebrow newspaper and magazine publishing. Sir George Sutton considered rights to Woodward's *Queen Mary* important enough to announce at the Amalgamated Press's Annual General Meeting in 1926, confident that serialization in *Woman's Pictorial* would "enhance the prestige and popularity of this valuable property." As magazine publishing expanded, these opportunities grew.[32] "I could not write 'Royalty' articles quickly enough," Graham observed, "so to cut down my output I put up my prices to figures that compared favourably with those of the most eminent writers of the day"—fifty pounds for two thousand words, he claimed. Writing for magazines accounted for a third of his income.[33]

Graham's work thus became ubiquitous in titles oriented toward a domestic or feminized audience. Ward Lock's quality monthly *Windsor* included an aspirational mixture of fiction and nonfiction for one shilling.[34] Graham contributed a whimsical piece on "Pets of Royal Personages" in May 1929.[35] The next month the *Windsor* began to serialize "Edward P.: The Story of H.R.H. the Prince of Wales." Notable for its high production values and lavish illustration, the series was hugely successful (fig. 15).[36] High-profile contributions to other magazines followed: "Intimate Studies of Royal Princesses" in *Pearson's*, "Chapters of Royal Life" in *My Home*, portraits of the Duke and Duchess of York in *Modern Home* and the *Hartford Courant* in the United States.[37]

Graham was clever, energetic, and lucky. He was also able to navigate the mediating agencies that emerged to address the growing complexity of literary markets in the late nineteenth century. He readily acknowledged the importance of his relationships with prominent literary agents. Attacked as "the happy hunting ground of the unscrupulous adventurer" by organizations like the Society of Authors, agency caused concern well into the twentieth century. By the 1930s, however, renewed efforts to establish a professional code of practice made it more respectable.[38] A driving force in those efforts was Raymond Savage. Acting for clients who included T. E. Lawrence and Leslie Charteris, creator of the popular "Saint" novels, Savage stressed the "personal and individual attention" he provided. While he emphasized the quality of his

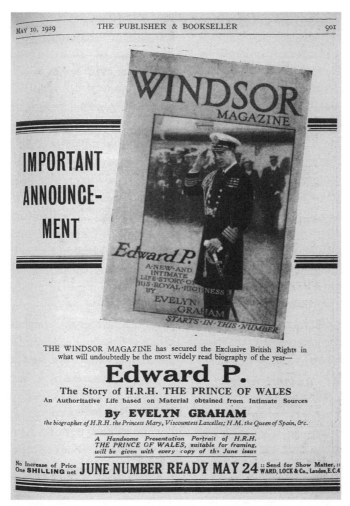

IMPORTANT
ANNOUNCE-
MENT

THE WINDSOR MAGAZINE has secured the Exclusive British Rights in
what will undoubtedly be the most widely read biography of the year—

Edward P.

The Story of H.R.H. THE PRINCE OF WALES

An Authoritative Life based on Material obtained from Intimate Sources

By EVELYN GRAHAM

the biographer of H.R.H. the Princess Mary, Viscountess Lascelles; H.M. the Queen of Spain, &c.

A Handsome Presentation Portrait of H.R.H.
THE PRINCE OF WALES, suitable for framing,
will be given with every copy of the June issue

No Increase of Price
One **SHILLING** net **JUNE NUMBER READY MAY 24** :: Send for Show Matter, ::
WARD, LOCK & Co., London, E.C.4

FIGURE 15. Evelyn Graham, a new star in the literary firmament. From "Important Announcement," *Publisher and Bookseller*, 10 May 1929, 901. Published courtesy of The Bodleian
Libraries, The University of Oxford, per. 2585 d. 14, 10 May 1929, 901, and *The Bookseller*.

list, that did not mean he only worked with highbrow writers. Graham became
a client in 1928.[39]

Savage placed Graham's work, negotiated contracts, and cultivated publicity.[40] The agent launched his client's career, securing a lucrative contract
for the serialized "Lifestory of Princess Mary" in the *Daily Mail* in November 1928. This "specially written and authoritative account" was vigorously

promoted, with details of "delightful glimpses of [Princess Mary's] family life" "splashed" on advertising hoardings and newspaper headlines.[41] Such publicity suggests both the salability of royal lives and Savage's talents. That his name first appeared in print "through the most widely read of newspapers," Graham recalled, "was an achievement for which I do not take any credit, for it was due to the skillful 'agenting' of my man of affairs."[42] Savage did not stop there: he sold serial rights to the *Ottawa Evening Citizen* and *Washington Post*. As Graham realized that his "new 'racket'" was a "gold-mine," his "'live wire' of an agent" secured a book contract and five-hundred-pound advance: *Princess Mary* was published by Hutchinson in 1929.[43]

Savage was Graham's main link with publishers and editors over the next two years, and an increasingly close friend. Graham also worked with other agents, particularly when seeking new markets. In November 1928 he approached William Bradley. Having been commissioned to write an "intimate personal biography" of the queen of Spain "in personal collaboration with Her Majesty," he asked:

> Do you think that this would have any interest for a French publisher and one of the better French reviews for Serial Rights? Queen "Ena" is . . . a frequent and welcome visitor to France—is handsome and is the best dressed Queen in Europe.[44]

Bradley was a prominent figure in the literary expatriate world in Paris, acting for writers who included Henry Miller and Edith Wharton. His reply was unrecorded—there was no French version of the book—but Graham's letter gives some indication of his international ambitions.

These were the foundations of Graham's success. His books were published in Britain, the empire, and the United States. They were serialized, advertised, and reviewed in reputable journals and broadsheet and popular newspapers. They sold well. Many readers would have found them in local lending libraries and circulating libraries, but they were within the budget of ordinary middle-class readers. Books like the *Duke of Connaught* cost twenty-one shillings. Serialized in the *Daily Chronicle*, it became one of the *Publisher and Bookseller*'s best-selling titles in March 1930.[45] Balancing affordability and quality, this pricing gives some sense of the audience publishers addressed. The exceptions were cases in which publishers saw opportunities to exploit interest in the more glamorous royals, reducing prices to boost sales and publicity. Although it was printed and bound in the publisher's standard format, at seven shillings sixpence, *Princess Mary* cost the same as a new novel.[46]

Graham's best-known biography focused on the most feted British royal: *Edward P.: A New and Intimate Life Story of H.R.H. the Prince of Wales* was published in November 1929 by Ward Lock and serialized in Australian newspapers like Adelaide's *Register*.[47] Priced at twelve shillings sixpence, it was "handsomely bound, lavishly illustrated," and advertised as "The Outstanding Biography of the Year."[48] *Edward P.* was rich pickings for journalists, who followed the conventions of contemporary reviewing and mined it for newsworthy anecdotes. Extracts describing the prince's views on love were reprinted across the English-speaking world under headlines like "Don't Grieve Girls: Here's Why the Prince Doesn't Marry."[49] When considering the book's merits, reviewers were positive. In December 1929, the *Illustrated London News* praised this "interesting and companionable book," noting how the "gossipy style and fund of anecdote lure the reader on from page to page."[50] A "gossipy style" and "anecdote" was not damning with faint praise: these were deemed essential components of an authentic royal life. Reviewers were also impressed by the ease with which *Edward P.* navigated the competing demands of "discretion" and "false adulation."[51]

There were dissenting voices. Yet criticism treated Graham's work less on its own terms than as exemplary of popular life-writing. The *Guardian* described how *Edward P.* "falls between two conventions." Disdainful of the traces of an "old convention of just 'burbling' about royalty," it was more positive toward "a saner tradition which leads Mr Graham to see that monarchy to-day 'is merely a form of Constitution that is in itself no better than any other, and must be judged solely on results.'"[52] It was usually broadsheet newspapers or literary periodicals that were antagonistic, understanding a "gossipy style" as an obstacle to understanding royal lives in their historical and political contexts. Questions of form, in other words, were approached through different understandings of biography's intellectual objectives. While most reviewers praised *Albert of the Belgians* as a judicious balance of historical narrative and personal anecdote, the *Times Literary Supplement* found it "none too well informed," highlighting Graham's "astonishing" ignorance of Belgian military defenses in 1914.[53] Such divisions mapped onto emerging fault lines between the popular, middlebrow, and highbrow. The *Daily Mirror* praised the "fascinating close-ups" that made *King Alfonso* an accessible introduction to Spanish politics, but others dismissed Graham's focus on the personal.[54] The *New York Times* commented: "What frosting is to solid food this book is to real biography." At a moment when the political crisis in Spain created a "craving among non-Spaniards to learn something about Spain's King," the failings of *King Alfonso* could only result in the "great resentment of the reader!"[55]

Critical reviews were outweighed by positive ones. Graham's rising star reflected the growing importance of authorial identity to commercial publishing. Integral to publishing, advertising, and the reading habits of ordinary Britons, the celebrity writer was as much a product of the literary marketplace as the best seller. By September 1929 the *Queenslander* could comment: "Evelyn Graham is known as the 'Official Royal Biographer.'"[56] That names sold was illustrated through the launch of British National Newspapers' *Britannia and Eve* magazine in 1929. Readers were promised "articles from famous pens," a home section, and "exclusive models" from Paris.[57] While the magazine placed a premium on quality, its main selling point was its contributors. In a who's who of 1920s publishing, Graham appeared alongside Lord Birkenhead, P. C. Wren, Clemence Dane, and Warwick Deeping, an unlikely list that underscored the slippage between popular, middlebrow, and highbrow.[58] In the first twelve issues of *Britannia and Eve*, Graham published five pieces. "Royal Romances" appeared alongside contributions from Beverley Nichols and Storm Jameson in the summer of 1930. Apparently considered in the same terms as such luminaries, his name's prestige was clear.[59] With Graham's reputation secured, his appreciation of "Our Gracious Queen Mary" was solicited by the *Illustrated London News* for the "Thanksgiving Number" that marked George V's recovery from illness in July 1929. This was an "honour" he "treasured . . . more than many of the others which I received at this time."[60]

Graham presented his success as a mystery that captivated readers and those in publishing and journalism:

> Interest in Evelyn Graham reached fever pitch at this time. "Who is Evelyn Graham?" everyone in the street of Adventure was asking. "Where does he come from? What is he like? Does he really exist?" . . . Wild and woolly rumours flew round. . . . Some said I was the illegitimate son of a royal personage, others that my father was a Cabinet Minister.[61]

Rumor is difficult to trace, but interest in Graham's work (if not his private life) was striking. His name became part of the currency of celebrity. "Evelyn is not uncommon as a man's name, but it is so much commoner as a woman's name that one instinctively supposes anyone bearing it to be a woman," observed the *Canberra Times*, which continued: "Mr Evelyn Waugh, the novelist brother of Mr Alec Waugh, the novelist, and Mr Evelyn Graham, Princess Mary's biographer, are two Evelyns commonly referred to as 'she' by innocent readers."[62]

All this reflected Graham's entrepreneurial energy. When the royal household announced George V's recovery in April 1929, Graham wrote to his private secretary, Sir Bryan Godfrey-Faussett:

> I am asked by an All-British Talking Film organisation covering the whole of the British Empire to humbly suggest that His Majesty should consider the question of issuing to his subjects in all parts of the Empire a message, similar to that published today, through the medium of the talking picture.[63]

The BBC had begun broadcasting speeches by the Prince of Wales and other royals on the wireless five years earlier; it would be three years until the ritual of the king's Christmas address to the nation began; the first British all-talkie film, Alfred Hitchcock's *Blackmail*, was only released the previous year. Here was Graham, proposing a new departure in public relations. Rather than "financial gain," Graham stressed, his proposal was "inspired by loyalty." Engaging with the philanthropic work central to monarchy's refashioning, he promised profits would be given to the "Miners Fund or any charity which His Majesty might name." The proposal to render the king audible and visible was presented as a powerful instrument of democratic nation building. Graham concluded: "His Majesty's subjects would acclaim with enthusiasm a film message from their Sovereign, and this would especially apply to those far flung corners of the Empire where as yet His Majesty's own spoken word is unknown and unheard."[64] Godfrey-Faussett took two days and one sentence to refuse the request, but it encapsulated Graham's imagination and anticipated a defining development in modern monarchy.[65]

By 1930 Graham had found rewards uncommon for contemporary writers. "I was now a rich man," he recalled, "earning something like £500 a month."[66] While we might be skeptical of such claims, Graham presented celebrity as something that brought tangible opportunities. Literary success was elided with social advancement. Never fully part of London Society, he inhabited a cosmopolitan world on its fringes, frequenting West End nightclubs and shadowing the movements of the season from London to the Riviera. Never part of literary and journalistic networks, as a popular biographer his focus was reward rather than reputation. Raffish and indulgent, he never sought access to the patrician clubland with which he came into contact. Often estranged from his wife, he savored the delights of conspicuous consumption, drinking cocktails with chorus girls at the Piccadilly Hotel.[67] Entertaining the cast of the musical comedy of the Great War *Sons O' Guns*, he took the Royal Box at the Hippodrome Theatre, recounting how the orchestra played the national anthem as he entered—perhaps, he suggested, mistaking him for the Prince of Wales. Europe was his playground. Falling in love with "the most lovely creature I had ever seen," Graham pursued romance across national borders: "Most week-ends we flew to the Continent, either to Paris or Berlin, or, in the season, to Deauville."[68] Shipping records show Leslie Evelyn Graham and his wife, Elsie, returning to Southampton from Malta on the SS *Largs Bay* in April 1928.[69] In July 1930 Graham traveled first-class to Tenerife. Two weeks later he returned, boarding the *Dunluce Castle* to meet Elsie, who been on board since Mozambique.[70] Graham might have been rich, but his "living expenses were colossal."[71]

Graham's peripatetic residential movements also suggest his upward social mobility. He moved six times in three years. At the start of 1928, he lived in Colebrooke Drive in Wanstead, a new development of mock-Tudor houses built around an arterial road.[72] The sale of *Princess Mary* allowed Graham to leave both the tedium of bourgeois suburbia and his wife. That summer he took a flat in Wymering Mansions, an elegant block in leafy Maida Vale.[73] By December 1929 he had moved again to Dulverton Mansions, a luxury apartment block on Gray's Inn Road.[74] Affluent and respectable, Maida Vale and Gray's Inn Road still lacked the cachet of central London. As his star continued to rise, Graham moved to what Muirhead's *Blue Guide* called the "most luxurious and expensive quarters" to be "found in St James and the streets off Piccadilly." Here wealthy men could find "furnished apartments" in a "quiet and select neighbourhood" for between two and three pounds a week.[75] At the start of 1930 Graham did just that, moving first to Clarges Street and then to a "beautiful flat" farther east in Sackville Street. The neighborhood's quiet might have been disturbed: it "was the scene of many wild parties."[76] Graham's final recorded address in this period was Chalfont Court, an imposing Edwardian mansion house overlooking Regents Park.[77]

Where Graham chose to live was an index of literary success and its rewards. It was also a kind of self-fashioning through which the parvenu biographer claimed the material trappings of his newfound status. Aspiration as much as achievement drove his movements. Graham always conducted his literary affairs from a separate office. At first, he took premises in Empire House on Piccadilly, sharing these with South African Brandy Distilleries and the publisher Albert Marriott.[78] He moved at the start of 1929, taking an office almost next door in Egyptian House, a modern block of expensive flats with a "spacious front office" overlooking one of London's main thoroughfares.[79] The location alone showed Graham's success, bringing him close to the center of patrician sociability and power. Above the exclusive retail premises of the

Piccadilly Arcade, his offices were opposite the Royal Academy and the grand Burlington House. Close to his Sackville Street flat, Graham worked and lived on the border between the clubs of St. James's and Mayfair. His offices were on the same block as the luxury shopping of Fortnum and Mason and near Jermyn Street's upscale gentlemen's outfitters. He was a short walk from the theaters of Piccadilly Circus and Soho's dubious delights. Immediately south was the monumental topography of monarchy: the Royal Parks and Buckingham Palace. This was a successful royal biographer's natural habitat.

THE MARRIOTT COMET

Graham was not the only publishing sensation of the late 1920s. His star was shadowed by what was called the "Marriott comet." Albert E. Marriott and Son was registered as a private company in November 1929.[80] After first occupying rooms on Piccadilly, the company quickly moved to a modern office block in Golden Square, Soho (a tenancy held by Leslie Evelyn Graham).[81] The directors, Albert Marriott and Richard Dent, employed a secretary, Winifred Ococks, and a typist, messenger, and office boy. Three commercial travelers represented their interests to retailers across Britain.[82] Much of this was unremarkable. Marriott was one of countless small concerns drawn into publishing by the opportunities created by what Stanley Unwin called the "commercialization of literature."[83] Yet Marriott presented itself as something different. Embracing the market, its extensive publicity fashioned a compelling story of the rise of a pioneering publishing house. Cultivating the confidence of booksellers and editors and the attention of readers, Marriott's enterprise was ostentatious, its innovations self-promoting, its focus profit rather than reputation. Soon the Marriott comet would focus scrutiny on the tensions within commercial publishing.

Marriott's first advert in the *Publishers' Circular* set modesty aside to herald "A New Era in Publishing!" The company promised a "uniform series of intimate biographies of the World's greatest men and women" for ten shillings sixpence. Forthcoming titles included *King George V through American Eyes*; "in preparation" were biographies of King Amanullah of Afghanistan, Charlie Chaplin, and Edith Cavell.[84] Marriott published biographies throughout its existence: Walter Townsend and Leonard Townsend's work on *Pope Pius XI* and A. M. K. Watson's *Biography of President von Hindenburg* appeared in 1930.[85] Its list was remarkably diverse, however. William Mackay's autobiographical novel *Ex-Soldier* (1930) was well received as a searing indictment of the "growing callousness of a social system to the pitiable status of the ex-serviceman."[86] The firm reprinted best-selling American comedies and sex novels.[87] It published the British edition of Otto Nückel's groundbreaking graphic novel *Destiny: A Novel in Pictures* (1930), a dystopian account of poverty, prostitution, and murder rendered entirely through leadcuts.[88] Donald Sinderby's *Mother-in-Law India* (1929) was rushed into print to exploit the international sensation caused by Katherine Mayo's notorious *Mother India* (1927). Anticipating the violence following a socialist government's granting of Indian independence, Sinderby's novel was, the *Times Literary Supplement* noted, a "good idea spoiled by lack of care in the handling" (fig. 16).[89]

Marriott first drew attention for *The Biography of H.R.H. the Prince of Wales* (1929), by the young journalists Walter Townsend and Leonard Townsend.[90] This was, Marriott remembered, the "sensation of the publishing season."[91] *H.R.H.* entered the *Publisher and Bookseller*'s best-selling lists for Leeds, Paris, Bath, Hastings, and Hull.[92] Serial rights were sold to periodicals across the world: the Amalgamated Press in Britain for £580; Hearst Publications in the United States for £714; and the Australian Press and *Montreal Star* for £250 each. Indian serial rights were sold for £75 to the *Englishman* in Calcutta, and Swedish rights for £100 to Albert Bonnier. Most profitably, the book was licensed to Macmillan in New York: by April 1931 this edition had sold 10,376 copies.[93]

Much of this reflected the prince's global celebrity. Yet the intricate contracts were symptomatic of Albert Marriott's sophisticated commercial practices. Acting as publisher and agent, he presented himself as a dynamic entrepreneur and argued that the "only way in which to be a success as a publisher was to break all the accepted rules of the game." Marriott's "system" included a clientelistic relationship with his authors. Rather than an advance, the company paid 10 percent royalties on sales to protect itself against potential losses. If this limited writers' ability to profit from their labor, their creative opportunities were already attenuated. Marriott himself sketched out initial ideas for the firm's books, using agents to identify a suitable writer, then sharing royalties.[94] This gave the company the flexibility to respond to demand and controversy. Maximizing profits was Marriott's concern: "Usually I planned a book which would sell easily to a newspaper as a serial, having an appeal to the American public [and] dramatic and motion picture possibilities." With the author at work, "I would sit spider-like in my office . . . and get busy in selling the subsidiary rights." Such innovations brought the company close to the "shark publishers" condemned in the trade press.[95]

Consider Marriott's most enduring legacy: Helen Zenna Smith's novel *Not So Quiet: Stepdaughters of War* (1930) is now part of the canon of women's

482   The Publishers' Circular and Booksellers' Record   October 4, 1930

THIS SEASON'S MARRIOTT BOOKS

MOTHER-IN-LAW —INDIA
by Donald Sinderby
Crown 8vo, cloth   7/6 *net*

DRESS OF THE DAY
by W. B. Logan
Crown 8vo   7/6 *net*

FAMINE ALLEY
by Prudence O'Shea
Crown 8vo, cloth   7/6 *net*

DESTINY
by
Otto Nückel
Large Crown 8vo   8/6 *net*
" Destiny," a novel in pictures, will make a unique gift book for the whole of this season. The story portrayed in lead cuts is powerful and also beautiful. It will sell !
(Fully cloth bound)

MEET JANE
by Evadne Price
Crown 8vo, cloth   5/- *net*

THE INTIMATE LIFE OF THE QUEEN OF SHEBA
by Norman Hill
Demy 8vo   12/6 *net*

EX-HUSBAND
Anonymous
Crown 8vo, cloth   7/6 *net*

EX-MISTRESS
by Dora Macy
Crown 8vo, cloth   7/6 *net*

EX-SOLDIER: WE ARE DEAD
by W. Mackay
Crown 8vo, cloth   7/6 *net*

The Child's Gift Book which is in the centre

Crown 4to   7/6 *net*   *Crown 4to*   7/6 *net*

Lavishly illustrated—printed in colour —with five colour plates.
(Fully cloth bound)

BLACK CAP: Murder Will Out
by W. & L. Townsend
Demy 8vo   10/6 *net*
(Fully Illustrated)

The Biography of POPE PIUS XI
by W. & L. Townsend
Demy 8vo   10/6 *net*
(Fully Illustrated)

The Biography of PRESIDENT VON HINDENBURG
by A. M. K. Watson
Demy 8vo   10/6 *net*

THE AIRWAY TO SEE EUROPE
by Eleanor Elsner
Crown 8vo, cloth   6/- *net*

THE LIFE STORY OF FRIDTJOF NANSEN
by C. Marcotty
Demy 8vo   12/6 *net*

THE ITALIAN ARTISTS AS MEN
by Norman Hill
Crown 4to   12/6 *net*
Beautifully bound, with thirty-three full plate illustrations
All the great painters and sculptors are included, from Cimabue and Giotto to Raphael and Leonardo. Mr. Hill carries on the story from the primitives to the triumph of the sugary and sentimental in the works of Carlo Dolci.

A New and Illustrated Edition of

H.R.H. PRINCE OF WALES
The Biography Sensation of the Last Season
Demy 8vo   10/6 *net*

ALBERT E. MARRIOTT LTD., 37/38 Golden Square, LONDON, W.1

FIGURE 16. The Marriott comet, and the commercialization of publishing. From "This Season's Marriott Books," *Publishers' Circular*, 4 October 1930, 482. Published courtesy of The Bodleian Libraries, The University of Oxford, per. 2585 d. 14, 4 October 1930, 482.

Great War writing. It was Marriott's idea. Envisaged as a satirical response to Erich Maria Remarque's *All Quiet on the Western Front* (1929), it was first attributed to "Erica Remarks."[96] The book was eventually written by Evadne Price, a prolific Australian children's writer. Price recalled being invited by her agent, Audrey Heath, to meet "a new publisher, [who] seems to have packets of money." Having read Remarque's powerful antiwar message and Marriott's prospectus, Price told him that "anybody who writes a skit on this book wants their brains dusted. . . . What you want to do Mr Marriott, is to get an experienced author who could write the woman's war book of the trenches." His response was, "Fine, you do it for me." While Price was uneasy over her qualifications for this project, noting readers "wouldn't take a book on the war by Evadne Price," Marriott was insistent:

> He said, "We'll get you a pseudonym. I'll think out one by the morning. I know you can do this. . . . I think that you're a marvellous writer and you've got great potential," and I looked at him in a very old-fashioned way and I thought he's mixing me up with somebody else but I do need the job.[97]

Accepting the contract, Price wrote the unflinching depiction of modern war that, she claimed, drew on the diary of a member of the Women's Army Auxiliary Corps.[98]

Not So Quiet was a critical and commercial success. It was awarded the Prix Severigne in France as the "novel most calculated to promote international peace." The first edition sold fifteen thousand copies in Britain and became one of the *Publisher and Bookseller*'s best-selling fiction titles.[99] Price claimed film rights were sold to Paramount, though the project was shelved "because they had a film called War Nurse and they wouldn't use it."[100] It was serialized in *Collier's* in the United States and the *People* in Britain, whose editor described it as a "narrative that will stir every human emotion [and that] has the supreme value of truth."[101] *Not So Quiet* was simultaneously understood as fiction and documentary. Some readers were skeptical, but it was usually accepted as a first-person account and what the *Daily Herald* called "the greatest War book yet written."[102]

Titles like *H.R.H.* and *Not So Quiet* meant that Marriott was "considered to be a very live publishing firm." Challenging the "snobbery" in British publishing, the iconoclastic publisher broke down boundaries between intellectual and commercial production by lunching with booksellers and the managers of department stores. "I applied to publishing my knowledge of human psychology," he recalled, "and adopted quite unorthodox methods of selling the firm's books."[103] While George Harrap claimed to have pioneered innovations like a professional publicity department and newspaper editorial paragraphs, he and other established publishers were skeptical about their utility. Advertising was often driven by "newer publishers [seeking to] purchase an earlier 'place in the sun.'"[104] Harrap might have had the "Marriott comet" in mind: the company's brash publicity defined its public image. Cultivating the confidence of librarians, booksellers, agents, and readers, Marriott became a driving force in the commercialization of literature.[105]

Newspaper advertising was central to Marriott's publicity. Full- or half-page outlines of its list appeared in newspapers and periodicals, including the high-brow *Dublin Review*, popular titles like the *Sunday Referee*, periodicals like the *Illustrated London News*, and trade publications like *All about Books* in Australia.[106] The company staged flamboyant publicity stunts. Evadne Price attributed *Not So Quiet*'s "tremendous sale" to Marriott's "genius" for publicity—a gift for the spectacular that included "hav[ing] girls in ambulances driving army ambulances around London with 'Prize £5000 novel' and all that sort of thing."[107] At Christmas 1930, promotional material for *The Princess Elizabeth Gift Book* included a halftone photograph, color show cards, and glossy advertising circular.[108] Between January and November 1930, Marriott spent eleven hundred pounds on advertising. This was around 11 percent of total expenditure and its third largest outlay after printing and binding and royalty payments.[109] As W. G. Taylor observed, advertising was essential, but also "the heaviest item in [the publisher's] overhead expenses" and "one of the causes of their high rate of mortality."[110]

Much of the company's energies focused on cultivating relationships with booksellers and commercial libraries and encouraging outlets to stock Marriott books. Marriott was the first company to submit its autumn list to the *Publishers' Circular* in 1929, drawing the approving comment that "this young but enterprising firm is making rapid progress."[111] Between July 1929 and November 1930, eighty quarter-, half-, or full-page adverts for Marriott titles appeared in the *Publishers' Circular* and *Publisher and Bookseller*. Alongside extensive publicity campaigns, booksellers were offered incentives to stock books: discounts for buying early and posters to help them sell to readers. A double-page advert (including the company's stylized colophon) for *H.R.H.* offered a special Christmas gift edition that included a "loosely inserted autographed portrait."[112]

Bold slogans like "Publicity Pays! Our Half Guinea Biographies Are Selling Like Hot Cakes!" emphasized the rewards Marriott books could bring. Adverts reprinted positive reviews and provided evidence of strong sales.[113] Growing in confidence, Marriott's publicity informed an ostentatious narrative of its role in the development of modern advertising. In August 1930, adverts announced a "display competition for the trade," offering a fifty-pound prize for the bookseller who created the best display of the company's publications.[114] Quoting its description as a "young and enterprising firm," the advert observed, "Here is Another Unique Step Forward!" Conditions stipulated that each display should include the *Princess Elizabeth Gift Book* and reminded booksellers that the "selling power of the position you chose will be taken into account."[115] Assuming the role of adviser to other publishers, Marriott blurred innovation and altruism. In October 1929 he drew the attention of *Publishers' Circular* to a "rather unique publicity precedent" created by *H.R.H.*:

> We were approached by the Topical Press Agency with the suggestion that we should pose members of our staff reading the above-mentioned book and they would photograph them and circulate the picture free of any cost to us to the newspapers. We . . . naturally did not wish to impress our staff into a service that might mean distasteful publicity for them. However, we supplied the photographic agency with books with the intimation that they found their own young ladies.

The result was an "attractive picture"—"unique free publicity" that Marriott now shared with his commercial rivals.[116]

Such innovations reflected the competition driving the development of professional advertising in publishing. Marriott broke new ground, but by the 1930s Frank Swinnerton observed how even the established publisher "vies with his competitor in the use of every legitimate means of publicity."[117] Advertising remained controversial, however, and created ferocious debate over the market's effects on literature.[118] Key figures like W. G. Taylor, president of the Publishers' Association, considered advertising inappropriate. Taylor argued that books "cannot be 'marketed' like mass-produced commodities" and attacked those who treated them like "soap and toothpaste."[119] Swinnerton was uneasy about the loss of the "fine relish in a book for its own sake" and the growing "preference on the part of publishers and booksellers for the book which has 'advertising' or 'sales' value." Never a straightforward critic of mass culture, however, he was equally concerned with the limited appeal of "a self-conscious and a self-righteous literature" distanced from readers as with the "commercialized literature" emblematized by Marriott.[120]

Marriott's innovations made the company a global publishing sensation. The company's books were available through all main booksellers and libraries in Britain, including Foyles, W. H. Smith, and Boots, with its huge lower-middle-class clientele. In Europe it dealt with booksellers in Finland, Paris, Stockholm, and Berlin. It worked through imperial outlets for syndication and established relationships with stores that included Albert and Sons in Perth, Himla Libraries in Calcutta, the China News Company in Shanghai, the Bermuda Book Stores, and Plaida in Malta.[121] The company's expenses between January and November 1930 totaled £9,785, but it returned £5,430 on book sales and £3,010 on serial rights. Including stock in hand, this represented an income of £9,755. The Marriott comet was a profitable concern.[122]

PRIVATE LIVES

Looking back, Graham attributed his success to an "astounding piece of good fortune" in the autumn of 1928: "meeting with a ruling Queen in the intimacy of her own boudoir within the walls of a Royal Palace."[123] Taking readers behind the scenes, he showed a royal biographer at work. Writing to the queen of Spain "soliciting the honour of being permitted to write her life story," he was invited to Madrid for a "personal interview." The journey south was eased by "documents which gave me freedom of frontiers and customs and the courtesy of governments." He carried a "letter of authorisation" from the queen's private secretary and, after a meeting at the Foreign Office, an introduction from His Majesty's government; in Madrid he was introduced to the queen's chamberlain by the British ambassador, Sir George Grahame. Unnerved by the demands of protocol, Graham was set at ease by the welcoming queen.[124] Passing her his manuscript, he watched as she went through it with a "gold pencil." " 'You are very well informed about me' said the Queen eventually." The veracity of his manuscript confirmed, Graham "quietly asked questions about her childhood and her marriage."[125]

The Queen of Spain (1929) did not describe Graham's meeting with Queen Ena, but it framed the book for readers. The frontispiece recounted how it was written "from material supplied by her Majesty to the author in audience at the Royal Palace." Explaining her reforms of Spain's hospitals, he quoted "Her Majesty's account of this great undertaking, given to me recently."[126] The interview allowed readers "to penetrate . . . into that misty haze which inevitably surrounds the early childhood even of a Princess."[127] The Queen had

> a supremely happy domestic life; she has had the satisfaction of seeing her children grown up healthily and happily under her watchful care, and the joy of knowing her efforts for the good of her country had been crowned with success and rewarded by the love of her people.[128]

Saccharine and hagiographic, *The Queen of Spain* was typical of contemporary royal biography. Read alongside Graham's other work, it allows us to understand changes in the writing of royal lives. Highlighting the queen's national service suggests a continued focus on monarchy's tireless philanthropy. Foregrounding her domestic happiness suggests the growing emphasis upon private lives. A personal audience also secured Graham's position as a knowledgeable observer. In this "authorized life-story," the queen herself marked Graham's facts as "correct." A growing preoccupation with monarchy's "personality" was worked out as both the ways in which an "authentic" life was produced and the themes on which biographers focused.[129]

Historians have suggested that "uncritical" nineteenth-century works were replaced by "muckraking biographies based on unsubstantiated and unattributable gossip" in the 1950s. Unattributed anecdotes were the stuff of royal lives in the 1920s and 1930s, however.[130] In 1930 the *Daily Mail* noted "the voracious appetite of the Transatlantic reading public for 'inside details' of the lives of members of the Royal Family."[131] Never simply a challenge to deference, such storytelling reflected the shifting concerns of writers and the generic conventions that defined biographical "truth." "Inside details" had to be balanced with respect, but "gossip" was not always problematic.

Charlotte Cavendish's *Biography of H.M. Queen Mary*, published by Marriott in 1930, thus identified a radical transformation since Queen Victoria's reign:

> Our ideas concerning Royalty and their duties have changed somewhat since those days. The growth of democracy has forced members of the Royal House into closer contact with the people, the popular Press has given them a hitherto undreamed-of publicity, with the result that today we are inclined to look upon them not so much as a race apart, but as human beings, very like ourselves, and with much the same hopes, fears and desires as animate the bulk of mankind.[132]

Such comments evinced increasing scrutiny of the monarchy's private lives. Foregrounding an interior realm of "hopes, fears and desires" effaced inequalities of wealth and power. Cavendish presented this shift as the inevitable result of evolving ideas. Highlighting the relationship between mass democracy and mass culture, however, gestured toward the deliberate construction of royalty as "like ourselves."[133] Rather than describing historical changes, Cavendish was commenting on processes to which her work contributed. Distancing herself from earlier life-writing, she noted that "I have striven . . . to avoid stressing those aspects of [Queen Mary's] character usually emphasised by those who write on this subject." Cavendish criticized depictions of "a paragon of all the virtues . . . entirely lacking in any faults common to all humanity," insisting instead on setting aside the public mask to explore the queen's private life and personality.[134]

The idea of monarchy as both domestic and public had shaped images of Victoria since the 1860s. In the decades around the Great War, these ideas became increasingly important to biographers. New forms of personal journalism remade royals as modern celebrities. No longer distant figures defined by public duty, individuals like the Prince of Wales were treated like the Hollywood starlet—their private lives dissected, their looks and personality scrutinized. Yet monarchy was a particular kind of celebrity. The Prince of Wales and Duchess of York were often portrayed as glamorous, but the emphasis on what the *Empire News* called their "gentle homely moods" suggests how closely privacy and domesticity were entwined.[135] When Graham sought to provide an intimate portrait of his subjects, he looked first to the home. It was here, he suggested, rather than in public forms of ceremony and philanthropy, that personality could be seen most vividly. Graham remembered visiting the private rooms in St. James's Palace, seeing in their fabric "an impression of the Prince of Wales' character that I had never obtained in half a dozen meetings with him in his public life."[136]

These ideas had informed earlier profiles like *Homes and Haunts of Famous Authors* (1906), but were given renewed impetus after the Great War.[137] Psychology and psychoanalysis constructed the family as the quintessentially private sphere and childhood as a formative stage in the development of character. After the disruptions of war, didactic literature and social policy cohered around the assumption that the domestic unit was the bedrock of private lives and postwar reconstruction. "The only secure basis for a present-day State is the welding of its units in marriage," argued Marie Stopes, "but there is rottenness and danger at the foundations of the State if many of the marriages are unhappy." The family was a ubiquitous presence in the 1920s and 1930s, shaping notions of Britishness and the nature of national politics.[138]

The privatization of royal life-writing was thus entwined with changes in public life and political culture.[139] In focusing on the home, biographers echoed how courtiers emphasized the royal family's ordinariness to citizens and sought to enable emotional bonds between monarchy and subject. It was no accident that George V's first Christmas broadcast equated "the family audience, the royal family, the nation as family." Characterized by domesticity and duty, monarchy was marked by the demands of mass democracy.[140]

Ideas of domesticity also shaped attempts to understand the monarchy's continued popularity. Observing the crowds watching George VI's coronation in 1937, Mass Observation argued: "So far as the King himself becomes an object of emotion he is conceived in family or 'Freudian' relations, not as a person who might do anything and hardly even as representing a country or a class." Family, it suggested, elided social hierarchies and elevated the monarchy above sectional differences.[141] The psychoanalyst Ernest Jones suggested that constitutional monarchy decomposed the figure of the ruler into the two persons of king and prime minister. This meant the "murderous potentialities" in the relations between son/father and governed/governing were satisfied by the opportunities for "destruction" of the prime minister provided by democratic elections and a free press. "Guarded from adverse criticism," monarchy presented an "idealized picture of the most homely and familiar attributes" and released citizens from the "harassing exigencies of mundane existence." Jones's comments evoked a pervasive theme in cultures of monarchy.[142]

Despite Jones's language of father/son relations, the privatization of royal biography reflected a longer process through which monarchy was feminized. A focus on domesticity displaced traditional forms of authority. In the 1920s this was reinforced by the close association between life-writing and women's magazines. The space given to Graham's work in publications like *Woman's Journal,* and the money invested in serial rights and advertising, suggests editors had a strong sense of the genre's appeal to female readers.[143] Graham's "At Home with the Duke and Duchess of York," published in *Modern Home*, suggests writers also knew what editors and readers wanted. The duchess took great "pride in her home" at 145 Piccadilly. "Public engagements" often took her away from "the normal course of domestic routine," but it was "surprising how much she manages to get done." Supervising the monthly household accounts, she was "careful to see that there is not extravagance." Monarchy was brought closer to the concerns of ordinary middle-class women.[144]

While interviewing the queen of Spain, Graham was shown "charming and amusing photographs" of her family.[145] Reproduced in print, snapshots from a private album collapsed the distance between monarch and subject, offering readers a window through which to glimpse intimate domestic lives. In *Modern Home*, the idyllic portrait "Bringing Up Princess Elizabeth" was accompanied by " 'Lillabet' among the lilies: surely the sweetest picture ever taken by a proud father."[146] Photographic conventions could also disrupt the image of the royal family. Since photojournalism was in its infancy, images of monarchy were dominated by spectacular state ceremonial and formal studio portraits. Graham's portrayal of Princess Mary in *Pearson's* was accompanied by the work of court photographer Richard Speaight. "Princess Mary in the nursery at Goldsborough Hall" confirmed the domestic qualities Graham evoked, but the family's awkward pose and grand surroundings distanced them from readers.[147]

The monarchy became most distant when portrayed in its public ceremonial roles. Infused with ideas of hierarchy and tradition, this vision of monarchy was played out in Cecil Beaton's work in the 1930s. Photographing the Duchess of York in opulent settings and costumes, and retouching his images while developing them, Beaton created images marked by the magnificence of the past and the dreamlike reveries of the fairy tale.[148] Graham attributed the "imaginative appeal of a Princess" to her status as "personification of all those beautiful qualities" associated with the word through children's stories. His efforts to describe Princess Mary "from the human point of view" were undercut by alternative visions of monarchy.[149] Naturalizing the process in which she and Beaton were complicit, Lascelles invoked the justifiable "hero-worship" of a couple who "stood out conspicuously from those of their fellows . . . simply on account of their fairy-tale atmosphere." The duke and duchess "stood out" because of the efforts of biographers and photographers; the "fairy-tale atmosphere" was constructed, not natural; ordinariness was always compromised.[150]

The monarchy's changing image reflected the changing nature of 1920s life-writing. Rich detail and the illusion of closeness to their subjects authorized the claims of biographers. This mattered. Biographical "truth" was a valuable commodity. Evoked in book titles through words like *authorized* and *intimate*, it was a prominent motif in the adverts that cultivated readers' interest and confidence. Authenticity effects were carefully constructed through the paratextual apparatus of titles and frontispieces that framed a book for readers. Graham's coauthored work with Sir George Aston included a preface:

> It is a great privilege to place before the public this life of His Royal Highness the Duke of Connaught and Strathearn. Grateful thanks are due to Lieutenant-Colonel Sir Malcolm Murray, KCVO, Comptroller of His Royal Highness's Household, for reading and passing the proofs on behalf of the Duke.[151]

As well as an expression of gratitude for Murray's help, this was an authorizing statement marked by the imperatives of commercial publishing. Murray had read the proofs, stamping them with the duke's imprimatur; Aston's title intimated personal and professional acquaintance with his subject.

These effects were furthered by the forms of biographical storytelling. Graham wrote with a doubled perspective, establishing a panoramic view of historical and political context, then teasing out character through telling vignettes. *Princess Mary* reflected on how "a definite and authentic idea of any personality" demanded what was described as the "inspection of collected evidence."

> We must examine in detail the habits, inclinations, likes and dislikes of the individual in question, together with the impressions received by others; for any idea of personality can only be built up by degrees, from small mosaic-like parts—namely the tastes and habits wherein we may see a reflection of that personality.[152]

Graham sketched out a meticulous method predicated upon accumulating detail, weighing the impressions of observers against the revealing traces of "personality," and scrutinizing ostensibly "trivial" fragments. Worked out in his writing, here we see the importance of "anecdote" and "inside details" to contemporary biography.

Certain sources carried most weight, particularly firsthand "impressions" and experience. Biographers often worked hard to place themselves in the scenes they described. *Edward P.* staged a meeting between biographer and prince: "Not so long ago I shook hands with the Prince of Wales, at the end of a day that had been . . . arduous in its variety of engagements." While the prince "looked fagged out . . . that did not in any way diminish the heartiness of his handshake."[153] A simple touch secured Graham's authority, just as the ostentatiously colloquial "fagged out" brought him closer to ordinary readers. His sketch stockpiled details about the prince's day: driving from St. James's Palace to Paddington and on to Birmingham; talking to ex-servicemen on an "experimental farm."[154] Elsewhere Graham attributed anecdotes to those close to his subjects. Noting how "I have it on excellent authority that all the children of King George and Queen Mary were mischievous," he cited a conversation with Lady Bertha Hawkins. This informant "talks with some knowledge since she was . . . one of Queen Mary's ladies-in-waiting, and was constantly in sole charge of the children of their Majesties in their infancy and until they left the nursery for the schoolroom."[155]

The biographer's craft rested in diligent research. Graham spent hours in the British Museum reading newspapers and books.[156] Marriott subscribed to the Harris Press Agency and International Press Cuttings, and made these resources available to authors.[157] Commissioned to write a biography of the Prince of Wales, Walter Townsend and Leonard Townsend wrote to the officer commanding the First Battalion of the Grenadier Guards, asking for "any information respecting the period during which HRH was at Warley

Barracks."[158] If not always accurate, details were attributed to authoritative sources. Graham rarely used footnotes, but his work could deploy something approaching a scholarly apparatus. *Albert of the Belgians* quoted "Wauters's book *L'État Indépendant du Congo*" and Roger Casement's report on colonial atrocities in the Belgian Congo. Knowledge was performed for readers.[159]

Above all, biographies were presented as an exercise in truth telling, challenging the mistakes of the ignorant and uninformed. *Edward P.* dismissed accounts of the Prince of Wales being "smitten with the charms of various 'Dollar Princesses'" in the United States, disdainfully attributing these stories to "reporters' fertile imagination." Identifying the falsehoods of others called attention to a book's veracity.[160] Charlotte Cavendish thus presented her description of Queen Mary as a critical intervention in debates over life-writing. It "is often the custom," she observed, "to endow [members of the Royal family] . . . with all the arts . . . to depict them as bibliophiles, art connoisseurs, patrons of music, and of the sciences." Cavendish rejected such clichés, observing pointedly how the queen "would be the first to repudiate such claims to artistic omniscience." This created the illusion of critical perspective and truth, but Cavendish did exactly what she criticized in others when she described the queen's "knowledge of pictures."[161]

This ironic doubling was elaborated in *Princess Mary*. Graham offered intimate details of the princess's romance, but distanced himself from the excesses of popular biography. A detailed account of her courtship was "both impossible and undesirable." The demands of "good taste compel us to leave the Princess alone at this point in her history—to allow her the privilege . . . of enjoying the beauty of her own happiness in a quiet privacy." While "inferences" could be drawn from the "external facts," it was "unnecessary to translate these into words and far more satisfactory that they should be left to the individual imagination." Saying nothing—drawing attention to the limitations of biographical knowledge—paradoxically secured the truth of Graham's life.[162]

Graham, Cavendish, and Lascelles were all British—that was essential to the proximity to monarchy they claimed—but their work was published throughout the English-speaking world. There were marked differences across national borders in the practices in which authenticity was located: biographical "truth" meant different things in different places. British versions of the life of the queen of Spain acknowledged but effaced Graham's audience in Madrid. Reworked in the United States, the interview allowed Graham to retell familiar stories. In the *San Antonio Light*, a character sketch became a conversation between biographer and subject, as Graham described his "first impression" of seeing a "slim figure standing in a doorway through which streamed the morning sunlight . . . wearing a light summery frock of beige that fell gracefully in lines that betrayed the art of its creator." Readers learned about the queen through her replies to Graham's questions. Asked about reports of an imminent royal visit, she replied: "It is possible, but not as yet probable. . . . No definite arrangements have been made for us to visit the United States." Graham's departure ended the audience and the article. Identical in content to the book published in Britain, the interview form pointed toward the different ways in which authenticity effects were constructed.[163]

I think the prominence of the interview suggests that the proximity of biographer and subject mattered more in life-writing and journalism in the United States. Less invested in the conventions of deference, less dependent on the royal household's goodwill, newspapers demanded more explicit intimacy and revelations. Consider Richard Dent's sketches of the Prince of Wales in *Collier's Weekly*. Described as a "former member of the Press Department at Buckingham Palace," Dent wrote as an inside witness who had "travelled with the Prince of Wales [and] . . . had unusual opportunities to observe him at close range." This allowed him to present "HRH not as the press department shows him, but as he really is." Quoting the prince's conversations and salacious revelations created the illusion of authenticity:

> Wales has had his little affairs and who can blame him for that? He likes pretty women—he likes the cabaret—in fact he likes to see a good chorus with plenty of leg. He much prefers vaudeville to straight plays and I have sat next to him when he has openly admired the charms of some star or showgirl.[164]

Dent would later publish the *Life Story of King George V* (1930) in New York. Here he also claimed intimacy with the king, recounting private conversations in which the monarch worried about his children's future. Where Graham used the interview, Dent deployed a different device to convey knowledge. The period after the Great War was "so crowded with engagements that, to give my readers some idea of them, I quote them as they were jotted down in my diary at the time."[165]

It was in this context that the editor of *Truth* criticized what he called the "profusion of apparently intimate personal details and imaginary conversations" that characterized royal biography in 1931. While such details were "mostly harmless nonsense," it was "extremely undesirable . . . that such stuff should be foisted on the public as true." This was a rare dissenting voice: they might have been fictitious and undesirable, but "personal details" were read "as true" by readers and reviewers alike.[166] Vivid storytelling defined the monarchy as ordinary domestic subjects and authorized such accounts. Intimacy was simultaneously about content, authorial voice, and form.

Reviewers emphasized how Graham successfully navigated expectations of the genre. He had a keen eye for the minutiae of monarchical ritual and philanthropy, but was always more interested in the ordinariness of royal lives. Mining his books for newsworthy anecdotes, journalists reinforced this shift in emphasis. Graham's account of the king and queen's children, the *Scotsman* observed, "presents a process of development and education which might well serve as an example in other families." This was "an attractive picture of healthy happy British childhood . . . not immune from the promptings to innocent mischief common to all normal children."[167] A royal childhood was deliberately linked to the playful "mischief" of "normal children," echoing Graham's reworking of monarchy. Telling details of Mary's childhood were elided with the truthfulness of Graham's book. Its claims to be authorized were accepted on face value; its veracity was taken for granted. As his reputation grew, Graham's name became synonymous with authority. The *Bookman* concluded: "In the preparation of his various royal biographies Mr Evelyn Graham must have had exceptional opportunities for gleaning an enormous amount of relevant material."[168]

CONCLUSION

Graham's star and Marriott's comet rose because both men identified and reproduced a powerful formula for writing royal biographies. The effects of authenticity were secured through interlocking processes of authorization and authorship, and paratextual and textual conventions that placed a premium on intimate details and private lives. Characterized by intensely detailed observations and an emphasis on the social, material, and emotional fabric of home life, royal biography echoed the work of middlebrow novelists like Arnold Bennett and the detective fiction of Agatha Christie. This realist aesthetic is usually associated with the valorization of everyday life and the feminization of national culture. Thick description of private lives cut across boundaries between genres, and between "factual" and "fictional" modes of writing, however, suggesting an understanding of how to evoke character independent of the democratic and feminine sensibilities in which it is often grounded. In Graham's hands this was a more general modern conception of personhood that could be harnessed to the dual task of securing the authority of the royal biographer and royal family. Processes that brought the royal family closer to ordinary life reified their distance from it.[169]

If authenticity was valorized, it always needed protecting. That is why newspapers were so quick to correct mistakes in Graham's work. In October 1928 the *Daily Mail* included an erratum:

> In a recent installment of Mr Evelyn Graham's story of Princess Mary he referred to "her clever music master, Mr Hutchinson." Actually Princess Mary's musical education was, of course, in the hands of Mrs W.L. Hutchinson, the well-known teacher of music.[170]

Paradoxically, perhaps, biographical "truth" coexisted with an implicit recognition that authenticity was insecure. There was a pervasive culture of knowingness around the veracity of gossip columns, newspaper reports, and life-writing in the 1920s and 1930s. *Truth* described the "pleasing" yet fictive "journalistic fairy stories" that greeted Princess Margaret's birth.[171] Addressing the annual dinner of the Newspaper Press Fund, the Duke of York wryly observed: "If I am ever in doubt . . . what is happening in my own home I need only turn to the gossip column in the 'Daily wonder' and I find all the information I need, whether it be the latest remark or action of my daughter . . . or that we have changed the decoration of our London house some ten or twelve times since we first occupied it three years ago."[172]

Within this cynical humor we can see how popular life-writing depended upon a complicity of interest between producer and consumer. To enjoy the pleasures of royal biography, readers were invited to suspend disbelief, temporarily immersing themselves in works that adhered to the conventions of authenticity at the same time as their romantic aesthetic might tax the credulity of an excessively critical reader. As biographers mobilized this "ironic imagination," it gave them a doubled perspective on their work that many were willing to play with.[173] Graham worked hard to ensure the "authenticity" of his writing, but was also mischievous enough to ridicule the clichés of mass-market monarchism. In the *Woman's Journal*, "Things They've Neither Done nor Said" lightheartedly exposed the myths and made-up stories contained in a press-cutting album that was the royal family's "favourite source of amusement." Rather than "flattering references," it contained "nothing except cuttings of stories and incidents that have appeared in the press all over the world, and in which there is not one word of truth."[174]

The "family joke" of the album allowed Graham to expose untruths while still acknowledging the imperatives of biographical truth telling. Learning of the falsehoods that filled their newspapers, readers were asked to believe *he* was a reliable narrator. It was on this basis that Graham identified imagined quotes and fictitious incidents. The inconsistencies of popular life-writing were laid bare:

> The Duchess of York has been described as blonde, brunette, petite, majestic, blue-eyed, grey-eyed, brown eyed, shy, self-possessed. In America she has been the daughter of the Duke of Strathmore, Lord Bowes-Lyon, on one occasion Lord Bowes of Lyon, England's Premier Duke, Count Strathmore, one of the Barons who was present at the signing of the Magna Carta and a descendant of the Young Pretender.[175]

It was daring for Graham to suggest "there is not a word of truth" in these stories: the same could have been said of his work. Knowing and subversive, the article played with literary forms he had exploited. Readers saw the paradox of a successful biographer revealing the genre's expediencies and threatening the conspiracy of knowingness on which it depended.

CHAPTER 7

The Courtier and the Con Man

INTRODUCTION

How much was the stamp of official authorization worth to a royal biographer? It might have been £1,050: that was the advance against royalties the publisher Harrap paid to Evelyn Graham and Sir George Aston for *His Royal Highness the Duke of Connaught and Strathearn* in 1929. Harrap deemed that imprimatur valuable enough to write it into the contract negotiated through the men's agent, Audrey Heath. The second clause stipulated:

> The Authors guarantee that the said work shall be an authentic biography and that it shall be read and passed for publication by H.R.H. The Duke of Connaught or a member of his staff *authorised to do so on his behalf* and that it shall be the *only biography approved by His Royal Highness.*

So pronounced was the demand for "true" portraits of monarchy's private lives that an "authentic biography" required a formal guarantee. Authenticity was rooted in the forms and conventions of biographical storytelling, but also secured by processes of social, political, and legal accreditation. When a manuscript was "read and passed for publication," its accuracy and the royal household's "approval" were confirmed. Harrap even sought to indemnify itself against the possibility that approval was not forthcoming: clause thirteen of its contract provided that Aston and Graham should return the £250 they received on signing if they did not deliver the work as specified.[1]

The value of the authorized royal life drew biographers and publishers into contact with the sprawling bureaucracy of Britain's royal household. Like many others, Albert Marriott and Evelyn Graham went to extraordinary lengths to secure coveted official sanction. Corresponding with the private secretaries of George V, the Prince of Wales, and the Duke and Duchess of York, they sought endorsement for their work. Official authorization also became a valuable commodity for courtiers. Their dialogue with figures like Marriott and Graham presented challenging new opportunities to manage the monarchy's public image. Commercial publishing and personal journalism threatened social hierarchies, but also made courtiers' goodwill priceless. Traditional forms of patrician power could be elaborated through ostensibly modern consumer markets.

After the birth of their daughters Elizabeth and Margaret, for example, the Duke and Duchess of York's family life was insistently repackaged for the reading public. In 1930 the prestigious publisher John Murray released *The Story of Princess Elizabeth* by Anne Ring, a former member of the duchess's household. Ring's intimate account of Elizabeth's childhood was "told with the sanction of her parents." The conventions of authorized biography created an idyllic vision of the "simple happiness of a royal home life" and allowed courtiers to fashion a modern monarchy for a democratic age.[2] Officially commissioned royal biographies are usually associated with the works overseen by Alan Lascelles after the Second World War. In the 1920s and 1930s, however, biographers and courtiers were bound together by intricate yet informal webs of correspondence and cooperation. Well-received books by authors like Gertrude Lascelles and Lady Cynthia Asquith were not labeled "official," but were shaped by the tacit authorization, encouragement, and assistance of the royal family and those close to them.[3]

When Graham and Marriott wrote to the royal household, they engaged with an institution undergoing profound change. After the Great War and the expansion of the franchise in 1918, the shifting foundations of monarchical authority and growing importance of public opinion meant courtiers were drawn into forms of public relations often characterized as antithetical to monarchy. The biographer Kenneth Rose has noted how George V found the idea of "propaganda" repugnant; his private secretaries lacked "experience . . . in such artifice" and were "men of conservative tastes, set in their ways."[4] The king's household was overseen by the domineering Lord Stamfordham until his death in 1931. A former Royal Artillery officer and staunch Tory, Stamfordham had become private secretary to Queen Victoria in the 1890s before serving George V and was in his seventies in the 1920s. Stamfordham's assistant was the engaging Sir Clive Wigram, son of a military and imperial family.[5] The Prince of Wales's household included Sir Godfrey Thomas and Alan Lascelles as private secretaries, and Admiral Sir Lionel Halsey as comptroller, treasurer, and equerry. This was a patrician world, in which men like Lascelles and Thomas shared a social background, public school and Oxbridge education, military service, and aristocratic interests. Lascelles was nephew of the Earl of Harewood. Educated at Marlborough and Oxford, after serving in the Great War he became aide-de-camp to the governor of Bombay, his brother-in-law, and was invited to join the prince's staff through a personal contact in 1920. There were always internal tensions, but the royal household remained discreet in how it appeared to the outside world.[6]

Rather than impermeable and unchanging, however, in the 1920s the royal household built upon Victorian precedents to engage assiduously with emerging forms of modern mass culture.[7] Stamfordham was acutely aware of the importance of cultivating public opinion. Wigram was a driving force in attempts to secure a "good press" and the support of a democratic citizenry. In 1917 he noted how "in the past there has been a tendency to despise and ignore, if not insult, the Press, which is a powerful weapon in the twentieth century."[8] Despite some concern over the perceived erosion of monarchical dignity, their awareness of the power of the press drew courtiers into more proactive media relations. Touring the United States and Canada with the Prince of Wales in 1924, Lascelles briefed journalists every day, feeding them "a sufficient quantity of harmless rot" in exchange for respect for the prince's privacy. Press releases, accrediting correspondents, and pressure on editors shaped how other tours were reported. All the time, Lascelles's letters and diaries attest to his distrust of journalists and adversarial relationship with those "poor wretches."[9] Courtiers were also drawn into protracted correspondence with writers, publishers, journalists, and editors about the form and content of royal biographies. Tracking their correspondence with (and about) Marriott and Graham allows us to explore the informal everyday processes through which an "authentic" royal life came into being. Focusing on moments at which courtiers moved to publicly identify work that was unauthorized, inaccurate, or intrusive suggests how mass culture was politicized in the 1920s and 1930s. The traces left by Graham's star and Marriott's comet allow us to understand the transformation of monarchical power and authority, its effects on popular life-writing, and the growing scandal around the bogus biography factory.

ALL WRITING IS COWRITING

Albert Marriott first wrote to Sir Godfrey Thomas, the Prince of Wales's private secretary, in May 1928. He was deferential. Submitting an outline of what became the Townsends' biography of the prince, he asked "if you would glance at this and advise us if you see any point which might cause His Royal Highness any pain or annoyance." Seeking Thomas's goodwill and support, Marriott deliberately set out how his company was "taking the most stringent steps to verify every fact and point in the manuscript."[10] The correspondence that followed was symptomatic of the informal dialogue between courtiers and biographers. Thomas met Leslie Graham, then apparently working with Marriott, at St. James's Palace. Their discussion was amicable and governed by the conventions of polite understatement. Despite this, there were underlying tensions between Graham's desire to profit from the prince's celebrity and Thomas's wish to control his public image. He was never explicit, but Thomas did not want another book about the prince. So much had been published that he "could not see any profitable market for another biography." Thomas "did my best to dissuade him from publishing anything," but his notes of the meeting acknowledged the limits of his power: "There was nothing to prevent anyone writing a book about H.R.H. should they so desire." In conversation, Thomas thus added, "If he decided to go on with the idea, I would be prepared to read through, and give my <u>private</u> opinion on any manuscript he cared to send me."[11]

Graham and Marriott ignored Thomas's hints. Continuing with their plans, they drew him into correspondence that lasted several weeks. Chapter by chapter, Thomas read the manuscript, replying to questions, verifying facts, and making "a certain number of marginal notes and alterations."[12] Graham asked "if the part of Chapter 17 making mention of the question of marriage and the Prince is in quite good taste, or whether you think this ought to be deleted." Thomas did "not think exception could be taken."[13] While he was satisfied with the manuscript's discretion, he had doubts about its accuracy: "There are so many incorrect statements in the last few chapters that I have found it difficult to deal with these short of rewriting the paragraphs in question, but I leave it to you to do what you think best from my marginal notes."[14] Responding to an earlier letter, Graham commented: "I have noted very carefully the remarks pencilled by you on previous chapters and have altered the manuscript accordingly." Royal life-writing became a collaborative exercise between courtier and biographer.[15]

Throughout these exchanges, Thomas sought to distinguish between his private and professional roles, emphasizing that correcting mistakes did not represent official sanction—something that would later cause considerable embarrassment. George V's private secretaries, by contrast, refused to engage with the substantive process of writing. In August and September 1928, Graham and Marriott wrote to Stamfordham and the king regarding a proposed biography. To "Your Majetsy [*sic*]," Marriott asked that we may submit the manuscript to a member of Your Majesty's staff for reading, or to Your Majesty's Royal Histographer and Keeper of the Archives, as we feel that a book which is not entirely correct and sympathetic might bring about the disapproval of Your Majesty's Government after publication.[16]

Stamfordham refused Graham's request but asked to see "any hitherto unpublished letters from or to the King" before publication.[17] This meant he was irritated by Marriott's subsequent letter—Wigram called it "an impertinent request because Evelyn Graham had already been told that this could not be done."[18] Their reply was polite but definite. It was "contrary to rule" for a courtier to be associated with this biography.[19]

Thomas's goodwill blurred boundaries between private and professional life. While Graham's incessant questions underscored the importance of accuracy to contemporary life-writing, his contract with Harrap suggests how the value of tacit authorization was public and commercial: an "authentic" life was a valuable commodity when negotiating with publishers or editors. When Thomas read the manuscript, he relied on Graham and Marriott's good faith that they would not seek to profit from his corrections. In August 1928 he was horrified to receive a letter from the publisher Hutchinson. Marriott had offered the firm a biography that, Hutchinson claimed, Thomas had approved. Having published Kathleen Woodward and Lady Cynthia Asquith's biographies of Queen Mary and the Duchess of York with the household's tacit support,

> Messrs. Hutchinson & Co. would be very greatly obliged if Sir Godfrey Thomas would let them know whether this life story of His Royal Highness the Prince of Wales could be included in the same category, that is to say that the publication would have His Royal Highness's approval in the same way that the other biographies have received Royal approval.[20]

Defensive and anxious, Thomas replied within hours. Summarizing his negotiations with Marriott, he stressed how "any fresh biography . . . could only be a repetition of several books" published recently. Acknowledging he had read the manuscript, he nonetheless emphasized that this was "in my spare time" and "my purely private opinion." Just as "the Prince himself felt very strongly that his 'Life Story' had been . . . sufficiently written up," so there was "no question of this projected biography being published 'by permission' or regarded in any way as officially authorized."[21] Unwilling to incur the royal household's disapproval, Hutchinson returned the manuscript to Marriott.[22]

The exchange between Thomas and Hutchinson underscores how courtiers could influence the operations of commercial publishing and control the royal family's public image. A complicity of commercial and political interest bound publishers and editors to the royal household. Reputable firms like Hutchinson depended upon the household's goodwill for their lucrative authorized biographies. As much as deference, simple commercial considerations meant they responded quickly to polite suggestion and informal pressure by declining, suppressing, or revising manuscripts before publication. When Graham later sold rights to *Edward P.* to Ward Lock, claiming it was authorized by St. James's Palace, Thomas again had to explain his objections to Harry Golding, editor of the *Windsor*, in which it was serialized:

> I fear exception will be taken to the use of the word "authoritative" in connection with this life, as all whom I have consulted agree that this gives the impression that the book has been written with His Royal Highness's approval.[23]

Graham's work was "purely unofficial." What he presented as an "authoritative" life was calculated to deceive publishers and readers.[24] Ward Lock's misplaced confidence meant it had already signed a contract for *Edward P.* Golding was embarrassed and apologetic, but could do nothing to stop publication. He still sought to make amends. Thanking Thomas for his "courtesy and consideration," he promised "the word 'Authoritative' will not be used" in the forthcoming book:

> We have already modified the heading in the Magazine instalments which have still to appear. I think you fully understand that we have been given very wrong impressions from the outset. In the unfortunate circumstances it is our wish to do everything we can to remove every possible objection, either in the letterpress itself or in the manner of presentation.[25]

"Edward P." first appeared in the *Windsor* as "an authoritative lifestory" in June 1929; in July and August it was "an intimate lifestory." The final installment was simply "The Story of His Royal Highness the Prince of Wales."[26] Golding later offered a more tangible apology:

> I am wondering whether I dare ask you, as a slight mitigation of our crime, to accept a copy of a little book of "doggie" verse we have just published, which promises to have a great vogue as a Christmas gift. I fancy it will amuse you, but if not you have a waste-paper basket.[27]

If the royal household's ability to deal with men like Graham was under-pinned by the logics of a commercial literary market, it also reflected the personal and social ties that courtiers invoked to bind themselves to key cultural power brokers. Thomas and Golding's cordial exchange highlights how enduring forms of elite sociability shaped ostensibly modern forms of public relations. Thomas was close friends with both Sir Ernest Benn, the publisher, and Alice Head, manager of the National Magazine Company and the Hearst syndicate's representative in Britain. Personal ties provided inside knowledge of publishing and journalism. In February 1929 Graham offered the publisher Williams and Norgate what he claimed was an authorized life of the Prince of Wales. Its director, E. L. Skinner, wrote to Alan Lascelles, addressing "Dear Tommy" at the Travellers' Club on Pall Mall: "I wish you would let me know, in confidence, anything you know about Mr E. Graham, and whether his book is likely to be any good."[28] Lascelles forwarded Thomas's letter to Hutchinson to Skinner and observed that Graham "received no encouragement at all in this quarter" for his proposed book on George V.[29] For Skinner, Lascelles's word "tells me everything I wanted to know." Friendship and acquaintance allowed courtiers to extend their influence.[30]

Of course, there was something else going on here. As much as this correspondence allows us to trace how courtiers shaped the monarchy's public image, these were moments at which their attempts to control Graham and Marriott broke down and were reestablished. By autumn 1928 courtiers were increasingly aware that neither man was entirely willing to play the game. Biographer and publisher resisted the conventions of polite communication within which courtiers worked. Obsequious and sycophantic when it suited them, they could also simply ignore Stamfordham and Thomas's deliberate hints and continue with projects that the household did not welcome. Persistent in seeking official support yet sometimes rude and abrupt in manner, their "impertinent" requests alienated courtiers. Above all, while they went to considerable lengths to ensure their manuscripts were accurate and authentic, Graham's approach to Williams and Norgate suggests how both were prepared to lie to publishers, editors, and agents. If official authorization was not forthcoming, it could always be mimicked. Thomas summed up: "I have had a lot of trouble with them over a 'Biography' of the Prince of Wales which they brought out recently and which they pretended was an 'Authorised' work."[31] For the unscrupulous entrepreneur, the authorized royal life had a crude commercial value that overwhelmed the household's influence. Profit came before deference.

After the autumn of 1928, the relationship between the royal household, Graham, and Marriott deteriorated. Their correspondence was now marked by conflict rather than cooperation. Faced with another letter from Graham, the exasperated Thomas worked out his frustration in a handwritten annotation, railing against Graham's "effrontery" and duplicity.[32] For over a year he was repeatedly forced to deny Marriott's claims in adverts in *Publishers' Weekly* in the United States and *Publishers' Circular* in Britain that he had authorized the Townsends' *H.R.H.*[33] Sent a copy of the book's promotional jacket, he angrily marked one passage:

> We should not have cared to accept the responsibility of publishing this book without taking every step to ensure its accuracy. <u>Therefore the manuscript was forwarded to St James's Palace and kindly read by Sir Godfrey Thomas, KCVO, Private Secretary to the Prince of Wales</u>.[34]

Looking out for adverts and reviews, Thomas identified and then denied unwarranted claims to authorization. In July 1928 he wrote to Graham in response to an announcement that *H.R.H.* was forthcoming in a provincial newspaper pointing out "that though I was only too pleased to help you by reading through the proofs, there is no question whatever of the book being published under 'official auspices.' Nor do I wish my name to be mentioned again in this way."[35] In response Marriott was apologetic but disingenuous, claiming "the information did not emanate from us."[36] Still, it continued to present *H.R.H.* as an authorized life. In October 1929 Thomas issued a public statement to *Publishers' Weekly*. He was "frequently" asked to read manuscripts and did so to "prevent inaccuracies from appearing." While he had read *H.R.H.* "in the usual way," he insisted this was "done in my private capacity and does not give any official recognition to the work." The private squabbles between courtier and publisher spilled out into the public domain.[37]

Thomas was deeply embarrassed by his association with *Edward P.* and *H.R.H.* All his later dealings with Marriott and Graham were marked by a desire to compensate for his naïveté and ensure colleagues were not also tricked. Despite his frustration, the household ultimately "decided to take no action about this tiresome book." Despite Marriott's "gross breach of faith," the publisher "could slip out of it by stating that the guarantee given that my name should not be mentioned in the book has been technically observed." Moreover, Thomas had received this guarantee from Evelyn Graham, who "I understood quarreled with and parted from Marriotts." Both *Edward P.* and

H.R.H. were of "trivial importance, have had no sale to speak of, & are already forgotten. It is far better to let sleeping dogs lie but to be careful of Messrs. Marriott & especially the elusive Evelyn Graham in the future."[38]

Marriott and Graham's behavior was in many ways symptomatic of their mercenary approach to commercial publishing. At times, paradoxically, they responded positively to the royal household. At the start of 1930 a conciliatory Marriott abandoned his plans for "The Prince of Wales Series of Sporting Books" after letters and a telephone call from Thomas.[39] A month later Stamfordham wrote to Marriott about the prospectus for Major C. F. L. Kipling's forthcoming biography of the king.[40] His approach was deliberate and precise:

> You state that it is an "<u>authoritative</u> record of the life and reign of our beloved Sovereign" and that the author "traces soberly and <u>authoritatively</u> the intimate life of King George." Will you be good enough to inform me who, or what, is the "authority" from which Major Kipling "<u>authoritatively</u> traces" the details of the intimate life of King George, or which justify the book being described as "an <u>authoritative</u> record."[41]

The repeated quotation marks and underlining made the focus of Stamfordham's ire clear: this life was neither authorized nor authoritative, and Marriott was deceiving the public for commercial gain. The publisher was evasive—it claimed the material had been provided by Kipling, who was in Cairo and could not be contacted—but backed down under Stamfordham's unrelenting pressure. The prospectus was canceled; the word *authoritative* was removed from publicity materials. Kipling's work was serialized in *Home Magazine*, but the advertised book never appeared.[42]

Providing or withholding official endorsement gave courtiers a way to control what was written about members of the royal family. When dealing with reputable publishers, intimating that a life was unwelcome usually ensured it would not be published. Courtiers also made effective use of their control of the iconography of monarchy. Studio portraits, family snapshots, and royal coats of arms were integral to the authenticity effects of contemporary life-writing. The value of images and symbols meant their use was licensed carefully. When Ward Lock began production of *Edward P.*, it had a specific portrait in mind for the jacket—the only one "befitting the dignity and importance of the subject." While copyright was held by Messrs. Foulsham and Banfield, it could only be used with the "express sanction" of the prince's household. Harry Golding thus wrote to Sir Lionel Halsey asking permission to use this image "rather than . . . one of the more ordinary and commonplace photographs." The company was conciliatory—"we pledge ourselves not to use the portrait in any advertising sense whatever except that directly concerned with the book"—but in refusing permission, Thomas was able to signal his disapproval of Graham's work.[43] Dispensing favor and disfavor through the symbols of monarchy was commonplace. Thomas refused to allow Graham to use the Prince of Wales's "Coat of Arms and Feathers" on the cover of *Edward P.*, since they were "the private property of His Royal Highness." A later letter noted how they were "protected by Act of Parliament." The legal status afforded the prince's coat of arms hinted at the sanctions its unauthorized use might draw.[44]

Courtiers faced several problems in dealing with Marriott and Graham. Both men were unpredictable and energetic. At times, courtiers seemed overwhelmed by the scale of their activities and the correspondence they received—to say nothing of their deceit and sharp practice. They were often unsure whom they were dealing with. In July 1929 Thomas admitted: "I am still not clear whether this is the same story written by 'Walter and Leonard Townshend' which Mr L. Evelyn Graham submitted to me some time ago, or another version compiled by the latter gentleman."[45] The household's problems were also structural, reflecting the diffuse bureaucracy around the monarchy. The staff of the king and queen, Prince of Wales, and Duke and Duchess of York were notionally discrete and dispersed among different locations, including Buckingham Palace and St. James's Palace. The peripatetic nature of monarchy meant courtiers were constantly on the move, following the king between Buckingham Palace, Windsor Castle, and Balmoral, or accompanying the Prince of Wales on his global tours. This made it difficult to accumulate knowledge consistently. Graham and Marriott exploited the gaps in communication, approaching different offices with the same proposal, concealing earlier correspondence with other officials and publishers, playing courtiers off against one another.[46]

Tracking the royal household's dealings with Graham and Marriott, however, suggests the material networks of power they elaborated in the 1920s and 1930s. As well as exploiting the ties of friendship and class that bound them to key cultural power brokers, courtiers' power was also increasingly bureaucratic. Underpinned by meticulous processes of annotating, copying, and filing, it took material form in the bulging brown files that ordered their negotiations with writers and publishers. George V's staff annotated letters from prospective biographers: "Please card this under applications to write the King's life."[47] Thomas and Halsey retained all correspondence they received and sent, placing it alongside memoranda and notes of meetings in reverse chronological order in individual subject files. When Stamfordham was moved to send a memorandum on Graham's activities to the Prince of Wales's staff in September 1928, Halsey replied: "We have got quite a big file here concerning him."[48] As that file grew, officials added a cover sheet: a table set out the chronology of their correspondence with Marriott, placing the date and purpose of each letter next to notes on "How dealt with." The neat rows and columns sought to impose coherence on communications that could otherwise seem bewildering.

Stamfordham and Halsey's exchange suggests how these files allowed courtiers to accumulate knowledge of Graham and Marriott's activities and, in so doing, deal with them. Circulated with covering letters and memoranda, files moved along circuits that bound the households together. As knowledge was diffused, the men's opportunities were slowly shut down. In May 1928 Marriott approached Lady Helen Graham, lady-in-waiting to the Duchess of York, seeking permission to write the duchess's biography: Graham forwarded his letter to Thomas, seeking further information and noting, "The Duchess does not feel very keen."[49] Thomas described his dealings with Graham and Marriott, suggesting she explain that the number of recent biographies meant the duchess "would therefore prefer that, for the moment at any rate, another did not appear." Lady Graham terminated the correspondence.[50]

It was on this basis that members of the household gradually pieced together the connections among the disreputable biographers, publishers, and journalists causing them so much trouble. The relationship between Graham and Marriott was often uncertain, but itemizing their correspondence in a table isolated them as a common problem. In February 1930 publication of a biography of George V in New York prompted Stamfordham to ask Thomas: "Have you anything in your files about a Mr Richard Dent, who seems to be describing himself as one of the Staff of the Press at Buckingham Palace?"[51] Thomas could find no relevant correspondence but had discussed Dent's articles in *Collier's Weekly* with his colleague Mitchell. Mitchell had shared reports of Dent's activities with Wigram. Thomas was able to confirm, "No such person was ever with the various Press parties that accompanied us on our Overseas Tours," but admitted Dent "may have been a free lance reporter hanging around."[52] He had another theory: on Marriott's headed notepaper, he had annotated "R. Dent," listed as one of the company's directors: "? The author of the Colliers Magazine stories."[53] Such ad hoc exchanges gave material form to the bureaucratic processes through which courtiers sought to protect the monarchy's public image.

The circuits through which this information moved extended outside the royal household. Files, letters, cuttings, and telegrams established networks that bound courtiers to publishers and editors. Having been offered Graham's manuscript *Behind the Scenes in Buckingham Palace*, the publisher John Murray wrote to Stamfordham in 1929. While the title did not suggest "very high class literature," the "position is changed" by Stamfordham's inclusion among "those who are assisting with information."

> Could you tell me in strict confidence how far there is any authority for this and whether you are really lending your name in any way. You will realize what a difference it makes in the "standing" of the book and I hope that you will forgive my asking.[54]

Their familiar correspondence suggests the men knew each other. Stamfordham addressed "My dear Jack," noting how this letter "astounds me!" There was more to their exchange than the mobilization of elite social relations. Stamfordham replied: "I send you in confidence our file . . . with regard to this impudent fellow"—the loose collection of papers labeled PS/PSO/GV/PS/MAIN/48600. Amazed and entertained, Murray withdrew from his correspondence with Graham; his letters were added to the file he had been sent to read.[55]

Receiving information *from* publishers and editors also allowed courtiers to monitor the publishing industry from within. Harry Golding at Ward Lock shared details of Graham's activities with Thomas. He apologized "that I have been unable to get nearer to Mr Graham than the end of the telephone," and observed "at the risk of giving you nightmare[s] I am bound to pass on the intelligence that apparently yet another life of the Prince is on the way!"[56] Approached by Stamfordham after advertising Marriott's biography of the king, E. W. Shepherd, manager of Hatchards Booksellers, took it upon himself to act as courtiers' eyes and ears. Eager and sycophantic, he made inquiries among publishers and booksellers and sent Stamfordham copies of Marriott's prospectus. By the end of 1929, courtiers usually had some idea what Graham and Marriott were doing.[57]

All of these strategies coalesced in the household's response to a more unusual Marriott title: Ida May's illustrated *Princess Elizabeth Christmas Book*. This saccharine "child's biography of Her Royal Highness" depicted an ordinary child in a fairy-tale environment. "The British nation loves the little Princess because she is a sweet and pretty baby," observed May, "but as she grows up they will go on loving her because she has been brought up to be gracious and kind and true." Simple morality tales stressed the importance of selflessness and humility. Stories and verses riffed on Elizabeth's supposed childhood: "Peter, the Puppy: The Story of a Cairn Terrier," or meeting the talking monkey Jingle Jinks in "The Enchanted Garden."[58]

There was little here that could be considered offensive, but the book clearly angered courtiers. Having learned of its publication from an advert in the trade press, Sir Basil Brook, the Duke of York's comptroller, wrote to Marriott in July 1930: "I would point out that Their Royal Highnesses the Duke and Duchess of York have given no authority for this work to be published nor can the book have official recognition."[59] Marriott promised to change the title to *The "Princess Elizabeth" Children's Gift Book*, assuring Brook that "no indication whatever shall be given that the book is published by the authority of Their Royal Highness."[60] This was not enough. A further letter repeated the Duchess's "hope . . . that the name 'Princess Elizabeth' will be deleted entirely from the title." As the correspondence continued, Brook interwove persuasion and pressure in seeking to prevent publication. "I hope very much that you will see your way to acceding to the Duchess," he concluded. Publication would create a "difficult situation" and "might necessitate an official statement being issued from here to the effect that it has been done without the approval of Their Royal Highnesses."[61] When Marriott ignored such hints, the book's publication was met with a notice in the *Morning Post*:

> The "Morning Post" is authoritatively informed that the book contains many inaccuracies and has no official sanction. The original manuscript . . . was submitted to the Duke of York's Household with a request for permission for the book to be dedicated to Princess Elizabeth. This request was refused on the ground of the extreme youth of the Princess.[62]

When informal pressure did not work, their close relationship with the editor of the *Morning Post* allowed courtiers to make their displeasure public and reveal the shoddy expediencies and deceptions on which the *Princess Elizabeth* book rested.[63]

CONTROLLING

The authoritative statement in the *Morning Post* underscores both how the press might serve to elaborate monarchical power and the relationship between literary scandal and the private negotiations among courtiers, publishers, biographers, and editors. Official statements and off-the-record briefings prompted public scandals that discredited disreputable writers and unwanted books. The response to *Princess Elizabeth* was muted, but in different circumstances such interventions had dramatic effect. In the spring of 1929, the exchanges among Graham, Marriott, and George V's private secretaries exploded into public view. Stamfordham had corresponded with both men over a prospective biography of the king in 1928. Nothing happened, but the following year he faced a new challenge. In February, George Sutton, manager of the Amalgamated Press, visited Wing Commander Louis Greig, stockbroker and gentleman usher to the king, at his offices in the City. Sutton had been offered the manuscript "His Majesty, by a Gentleman of England" by the agent Raymond Savage. He approached Greig asking whether it included anything "likely to be criticized or contentious." There was, Greig wrote, "something mysterious about the authorship," but Savage "thinks it good."[64] At Greig's suggestion, Sutton approached Wigram. Neither Sutton nor Savage could "disclose the name of the writer of the work," though he had "no doubt about the bona-fides of the people with whom he is dealing."[65] When the manuscript arrived, Sutton forwarded it to Wigram, noting disappointedly, "It does not appear to be very good, [and] much of it seems to me to have been published before."[66]

Wigram was furious. A handwritten note—the repeated crossings out and reworking symptomatic of his anger—summed up his position:

I must confess that I do not think much of the production.

~~A good deal~~ Most of the story is scissors and paste and a dish up of what has been published already.

This is enlivened by a series of romantic and fanciful pictures fabricated by the writer and his informants. Most of the ~~special utterances~~ tit bits put into the mouths of the King and Queen and their children are pure fiction.

I am fairly certain I ~~know~~ can trace the author of these tales. He is ~~reported~~ known to ~~keep~~ have kept a diary and has been a servant in the Royal Household for many years and ~~at present holds a responsible position~~ worked his way to the higher grades. He knows as well as I do that as a trusted servant he has no business to sell his conscience outside.

There is nothing offensive in the manuscript but the King ~~would resent~~ I am sure would rightly resent such a garbled account of the domestic life of himself and his family being given to the world.

The so-called "Gentleman of England" was a "miserable ~~individual~~ creature out for filthy lucre."[67]

If the manuscript was "pure fiction," then the idea of a "trusted servant" revealing intimate details of monarchy's "domestic life" was an intolerable transgression of their privacy. Protecting the monarchy from a potentially intrusive mass media was a pressing issue for Wigram and his colleagues. It was also a personal concern for George V: biographies were among the king's favorite reading, but he "displayed an angry contempt for those who abused the confidences of friends or the trust of an official position in return for money."[68] Demanding discretion from his staff, the king also—as Wigram confided to Greig—had "an insuperable objection to any biography being written during [his] lifetime."[69] Wigram's anger reflected the cumulative frustrations of dealing with Marriott and Graham. A handwritten note by Alexander Hardinge linked the book to "the man who behaved so badly about the life that he intended to write of The King."[70] News of "His Majesty," finally, coincided with George V's return to Windsor after a long and traumatic recovery from illness in Bognor, characterized in the media as a poignant moment in national life. An unwanted biography was an affront to monarchical prestige just as the body of the king and the politics of succession were freighted public issues. Graham had been solicited to write a contribution for the *Illustrated London News*'s special "Thanksgiving" issue, but at his greatest success, he fully alienated the royal household.[71]

Sutton refused to publish the manuscript. He was careful to exonerate Savage from blame, reiterating to Wigram that he was a "perfectly reputable man, and has published some extraordinarily high-class books," and had himself been "misled." Yet there was bad news: Hutchinson had signed a contract to publish the book.[72] Wigram received Sutton's letter on 7 May. Nine days later, readers of the *Star* were confronted with a front-page "Royal Biography Sensation."

The Star is able to reveal the fact that publication of a story of the King's life, written by "someone in very close association with the Royal Family," has been officially prohibited on two grounds:

1. That the identity of the author could be detected without much difficulty on account of the intimacy of the matter
2. That the material of the book trespassed to an undesirable degree on HM privacy.[73]

Deploying the tropes of investigative journalism and the exclusive "special," the newspaper set out the "history of this remarkable event, obtained by one of our well-informed correspondents." Rather than the commercial details of contracts and word counts, publishing was now retold as a conspiratorial drama: a mysterious writer whose name was "kept a close secret" yet was in "most intimate touch with the Court"; contracts to publish "in serial form in the columns of a London daily newspaper," in India, America, and Australia; a book scheduled to appear with "a well-known London publishing company." The "most careful arrangements to ensure absolute secrecy were made," since "a sum in five figures was to have been paid for the serial rights." When proofs were submitted to the royal household upon the king's recovery, their content "produced prompt action."

> The company responsible for the distribution of the publishing rights were at once communicated with and asked to cancel all contracts entered into and to end all negotiations for further contracts. The matter was regarded as so urgent that messengers were actually sent round to the newspaper concerned instead of canceling the contracts by letter.[74]

Shaped by a keen sense of the relationship among discretion, deference, and the boundaries between public and private life, the *Star* presented "His Majesty" as an intolerable insult to monarchical prestige. More than this: "the intimacy of the matter" obtained through a gross breach of faith meant the book "trespassed to an undesirable degree on His Majesty's privacy as an individual."[75] The *Star*'s public account of a literary scandal resonated with Wigram's comments on the manuscript. When the *Daily Chronicle* later suggested that "news leaked out," it perhaps effaced the deliberate communications that prompted the "Royal Biography Sensation." Other reports hinted that a "statement circulated" about the book's suppression.[76]

The *Star* broke the initial scandal and its report framed how it would be reported, yet the dramatic story of a "banned" biography was elaborated in newspapers including the *News of the World*, *Telegraph*, *Irish Times*, and *New York Times*.[77] Those associated with the affair were forced to explain their role. In a statement to the Press Association, Walter Hutchinson, the company's managing director, stressed that his contract was conditional on the royal household's approval. When "this condition could not be fulfilled," he "refused to have anything to do with the publication." Seeking to protect his company's reputation, he was quick to add that Hutchinson "always make it a condition that nothing displeasing to royal circles shall appear in any of their publications."[78]

Raymond Savage issued a statement the next day. Reasserting his credentials as a deferential subject, he insisted his role in negotiating the manuscript was "on the assurance that the work would be read privately by someone in Court circles." Elaborating this premise, he quoted the clauses he inserted in the publication agreement—a legal guarantee that the "said work will not be libellous . . . and that it shall not contain anything scandalous or which may cause offence to his Majesty." Savage had been privately told the "manuscript was not what it was alleged to be" earlier that week. Realizing the manuscript was fictitious, he canceled his contracts with the author, passed the information to Hutchinson, and "mailed to America prohibiting publication in that country."[79] Hutchinson and Savage endured considerable embarrassment, but the author of "His Majesty" was usually unnamed. The exception was the newspaper most closely associated with the royal household. Ostensibly reflecting upon gossip and rumor, the *Morning Post* reported: "Many possible authors have already been named, among them Mr Everard Graham, who has had some success with authorized biographical work of a similar nature." The *Morning Post* got his name wrong, but this was the first time the famous biographer was implicated in a scandal over royal life-writing.[80]

The "Royal Biography Sensation" was followed by another scandal over what Graham presented as the authorized *War Diary of the Prince of Wales*. Courtiers again learned of this book from their publishing contacts. Graham had cabled the manager of the Cosmopolitan Book Corporation in the United States in May 1930 offering book and serial rights for one thousand dollars.[81] The cable was passed to Alice Head, manager of the National Magazine Company. Head was also close to Godfrey Thomas: her letter asking if the *War Diary* was genuine was annotated: "This is Miss Head—a friend of mine who looks after W.R. Hearst's affairs in England. G.T."[82] Thomas "had not heard anything for some time about . . . that indefatigable Royal Biographer, and had hoped that he was busy on a life of the King of Siam or some other minor foreign royalty." He was grateful for the warning. To Head, he explained that the book was unauthorized and "distasteful." It was a "barefaced untruth" that it had been read by a court official. Thomas had "nothing against" a book that used published sources to describe the prince's military service, even if it would "require a good deal of imaginative padding." Instead, "I chiefly take exception to the title which, with obvious intent, gives the impression that his production is actually 'The Prince's War Diary.'" Since Graham's approach amounted to a confidence trick on publishers and readers, he "ought to be had up for attempting to obtain money under false pretences." While Thomas was confident he could suppress publication in Britain, he remained concerned at the prospect of Graham finding a publisher in the United States: "I fear the fraudulent impression he gives as to its authenticity may take somebody in, and I only wish there were means of letting it be known over there that the whole proposition is just a big bit of bluff."[83] Picking up the intimation in Thomas's musings, Head shared "all the information [with] my American people so that they will know what an impudent fellow they are up against."[84]

Thomas had also been warned about the *War Diary* by the British publisher Sir Ernest Benn, "a publisher friend of mine."[85] In writing and in a personal meeting, he sought Benn's help in finding "any way of letting it be known privately in the publishing world that Mr Graham has no authority to write The Prince's Diary, and that such a publication from his pen would not be welcomed by St James's Palace."[86] Within six weeks a private problem had become a public scandal—reported on the front page of the *Daily Express* as "Fake War Diary of the Prince." Journalists had clearly seen Graham's correspondence with Benn and the Cosmopolitan Company, summarizing the proposal "signed by a man who has written several biographies." It was, they noted, our "understand[ing] that the publication of any manuscript which purports to be a diary kept by the Prince during the war years is entirely unauthorized and . . . a 'fake.'"[87] Responding to this "impudent" deception, the editor of *Truth* railed against the "imaginative writer" responsible. Rather than a biographer, he was an "impostor" seeking to turn the prince's "unique popularity" to "financial account." "Publishers may be simple people," the editor concluded, "but they are not so easily deceived as the egregious person thinks."[88] Uncompromising and widely reported, such interventions echoed courtiers' private correspondence and publicly revealed the *War Diary* as fictitious.

Taken together, the *War Diary* and "His Majesty" are a kind of limit case that allows us to understand what Stamfordham, Wigram, and Thomas sought to achieve through their negotiations with biographers and publishers. Reading and correcting manuscripts was ostensibly a way of ensuring accuracy and biographical truth. Yet the household's concern with these questions was neither universal nor consistent. Even Thomas thought *Edward P.* and *H.R.H.* "harmless, but the usual kind of trash." He had tried to prevent publication and correct mistakes, but was sanguine about their threat to the monarchy's reputation.[89] Reading a manuscript was thus shaped by a broader understanding of the status of the authorized life. Granting or withholding official sanction could allow courtiers to influence how publishers and agents responded to a manuscript; it might affect a book's popularity with readers. Underpinned by the imperatives of commercial publishing, such practices could be derailed by a cynical publisher or deceitful writer. Still, they were the basis upon which courtiers influenced the literary marketplace.

As the furore over "His Majesty" suggests, courtiers were most concerned with the royal family's privacy. In their correspondence and interventions in sensational scandals, they effectively policed boundaries between public and private life. It was no accident that they were most angry when the integrity of those boundaries was disrupted. The "Gentleman of England" affair highlighted the threat of "intimate details" of royal life being revealed from within. It had been anticipated by an angry exchange in the autumn of 1928. Graham had written directly to the queen explaining how "material of an intimate nature relating to Your Majesty's private life and family circle has come into my possession." This included the queen's "private correspondence" and "some facts about the early life of Your Majesty's sons supplied by a late member of the Household of Her Majesty Queen Alexandra." Managing to combine veiled threat with sycophancy, Graham asked if an official would read the manuscript "to prevent the publication of material that might cause Your Majesty displeasure."[90] Stamfordham was furious, astonished that Graham had secured such material, and demanded a list of letters. He concluded: "I beg to point out that no such correspondence could be published without the Queen's sanction."[91]

In an ongoing struggle in which the bounds of discretion were constantly rent and repaired, Wigram, Lascelles, and Stamfordham worked to reconcile the imperatives of modern mass culture with monarchical deference and patrician power. Rather than the established brows that notionally ordered questions of literary taste and reading, such discussions were shaped around a simple binary predicated upon values of loyalty, respect, and discretion. Deference transcended divisions of brow and nation. Despite this, courtiers always had a clear sense of who was suitable to write or publish royal lives. The prestigious John Murray was thought an appropriate publisher; courtiers were prepared to work with Asquith and Ring. The parvenu commercial publisher and biographer were thought beyond the pale, even before their duplicity became clear. "It does not appear that Mr Marriott is a publisher of any note," Thomas observed in 1928, "and I see no reason whatever why Her Royal Highness should consent to his request."[92]

These decisions were animated by a sense of the dignity of modern monarchy for which the audience was global. Just as Graham and Marriott operated across national borders, so the household sought to manage the monarchy's image across the empire and the Atlantic world. Thomas's correspondence with Head reflected his anxiety at his limited ability to engage publishers and editors outside Britain. In 1930, similarly, George V's staff became increasingly frustrated at Richard Dent's publishing activities in Canada and the United

States. In January, Mitchell wrote in confidence to Wigram: "As this appears in a Canadian Magazine cannot we do something through the Dominions Office or through the Governor General?" There is no evidence that this proposal ever came to anything, but it underscores courtiers' unease over their comparative impotence overseas.[93]

Graham and Marriott knew this. As their publishing opportunities in Britain were shut down, they looked elsewhere. Brazen and cynical, Dent wrote to Wigram after the "His Majesty" scandal. Having been asked to sell the manuscript in New York, he knew of "conflicting reports in the press to the effect that it was banned officially." Anxious (he claimed) to avoid drawing action by the British ambassador, Dent sought to clarify "whether the ban precludes the sale of the work for publication in the United States of America." Again seeking official approval, he promised to delete "all objectionable parts" and asked if a revised manuscript could be read by the royal household.[94] While Dent was ostensibly conciliatory, he was trying to ascertain if there would be any fallout from publishing in the United States. Wigram reiterated his position: the book was unauthorized and unacceptable. There was "nothing objectionable in the historical part of this narrative," but it included "a series of romantic and fanciful tales," the "reported sayings of Their Majesties" were "pure fiction," and the book was intrusive and "in bad taste." This position was clear, but Dent still published the book in New York.[95]

Despite the limits of the household's power, the furore over the *War Diary* and "His Majesty" dramatized the success with which courtiers could suppress unauthorized biographies in Britain. Public scandal and private representation destroyed the confidence essential to Graham and Marriott's work and marginalized them within commercial publishing. By the summer of 1930, officials had systematically shut down their publishing opportunities and revealed the shabby expediencies that sustained their success. In May 1930, Head explained to Thomas:

> I personally have had two difficulties over Evelyn Graham and should not think of publishing anything more by him. Both Her Majesty the Queen and HRH the Duchess of York wrote to me saying that his material used in articles which I had published was unauthorised and incorrect.[96]

Having read Stamfordham's file on Graham, John Murray similarly commented: "I shall have nothing whatever to do with the book. . . . The author seems to be an entirely undesirable kind of person and a most pertinacious one!"[97] It was on this basis that even Thomas became more confident in his ability to manage the disreputable biographer. His reply to Head was satisfied: "I doubt whether any publisher in London, most of whom know something of Mr G. by now, would purchase [his work] without first verifying the facts with St James's Palace."[98]

These interventions also destroyed Graham's relationship with Raymond Savage. Much of Graham's success depended on Savage's ability to negotiate the literary marketplace. Now his deceit and brazen pursuit of profit threatened the agent's professional credibility and undermined the trust necessary to his dealings with publishers, editors, and courtiers. The public disclaimer he had to issue for his role in the king's biography was humiliating and damaging. Graham and Savage's relationship was already under considerable stress. Graham had sought authorization for a life of the Duke of Connaught from Sir Malcolm Murray, the duke's comptroller, but received a "polite note" intimating that the duke did not want his biography written.[99] Ignoring this hint, Graham pressed ahead with his plans, misleading his collaborator, Sir George Aston, into thinking their work was authorized. When he asked his agent to negotiate the sale of rights to the manuscript, Savage refused. The mediating networks that underpinned Graham's success were disrupted by the lingering bonds of military service and patrician sociability. During the Great War, then a captain and adjutant to a territorial battalion, Savage had been seconded to Connaught's staff in Egypt and Palestine. He himself had asked permission to write Connaught's biography in the mid-1920s but was told "HRH would not have his life written while he was alive." After Graham approached him, Savage telephoned the duke's comptroller. Murray "told him emphatically that the biography would not be officially recognised."[100] With his deceptions exposed and his practices unraveling, Graham remembered, "A break with Savage was inevitable."[101]

CONCLUSION

In the two years after Marriott first wrote to Thomas, courtiers became increasingly exasperated with the barrage of scandal and communication they endured. In February 1930 Thomas railed against "that very tiresome and obscure firm of publishers."[102] Writing to Ernest Benn in May, he commented, "I would dearly like to tackle [Graham] direct, and threaten him with an injunction."[103] As much as courtiers fantasized about legal action, and at times implicitly threatened prosecution in their correspondence, until 1931 Graham and Marriott's only brush with the law was a bankruptcy petition filed against the latter in November 1930. The household's reluctance to take formal action was partly a matter of need: personal correspondence and communication worked, allowing courtiers to apply pressure on publishers and editors to quietly suppress intrusions on the monarchy's privacy and to orchestrate (or at least initiate) high-profile public scandals. As well as risking undesired publicity, the prospect of associating the monarchy with a libel trial was unwelcome. In *Woman's Journal*, Graham observed that "tradition and dignity" meant the "remedies" available to "any ordinary citizen" when facing "a statement about himself or herself that is wholly untrue"—the laws of libel—were unavailable to the monarchy. To "insist upon a denial of the statement" remained theoretically possible.

> Yet it would not accord entirely with our national ideas of the respect due to members of the Royal Family if we found paragraphs in the newspapers reading: "The Comptroller of the Household of His Royal Highness the Duchess of York has requested us to publish a denial of the fact reported in yesterday's issue that Her Royal Highness Princess Elizabeth instructed His Royal Highness the Prince of Wales to 'hurry up and mawwy a lady like mummy'. The editor wishes to express his regret that such a statement should have been published."

The whimsical scrapbook "Things They've Neither Done Nor Said" was the "one answer that they can make to apocryphal anecdotes about themselves."[104]

In one sense, Graham showed a subtle grasp of the constraints on courtiers' power that made his writing possible. In public, however, he remained oblivious to the private strategies available to courtiers. In contrast to the monarchy, other members of the aristocracy *were* willing to resort to civil law. Lord Lonsdale was fiercely protective of his privacy. In 1931 he used the threat of libel action to force Putnam to suspend *The Memoirs of Prince von Bulow*, recalling copies and undertaking to "make such alterations as may be necessary."[105] Confronted with Theodore Daly's unauthorized biography, sold to the *News of the World* by Marriott, Lonsdale was similarly belligerent. Corresponding with publisher and newspaper through his solicitor, he expressed his "objection to the biography on the ground that much of the matter contained therein was inaccurate or untrue." When serialization was announced, a solicitor's letter forced the newspaper to withdraw publication to avoid a damaging court case.[106]

Their negotiations with and about Marriott and Graham allow us to tease out how the royal household and an emerging elite of cultural power brokers were bound together by a complicity of commercial and political interest and shared social experience. It was on this basis that courtiers extended their influence into emerging modes of cultural production. Editors and journalists constantly responded to the demands of courtiers; so did magazine proprietors and editors, and the heads of most publishing houses. What is significant is that such practices went unremarked. While discussion of the *War Diary* gestured toward the household's interventions, journalists were remarkably complicit in concealing the household's role in suppressing unwelcome books. The *Daily Mirror* began to develop a populist critique of the establishment around the abdication crisis, but it was only in the United States that what was presented as a conspiracy of silence received sustained criticism. Angered by the withdrawal of Geoffrey Dennis's *Coronation Commentary* (1937), the historian M. M. Knappen took up these issues in the *Journal of Modern History*. That publishers and editors responded with alacrity to royal pressure, Knappen argued, raised serious questions about the "rights and duties of free speech and a free press." Should publishers and press "tell the public all the truth"? Should elites enjoy the "privilege" of "apply[ing] informal censorship"? The answers to these questions, Knappen suggested, bespoke sharp distinctions between national democratic cultures. In Britain "the conduct of the British press has been treated as vastly superior to that of its undisciplined American counterpart." For Knappen, by contrast, valorizing discretion and deference was a pretext for "the grossest of misrepresentation." Democracy was compromised when social, cultural, and political leadership became entwined. A "little obscurantism may be necessary in a social system," he acknowledged, "but it is certainly a dangerous thing." The scandals around Marriott and Graham's activities had sometimes pointed toward them, but only in Knappen's hands were the silences on which the monarchy's authority rested fully exposed.[107]

CHAPTER 8

Stunts and Scandals

INTRODUCTION

The reception of *The War Diary of the Prince of Wales* underscores the power of the royal household. Extending their influence into commercial publishing and journalism, courtiers drove—or at least initiated—the growing furore around Evelyn Graham and Albert Marriott's activities in the late 1920s. While the news value of such scandals was huge, they also provided talking points through which journalists explored the broader issues at stake. By 1929 the *Star* could observe that the "field of Royal biographical literature holds rather more pitfalls than any other branch of writing, and even the best-known biographers of Royalty have been accused of indiscretion or exaggeration." Now, it seemed, "few intimate studies of Royal Personages . . . have not evoked criticism."[1]

These "intimate studies" provided a focus for an increasingly fractious debate over the ethics and practice of biography after the Great War. Lytton Strachey's *Eminent Victorians* (1918) intensified public discussion that had begun with the initial challenges to Victorian "devotional" traditions in the 1890s.[2] There were three strands to these debates. First, an issue of form and literary reputation: was biography an art or a craft? Second, what were the effects of new biographical practices on boundaries between public and private life? More than ever, commentators linked life-writing's "human appeal" to ideas that private life was *the* site of biographical truth.[3] Third, where did Strachey's "imaginative" method leave notions of authenticity? "In these days," noted Osbert Burdett in the *English Review*, "biography is a popular substitute for fiction, or the form in which fiction is preferred"—a comment that crystallized concerns that boundaries between truth and fiction were collapsing.[4]

Inspired to write by Strachey, in 1930 Hesketh Pearson asserted that a "biographer may justifiably tamper with the facts in order better to get at 'the essential truth' about his subject."[5] Eight years later, he repudiated this "inexcusable" youthful indiscretion and turned against Strachey's influence: "By sacrificing truth to effect, he became the progenitor of that bastard brood of biographers who make character subservient to story." Biography required "honesty . . . impartiality and absolute fidelity."[6] Pearson's volte-face reflected a more pervasive reassertion of biographical authenticity in the 1930s. Harold Nicolson and Lord David Cecil stressed the importance of dispassionate "scientific" research and the tools of popular psychology. Nicolson deemed "historical truth" biography's "primary essential." Calling for a "wider veracity of complete and accurate portraiture," he attacked both Victorian hagiography's "catastrophic failure" and the new biography's worst excesses. Despite this emphasis on discipline, Strachey's intervention generated creative tensions that neither Nicolson nor Cecil could reconcile.[7]

The form, method, and subject matter of life-writing were thus uncertain and contested. When H. M. Paull considered biography in *Literary Ethics* (1928), he did so with "hesitation," since "on no question . . . has so much been written: on none have the verdicts differed so much." Paull distanced modern writing from older traditions of deference and discretion that created work "about as truthful as an epitaph."[8] He was equally critical of "debunking" attacks on public figures, railing against "men of the Smellfungus type who enjoy raking up scandal about celebrities and publishing books which they label 'The *Real* So and So.'"[9] Paull recognized legitimate "public interest in the private life of the celebrity." Biographies that did not discuss private life were "absurd" and not "entirely true."[10] He envisaged a third way: "giving as true a portrait as possible: not concealing faults, but not exaggerating them." Truth should be balanced with respect.[11]

Graham and Marriott's success underscores the limited reach and influence of the new biography exemplified by *Eminent Victorians*. Modernist and psychoanalytic texts attract most attention today, but older biographical forms dominated popular and middlebrow culture after the Great War. What Pearson called the "romantic method of biographical pot-boiling" endured throughout the 1930s.[12] Yet the growing furore around Graham and Marriott's work was shaped by, and contributed to, debates over life-writing's ethics and practice. Their fixation upon royalty provided a bridge between the literary periodical, trade press, and popular newspaper. Refracted through the prism of monarchical dignity, concerns over the sanctity of private life and authenticity acquired powerful social and political resonance.

In a period of uncertainty for life-writing and personal journalism, the response to Graham and Marriott was inevitably defensive. For members of the royal household, they were an unwelcome affront to the dignity of the royal family and to courtiers' efforts to fashion a monarchy for the modern world. More than this: when journalists from the *Daily Mail* retold the story of Graham's rising star as a confidence trick on publishers and readers, the precarious foundations of commercial publishing were revealed for all to see. The spectacle of a celebrated biographer whose success was founded on fakes and frauds suggested that the authenticity effects on which popular publishing and journalism rested were illusory. It took a sustained exercise in investigative journalism, a newspaper "stunt," an international manhunt, and the imprisonment of a famous royal biographer before the threat of the bogus biography factory could even partly be contained.

ANATOMY OF A STUNT

In April 1930 Marriott published *The Biography of H.M. Queen Mary*, by Charlotte Cavendish, reportedly the widow of a colonel in the Indian army. Cavendish's book was typical of the company's output. It was offered to readers as an intimate account of the queen's public and private lives, acknowledging her hauteur and exploring sensitive issues like the Prince of Wales's bachelor lifestyle. Cavendish did not explicitly claim firsthand knowledge, but recounted conversations verbatim and described the king's coronation "from my seats in the abbey."[13] The book was received warmly. The *Daily Chronicle* reprinted "piquant passages" in which the queen reflected on her son's marital prospects, praising Cavendish for a "portrait which appears to be that of a human being" rather than the "mere effigies" characteristic of many books.[14] In the *Evening Standard*, Horace Thorogood was unstinting in his praise. *H.M. Queen Mary* should "serve as a model for royal biographies. [Cavendish] has treated her august subject with profound respect, but without embarrassment. There is nothing fulsome, trivial or inanc. It is an intimate, truthful study."[15]

Not everyone agreed. The Royal Archives include Queen Mary's own copy of Cavendish's book. Reminiscent of Graham's whimsical "Things They've Neither Done nor Said," a handwritten note on the frontispiece comments: "I have annotated this book to show what a number of inventions are written about one. Mary R, 1930." Penciled comments in the margin and deliberate crossings out marked the limits of the biographer's knowledge. Where Cavendish described how "Prince Edward ~~behaved well~~ at his christening," the queen crossed out two words and scribbled, "He cried all the time." A paragraph describing how the queen did not enjoy "some of the native dances she witnessed" on an official visit to India is scored through by two diagonal lines and annotated "I never saw any." In private, at least, the shabby expediencies and inventions of popular life-writing were meticulously revealed.[16]

The initial success of *H.M. Queen Mary* quickly turned into explosive controversy. Unlike Thorogood, others considered the book an intolerable affront to monarchy's privacy and dignity. The *Daily Mail* was complicit in the mass-market monarchism of the 1920s. While the paper reported extensively on royal affairs and serialized biographies, it greeted Cavendish's book with ostentatious silence: "As the Press Association states that the book has not been officially submitted to the Queen for her approval we refrain from publishing any extracts."[17] The next day journalists began a sustained attack on this "impertinent biography." Unauthorized and intrusive, *H.M. Queen Mary* was "in the worst of taste . . . [and] most offensive to the Royal Family."[18]

If the biography was unacceptable in scope, then its provenance was also questionable. Journalists searching for Cavendish visited Marriott's offices in Golden Square. Cavendish was apparently in Cairo. While the directors were away, the secretary, Winifred Ococks, explained that the author was unconnected with the court but "has done some writing for the newspapers."[19] The names linked to the book multiplied: "One copy of the manuscript recently appeared in publishing circles in London; another copy bore the name of a male author who has specialised in writing 'biographies.'" Journalists questioned the unnamed man: "I had been associated with Mrs Cavendish in writing the book, but when I learned that it was to be published without the authority of Buckingham Palace I disassociated myself." Still the names proliferated. Articles in a magazine in the United States were attributed to a "late member of the Buckingham Palace Press Bureau." Not only was this claim "unfounded," but the "name of the writer of this book is identical with that of one of the partners in the firm of publishers responsible for the work on the Queen." A cluster of mysterious publishers and writers was merging together.[20]

The *Daily Mail*'s outrage was driven by the commercial rewards of stunt journalism. In attacking *H.M. Queen Mary*, however, it assumed the critic's role in adjudicating literary value and "truth," echoing yet questioning the integrity of processes of cultural production and accreditation, and highlighting the failings of agents, reviewers, and publishers.[21] Its search for Cavendish suggests the book was deemed problematic because it lacked the necessary inside perspective for biographical authenticity. "Biography is a branch of literature for which a first requisite is an intimate and exact knowledge by the author of the subject portrayed," it argued. Neither "Mrs Cavendish" nor her collaborator had these "essential qualifications to write a 'Life' of the Queen."[22]

As the controversy deepened, it prompted a wider debate over royal life-writing. After reprinting salacious extracts about the Prince of Wales, the *Daily Mirror* asked: "Should biographies of Royal personages be written and published without their consent?"[23] *H.M. Queen Mary*'s "outspoken nature," it noted, "resulted in general criticism of all books which deal with the lives of Royalty and which are published without authority." It set an interview with Marriott against hostile comments from the *Daily Mail*. Accepting the importance of "intimate and exact knowledge," Marriott ironically pleaded extenuating circumstances when dealing with the monarchy. "It was useless to submit books to Buckingham Palace," since "books . . . are promptly returned to the senders because their majesties cannot be associated with any particular book." Denying that Cavendish's book was "offensive," he now implied that authorized biography was impossible: "If her Majesty had perused the book before publication it is possible that she would have eliminated some passages—those which are the most interesting."[24] Repeating his comments in the *Star*, Marriott concluded: "The interesting matter justified publication, since the lives of reigning monarchs are matters of public interest."[25]

Marriott's emphasis on the "public interest" was prescient. Having secured serial rights to *H.M. Queen Mary*, the *Sunday Express* responded to the controversy by going on the offensive. Caught up in the commercial rivalry between the Beaverbrook and Rothermere presses, Marriott's work ignited a renewed debate over royal life-writing.[26] In the *Daily Express*, a full-page advert for "The Real Queen Mary" attacked its "anonymous critics" and approvingly quoted Thorogood's review. Vivid and colorful, Cavendish's book contained the "real picture of the Queen," which "every man and woman, and every girl and boy in the Empire ought to read." Several months later the *Express* newspapers would retreat quietly from their support for Marriott. In the spring of 1930, their argument with the *Daily Mail* was rooted in alternative ideas of biographical value, prioritizing the veracity of an unauthorized work above the deference of one with official approval.[27]

If the *Daily Mail* sought to suppress Cavendish's biography, the furore brought it to public attention and made it "an astonishing success." The first edition of *H.M. Queen Mary* "sold out in a day" and became one of the *Publisher and Bookseller*'s best-selling books of 1930.[28] While Marriott could have been surprised by the *Daily Mail*'s attack, I wonder if we might think of the controversy as another publicity stunt. Trade adverts promised that

publication would be "supported by wide Press Publicity."[29] As the controversy deepened, they exploited the opportunity to bring the book to public notice: "Publicity Pays!" drew attention to the "book that became world famous
in a single day."[30] An unexpected source lends support to this reading. On
14 April, Godfrey Thomas wrote to Sir Harry Verney, Queen Mary's private
secretary, urging caution:

> I know "Messrs. Marriott" and their methods too well to be drawn [in], and,
> by contradicting them, to keep the controversy going and help advertise their
> book.
>
> The only way they induced anyone to buy a single copy of their so-called
> Biography of The Prince was to engineer a similar controversy in a couple of
> newspapers, hinting that although the book had received official sanction, (lie
> No. 1) it was nevertheless full of sensational revelations, (lie No. 2).[31]

The queen's household refused to be drawn into the controversy. Approached
by journalists, Verney "had no statement to make on the matter." Despite sum-
moning Marriott's directors to a private interview, he publicly distanced himself from the distasteful spectacle.[32]

Such controversies coalesced around the boundaries between public and
private life, and individuals' control over their own life stories. A *Daily Chronicle* editorial considered Marriott's titles part of a growing number of "Smash
and Grab Memoirs," praising those who took a stand and hoping this would
"establish the obvious right of anyone, however public his (or her) position, to
keep some check on the disposal of his 'life' for public consumption."[33] In the
Publisher and Bookseller, Jacob Omnium was more uneasy. Identifying *H.M.
Queen Mary* only as "a recently issued book devoted to apparently intimate
details about the personality and life of a very exalted lady," he argued that
it could not be considered offensive, since it "elicited no complaint or protest from the high quarter concerned." Challenging the *Daily Mail*'s "drastic
and indignant condemnation," Omnium noted that "it can hardly be seriously
contended that no book having as its subject any of the great ones of the land,
should be published unless it has previously received the imprimatur of the
personage to whom it refers."[34]

Writing from within the world of letters, Omnium characterized the
Daily Mail's position as an implicit restriction upon literary expression—
problematic because the lives of reigning monarchs were of legitimate public
interest. Members of the reading public were able to distinguish "real" from
fake, and were "content to take their chance of being misinformed in this or

that particular by an author who may be a little less intimate with the subject than he or she affects to be." He had confidence in the gatekeepers to the literary marketplace. Readers "have at least the guarantee that the publisher would have been bound to be satisfied that . . . he was dealing with an author who could at least show some substantial qualification for undertaking a work of that special kind."[35]

MEANDERING ABOUT THE WORLD

At the end of 1930, public scandals and private correspondence meant the outline of the bogus biography factory had begun to take shape. As Graham and Marriott enjoyed some of their greatest successes, they came under increasing scrutiny. On 1 December, suspicion became a question:

> Who is Evelyn Graham?
> The answer to this apparently simple question is . . . eagerly sought by the leading publishers and literary agents, to say nothing of other people, in this country, in America, and on the Continent.[36]

Published in the *Daily Mail*, the article that followed charted the rise of an international celebrity. Graham "appeared like a meteor in the sky of the literary world," astonishing agents and publishers with "offers of authentic and most intimate biographies of illustrious and famous living persons." Synopses and published work "gave the impression that he possessed the entrée into the most exclusive circles" in Britain and Europe. Graham's ambition was bewildering: a table set out twenty-seven biographies he had either proposed or published. As interest rose "to fever pitch," he "disappeared as suddenly as he appeared." This was "The Mystery of Evelyn Graham."[37]

Staged through the characteristic forms of investigative journalism, the search for a mysterious missing writer was elaborated as the systematic untangling of names and stories. Its sensation rested in the unlikely connections between putatively discrete social worlds. "Intensive and careful inquiries" had "unearthed a curious tale" and "reveal[ed] to the general public a story almost unparalleled in its audacity and effect." Who was Evelyn Graham? Manuscripts submitted in his name in Britain were published in America by Richard Dent; Dent—one of Marriott's directors—claimed to be a member of the Buckingham Palace Press Bureau; this "had not the slightest foundation." A magazine declined Graham's life of Queen Mary; Marriott published an identical manuscript attributed to Charlotte Cavendish. The most dramatic revelation was to come: "The Daily Mail . . . is able to add yet another name to those used by this man—it is Netley Lucas." Literary agents identified the biographer from photographs of a convicted gentleman crook. This was a "remarkable chain of circumstances, the explanation of which will be awaited with interest by the public from Evelyn Graham, otherwise Charlotte Cavendish, otherwise Netley Lucas, by whichever name he chooses to disclose himself."[38]

"The Mystery of Evelyn Graham" continued over several weeks. Revealing and concealing, unpacking the stories layer by layer, journalists orchestrated moments of suspense to draw in readers. Articles gestured toward the "truth" of Graham's identity yet always held back, creating a desire to know that was never entirely gratified. Until the series petered out in February 1931, another revelation always seemed imminent. "Evelyn Graham Unmasked" set out a biographer's unlikely life story on 2 December. While Graham had "used many names," Scotland Yard's records suggested that Netley Lucas was "that to which he has best title." Rooted in authorities and archives, an alternative biography undercut his flamboyant claims. Graham appeared in prison records in London and Canada as Robert Clarke and Armstrong McKenzie.[39] "New disclosures" followed on 5 December: Graham was also the disreputable publisher Albert Marriott; Dent was the "convicted thief, Guy Hart."[40]

A publishing house run by ex-crooks, a biographer with a criminal record, a "borstal boy" interviewing the queen of Spain: here was the bogus biography factory. The number of names linked to Graham made it difficult to maintain coherence. Journalists listed eight, though acknowledged how "names . . . are small things in Lucas's life; he assumes and discards them like a coat."[41] This frustrating multiplicity enhanced the intrigue that animated the series and made the journalist an indispensable guide through a tangle of deceit. Rather than a literary sensation, Graham and Marriott's rise now appeared as an audacious confidence trick on publishers, editors, and readers. Bringing together Graham's many names transformed their significance. A rising star was aligned with Lucas's deceptive criminality: a "convicted swindler" had "victimised many people" with his "so-called authorised biographies."[42] Exercised by the Queen Mary affair, and furious at realizing that publishing "Princess Mary" made it complicit in fraud, the *Daily Mail* stepped forward to protect the public interest and literary truth.[43]

As well as "unmasking" Graham, journalists drew on documentary evidence and personal testimony to reconstruct his biography factory. Graham had claimed intimacy with his subjects: as a "borstal boy," he lacked social connections.[44] He had presented himself as a successful biographer: "Although so

free in affixing one or other of the names he used to the title page of a manuscript, Lucas had no merit as a writer and almost always secured the collaboration of someone else in his literary efforts."[45] Marriott had acted as a literary
agent: now the prefect of police in Paris, Alfred Morain, "complains bitterly
that certain literary transactions he entrusted to . . . [him] have not been completed."[46] Graham had claimed his work was authorized and authentic. Now
a literary agent described their collaboration. When he sold a biography of
Lord Lonsdale, Graham delivered the manuscript late and short; Lonsdale
threatened legal action, since it was "grossly inaccurate." Alice Head, manager of the National Magazine Company, declined the offer of Graham's work.
Having published his articles on Queen Mary and the Duchess of York, she
"received communications denying their authenticity. The letter on behalf of
the Duchess said that to her certain knowledge Mr Graham had never been
inside the house."[47]

Inexorably readers were shown glimpses of what was presented as a fictitious publishing enterprise. Yet the distance between deception and legitimate
literary success was never as great as the *Daily Mail*'s language of exposure
allowed. Journalists traced how "Lucas was building up his bogus reputation
as Evelyn Graham, the 'great biographer,'" yet never quite specified what was
bogus about it. Graham was an assumed name, but by 1930 his reputation was
beyond question.[48] Observing that Lucas "poses as the intimate and biographer of famous people" effaced the fact that he *was* the biographer of "famous
people." Characterizing biographer and biographies as bogus or forgeries suggested the extent of their transgression, yet gave them a resonance that was
difficult to pin down.[49]

The *Daily Mail*'s investigations isolated the biography factory as a social,
cultural, and political problem. By December 1930 Graham was a famous yet
controversial writer. As this "exclusive" scoop gathered pace, it was elaborated
elsewhere. Reflecting on a "first class literary sensation," the *Ottawa Evening
Citizen* concluded: "The literary world and newspaper reading public will
await an explanation with intense interest, for 'Evelyn Graham's' biographies
of royal personages have been eagerly read and discussed by millions."[50]

There was a problem: Graham, Marriott, Dent, and Lucas were nowhere to
be found. Evadne Price later reflected on this episode with affection and admiration. When his affairs came under scrutiny, the man she knew as Marriott
"absconded." A literary scandal became an international manhunt. The "most
impudent literary hoaxer for many years is meandering about the world with his
usual effrontery and show of affluence," noted the *Daily Mail*. The biographer

was now a flamboyant man of mystery—Price breathlessly recalled, "Oh he was daring, he was like a daring crook"—chased across the world by journalists.[51]

Realizing that the "game was up" when journalists visited the Golden Square offices in the autumn of 1930, Marriott and his fellow director decided to "flee the country" with all the money they could withdraw.[52] Later retold as an increasingly "hectic life of dissipation," their journey was marked by drunkenness and dalliances with beautiful women. From London the men traveled through Paris, the Riviera, and Madrid to Malta.[53] After a scheme to open a nightclub in Valetta failed, they continued to Port Said. Having outfitted with tropical kit, they transferred to the *Llangibby Castle* before voyaging through the Suez Canal and down the coast of Africa. Christmas 1930 found them in Durban, where, despite the city's provincial dullness, they "lived the lives of wealthy young globe-trotters, doing little beyond motoring, playing midget golf . . . drinking, dancing and making love. It was an ideal existence, and one which we should have liked to continue indefinitely."[54]

The idyll of Durban was short-lived. As finances dwindled, the searching gaze of the *Daily Mail* drew nearer. Crisis began when a transcript of the report "England's Mystery Writer" appeared on the ship's notice board: "If you get a big newspaper after you, there is no place on this earth where you can hide. It is the greatest and surest force in the world for finding a missing man."[55] Rumors that Marriott's directors had fled Britain first appeared on 9 December, although they were reportedly in New York.[56] Three weeks later Graham reappeared several thousand miles away across the Atlantic: calling "himself Stewart-Murray," he was "basking in the favour of pretty women at Durban." Dent was with him, traveling as Abbott. Its "worldwide circulation" meant the *Daily Mail* could reveal the men's stay at the Majestic Hotel. The "well-known Rhodesian tobacco farmer" Mr. Stedman had cabled the paper's editor. In July 1930 Stedman had met "Mrs Evelyn Graham . . . who made a great parade of books by her husband" while sailing to Britain on the *Dunluce Castle*; Graham himself joined the ship at Las Palmas. A year later he was "surprised to see Evelyn Graham walk in[to Durban's Palace Hotel] and inquire the whereabouts of a woman." Interviewed by a *Daily Mail* "representative," Stedman commented: "I knew him instantly . . . and I am certain he recognised me for he left very hurriedly." Inquiries filled in the details. The young woman had recently arrived on the *Llangibby Castle*:

> Stuart-Murray, she says, joined the ship at Port Said, and had described himself to her as a dilettante novelist and a man of means, his income being £4000 a year. He declared to her that he has a large house in Piccadilly with

30 bedrooms and a villa at Nice. He proposes to set out for Nice by way of Tenerife and Marseilles by a ship sailing from Durban early next month.[57]

Having learned of the collapse of his empire and the newspaper reports following his journey south, Graham had reluctantly decided to return to London. Now he was tracked along the circuits of Britain's maritime empire. His journey to Tenerife on the *Themistocles* was "the only voyage that I can recall during which I remained quite virtuous." Lacking any opportunities for flirtation, he "sought solace" in the bar.[58] At the end of January, the *Daily Mail*'s "own correspondent" reported Graham's arrival in Las Palmas.[59] He was summoned to a meeting with the British vice-consul, now apparently the newspaper's "special commissioner." Talking "airily" of chartering a "special steamer" to Madeira, he was left "somewhat abashed" when told this would cost one thousand pounds and "finally left Tenerife in a German fruit boat."[60] By 3 February "this elusive young man"—now traveling as Leslie Murray—had reached Hamburg. Amazed at the easy "manner in which this man is able to move about the world," reporters wondered "how he obtained the necessary documents in the name of Stuart-Murray."[61]

What proved the last update in the *Daily Mail*'s manhunt appeared the following day. It included an anecdote—evidence of the investigative journalist's all-seeing gaze—told by "fellow passengers" on the *Themistocles*:

> One day in the smoking room the men were discussing public schools. Lucas was asked to what school he belonged, and quick as a flash replied "Borstal."
>
> The answer was treated as a bon mot and the passengers roared at his wit, little realising that Lucas had spoken the truth and was probably laughing at them.[62]

It was in Hamburg, finally, that Graham eluded the journalist following him: pretending to book a flight to Croydon airport, he boarded a train before returning through the Channel Islands to London.[63] Relieved to learn his activities had not prompted a police investigation, he was nonetheless affronted that the "Daily Mail had ceased to take any interest in me." Approaching its solicitor, he was told: "Evelyn Graham missing and running away abroad was a good story. Evelyn Graham returned is of no interest to us!"[64] The biographer was left despondent and almost destitute: "Fallen from my pinnacle as Evelyn Graham, besieged on all sides by debtors, owing thousands of pounds, I began to drift and to become callous. I lived for the moment, and my only solace was alcohol—and women."[65]

FALLOUT

Under this unrelenting scrutiny, the bogus biography factory first emerged only to then immediately unravel. Editors who had bought rights to Graham's writing faced financial loss and public humiliation. In October 1930 *Modern Home* boasted of Graham's "Exclusive New Series" on the Duke and Duchess of York. After the *Daily Mail* exposé, an intimate portrait by a renowned biographer became a shoddy fake. After three articles under Graham's byline, a final installment was published anonymously in January before the series was withdrawn.[66] For those not complicit in Graham's success, here was an excuse to delight in the failings of rivals. *Truth* reflected on the "embarrassing and expensive situations" that faced "dupes . . . more anxious for meaty disclosures than accuracy."[67] Ironically, this later allowed Graham to insist on his work's merits: that it was published "after I was exposed, although without my name on it, is proof surely that there was nothing wrong with the material in itself?"[68]

The transformation of the man of letters into a fraudulent trickster was paralleled in the transformation of his work. Rather than "authentic" and "intimate," his biographies were now "spurious" and "bogus." Such terms disrupted notions of individual authorial production but left the nature of his offense undefined. Were his deceptions a mischievous hoax, a mercenary forgery, or a criminal fraud? Were the biographies ghosted, plagiarized, or the product of individual craft?[69] The provenance of Graham's writing had been questioned, but its intrinsic properties remained unchanged. It still conformed to the conventions of biographical authenticity; it still drew on research in published sources; it was still based on personal acquaintance with its subject in at least one case. This was why magazines could still publish his anonymized articles. Yet the *Daily Mail* exposé shifted how Graham's work could be apprehended. Just as authenticity was secured through particular processes of artistic accreditation, so a very public dis-accreditation marked his work as fraudulent and deprived it of its literary qualities.[70]

At the same time as Graham's byline vanished, A. E. Marriott collapsed. Ambition and profligacy left the company with crippling debts. Partly concealed under "miscellaneous expenditure," the company's accounts recorded £50 on "Travelling Expenses" and a check for £300 cash drawn for "A.E. Marriott's American expenses" in a period when there is no evidence he visited the United States. In October the huge sum of £993 25s was paid to a man named Daly. Ostensibly for writing Lord Lonsdale's life, the expenditure coincided with Marriott and Dent's departure from Britain.[71] While the directors siphoned off money, Marriott owed £1,250 to the company's printers and £473 in royalties to Evadne Price. After creditors petitioned for bankruptcy, the case was heard at the High Court of Justice on 21 November 1930. Called to give evidence, Price recounted her fear of being forced to pay back her earnings from *Not So Quiet*: "I had spent the money as it came in. I had a mink coat, a car, I bought a Rolls Royce, I went mad."[72] Placed under careful examination, the company's accounts showed gross liabilities of £5,174 and assets of only £1,786.[73] It was on this basis that Mr. Justice Maugham granted a compulsory winding-up order on 8 December.[74]

The case was unopposed. When the creditors first assembled, the official receiver explained what he had learned about Marriott's accounts: "I am not going to say that there has been fraud . . . because my investigations are not yet complete. But . . . there are certain circumstances connected with this business of a very suspicious nature."[75] Marriott later appeared before the receiver and attributed the company's collapse to "insufficiency of working capital, aggravated to an extreme degree by press articles attacking him as chief director which, he states, were unjustified." When the company collapsed, he was "abroad urgently seeking further capital and negotiating the sale of the foreign rights of the company's publications." This "could have saved the situation."[76]

A skeptical receiver blamed Marriott's failure on "mismanagement"—its "working capital . . . totally inadequate to its requirements [and] overhead expenses."[77] Putting the company's affairs in order, he sold the furniture and typewriter from Golden Square and settled the debts to printers, publishers, and agents. The Townsend brothers and Price demanded unpaid royalties; left two thousand pounds out of pocket and with a worthless life of Lord Lonsdale, the *News of the World* claimed damages for breach of contract. Still, Marriott books sold: receipts of two thousand pounds were taken from booksellers after the company was wound up.[78] The *Princess Elizabeth Gift Book* appeared in best-selling lists in December 1930 and January 1931; *H.M. Queen Mary* was among the "Best Selling Books in 1930." Now the publisher responsible for these phenomenally successful titles went unnamed.[79]

The bogus biography factory scandals provided opportunities to rehearse debates around the ethics of popular life-writing and the boundaries between public and private life. Newspapers usually prioritized the responsibilities and regulation of author, editor, and publisher. The trade and periodical press, by contrast, developed a more wide-ranging critical analysis of the relationship between reading and the market. In the *Publisher and Bookseller*, Jacob Omnium attributed biography's popularity to a "modern craving for 'personalia' at all costs." Uneasy at its "vulgar" tendencies, Omnium was still optimistic that "love of personal detail . . . cannot in itself be otherwise than right and commendable." Life-writing provided lessons in citizenship for an emerging mass democracy.[80]

Others were less sanguine. *Truth*'s editor launched a vitriolic attack on contemporary reading habits. "Provided the literary fare is sufficiently spicy or sensational," he argued, "a large part of the public . . . do not bother their heads about the credentials of the chef." It was this "attitude of indifference" that sustained the "intense activity in the manufacture (one cannot call it anything else) of all sorts and conditions of 'memoirs' and 'character sketches.'"[81] Claiming that the "credentials of the chef" were unimportant was paradoxical: if nothing else, the discussion above shows the value of an authorized life and an author with firsthand knowledge. Yet the premise was clear. Readers got the kind of biography they deserved, and responsibility for Graham's success rested with those "whose purpose in reading is not to inform what they call their minds or to widen what does duty for their understanding, but to stimulate their coarse palates with the most vulgar sensationalism."[82]

Much of this was familiar from the critique of mass culture that gathered impetus in the 1920s and 1930s. Both *Truth* and the *Publisher and Bookseller* agreed that unmanaged demand from new mass readerships had distorting effects on publishing and journalism. This "marked and insistent taste," Omnium suggested, "places certain temptations in the way of authors who . . . are 'out' to minister to it, and certain difficulties in that of publishers who undertake of putting their works upon the market." Graham showed what could happen if profit was placed above good practice and greed above discretion. Omnium warned the trade: "The keener the public appetite for 'personalities' . . . the more necessary it becomes for both authors and publishers to walk warily and exercise vigilant discretion in supplying the demand." This was a call to arms to those in publishing to be alert to the dangers of the predatory trickster.[83]

Elsewhere the problematic relationship between public "taste" and the market was elaborated into criticisms of British democratic culture that were shaped by the centrifugal pressures of empire. In January 1931 the columnist "Marion" used her regular "Woman's Way" feature in Brisbane's *Worker* to invoke both the growing demands for Australian self-determination that culminated later that year in the Statute of Westminster and a socialist analysis of mass-market monarchism. Here was a case of "British snobbery taken in" and a society mired in hierarchy and tradition.[84] Australian publishers had also invested in Graham's work, yet the "amazing sequel" to Graham's success gave Marion opportunity to delight in how the trickster punctured a particularly British pomposity. Rather than endorse the *Daily Mail*'s intervention, Marion savored the irony that this knowledge had been "provided by such an authority in the world of British society." Scandal was now a moment of crisis in social relations. What had the *Daily Mail* revealed? "Evelyn Graham . . . is not a lady at all. Also—and still more dreadful—according to society conventions, Evelyn Graham is not a gentleman either." A patrician biographer was a convicted crook. Little wonder "British snobbery is slowly recovering from the shock."[85]

The biography factory scandals also drew attention to points of conflict within the literary marketplace. As well as a deceptive biographer, the scandals exposed an exploitative publisher and disreputable agent profiting from the labor of unwary victims. Such figures embodied the folk devils that had exercised professional organizations like the Society of Authors since the late nineteenth century. Lobbying for copyright law reform to protect members' literary and commercial interests, the society also helped writers navigate increasingly complex markets, worked to "make [them] more aware of their rights," and offered legal representation.[86] The society's solicitors handled twenty cases in the first three months of 1931. In forty other cases, informal mediation or pressure on publishers and agents allowed the secretary to "obtain . . . full satisfaction for members' claims or arrange . . . equitable settlements." Some of these cases involved infringement of copyright and breach of contract; most followed "the liquidation of certain publishing firms."[87]

The society was drawn into the recriminations that followed Graham's exposure and Marriott's bankruptcy. Surprisingly, neither man was ever a member. Many of their authors were—Leonard and Walter Townsend's election in 1929 coincided with publication of *H.R.H.*—and they often turned to the society for help.[88] The *Daily Mail* journalist Hugh Pilcher had signed a publication agreement for *Who's Who in 1950* in March 1930. Having delivered the manuscript, Pilcher unsuccessfully pushed Marriott to publish his work before contacting the society in desperation eight months later. In November, the solicitor C. D. Medley wrote to remind Marriott of its contractual obligations. He received no reply, noting, "From the information that is available it is tolerably clear we shall not hear anything." Medley concluded that publication was unlikely, since Pilcher "has never had any proofs and . . . the work has never been set up by the printers." He wrote again to demand return of his client's work but was not optimistic, advising Pilcher to "drop this whole concern and start afresh with someone else."[89] With his work caught up in bankruptcy proceedings, Pilcher petitioned for his manuscript's return, emphasizing the "pecuniary loss and embarrassment" he had suffered when the book did not appear: he had already cultivated publicity through a series of newspaper articles.[90]

Then in his seventies, Sir George Aston also contacted the society, fretful and facing angry demands from Harrap for return of the advance for his supposedly authorized life of the Duke of Connaught. Aston and Graham's contract included the proviso that they should return their initial advance if they failed to deliver an "authentic biography."[91] Aston had been deceived by his coauthor, but Harrap still demanded recompense: the society's secretary advised him that it was the "very strong custom" that advance royalties "are not returnable in any event" *unless* stipulated in the contract.[92] Still, Aston sought help. Writing to Clive Wigram, he asked for his cuttings on "the amazing 'Evelyn Graham' developments" so he could pass them to the society's solicitors. Harrap was "inclined to the view that my implicit trust in 'Evelyn Graham' . . . involved me in responsibility to bear a share in their loss."[93] While the publishers "seem to be wanting their 'pound of flesh' . . . the Society of Authors are helpful."[94]

While the society and other professional organizations may have worked effectively for Aston and Pilcher, its failure to be more proactive in protecting members caused discomfort. Trade periodicals regularly warned against the predators inhabiting the "pirate-and-parasite-ridden world of books."[95] "Shark Publishers" preyed on young writers; agents stole intellectual property.[96] In the month Graham was arrested, the *Publishers' Circular* had to address accusations it had failed to deal with such parasites and "explain why invariably we have to refuse to pillory the scamps." Graham and Marriott were unnamed but haunted these discussions. A defensive editorial noted "many occasions" on which the publication had "been asked to 'show up' Mr So and So of Such and Such a firm." Despite this pressure, it could do nothing "beyond refusing advertisements, returning subscriptions and giving confidential warnings." A blacklisting process adopted before the Great War had not been revived. While the periodical was often "roundly abused for not 'exposing' some particularly tricky individual," it argued that even the most "thoroughgoing scamp" could "bring an action for libel against any newspaper bold enough, or perhaps rash enough, to pillory his name."[97] Newspapers often hid behind the restrictive effects of the laws of libel, but the *Daily Mail*'s stunt journalism revealed the disingenuous nature of this position—special pleading in a case that exposed the limits of professional organizations.[98]

We can only understand the furore over publications like the *War Diary* within the context of the established relationships between the royal household and publishers and editors. By the time the *Daily Mail* scandal broke, courtiers had been dealing with Graham and Marriott for over two years. It still took them by surprise. Clive Wigram and Godfrey Thomas watched bemused and "amused" as the impertinent men who had caused them such trouble were exposed, sharing newspaper cuttings and seeking inside information from their contacts. Their fellow courtier Frank Mitchell was skeptical about the prospect of legal proceedings but was amazed: "It seems clear that Marriott, Dent, Graham and others are extremely likely to be one and the same person!"[99] As the scandal continued, Wigram invited Aston to St. James's Palace—something Aston described as "the nicest luncheon party I can remember." Symptomatic of the patrician sociability through which the household operated, here and in their confiding letters, the men shared their experiences of dealing with the biography factory. Aston was worried, but Wigram reveled in every revelation.[100]

Scandal was also an opportunity to increase pressure on editors and publishers. In December 1930 the Amalgamated Press's *My Home* published the first of Graham's series "Chapters of Royal Life." Within days, Thomas wrote to the company's manager, James Brown. Delicately but pointedly, he drew attention to the *Daily Mail*'s "exposure" and Graham's link to the "obvious fake" of the *War Diary*. "I do not know whether you are proposing to publish any further articles about The Prince of Wales," he observed, "but I felt it only right to let you know that his claim to have had an interview with HRH at St James's Palace is an impudent falsehood."[101] An apologetic Brown replied immediately: the company had canceled publication of "all matter . . . which we had in hand" when the *Daily Mail* exposé began. Since "these monthly magazines . . . go to press very far ahead of publication . . . [it] was unfortunately impossible to stop" the December and January articles. Readers anticipating the "interesting account of Queen Ena's life in Spain" promised for February 1931 were disappointed.[102]

EVELYN GRAHAM'S WATERLOO

For several months after the *Daily Mail* chased Graham across the globe, the biography factory disappeared. Then in the spring of 1931, rumors of another mysterious royal life began to circulate. By June *Truth*'s editor felt compelled to speak out: "It may be useful if I remind literary agents, publishers and editors of the exposure some time ago of one Netley Lucas, otherwise 'Evelyn Graham,'" since "there is reason to believe that some of his effusions about members of the Royal Family are again being hawked round for publication." The editor's hope "that this impostor will not find a fresh market for his inventions" was ill founded.[103] As the *Daily Mail* renewed its interest in the elusive biographer in July, the *Empire News*'s "Week-end Gossip" enigmatically commented: "There may shortly be sensational revelations concerning a literary man, once much in the public eye, who has not been seen in his usual haunts for many months."[104]

Two weeks later Detective Inspector Percy Smith arrested Graham in his Fulham studio. His crime? Obtaining money by false pretenses from a literary agent and magazine editor for what, officers now suspected, was a spurious life of Queen Alexandra. With Graham exposed as a fraud, his empire had collapsed. His reputation in tatters, his debts insurmountable—he had been forced to leave his flat in Chalfont Court, since "he could not pay the rent and the bailiffs were in"—he sought escape through one of the ostensibly worthless manuscripts he still possessed.[105] In hindsight, Graham was evasive, acknowledging only "that I desperately needed a couple of hundred pounds, and, by hook or by crook, had to get it immediately. I chose the crook."[106]

In May 1931 the agent James Seabrooke Pinker received a short note:

> Lady Angela Stanley presents her compliments to Mr Pinker and would be glad to know if he thinks he could find a publisher for a life of the late Queen Alexandra. Lady Angela was formerly one of her Ladies-in-Waiting.[107]

His interest piqued, Pinker agreed to pay £225 if the manuscript could be proved genuine. Stanley's "authenticity was vouched for by a letter purporting to have been written by the late Lord Stamfordham, Private Secretary of Edward VII, on Buckingham Palace notepaper."[108] Observing, "I have read your book about her late Majesty with great interest," Stamfordham acknowledged a "beautiful picture of the Queen Mother we both knew and loved so well. . . . Those who enjoyed her Majesty's friendship will welcome your book."[109] Reports later suggested the "coroneted notepaper" came from a West End stationer, but the agent was taken in, buying the manuscript and securing a contract with Harrap.[110] James B. Pinker had been a leading figure in the professionalization of authorship since founding his agency in 1895. Fashioning a reputation as an innovative literary power broker, he supported the emergence of modernism through a list that included Joseph Conrad and James Joyce.[111] By 1931 Pinker had been dead for almost a decade. Until the mid-1930s, the firm "limped along" under his sons, who lacked their father's ability to identify new talents and markets. Stanley's contract for a potboiling biography was symptomatic of and contributed to Pinker's decline.[112]

By the summer of 1931, Graham was a famous biographer and notorious fraudster. His arrest attracted huge attention from newspapers in Britain, the empire, and the United States.[113] After Graham was first charged before the

Bow Street magistrate, his trial was eventually heard over two days in September before the recorder of London, Sir Ernest Wild, at the Central Criminal Court at the Old Bailey. The court was "packed with society people and members of the literary world."[114] In this short period the intersection between law and press created a public space in which journalists, lawyers, and representatives of the publishing industry explored the mediating practices of the literary market, the nature of biographical truth, and the relationship between authenticity and authorship. Prompted by a manuscript royal biography, these discussions nonetheless effaced questions of monarchical authority and the boundaries between public and private. In contrast to earlier scandals, the biography factory was isolated as a problem of cultural production that could be held apart from social and political life.[115]

Presented at the Old Bailey by the barrister Sir Percival Clarke, the case brought by the director of public prosecutions against Graham took shape around three premises. First, Angela Stanley was a "mythical personage."[116] In court, Arthur Smalley, former chief clerk to the comptroller of Queen Alexandra's household, produced a list of the queen's ladies-in-waiting that did not include Stanley.[117] Second, the Stamfordham letter was a forgery. Smalley suggested that it was neither "the style of letter Lord Stamfordham was in the habit of writing" nor written on Buckingham Palace paper; there was no copy in Smalley's files.[118] The third strand of the prosecution case sought to establish the materiality of Graham's masquerade as Angela and Victor Stanley. Letters from Angela and Victor (who wrote to Pinker on his mother's behalf) were addressed from Chalfont Court; imprints of their signatures were on the blotting pad on Graham's desk; Pinker's money was paid into an account opened by Angela Stanley in a Japanese bank, but two hundred pounds found its way into an account in Graham's name.[119]

Graham disputed this. Regarding the evidence Graham gave at the Old Bailey, the *Empire News* commented:

> It all seemed plain sailing for a while. He told, in suave tones, of his chronicles of the great—of a summons to the Royal Palace in Madrid, of Lord Darling lending him his casebooks, of distinguished collaborations, of lives of the Prince of Wales and Princess Mary. . . . He seemed to have the perfect manners for these aristocratic tasks.

Graham described meeting Stanley in "the luxurious surroundings of a great Berlin hotel," and their negotiations over lunch at the Berlin Yacht Club. Despite Graham's poise, such claims came under close scrutiny from Clarke:

"searching and remorseless, rolling each answer about and about and always dissatisfied until he pounced on an admission: 'Can you produce in this court anybody who ever saw Lady Angela?'"[120] However much he blustered, Graham could not. The "puzzle of Lady Angela Stanley" was insolvable. The porter at Chalfont Court testified to the arrival of letters addressed to the Stanleys. He knew there was a woman living in the flat but could not confirm her identity. The "young stylishly dressed woman" later identified in court did not match Graham's description of the older woman he met in Berlin.[121] Challenged on the similarities between Victor Stanley's handwriting and his own, he claimed to have written letters that Stanley—his arm "crippled" by an accident on his plantation in Malaya—dictated. Retreating rapidly, Graham offered the familiar defense that he had been tricked. His counsel summed up: Graham was "deceived by a plausible lady just as these people were by her letters. . . . He is a person to whom a rogue might go for this purpose because of his association with books of a biographical nature."[122]

Here was ironic confirmation of the biography factory's success. By 1930 Graham was a plausible "Royal Biographer." His disreputable past was public knowledge, but such performances could still convince and confuse. Newspapers and court registers identified him as an "author" throughout the trial.[123] In print and the official record, Graham was confirmed in the professional identity he had claimed just as he was discredited. Netley Lucas and Evelyn Graham coexisted, an unnerving doubling crystallized in the difficulties journalists and officials faced in dealing with what Percy Smith called the "intriguing nature of [his] dual personality."[124] Who was he? The defendant was first charged as "Evelyn Graham"; only later was the charge sheet amended to identify the defendant as either "Netley Lucas" or "Evelyn Graham (or Netley Lucas)."[125] Subeditors at the *Sunday Dispatch* switched between "Netley Lucas" and "Evelyn Graham" in their headlines often enough to baffle readers.[126] How were Lucas and Graham related? Linking the names with "alias" underscored a troubling multiplicity. This was the formal terminology of the Criminal Record Office. "Lucas" was the deviant subject's "real" identity; "Graham," the fraudulent mask assumed to work his criminal deceptions.[127] The *Empire News* placed "'EVELYN GRAHAM'" in quotation marks: the punctuation simultaneously contained yet marked identity as indeterminate and fictive.[128]

These uncertainties were reinforced by the tensions between newspaper reports and the photographs accompanying them. The *News of the World* and *Empire News* juxtaposed Graham's criminal past with the publicity portraits distributed to publishers. Debonair, alert, and thoughtful, caught unawares at his desk in a moment of literary inspiration—the pen in his hand hovered above the papers representing his next masterpiece—here was the refined man of letters.[129] Now Graham's claims to status were playfully subverted by headlines that screamed of his criminal past and of his having "BEGGED IN WEST END." No longer a tool of literary inspiration, the instrument in his hand was "his pen of deceit." There was a problem: he still looked like a "royal biographer," and it was impossible to square his carefully crafted image with the lives revealed in print. The biographer and ex-crook defied easy categorization.[130]

Viewed through the prism of the law, multiple names and stories were elided with deceptive criminality and the offense of "obtaining money by false pretences." While the prosecution focused on establishing the mechanics of Graham's fakery, his defense set out alternative ways of understanding the putative Angela Stanley. Moving from the criminal to the literary, the solicitor Daniel Hopkin, MP, worked to exculpate his client from the charges. Consider this cross-examination of Pinker at Bow Street:

HOPKIN: In *Who's Who in Literature* 33 pages are devoted to names of authors with noms de plume. It is a common thing for plain Mr Jones to call himself the Count de Paris or something of that sort, and it add[s] to his selling value?

PINKER: Yes, sometimes.

HOPKIN: Is it quite a common thing for authors to adopt assumed names?

PINKER: Yes.

HOPKIN: You do not make the complaint that Evelyn Graham called himself "Lady Angela Stanley"?

PINKER: I do.

HOPKIN: Take the case of George Eliot, who was a Miss Evans. Now, if you were a literary agent in her town would you have objected to her calling herself George Eliot?

PINKER: No.

HOPKIN: Then why do you object to Graham taking the name of "Lady Angela Stanley"?

PINKER: Because the book is a non-fiction book and its only value would be if it were written by a genuine Lady Angela Stanley.[131]

In Hopkin's analysis (undertaken before Stanley's existence had been questioned) pseudonyms were commonplace rather than criminal; "Evelyn Graham" was a "nom de plume" rather than an "alias"; "Angela Stanley" was a ghosted identity rather than fraudulent. Graham reiterated such arguments at the Old Bailey: Graham was a "nom de plume; his real name was Netley Lucas. Many years ago he had written under other names. He had done a lot of 'ghosting'" and had done so again, since "Lady Angela's name was more powerful than his own."[132]

Such exchanges gestured toward the difficulties of defining Graham's criminality and competing ways of understanding the names and stories around him. His behavior was problematic precisely because it was ubiquitous. The *Publisher and Bookseller* argued, "There is hardly an author of any standing who has not at one time or another sought to hide his identity and has used a pseudonym," and thought it "easy to understand the motive." Reference works like the *Dictionary of Anonymous and Pseudonymous English Literature* addressed "questions of concealed authorship" as a problem of literary history. Reworking these positions in court, Hopkin challenged narratives of criminal deception and moved Graham closer to the accepted conventions of literary practice.[133]

In linking "value" to a "genuine" authorial identity, Pinker gestured toward broader tensions around the status of authorship. These tensions crystallized in Hopkin's courtroom exchange with Marjorie Hammerton, editor of *Weldon's Ladies' Journal*. It was Hammerton's "detective ability" that frustrated the attempt to sell serial rights to Queen Alexandra's biography. Finding no trace of Angela Stanley in "any reference book" or the records of the lord chamberlain, and learning from a street directory that Stanley shared an address with "Mrs E. Graham," Hammerton contacted the police.[134] In cross-examination, she disingenuously insisted, "It was not common for writers of biographies to use fictitious names." Asked "How would it hurt your journal if Lady Angela Stanley was a fictitious person?" she replied: "Because we never touch any article concerning the Royal Family which is not authentic."[135] The commercial value of the authentic life was not defined by aesthetics, form, or content, but was subsumed fully into authorial identity. Names rather than books were increasingly sold to readers in the early twentieth century. Just as anonymity declined sharply, so Hammerton's comments suggest how authorship collapsed into biographical truth and personal knowledge. When the author provided a "short cut to interpretation," processes of identification became increasingly important. Graham's recognition of the "power" of a name not his own underscores the economic incentives underpinning the emergence of figures like Stanley.[136]

The problematic status of authorial identity was exacerbated by the difficulties of untangling the work of Graham, Marriott, Dent, Cavendish, Stanley, and others, and the unknowable literary capacities of the man on trial. What had

Graham written? Percy Smith had no doubt that he was an educated gentle-man. Graham was untrustworthy, but "although he often stole manuscripts or employed 'ghosts' he did have a good brain and a ready pen. He spent many hours writing and editing."[137] Smith's grudging respect for Graham's intelli-gence and dedication was undercut by other depictions of him as an ignorant parasite, swindling readers and profiting from others' labor. *Truth* called him "barely literate," and described how he "employed wretched literary hacks" to write manuscripts sold "as his own work."[138] From this perspective, Graham disrupted conventions of the biographer's professionalism and craft. His as-sociation with ghosting ensured that "doubts were cast on his authorship."[139]

Deeply invested in his own authorial status, Graham nonetheless always acknowledged the collaborative foundations of his success. Elaborating a line of defense implicit in court, *My Selves* observed:

> I employed what is known in the literary world as "ghosts"—men and women who did the "donkey work" for me, spending their days in the British Museum digging out facts and data which they collected together under chapter head-ings with which I supplied them. On this foundation I worked, adding and deleting, transposing and altering, until I had knocked the rough draft into proper form, ready for the press.[140]

Were these freelance writers "ghosts" or "literary hacks"? Paid research as-sistants or unwitting victims? Was Graham working within accepted conven-tions of modern authorship or criminally duplicitous? Unanswered—perhaps unanswerable—such questions encapsulated the fault lines within contem-porary publishing that the trial brought under scrutiny. Summarizing the prosecution case, Clarke addressed these uncertainties: "It may be said by the defence that it is a well known practice in the literary world for persons to adopt names other than their own, but in our submission it must not be done for fraud."[141]

At the conclusion of the trial, the "man of mystery" was apparently put in his place. When the *Police Gazette* prosaically recorded the reconviction of a known criminal, there was no room for ambiguity—certainly no mystery.[142] The jury did not even have to leave the courtroom to reach a unanimous ver-dict. After sentence was passed, Smith offered an "official" version of Lucas/ Graham's life story: the orphaned "son of a man of means," previous convic-tions, repeated spells in prison. Alongside this criminality, Smith suggested, ran a period of literary success built on deception and plagiarism. Graham's work on the queen of Spain and Lord Justice Darling had official sanction;

biographies of the Prince of Wales and the Duke of Connaught did not. He had swindled the *News of the World* over Lonsdale's putative biography and secured six hundred pounds from Hutchinson for lives of Mr. Justice Avory, the Duke of Gloucester, and Queen Alexandra—the latter first attributed to Charlotte Cavendish before it was offered to agents under Stanley's name. His life of George V sold to Macmillan in the United States was "identical" to Dent's *Life Story of King George V* (1930). Forced to cease publication of the book, Macmillan lost one thousand pounds.[143]

For newspapers that had fallen victim to Graham's schemes, this was an opportunity to enjoy the exposure of an "audacious swindler." Effacing its complicity in the biography factory, the *Daily Express* noted how

> an old public school boy, who has obtained thousands of pounds as the biographer of royalty and world famous celebrities, was unmasked at the Old Bailey yesterday as an impostor with a long record of crime and trickery.[144]

Stunt journalism and legal scrutiny constituted the process through which the truth was unearthed and the authentic subject brought into the public gaze. Characterizing the trial as "Evelyn Graham's Waterloo," *Truth* welcomed the demise of "a literary shark of the most unscrupulous kind."[145]

This analysis was difficult to sustain. Ernest Wild's summation in court evinced a striking lack of closure. Wild described this as "a very bad case, foisting on the public literary matter that was really trash." In so doing, he talked more like a critic than a judge, compelled by his self-image as a champion of literary values to treat the biographies on their aesthetic merit—never at stake during the trial—yet failing to address the issues of provenance and authenticity encapsulated in the offense of obtaining money by false pretenses. Wild described Graham as "a young man who had led a very bad life," but thought it "in his defence that he had done a certain amount of literary work," sentencing him to hard labor rather than penal servitude in recognition of the seven years in which Graham had, he believed, followed the highway of honesty.[146]

More than this: Graham was still described as an author. He still looked the part: the *Empire News* called him a "bluffer" but described a "well-spoken . . . easily mannered, spruce and debonair" man who left the dock smiling.[147] Smith's biography of Graham interwove official files with the published "confessions" of Netley Lucas. Still, Graham retained control of the stories told about him. Newspapers "exposed" Graham's past but evaded the fact that Lucas had done most of the exposing himself. Finally, Graham continued to protest his innocence, revealing the illusory authenticity effects on which mass culture was premised. After sentencing, he claimed to have "done nothing that was not habitually done in Fleet Street and in common practice in the literary world."[148] Elaborating this position later, he "state[d] emphatically . . . that in every case the manuscript was submitted to, read and passed for press by those concerned." These claims sat uneasily against his correspondence with the royal household but left questions of authorization and authorship open. Graham admitted, "I did not reveal my real identity," but asked, "Was it a very great crime to try to live down my criminal past by adopting a nom-de-plume, the Christian name of which was my own?"[149]

Graham's Waterloo was prompted by a spurious royal life, fictitious lady-in-waiting, and forged letter from George V's private secretary. Compared to earlier scandals, the disappearance of questions of monarchical authority from public discussion is striking. Apart from the evidence given by Smalley, a minor official, no courtier engaged directly in the trial. The staff of George V, the Prince of Wales, and Duke and Duchess of York who had dealt with Graham and Marriott distanced themselves from the distasteful spectacle of a criminal prosecution. There were two exceptions. Sir Malcolm Murray, equerry to the Duke of Connaught, was in court throughout the trial. As Smith recounted Graham's life story, Murray passed the recorder a letter confirming that Graham and Aston's biography was published "without the Duke's consent and in spite of protests."[150] In cross-examination, Graham claimed to have discussed Queen Alexandra's biography with Lady Haig. Haig refuted this in a furious letter to the *Guardian*: "I had the privilege . . . of serving Queen Alexandra as Maid of Honour for seven years, and it is recognised among those who serve in the Royal Household that it is not correct to write about the intimate and private life at court." Her comments suggested that intimate royal biographies were impossible. Such interventions were exceptional, however. The agnotology of modern monarchy made this a straightforwardly literary scandal.[151]

The disappearance of these questions did not mean monarchical authority was not important in shaping the scandal of 1931. Far from it. We can make more sense of the furore surrounding Graham by comparing it to moments at which questions of literary ethics did not provoke controversy. Like Graham, Evadne Price wrote under a pseudonym and claimed firsthand knowledge of the Great War. Although some reviewers questioned the "truth" of *Not So Quiet*, this was never considered grounds for castigation. When a book was "exposed" as fake, the responses could be very different. In 1929 Joan Lowell's *Child of the Deep* prompted "a general set-to on the ethics of literary hoaxing" that emphasized the tensions between "artistic license" and "actual experiences" in an autobiographical novel.[152] Lowell's book was often condemned as a confidence trick on readers. Magdalen King-Hall's *Diary of a Young Lady of Fashion, 1764–65* (1925), by contrast, was greeted gleefully as the "Cleverest Hoax of the Century." A "hoax" might prompt outrage for disrupting the integrity of literary production and betraying the confidence of readers or delight for mischievously puncturing highbrow pretension.[153]

These examples underscore how scandal was overdetermined by what we might think of as the politicization of culture. That *Not So Quiet* did not cause controversy suggests different generic expectations of the popular novel and biography. It also suggests the importance of identifying the processes through which scandal was called into being. The journalistic stunts that isolated Graham and Marriott's activities were often mobilized by the insistent demands of the royal household. Courtiers prompted and cajoled cultural power brokers into action. Unfolding in public through the national and imperial press, each scandal was shaped by private correspondence and anonymized "official sources." Literary ethics became most pressing—most newsworthy—when entwined with freighted questions of social leadership and monarchical authority. It was no accident that the only scandal that approached the biography factory in scale followed publication of *The Whispering Gallery: Leaves from a Diplomat's Diary* (1926). Attributed to the former ambassador Sir Rennell Rodd, yet written by actor and journalist Hesketh Pearson, these irreverent imagined accounts of international politics provoked a vituperative attack from the *Daily Mail*, a sensational court case (in which Pearson was acquitted of false pretenses), and furious debate over the relationship between truth, authorial responsibility, and the reputation of public figures in life and death.[154]

CONCLUSION

In the late 1920s and early 1930s, Evelyn Graham and Albert Marriott intruded onto increasingly fraught attempts to establish the bounds of legitimate publishing. Addressing the Annual Conference of Associated Booksellers in June 1931, just before Graham was arrested, the highbrow publisher Geoffrey Faber looked for a solid ethical foundation on which to ground commercial forms of cultural production in a period of rapid change:

> There is a standard—on one side of it there is the genuine article, the honest book, on the other the imitation, the fake, the shoddy insincere book. I would define our job . . . as that of giving the genuine article its best chance. . . . Of course the thing isn't quite as simple as all that. For one thing the great majority of books, like the great majority of human beings, are neither wholly genuine

nor wholly fake. For another, most of us fall for the fake oftener than we know. And for a third, the great British public, by whose patronage we live, hasn't yet begun to learn to distinguish between the fake and the genuine article. But that's what makes the whole business so uncommonly interesting.[155]

The traces of the biography factory mark this analysis. Had he been drawn into its operations like Harrap or Hutchinson, Faber might have found it an "interesting" challenge. His comments simultaneously underscore the factory's transgressive capacities. Aggregating to the bookseller and publisher a gatekeeping role in the market, Faber nonetheless recognized their constrained ability to distinguish "genuine" from "fake." Expert knowledge and professional judgment were inexact. That books were "neither wholly genuine nor wholly fake" gestured toward the illusory nature of the binary oppositions Faber initially sought to mobilize. Above all, in an industry increasingly oriented toward the "patronage" of new mass readerships, the vagaries of public taste undermined the drive to give "the genuine article its best chance," devaluing authenticity in powerful and bracing ways.[156]

Faber's cynically honest analysis offers a way of thinking about the bogus biography factory. It confounded distinctions between "genuine" and "fake" in the intersecting realms of production, distribution, and reception. Just as the autobiographical experiments of modernist writers blurred boundaries between "fact" and "fiction," so did the conventions of potboiling popular life-writing. The furore over Graham's work suggests how that process could represent something troubling rather than an expression of literary genius.[157] Forgeries hold the power to "destabilise the fragile economy of literary accreditation by drawing attention both to its conceptual shoddiness and the expediencies that characterise its operations." Graham and Marriott's deceptions disrupted the precarious foundations of newspaper and literary culture, undermining the nexus of cultural and commercial practices through which a work was produced for public consumption. What they did questioned the sanctity of the (auto)biographical author, the power of the agent, the taste of the publisher or editor, the perceptiveness of the reviewer, and the intelligence of readers who often took "forgeries" as "real" long after they were exposed.[158] In questioning the processes through which authenticity was called into being, the life-writing scandals showed how it was illusory and contingent. What were the differences between Graham's factory and established (albeit controversial) practices like ghostwriting and "signed interviews"? It was the porousness of these boundaries that meant, as H. M. Paull acknowledged, that when faced with the fake or fraudulent, "one's natural attitude is that of condemnation. The forger renders history, biography, in fact every form of literary work, untrustworthy: he 'fouls the very wells of truth.'"[159]

The *Daily Mail* presented its exposé as a necessary defense of literary "truth" undertaken in the public interest. Such interventions were always defensive and anxious. Seeking to secure the integrity of authorized forms of life-writing and personal journalism, journalists, critics, publishers, and editors mobilized a supposedly stable distinction between legitimate and illegitimate forms of writing. With Graham discredited, the fake (and faker) was contained and the respectability of press and publishing reiterated.[160] As Faber implied, however, the opposition between "real" and "fake" set out through stunt journalism and the literary periodical remained fictive and unstable. Like authenticity itself, the fake was also contingent and constructed. Rather than discrete and bounded, it was called into being through an interlocking apparatus of cultural nonproduction, literary dis-accreditation, and legal intervention.[161] Treating "genuine" and "fake" as both constitutive and coterminous allows us to understand how "literary forgery is not so much the disreputable Other of 'genuine' literature as its demystified and disreputable Self." In a "culture of the factitious," defining Graham's biographical potboiling as fraudulent was necessary to delineate a canonical royal life-writing. This was a way of policing the limits of the literary.[162]

While designating this a literary scandal established bounds within which to confine the biography factory, its ambition intruded on realms beyond cultural life. Graham described the furore created by his account of the queen of Spain's criticisms of her nation's religious hospitals in the *Sunday Dispatch* as "the only occasion that I . . . have ever unwittingly stirred up strife politically."[163] Such comments glossed over the charged politics surrounding his biographies and his fractious relationship with Britain's royal household. Often anodyne and cloying, Graham and Marriott's work reinforced the monarchy's own self-fashioning as domestic and dutiful. Its threat was more than muckraking or revealing intimate details. Instead, the factory disrupted courtiers' ability to manage monarchy's public image at a formative moment when the mediated relationship between monarch and subject acquired growing political significance.

Graham managed to insinuate himself into networks of patrician power with striking ease. Communicating with courtiers and publishers in writing and person, he cultivated their confidence and operated as a respectable man of letters for long periods. He moved dangerously close to the centers of social and cultural leadership in 1920s and 1930s Britain. In different guises Graham met and charmed the queen of Spain, a British ambassador, and at least two courtiers. While his Piccadilly offices were some distance from the focal points of publishing and journalism around Paternoster Row and Fleet Street, their location emblematized his successful penetration of a notionally impermeable elite. The Duke and Duchess of York lived on the same street at 145 Piccadilly; the royal palaces were a short walk away; so was the Travellers' Club in Pall Mall, from where Alan Lascelles corresponded with editors and publishers. The prestigious publishers and booksellers Graham sought to work with were equally close: John Murray had offices across the road in Albemarle Street; Hatchards booksellers was almost next door.

In entering these circuits of power and authority, Graham disrupted them. Exposed as a convicted trickster, he undermined the trust—the confidence— that was an essential currency of communication within this close-knit world. Always unpredictable, Graham exposed the contradictions of contemporary culture and politics. This is why courtiers and publishers found him so "impertinent"—a recurrent term in correspondence about him. Depicted as a parvenu interloper, Graham himself fashioned an identity as a dynamic entrepreneur pushing the logic of the marketplace to its inevitable conclusion. Different in degree rather than kind, operating within rather than without publishing conventions, this is why he was dangerous.

In *The Twilight of the British Monarchy* (1937), "An American Resident" identified two paradoxes about Britain's relationship with the monarchy. First, despite the nation's newfound democracy, nowhere else was the royal family such an "object of adulation, adoration and sentimentality." Second, despite the loss of formal political power, the monarchy retained huge "influence over the minds and social life of a great portion of the people."[164] The monarchy's renewed stability in the 1920s and 1930s was neither accidental nor a product of innate national deference. Instead, its refashioning was carefully managed through courtiers' interactions with cultural power brokers. Polite and familiar, threatening and insistent, patrician power was extended into new forms of mass culture. A complicity of political and commercial interest meant public adoration and monarchical influence—deference and tradition—were embedded in modern consumer cultures. Although members of the royal household were often uneasy about the forms of public relations they were drawn into, their interactions with Graham and Marriott underscore their success in establishing a productive, albeit temporary, rapprochement between established social hierarchies and the potentially disruptive practices of commercial life-writing. Graham's racket was exceptional in many ways, but the process through which he was discredited might stand as a limit case for modern forms of commodified monarchism.

observed, "Here is Another Unique Step Forward"? Conditions stipulated that each display should include the *Princess Elizabeth Gift Book* and reminded booksellers that the "selling power of the particular window will be taken into account."[19] Assuming the role of adviser to other publishers, Marriott blurred innovation and altruism. In October 1929 he drew the attention of *Publishers' Circular* to a "rather unique publicity precedent" created by *H.R.H.*:

> We were approached by the Topical Press Agency with the suggestion that we should pose typists of our staff reading the above-mentioned book and they would photograph them and circulate the picture free of any cost to us to the newspapers [etc.] . . . naturally did not wish to in any case countenance a service that might interfere in its use in publicity for them. However, we combined the photographing press with books with the indication that they were our own young ladies.

The result was an "attractive picture"—"unique free publicity" that Marriott now shared with his commercial rivals.[20]

Such innovations reflected the competition driving the development of professional advertising in publishing. Marriott broke new ground, but by the 1930s Frank Swinnerton observed how even the established publisher vied with his companies in the use of every legitimate means of publicity. Advertising remained controversial, however, and created ferocious debate over the market's effects on literature.[21] Key figures like W. G. Taylor, president of the Publishers' Association, considered advertising inappropriate. He argued that books "cannot be marketed" like mass-produced commodities and attacked those who treated them like "soap and new tyres." Swinnerton was uneasy about the loss of the "true relish in a book for its own sake" and the growing "preference on the part of publishers and booksellers for the book which has 'advertising' or 'sales' value." Never a straightforward critic of mass culture, he was even here essentially concerned with the limited appeal of books and their influence on literature. That nexus also gave rise to the "commercialized literature" commented on by Marriott.

Marriott's own short books, the record of a global publishing enterprise. His company's books were available throughout its network of booksellers and its exhibitions, competition society. W. H. Smith, and a successful strategy toward middle-class clientele. In its time it dealt with concerns in New York, Paris, Stockholm, and Berlin. It worked through ties of a disparate kind. It extended its own estimation of relationships with societies that included Allied and Associated North Library Libraries in Italy, the Oxford Press Company in Shanghai,

* 4 *

Denouement

CHAPTER 9

My Selves

INTRODUCTION

The author Evelyn Graham was admitted to Wormwood Scrubs Prison on 22 September 1931. Having earned a remission of his sentence, he was discharged fifteen months later. Graham was still in his twenties, but confinement had aged him. Gaunt and haggard, he had lost weight and gained new lines of tiredness in his face. The pounds came back, but he would never really recover the vitality that marked his work as a gentleman crook and writer. Physically and emotionally drained, Graham was also publicly humiliated by the collapse of his biography factory. It was perhaps inevitable that he tried to write his way out of financial ruin. A new autobiography took up defenses he offered in court in 1931. Rather than refute his notoriety, Graham embraced it. Scandal was an opportunity—the only one for an author convicted of false pretenses. Reprising forms of storytelling that had served him well in the 1920s, Graham again recounted his criminal and literary deceptions. More than a straightforward confession, he now emphasized the bewildering names and stories that had unsettled contemporaries for fifteen years. The manuscript he called "My Selves" was coauthored by Netley Lucas and Evelyn Graham.[1]

My Selves was published in 1934. It was in this book that I first glimpsed Lucas's astonishing ambition and was unnerved by the challenges his lives posed. I came to Lucas as a historian interested in the ways in which individuals made sense of their lives, and how ideas of selfhood might be seen as fractured and changeable. A coauthored "autobiography" called *My Selves* pointed toward those preoccupations. Reading it, I became absorbed and excited by its stories and possibilities. Lucas's lives still absorb my attention, but excitement has often been tempered by unease. How can we trust a calculating storyteller? *My*

Selves's wildest claims find echo in the archives; mundane details are uncorroborated. How can we know anything about someone who changes names so often? Neither coauthorship nor the scams the book describes come close to capturing the number of "selves" he claimed. Aliases were to the trickster what pseudonyms were to the freelancer. I think I have seen him in thirty-eight guises, but I am not sure, and there may be more. A simple change of name might temporarily deceive detectives; it certainly frustrates the historian pursuing an unpredictable subject through archives and libraries. Perhaps I have no subject to pursue. There are so many names that I do not really know what to call him. He is a specter in the distance, a flicker of light, a will-o'-the-wisp.

These uncertainties became particularly pronounced in the period between Evelyn Graham's discharge from prison and Robert Tracy's death in 1940. Publication of *My Selves* prompted a flash of publicity, but the *Empire News* noted how he then "faded out for a time."[2] Perhaps I have become too suspicious, but we might think carefully about what this means. "Fading out" might suggest the desperate struggles of someone trying yet failing to rebuild his life, and anticipate his early death. It might be a deliberate response to being exposed as untrustworthy. Are we falling victim to yet another trick? Vanishing was the precondition for resuming a literary career; new names in the present surmounted the constraints of a criminal past. Nor was it quite the case that Lucas disappeared into his own "Hungry Thirties." We see him fleetingly—a trace in a fading letterhead rather than fully realized, at moments of crisis when a mask slips and someone we half recognize passes across the edge of a courtroom. These are all uncertain fragments, and it is difficult to order them into a coherent narrative. The trickster calls attention to the limits of what we can know, and the impossibility of finding the "real" biographical subject.[3]

This chapter picks up the threads of Lucas's lives after prison. *My Selves* is a starting point to explore the ways in which he made sense of the many "selves" that marked his career. The book was characterized as a final revelation of autobiographical "truth." This was a cliché he had peddled many times—a cynical ploy to secure the confidence of readers. We might well be skeptical, focusing instead on the stories available to an ex-crook trying to make money and make his lives intelligible to a popular audience. *My Selves* simultaneously resisted and embraced the indeterminacy of its title. At times the names and stories proliferated. It was always written in a singular authorial voice, however, and the doubling of identity was constrained within a linear narrative through which Netley Lucas *became* Evelyn Graham. The perspective from which Lucas/Graham described the social and psychological effects of many "selves" shifted constantly. At times *My Selves* revels in the rewards deception brings, savoring the pleasures of crime and literary success. Elsewhere Lucas/ Graham struggles under the anxieties of a dual life. Success is precarious; a criminal past always risks exposure; self-naming demands constant pretense and carries huge psychological costs. Torment can only be escaped through alcohol and sex. Ludic and melancholic, playful and anguished, *My Selves* shakes off our efforts to know its author.

In this sense, *My Selves* offers a framework through which to understand Lucas/Graham's lives in the later 1930s. The ludic and the melancholic provide ways of seeing through which we might make sense of fragmented and uncertain archival traces. The flashes of Lucas's continued literary endeavor and tortuous personal relationships—he divorced and remarried—can be read as evidence of both his renewed enterprise and inexorable decline. These tensions played out in the circumstances of his death in a smoke-filled room in June 1940. The horrific testimony of his second wife and a detailed postmortem report outlined the sordid demise of a violent alcoholic. Out of control and unpredictable, Lucas alienated those closest to him. He drank himself to death. Those who wrote his obituaries and later retold stories of his lives occasionally noted this. But because his exploits retained their capacity to intrigue, Lucas lived on in popular crime writing, fixed forever as the debonair gentleman of 1920. His lives and afterlives took shape within the tensions between the ludic and the melancholic.

A LITERARY SENSATION (IN A MINOR TONE)

In *My Selves* Lucas/Graham recounted his successive rise and fall as a gentleman crook, crime writer, and biographer. The manuscript first drew attention because his personal narrative was interwoven with recycled "intimate stories of . . . royalties" and "other famous persons," including Lord Lonsdale, Sir Bernard Spilsbury, Earl Haig, and Queen Marie of Rumania.[4] Reducing different genres into a single manuscript, *My Selves* was unusual. Sensing a profitable opportunity and keen to "help 'Graham' to make a fresh start," the British publisher Arthur Barker accepted the book, and it was considered by Harpers in the United States.[5] Barker's interest was tempered by his knowledge of Graham's past. Concerned to avoid a damaging scandal, he sent the manuscript to those mentioned in the book, including Sir Clive Wigram and Sir George Aston.[6] Wigram and Sir Frederick Ponsonby, keeper of the privy purse, read the manuscript. Ponsonby found the discussions of George V and Lord Stamfordham "innocuous" and was "inclined to leave the book alone, as a man who owns himself to be a crook . . . cannot carry much weight with the public."[7] Wigram could admire this "incredible chronicle of nerve," but after five years dealing with Graham, his patience had gone and his response was less sanguine: "I am certain [this book] should not be circulated at home or abroad."[8]

In moving to stop publication, courtiers again mobilized the connections of elite sociability. Vouching for Barker, Aston described him to Wigram as "a white man (Harrow and Oxford etc.)." Aston read the manuscript with Barker, showing him how a "large proportion of the statements were untrue and . . . objectionable."[9] After a tense telephone conversation with a court official, Barker wrote to Wigram. He had decided not to publish the book: "I can no longer feel confident of anything that I am told by [Evelyn Graham]."[10] *My Selves* was withdrawn a week before it was due to go on sale; advance copies had already circulated. Furious at the damage to his reputation, Barker "got hold of Graham and tore up his Contract."[11]

Newspapers suggested Barker changed his mind because the manuscript trespassed on the royal family's privacy. This was an explanation Graham encouraged: his first response to the crisis of his "banned book" was to go on the offensive in the *Daily Express*:

> I have a story that no one will let me tell. It is a chronicle of the most colossal piece of bluff that has ever been perpetrated in the literary world; but because it involves the names of the highest in the land the most elaborate steps have been taken to prevent the story appearing.

Embroiled in scandal, Graham tried to expose the hidden hand of Britain's elites, anticipating the *Daily Mirror*'s populist stance on the abdication crisis three years later. He was a self-serving whistle-blower, linking the "names of the highest in the land" to efforts to stop him telling the "truth about Evelyn Graham." *My Selves*, he suggested, was an intolerable affront to patrician power. Lucas had exposed the corruption of the honors system and aristocratic immorality in the 1920s, but not with such bitterness. Perhaps his diatribe reflected the growing criticism of Society after Evelyn Waugh's *Vile Bodies* (1930). Yet Graham was desperate in 1933. Presenting *My Selves* as victim of an establishment conspiracy raised the stakes of publication and mobilized public interest. He had "a story that ought to be told—because so many people have tried to stop it from appearing."[12]

In private Graham was more measured. Having found a new publisher in the Unicorn Press, he wrote to Wigram. Disingenuously he admitted he "may, wittingly or unwittingly, have made some slight inaccurate statements" and promised to delete any "objectionable" passages if a courtier read the manu-script.[13] Writing to the publisher, Wigram drew attention to the manuscript's mistakes and the "character both of the author and book which his Firm pro-poses to sponsor."[14] Apologetic and anxious, the chair, Captain W. J. Hunter, hastily withdrew from the contract and "endeavoured to persuade [Graham] to suppress this book, and turn his undoubted literary talent in other direc-tions." He was not optimistic: "His book would obviously sell, and . . . there can be little doubt that he will succeed in getting it published by somebody or other."[15] Hunter was right. When Graham tried to publish *My Selves* privately, courtiers intervened with British printers and booksellers. After a printer was found in Finland, in the autumn of 1933 adverts appeared for the Bantam Press book *My Selves*.[16] The book was never released: it was May 1934 before *My Selves* was published by the obscure Arthur Barron, and serialized in the popu-lar women's story paper *Red Letter* in Britain and the Hearst newspapers in the United States.[17]

Recently released from prison, Lucas/Graham returned to questions of criminality and citizenship he had explored in the 1920s. *My Selves* was a dif-ferent book, though: more introspective, franker in dealing with his drinking and infidelities. It was presented as a moment of unflinching revelation:

> I am being, perhaps for the first time in my life, perfectly honest with myself and the world. I am attempting to hide nothing, and if some of the things I have already told and shall tell in the following chapters shock people into a state of moral horror, or exasperation at the absolute unscrupulousness of my life, then I can only urge in extenuation that I have told the truth and nothing but the truth.[18]

Confession was a device to secure the effects of authenticity, cultivate "moral horror," and draw interest: it is more useful to consider the book within the changing conventions of 1930s life-writing. Any introspection was episodic rather than sustained, since Lucas/Graham again focused as much on reveal-ing hidden social worlds as exploring the psychological origins and effects of crime.

Much of this echoed Lucas's earlier writing, but this was the first time he at-tributed his work to two authors. He never explained why. Along with the enig-matic title, it might denote the masks that enabled his deceptions or a desire to pique interest through the unlikely pairing of an ex-crook and royal biogra-pher. While the possibilities for names to proliferate were endless, the number of "selves" was bounded. He had used almost forty names, but appeared in only two guises as the book's authors, and a handful more in its pages. Nor were Lucas and Graham depicted as coexisting dual personalities. Leaving New York in January 1928 "was not only the death of all my hopes for a new life in a new world, but it was the death of my real self, that is to say, Netley Evelyn Lucas." In London, however, "Out of the ruins of Netley Lucas arose 'Evelyn Graham,' a mysterious individual who was to take the literary world of London by storm."[19] Discredited on both sides of the Atlantic, Lucas "died" and Graham was "born." Dual "selves" were successive phases of an individual life. Graham's "mysterious" rise was a deliberate decision to pursue literary success under a new name. "My selves" were framed by the opposition between "reality" and "mask." The misleading title concealed an unchanging and reliable narrator: "I—Netley Evelyn Lucas."[20]

Despite this, *My Selves* betrayed traces of an uncontrollable multiplicity. A knowledgeable reader might have recognized the presence of different texts and voices. The book was a collage. Rushing to exploit his notoriety, Lucas/Graham plundered his earlier work, cutting and pasting, retelling stories verbatim or with names changed slightly, and stitching them together. A new account of his career as a biographer formed the final third of the book. *My Selves* was made up of accreted stories written over a decade. The singular voice concealed ghosts known and unknown. Parts of the book first appeared under Lucas's own byline; others were first attributed to Lucas and Guy Hart. Commander R. L. Dearden's pointed letter to the *Daily Express* revealed his role in writing the *Autobiography*. It was never clear whose selves were on display.[21]

Although we might be tempted to try to read through this mutivalent tangle in search of biographical "truth," *My Selves* pushes us to instead be more open-ended and provisional in exploring how Lucas/Graham made sense of his lives. Proliferating stories generate both exciting new pleasures and powerful psychological anxieties. At times the ludic or the melancholic appears fleetingly, then fades out. Elsewhere the two remain entangled, only to coalesce in passages of startlingly poignant clarity. However skeptical we might be, at such moments new forms of psychoanalytic autobiography allowed Lucas/Graham to stage an excess of raw emotion.

In its ludic moments, *My Selves* is reminiscent of the *Autobiography*: a breathless account of the pleasures of crime and social mobility. Crimes of confidence are an exciting game; a gentlemanly demeanor opens up the delights of the West End. The reader is invited to experience those delights vicariously, guided through underworld and overworld, transatlantic liner and upscale nightclub. As a young midshipman,

I lived from day to day taking no heed of the morrow, and if I had been asked at that time what the future held I should merely have replied that life was just the space between each different woman—the days merely *entre actes* of the nights.[22]

Sexualized and enticing, the life of a man-about-town is presented as a natural aspiration.

My Selves also evoked the particular pleasures of a double life. Recounting Evelyn Graham's success, the book delighted in the unlikely juxtapositions between past and present, finding ironic humor in an ex-crook passing as a celebrated biographer, puncturing snobbery and pretension. Dining with Raymond Savage, Graham asks "with an inward smile" if the agent had read the work of Netley Lucas.[23] Graham is sometimes apologetic—often not—the joke always on the unsuspecting people he meets. It can only work with an omniscient storyteller. Recounting his interview with the queen of Spain dramatizes how the mask of literary respectability concealed "the amazing phenomenon of a young crook who, chameleon-like, had succeeded in changing his colour from that of a 'known to Scotland Yard' to the favoured, not only of the great, but even of royalty!" Readers were invited to "imagine the piquancy of the situation," and Lucas/Graham "had to hold my sides with laughter when I realized how I was 'getting away with it.'"[24]

At moments like this, *My Selves* was playful and knowing. Yet the ludic mood was unsettled by repeated moments of anguish. The mischievous trickster was also tormented by the emotional costs of his double lives:

It was a difficult life . . . running Evelyn Graham, keeping the skeleton of Netley Lucas out of the way, and also supporting a wife and two mistresses in happy mood. It called for not a little organisation and staff management, as well as a good deal of physical energy. Before long I found that my health was beginning to suffer. . . . I realised that unless I was always on the *qui vive* something might go wrong at any moment.[25]

Graham's success meant concealing all traces of Lucas, Marriott, and his many infidelities. Keeping discrete "selves" apart was a constant struggle; multiplicity meant always fearing discovery. Soon the "strain of my dual personality was telling on me dreadfully, and the only way I could keep my nerves in order was to drink, usually whiskey, and a bottle of that a day, sometimes in the evening a bottle of brandy."[26] Lucas/Graham narrowly avoided crisis when a drunken scene outside his mistress's house led to his arrest and appearance at Marylebone Police Court. Fined for causing willful damage, he thought himself lucky no journalists were in court.[27] Under the scrutiny of the *Daily Mail*, bankruptcy courts, and police, the tensions grew and Graham's condition deteriorated. At the start of 1931, "I began to drift and to become callous. I lived for the moment, and my only solace was alcohol—and women." Never simply the hedonistic pleasures of a man-about-town, alcohol and affairs were his desperate search for "solace."[28]

Lucas/Graham thus described his relief when his double life ended. "When my bubble burst I was not particularly upset," he recalled. Indeed, arrest, humiliation, and imprisonment also marked the "end of a long period during which I had suffered such a strain that I was practically a nervous wreck, and drinking myself to death, for artificial stimulants alone had kept me going." A "dual existence" represented emotional pain rather than pleasure; "riches did not bring me happiness."[29] Even this remorse was unsustained, however: the next chapter began with the "amusing" joke of linking Lucas to a book on the Secret Service.[30]

The melancholia of *My Selves* was enhanced by Lucas/Graham's frustration at being unable to leave his past behind. After his sixth prison sentence, the *Autobiography*'s jaunty optimism evaporated. Time in Wormwood Scrubs prompted a profound crisis. "Going absolutely to pieces, morally and physically," Lucas/Graham was sustained in his "psychological agony" only through the love of Lucy, his most recent mistress. Hope vanished on his first night of freedom, when she ended their relationship. Leaving her, "I thought how analogous that exit was to my own life at the moment . . . for not only was I stepping out from the bright lights of the restaurant into the darkness of the night—but from the brightness of the future I had looked forward to for so many months . . . to the blackness of a future alone . . . alone."[31]

This is how *My Selves* ends. The bleak and uncompromising conclusion was anticipated in Lucas/Graham's reflections on the nature of his criminality. Moving between environmental, hereditary, and psychoanalytic explanations, he now considered his behavior innate. Hubert Lucas had "left me a legacy of mental misery which a million years of purgatory could never wipe out." The "sins of the father" were "reincarnated" in the son's "looseness of moral conduct." Echoing the preoccupations of contemporary criminologists, Lucas/Graham reflected on the tragedy of his broken family. Gesturing toward a kind of popular Freudianism, he highlighted his "total lack of that maternal affection which most people are fortunate to experience." Falling back on older notions of familial discipline, he described how his youthful exuberance ran riot without "parental control."[32]

Lucas/Graham was desperate—almost incoherent—in trying to explain the "irregularities" of his lives. At times he rejected the insights of "Criminologists or disciples of Freud," claiming to have "given up speculating . . . why I was, and still am, thus mentally constituted." A paragraph later, he returned to the language of popular psychology: "No one realises that my inversion is deep rooted and that subconsciously I react to all the usual restrictions and conventions of life inversely."[33] Increasingly he fixated on the idea that his predispositions to crime were irrevocable. Little wonder his life had followed its peculiar course when "you cannot cure hereditary tendencies if they are really and truly inherent." He was "inherently crooked—and I am perfectly well aware that there is a criminal 'kink' in my brain." What else could he do but defraud and deceive?[34]

This was very different from the *Autobiography*. In the mid-1920s Lucas insisted on the possibility of leaving the past behind, finding hope for the future in the idea of the "Highway of Honesty." For a time he followed that path, but by 1934 reform seemed a cruel joke. Lucas/Graham's sense of being trapped by psychology, physiology, and environment illuminated the origins of his criminality, but was profoundly debilitating. Turning his self-pity outward, he displaced some blame onto a society ill equipped to sustain a reformist state:

> It is said that the past can be lived down, but the statement is a scandalous fallacy. . . . I have tried again and again to bury the past, but always the fact that I am Netley Lucas, ex-crook and ex–Borstal boy, has levelled me again to the foot of the ladder, a position which the world believes to be my due.

Presenting himself as a victim meant saying nothing about lying to publishers, editors, and courtiers. Having been exposed as a fraud by *John Bull* and revealed as an "ex-crook" in the *Daily Mail*, he now insisted his past lives were insurmountable obstacles to the "eminence of respectability" he so desired. Discredited and impoverished, he could do nothing other than "make capital out of my very notoriety."[35] For someone reaching his thirties, the telltale signs of aging were a ready metaphor: "A criminal past is something it is as easy to be rid of as to prevent hair turning grey with old age. It may be camouflaged, just as hair can be dyed but, like the hair, it will grow through the falseness of self-deception and betray itself."[36]

My Selves's claustrophobic misery thus reflected an impossible struggle with self and society. The truism "Once a crook, always a crook" challenged the "cranks who try to reform criminals." Bitter experience taught Lucas/Graham "that no one can reform anyone else, unless there is the will to be reformed.

How many crooks will to be turned into honest citizens?"[37] The freelance journalist of the 1920s might have responded positively; the discredited writer of 1934 clearly thought the answer was very few. There was no escape:

> In quieter moments, when I have lain on my back on the plank bed of a prison cell, or in the soft bed of some mistress, my mind has often played with the "might have been."
>   If only . . . That's just it . . . IF![38]

These moving reflections are offered by a narrator engaged in the necessarily painful task of weighing up the costs of multiple lives. They exemplify the shifting preoccupations of contemporary life-writing and (perhaps) an emerging sense of interiority. The problem with *My Selves* is that melancholy is interwoven with an equally compelling sense of the pleasures of crime. Perhaps these jarring movements reflect the competing demands of personal reform and commercial publishing. Perhaps the dissonant voices reflect how *My Selves* was a collage. How can we know? Lucas/Graham resisted any urge to reconcile the different positions he occupied.

At least some later observers sought to isolate Lucas/Graham as a pathological psychological type. By the 1950s, the influence of psychoanalytic ideas meant that his "selves" could be diagnosed as symptoms of an interiorized dual personality or "schizophrenic life."[39] This analysis echoed possibilities first outlined in the foreword to *My Selves* written by Sir James Purves-Stewart. Lucas later told his second wife he had "only one living relative, an Uncle Sir Purove [*sic*] Stewart, a Psycho Analyst."[40] There is no evidence to support this claim: it seems more likely that Lucas approached Purves-Stewart because of his reputation as a prominent neurologist and his work on *The Diagnosis of Nervous Diseases* (1906). Already known as an expert witness on the effects of alcohol on self-control, Purves-Stewart drew further attention in the 1930s through his contribution to debates over euthanasia and the scandal over Kathleen Chevassut's disputed research on disseminated sclerosis.[41] In one sense, Purves-Stewart fulfilled the same role that Eustace Jervis, John Goodwin, and Edmond Locard had for Lucas's earlier work. Yet his foreword was also an exercise in diagnosis, treating the autobiographer as a patient and the autobiography as a case history. "After studying *My Selves* and talking with the author," Purves-Stewart provided an analysis that was the closest Lucas/Graham came to a sustained scientific evaluation of his "selves." Read alongside *The Diagnosis of Nervous Diseases*, it suggests alternative ways of seeing his lives.[42]

Purves-Stewart's published work suggests he could have placed *My Selves* within pathological categories of schizophrenia or multiple personality disorder. His foreword acknowledged that diagnosis, but quickly closed it down: there was "no sufficient evidence of the existence of two distinct or alternating personalities." Purves-Stewart discerned an essential unity of character defined by "exactly the same defects in social responsibility."[43] Lucas/Graham was still "congenitally abnormal." Rather than psychological duality, abnormality was defined as the transgression of behavioral norms and social codes. Rather than an "ordinary degenerate," Lucas/Graham was

> one of those "deviates" whose variation from the normal is not exclusively in a downward direction, but in some respects upwards, or even . . . sideways, so that there is a combination of superior intelligence together with a deficiency of self-control. The result is that under certain circumstances, the deviate's behaviour becomes abnormal and anti-social.[44]

What caused this antisocial behavior? Elsewhere Purves-Stewart outlined how "modern psychological thinking" defined behavior as a conflict between "elemental instincts" and social codes that could be understood through "study of the patient's past emotional history." Here he resisted these diagnostic processes and refused to subject Lucas/Graham to "mental exploration."[45] Rather than the unconscious, he focused on the organic and hereditary origins of crime. Lucas/Graham's family and father meant he had "inherit[ed] . . . a certain pattern of brain cells," which meant his lives reflected a "deficiency of self-control, in combination with outside circumstances of environment or temptation," that was exacerbated by his dissipation.[46]

> Alcohol is a drug which, even in ordinary people, diminishes self-control, and is specially deleterious to a highly strung or nervous subject. Alcohol has been one of Evelyn Graham's most serious failings. Although sexual athletics have also been a frequent feature in Evelyn Graham's career, they do not appear to have been the exciting cause of any of his criminal actions.

The foreword's silences were striking. Purves-Stewart implied that Lucas/Graham was "highly strung," but ignored the multiplicity central to *My Selves* and contradicted his careful analysis of dual personality in *The Diagnosis of Nervous Diseases*. There was much of Graham in his "psychasthenic" type—unable to adapt to the "realities of his ordinary life," experiencing "a feeling of double personality."[47] Like Lucas/Graham's criminality, psychasthenic symptoms were endogenous and the "culmination of an ingrained neuropathic heredity."[48] *My Selves* could be read as a catalog of those symptoms, particularly the lack of self-control, which meant that for the psychasthenic, "obsessions to steal (kleptomania), to drink (dipsomania) and to perform sexual acts are more difficult to resist."[49] Crime, alcohol, and promiscuity were recurrent themes in Lucas/ Graham's writing, but Purves-Stewart treated them as an "exciting cause" of his behavior rather than symptoms of a pathological neurosis. The categories he deployed were incoherent and provisional. Describing alcohol as an "exciting cause" aligned Lucas/Graham with the "neurasthenic" personality. Defined as the antithesis of psychasthenia, neurasthenia was an exogenous disease caused either by "over-strain, mental or physical, combined with some emotion of a disagreeable kind," or the "abuse of drugs such as alcohol, tobacco or cocaine."[50]

There are striking resonances with Lucas/Graham's account of emotional "strain" and the effects of drinking and "sexual excess." We might even read *My Selves* as a neurasthenic book, betraying a sense of being out of control and a "general gloominess and depression."[51] Drawing together competing narratives, Purves-Stewart tried but failed to integrate them. His foreword simultaneously deployed and denied his own scientific research, and suggested that a coherent diagnosis of Lucas/Graham's "selves" was impossible. The unruly subject eluded classification.

Lucas/Graham glossed over these tensions, citing a conversation with the "famous brain specialist and neurologist" to support his sense of entrapment.[52] Purves-Stewart, by contrast, saw "no reason for pessimism." Encouraged by Lucas/Graham's "outstanding intellectual ability," he hoped he would "realise that honourable literary success is more than probable." Heredity was unavoidable, but "suitable exercises" and the "avoidance of alcohol" would "help to strengthen [his] deficient powers of self-restraint" as he sought to rebuild his lives.[53]

My Selves echoed the cycle of publicity and scandal that characterized the biography factory. Despite the affinities with earlier scandals, this was a different moment. In the late 1920s observers suggested Marriott was cultivating scandal to secure sales. Graham's bombastic response to the "banning" of *My Selves* made that explicit: he sought public attention by presenting himself as victim of an establishment conspiracy. Bluster belied the desperation of a man recently released from prison. Read against the melancholia of *My Selves*, it was marked by the trial that left him discredited and impoverished. Unable to relinquish his literary pretensions, Graham sought to rebuild his life by renewing his writing. Scandal and imprisonment precluded any easy return to biography but were themselves potential sources of profit. The ex-crook was now also an ex–crime writer and ex-biographer, claiming a privileged position from which to dissect discrete social worlds from the inside. This individualized focus was secured through the dialogue between courtiers and publishers. Graham's account of his literary career included a saccharine portrait of the queen of Spain but remained silent about the British monarchy: promised revelations about the king and Lord Stamfordham were removed before publication, and *My Selves* was no threat to monarchical prestige. Publication drew some attention, but little of the anger of 1928–31. Most newspapers seem to have decided simply to ignore Graham. Starved of the publicity he craved, this was what the *Straits Times* called a " 'literary' sensation . . . (in a minor tone)."[54]

IN PIECES

This was the last time Lucas/Graham drew sustained public scrutiny until his death. When journalists looked back from 1940, their obituaries confronted what was usually understood as his disappearance for much of the previous decade. The *Daily Express* observed Lucas's youthful confidence when he left prison in 1932, "determined to resume his writing activities." Seven years later, however, they could note how "Lucas had no more luck."[55] This contrast figured his later life as a story of pathos and tragedy. Hindsight suggested his aspirations were frustrated, hopes undermined by ill luck, desperate quest for literary success unfulfilled. Graham's fall from grace in 1931 now seemed a fitting denouement. The melancholic *My Selves* was the faint echo of disreputable lives long forgotten.

These sketches were only partial, and Lucas's "fading out" was illusory. The ludic and melancholic moods of *My Selves* give us a framework through which to understand the traces of his lives after 1932. The archival fragments suggest undaunted ambition, imagination, and the pursuit of advancement; they exist because of recurrent moments of crisis. We cannot easily resolve these tensions nor contain them within a singular story of decline: the pieces of lives we see are always-already marked by success and failure. After prison, said the *News of the World*, Lucas

returned to Fleet Street and started a number of literary agencies and journalistic enterprises. By this time he was so well known that his contributions were barred by most reputable newspapers and publishers. By adopting various devices however, he succeeded in selling a number of "dud" stories.[56]

The disgraced writer was excluded from "reputable" publishing and journalism. Elusive and unruly, however, his "devices" could not be defined, his "dud" stories could not be identified. In the 1930s Graham found precarious opportunities through the imperatives of commercial publishing and the personal exigencies of the masquerade.

Consider the London United Press, a "news and feature agency which met with some success" after July 1934. This was a solo venture, but eleven months later Graham apparently became a partner in the new British General Press, a "Literary Agents and Brokers" with offices in Fleet Street.[57] Many names were associated with these agencies. Graham was later linked to Ian Walpole and Richard or Spencer Tracy, described on headed notepaper as "Company Director" and "Managing Editor." For around a year, Arthur Hutchinson was listed as a fellow director. Probably Graham's brother-in-law, Guy Hart, Hutchinson somehow provided the agency's capital.[58] The third partner in the press was a likely associate for Walpole and Hutchinson: Allan Eidenow was a freelance journalist with a criminal record. In the early 1930s he contributed regular opinion pieces on American society, economy, and politics to newspapers in Britain and Australia. A staunch advocate of President Franklin D. Roosevelt, he claimed to have spent ten years working at the New York Stock Exchange.[59]

Graham did not immediately know it would be impossible to return to royal biography. The London United Press began by reviving the formula of the "Marriott comet." Exploiting news of the Duke of Kent's marriage to Princess Marina of Greece, it solicited a manuscript from Grace Ellison. A redoubtable journalist, suffragette, and traveler, Ellison had made her name as a sympathetic authority on the contradictions of modern Turkey through titles like *An Englishwoman in a Turkish Harem* (1915). During the Great War, she served as a nurse, throwing her energies into the formation of the French Flag Nursing Corps.[60] Her involvement with Walpole was unlikely, to say the least: the *Authorised Life Story of Princess Marina* (1934) drew upon her friendship with the Greek royal family, but was the only biography she ever wrote. Like Sir George Aston, she was apparently unaware of whom she was dealing with and was exploited for her name and knowledge.[61] The *Observer* described *Princess Marina* as cynical and opportunistic. Written in three months, published three days before the wedding, it bore "signs of hurry in the writing and the printing."[62]

The new biography factory was quickly frustrated. Graham, Tracy, and Walpole only appear within the same frame because courtiers identified the connections among them. In November 1934 Thomas urged "extreme caution" upon his colleagues: "I have just been warned that Mr Evelyn Graham (alias Netley Lucas) the notorious 'Royal Biographer' . . . is on the warpath again."[63] In December, Richard Tracy wrote to Wigram asking permission to photograph George V's horses for a series about famous racing stables for the *Field*. Wigram knew whom he was dealing with, rejecting the request and repeating Thomas's warning.[64] Courtiers were incredulous when "R. Cameron"—"our old pal Evelyn Graham"—wrote to Wigram, Thomas, and others in February 1935 asking for a "special sitting" for an "exclusive picture for inclusion in the Special Jubilee Supplement which we are preparing." Wigram shut down a correspondence that had begun six years earlier. Graham's final letter in the Royal Archives, dated 14 February 1935 and signed Cameron, was brusquely annotated: "<u>No reply</u>: The London United Press is the firm Evelyn Graham is connected with."[65]

The British General Press could not shake off its association with the "notorious" biographer. Ingenious and adaptable, Graham and Eidenow changed focus. Eidenow became the agency's public face, and the firm now "made a speciality of obtaining articles from well-known people which they resold to newspapers."[66] Profit came from exploiting the newsworthy and the celebrity. That spring Eidenow approached the African American singer and actor Paul Robeson, asking him to write six articles "on his views about life, his film work and his experiences in Europe and America." Robeson was then at the height of his fame: Eidenow's letter arrived in the same week that Alexander Korda's epic *Sanders of the River* was released in British cinemas, and alongside more prestigious invitations from the Royal Institute of International Affairs and National Liberal Club for Robeson to speak on "the future of the Negro race" and "the conservation of true African culture."[67]

Eidenow's approach to Robeson was symptomatic of 1930s personal journalism, but the press's understanding of "well-known people" went beyond stage and screen. In an emerging mass democracy, the press sought to bring political debate to readers through both rigorous analyses of international and domestic affairs and ideas of personality.[68] In April 1935 Eidenow began a lengthy correspondence with Winston Churchill, soliciting "a powerful series of articles on the armaments and internal policy of the great nations of the world." Eidenow envisaged an "authoritative 'on the spot' world survey," but was increasingly interested in how focusing on personality could mobilize interest in politics. In May he offered Churchill one thousand guineas for ten articles on Ramsay MacDonald's premiership.[69]

In the mid-1930s, Churchill was in the political wilderness, mercenary and prickly over his reputation. His correspondence with Eidenow was partly driven by his negotiation of word counts, deadlines, contracts, and money.[70] Having agreed upon terms, the men argued about the relationship among politics, personality, and the press. Rather than "merely a political series of articles," Eidenow wanted "a colourful and intimate study" that would emphasize "the human side of the National Government" and bring politics to life.[71] For Churchill, by contrast, this approach threatened the dignity of public life and the possibility of understanding MacDonald's significance. The National Government only made sense when compared to the "first socialist administration."[72] He resisted Eidenow's suggestion that party conflict and ideological debate be reworked as questions of personality. MacDonald and his ministers were "small people though called upon to deal with momentous issues." Protective of his authorial independence, Churchill concluded tersely: "You can safely leave the matter to me."[73]

Despite this friction, Churchill was inclined to accept the commission. In June, however, he abruptly withdrew from the correspondence.[74] Eidenow and Churchill's exchanges encapsulated the strengths and weaknesses of the British General Press. Approaching a prominent politician suggests the company's ambition. The articles Eidenow envisaged placed it at the leading edge of the shifting relationship between politics and journalism. In the firm's correspondence with Robeson and Churchill, we see its orientation toward the market. All this came at a cost. Eidenow often misunderstood the subtleties of patrician communication: ignoring Churchill's polite hints—not taking no for an answer—meant alienating him. Ambition was risky. Eidenow made grandiose proposals with little substance. Churchill's fee for the MacDonald articles would have been fifteen hundred pounds. Securing articles from well-known figures was lucrative but expensive. The pressures of commercial publishing meant that the British General Press was always on the brink of overreaching itself.[75]

Its pursuit of profit meant that the British General Press blurred the line between brash commercialism and sharp practice. Marriott had shown how it was common for agents to use publicity circulars to seek contracts with publishers and editors. Such circulars were problematic when they sold work to which the agent did not yet hold rights. In December 1935 these tensions drew Eidenow into a disastrous public conflict. He had sold rights to the Aga Khan's "reminiscences and experiences on the Turf" to the *News of the World* on the strength of a circular.[76] As Eidenow pushed to secure agreement, their correspondence became increasingly heated until the Aga Khan rejected the proposal.[77] Desperate for money, the British General Press and its irascible director sued the Aga Khan for breach of contract. It was Eidenow's probity that

that was the only resolution to the legacies of past lives. Unlike Eidenow, Lucas continued to find some reward through writing. The archive records only failure, but the stories he sold successfully simply appeared unmarked by their conditions of production. Reputable publishers still found value in his earlier work; continued sales meant royalties. When opportunity arose, publishers set scruples aside and reissued biographies denounced as "fake" a few years earlier. In 1934 Hutchinson reprinted his life of the king of Belgium as *Albert the Brave*, adding two chapters on Albert's "tragic death" while climbing in the Ardennes. The title changed, the author's name was removed, but the book repeated the disingenuous claim that it had been read by Albert's adjutant.[93] In 1936 the accession of Edward VIII prompted Ward Lock to reissue *Edward P.* The company had been tricked into publishing the book but had no qualms about exploiting interest in Britain's new monarch. Identical to the first edition, the rereleased book included no fresh material dealing with the period since 1930.[94]

In 1939, finally, rights to *My Selves* were sold to the leading French publisher Gallimard. Gallimard's list included many prestigious writers, but its most profitable title was the seamy *Detective* magazine, a compendium of the everyday crime stories known as "faits divers." The autobiography of a British crook must have been an attempt to exploit demand for this kind of material, but there were other connections.[95] *My Selves* was translated into French as *Moi et Moi* by the surrealist poet René Daumal. Daumal had worked for Gallimard before, translating Ernest Hemingway's *Death in the Afternoon* (1938), and this might have been what Patrick Mouze calls "*travaux alimentaires* [work done for food]." *Moi et Moi* was also the title of a 1929 poem by Roger Gilbert-Lecomte, published in *Le Grand Jeu*, the magazine with which Daumal was associated.[96] Other leading surrealists including André Breton and Man Ray were avid readers of the *Detective*, finding rich terrain on which to explore the power of hidden fantasies and repressed desires. Taken up by French surrealists, the intriguing *Moi et Moi* perhaps crystallized growing interest in the fracturing of subjectivity and the relationship between the conscious and unconscious mind.[97]

In tracing Graham's lives after 1932, I have resisted straightforward narratives of decline or disappearance. While his literary efforts have left few signs, his private life is more opaque still. For almost a decade, he had lived in the public gaze, selling his selves to the highest bidder. *My Selves* was his last autobiography. It was a partial account narrated by an evasive subject, but with nothing similar covering the period before his death, it is even harder to understand the personal relationships within which his lives took shape. There are hints. Guy Hart had been Graham's pal and partner for over a decade. He remained involved with Graham's efforts at literary agency after leaving prison, but *My Selves* suggested that the men had begun to grow apart. A devoted spouse and "father of a fine boy (my nephew)," the man he called Dick had left his own criminal past behind. He was poorer, Lucas/Graham noted, but "I am certain that he is happier today with his wife and son, than during the time he played shadow to me."[98] In court in 1936, he quietly agreed that "Mr Dent" had "faded away . . . by mutual consent."[99]

Dent's disappearance reflected a more pervasive fracturing of Lucas/Graham's relationships. In the years after Lucas/Graham came out of prison, this serial adulterer left a trail of failed affairs and broken marriages behind him. The records of London's divorce courts provide the fullest traces of his lives. Suing his wife, Dorothy, for divorce in 1936, Cedric Hill named "Netley Lucas otherwise Leslie Evelyn Graham" as corespondent: Cedric won the case (and custody of his young child) on grounds of his wife's adultery.[100] A year later, Elsie Lucas finally sued her husband for divorce, citing his adultery with Dorothy Hill. Long estranged from Lucas/Graham, she still lived in the Colebrooke Road house they had shared in the late 1920s but was poor enough to qualify for legal aid. Her suit was uncontested, and a decree absolute was granted in May 1938.[101] Taking chambers in fashionable residential districts had suggested Graham's literary success, but now his movements told a different story. Between 1935 and 1938, he never stayed in one place for more than a few months. No longer at the heart of metropolitan Society, he could be found on London's growing suburban fringes: Wembley Park, where he lived with Dorothy Hill; Pinner; Twickenham. He was a long way from Piccadilly.[102]

Consider this, though: on 13 December 1938 Netley Evelyn Lucas married Mavis Jessie Cox in Westminster Register Office. Mavis was twenty-five, ten years younger than her husband. Described as a "smartly dressed blonde," she was attractive and fashionable. She was also independent. Born in India, daughter of a civil engineer, in 1935 she had traveled from Bombay to London in search of a new life. Working as a sales representative, she forged a successful career and lived in the respectable neighborhood around Great Portland Street. Despite his struggles, Lucas must have seemed glamorous and charming: they married after a whirlwind four-day romance. He was living in a flat in Duncan House, part of the recently completed complex of luxurious art deco apartments in Dolphin Square, Pimlico. The couple moved there after their wedding, living in the largest self-contained block in Europe, complete with swimming pool, tennis courts, bar, and restaurant. Lucas's marriage certificate described him as an author. His living arrangements suggested renewed prosperity and the life of a fashionable man-about-town. Marriage suggested the prospect of romantic fulfillment.[103]

Yet you already know that this story has no happy ending, don't you?

HYMN FOR THE ALCOHOL

Netley Lucas was found dead on the Chesterfield sofa in the lounge at St. Mary's Lodge in Bell Lane in Fetcham at around six o'clock on the morning of Sunday 23 June 1940. Set back from the road in a large garden, it was an imposing semidetached house recently built in dark red brick. In 1940 it must have been on the very edge of this leafy Surrey town: the lounge windows looked out over open fields down to Great Bookham Common.[104] Lucas had moved there with his wife at the end of April, calling himself Robert Tracy. It was Mavis who found him. Asleep in bed, she had been drawn downstairs by the smell of smoke. After trying to put the fire out, she called Alan Easton, the local doctor, from the telephone box at the top of the road. Easton was soon followed by Police Sergeant Frederick Smith. Easton and Smith later sketched plans of the disordered room they found (figs. 17 and 18). Each drew Lucas's body on the sofa in the corner—an ungainly composition of scribbled lines and a faceless stick figure. "Half lying, half sitting," he faced a small table in the window on which his typewriter sat. Near his feet "were two portions of metal broken from the typewriter." Easton marked them on his plan.[105]

Lucas had been smoking and drinking: there was a full ashtray and empty siphon beside the typewriter. The bureau next to the table was open. On the flap there was a blotting pad and "papers and envelopes." The material evidence of literary endeavor was covered by bottles and cigarette packets; there was an "empty glass and the top of a Haig Whisky Bottle on the pad"; above was "a bowl of Roses which were all shriveled up." Elsewhere the plans identified more evidence of heavy drinking. On a table to the left, Smith found half a bottle of Haig, a broken and almost empty bottle of ale, a bottle of tonic water, a half-drunk glass of beer, and two decanters with spirits in the bottom. On the lower shelf of the table were four bottles of lager (three full, one empty), more tonic water, and two wineglasses. There was an empty glass on the floor.[106] The room was full of smoke and the window coated in brown film, but Smith and Easton carefully marked the extent of burning, indicating "Fire Remains" and "Burned Chair" in a corner. The wall paneling and bookshelves were burned; the electric light shade had melted and fallen to the floor.[107]

Statements collected by police supported the material signs of dissipation.

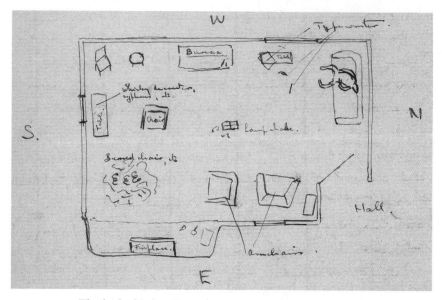

FIGURE 17. The death of Robert Tracy, part 1. Surrey History Centre: 606/2/1/1/53, Western Surrey Coroner's Report, no. 33, Netley Lucas: plan drawn by Dr. Alan Easton (23 June 1940). © Surrey History Centre. Reproduced by permission of Surrey History Centre.

Smith noted that the couple had "been known to drink heavily and visit Licensed premises in Leatherhead and Fetcham frequently."[108] Although the couple was cautioned for breaching the blackout regulations two days earlier, the constable who called at the house found Tracy "too drunk for me to obtain particulars."[109] Mavis Lucas gave the most harrowing account of her husband's death. The charming gentleman was now a violent drunk, abusive, unpredictable, and short-tempered. Mavis's statement was almost identical to accounts of Hubert Lucas's brutality thirty years earlier. A week after they married, her husband "came home the worse for drink and very violent. He dragged me about by my hair and tore my clothes off. . . . I sustained a broken nose and a black eye." A few months later, they were living above a shop in Paddington. There he "made my nose bleed and blackened both my eyes." When Mavis escaped to a friend, an insensible Lucas "phoned the Paddington Green Police and said that he had murdered me." He was arrested and only released when she went to the police station. He was often violent—"always when he was in drink." A fortnight before his death, he left Mavis unconscious in the lounge, hitting her over the head with a beer bottle "for no apparent reason." She had left him six times, but "I was very much in love with him and have always returned to him."[110]

None of this stopped when they moved to Surrey. They passed "most evenings" in the Bell Inn or Bull Hotel, and spent "£5 a week on liquor" at Burkwood's Off Licence. Lucas "used to drink Beer but latterly it was mainly Whisky. I used to drink a fair bit myself." On Saturday evening they spent several hours in local pubs. Returning home at ten o'clock, they continued to drink until Mavis went to bed at midnight. Mavis claimed Lucas was "comparitively [*sic*] sober" and listening to the wireless, but she woke to see him in the doorway holding burning pillows. He threw them at her, then disappeared. When Mavis moved to the second bedroom, Lucas reappeared, dragging off the bedclothes and pushing over the furniture. While Mavis managed to sleep, she woke to smell burning. The lounge was full of smoke. At first she thought Lucas was "merely in a drunken coma," though she quickly realized he was dead. Reflecting on the cause of the fire, she observed it was "a peculiarity of his to sleep on the floor with his head within inches of a fire. In this way he has on several occasions started fires, but we have always been able to extinguish any fires so started."[111]

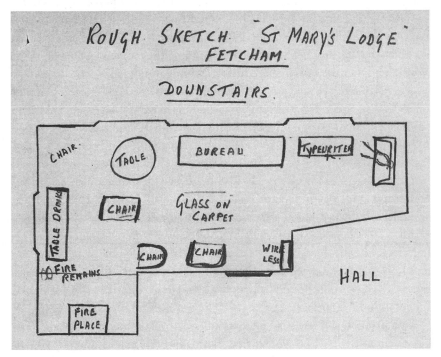

FIGURE 18. The death of Robert Tracy, part 2. Surrey History Centre: 606/2/1/1/53, Western Surrey Coroner's Report, no. 33, Netley Lucas: plan drawn by P. S. Smith (23 June 1940). © Surrey History Centre. Reproduced by permission of Surrey History Centre.

Like her married life, Mavis's statement was brutal. Yet she went some way toward explaining her husband's horrific behavior. A hesitant medical diagnosis echoed *My Selves* and drew upon pathological categories reminiscent of the man she knew as Lucas's uncle, "Sir Purove [*sic*] Stewart." Her husband, she volunteered, was "definitely a dipsomaniac and when in drink had Sadistical tendencies." In reflecting on Lucas's life, she told a melancholic story of the emotional costs of frustrated ambition. Mavis knew of his criminal past and bankruptcy but also suggested his continued aspirations: "My husband was an Author and at times financially well off." She continued: "At the moment my husband has no money at all, but was hoping to get payment in respect of several books he was expecting to get published."[112] Still Lucas told his stories; still he hoped to find success. Smith and Easton's plans show him facing his desk and typewriter. The mechanical and material tools of literary endeavor were now both broken and overwhelmed by the detritus of a life in turmoil. Fragments of the typewriter were on the floor as if thrown there in anger or frustration; his papers and blotting pad were covered in a mess of empty bottles and glasses and overflowing ashtrays; the flowers slowly rotted above his body.

Throughout this book I have presented Lucas in the way I have known him—as part of the warp and weft of British society and culture, and as a flawed yet characteristic product of his time. In tracking the months leading up to his death, mapping the room where he was found, and detailing the diagnostic processes of modern science, the file compiled by the West Surrey Coroner offers a more visceral way of understanding his lives. Witness statements and medical expertise enabled the systematic accumulation of knowledge, typed or handwritten into the standardized forms of the police and coroner's office. In a loosely bound file of twenty-two pages, this collective analysis moved from time to space to the body. Here we might see the manner of Lucas's lives embodied at his death. Doctor Easton had seen the man he knew as Tracy several weeks before he was called to St. Mary's Lodge. From Mavis, "I understood . . . that he was a 'paroxysmal dypsomaniac.'" After subsequently meeting Tracy, he concluded: "There was a history of considerable alcoholic excess and I diagnosed advanced alcoholic cirrhosis of the liver." Easton's diagnosis reflected Tracy's description of symptoms and behavior, and a brief examination of his body's surfaces.[113]

The processes of scientific investigation were elaborated the day after Lucas was found, when his body underwent postmortem examination by Doctor Eric Gardner at the Leatherhead Mortuary. It was 12:15 p.m., and the temperature in the room was sixty-nine degrees Fahrenheit. Following procedures standardized in the late nineteenth century, Gardner's examination began "Externally." The left side of Lucas's body was stained pink. First- and second-degree burns betrayed the circumstances of death and position in which he was found: "lobe of the Left ear, under the chin on the Left side (linear 2 inches long) the Left eyebrow, the back of both hands, and on the inner side of both legs between the knee and the ankle." Methodically Gardner's attention shifted inward, first to the "Head and Brain" before moving lower to the "Abdomen." While he initially focused on what he could see through the body's orifices—the "excess of carbon" in the nose, glottis, and trachea—his scrutiny became more invasive. With a short, broad-bladed knife, scalpel and forceps, saw, and mallet, he opened up Lucas's body, weighing the brain, lungs, heart, stomach, intestine, liver, spleen, and kidneys, and noting their appearance and condition. The stomach "contained some fluid which smelt of whisky . . . very perceptible in the post mortem room." The spleen weighed eight ounces. "Large, smooth, tense, and deeply engorged," it could be read as a symptom of the cirrhosis Easton had diagnosed. Still Lucas resisted definitive diagnosis: his kidneys were "engorged, but otherwise normal to the naked eye."[114]

Gardner did not treat the body in isolation. Analysis of Lucas's organs was situated in a "History" of the weeks before death and a panoramic view of what he saw when he visited St. Mary's Lodge. The "colour of his skin, the muscles and all the organs was of the intense pink suggestive of Carbon Monoxide poisoning." Laboratory tests showed carbon monoxide in his blood. "Smoke particles" in his windpipe indicated this was "derived from the fumes of the burning room"—Gardner noted traces of the "intense fire" in the lounge. Lucas's dissipation was apparent on the mortuary slab. His body showed evidence of "a considerable degree of chronic alcoholism and a large quantity of alcohol had certainly been taken immediately before death." It was visible in a more immediate sense. The gentleman crook and predatory rake had relied upon his trim figure and good looks; now his body was "that of a rather stout man." In identifying the cause of death, Gardner was clear: Lucas had died of carbon monoxide poisoning and smoke inhalation while showing symptoms of "acute and chronic alcoholism."[115]

In death, formal diagnostic procedures and the demands of legal process framed Lucas as an object of scientific knowledge and invested him with a fixity that he eluded in life. I have emphasized the mutability of his lives in the 1930s. Perhaps here, in the passage of time and the deteriorating disassembled body of a washed-up alcoholic, there is biographical "truth." This analysis might be too easy, though. Perhaps we see him more clearly in Mavis's blackened eyes or the "mass of dried blood" that still matted her hair a week after he struck her with a bottle.[116]

Newspapers reported Lucas's death and the coroner's verdict, but said little beyond noting his drinking and "mania for fires."[117] The *News of the World* concluded: "Few people in Fleet Street . . . will mourn the passing of this prince of tricksters, for despite his personal charm, his plausible tongue and his undoubted cleverness, Lucas was a crook and a rogue at heart."[118] The paper was right, of course: defrauded over the lives of Lord Lonsdale and the Aga Khan, it had good reason to welcome the unscrupulous trickster's passing. Using his death as a prompt to recount his criminal and literary deceptions, however, sketched out the terrain upon which Lucas could survive long after 1940. The drama of his lives remained a lucrative commodity, compelling the attention of journalists and crime writers into the 1950s and beyond. Absorbed into pleasure cultures of crime of which his confessions had been formative, Lucas's afterlives were animated by particular forms and genres of popular culture.

The most striking retelling of his lives was broadcast on the Australian commercial radio channels 2GB in Sydney and 3UZ in Melbourne in May 1956. "Netley Lucas. Forger. Confidence Man" was the forty-fifth episode of the long-running series *The Outlaw*, produced by Artransa and the Macquarie Broadcasting Service. This "true dramatization" was written by John Crane and produced by Walter Pym, well-known radio actors and producers. Twenty-five minutes long, and recorded in just over two hours, it was inevitably trashy and formulaic. It was also the most detailed version of Lucas's lives. Going beyond the biographical sketches that appeared in 1931 and 1940, it considered his journalism, criminology, and alcoholism, as well as the crimes of confidence on which his notoriety rested. The production notes give no explanation for their interest in Lucas, but Crane and Pym knew what they were talking about.[119]

Played by the prolific John Bushelle, Lucas was described as "debonair, plausible, a terrific con man. English and well-educated. Quite charming." The script followed him from birth to death, an omniscient narrator interweaving dramatic vignettes and imposing coherence on Lucas's many "selves." A spiraling theme tune created the "atmosphere of a 'manhunt,'" and the story began:

> Netley Evelyn Lucas is a name well known in English criminal history . . . as an impostor, fake, cheat and thief. If titles were given to those who lived unscrupulously by their wits, Nestley [*sic*] Lucas would certainly bear the title of Prince,

if not King, for by his charm, personality and plausible tongue, he worked his way through Europe and pocketed a fortune![120]

This was a melodrama of transnational criminality. Reworking a scene from the *Autobiography*, Crane showed Lucas teaming up with a beautiful vamp to rob "Mrs Andrew Carlyle, wife of a wealthy South African diamond trader." The "handsome young escort" seduced Carlyle to find her jewels:

NARRATOR: It took Netley Lucas just two days to meet and win over Mrs Andrew Carlyle—two rather hectic days for both of them. Milly Carlyle was enraptured with the fresh-faced young midshipman, and Netley—well, Netley was never one to let the side down—with a practiced art he made sure Milly confided to him the information he wanted.
MILLY (DARE WE RISK A RATHER NAUGHTY GIGGLE) Gerald, you're very sweet.[121]

The thrills of crime were never unequivocal. "Time and circumstance caught up with Netley Lucas": a dissonant "MUSIC STAB" heralded a stentorian judge sending him to Borstal. His "criminal tendencies still uncurbed, Netley Lucas danced around London as 'Lord,' 'Honourable,' or 'Colonel' as the fancy took him—still spending wildly" until sent to prison in 1920. The script echoed reports of his insouciance in court: "NETLEY (AMUSED). Thank you, Your Honour. I appreciate your concern for my future welfare."[122] Unlike most biographies, the play acknowledged Lucas's abortive moves along the highway of honesty in the mid-1920s. In the second act, a reformed Lucas "married and settled down to write his autobiography . . . enjoy[ing] a good living writing crime articles" until he was "discredited by Fleet Street" and in New York.[123] Lucas's "most profitable idea" was still to come: the rise and fall of the bogus biography factory, his global flight, and arrest and imprisonment in 1931 were staged through a series of dialogues.[124]

It was in the death of a "prematurely old Lucas" that Crane found the most powerful drama. The final scene, in which Lucas argues with his wife, now renamed Freda, is worth quoting in full:

FREDA (FADING IN) Now for Heaven's sake, forget about the glory of rich and extravagant living, Netley. You're not meant for it, and as long as you try to get it, it'll only lead you into trouble.

NETLEY (JUST SLIGHTLY TIPSY) I've been unlucky, Freda—that's what it is—unlucky.

STUDIO CLINK OF BOTTLE AGAINST GLASS

FREDA That drink's not going to do you any good either.
NETLEY But they haven't beaten me yet. (DRINKS) I can't be unlucky all the time. My chance will come—
FREDA You're a fool—that's the only word to describe you. Surely you should've learnt your lesson by now.
NETLEY I've learnt a lesson all right. Never trust other people in this game. Work as a solo operator.

. . .

[They continue to argue until Freda retreats to bed.]

STUDIO (OFF MIKE) DOOR OPENS AND CLOSES

NETLEY (DROWSY) Idiotic woman—suburban mentality!—always has been a parochial little fool. Next time, when I get some money, I'll get away from her for good (YAWNING). Next time—(GOING OFF TO SLEEP)—when I have some money—.

CO MUSIC

CO SMALL FIRE CRACKLING

CLOCK CHIMES HALF HOUR

STUDIO (PAUSE) (OFF MIKE) DOOR OPENS

FREDA (OFF MIC) Netley what on earth are you sit . . . (SHOCKED BEAT—SCREAMED) Netley![125]

As the music crescendoed, the narrator intervened for a final time. Death was a tragedy of frustrated aspiration—the impossible desire for "rich and extravagant living" and escape from a narrow "suburban mentality." A "career as one of England's most famous confidence men" ended not in glamour but with an insensible drunk consumed by a fire he had started. The play glossed over Lucas's violence. Perhaps it had to. Death then could be marked by pathos: "an ignominious end for the once handsome young man who thought he could beat the world." The melodramatic forms of a radio play were different from the methodical processes of postmortem autopsy; the dramatic sound effects evoking the scene of death were different from Easton and Smith's plans. In death as in life, however, Lucas confounded boundaries between fact and fiction. Whether dramatized as a cautionary tale or filed as accumulated medical knowledge, we see and hear the same death.[126]

This emphasis on death and melancholia was unusual. Yet Lucas became a compelling subject for an Australian radio play because his lives remained thrilling. That was why he attracted the attention of other commentators after the Second World War, and why they worked so hard to create resolutely ludic accounts of his exploits as a gentleman crook. Percy Smith had arrested Evelyn Graham and testified at his trial in 1931. In retirement he reflected on their encounters in *Plutocrats of Crime* (1960). Lucas was "one of the astutest and coolest rogues I have ever met," who demanded all the senior detective's experience. Smith briefly acknowledged the manner of Lucas's death, but was more preoccupied with his deceptions. Like so many other writers, he uncritically repeated stories Lucas told in his *Autobiography* and journalism, glossing over their uncertain authenticity and the period when Lucas found success as a writer on crime. As time was compressed, the gentleman crook morphed seamlessly into the royal biographer. Troubled and excited by his many "selves," accounts like this effaced the sordid realities of his early death.[127]

Lucas's storytelling thus provided rich material for a new generation of crime writers after the Second World War. Lucas claimed association with notorious crooks to secure his status as a privileged underworld observer. Now he played the same role for a new generation of writers: a duplicitous trickster authorized "true" accounts of London's underworld. Harold Castle was a prolific writer in the 1950s, best known for popular children's titles like *The Boy's Book of Sailing* (1956). Turning his attention to crime in *Case for the Prosecution* (1956), he sought to establish his credentials as an experienced observer who had published "several books on crime, criminology, and detection."[128] Castle described the unusual origins of his expertise in "a first-hand acquaintance with one of the arch-criminals of our time. He was known as Netley Lucas, alias Evelyn Graham and half a dozen other names."[129] Castle's calling Lucas an "arch-criminal" was both hyperbole and evidence of Lucas's ability to shape the stories others told about him. Castle "spent a good deal of my time with Lucas" when working with him on what became *Crooks: Confessions*. Just as Etienne Gaspard had conducted Lucas around Paris, so Lucas himself now guided Castle through London, where Castle observed that "because I was in his company, I was persona grata in that strange world." In the reminiscences of Smith, Castle, and others, Lucas lived on through the imperatives of commercial publishing and journalism.[130]

WE NEED TO TALK, NETLEY

It's not me—not this time; it's you. Because I've tried so hard and for so long to make this work only for you to do something that makes me realize we don't understand each other at all. Even that isn't right: you have no interest in understanding me, do you? Part of me has known that all along. That hasn't stopped me becoming obsessed with you. All this time, you have been on my mind as I fall asleep and as I wake up; I try to escape for a few hours on the bike and still I find you playing on my mind; your photo—that photo, where you're oh, so debonair—is my screen saver. Yes, it's safe to say that I'm obsessed with making sense of you. Somehow I think you get off on that.

What do I get in return? You're charming, for sure; you can be good company when you want to be; when the mood takes you (and the money's there), you're certainly generous. You're a right gentleman, aren't you? That isn't enough anymore. Being charming only goes so far when I don't know who you are. Is Netley even your name? I thought I knew that, at least; then I found all the traces of paper you left behind, and the names multiplied one upon the other. What have I not seen? What are you hiding from me? I cannot trust you now. All this time I have pursued you. Just when I thought I was getting somewhere, you had to go and fuck it up. Inscrutable doesn't come close, you lying bastard.

I used to enjoy it; I used to like you. It was frustrating yet exciting when you disappeared. Playing hard to get made you more alluring. As I watched you teasing colonial outfitters and courtiers, I found myself cheering you on, hoping you would get away with it. When things started to go wrong and you began drinking so heavily, I felt sorry for you; I even saw a bit of myself in you, and that isn't something I care to admit. You know that too, though, don't you? You've seen what I've written about you. Then something happened, and I'm not sure I can like you anymore. Yes, you're a <u>gentleman</u>: the sort that lies, cheats, and doesn't care about hurting those closest to him (like me, maybe) who have sustained him through the hard times and the wild successes. You're that sort of gentleman: self-absorbed, misogynist, a violent washed-up alcoholic. None of those rackets really came to anything, did they? You're a failure. What was I thinking?

I made you, Netley. You are nothing without me and without the stories that I have told about you.

Still it <u>is</u> me and it <u>is</u> you, Netley. After all this time, I have too much invested in you to walk away. I still fucking love you and want you. Work with me, just this once?[131]

Cooling Out:
Has the World Changed,
or Have I Changed?

If you have made a life for the dead and gone, then they can see you. You, the biographer, are real to them, in their obdurate, irritating individuality (which you have constructed).

CAROLYN STEEDMAN, "On Not Writing Biography,"
New Formations 67 (2009): 24

The man born Netley Evelyn died just before his thirty-seventh birthday. It was as Netley Lucas that he was cremated in Woking on 26 June 1940. There is no record of who attended his funeral. I am sure Mavis Lucas was there. She had loved him enough to endure his brutality and return each time she tried to leave; she described herself as "widow of Richard Lucas, a Writer" until she died in a London hospital in 1962, aged forty-nine, after an operation to remove a tumor from her mouth went wrong.[1] What about the others? What about Elsie, his first wife? What about Guy Hart and Florence, and their fifteen-year-old son, Lucas's nephew? I cannot tell if they remained in his life. Nothing in Lucas's writing suggests he knew he had two half brothers, let alone that they were in contact. Nor do I know if Lucas had friends to mourn him. He so rarely referred to significant relationships that it is difficult to imagine he had any friendships strong enough to survive his relentless pursuit of self-destruction in the 1930s. Stanley Scott could testify how he betrayed so many of those who sought to help him. Lucas was often bitter toward the women who won his affections then dropped him, but his infidelities left a trail of heartbreak. Did any old lovers read of his death and come to pay their respects? In the mid-1920s he might have had an affair with Josephine O'Dare. Like Lucas, O'Dare faded from view in the 1930s, living under different names and dying after an overdose of sleeping tablets in 1951. Perhaps she was moved to say farewell to a man whose lives were entwined with her own.[2] The gregarious man-about-town was often at the center of an admiring circle of raffish acquaintances. It was all transient, however. When Lucas died, it seems most likely that he was orphaned, estranged from what little family he had, and isolated. Wealth and luxury were distant memories. Impoverished, depending on his wife's salary, Lucas left no estate. As far as I can tell, Mavis received nothing more than the handkerchief and ten-shilling note in his pockets when he died. Death was ignominious.[3]

Lucas died weeks after the British Expeditionary Force was evacuated from Dunkirk, and just as the Battle of Britain was taking shape over the English Channel. Notices of "Trickster Prince's Fate in Fire" were contained within reports of the worsening course of the war in Europe and the threat of invasion, and printed alongside photographs of evacuated children.[4] Contrasted with such news, his obituaries suggested Lucas was a man out of time. He embodied the brittle flamboyance of the 1920s; his pretensions sat uneasily against wartime austerity; he was ill suited for the egalitarian stoicism then being demanded through ideas of the People's War. At the end of the Great War, he fraudulently claimed military rank. As a second conflict gathered force, he again evaded the responsibilities of patriotic citizenship. Lucas and Mavis left London just as the risk of air raids grew; he was cautioned for breaching the blackout regulations days before he died. He was one of the quintessential people of the aftermath of another conflict, but by 1940 that moment had gone. Lucas was within living memory, but part of the distant past.[5]

War changed the meaning of news; paper rationing reduced the space available to journalists; it was harder to sensationalize a dissolute life while also mobilizing comforting ideas of national character and civilian morale. More than this: the epidemic of bogus honorables Lucas exemplified was a postwar phenomenon, crystallizing as the Great War's disruptive legacies were intensified by the quickening pace of peacetime change, and dramatized by the upheaval of race riots and strikes in the immediate aftermath. While the gentleman crook provided one focus for an acute crisis of confidence in the stability of social hierarchies, by the mid-1920s the sense of a world in turmoil that made him so threatening had dissipated. The exploits of Lucas and his like continued to suggest no one was necessarily what he or she seemed, and questioned the status of established elites. By the 1930s, however, observers like the retired detective Percy Smith believed that the trickster's heyday was over. The frenetic energies of the postwar reaction had evaporated, Smith argued, and the "confidence squad" consigned them to the recent past. The knowledge enshrined in the *Illustrated Circular of Confidence Tricksters* was essential to this process, but in redefining crimes of confidence, it made Lucas anachronistic in his own lifetime.

Whatever literary success Lucas found reflected his ability to improvise with the characteristic forms of commercial mass culture. Whether reporting on crime for the *Sunday News* or through Albert Marriott's publicity stunts, he worked at the leading edge of processes by which journalism and publishing were remade in the 1920s and 1930s. Entrepreneurial and dynamic, his experiments with film and forays into the business of publishing and news agency suggest he was attuned to a commercial landscape then changing rapidly. As much as contemporaries dismissed Lucas as a duplicitous fraud, it was often difficult to separate his activities from dominant forms of cultural production. This was what made him both successful and dangerous.

Ironically, the far-reaching effects of these shifts left Lucas behind. "Netley Lucas. Forger. Confidence Man" was anomalous in the *Outlaw* radio series of the 1950s, an ostensibly modern crook included alongside tales of smugglers, pirates, and bushrangers. Sixteen years after his death, Lucas was already part of history. The uncompromising crime stories of the 1950s had little place for the leisured gentlemanly trickster; the changing conventions of social realism and crime reporting sat uneasily against an ex-crook's melodramatic confessions. After the Second World War, sensation was reworked as the meticulous investigations of hard-bitten newspapermen. Lucas had anticipated some of these shifts, but this was crime writing in a different register. Firsthand accounts of a life in crime could still intrigue, but Duncan Webb's career suggested that the value of the journalist's byline was exceeding that of the ex-crook's signature in securing readers' confidence.[6]

Evelyn Graham's abortive proposal to film George V's address to the empire anticipated a vital development in the making of modern monarchy and showed how new media could serve old institutions. After the Second World War, the official royal biographies overseen by Sir Alan Lascelles built upon the authorized lives that brought Graham and Marriott success. Working with chosen biographers and extending the explicit imprimatur of royal approval, courtiers like Lascelles protected the monarchy's privacy and public reputation through strategies honed during their fraught interactions with the biography factory. In the conventions of royal life-writing and the conditions in which biographers worked, Graham and Marriott's ostensibly discredited work was also part of the genealogy of Harold Nicolson's monumental *King George the Fifth* (1952).[7]

In the new Elizabethan age, however, official biographies and technological change transformed how intimacy and authenticity could be evoked. Written accounts of the royal nursery cultivated the illusion of personal knowledge, but competed with vibrant color television images of Elizabeth II's coronation and later scenes of the family at home. After Marion Crawford's *The Little Princesses* (1950), written by Elizabeth and Margaret's former nanny, accounts of the household from within appeared in growing numbers. Crawford's sentimental book was still considered an affront to the family's privacy.[8] The muted criticisms of Charlotte Cavendish's *H.M. Queen Mary* (1930) were exceeded by unauthorized lives more strident in tone and more consciously muckraking. Graham anticipated this, but from the 1950s the complicity of interest between the royal household and cultural power brokers began to break apart. Just as courtiers intensified their efforts to manage monarchy's public image, so a commercial mass media challenged their ability to do. Taking the biography factory seriously suggests how the erosion of deference and challenges to the establishment were animated by the imperatives of the market as much as the effects of generational social change or radical politics in midcentury Britain.

We might think of Lucas as extraordinarily prescient, and draw attention to the ways in which he anticipated and animated many of the changes that defined twentieth-century Britain. His lives sit uneasily within these genealogies, however, and frustrate any easy understanding of the relationship between then and now. From the moment of his death, Lucas was situated within a past that was bounded and distant. What looks familiar can be deceptive, and the stories Lucas told were embedded in social relations and cultural forms characteristic of the 1920s and 1930s. I have suggested how his lives informed, and were informed by, far-reaching historical processes, but have been just as interested in how Lucas inhabited postwar worlds that are not (and cannot be) our own, revealing ways of seeing and being that we might now understand as pathways not taken. It was the "radical strangeness" of his lives that first prompted me to use them to understand British society, culture, and politics after the Great War. The pathos of Lucas's death and anachronism of his lives have been my opportunity.[9]

In pursuing Lucas, I have become increasingly aware of how he also appears as an apparitional figure, a "specter outside of history," who retains the capacity to unsettle that disturbed and entertained his contemporaries. He is out of time and without time, anachronistic and achronistic.[10] Dilemmas of confidence in a society of strangers recur with new vigor in our mediated, mobile, and virtual world; the pressures of modern consumerism and popular cultures of psychology make being true to oneself a compelling personal challenge. Recent scandals over the criminal conduct of tabloid journalists, and newspaper and television images of the British royal family, have again turned journalistic ethics and practices, the beleaguered status of truth in the hands of a rapacious commercial media, and the boundaries between public and private life into hot political issues. None of these are timeless questions. The conditions in which they acquire force, the stakes they raise, and the basis on which trust can be defined and extended are configured differently in different times and places. Cultures and crises of confidence bear passing resemblance but remain always historically specific. Still, we can make the trickster's purposeful stories and the freelancer's scandalous writing carry haunting resonances for our contemporary world, if that is really what we want.

Lucas has been dead for seventy-five years but is still an uncanny presence. He vexes the work of criminologists, biographers, and historians who have enlisted him in support of their claims to knowledge. Helen Zenna Smith's *Not So Quiet* remains a touchstone of scholarship on women's writing of the Great War. Painstakingly compiled over a decade earlier this century, the *Oxford Dictionary of National Biography* includes Graham's work in the "sources" for entries on Princess Alexandra, the Duke of Connaught, and Princess Mary. The scholarly apparatus is monumental, but how much weight can it hold when it rests on case studies identified as fake?[11] Hiding deep in footnotes and bibliographies, the trickster, ghost, and discredited writer bedevils arguments he has been impressed to support, punctures the authority of those who invoke him as evidence, and draws attention to our precarious knowledge of the past. In a ludic mood, Lucas might have delighted in the irony of appearing in scholarly monographs and reference works, finding confirmation of the literary distinction he claimed. For the rest of us, his specter causes only trouble.

I have characterized Lucas's lives through words like *remarkable, audacious, success*. Perhaps my writing has taken on the clichés of 1920s journalism; perhaps I grasp instinctively for these words because they carry the story I want to tell about him. Despite the drama of his celebrity and hedonism, Lucas was not successful, however. The opportunities he found were short-lived and fragile. He might have enjoyed the rewards of crime or journalism for several weeks or months, sometimes a couple of years. Yet pleasures ended in prison, success in scandal; affluence was tempered by anxieties that would not fade. Exchanging names and stories was evidence of his creative energies and capacity for reinvention. It was also a sign that stories he had told could go no further. Notoriety, humiliation, disgrace; failed scams, failed relationships, failed lives: these also characterize his path through the 1920s and 1930s. A success? Lucas died a violent drunk, consumed by self-pity and a fire he started.

Is failure a queer art? It might be the trickster's final "refusal of mastery"— death a dramatic statement of his unwillingness to meet society's expectations. I think it also reflected an inescapable sense that the possibilities of a future had gone.[12] Storytelling was the substance of Lucas's lives. Whether charming shopkeepers or entertaining readers, stories could bring the distinction he desired and sustenance he needed. Telling stories allowed him to turn time into precarious and changeable selves.[13] For most of his adulthood, the demands of the market and interventions of the state forced Lucas to tell the same stories over and over again. Precluding any sense of lives in progress, repetition made autobiography impossible. Repeated dramas of scandal and imprisonment might have been debilitating; they also made everything Lucas tried to sell—himself included—a liability. By the mid-1930s, he could neither support himself nor understand himself, remake his lives or make sense of them. When the stories ran out, there could be no future. The claustrophobic melancholy of *My Selves*, and the violence and alcoholism of his hungry thirties, might have betrayed an impossible sense of being trapped by circumstances not entirely of his own making. Lucas's lives could be remarkable, but in the end he and they could go nowhere.

Think of Lucas as a modern Penelope. He was not waiting for an absent lover, nor did he exemplify the virtues of fidelity and patience, but for at least two decades he never stopped weaving stories only to then undo them. The threads of Lucas's lives unraveled at the end of his needle. Around 1920 he worked images of the debonair gentleman and the resources of everyday consumerism into credit and stories of aristocratic status. Later he ventriloquized contradictory ideas of the reformed criminal and aristocrat of crooks. He improvised compelling effects of authenticity that brought huge rewards yet always threatened to break apart. All the time, Lucas compulsively undid his own stories. Playful and knowing, he teased readers and hinted at the shortcuts on which those stories rested. In his frenetic haste, he left frayed edges and loose ends that others later unraveled. Following the threads of ghosted lives, fabricated news, and bogus biographies, detectives and journalists found evidence of his cynical deceptions. Lucas's stories were also unstitched publicly and catastrophically. Over and over again he recommenced his labors, only to run out of time in June 1940. Now I am the one unraveling Lucas's stories. I weave the gossamer of his lives into my own histories, only for the threads to melt into air just as I try to pull them apart again by showing you what I am doing.[14]

I have made Netley Lucas to suggest new ways of thinking about Britain in the 1920s and 1930s, and used him to explore how we might do history differently. The Prince of Tricksters is still an apparitional subject. He changes shape, then disintegrates as we approach, exposing the limits of what we can know and unsettling the foundations upon which we work. I have found myself occupying the same terrain as Erving Goffman's account of the confidence trick. All I offer is a gambit, plausible histories and effects of verisimilitude, and something approaching a reveal. Negotiating that uncertain space where front becomes backstage, the artifice of the storytelling historian at work is betrayed in my deliberately inopportune slips.[15] This book is still weighed down by the conventional apparatus of historical scholarship, however, and I have taken care to leave behind the dust of my archival labors. Each numbered note stands in for research I want you to know I have done, for my professional training and accumulated knowledge. Together this hall of mirrors creates the basis upon which I seek your trust. Of course, if you look carefully, you will see the forgeries that fill my references, and realize how the numbers only really guarantee that I know how to play the game: Netley Lucas has taught me well.[16]

I am done with him now. He is out of my hands—he is your problem, and you have to consider the claims I am making on your confidence. You can trust me; I'm telling you stories.

GAMBIT

1. The most interesting sketches of Lucas's life are Percy Smith, *Plutocrats of Crime: A Gallery of Confidence Tricksters* (London: Frederick Muller, 1960), chap. 8; and Steve Holland, "Netley Lucas," *Bear Alley*, 24 September 2008, accessed 3 December 2013, http://bearalley. blogspot.co.uk/2008/09/netley-lucas.html. See also Richard Whittington-Eagan, "The Netley Lucas Story," *New Law Journal* 150, no. 6942 (2000): 1–2; and "Lucas, Netley Evelyn (1903–1940)," *Scoop*, accessed 27 August 2014, http://www.scoop-database.com/bio/lucas_netley _evelyn. Lucas appears in James Morton and Hilary Bateson, *Conned: Scams, Frauds and Swindles* (London: Portrait, 2007), 156–57; James Morton, *Gangland Soho* (London: Piatkus, 2008), 44; and Nuala O'Faolain, *The Story of Chicago May* (London: Michael Joseph, 2005), 264–75. For Patrick Kennedy's 2012–13 production *Halbwelt Kultur*, see *Halbwelt Kultur*, accessed 1 September 2014, https://www.facebook.com/HalbweltKultur/info.

2. Paul Ricoeur, *Time and Narrative*, vol. 1, trans. Kathleen McLaughlin and David Pellauer (Chicago and London: University of Chicago Press, 1984), 3, 52; Stephanie Newell, *The Forger's Tale: The Search for Odeziaku* (Athens: Ohio University Press, 2006); and Partha Chatterjee, *A Princely Impostor? The Strange and Universal History of the Kumar of Bhawal* (Princeton, NJ: Princeton University Press, 2002), 128–31.

3. Patrick Balfour, *Society Racket: A Critical Survey of Modern Social Life* (Leipzig: Bernard Tauchnitz, 1934).

4. Ann Fabian, *The Unvarnished Truth: Personal Narratives in Nineteenth-Century America* (Berkeley and Los Angeles: University of California Press, 2001), 98; Nicholas Owen, "'Facts Are Sacred': The *Manchester Guardian* and Colonial Violence, 1930–32," *Journal of Modern History* 84, no. 3 (2012): 643–78; Ann Laura Stoler, *Along the Archival Grain: Epistemic Anxieties and Colonial Common Sense* (Princeton, NJ: Princeton University Press, 2009); Ken Alder, "A Social History of Untruth: Lie Detection and Trust in Twentieth-Century America," *Representations* 80, no. 1 (2002): 1–33; Hagen Schulz-Forberg, *London-Berlin: Authenticity, Modernity, and the Metropolis in Urban Travel Writing from 1851 to 1939* (Brussels: PIE-Peter Lang, 2006); Stephen Casper, "Trust, Protocol, Gender, and Power in Interwar British Biomedical

Research: Kathleen Chevassut and the 'Germ' of Multiple Sclerosis," *Journal of the History of Medicine and Allied Sciences* 66, no. 2 (2010): 180–215; Steven Shapin, *A Social History of Truth: Civility and Science in Seventeenth-Century England* (Chicago: University of Chicago Press, 1994); and Michael Pettit, *The Science of Deception: Psychology and Commerce in America* (Chicago: University of Chicago Press, 2013).

5. David Trotter, *Literature in the First Media Age: Britain between the Wars* (Cambridge, MA: Harvard University Press, 2013).

6. "Exploits of Prince of Pretenders," *Empire News*, 2 May 1920, 2; and Ronald Blythe, *The Age of Illusion: England in the Twenties and Thirties* (London: Hamish Hamilton, 1963), 15. On the confidence trickster, see William Meier, *Property Crime in London, 1850–Present* (Houndmills, UK: Palgrave Macmillan, 2011), chap. 4.

7. Todd Herzog, *Crime Stories: Criminalistic Fantasy and the Culture of Crisis in Weimar Germany* (New York and Oxford: Berghahn Books, 2009), 95–100. The interdisciplinary and transnational literature on the confidence trickster is vast. On the United States, see, e.g., Marshall Berman, *The Politics of Authenticity: Radical Individualism and the Emergence of Modern Society* (London: George Allen and Unwin, 1971), 323; Jonathan Cook, *Satirical Apocalypse: An Anatomy of Melville's "The Confidence-Man"* (Westport, CT, and London: Greenwood Press, 1996); Kathleen De Grave, *Swindler, Spy, Rebel: The Confidence Woman in Nineteenth-Century America* (Columbia and London: University of Missouri Press, 1995); Karen Halttunen, *Confidence Men and Painted Women: A Study of Middle-Class Culture in America, 1839–1870* (New Haven, CT, and London: Yale University Press, 1982); T. J. Jackson Lears, *Fables of Abundance: A Cultural History of Advertising in America* (New York: Basic Books, 1994); Gary Lindberg, *The Confidence Man in American Literature* (Oxford and New York: Oxford University Press, 1982); Stephen Mihm, *A Nation of Counterfeiters: Capitalists, Conmen and the Making of the United States* (Cambridge, MA: Harvard University Press, 2007); and Pettit, *Science of Deception*. Other work includes Golfo Alexopoulos, "Portrait of a Con Artist as a Soviet Man," *Slavic Review* 57, no. 4 (1998): 774–90; Natalie Zemon Davis, *Trickster Travels: A Sixteenth-Century Muslim between Worlds* (London: Faber and Faber, 2007); Ian Duffield, "Identity Fraud: Interrogating the Impostures of 'Robert de Bruce Keith Stewart' in Early Nineteenth-Century Penang and Calcutta," *Journal of Social History* 45, no. 2 (2011): 390–415; Sheila Fitzpatrick, *Tear Off the Masks! Identity and Imposture in Twentieth-Century Russia* (Princeton, NJ: Princeton University Press, 2005); Sheila Fitzpatrick, "The World of Ostap Bender: Soviet Confidence Men in the Stalin Period," *Slavic Review* 61, no. 3 (2002): 535–57; Valentin Groebner, *Who Are You? Identification, Deception and Surveillance in Early Modern Europe* (New York: Zone Books, 2007); Jennine Hurl-Eamon, "The Westminster Impostors: Impersonating Law Enforcement in Early Eighteenth-Century London," *Eighteenth-Century Studies* 38, no. 3 (2005): 461–83; Paul Jankowski, *Stavisky: A Confidence Man in the Republic of Virtue* (Ithaca, NY: Cornell University Press, 2002); Thomas Kidd, "Passing as a Pastor: Clerical Imposture in the Colonial Atlantic World," *Religion and American Culture* 14, no. 2 (2004): 149–74; James Lander, "A Tale of Two Hoaxes in Britain and France in 1775," *Historical Journal* 49, no. 4 (2006): 995–1024; Kirsten McKenzie, *A Swindler's Progress: Nobles and Convicts in the Age of Liberty* (Cambridge, MA: Harvard University Press, 2010); Newell, *Forger's Tale*; Hershel Parker, *The Powell Papers: A Confidence Man Amok among the Anglo-American Literati* (Evanston, IL: Northwestern

University Press, 2011); and Keith Walden, *Becoming Modern in Toronto: The Industrial Exhibition and the Shaping of a Late Victorian Culture* (Toronto: University of Toronto Press, 1997).

8. James Vernon, *Distant Strangers: How Britain Became Modern* (Berkeley: University of California Press, 2014).

9. Erving Goffman, "On Cooling the Mark Out: Some Aspects of Adaptation to Failure," *Psychiatry* 15, no. 4 (1952): 451–63; and Erving Goffman, *The Presentation of Self in Everyday Life* (New York: Anchor Books, 1959). For the association with advertising, see Guy Debord, *Society of the Spectacle* (Detroit: Black and Red, 1970); and Jean Baudrillard, *Simulacra and Simulation* (Ann Arbor: University of Michigan Press, 1994).

10. Modris Eksteins, *Rites of Spring: The Great War and the Birth of the Modern Age* (London: Bantam Press, 1989); Nicoletta Gullace, *The Blood of Our Sons: Men, Women, and the Renegotiation of British Citizenship during the Great War* (Basingstoke, UK: Palgrave, 2002); David Hendy, "Representing the Fragmented Mind: Reinterpreting a Classic Radio Feature as 'Sonic Psychology,'" *Radio Journal* 11, no. 1 (2013): 29–45; Samuel Hynes, *A War Imagined: The First World War and English Culture* (London: Pimlico, 1990); Susan Kingsley Kent, *Aftershocks: Politics and Trauma in Britain, 1918–1931* (Houndmills, UK: Palgrave Macmillan, 2009); Seth Koven, "Remembering and Dismemberment: Crippled Children, Wounded Soldiers, and the Memory of the Great War in Great Britain," *American Historical Review* 99, no. 4 (1994); and Katy Price, *Loving Faster Than Light: Romance and Readers in Einstein's Universe* (Chicago: University of Chicago Press, 2012).

11. I draw on Laura Doan, "Topsy-Turvydom: Gender Inversion, Sapphism, and the Great War," *GLQ* 12, no. 4 (2006): 517–42. On selfhood and authenticity, see, e.g., Richard Sennett, *The Fall of Public Man* (New York: Knopf, 1977); Lionel Trilling, *Sincerity and Authenticity* (Oxford: Oxford University Press, 1972), 93; Theodor Adorno, *The Jargon of Authenticity* (London: Routledge and Kegan Paul, 1973); Debord, *Society of the Spectacle*; Berman, *Politics of Authenticity*; Charles Taylor, *Sources of the Self: The Making of Modern Identity* (Cambridge: Cambridge University Press, 1989); and Charles Taylor, *The Ethics of Authenticity* (Cambridge, MA: Harvard University Press, 1991), 39–41.

12. Miles Orvell, *The Real Thing: Imitation and Authenticity in American Culture, 1880–1940* (Chapel Hill: University of North Carolina Press, 1989), xv, xxiii. See also Hillel Schwartz, *The Culture of the Copy: Striking Likenesses, Unreasonable Facsimiles* (New York: Zone Books, 1996), 17; Lara Kriegel, "Culture and the Copy: Calico, Capitalism and Design Copyright in Early Victorian Britain," *Journal of British Studies* 43, no. 2 (2004): 233–65; and Timothy Brown, *Weimar Radicals: Nazis and Communists between Authenticity and Performance* (New York and Oxford: Berghahn, 2009).

13. Henry Rhodes, *The Craft of Forgery* (London: John Murray, 1934), 39.

14. Robert Graves and Alan Hodge, *The Long Week-End* (London: Faber and Faber, 1940), 180, 283–84.

15. Balfour, *Society Racket*, 176; and Herbert Cescinsky, *The Gentle Art of Faking Furniture* (London: Chapman and Hall, 1931).

16. Bernard Wasserstein, *The Secret Lives of Trebitsch Lincoln* (New Haven, CT, and London: Yale University Press, 1988). See also Andrew Cook, *Cash for Honours: The Story of Maundy Gregory* (Stroud, UK: History Press, 2008); Richard Rayner, *Drake's Fortune: The*

Fabulous True Story of the World's Greatest Confidence Artist (New York: Anchor Books, 2002); and Martyn Downer, *The Sultan of Zanzibar: The Bizarre World and Spectacular Hoaxes of Horace de Vere Cole* (London: Black Spring Press, 2011). On the masquerade, see Lucy Bland, "British Eugenics and 'Race Crossing': A Study of an Interwar Investigation," *New Formations* 60 (2007): 66–78; Angus McLaren, "Smoke and Mirrors: Willy Clarkson and the Role of Disguises in Inter-war England," *Journal of Social History* 40, no. 3 (2007): 597–618; Alison Oram, *"Her Husband Was a Woman!" Women's Gender Crossing and Modern British Popular Culture* (London: Routledge, 2007); and James Vernon, " 'For Some Queer Reason': The Trials and Tribulations of Colonel Barker's Masquerade in Interwar Britain," *Signs* 26, no. 1 (2000): 37–62.

17. Alison Light, *Forever England: Femininity, Literature and Conservatism between the Wars* (London and New York: Routledge, 1991), 97, 61–97; Linden Peach, *Masquerade, Crime and Fiction: Criminal Deceptions* (Houndmills, UK: Palgrave Macmillan, 2006), 54–55; and *Rich and Strange*, directed by Alfred Hitchcock (1931).

18. "The Human Machine," *John Bull*, 3 July 1926, 8; and "Have They No Shame?" *John Bull*, 16 January 1926, 21.

19. Joan Scott, "Storytelling," *History and Theory* 50, no. 2 (2011): 205. See also Alain Corbin, *The Life of an Unknown: The Rediscovered World of a Clog Maker in Nineteenth-Century France* (New York: Columbia University Press, 2001); Zemon Davis, *Trickster Travels*; Seth Koven, *The Match Girl and the Heiress* (Princeton, NJ: Princeton University Press, 2015); Sarah Maza, *Violette: A Story of Murder in 1930s Paris* (Berkeley and Los Angeles: University of California Press, 2011); Carlo Ginzburg, *The Cheese and the Worms: The Cosmos of a Sixteenth-Century Miller* (Baltimore: Johns Hopkins University Press, 1992); McKenzie, *Swindler's Progress*, 294; Carolyn Steedman, *Landscape for a Good Woman* (London: Virago, 1986), 5; and Mrinalini Sinha, *Specters of Mother India: The Global Restructuring of an Empire* (Durham, NC: Duke University Press, 2006).

20. The most powerful statement of this position is still Ross McKibbin, *Classes and Cultures: England, 1918–51* (Oxford: Oxford University Press, 2000). See also Selina Todd, "Class, Experience, and Britain's Twentieth Century," *Social History* 39, no. 4 (2014): 489–508. For an alternative, see James Hinton, " 'The "Class" Complex': Mass Observation and Cultural Distinction in Prewar Britain," *Past and Present* 199, no. 1 (2008): 207–36; and Dan LeMahieu, *A Culture for Democracy: Mass Communication and the Cultivated Mind in Britain between the Wars* (Oxford: Clarendon Press, 1988).

21. Luisa Passerini, *Europe in Love, Love in Europe: Imagination and Politics in Britain between the Wars* (London: I. B. Tauris, 1999); and Judith Walkowitz, *Nights Out: Life in Cosmopolitan London* (New Haven, CT, and London: Yale University Press, 2012).

22. George Orwell, *Down and Out in Paris and London* (London: Victor Gollancz, 1933).

23. Max Saunders, *Self Impression: Life-Writing, Autobiografiction, and the Forms of Modern Literature* (Oxford: Oxford University Press, 2010), 510.

24. Stefan Collini, "Plain Speaking: The Lives of George Orwell," in Stefan Collini, *Common Reading: Critics, Historians, Publics*, 72–83 (Oxford: Oxford University Press, 2008); Robert Colls, *George Orwell: English Rebel* (Oxford: Oxford University Press, 2013); and Bernard Crick, *George Orwell: A Life* (London: Penguin, 1992).

25. Raymond Williams, "Culture Is Ordinary" [1958], in Raymond Williams, *Resources of Hope: Culture, Democracy, Socialism*, 3–14 (London: Verso, 1989).

26. Lawrence Napper, *British Cinema and Middlebrow Culture in the Interwar Years* (Exeter, UK: Exeter University Press, 2009), 7, 8. See also Jane Shaw, *Octavia, Daughter of God: The Story of a Female Messiah and Her Followers* (London: Jonathan Cape, 2011); Elizabeth Darling, *Reforming Britain: Narratives of Modernity before Reconstruction* (London: Routledge, 2007); Richard Hornsey, "Listening to the Tube Map: Rhythm and the Historiography of Urban Map Use," *Environment and Planning D* 30, no. 4 (2012): 675–93; Richard Hornsey, "'He Who Thinks, in Modern Traffic, Is Lost': Automation and the Pedestrian Rhythms of Interwar London," in *Geographies of Rhythm: Nature, Place, Mobilities and Bodies*, ed. Tim Edensor (Aldershot, UK: Ashgate, 2012); John Lucas, *The Radical Twenties: Aspects of Writing, Politics, and Culture* (London: Fives Leaves Publications, 1997); and Trotter, *Literature in the First Media Age*. Traditional accounts of the period include Juliet Gardiner, *The Thirties: An Intimate History of Britain* (London: Harper, 2011); Graves and Hodge, *Long Week-End*; Roy Hattersley, *Borrowed Time: The Story of Britain between the Wars* (London: Abacus, 2009); Kingsley Kent, *Aftershocks*; Richard Overy, *The Morbid Age: Britain and the Crisis of Civilization, 1919–39* (London: Penguin, 2010); and Martin Pugh, *We Danced All Night: A Social History of Britain between the Wars* (London: Vintage, 2009).

27. Saunders, *Self Impression*, 508–9; Ricoeur, *Time and Narrative*, 1:3, 1:52; and Todd Herzog, "Crime Stories: Criminal, Society, and the Modernist Case History," *Representations* 80, no. 1 (2002): 34–35.

28. "Public Schoolboy's Own Story of Exploits as a Crook," *People*, 1 July 1923, 7.

29. *Autobiography*, frontispiece, 18; and *My Selves*, 2.

30. Netley Evelyn, certified copy of an entry of birth, Fawley, New Forest (21 July 1903), number 490; General Register Office application number 1388087-1; and "Deaths Registered in July, August and September 1903," *FreeBMD Death Index, 1837–1915*, vol. 2b, p. 391, accessed 5 August 2014, www.ancestry.co.uk. On the *Scorpion*, see *My Selves*, 2; and "Auctions," *Evening News*, 29 March 1904, 4.

31. *My Selves*, 1.

32. "The Great Gale," *Sheffield Daily Telegraph*, 12 September 1903, 8; and "Auctions," *Evening News*, 29 March 1904, 4.

33. Netley Lucas, "Four Years of My Life-Story," *World's Pictorial News*, 12 August 1922, 14.

34. This account draws upon *Census Returns of England and Wales, 1851*, class HO107, piece 1605, folio 490, p. 20, accessed 13 March 2015, www.ancestry.co.uk; *Census Returns of England and Wales, 1861*, class RG9, piece 461, folio 10, p. 19; *Census Returns of England and Wales, 1871*, class RG10, piece 864, folio 65, p. 3; *Census Returns of England and Wales, 1881*, class RG11, piece 85, folio 83, p. 7, accessed 13 March 2015, www.ancestry.co.uk; *Census Returns of England and Wales, 1891*, class RG12, piece 62, folio 4, p. 4, accessed 13 March 2015, www.ancestry.co.uk; *Post Office London Directory* (London: Kelly's Directories, 1902), p. 1887; "Commissions," *Times*, 12 June 1858, 5; "The Levee," *Times*, 7 April 1870, 10; "Levee at St James's Palace," *Standard*, 13 March 1883, 3; "The Queen's Levee," *Morning Post*, 18 March 1884, 3; "Creditors' Meetings," *Times*, 19 December 1905, 13; and "Bankruptcy Notices," *Daily Express*, 2 December 1905, 2.

35. Hubert Lucas and Mina Cresswell, Register of Marriages in St George Hanover Square (26 November 1892), no. 113; General Register Office application no. 1389929/1; *Census Returns of England and Wales, 1891*, class RG12, piece 62, folio 4, p. 4, accessed 13 March 2015, www

.ancestry.co.uk; TNA, J/77/585/17879: *Herbert Lucas versus Mina Lucas* (1896); "Mina Leigh's Tour," *Era*, 9 February 1895; "Provincial Theatricals," *Era*, 30 March 1895; "*La Tosca*," *Isle of Wight Observer*, 8 June 1895, 5; and "The Stage and the Age," *Newcastle Weekly Courant*, 28 December 1895.

36. "Theatrical Gossip," *Era*, 18 March 1899; "Globe Theatre," *Daily News*, 3 October 1899; and "On Tour," *Daily Mail*, 13 June 1902, 7.

37. "Mystery of an English Actor's Death," *Nottingham Evening Post*, 5 February 1907, 3.

38. "Are Silk Shirts Necessaries?" *Birmingham Daily Post*, 9 February 1893; "In the Bankruptcy Court Today," *Pall Mall Gazette*, 24 February 1894; and "Receiving Orders," *Standard*, 24 January 1894, 7.

39. "Tragedy-Romance of Actor-Sailor," *Daily Mirror*, 5 February 1907, 3, 5; and "Actor's Death," *Daily Chronicle*, 5 February 1907, 5.

40. "Tragedy-Romance of Actor-Sailor," *Daily Mirror*, 5 February 1907, 3, 5; and "Tragedy-Romance of an English Actor-Sailor," *Daily Mirror*, 6 February 1907, 1.

41. *My Selves*, 2.

42. "Tragedy-Romance of Actor-Sailor," *Daily Mirror*, 5 February 1907, 3, 5; and "Actor's Romance," *Eastern Daily Mail*, 5 March 1907, 6.

43. "Funeral of 'Hubert Evelyn,'" *Daily Mirror*, 7 February 1907, 3.

44. "Actor's Tragic End," *Daily Mail*, 5 February 1907, 7; and "The Paris Tragedy," *Sussex Express*, 9 February 1907, 6.

45. TNA, J/77/582/17804 (1896).

46. "Actor's Death," *Daily Chronicle*, 5 February 1907, 5.

47. Ibid.

48. "Tragedy-Romance of an English Actor-Sailor," *Daily Mirror*, 5 February 1907, 1.

49. "Tragedy-Romance of Actor-Sailor," *Daily Mirror*, 5 February 1907, 3, 5.

50. Hubert Lucas, Certified Copy of an Entry of Birth in St Giles and Bloomsbury (26 July 1907), no. 494; and General Register Office application no. 1426806-1.

51. "Tragedy-Romance of Actor-Sailor," *Daily Mirror*, 5 February 1907, 3, 5.

52. *My Selves*, 1.

53. *Autobiography*, 18.

54. *My Selves*, 2, 5.

55. Deborah Cohen, *Family Secrets: Living with Shame from the Victorians to the Present Day* (London: Viking, 2013), 122–23; and Nadja Durbach, "Private Lives, Public Records: Illegitimacy and the Birth Certificate in Twentieth-Century Britain," *Twentieth Century British History* 25, no. 2 (2014): 305–26.

56. *Autobiography*, 19–22; *My Selves*, 5–6; and Netley Lucas, "Story of Netley Lucas," *World's Pictorial News*, 8 July 1922, 12.

57. *Calendar of the Grants of Probate and Letters of Administration*, p. 88: Alice Evelyn Lucas (28 June 1911); Bedford School, *Headmaster's Class List*, vol. 4 (17 January 1911); and *Bedford Grammar School Register* (17 January 1911).

58. *Census Returns of England and Wales, 1911*, class RG14, piece 8840, schedule no. 116, accessed 13 March 2015, www.ancestry.co.uk; Bedford School, *Headmaster's Class List* vol. 4 (17 January 1911); and *Bedford Grammar School Register* (17 January 1911).

59. BSA: Bedford School, *Headmaster's Class List*, vol. 4 (17 January 1911); BSA: *Bedford Grammar School Register* (17 January 1911); BLAS, HT/9/17/4: Bedford Grammar School Register, 1911; BLAS, HT/9/13/1: Bedford Grammar School Admission Register, 1911, accessed 13 March 2015, www.findmypast.co.uk; LMA, LCC/CH/D/PEN/1: Pentonville Remand Home, Admission and Discharge Registers (July 1917–June 1918), 461 and 468, suggests this was the highest standard Lucas reached.

60. Netley Evelyn, certified copy of an entry of birth, Fawley, New Forest (21 July 1903), no. 490; General Register Office application no. 1388087-1; "Deaths Registered in October, November and December 1913," *England and Wales, FreeBMD Death Index: 1837–1915*, vol. 3a, p. 907, accessed 5 August 2014, www.ancestry.co.uk; and D. Cohen, *Family Secrets*, 122–23.

61. *My Selves*, 8.

62. Stoler, *Along the Archival Grain*; and Patrick Joyce, *The State of Freedom: A Social History of the British State since 1800* (Cambridge: Cambridge University Press, 2013).

63. See A. Cook, *Cash for Honours*; Rayner, *Drake's Fortune*, 29; and Wasserstein, *Trebitsch Lincoln*.

64. Morris Kaplan, *Sodom on the Thames: Sex, Love and Scandal in Wilde Times* (Ithaca, NY: Cornell University Press, 2005), 287.

65. Carolyn Steedman, "On Not Writing Biography," *New Formations* 67 (2009): 17.

66. Newell, *Forger's Tale*, 18–19. See also Yirmiyahu Yovel, *The Other Within: The Marranos: Split Identity and Emerging Modernity* (Princeton, NJ: Princeton University Press, 2009), 333; Vernon, "For Some Queer Reason," 37–62; Zemon Davis, *Trickster Travels*; Lisa Cohen, *All We Know: Three Lives* (New York: Farrar, Straus and Giroux, 2012), 11; and Laura Doan, *Disturbing Practices: History, Sexuality, and Women's Experience of Modern War* (Chicago: University of Chicago Press, 2013).

67. Kali Israel, *Names and Stories: Emilia Dilke and Victorian Culture* (Oxford: Oxford University Press, 2002), 13, 9.

68. See Newell, *Forger's Tale*, 18.

69. Lauren Berlant, "What Does It Matter Who One Is?" *Critical Inquiry* 34, no. 1 (2007): 1–4.

70. Alun Munslow, *A History of History* (London and New York: Routledge, 2012), 9, 6. See also Jeremy Popkin, *History, Historians, and Autobiography* (Chicago: University of Chicago Press, 2005); Hayden White, *Metahistory: The Historical Imagination in Nineteenth-Century Europe* (Baltimore: Johns Hopkins University Press, 2014); and Hayden White, *The Content of the Form: Narrative Discourse and Historical Representation* (Baltimore: Johns Hopkins University Press, 1987).

71. Aaron Sachs, "Letters to a Tenured Historian: Imagining History as Creative Nonfiction—Or Maybe Even Poetry," *Rethinking History* 14, no. 1 (2010): 20; Greg Dening, "Writing, Rewriting the Beach: An Essay," *Rethinking History* 2, no. 2 (1998): 170; O'Faolain, *Chicago May*; and Helen Rogers, "Blogging Our Criminal Past, Part 3: Public and Creative History," *Conviction: Stories from a Nineteenth-Century Prison*, accessed 28 August 2014, http://conviction blog.com/2014/08/24/blogging-our-criminal-past-part-3-public-and-creative-history/.

72. Fraser MacDonald, "The Ruins of Erskine Beveridge," *Transactions of the Institute of British Geographers* 39, no. 4 (2014): 478.

73. On the historian as trickster, I draw on the wonderful discussion in Helen Rogers, "Blogging Our Criminal Past: Social Media, Public Engagement, and Creative History," *Law, Crime, and History* 1 (2015): 54–76; Natalie Zemon Davis, *A Passion for History: Conversations with Denis Crouzet* (Kirksville, MO: Truman State University Press, 2010), 11. On "impossible" subjects, see Martha Umphrey, "The Trouble with Harry Thaw," *Radical History Review* 62, no. 9 (1995): 12; and Claire Potter, "Queer Hoover: Sex, Lies, and Political History," *Journal of the History of Sexuality* 15, no. 3 (2006): 355–81.

74. Joan Scott, "History-Writing as Critique," in *Manifestos for History*, ed. Keith Jenkins, Sue Morgan, and Alun Munslow (London: Routledge, 2007), 34–35.

75. Munslow, *History of History*, 125.

76. See, e.g., *Autobiography*, 44–45.

77. Neil Bartlett, *Who Was That Man? A Present for Mr Oscar Wilde* (London: Serpent's Tail, 1988), 169.

78. I draw on Sharon Marcus, *Between Women: Friendship, Desire, and Marriage in Victorian England* (Princeton, NJ: Princeton University Press, 2007), 21–22.

79. Emily Robinson, "Touching the Void: Affective History and the Impossible," *Rethinking History* 14, no. 4 (2010): 503–4.

80. Jacques Derrida, *Archive Fever: A Freudian Impression* (Chicago: University of Chicago Press, 1995); Carolyn Steedman, *Dust* (Manchester, UK: Manchester University Press, 2001); Antoinette Burton, ed., *Archive Stories: Facts, Fiction and the Writing of History* (Durham, NC: Duke University Press, 2005); Christine Stansell, "Dreams," *History Workshop Journal* 62 (2006): 241–52; Mark Salber Phillips, "Distance and Historical Representation," *History Workshop Journal* 57, no. 1 (2004): 123–41; and Herman Paul, "Performing History: How Historical Scholarship Is Shaped by Epistemic Virtues," *History and Theory* 50, no. 1 (2011): 1–19.

81. Michael Roper, "The Unconscious Work of History," *Cultural and Social History* 11, no. 2 (2014): 169–93.

82. Frank Ankersmit, *Sublime Historical Experience* (Stanford, CA: Stanford University Press, 2005), 9. For a critical discussion, see Munslow, *History of History*, chaps. 7 and 8.

83. I am thinking here of Rachel Moss's fantastic blog "The Messy Intimacy of Writing History," *Meny Snoweballes*, accessed 1 September 2014, http://menysnoweballes.wordpress.com/2014/03/07/the-messy-intimacy-of-writing-history/. See also Mark Salber Phillips, "Rethinking Historical Distance: From Doctrine to Heuristic," *History and Theory* 50, no. 4 (2011): 11–23; and Reinhart Koselleck, *The Practice of Conceptual History: Timing History, Spacing Concepts* (Stanford, CA: Stanford University Press, 2002), 120–23.

CHAPTER ONE

1. Percy Smith, *Plutocrats of Crime: A Gallery of Confidence Tricksters* (London: Frederick Muller, 1960), 184–92.

2. "Boy 'Peer's' Motor Trips," *Empire News*, 1 August 1920, 1.

3. P. J. Smith, *Con Man: The Personal Reminiscences of Ex–Detective Inspector Percy Smith* (London: Herbert Jenkins, 1938), 38.

4. P. Smith, *Plutocrats of Crime*, 14, 15.

5. Henry Rhodes, *The Criminals We Deserve: A Survey of Some Aspects of Crime in the Modern World* (London: Methuen, 1937), 105.

6. Ibid., 105, 91.

7. Ibid., 94.

8. Mary Bertenshaw, *Sunrise to Sunset: A Vivid Personal Account of Life in Early Manchester* (Manchester, UK: Pan Visuals, 1980), 98–101.

9. H. Rhodes, *Criminals We Deserve*, 87–88.

10. Robert Graves and Alan Hodge, *The Long Week-End: A Social History of Great Britain, 1918–1939* (London: Faber and Faber, 1940), 95; and Katy Price, *Loving Faster Than Light: Romance and Readers in Einstein's Universe* (Chicago: University of Chicago Press, 2012).

11. Patrick Balfour, *Society Racket: A Critical Survey of Modern Social Life* (Leipzig: Bernard Tauchnitz, 1934), 254.

12. Cecil Chapman, *The Poor Man's Court of Justice: Twenty-Five Years as a Metropolitan Magistrate* (London: Hodder and Staughton, 1925), 246.

13. *Autobiography*, 31–36; *My Selves*, 10–15; Stanley Scott, *The Human Side of Crook and Convict Life* (London: Hurst and Blackett, 1924), 123; and LMA, PS/IJ/W1/8: Westminster Juvenile Court, Registers (11 and 18 December 1917).

14. *Autobiography*, 38.

15. *My Selves*, 15.

16. See, e.g., "Posed as a WACC," *Daily Mail*, 26 April 1920, 10; "The Concealed Arm," *Empire News*, 27 June 1920, 3; and "Bogus Officer VC," *Evening Standard*, 3 January 1922, 5.

17. *Autobiography*, 7–8.

18. Quentin Coleville, "Jack Tar and the Gentleman Officer: The Role of Uniform in Shaping the Class and Gender Identities of British Naval Personnel, 1930–1939," *Transactions of the Royal Historical Society* 6, no. 13 (2003): 108.

19. Ibid., 113.

20. "Bogus Officers," *Empire News*, 3 February 1918, 6.

21. *Autobiography*, 38–39.

22. Ibid., 40, 42.

23. Netley Lucas, "Four Years in My Life," *World's Pictorial News*, 15 July 1922, 12.

24. *Autobiography*, 43.

25. Ibid., 43–44.

26. "A Crowded Life," *News of the World*, 1 July 1923, 5.

27. Chapman, *Poor Man's Court of Justice*, 246.

28. LMA, LCC/CH/D/PEN/1: Pentonville Remand Home, Registers (July 1917–June 1918), 461; and LMA, LCC/CH/D/PEN/7: Register of Children (October 1917–March 1918), 142.

29. Chapman, *Poor Man's Court of Justice*, 246–47. LMA, PS/IJ/W1/8 (11 and 18 December 1917; 18, 22, and 29 January, 5 February, and 12 March 1918); and LMA, LCC/CH/D/PEN/1 (July 1917–June 1918), 461.

30. LMA, LCC/CH/D/PEN/1 (July 1917–June 1918), 461.

31. *My Selves*, 31.

32. LMA, PS/BOW/A/01/68: Bow Street Police Court Register (11 and 18 January 1918).

33. LMA, LCC/CH/D/PEN/1 (July 1917–June 1918), 468; LMA, LCC/CH/D/PEN/7

(October 1917–March 1918), 159; LMA, PS/IJ/W1/8 (11 and 18 December 1917; 18, 22, and 29 January, 5 February, and 12 March 1918). I cannot find any official record of Lucas's time on the *Cornwall*. Gordon Brown, *Mate of the* Caprice (London: Seafarer Books, 1995), chap. 1; and Steve Humphries and Pamela Gordon, *Forbidden Britain: Our Secret Past, 1900–1960* (London: BBC Books, 1994), 29–35. On Lucas's escape, see *Autobiography*, 91–95.

34. S. Scott, *Human Side*, 123.

35. *Autobiography*, 140.

36. N. Lucas, "Four Years of My Life-Story," *World's Pictorial News*, 12 August 1922, 14.

37. LMA, LJ/SR/602, County of London Quarter Sessions Roll (27 July 1920); LMA, PS/WES/A/01/103 (9, 16, and 23 July 1920); and "Criminal at Seventeen," *Western Daily Press*, 28 July 1920, 8.

38. "Public Schoolboy's Own Story of Exploits as a Crook," *People*, 1 July 1923, 7.

39. LMA, LJ/SR/602 (27 July 1920).

40. Sir Harry Wilson and Edward Salmon, *United Empire: The Royal Colonial Institute Journal* (London: Isaac Pitman, 1920), 57, 370, 513.

41. N. Lucas, "Four Years of My Life-Story," *World's Pictorial News*, 12 August 1922, 14.

42. Wilson and Salmon, *United Empire*, 134, 222, 271, 401.

43. LMA, LJ/SR/602 (27 July 1920); LMA, PS/WES/A/01/103 (9, 16, and 23 July 1920); and "Posed as Peer," *Devon and Exeter Gazette*, 28 July 1920, 1.

44. "Boy 'Peer's' Motor Trips," *Empire News*, 1 August 1920, 1; and "Boy Posed as Peer," *World's Pictorial News*, 30 July 1920, 3.

45. *Autobiography*, 141.

46. Ibid., 141.

47. Ibid., 140.

48. N. Lucas, "Four Years of My Life-Story," *World's Pictorial News*, 12 August 1922, 14.

49. "Public Schoolboy's Own Story of Exploits as a Crook," *People*, 1 July 1923, 7.

50. LMA, LJ/SR/602 (27 July 1920); and LMA, PS/WES/A/01/103 (9, 16, and 23 July 1920). I have calculated the modern value of these goods using the Retail Price Index at *Measuring Worth*, accessed 19 May 2014, http://www.measuringworth.com/ukearncpi/.

51. "Supplement A: Expert and Travelling Criminals," *Police Gazette*, 18 July 1924, 1.

52. Balfour, *Society Racket*, 21, 25, 32; and Sarah Newman, "The Talk of London: Interpreting Celebrity in the British Newspaper Gossip Column, 1918–1939" (DPhil thesis, University of Oxford, 2013).

53. Marcus Collins, "The Fall of the English Gentleman: The National Character in Decline, c. 1918–1970," *Historical Research* 75, no. 187 (2002): 90–111; Eloise Moss, "'How I Had Liked This Villain! How I Had Admired Him!': A.J. Raffles and the Burglar as British Icon, 1898–1939," *Journal of British Studies* 53, no. 1 (2014): 136–61; Sarah Newman, "Gentleman, Journalist, Gentleman-Journalist: Gossip Columnists and the Professionalization of Journalism in Interwar Britain," *Journalism Studies* 14, no. 5 (2013): 698–715; Penny Corfield, "The Democratic History of the English Gentleman," *History Today* 42, no. 12 (1992): 40–47; Christine Berberich, *The Image of the English Gentleman in Twentieth-Century English Literature* (Aldershot, UK: Ashgate, 2007); and Peter Mandler, *The English National Character: The History of an Idea from Edmund Burke to Tony Blair* (New Haven, CT: Yale University Press, 2006), 165–68.

54. Andrew Miles and Mike Savage, "The Strange Survival Story of the English Gentleman, 1945–2012," *Cultural and Social History* 9, no. 4 (2012): 603.

55. "Public Schoolboy's Own Story of Exploits as a Crook," *People*, 1 July 1923, 7; and "Colonel, Captain, and Peer," *Aberdeen Journal*, 28 July 1920, 6.

56. "Supplement A: Expert and Travelling Criminals," *Police Gazette*, 18 July 1924, 1.

57. Netley Lucas, "Sidelights on Crime," *Detective*, 1 August 1924, 580; and *Autobiography*, 140.

58. *My Selves*, 41.

59. Catherine Horwood, *Keeping Up Appearances: Fashion and Class between the Wars* (Stroud, UK: Strutton Publishing, 2006), 120.

60. "West End Suits," *John Bull*, 23 February 1929, 5; and Christopher Breward, *The Hidden Consumer: Masculinities, Fashion and City Life, 1860–1914* (Manchester, UK: Manchester University Press, 1999).

61. "Boy Posed as Peer," *World's Pictorial News*, 30 July 1920, 3; and *Autobiography*, 123.

62. "Apprehensions Sought," *Police Gazette*, 2 July 1920, 1; and "Person in Custody Who May Be Wanted Elsewhere," *Police Gazette*, 6 July 1920, 8.

63. "Apprehensions Sought," *Police Gazette*, 2 July 1920, 1.

64. Eustace Jervis, *Twenty-Five Years in Six Prisons* (London: T. Fisher Unwin, 1925), 82–83.

65. Graves and Hodge, *Long Week-End*, 178; Joe Moran, "Vox Populi? The Recorded Voice and Twentieth-Century British History," *Twentieth Century British History* 25, no. 3 (2014): 461–83; and Alison Light, *Forever England: Femininity, Literature and Conservatism between the Wars* (London and New York: Routledge, 1991), 215–16.

66. *My Selves*, 162.

67. "Boy Posed as Peer," *World's Pictorial News*, 30 July 1920, 3.

68. "Boy 'Peer's' Motor Trips," *Empire News*, 1 August 1920, 1.

69. *Autobiography*, 138. On "plausibility," see, e.g., Chief Inspector William Gough, "Confidence Men," *Detective*, 2 February 1923, 46; James Berrett, *When I Was at Scotland Yard* (London: Sampson, Low, Marston, 1932), 28–29; and "Lived a Gay Life," *Empire News*, 1 February 1920, 7.

70. "Archibald Ford's Exploits," *Empire News*, 14 November 1920, 4.

71. Nina Vane, "Those Too Charming People," *Daily Mail*, 9 February 1931, 16.

72. Jervis, *Twenty-Five Years*, 170.

73. *Autobiography*, 88.

74. "Swindling of Visitors to London," *World's Pictorial News*, 10 June 1922, 11; Roy Hinds, "Treat 'Em Soft," *Detective*, 19 January 1923, 77–84; and Bruce Graeme, *Mystery on the Queen Mary* (London: Hutchinson, 1937). On the Riviera, see "Crime at Monte Carlo," *Granta*, 3 June 1927, 480. On British resorts, see Leonard Armstrong, "Swindlers of the Seaside," *Popular*, August 1925, n.p.; and Henry Leach, "The Heart of Things," *Chambers's Journal*, 30 August 1930, 610. On detective fiction, see Keith Snell, "A Drop of Water from a Stagnant Pool? Interwar Detective Fiction and the Rural Community," *Social History* 35, no. 1 (2010): 21–50; Warren Chernaik, ed., *The Art of Detective Fiction* (Basingstoke, UK: Macmillan, 2000); and Susan Rowland, *From Agatha Christie to Ruth Rendell: British Women Writers in Detective and Crime Fiction* (Houndmills, UK: Palgrave, 2001). For the association between crimes of confidence and societies of strangers, see above, p. 5.

75. P. Smith, *Con Man*, 41–42.

76. John Daniell, "The Wild West End of London," *Daily Mail*, 20 May 1919, 6; and Sidney Felstead, *The Underworld of London* (London: John Murray, 1923).

77. "Hotels and Shops Defrauded by Boy," *Register* (Adelaide), 30 October 1920, 10. Amy Milne-Smith, *London Clubland: A Cultural History of Gender and Class in Late-Victorian Britain* (Houndmills, UK: Palgrave Macmillan, 2011); and Matthew Sweet, *The West End Front: The Wartime Secrets of London's Grand Hotels* (London: Faber and Faber, 2012).

78. Basil Tozer, *Confidence Crooks and Blackmailers: Their Ways and Methods* (London: T. Werner Laurie, 1929), 135.

79. *My Selves*, 63. Netley Lucas, "Four Years of My Life-Story," *World's Pictorial News*, 12 August 1922, 14.

80. N. Lucas, "Sidelights on Crime," *Detective*, 1 August 1924, 580.

81. *London and Its Criminals*, 110.

82. "Lord Clancarty Summoned," *Times*, 13 May 1920, 13.

83. "Lord Clancarty Sent to Prison," *Times*, 24 July 1920, 7. Clancarty was imprisoned and stripped of his role as deputy lieutenant of Galway. See TNA, B/9/847: Earl of Clancarty, Court of Bankruptcy (1918); TNA, HO/144/22335: Recommendations for Displacement of Deputy Lieutenants, Earl of Clancarty (1920–39). Other cases included the Duke of Leinster, the Honourable Reginald North, George Master-Byng, Viscount Torrington, and the prominent Fascist Lady Esther Makgill: TNA, CRIM/1/237: Edward Fitzgerald (Duke of Leinster), Obtaining Money by False Pretences (1923); "Squandered £15,000," *Empire News*, 13 April 1919, 2; "Lord Torrington Acquitted," *Times*, 23 October 1925, 11; and TNA, CRIM/1/796: Lady Esther Makgill, False Pretences (10 September 1935).

84. Felstead, *Underworld of London*, 254–55.

85. *Autobiography*, 147. On this material culture, see, e.g., TNA, MEPO/3/1527: "Flash" Notes Used in a Confidence Trick (1932); and TNA, MEPO/3/1425: Assistant Commissioner Crime's Observations on "The Con Man," a *Police Journal* article (1939).

86. Jon Agar, "Modern Horrors: British Identity and Identity Cards," in *Documenting Individual Identity: The Development of State Practices in the Modern World*, ed. Jane Caplan and John Torpey, 101–20 (Princeton, NJ, and Oxford: Princeton University Press, 2001); John Torpey, *The Invention of the Passport: Surveillance, Citizenship and the State* (Cambridge: Cambridge University Press, 1999); and Valentin Groebner, *Who Are You? Identification, Deception and Surveillance in Early Modern Europe* (New York: Zone Books, 2007).

87. "A Youth's Alleged Masquerade," *Times*, 2 July 1920, 9; and "Apprehensions Sought," *Police Gazette*, 2 July 1920, 1.

88. "Traders Robbed of Millions," *News of the World*, 17 June 1923, 1; and "£1000 Long Firm Swindlers," *News of the World*, 24 June 1923, 1. For a different perspective, see Sean O'Connell, *Credit and Community: Working-Class Debt in the UK since 1880* (Oxford: Oxford University Press, 2009); and Margot Finn, *The Character of Credit: Personal Debt in English Culture, 1740–1914* (Cambridge: Cambridge University Press, 2003).

89. N. Lucas, "Four Years of My Life-Story," *World's Pictorial News*, 12 August 1922, 14.

90. *Autobiography*, 44–45.

91. "Boy 'Peer's' Motor Trips," *Empire News*, 1 August 1920, 1; and "Boy Posed as Peer," *World's Pictorial News*, 30 July 1920, 3.

92. *Autobiography*, 97.

93. "Boy 'Peer's' Motor Trips," *Empire News*, 1 August 1920, 1.

94. *Autobiography*, 148.

95. *My Selves*, 50; and *Autobiography*, 146.

96. "Colonel, Captain, and Peer," *Aberdeen Journal*, 28 July 1920, 6.

97. *My Selves*, 65.

98. "Boy 'Peer's' Motor Trips," *Empire News*, 1 August 1920, 1; "Colonel, Captain, and Peer," *Aberdeen Journal*, 28 July 1920, 6; and "Youth Who Masqueraded as a Peer," *Gloucester Journal*, 14 August 1920, 7.

99. "Boy Posed as Peer," *World's Pictorial News*, 30 July 1920, 3.

100. Ex-Detective Mark Harrison, "Dark Mysteries of Great Hotels," *Popular*, 9 May 1925, 523.

101. Netley Lucas and Guy Hart, "Two Crooks Confess," *Popular*, 25 April 1925, 415.

102. *Autobiography*, 97.

103. John Goodwin, *Sidelights on Criminal Matters* (London: Hutchinson, 1923), 48; "Gaby's Jewels Make £92,000," *People*, 4 July 1920, 4; and James Gardiner, *Gaby Deslys: A Fatal Attraction* (London: Sidgwick and Jackson, 1986).

104. N. Lucas and G. Hart, "Two Crooks Confess," *Popular Magazine*, 25 April 1925, 417.

105. Netley Lucas, "Story of Netley Lucas," *World's Pictorial News*, 8 July 1922, 12; Netley Lucas, "Pearls and the Woman," *Detective*, 15 August 1924, 637–42; "Crooks' Plot to Steal Dancer's £30,000 Pearls," *People*, 27 August 1933, 4; and *My Selves*, 42–48.

106. *My Selves*, 49.

107. *Autobiography*, 86.

108. TNA, MEPO/3/441: Theresa Agnes Skyrme alias Josephine O'Dare and others: forgery and uttering will of Edwin Docker, Minute 4BV: William Cook to Commissioner of Police (15 January 1927).

109. "Lived by His Wits," *Empire News*, 15 August 1920, 4.

110. "Youth Who Masqueraded as a Peer," *Gloucester Journal*, 14 August 1920, 7.

111. "A Crowded Life," *News of the World*, 1 July 1923, 5.

112. For Lucas's trial, see LMA, ACC/3444/PR/01/186: Wandsworth Prison, register (June–December 1920), 95–96; LMA, PS/WES/A/01/103 (1, 9, 16, and 23 July 1920); LMA: LJ/SR/602 (27 July 1920); and TNA, HO/140/361 (27 July and 10 August 1920).

113. TNA, MEPO/3/441: Minute 8e, Edward Waring Martyr (27 October 1926).

114. "My Partnership with Josephine O'Dare," *World's Pictorial News*, 5 June 1927, 3.

115. TNA, MEPO/3/441: Yandell (May 1926); Josephine O'Dare: alleged blackmail, history of inquiry (31 August 1926); and Minute 26a, Yandell to CI (29 March 1927).

116. TNA, MEPO/3/441: Minute 20d, Dolita Morton; Minute 26a, Yandell to CI (29 March 1927); and TNA, CRIM/1/394: Adrian Morton (17 February 1927).

117. TNA, MEPO/3/441: Minute 8e, Edward Waring Martyr (27 October 1926); and "British Model House: Opening Ceremony," *ITN Source*, accessed 19 July 2014, http://www.itnsource .com/fr/shotlist//RTV/1926/01/26/BGT407110816/?s=*.

118. TNA, CRIM/1/393: George Poole (23 January 1927).

119. "Secret of Society Girl's Wealth," *Reynolds's*, 19 December 1926, 8. There are longer biographies in George Dilnot, *Getting Rich Quick: An Outline of Swindles Old and New* (London:

G. Bles, 1935), chap. 14; R. Thurston Hopkins, *Famous Bank Forgeries, Robberies and Swindles* (London: Stanley Paul, 1936), chap. 7; and Mary Sophia Allen, *Lady in Blue* (London: Stanley Paul, 1936), 182–91. Jennifer Green, *Whatever Happened to Trixie Skyrme?* (Leominster, UK: Green Grass Enterprises, 2011), offers a more recent fictionalized version of O'Dare's life. For O'Dare's trial, see, e.g., TNA, MEPO/3/441 (1927); TNA, CRIM/1/393 (March 1927); TNA, CRIM/1/394 (March 1927); and HRO, CM16: Research on Theresa Skyrme, aka Josephine O'Dare (1980–2002).

120. "The O'Dare Case," *Daily Telegraph*, 2 June 1927, 6.

121. Guy Hart, "Why Trixie Skyrme Became Josephine O'Dare," *World's Pictorial News*, 19 June 1927, 1–2.

122. Guy Hart, "Josephine Tricked by Bogus Prince," *World's Pictorial News*, 26 June 1927, 11–12; and Guy Hart, "Why Trixie Skyrme Became Josephine O'Dare," *World's Pictorial News*, 19 June 1927, 1–2. See Andy Bielenberg, "Exodus: The Emigration of Southern Irish Protestants during the Irish War of Independence and the Civil War," *Past and Present* 218, no. 1 (2013): 199–233; Mo Moulton, *Ireland and the Irish in Interwar England* (Cambridge: Cambridge University Press, 2014); and Peter Martin, "Unionism: The Irish Nobility and the Revolution, 1919–23," in *The Irish Revolution, 1919–23*, ed. Joost Augusteijn (Basingstoke, UK: Palgrave, 2002).

123. TNA, MEPO/3/441: Minute 15a, Inspector Yandell to CI (18 December 1926).

124. "The Adorable Swindler Unmasked," *People*, 5 June 1927, 5; and "Miss Josephine O'Dare," *Bystander*, 9 December 1925, cover. See, e.g., "Society Girl's Adventure," *Dundee Courier*, 2 April 1925, 5; and Netley Lucas, "Country Girl Who Duped Mayfair," *Sunday News*, 5 June 1927, 5.

125. "Woman with a Derby Horse," *Daily Express*, 9 June 1926, 6; and "Beautiful Girl and Moneylenders," *People*, 13 June 1926, 3.

126. "Dress Parade at Miss O'Dare's," *Daily Express*, 11 June 1926, 6.

127. "Pursued at Monte Carlo," *Reynolds's*, 19 June 1927, 5. For this image, see "Lady Warrender and Lady Kathleen Rollo," *Tatler*, 28 January 1925, 174; and "The New Luxury Soap," *Daily Mail*, 2 October 1926, 1.

128. "Peer Thrashed in My Mayfair Flat," *Reynolds's*, 26 June 1927, 5; and Hugh Cecil, *Book of Beauty* (London: Philip Allan, 1926), 5.

129. Netley Lucas, "Country Girl Who Duped Mayfair," *Sunday News*, 5 June 1927, 5; and TNA: MEPO/3/441: Minute 4BG, Yandell to CI (4 February 1927).

130. "'Vamp' Wife Play," *Daily Mirror*, 12 August 1924, 2; "Hard to Vamp a Briton," *Daily Mirror*, 29 November 1929, 18; and R. Brimley Johnson, *Moral Poison in Modern Fiction* (London: A. M. Philpot, 1922), 28–30. For the "vamp" in crime, see, e.g., "Amazing Underworld Queen," *Sunday News*, 17 July 1927, 2.

131. TNA, MEPO/3/441: Respecting Trixie Skyrme (May 1926).

132. "The Adorable Swindler Unmasked," *People*, 5 June 1927, 5.

133. Ibid.

134. "The O'Dare Case," *Daily Telegraph*, 2 June 1927, 6.

135. "Are Men Deceived by Beauty?" *Daily Mirror*, 12 December 1921, 7.

136. M. Allen, *Lady in Blue*, 189.

137. John Goodwin, *The Soul of a Criminal* (London: Hutchinson, 1924), 213–15.

138. Frederick Wensley, *Forty Years of Scotland Yard* (London: Doubleday, 1930), 150. See

Eloise Moss, "The Scrapbooking Detective: Frederick Porter Wensley and the Limits of 'Celebrity' and 'Authority' in Interwar Britain," *Social History* 40, no. 1 (2015): 58–81.

139. See, e.g., "Girl's Sensational Career in London," *Empire News*, 1 August 1920, 1.

140. *Crook Janes*, 9–10. See also Mark Silence, "Queens of Crime," *Detective*, 18 January 1924, 485–88.

141. "A Flaxen Haired Fraud," *John Bull*, 16 February 1929, 11; and "A Rogue's Life Story," *John Bull*, 4 December 1926, 30.

142. "Bogus Peer's Love Adventures," *Daily Sketch*, 1 February 1922, 15; "Posed as a Peer," *Daily Sketch*, 4 March 1922, 2; "Love Adventures of Bogus Peer," *Evening Standard*, 31 January 1922, 8; "Lordly 'Baronet,'" *World's Pictorial News*, 4 February 1922, 2; "Ex-Convict 'Earl,'" *Weekly Dispatch*, 19 October 1924, 3; "Impersonation of a Scottish Peer," *People*, 20 August 1922, 9; and "The Mystery Laird of Drumblair," *Empire News*, 1 January 1922, 2.

143. "Letters in Little," *Daily Mail*, 3 July 1918, 2.

144. "Baroness in Bad Company," *John Bull*, 6 March 1926, 15; "The Baroness de Bunkum," *John Bull*, 1 May 1926, 17; and "Unscrupulous Frauds," *News of the World*, 8 April 1923, 5.

145. Michael Miller, *Shanghai on the Metro: Spies, Intrigue and the French between the Wars* (Berkeley and Los Angeles: University of California Press, 1994).

146. "Bogus Baron's Victims," *News of the World*, 29 April 1923, 3.

147. "'Prince of Kurdistan,'" *News of the World*, 15 April 1923, 5; and "Mystery of a 'Prince,'" *News of the World*, 8 April 1923, 3.

148. "'Prince of Kurdistan,'" *News of the World*, 15 April 1923, 5. See also "'Prince of Kurdistan' Sentenced," *Times*, 13 April 1923, 9; "Story of 'Untold Wealth,'" *People*, 2 March 1923, 3; and "Bogus Emir's New Exploit," *Sunday News*, 28 August 1927, 9.

149. "Exploits of Prince of Pretenders," *Empire News*, 2 May 1920, 2.

150. *Report of the Commissioner of Police of the Metropolis* (London: HMSO, 1900–40).

151. Dilnot, *Getting Rich Quick*, 39.

152. Hermann Mannheim, *Social Aspects of Crime in England between the Wars* (London: George Allen and Unwin, 1940), 6.

153. Ibid., 117. H. Rhodes, *Criminals We Deserve*, 91–92.

154. See "Gambit," n. 16.

155. Edgar Wallace, "Kennedy the Con Man," *Thriller*, 23 February 1929; Roy Hinds, "Treat 'Em Soft," *Detective*, 19 January 1923, 77–84; Gerald Verner, *The Con Man* (London: Wright and Brown, 1934); George Scott Moncrieff, *Café Bar: A Novel without Hero or Plot* (London: Wishart, 1932); Michael Crombie, *The Gentleman Crook* (London: Gramol, 1935); and "Confessions of a Confidence Man," *Adventure Story*, May 1927, 15–24. Light, *Forever England*, 88–98, explores these questions in middlebrow fiction.

156. TNA, MEPO/3/1457: Ernest Jacob Crane, conspiracy and attempting to obtain £11,000 by confidence trick (1931–34); TNA, MEPO/3/3050: The "Spanish Prisoner" Type Fraud (1934–51); TNA, MEPO/3/1451: James Mann, international crook, concerned in stealing from Prince Sapieha by confidence trick (1936–40); "King of the 'Con' Men Is Caught," *People*, 12 July 1931, 9; "Gang of Tricksters," *Daily Mail*, 4 September 1928, 6; "Crook Who Speaks Seven Languages," *People*, 9 April 1922, 17; "Confidence Men's £15,000 Haul," *Daily Express*, 11 August 1933, 9; and "Patsy: King of Confidence Tricksters," *Lloyd's Sunday News*, 3 June 1923, 7.

157. TNA, HO/144/22296: Gerald Francis Riviere, notorious confidence trickster and thief

who operated in England and the continent (1921–44); "Five Years for the Amazing Corrigan," *Evening News*, 17 September 1930, 1; and TNA, HO/144/22540: Michael Dennis Corrigan, confidence trickster (1926–46).

158. John Blunt, "The Confidence Trick," *Daily Mail*, 2 June 1924, 7.

159. "How to Foil Tricksters," *Daily Mail*, 24 May 1933, 9; "Trick the Confidence Trickster," *Daily Mirror*, 24 May 1933, 2; and TNA, MEPO/3/1443: Harry Ryan and Victor Brambley arrested for loitering, found to be confidence tricksters: issue of press warning to the public (1933).

160. "Doped and Robbed," *People*, 7 May 1922, 12; "Confidence Trickster Sentenced," *Times*, 9 August 1923, 5; "Taken In," *Daily Mirror*, 30 June 1926, 7; "Credulity," *Daily Mail*, 5 August 1930, 8; "Age-Old Crime," *Daily Mail*, 5 May 1923, 13; and "An Ever-Green Fraud," *Daily Mail*, 6 September 1926, 8.

161. "Polished Rogues with Raffles Touch," *World's Pictorial News*, 11 February 1922, 9.

162. H. Rhodes, *Criminals We Deserve*, 105.

163. John Collier and Iain Lang, *Just the Other Day: An Informal History of Great Britain since the War* (London: Hamish Hamilton, 1932), 29.

164. Ibid., 29. Martin Petter, " 'Temporary Gentlemen' in the Aftermath of the Great War: Rank, Status and the Ex-Officer Problem," *Historical Journal* 37, no. 1 (1994): 127–52.

165. Louise Heilgers, "The Glamour of Khaki," *Empire News*, 12 January 1919, 2.

166. Petter, "Temporary Gentlemen," 133–35.

167. J. Collier and I. Lang, *Just the Other Day*, 29.

168. P. Smith, *Con Man*, 38.

169. "A Carnival of Crooks," *Empire News*, 22 June 1919, 2.

170. Frank Mort, *Capital Affairs: London and the Making of the Permissive Society* (New Haven, CT: Yale University Press, 2010), chap. 2; and Ross McKibbin, *Classes and Cultures: England, 1918–51* (Oxford: Oxford University Press, 2000), 22–37.

171. Charles Jennings, *Them and Us: The American Invasion of British High Society* (Stroud, UK: Sutton Publishing, 2007), 142; Marcus Scriven, *Splendour and Squalor: The Disgrace and Disintegration of Three Aristocratic Dynasties* (London: Atlantic Books, 2009), 6; and D. J. Taylor, *Bright Young People: The Rise and Fall of a Generation, 1918–1940* (London: Chatto and Windus, 2007).

172. "The Back Stair Traffic in Titles," *John Bull*, 11 November 1922, 9. Andrew Cook, *Cash for Honours: The Story of Maundy Gregory* (Stroud, UK: History Press, 2008), 4.

173. Mort, *Capital Affairs*, chap. 2.

174. Balfour, *Society Racket*, 59–60.

175. Ibid., 80.

176. Ibid., 227.

177. Ibid., 232.

178. Ibid., 231.

179. D. Taylor, *Bright Young People*, 38.

180. Ibid., 51, 145.

181. Ibid., 241.

182. "A Crowded Life," *News of the World*, 1 July 1923, 5.

183. Collins, "Fall of the English Gentleman," 99.

184. Jervis, *Twenty Five Years*, 39. I draw here on Stephanie Newell, *The Forger's Tale: The Search for Odeziaku* (Athens: Ohio University Press, 2006), 27–28.

185. H. V. Morton, *The Nights of London* (London: Methuen, 1926), 63.

186. Baedeker's *London and Its Environs* (London: T. Fisher Unwin, 1923), 61. See also A. R. Hope Moncrieff, *London* (London, A. and C. Black, 1910), 128; and A. Staines Manders, *Colonials' Guide to London* (London: Fulton-Manders, 1917), 165–69.

187. John Laurence, *Everyday Swindles and How to Avoid Them* (London: C. Arthur Pearson, 1921), 9. See James Vernon, *Distant Strangers: How Britain Became Modern* (Berkeley: University of California Press, 2014), chap. 1. Detective, *The Ways of Swindlers* (London: T. H. Shepherd, 1879), is an early example.

188. Laurence, *Everyday Swindles*, 9.

189. "Gossip of London and Paris," *Empire News*, 23 May 1920, 6.

190. P. Smith, *Con Man*, 38.

191. Max Pemberton, "New Criminals and New Crimes," *Sunday Pictorial*, 29 January 1922, 7.

192. Kathy Peiss, "Making Up, Making Over: Cosmetics, Consumer Culture and Women's Identity," in *The Sex of Things: Gender and Consumption in Historical Perspective*, ed. Victoria de Grazia and Ellen Furlough (Berkley and Los Angeles: University of California Press, 1996), 312, 323; and Warren Susman, " 'Personality' and the Making of Twentieth Century Culture," in *Culture as History: The Transformation of American Society in the Twentieth Century*, 271–86 (New York: Pantheon, 1984).

193. J. Collier and I. Lang, *Just the Other Day*, 163–64.

194. Ibid.

195. Kathlyn Rhodes, "Only the Rich Are Shabby," *John Bull*, 14 September 1929, 16.

196. Judith Walkowitz, *Nights Out: Life in Cosmopolitan London* (New Haven, CT, and London: Yale University Press, 2012), chap. 5; Richard Hornsey, *The Spiv and the Architect: Unruly Life in Postwar London* (Minneapolis: University of Minnesota Press, 2010); and Mark Roodhouse, *Black Market Britain, 1939–1955* (Oxford: Oxford University Press, 2013).

197. H. Rhodes, *Criminals We Deserve*, 104. Michael Pettit, " 'The Joy in Believing': The Cardiff Giant, Commercial Deceptions, and Styles of Observation in Gilded Age America," *Isis* (2006): 97, 206, 659–77, explores these connections.

198. Graves and Hodge, *Long Week-End*, 188–89.

199. "How to Size People Up from Their Looks," *John Bull*, 31 May 1919, 15.

200. "£100 Hidden in Lines on Man's Face," *Sunday News*, 22 August 1926, 4.

201. "Your Character from a Photograph," *Popular*, 28 March 1925, 264.

202. "Develop Your Personality," *Sovereign*, November 1925, contents page.

203. "The Secret of Being a Convincing Talker," *Sovereign*, June 1925, x.

204. "Your Unsuspected Self," *John Bull*, 20 September 1919, 9.

205. Ibid.

206. "Sir John Foster Fraser's Appeal," *Weekly Dispatch*, 29 January 1928, 9.

207. "How Girls Can Cultivate the Charm of a Sweet Expression," *World's Pictorial News*, 15 June 1922, 17; and Michael Pettit, *The Science of Deception: Psychology and Commerce in America* (Chicago: University of Chicago Press, 2013), 214.

208. Graves and Hodge, *Long Week-End*, 222.

209. W. C. Gough, *From Kew Observatory to Scotland Yard* (London: Hurst and Blackett, 1927), 72.

210. Percy Smith, "They're All Here for the Confidence Trick," *Daily Mail*, 2 July 1938, 10.

211. Dilnot, *Getting Rich Quick*, 39.

212. John Goodwin, *Crook Pie* (London: Alston Rivers, 1927), 315; Angus McLaren, *Sexual Blackmail: A Modern History* (Cambridge, MA: Harvard University Press, 2002); and Angus McLaren, *The Trials of Masculinity: Policing Sexual Boundaries, 1870–1930* (Chicago: University of Chicago Press, 1997), chap. 3.

213. "Public Schoolboy's Own Story of Exploits as a Crook," *People*, 1 July 1923, 7.

214. Netley Lucas, "Four Years of My Life," *World's Pictorial News*, 29 July 1922, 12.

215. Netley Lucas, "Story of Netley Lucas," *World's Pictorial News*, 8 July 1922, 12.

216. Netley Lucas and Guy Hart, "Two Crooks Confess," *Popular*, 23 May 1925, 56; *Crooks: Confessions*, chap. 5; *My Selves*, 84–97; Gertrude Lythgoe, *The Bahama Queen: The Autobiography of Gertrude "Cleo" Lythgoe* (Mystic, CT: Flat Hammock Press, 2007), 57–58; and H. de Winton Wigley, *With the Whiskey Smugglers* (London: Daily News, 1923).

217. "Supplement A: Expert and Travelling Criminals," *Police Gazette*, 18 July 1924, 1.

218. "The Craving Weakness of Netley Lucas," *World's Pictorial News*, 30 June 1923, 2. *My Selves*, 98–99, describes his being taken back into custody but does not explain why.

219. "Trickster Prince's Fate in Fire," *News of the World*, 30 June 1940, 2.

220. "Whirled into Crime," *Hawera and Normanby Star*, 31 August 1923, 6.

221. *Autobiography*, 181; and *My Selves*, 115.

222. "How I Crossed the Atlantic for Nothing," *People*, 8 July 1923, 7.

223. *Autobiography*, 214.

224. Ibid., 191, 200.

225. Ibid., 194. The claim first appeared in "How I Crossed the Atlantic for Nothing," *People*, 8 July 1923, 7.

226. "Whirled into Crime," *Hawera and Normanby Star*, 31 August 1923, 6. S. Scott, *Human Side*, 124.

227. "How I Crossed the Atlantic for Nothing," *People*, 8 July 1923, 7.

228. "Apprehensions Sought," *Police Gazette*, 19 March 1923, 3–4; and "Portraits of Persons Wanted," *Police Gazette*, 21 March 1923.

229. "Apprehensions Sought," *Police Gazette*, 14 March 1923, 14.

230. "Apprehensions Sought," *Police Gazette*, 19 March 1923, 3–4.

231. "The Craving Weakness of Netley Lucas," *World's Pictorial News*, 30 June 1923, 2.

232. "Apprehensions Sought," *Police Gazette*, 19 March 1923, 3–4.

233. *Autobiography*, 224; and *My Selves*, 147.

234. "Swaggering Fool," *Empire News*, 1 July 1923, 4; and "A Crowded Life," *News of the World*, 1 July 1923, 5.

235. LMA, PS/WES/A/01/113 (11, 18, 22, and 23 May 1923); LMA, PS/WES/A/01/112 (5 June 1923); LMA, ACC/2385/163: Central Criminal Court: Calendar of Prisoners (26 June 1923); and "Monthly Index," *Police Gazette*, May 1923, viii.

236. H. G. Castle, *Case for the Prosecution* (London: Naldrett Press, 1956), vii.

237. P. Smith, *Plutocrats of Crime*, 185.

238. P. Smith, *Con Man*, 204.

239. Neil Bartlett, *Who Was That Man? A Present for Mr Oscar Wilde* (London: Serpent's Tail, 1988), 169.

240. *My Selves*, 41.

241. Victor Hicks, "The Only Way," *Sunday News*, 14 August 1927, 8.

242. McLaren, *Trials of Masculinity*, 109.

243. Christine Grandy, " 'Avarice' and 'Evil Doers': Profiteers, Politicians, and Popular Fiction in the 1920s," *Journal of British Studies* 50, no. 3 (2011): 689.

CHAPTER TWO

1. Stanley Scott, *The Human Side of Crook and Convict Life* (London: Hurst and Blackett, 1924), 122–23, 124.

2. Ibid., 255–56.

3. I draw on John Akomfrah's interview with Stuart Hall, *The Unfinished Conversation* (2013), accessed 22 July 2014, http://www.nae.org.uk/exhibition/the-unfinished-conversation-john/5.

4. "Apprehensions Sought," *Police Gazette*, 2 July 1920, 1; and "Apprehensions Sought," *Police Gazette*, 19 March 1923, 3–4.

5. LMA, LCC/CH/D/PEN/1: Pentonville Remand Home, registers (July 1917–June 1918), 461, 468; and LMA, LCC/CH/D/PEN/7: Register of Children (October 1917–March 1918), 142, 159.

6. LMA, PS/WES/A/01/103: Westminster Police Court Register (1, 9, 16, and 23 July 1920); LMA, ACC/3444/PR/01/186: Wandsworth Prison, register (June–December 1920), 95–96; and TNA, HO/140/361: County of London Sessions, Calendar of Prisoners (27 July and 10 August 1920).

7. "Sham Peer and Colonel," *Times*, 28 July 1920, 14; and "Boy 'Peer's' Motor Trips," *Empire News*, 1 August 1920, 1.

8. "Swaggering Fool," *Empire News*, 1 July 1923, 4.

9. "Boy Posed as Peer," *World's Pictorial News*, 30 July 1920, 3.

10. "Boy 'Peer's' Motor Trips," *Empire News*, 1 August 1920, 1.

11. "Boy Posed as Peer," *World's Pictorial News*, 30 July 1920, 3.

12. "Colonel, Captain, and Peer," *Aberdeen Journal*, 28 July 1920, 6.

13. "Boy 'Peer's' Motor Trips," *Empire News*, 1 August 1920, 1.

14. *My Selves*, 26.

15. *Autobiography*, 165.

16. " 'Colonel' in the Car," *News of the World*, 1 August 1920, 3.

17. Joan Sutherland, "Why People Masquerade," *Daily Chronicle*, 17 May 1929, 7. Stephanie Newell, *The Forger's Tale: The Search for Odeziaku* (Athens: Ohio University Press, 2006), 28–30, discusses the association between deception and the clerk's ambiguous social position.

18. Hermann Mannheim, *Social Aspects of Crime in England between the Wars* (London: George Allen and Unwin, 1940), 110.

19. John Goodwin, *Sidelights on Criminal Matters* (London: Hutchinson, 1923), 295.

20. Ibid., 296.

21. "Public Schoolboy's Own Story of Exploits as a Crook," *People*, 1 July 1923, 7.

22. "Sham Peer and Colonel," *Times*, 28 July 1920, 14.

23. "Posed as Peer at 17," *News of the World*, 15 August 1920, 3.

24. "Youth Who Masqueraded as a Peer," *Gloucester Journal*, 14 August 1920, 7.

25. "Boy 'Peer's' Motor Trips," *Empire News*, 1 August 1920, 1.

26. Cecil Chapman, *The Poor Man's Court of Justice: Twenty-Five Years as a Metropolitan Magistrate* (London: Hodder and Staughton, 1925), 247.

27. " 'Colonel' in the Car," *News of the World*, 1 August 1920, 3.

28. "Boy 'Peer's' Motor Trips," *Empire News*, 1 August 1920, 1.

29. "The Craving Weakness of Netley Lucas," *World's Pictorial News*, 30 June 1923, 2.

30. "Whirled into Crime," *Hawera and Normanby Star*, 31 August 1923, 6.

31. "A Crowded Life," *News of the World*, 1 July 1923, 5.

32. *Autobiography*, 7.

33. *My Selves*, 69–70.

34. *Autobiography*, 11.

35. Eustace Jervis, *Twenty-Five Years in Six Prisons* (London: T. Fisher Unwin, 1925), 167.

36. *Autobiography*, 11.

37. Ibid., 12.

38. Ibid.

39. Netley Lucas, "Story of Netley Lucas," *World's Pictorial News*, 8 July 1922, 12.

40. Netley Lucas, "Four Years of My Life-Story," *World's Pictorial News*, 12 August 1922, 14.

41. "Swaggering Fool," *Empire News*, 1 July 1923, 4.

42. N. Lucas, "Four Years of My Life-Story," *World's Pictorial News*, 12 August 1922, 14.

43. "Public Schoolboy's Own Story of Exploits as a Crook," *People*, 1 July 1923, 7.

44. *Autobiography*, 18.

45. Ibid., 19.

46. Ibid., 20.

47. Ibid., 18–19, 21.

48. Ibid., 21.

49. Netley Lucas, "The Gentleman Crook," *Granta*, 27 February 1925, 301.

50. "Adventuress Fools London Society," *New York Times*, 2 June 1927, 6.

51. Williamina Shaw Dunn, "Pseudologia Phantastica, or Pathological Lying, in a Case of Hysteria with Moral Defect," *British Journal of Psychiatry* 62 (1916): 596.

52. C. W. Forsyth, "A Case of Pseudologia Phantastica," *British Journal of Psychiatry* 67 (1921): 82–83.

53. Hugh Grierson, "Memory and Its Disorders in Relation to Crime," *British Journal of Psychiatry* 82 (1936): 361. See also John Goodwin, *The Soul of a Criminal* (London: Hutchinson, 1924), 162–63; and William Norwood East, *Medical Aspects of Crime* (London: J. and A. Churchill, 1936), 338.

54. N. Lucas, "Four Years of My Life-Story," *World's Pictorial News*, 12 August 1922, 14.

55. *My Selves*, 199.

56. Dunn, "Pseudologia Phantastica," 597.

57. John Goodwin, *Insanity and the Criminal* (London: Hutchinson, 1923), 188.

58. Ibid., 186.

59. Goodwin, *Soul of a Criminal*, 153.

60. Ibid., 163; and William Norwood East and W. H. de B. Hubert, *Report on the Psychological Treatment of Crime* (London: HMSO, 1939), 71–72.

61. Goodwin, *Soul of a Criminal*, 163.

62. Michael Pettit, *The Science of Deception: Psychology and Commerce in America* (Chicago: University of Chicago Press, 2013), 176 and chap. 5.

63. Goodwin, *Sidelights*, 151.

64. Ibid., 152.

65. C. J. C. Earl, "Lying and Its Detection," *British Journal of Psychiatry* 79 (1933): 382; and Ken Alder, "A Social History of Untruth: Lie Detection and Trust in Twentieth-Century America," *Representations* 80, no. 1 (2002): 1–33.

66. *My Selves*, 14–15.

67. Netley Lucas, "My Life in Borstal," *Detective*, 8 May 1925, 1261.

68. *Autobiography*, 165.

69. Netley Lucas, "Four Years of My Life," *World's Pictorial News*, 29 July 1922, 12.

70. *Crooks: Confessions*, 227.

71. *My Selves*, 39. See Santanu Das, *Touch and Intimacy in First World War Literature* (Cambridge: Cambridge University Press, 2005), 99–102. George Orwell, *Homage to Catalonia* (Harmondsworth, UK: Penguin, 1962), 74–75, also discusses being lousy.

72. TNA, MEPO/3/441: Theresa Agnes Skyrme alias Josephine O'Dare and others: forgery and uttering will of Edwin Docker, Minute 48a: Josephine O'Dare to C.I. Yandell (6 August 1928).

73. *My Selves*, 31, 27.

74. *Autobiography*, 171–72, 178.

75. Ibid., 171.

76. *My Selves*, 37.

77. Ibid., 75–76.

78. *Autobiography*, 11–12.

79. *Red Stranger*, 155, chap. 11.

80. Ibid., 235.

81. Ibid., 237.

82. Ibid., 238, 245; and Netley Lucas, "The Boy Apache," *Golden*, 13 November 1926, 3.

83. "The Craving Weakness of Netley Lucas," *World's Pictorial News*, 30 June 1923, 2.

84. "Swaggering Fool," *Empire News*, 1 July 1923, 4.

85. *Autobiography*, 235–36.

86. *My Selves*, 147, 165.

87. Eustace Jervis, "Criminals All," *Detective*, 13 February 1925, 618.

88. *My Selves*, 147, 165. On romantic love, see Claire Langhamer, *The English in Love: The Intimate Story of an Emotional Revolution* (Oxford: Oxford University Press, 2013); and Marcus Collins, *Modern Love: An Intimate History of Men and Women in Twentieth-Century Britain* (London: Atlantic, 2003).

89. TNA, MEPO/3/441: Josephine O'Dare, William Davis and others: sentenced for forgery, larceny, fraud (18 June 1926); Guy Hart, "Pleading Guilty to Save Josephine O'Dare," *World's Pictorial News*, 12 June 1927, 1–2; and Guy Hart, "Josephine Tricked by Bogus Prince," *World's Pictorial News*, 26 June 1927, 11–12.

90. TNA, MEPO/3/441: Minute 19, D.I. Hoskins City of Hereford Police to Commissioner of Police (21 June 1923).

91. TNA, MEPO/3/441: Section 235/C/139 (1923).

92. Hart received fifteen months' hard labor; Hellier was sentenced to three years: TNA, HO/140/379: Central Criminal Court, Calendar of Prisoners (26 June 1923). I draw on "Hired Motor Car Mystery," *Evening Standard*, 5 June 1923, 6; "Collapse on Car Journey," *Evening Standard*, 12 June 1923, 2; "Like a Novelette," *News of the World*, 10 June 1923, 5; "'Penny Novelette' Court Story," *Daily Express*, 6 June 1923, 5; and TNA, MEPO/3/441: Section 222/BK/406 (18 June 1926).

93. *My Selves*, 147.

94. Hart also contributed to Lucas's series "Two Crooks Confess" and wrote about O'Dare for the *World's Pictorial News*. See, e.g., Netley Lucas and Guy Hart, "Two Crooks Confess," *Popular*, 16 May 1925, 9–13; Guy Hart, "Pleading Guilty to Save Josephine O'Dare," *World's Pictorial News*, 12 June 1927, 1–2; Guy Hart, "Josephine Tricked by Bogus Prince," *World's Pictorial News*, 26 June 1927, 11–12; and Guy Hart, "Josephine O'Dare Thrashes Countess," *World's Pictorial News*, 3 July 1927, 10.

95. *My Selves*, 166.

96. "Supplement A: Expert and Travelling Criminals," *Police Gazette*, 18 July 1924, 1.

97. TNA, MEPO/3/1605: Murder of Emily Kaye by Patrick Mahon, Statement 20: G. Armstrong Mackenzie to Patrick Mahon (5 May 1924). For Mahon's trial, see TNA, MEPO/3/1605 (1 January–31 December 1924); and TNA, HO/144/4100: Mahon, Patrick convicted at Lewes for murder (1 January–31 December 1924).

98. TNA, MEPO/3/1605: Statement 20: Mackenzie to Mahon (5 May 1924).

99. "Get-Rich-Quick Scheme That Failed," *Glasgow Weekly News*, 4 October 1924, 10.

100. "Crumble's Sensation," *Nottingham Evening Post*, 9 May 1924, 6.

101. "Get-Rich-Quick Scheme That Failed," *Glasgow Weekly News*, 4 October 1924, 10.

102. Ibid.

103. TNA, MEPO/3/1605: Statement 20: Mackenzie to Mahon (5 May 1924); and "Canadian Pacific Steamship Line: Names and Descriptions of British Passengers Embarked at the Port of Liverpool, 8 August 1924," accessed 22 August 2014, http://search.findmypast.co.uk/record?id=tna%2fbt27%2f1048000047%2f0016.

104. *My Selves*, 165.

105. Ibid., 171. Sally Gibson, *An Illustrated History of the King Edward Hotel*, accessed 6 February 2014, http://www.kingedward.ca/flash/assets/pdfs/king_edward_an_illustrated_history.pdf.

106. "Trickster Prince's Fate in Fire," *News of the World*, 30 June 1940, 2.

107. Ibid; and "Companion to a Countess," *Toronto Evening Telegram*, 30 August 1924, 1.

108. *My Selves*, 171.

109. A footnote to a silence: Christine Grandy and Steven Maynard generously gave up their

time and looked for traces of Mackenzie and Marriott in the Toronto City Archives and Ontario Archives but found nothing.

110. Netley Lucas, "Odd Tricks," *Detective*, 10 October 1924, 1008–10.

111. "Companion to a Countess," *Toronto Evening Telegram*, 30 August 1924, 1.

112. "Get-Rich-Quick Scheme That Failed," *Glasgow Weekly News*, 4 October 1924, 10; and "Companion to a Countess," *Toronto Evening Telegram*, 30 August 1924, 1.

113. "Situations Vacant," *Daily Telegraph*, 23 May 1923; and TNA, MEPO/3/441: Minute 9, Markham to D.D.I. (13 June 1923).

114. TNA, MEPO/3/441: Minute 3A, Markham to D.D.I. (30 May 1923).

115. TNA, MEPO/3/441: Minute 17, PC Fleetwood to Supt. Smith (16 June 1923); Minute 17a, R. W. Dammers to Henry Wayne (23 March 1923); and Minute 17b, Dammers to Wayne (18 May 1923).

116. TNA, MEPO/3/441: Minute 3d, C. F. Taylor to H. C. Taylor (25 May 1923); and Minute 3c, Dammers to Taylor (24 May 1923).

117. TNA, MEPO/3/441: Minute 3c, Taylor to Taylor (25 May 1923).

118. TNA, MEPO/3/441: Minute 3b, Taylor to Taylor (28 March 1923).

119. Netley Lucas, "Odd Tricks," *Detective*, 10 October 1924, 1008–10.

120. "The Palm Oil Dowager," *John Bull*, 15 November 1930, 2.

121. "Help Wanted—Female," *Toronto Daily Star*, 23 August 1924, 21; and "Companion to a Countess," *Toronto Evening Telegram*, 30 August 1924, 1.

122. "Film Beauty Contest Scandal," *John Bull*, 17 May 1930, 11.

123. "A Rogue's Resurrection," *John Bull*, 15 April 1922, 6; and "Men Who Prey on Revue Chorus Girls," *World's Pictorial News*, 11 February 1922, 11.

124. Basil Tozer, *Confidence Crooks and Blackmailers: Their Ways and Methods* (London: T. Werner Laurie, 1929), 16–17; and George Dilnot, *Getting Rich Quick: An Outline of Swindles Old and New* (London: G. Bles, 1935), 109–10.

125. "Higate the Hoaxer," *John Bull*, 19 December 1925, 14. For the new regulations, see "Cinema Schools," *Empire News*, 3 October 1920, 5. This brought the cinema into line with the licensing system used to regulate theatrical agencies. See "Stage Struck Girls," *Empire News*, 30 May 1920, 5.

126. "Learn to Act for the Cinema in Your Own Home," *John Bull*, 25 October 1919, 15.

127. "From Bank Clerk to Film Star," *Daily Mirror*, 10 April 1919, 15; and "Are You My Cinema Star?," *Empire News*, 5 September 1920, 6.

128. "Companion to a Countess," *Toronto Evening Telegram*, 30 August 1924, 1.

129. "Fooled the Girls," *Toronto Evening Telegram*, 10 September 1924, 9.

130. "Deportation of Netley Lucas," *World's Pictorial News*, 4 October 1924, 13; and "Undesirables Deported," *Advertiser* (Adelaide), 13 December 1924, 9.

131. Thanks to Steven Maynard for this point.

132. "Deportation of Netley Lucas," *World's Pictorial News*, 4 October 1924, 13.

133. "Undesirables Deported," *Advertiser* (Adelaide), 13 December 1924, 9; and "Fooled the Girls," *Toronto Evening Telegram*, 10 September 1924, 9.

134. "Companion to a Countess," *Toronto Evening Telegram*, 30 August 1924, 1.

135. "Deportation of Netley Lucas," *World's Pictorial News*, 4 October 1924, 13.

136. "Undesirables Deported," *Advertiser* (Adelaide), 13 December 1924, 9; and "Fooled the Girls," *Toronto Evening Telegram*, 10 September 1924, 9.

137. Netley Lucas, "Odd Tricks," *Detective*, 10 October 1924, 1008–10.

138. In the early 1920s, Cooper starred in films like *The Glorious Adventure* (1922), appeared on the cover of *Picturegoer*, and was featured in gossip columns like the *Evening Standard*'s "Woman's World." Philip Ziegler, *The Biography of Lady Diana Cooper* (London: Faber and Faber, 2011).

139. "Undesirables Deported," *News of the World*, 28 September 1924, 9.

140. "Companion to a Countess," *Toronto Evening Telegram*, 30 August 1924, 1.

141. *My Selves*, 172.

142. "Deportation of Netley Lucas," *World's Pictorial News*, 4 October 1924, 13; and "Companion to a Countess," *Toronto Evening Telegram*, 30 August 1924, 1.

143. *My Selves*, 172.

144. "Undesirables Deported," *Advertiser* (Adelaide), 13 December 1924, 9.

145. "Undesirables Deported," *News of the World*, 28 September, 1924, 9.

146. "Fooled the Girls," *Toronto Evening Telegram*, 10 September 1924, 9; and *My Selves*, 175.

147. "Pair Get 30 Days," *Toronto Daily Star*, 10 September 1924, 2.

148. "Fooled the Girls," *Toronto Evening Telegram*, 10 September 1924, 9.

149. "Get-Rich-Quick Scheme That Failed," *Glasgow Weekly News*, 4 October 1924, 10; and "Deportation of Netley Lucas," *World's Pictorial News*, 4 October 1924, 13.

150. "Get-Rich-Quick Scheme That Failed," *Glasgow Weekly News*, 4 October 1924, 10.

151. "Deportation of Netley Lucas," *World's Pictorial News*, 4 October 1924, 13.

152. *My Selves*, 175–80. No prison records survive, but a subsequent inquiry (prompted by concerns over the superintendent's corruption) documented conditions at Langstaff two years later. See ONT, RG 18-87, box 1: Inquiry into the Industrial Farm at Langstaff (1926).

153. "Returns of Passengers Brought to the United Kingdom in Ships Arriving from Places out of Europe: Names and Descriptions of British Passengers: S.S. *Melita*" (7 November 1924), accessed 22 August 2014, www.ancestry.co.uk. For the Pimlico address, see, e.g., TNA, MEPO/3/1605, Statement 20: Mackenzie to Mahon (5 May 1924).

154. "Supplement A: Expert and Travelling Criminals," *Police Gazette*, 18 July 1924, 1–2.

155. "Apprehensions Sought," *Police Gazette*, 2 July 1920, 1.

156. "Supplement A: Expert and Travelling Criminals," *Police Gazette*, 18 July 1924, 1–2; and Alyson Brown, "Crime, Criminal Mobility and Serial Offenders in Early Twentieth-Century Britain," *Contemporary British History* 25, no. 4 (2011): 551–68. Details of Mackenzie's Toronto conviction were added in "Supplement A: Expert and Travelling Criminals," *Police Gazette*, 21 November 1924, 7.

157. P. J. Smith, *Con Man: The Personal Reminiscences of Ex–Detective Inspector Percy Smith* (London: Herbert Jenkins, 1938), 157.

158. Ibid., 9–10.

159. TNA, MEPO/8/41: *Illustrated Circular of Confidence Tricksters and Expert Criminals* (1935), 1.

160. TNA, MEPO/8/41: *Illustrated Circular*, 6, 10. For this focus on commercial frauds and set-piece tricks, see, e.g., James Bone, *The London Perambulator* (London: Jonathan Cape,

1925), 51; and John Laurence, *Everyday Swindles and How to Avoid Them* (London: C. Arthur Pearson, 1921).

161. TNA, MEPO/8/41: *Illustrated Circular*, 3. On the prominence of Australian confidence tricksters, see, e.g., Jervis, *Twenty-Five Years*, 55–57; and TNA, MEPO/2/10108: Allegations that the Cafe Royal is frequented by known prostitutes and confidence tricksters (1910–20). On the productive nature of bureaucratic recording practices, see Julia Laite, *Common Prostitutes and Ordinary Citizens: Commercial Sex in London, 1885–1960* (Houndmills, UK: Palgrave Macmillan, 2012), chap. 6; and Stefan Slater, "Pimps, Police and Filles de Joie: Foreign Prostitution in Interwar London," *London Journal* 32, no. 1 (2007): 53–74.

162. TNA, MEPO/2/3173: Section 24/GEN/64 (8 March 1935).

163. Ibid., Section 235/GEN/3173 (20 October 1936). On crime and the coronation, see Judith Walkowitz, *Nights Out: Life in Cosmopolitan London* (New Haven, CT, and London: Yale University Press, 2012), 230–32.

164. TNA, MEPO/2/3173: *Illustrated Circular* (1935–40).

165. William Meier, *Property Crime in London, 1850–Present* (Houndmills, UK: Palgrave Macmillan, 2011), chap. 3; and George Robb, *White-Collar Crime in Modern England: Financial Fraud and Business Morality, 1845–1929* (Cambridge: Cambridge University Press, 1992), chap. 5.

166. *Report of the Commissioner of Police for the Metropolis for the Year 1937* (London: HMSO, 1938), 39.

167. Percy Smith, *Plutocrats of Crime: A Gallery of Confidence Tricksters* (London: Frederick Muller, 1960), 10.

168. Ibid., 14. On this, see Eloise Moss, "The Scrapbooking Detective: Frederick Porter Wensley and the Limits of 'Celebrity' and 'Authority' in Interwar Britain," *Social History* 40, no. 1 (2015): 58–81.

169. P. J. Smith, *Con Man: The Personal Reminiscences of Ex–Detective Inspector Percy Smith* (London: Herbert Jenkins, 1938), 37–38.

170. James Berrett, *When I Was at Scotland Yard* (London: Sampson Low, Marston, 1932), chap. 2; and Percy Savage, *Savage of Scotland Yard* (London: Hutchinson, 1934), chap. 25.

171. P. Smith, *Con Man*, 11.

172. Frederick Wensley, *Forty Years of Scotland Yard* (London: Doubleday, 1930), 153–54.

173. P. Smith, *Plutocrats of Crime*, 184.

174. Ibid. See Marcus Collins, "The Fall of the English Gentleman: The National Character in Decline, c. 1918–1970," *Historical Research* 75, no. 187 (2002): 90–111.

175. N. Lucas, "The Gentleman Crook," *Granta*, 27 February 1925, 301.

CHAPTER THREE

1. *My Selves*, 189; TNA, J/77/3711/3087: Elsie Lucas vs. Netley Lucas, wife's petition for divorce (1937): Marriage Certificate (11 June 1925); "Marriages Registered in April, May and June 1925," in *England and Wales, Marriage Index, 1916–2005*, vol. 1a, p. 992b, accessed 13 March 2015, www.findmypast.com; *Census Returns of England and Wales, 1911*, class RG14, piece 1422, accessed 13 March 2015, www.ancestry.co.uk; *England and Wales, FreeBMD Birth Index,*

1837–1915, vol. 1c, p. 178, accessed 13 March 2015, www.ancestry.co.uk; WEST, Register of Marriages (11 June 1925), accessed 13 March 2015, http://search.findmypast.co.uk/record?id=gbprs %2fm%2f492467366%2f2; and "Commercial Road 1921," accessed October 2013, http://www .stgite.org.uk/media/commercialroad1921.html.

2. *Criminal Paris*, frontispiece.

3. *My Selves*, 181.

4. Hans Rudolf Berndorff, *Espionage!* (London: Eveleigh, Nash and Grayson, 1930), 176–77.

5. "Exhibitions of the Royal Photographic Society, 1870–1915," accessed 28 October 2013, http://erps.dmu.ac.uk/exhibitor_details.php?year=1903&efn=F.+A.+Swaine; and "National Portrait Gallery: Frank Arthur Swaine," accessed 28 October 2013, http://www.npg.org.uk /collections/search/person/mp19222.

6. *Criminal Paris*, vii. For Lucas's visit to Paris, see "What They Tell Me," *T.P.'s and Cassell's Weekly*, 2 May 1925, 37.

7. *My Selves*, 181.

8. Alyson Brown, "Crime, Criminal Mobility, and Serial Offenders in Early Twentieth-Century Britain," *Contemporary British History* 25, no. 4 (2011): 560–61.

9. Shani D'Cruze, " 'Dad's Back': Mapping Masculinities, Moralities and the Law in the Novels of Margery Allingham," *Cultural and Social History* 1, no. 3 (2004): 265.

10. Sharon Marcus, *Between Women: Friendship, Desire, and Marriage in Victorian England* (Princeton, NJ: Princeton University Press, 2007), 37–38; Charles Taylor, *Sources of the Self: The Making of Modern Identity* (Cambridge: Cambridge University Press, 1989); Nikolas Rose, *Governing the Soul: The Shaping of the Private Self* (London and New York: Routledge, 1999); and Anthony Giddens, *Modernity and Self-Identity: Self and Society in the Late Modern Age* (Cambridge: Cambridge University Press, 1991).

11. N. Rose, *Governing the Soul*, 263.

12. Mathew Thomson, *Psychological Subjects: Identity, Culture and Health in Twentieth-Century Britain* (Oxford: Oxford University Press, 2006), chap. 1.

13. John Goodwin, *Crook Pie* (London: Alston Rivers, 1927), 312.

14. Mark Benney, *Gaol Delivery* (London: Longmans, 1948), 19.

15. Christopher Hilliard, *To Exercise Our Talents: The Democratization of Writing in Britain* (Cambridge, MA, and London: Harvard University Press, 2006), 5; Charles Hellier, "My Life as a Prince of Society Adventurers," *Glasgow Weekly Record*, 13 March 1926, 8, 9; George Richards, "A King of Pickpockets," *World's Pictorial News*, 12 August 1922, 12; George Smithson, *Raffles in Real Life* (London: Hutchinson, 1930); and Eddie Guerin, *Crime: The Autobiography of a Crook* (London: John Murray, 1928).

16. For earlier traditions of criminal (auto)biography, see, e.g., Helen Rogers, "The Way to Jerusalem: Reading, Writing and Reform in an Early Victorian Gaol," *Past and Present* 205 (2009): 71–104; Hal Gladfelder, *Criminality and Narrative in Eighteenth-Century England* (Baltimore: Johns Hopkins University Press, 2001); Anna Bayman, "Rogues, Conycatching and the Scribbling Crew," *History Workshop Journal* 63 (2007): 1–17; Eleanor Gordon and Gwyneth Nair, *Murder and Morality in Victorian Britain: The Story of Madeleine Smith* (Manchester, UK: Manchester University Press, 2009); Sean Grass, *The Self in the Cell: Narrating the Victorian Prisoner* (London: Routledge, 2003); and Gillian Spraggs, *Outlaws and Highwaymen:*

The Cult of the Robber in England from the Middle Ages to the Nineteenth Century (London: Pimlico, 2001).

17. Eloise Moss, "Notorious Thieves and Housebreakers: Burglary and Burglars in London, 1860–1939" (DPhil Thesis, University of Oxford, 2013).

18. *My Selves*, 186–87, 193–94.

19. "Crook, n. and adj.," *Oxford English Dictionary*, accessed 5 August 2011, http://www.oed.co.uk/viewdictionaryentry/Entry/44743; and Eric Partridge, *Dictionary of the Underworld* (London: Wordsworth, 1995), 163–64.

20. V. A. C. Gatrell, "The Decline of Theft and Violence in Victorian and Edwardian England," in *Crime and the Law: The Social History of Crime in Western Europe since 1500*, ed. V. A. C. Gatrell, Bruce Lenman, and Geoffrey Parker (London: Europa, 1980); Victor Bailey, "English Prisons, Penal Culture, and the Abatement of Imprisonment, 1895–1922," *Journal of British Studies* 36, no. 3 (1997): 285–324; and Martin Wiener, *Reconstructing the Criminal: Culture, Law and Policy in England, 1830–1914* (Cambridge: Cambridge University Press, 1990), 12–13, 190–97.

21. E. Moss, "Notorious Thieves and Housebreakers."

22. Major G. Harrison and F. C. Mitchell, *The Home Market: A Handbook of Statistics* (London: George Allen and Unwin, 1936), 100; and Press Group of Political and Economic Planning, *Report on the British Press* (London: Political and Economic Planning, 1938), 8.

23. Hamilton Fyfe, *Press Parade: Behind the Scenes of the Newspaper Racket and the Millionaires' Attempt at Dictatorship* (London: Watts, 1936), 138.

24. Tom Clarke, *My Northcliffe Diary* (London: Victor Gollancz, 1931), 199. See also John Carter Wood, *The Most Remarkable Woman in England: Poison, Celebrity and the Trials of Beatrice Pace* (Manchester, UK: Manchester University Press, 2012); Heather Shore, "Criminality and Englishness in the Aftermath: The Racecourse Wars of the 1920s," *Twentieth Century British History* 22, no. 4 (2011): 474–97; Heather Shore, "Constable Dances with Instructress: The Police and the Queen of Nightclubs in Interwar London," *Social History* 38, no. 2 (2013): 183–202; John Carter Wood, "Press, Politics and the 'Police and Public' Debates in Late-1920s Britain," *Crime, Histoire et Sociétés* 16, no. 1 (2012): 75–98; and John Carter Wood, "'The Third Degree': Press Reporting, Crime Fiction and Police Powers in 1920s Britain," *Twentieth Century British History* 21, no. 4 (2010): 464–85.

25. John Carter Wood, "'Those Who Have Had Trouble Can Sympathize with You': Press Writing, Reader Responses, and a Murder Trial in Interwar Britain," *Journal of Social History* 43, no. 2 (2009): 441.

26. Charles Pilley, *Law for Journalists* (London: Isaac Pitman, 1924), xiv.

27. Ann Fabian, *The Unvarnished Truth: Personal Narratives in Nineteenth-Century America* (Berkley and Los Angeles: University of California Press, 2001). On personal experience and literary capital, see Miles Orvell, *The Real Thing: Imitation and Authenticity in American Culture, 1880–1940* (Chapel Hill: University of North Carolina Press, 1989), xv; and Hilliard, *To Exercise Our Talents*, passim. For police memoirs, see, e.g., Haia Shpayer-Makov, "Explaining the Rise and Success of Detective Memoirs in Britain," in *Police Detectives in History, 1750–1950*, ed. Clive Emsley and Haia Shpayer-Makov, 102–7 (Aldershot, UK: Ashgate, 2006); and Paul Lawrence, "Images of Poverty and Crime: Police Memoirs in England and France at the End of the Nineteenth Century," *Crime, Histoire et Sociétés* 4, no. 1 (2000): 63–82.

28. Netley Lucas, "Vanity's Consequence," *Sovereign and Regent*, October 1925, 623.

29. *My Selves*, 104.

30. Ibid., 108; and Stanley Scott, *The Human Side of Crook and Convict Life* (London: Hurst and Blackett, 1924), 122.

31. *My Selves*, 110. The report was probably "Mrs Thompson Told of Appeal Failure," *People*, 24 December 1922, 1. See also "The Letters of Mrs Thompson," *People*, 29 October 1922, 16; and "Closing Scenes in Ilford Trial," *People*, 10 December 1922, 1, 20.

32. *My Selves*, 110. S. Scott, *Human Side*, passim. The articles began with "Life among Famous Convicts," *World's Pictorial News*, 7 October 1922, 13, and ran until "Last Days of Famous Convicts," *World's Pictorial News*, 25 November 1922, 16.

33. "Confessions of a Motor Car Bandit," *People*, 22 October 1922, 5; and *My Selves*, 112, 104–16.

34. *My Selves*, 105.

35. Ibid., 110, 112.

36. Ibid., 112–13.

37. Mike Ashley, *The Age of the Storytellers: British Popular Fiction Magazines, 1880–1950* (London: British Library and Oak Knoll Press, 2006), 66–67.

38. *My Selves*, 160. Netley Lucas, "Sidelights on Crime," *Detective*, 1 August 1924, 576–80. See also Netley Lucas, "Some Robberies I Have Committed," *Detective*, 29 August 1924, 743–52; and Netley Lucas, "Robbing the Continental Boat Trains," *Detective*, 12 September 1924, 889–91.

39. *My Selves*, 112, 105.

40. TNA, MEPO/3/441: Minute 31F, Wontner and Sons to CI (18 June 1927).

41. TNA, J/54/2130/2245: Josephine O'Dare vs. John Dicks Press (14 April 1932). The interview appeared as "Remarkable Romance of Young Mayfair Hostess," *Reynolds's*, 13 June 1926, 5.

42. The series began with Netley Lucas, "Story of Netley Lucas," *World's Pictorial News*, 8 July 1922, 12, and continued until Netley Lucas, "The Resolve of Netley Lucas," *World's Pictorial News*, 19 August 1922, 14. For a later version, see "Public Schoolboy's Own Story of Exploits as a Crook," *People*, 1 July 1923, 7; and "How I Crossed the Atlantic for Nothing," *People*, 8 July 1923, 7.

43. *Autobiography*, passim; and "A Swindler's Own Life Story," *Daily Mail*, 7 January 1925, 4. See also "Review," *Scotsman*, 11 May 1925, 2; and "Villainy of a Very Sordid and Petty Kind," *New York Times*, 9 August 1925, BR8.

44. *My Selves*, 186–87, 193–94.

45. Fergus Hume, *The Caravan Mystery* (London: Hurst and Blackett, 1926), 291; and "Hurst and Blackett," *Bookman*, May 1926, 127.

46. "Advert," *Canadian Bookman* 7, no. 5 (1925): 92; and "Advert," *Observer*, 14 November 1926, 14.

47. Mark Meredith, ed., *Who's Who in Literature* (Liverpool, UK: Literary Year Books Press, 1926), 270.

48. Netley Lucas, "The Underworld of Paris: I," *Oakland Tribune*, 1 November 1925.

49. R. L. Dearden, from material supplied by Netley Lucas, *The Autobiography of a Crook* (New York: Lincoln MacVeagh, 1925); Netley Lucas, *Crooks: Confessions* (New York: George H.

Doran, 1925); Netley Lucas, *Criminal Paris* (New York: George H. Doran, 1926); and Netley Lucas, *Ladies of the Underworld: The Beautiful, the Damned, and Those Who Get Away with It* (New York: J. H. Sears, 1927).

50. *My Selves*, 187.

51. Philip Harrison, *Free Lance Fallacies: Straight Talks to Young Writers* (London: Hutchinson, 1927); Michael Joseph, *Complete Writing for Profit* (London: Hutchinson, 1930); C. F. Carr and F. E. Stevens, *Modern Journalism: A Complete Guide to the Newspaper Craft* (London: Isaac Pitman and Sons, 1931); and Hilliard, *To Exercise Our Talents*.

52. Mark Meredith, ed., *What Editors and Publishers Want* (Liverpool, UK: Literary Year Books Press, 1924), 76, 106, 126.

53. P. Harrison, *Free Lance Fallacies*, 107; and Hilliard, *To Exercise Our Talents*, 16.

54. Ashley, *Age of the Storytellers*, 14–15, 127–29.

55. Netley Lucas, "How Bicycles Are Stolen," *Cycling*, 21 August 1925, vii.

56. Netley Lucas, "Prison Libraries," *Library World*, April 1926, 179–81.

57. Mark Meredith, ed., *Who's Who in Literature* (Liverpool, UK: Literary Year Books Press, 1927), 277.

58. Netley Lucas, "The Gentleman Crook," *Granta*, 27 February 1925, 301; Netley Lucas, "Humour behind Prison Walls," *Granta*, 12 March 1925, 340–41; and Netley Lucas, "Tragedy and Pathos in the City of Cells," *Humanist* (December 1925): 276.

59. Hilliard, *To Exercise Our Talents*, 3–4. On British authors, see Richard Altick, "The Sociology of Authorship: The Social Origins, Education and Occupations of 1100 British Writers, 1800–1935," *Bulletin of the New York Public Library* 66 (June 1962); Nigel Cross, *The Common Writer: Life in Nineteenth-Century Grub Street* (Cambridge: Cambridge University Press, 1985); Valentine Cunningham, *British Writers of the Thirties* (Oxford: Oxford University Press, 1988); Mary Hammond, *Reading, Publishing, and the Formation of Literary Taste in England, 1880–1914* (Aldershot, UK: Ashgate, 2006); Joseph MacAleer, *Popular Reading and Publishing in Britain, 1914–1950* (Oxford: Oxford University Press, 1992); Peter McDonald, *British Literary Culture and Publishing Practice, 1880–1914* (Cambridge: Cambridge University Press, 1997); David Reed, *The Popular Magazine in Britain and the United States, 1880–1960* (Toronto: University of Toronto Press, 1997); and Philip Waller, *Writers, Readers, and Reputations: Literary Life in Britain* (Oxford: Oxford University Press, 2008).

60. *My Selves*, 110, 160, 192.

61. Political and Economic Planning, *Report on the British Press*, 135, 138.

62. *My Selves*, 183, 188.

63. Netley Lucas, "The Convict's Prayer," *Pearson's*, September 1925, 228–34; and Ashley, *Age of the Storytellers*, 159–69.

64. "Bluff and Insolence," *News of the World*, 10 October 1926, 6.

65. "Armed Man," *Derby Daily Telegraph*, 27 August 1926, 1. See also Victor Carasov, *Two Gentlemen to See You, Sir: The Autobiography of a Villain* (London: Victor Gollancz, 1971).

66. "Man of Many Names," *Yorkshire Post*, 3 September 1926, 9.

67. Carasov, *Two Gentlemen to See You*, 33–35.

68. "Harrogate Hotel Theft," *Scotsman*, 3 September 1926, 9.

69. "Man of Many Names," *Yorkshire Post*, 3 September 1926, 9.

70. Carasov, *Two Gentlemen to See You*, 33–35.

71. "Mr Netley Lucas," *Yorkshire Post*, 3 September 1926, 9.

72. Sydney Moseley, *The Truth about a Journalist* (London: Isaac Pitman, 1935), 265.

73. Dan LeMahieu, *A Culture for Democracy: Mass Communication and the Cultivated Mind in Britain between the Wars* (Oxford: Clarendon Press, 1988), 22–25; Adrian Bingham, *Gender, Modernity and the Popular Press in Interwar Britain* (Oxford: Oxford University Press, 2004), 38; and Mark Hampton, "Inventing David Low: Self-Presentation, Caricature and the Culture of Journalism in Mid-twentieth Century Britain," *Twentieth Century British History* 20, no. 4 (2009): 482–512.

74. "The Sale of Scandal," *Saturday Review*, 27 November 1926; and Patrick Collier, *Modernism on Fleet Street* (Aldershot, UK: Ashgate, 2006), introduction.

75. Charles L. Ponce de Leon, *Self-Exposure: Human-Interest Journalism and the Emergence of Celebrity in America, 1890–1940* (Chapel Hill: University of North Carolina Press, 2002), 5, 29, and 40; and Paul John Eakin, *How Our Lives Become Stories: Making Selves* (Ithaca, NY: Cornell University Press, 1999), 165.

76. Paul John Eakin, *Fictions in Autobiography: Studies in the Art of Self-Invention* (Princeton, NJ: Princeton University Press, 1985), 10; and Orvell, *Real Thing*, xv.

77. Ann Fabian, "Making a Commodity of Truth: Speculations on the Career of Bernarr Mcfadden," *American Literary History* 5 (1993): 58–59.

78. *Crooks: Confessions*, 15. See Heather Shore, *London's Criminal Underworlds, c. 1720–c. 1930* (Houndmills, UK: Palgrave Macmillan, 2015).

79. George Dilnot, *Getting Rich Quick: An Outline of Swindles Old and New* (London: G. Bles, 1935), 163. The series began with Charles Hellier, "My Life as a Prince of Society Adventurers," *Glasgow Weekly Record*, 13 March 1926, 8, 9, and ran until Charles Hellier, "My Success in Guise of Rich Prince," *Weekly Record*, 29 May 1926, 20.

80. "Josephine O'Dare as She Was," *News of the World*, 5 June 1927, 1, 4. The series attributed to Hart began with Guy Hart, "My Partnership with Josephine O'Dare," *World's Pictorial News*, 5 June 1927, 3, and appeared weekly until Guy Hart, "Day in Life of Josephine O'Dare," *World's Pictorial News*, 3 July 1927, 12. The series published under O'Dare's name began with Josephine O'Dare, "My Life, My Lovers and My Love Letters," *Reynolds's*, 5 June 1927, 1, and ran weekly until Josephine O'Dare, "Mayfair Flat Scene That Ruined Josephine O'Dare," *Reynolds's*, 10 July 1927, 5; "My Life as Maid to Josephine O'Dare," *Glasgow Weekly News*, 11 June 1927, 12–14; "My Life as Maid to Josephine O'Dare," *Glasgow Weekly News*, 18 June 1927, 12–13; "Lovers Who Were Ruined by Josephine O'Dare," *Glasgow Weekly News*, 25 June 1927, 3–4; George Poole, "Never a Coward," *Sunday Mail* (Brisbane), 5 June 1927, 1; and Netley Lucas, "Country Girl Who Duped Mayfair," *Sunday News*, 5 June 1927, 5, 14.

81. "My Wasted Years," *People*, 6 July 1930, 5.

82. Ibid.

83. "Mayfair's Marriage Market," *People*, 3 August 1930, 3.

84. See below, p. 254.

85. TNA, MEPO/3/441: Minute 31a, Inspector Yandell to CI (22 June 1927).

86. "Public Schoolboy's Own Story of Exploits as a Crook," *People*, 1 July 1923, 7.

87. *Autobiography*, 7. Jervis's reminiscences were published as Eustace Jervis, *Twenty-Five Years in Six Prisons* (London: T. Fisher Unwin, 1925).

88. "A Swindler's Own Life Story," *Daily Mail*, 7 January 1925, 4.

89. Fabian, *Unvarnished Truth*, 30, 47.

90. "The Truth about My Mayfair Thieves Kitchen," *Reynolds's*, 3 July 1927, 5; "Mad-Cap Episodes," *Reynolds's*, 12 June 1927, 5, 8; and "Peer Thrashed in My Mayfair Flat," *Reynolds's*, 26 June 1927, 5, 17. On authenticity and the photo album, see Erika Hanna, "Reading Irish Women's Lives in Photo Albums: Dorothy Stokes and Her Camera, 1925–1923," *Cultural and Social History* 11, no. 2 (2014): 89–109.

91. "My Life and My Lovers," *Reynolds's*, 5 June 1927, 5, 17.

92. Netley Lucas, "Story of Netley Lucas," *World's Pictorial News*, 8 July 1922, 12.

93. Netley Lucas, "Four Years of My Life-Story," *World's Pictorial News*, 12 August 1922, 14.

94. *Crooks: Confessions*, 15–23.

95. *London and Its Criminals*, 156.

96. Ibid., vii–viii.

97. Ibid., 130, 105–10, frontispiece.

98. John Gregory, ed., *Crime from the Inside* (London: John Long, 1933), 153.

99. "In Memory of an Incident," *Daily Sketch*, 25 November 1926, n.p.; BI, WENSLEY/3/1: Scrapbook with Newspaper Cuttings (1898–1929); and Eloise Moss, "The Scrapbooking Detective: Frederick Porter Wensley and the Limits of 'Celebrity' and 'Authority' in Interwar Britain," *Social History* 40, no. 1 (2015): 58–81.

100. Frederick Porter Wensley, *Detective Days* (London: Cassell, 1930). See Hagen Schulz-Forberg, *London-Berlin: Authenticity, Modernity, and the Metropolis in Urban Travel Writing from 1851 to 1939* (Brussels: PIE-Peter Lang, 2006), 23.

101. "Advert," *Times*, 4 December 1925; and "Hurst and Blackett," *Bookman*, May 1926, 127.

102. "Stories of 'Crooks,'" *Aberdeen Journal*, 28 December 1925, 2.

103. TNA, MEPO/3/441: "Respecting Trixie Skyrme otherwise Josephine O'Dare" (May 1926).

104. "In Brief Review," *Bookman*, April 1927, 94.

105. N. Lucas, "Tragedy and Pathos in the City of Cells," *Humanist* (December 1925): 276.

106. Carolyn Steedman, *Strange Dislocations: Childhood and the Idea of Human Interiority* (Cambridge, MA: Harvard University Press, 1998), 4.

107. *Autobiography*, 18.

108. M. Thomson, *Psychological Subjects*, chap. 1; Victor Bailey, *Delinquency and Citizenship: Reclaiming the Young Offender, 1914–1948* (Oxford: Oxford University Press, 1987), 12–15; David Hendy, "Painting with Sound: The Kaleidoscopic World of Lance Sieveking, a British Radio Modernist," *Twentieth Century British History* 24, no. 2 (2013): 169–200; and David Hendy, "Representing the Fragmented Mind: Reinterpreting a Classic Radio Feature as 'Sonic Psychology,'" *Radio Journal* 11, no. 1 (2013): 29–45. John Goodwin, *Insanity and the Criminal* (London: Hutchinson, 1923), 150–53, is a good example of Freudian criminology.

109. Bailey, *Delinquency and Citizenship*, 12, 15. Cyril Burt, *The Young Delinquent* (London: University of London Press, 1925). For later life stories informed by a more rigorous and explicit psychoanalysis, see, e.g., Benney, *Gaol Delivery*, 19; and Mark Benney, *Low Company: Describing the Evolution of a Burglar* (London: Peter Davies, 1936).

110. *Autobiography*, 120.

111. Netley Lucas, "Four Years of My Life," *World's Pictorial News*, 29 July 1922, 12.

112. Bailey, *Delinquency and Citizenship*; Bailey, "English Prisons"; Katharine Bradley, "Juvenile Delinquency, the Juvenile Courts and the Settlement Movement, 1908–1950: Basil Henriques and Toynbee Hall," *Twentieth Century British History* 19, no. 2 (2008): 133–55; Alyson Brown, *Interwar Penal Policy and Crime in England: The Dartmoor Convict Prison Riot, 1932* (Houndmills, UK: Palgrave Macmillan, 2013); Pamela Cox, *Bad Girls: Gender, Justice and Welfare in Britain, 1900–1950* (Basingstoke, UK: Palgrave Macmillan, 2003); and M. Wiener, *Reconstructing the Criminal*.

113. Abigail Wills, "Delinquency, Masculinity and Citizenship in England, 1950–70," *Past and Present* 187 (2005): 159.

114. Rogers, "Way to Jerusalem," 71–104.

115. Frank Lauterbach, "From the Slums *to* the Slums: The Delimitation of Social Identity in Late-Victorian Prison Narratives," in *Captivating Subjects: Writing Confinement, Citizenship, and Nationhood in the Nineteenth Century*, ed. Jason Haslam and Julia Wright (Toronto: University of Toronto Press, 2005), 130.

116. "From Gaol to Grub Street," *Truth*, 16 December 1930, 949.

117. *Autobiography*, 11–13.

118. Ibid., 234, 254.

119. *My Selves*, 67; and *Crooks: Confessions*, 223.

120. *My Selves*, 69–70, 332.

121. Ibid., 183–84.

122. C. E. F. Rich, *Recollections of a Prison Governor* (London: Hurst and Blackett, 1932), 7–8.

123. Bailey, *Delinquency and Citizenship*, 196. On Paterson, see S. K. Ruck, ed., *Paterson on Prisons: The Collected Papers of Sir Alexander Paterson* (London: Frederick Muller, 1951).

124. Bailey, *Delinquency and Citizenship*, 192, 215.

125. TNA, HO/247/99: Borstal Association, Executive Committee Meetings Minutes (12 April 1923).

126. *My Selves*, 35–36.

127. Netley Lucas, "A Wonderful Prison," *Advertiser* (Adelaide), 18 January 1927, 17.

128. Netley Lucas, "Life at Wormwood Scrubs," *Detective*, 23 May 1924, 11–18; and Netley Lucas, "The Training Ship *Cornwall*," *Detective*, 24 October 1924, 1192–94.

129. *My Selves*, 36.

130. Juliet Gardiner, "'Searching for the Gleam': Finding Solutions to the Political and Social Problems of 1930s Britain," *History Workshop Journal* 72, no. 1 (2011): 107; and Max Saunders, *Self Impression: Life-Writing, Autobiografiction, and the Forms of Modern Literature* (Oxford: Oxford University Press, 2010), 510.

131. Sydney Moseley, *The Convict of Today* (London: Cecil Palmer, 1927), x.

132. Sydney Moseley, *The Truth about Borstal* (London: Cecil Palmer, 1926), 165.

133. Ibid., 123. Moseley's investigation was supported by the Borstal Association: TNA, HO/247/100: Minutes of Meeting (20 April 1926).

134. M. Wiener, *Reconstructing the Criminal*, 327–29.

135. Bailey, "English Prisons," 309.

136. TNA, HO/247/99: Minutes (21 January 1921). See also the letters in TNA, HO/247/99:

Minutes (29 May 1924, 14 October 1924); *Annual Report of the Borstal Association* (London: HMSO, 1922), 4–6; and *Annual Report of the Borstal Association* (London: H.M.S.O., 1924), 7.

137. D'Cruze, "Dad's Back," passim.

138. Netley Lucas, "The Only Way to Reform Criminals," *Humanist* (July 1926): 242.

139. Rich, *Recollections*, 95–97, 106.

140. N. Lucas, "Only Way to Reform Criminals," *Humanist* (July 1926): 242.

141. *Autobiography*, 174.

142. Ibid., 91.

143. Netley Lucas, "My Life in Borstal," *Detective*, 8 May 1925, 1264.

144. "From Gaol to Grub Street," *Truth*, 16 December 1930, 949.

145. N. Lucas, "The Resolve of Netley Lucas," *World's Pictorial News*, 19 August 1922, 14.

146. "The Craving Weakness of Netley Lucas," *World's Pictorial News*, 30 June 1923, 2.

147. "Public Schoolboy's Own Story of Exploits as a Crook," *People*, 1 July 1923, 7.

148. "The Editor," *Monster*, 10 April 1926, 8.

149. N. Lucas, "Four Years of My Life," *World's Pictorial News*, 29 July 1922, 12.

150. The series began with Netley Lucas, "The Borstal Boy," *Monster*, 17 April 1926, 3, 6, and ran until Netley Lucas, "The Borstal Boy," *Monster*, 3 July 1926, 2.

151. Michael Saler, " 'Clap If You Believe in Sherlock Holmes': Mass Culture and the Re-enchantment of Modernity, c. 1890–c. 1940," *Historical Journal* 46, no. 3 (2003): 620, 606–7.

152. N. Lucas, "Four Years of My Life," *World's Pictorial News*, 29 July 1922, 12; and N. Lucas, "Tragedy and Pathos in the City of Cells," *Humanist* (December 1925): 276. On photography and "authenticity," see Stephen Brooke, "Revisiting Southam Street: Class, Generation, Gender, and Race in the Photography of Roger Mayne," *Journal of British Studies* 53, no. 2 (2014): 453–96; Erika Hanna, "Photography, Truth, the State, and the Start of the Troubles," *Journal of British Studies* 54, no. 2 (2015); and Seth Koven, "Dr Barnardo's Artistic Fictions: Photography, Sexuality, and the Ragged Child in Victorian London," *Radical History Review* 69 (1997): 6–45.

153. "Supplement A: Expert and Travelling Criminals," *Police Gazette*, 18 July 1924, 1; and "Portraits of Persons Wanted," *Police Gazette*, 21 March 1923.

154. Alejandra Bronfman, "The Allure of Technology: Photographs, Statistics and the Elusive Female Criminal in 1930s Cuba," *Gender and History* 19, no. 1 (2007): 68.

155. Netley Lucas and Guy Hart, "Two Crooks Confess," *Cassell's Popular Magazine*, 25 April 1925, 415, 418.

156. Ibid., front cover.

157. *Criminal Paris*, 2–3.

158. Ibid., 117.

159. Netley Lucas, "Criminal Paris," *Hutchinson's Mystery Story Magazine*, October 1925, 23. These tensions became more pronounced in, e.g., N. Lucas, "The Underworld of Paris: I," *Oakland Tribune*, 1 November 1925.

160. Netley Lucas, "Four Years in My Life," *World's Pictorial News*, 15 July 1922, 12.

161. N. Lucas, "Vanity's Consequence," *Sovereign and Regent*, October 1925, 623. See also Netley Lucas, "Motor Car Thieving," *Detective*, 13 March 1925, 883–84.

162. *Autobiography*, 26. This discussion of domesticity draws on Deborah Cohen, *Household*

Gods: The British and Their Possessions (New Haven, CT: Yale University Press, 2006); and Matt Cook, *Queer Domesticities: Homosexuality and Home Life in Twentieth-Century London* (Houndmills, UK: Palgrave Macmillan, 2014).

163. *My Selves*, 191–92.

164. Goodwin, *Crook Pie*, 313–14.

165. *My Selves*, 191–92.

166. *Criminal Paris*, vii.

167. Ibid., 76.

168. Ibid., 76, 77, 79, 82. Netley Lucas, "Criminal Paris," *Hutchinson's Mystery Story Magazine*, December 1925, 31.

169. *London and Its Criminals*, 204, 205.

170. Ibid., 205–6. See Claire Langhamer, *The English in Love: The Intimate Story of an Emotional Revolution* (Oxford: Oxford University Press, 2013); and Marcus Collins, *Modern Love: An Intimate History of Men and Women in Twentieth-Century Britain* (London: Atlantic, 2003).

171. *London and Its Criminals*, 209.

172. *My Selves*, 192.

173. Ibid., 189.

174. Ibid., 24; and "Sociology," *Times Literary Supplement*, 5 July 1934, 479–80.

175. *Autobiography*, 53–54.

176. *My Selves*, 5–6.

177. Ibid., 16–17.

178. Ibid., 103, 77.

179. Ibid., 17.

180. Lucas, *Autobiography*, 35–36. This discussion draws on Laura Doan, *Disturbing Practices: History, Sexuality, and Women's Experience of Modern War* (Chicago: University of Chicago Press, 2013). For the queerness of the sites through which Lucas moved, see, e.g., Matt Houlbrook, *Queer London: Perils and Pleasures in the Sexual Metropolis, 1918–57* (Chicago: University of Chicago Press, 2005), passim; TNA, MH/102/170: *Cornwall*, Training Ship, Indecency among the Boys (1932); TNA, MH/102/161: Training Ship *Cornwall*, Case of Indecency by the Headmaster (1923); and TNA, MH/102/163: Training Ship *Cornwall*, Dismissal of Teacher Accused of Indecent Conduct with the Boys (1927).

181. *My Selves*, 13.

182. Ibid., 13.

183. Ibid., 14.

184. Ibid.

185. Ibid., 189.

186. *Crooks: Confessions*, 13.

187. *My Selves*, 189–90.

188. Ibid., 191.

189. Deborah Cohen, *Family Secrets: Living with Shame from the Victorians to the Present Day* (London: Viking, 2013), 183.

190. Ibid., 210.

191. P. Collier, *Modernism on Fleet Street*, 35.

192. *My Selves*, 68.

193. Cecil Chapman, *The Poor Man's Court of Justice: Twenty-Five Years as a Metropolitan Magistrate* (London: Hodder and Staughton, 1925), 247.

194. Meredith, *Who's Who in Literature* (1926), 270.

195. TNA, CRIM/1/393: George Poole (23 January 1927).

CHAPTER FOUR

1. "What They Tell Me," *T.P.'s and Cassell's Weekly*, 2 May 1925, 37.

2. Netley Lucas, *Criminal Paris* (London: Hurst and Blackett, 1926). The series began with Netley Lucas, "Criminal Paris," *Hutchinson's Mystery Story Magazine*, October 1925, 23–38, and ran over six months until N. Lucas, "Criminal Paris," *Hutchinson's Mystery Story Magazine*, March 1926, 51–59. For the *American Weekly* version, see, e.g., the series that began with N. Lucas, "The Underworld of Paris: I," *Oakland Tribune*, 1 November 1925, and ran until N. Lucas, "The Underworld of Paris: IX," *Oakland Tribune*, 6 December 1925.

3. The series began with Netley Lucas, "The Boy Apache," *Golden*, 28 August 1926, 3, and ran until N. Lucas, "The Boy Apache," *Golden*, 13 November 1926, 3.

4. Paul Fussell, *Abroad: British Literary Traveling between the Wars* (Oxford: Oxford University Press, 1980), 4.

5. J. Gerald Kennedy, *Imagining Paris: Exile, Writing and American Identity* (New Haven, CT, and London: Yale University Press, 1993); Harvey Levenstein, *Seductive Journey: American Tourists in France from Jefferson to the Jazz Age* (Chicago: University of Chicago Press, 1998); and Ernest Hemingway, *The Sun Also Rises* (New York: Scribner's, 1926).

6. Harry Greenwall, *The Underworld of Paris* (London: Stanley Paul, 1921); H. Ashton-Wolfe, *The Invisible Web: Strange Tales of the French Sûreté* (London: Hurst and Blackett, 1928); and Alfred Morain, *The Underworld of Paris: Secrets of the Sûreté* (London: Jarrolds, 1931).

7. "Starting Next Monday," *Golden*, 21 August 1926, 3. See, e.g., *Love Me Tonight*, directed by Rouben Mamoulian (1932).

8. *The Rat*, directed by Graham Cutts (1925). The film was followed by *The Triumph of the Rat*, directed by Graham Cutts (1926), and *The Return of the Rat*, directed by Graham Cutts (1929). For the "Apache dance," see also "Parisiana," *Britannia and Eve*, August 1930, 40–41, 124; and "Parisiana," *Bystander*, 30 June 1926, 838.

9. *Criminal Paris*, 16–17, 24.

10. "Underworld of Paris," *Oakland Tribune*, 1 November 1925, n.p.

11. Netley Lucas, "The Boy Apache," *Golden*, 28 August 1926, 3. The female Apache was a staple role for the biggest stars of the silent movie era, including Pola Negri in *The Shadows of Paris*, directed by Herbert Brenon (1924), and Gloria Swanson in *The Humming Bird*, directed by Sidney Olcott (1924).

12. *Queen of Hearts*, directed by Monty Banks (1934).

13. "Parisiana," *Britannia and Eve*, August 1930, 40–41, 124.

14. *The Rat*, directed by Graham Cutts (1925).

15. *Red Stranger*, 9–10.

16. Ibid., 25.

17. Ibid., 69.

18. Ibid., passim.

19. *Red Stranger*, 201.

20. Seth Koven, *Slumming: Sexual and Social Politics in Victorian London* (Princeton, NJ: Princeton University Press, 2004), 167; Diana Georgescu, "Excursions into National Specificity and European Identity: Mihail Sebastian's Interwar Travel Reportage," in *Under Eastern Eyes: A Comparative Introduction to East European Travel Writing on Europe*, ed. Wendy Bracewell and Alex Drace-Francis (Budapest and New York: Central European University Press, 2008), 297; and Anne Witchard, *Thomas Burke's Dark Chinoiserie: Limehouse Nights and the Queer Spell of Chinatown* (London: Ashgate, 2009).

21. *Criminal Paris*, 121.

22. Netley Lucas, "The Boy Apache," *Golden*, 18 September 1926, 3. If Lucas self-plagiarized, contemporaries did the same to him: H. Ashton-Wolfe, *Warped in the Making: Crimes of Love and Hate* (London: Hurst and Blackett, 1928), chap. 3, echoed the plot of the *Red Stranger*.

23. "New Books," *Aberdeen Press*, 15 September 1927, 2.

24. "The Underworld of Paris," *Dundee Courier*, 15 September 1927, 8.

25. "The Underworld of Paris," *Western Morning News*, 3 October 1927, 3.

26. "Editor's Secrets," *Monster*, 28 April 1927, 7.

27. Sydney Moseley, *The Truth about a Journalist* (London: Isaac Pitman, 1935), 289–90. See also C. F. Carr and F. E. Stevens, *Modern Journalism: A Complete Guide to the Newspaper Craft* (London: Isaac Pitman and Sons, 1931), 77; and Harold Herd, *The Making of Modern Journalism* (London: George Allen and Unwin, 1927), 99.

28. Michael Joseph, ed., *The Autobiography of a Journalist* (London: Hutchinson, 1929), 114–15.

29. Political and Economic Planning, *Report on the British Press* (London: Political and Economic Planning, 1938), 36.

30. Joseph, *Autobiography of a Journalist*, 114–15. See Mark Hampton, "Inventing David Low: Self-Presentation, Caricature and the Culture of Journalism in Mid-twentieth Century Britain," *Twentieth Century British History* 20, no. 4 (2009): 482; and Patrick Collier, *Modernism on Fleet Street* (Aldershot, UK: Ashgate, 2006), 26–27.

31. Moseley, *Truth about a Journalist*, 322–23.

32. Sidney Felstead, *The Underworld of London* (London: John Murray, 1923). On journalism and social investigation, see, e.g., W. Sydney Robinson, *Muckraker: The Scandalous Life and Times of W. T. Stead* (London: Robson Press, 2012); Koven, *Slumming*, chap. 3; and Judith Walkowitz, "The Indian Woman, the Flower Girl, and the Jew: Photojournalism in Edwardian London," *Victorian Studies* 42, no. 1 (1998): 3–46.

33. Tom Clarke, *My Northcliffe Diary* (London: Victor Gollancz, 1931), 20, 198.

34. Rob Mawby, "Chibnall Revisited: Crime Reporters, the Police, and 'Law-and-Order News,'" *British Journal of Criminology* 50, no. 6 (2010): 1068; Paul Willets, "Crime: Everything Old Is New Again," *British Journalism Review* 18, no. 2 (2007): 53–58; and Steve Chibnall, *Law-and-Order News: An Analysis of Crime Reporting in the British Press* (London: Tavistock Publications, 1977), chap. 3.

35. Political and Economic Planning, *Report on the British Press*, 17; and Judith Rowbotham,

Kim Stevenson, and Samantha Pegg, *Crime News in Modern Britain: Press Reporting and Responsibility, 1820–2010* (Houndmills, UK: Palgrave Macmillan, 2013).

36. *My Selves*, 195.

37. Ibid.

38. Ibid., 106.

39. Ibid., 195.

40. "Tragic Death at Seaside," *Sunday News*, 15 August 1926, 2; "'You Stole My Wife,'" *Sunday News*, 5 September 1926, 2; "Two Friends and a Fatal Shot," *Sunday News*, 21 November 1926, 3; and "Crowds Cheer Smith's Acquittal," *Sunday News*, 28 November 1926, 1.

41. "Boulogne Mystery," *Sydney Morning Herald*, 14 March 1927, 11.

42. *My Selves*, 195.

43. "Who Killed Nurse Daniels?" *Sunday News*, 6 March 1927, 1; "Nurse Daniels Life Story," *Sunday News*, 20 March 1927, 10, 12; "Nurse Daniels Sensation," *Sunday News*, 3 April 1927, 11; and "Nurse's Body Exhumed," *Sunday News*, 10 April 1927, 3.

44. Hamilton Fyfe, *Press Parade: Behind the Scenes of the Newspaper Racket and the Millionaires' Attempt at Dictatorship* (London: Watts, 1936), 36–37.

45. *My Selves*, 107.

46. See below, pp. 202–3.

47. *My Selves*, 195–96. For a fictional account of crime reporting, see Rose Macaulay, *Keeping Up Appearances* (London: William Collins, 1928), chaps. 20 and 11.

48. "Truth about My Husband and Myself," *Sunday News*, 5 December 1926, 11; "My Husband's Wild Escapades," *Sunday News*, 12 December 1926, 5; and "Our Early Married Life," *Sunday News*, 19 December 1926, 7.

49. "Newspapers and Contempt of Court," *Guardian*, 24 May 1924, 12.

50. Ibid.

51. Netley Lucas, "Yard Takes Gloves Off," *Sunday News*, 23 January 1927, 2.

52. Netley Lucas, "Country Girl Who Duped Mayfair," *Sunday News*, 5 June 1927, 5, 14.

53. Netley Lucas, "Big Traffic in Forged Passports," *Sunday News*, 30 January 1927, 2.

54. Netley Lucas, "Hawks of Hyde Park," *Sunday News*, 26 June 1927, 2.

55. Ibid.

56. Netley Lucas, "'Hell's Kitchens' in the West End," *Sunday News*, 27 February 1927, 2.

57. Netley Lucas, "Finger Prints Sensation," *Sunday News*, 6 February 1927, 11.

58. Netley Lucas, "Thugs of Waterloo," *Sunday News*, 13 February 1927, 11.

59. N. Lucas, "Hawks of Hyde Park," *Sunday News*, 26 June 1927, 2.

60. Carr and Stevens, *Modern Journalism*, 86.

61. Moseley, *Truth about a Journalist*, 322–23; and Mark Hampton, "Journalists and the 'Professional' Ideal in Britain: The Institute of Journalists, 1884–1907," *Historical Research* 72, no. 178 (1999): 183–201.

62. Joseph, *Autobiography of a Journalist*, 228.

63. Carr and Stevens, *Modern Journalism*.

64. Political and Economic Planning, *Report on the British Press*, 133, 12–13; Parliamentary Archives, Beaverbrook Papers BBK/H/19: wages on the *Evening Standard* and *Daily Express* (December 1930); and Sarah Newman, "Gentleman, Journalist, Gentleman-Journalist: Gossip

Columnists and the Professionalization of Journalism in Interwar Britain," *Journalism Studies* 14, no. 5 (2013): 698–715.

65. Political and Economic Planning, *Report on the British Press*, 14.

66. Ibid., 143.

67. Koven, *Slumming*, 153.

68. *My Selves*, 195.

69. Hampton, "Inventing David Low," 482; and Jean Chalaby, *The Invention of Journalism* (Houndmills, UK: Basingstoke, Macmillan, 1998).

70. Joseph, *Autobiography of a Journalist*, 18.

71. *My Selves*, 104, 106. Newman, "Gentleman, Journalist," discusses this from a different perspective.

72. Duncan Webb, *Deadline for Crime* (London: Frederick Muller, 1955), 9. For Webb see also TNA, HO/45/25638: Prostitution and Allied Offences, Messina Brothers (1947–51); TNA, MEPO/3/3037: Activities of Thomas Duncan Webb, Press Crime Reporter (1946–56); and Frank Mort, *Capital Affairs: London and the Making of the Permissive Society* (New Haven, CT: Yale University Press, 2010).

73. Duncan Webb, *Crime Is My Business* (London: Frederick Muller, 1953), 10, 95.

74. Harry Proctor, *The Street of Disillusion: Confessions of a Journalist* (London: Wingate, 1958); and Chibnall, *Law-and-Order News*, chap. 3.

75. TNA, MEPO/3/441: Minute 48, Yandell to CI (28 August 1927).

76. Ibid., Minute 20a: Yandell to CI (11 February 1927).

77. Ibid., Minute 23: A1 (19 February 1927); and Minute 24: ACC (22 February 1927).

78. "The Trapping of the Black Vampire," *Monster*, 24 July 1926, 3; and "The Case of the Kidnapped King," *Monster*, 19 February 1927, 3.

79. *Crooks: Confessions*, 91–100. Guy Hart told the same story in "Saved by Josephine's Quick Wits," *World's Pictorial News*, 19 June 1927, 2.

80. Netley Lucas, "The £10,000 Cheque Fraud," *Monster*, 12 February 1927, 3. The comment on Hellier is in *My Selves*, 148.

81. "Editorial Chit-Chat," *Golden*, 23 April 1927, 2.

82. "Wishing All Our Readers a Merry Xmas," *Golden*, 25 December 1926, 2. The series began with Netley Lucas, "Sea Dogs," *Golden*, 1 January 1927, 2, and ran until Netley Lucas, "Sea Dogs," *Golden*, 14 May 1927, 2.

83. The series began with Netley Lucas, "The Desert Watchers," *Monster*, 12 February 1927, 6, and ran until Netley Lucas, "The Desert Watchers," *Monster*, 11 June 1927, 2.

84. "The Editor's Secrets," *Monster*, 28 April 1927, 7; and W. O. G. Lofts and Derek Adley, *The Crime Fighters*, accessed 16 August 2013, http://www.philsp.com/homeville/CrFi/i0011.htm.

85. W. O. G. Lofts and Derek Adley, *The Men behind Boys' Fiction* (London: Howard Baker, 1970). This phase of the series began with "The Black Vampire," *Monster*, 10 July 1926, 3, and ran until "The Case of the Kidnapped King," *Monster*, 19 February 1927, 3.

86. "Editor's Secrets," *Monster*, 28 April 1927, 7. The series began with Netley Lucas, "Anthony Grex," *Golden*, 21 May 1927, 2 and 7, and ran weekly until Netley Lucas, "Anthony Grex," *Golden*, 28 January 1928, 3.

87. "Editor's Secrets," *Monster*, 28 April 1927, 7.

88. "Editor's Secrets," *Monster*, 2 July 1927, 7.

89. "Golden League Detective Bureau," *Golden*, 6 February 1926, 4–5.

90. "Editor's Secrets," *Monster*, 28 April 1927, 7.

91. Ibid.

92. "A Watch for Watching," *Monster*, 11 June 1927, 7.

93. "Editor's Secrets," *Monster*, 28 April 1927, 7.

94. Netley Lucas, "The Newcastle Necklace Theft," *Monster*, 18 June 1927, 6.

95. Netley Lucas, "Manchester Counterfeiters Outwitted," *Monster*, 25 June 1927, 6; Netley Lucas, "Glasgow Gunmen Foiled," *Monster*, 2 July 1927, 6; Netley Lucas, "Cardiff 'Tigers' at Bay," *Monster*, 9 July 1927, 6; and Netley Lucas, "Cradley Heath Adventurers Discover Bolshevist Secret Plant in the Steel Works," *Monster*, 1 October 1927, 6.

96. N. Lucas, "Manchester Counterfeiters Outwitted," *Monster*, 25 June 1927, 6.

97. N. Lucas, "Glasgow Gunmen Foiled," *Monster*, 2 July 1927, 6.

98. Netley Lucas, "Darky and Julia with Six Adventurers Raid a London Gambling Hell," *Monster*, 3 September 1927, 6.

99. "Editor's Secrets," *Monster*, 28 April 1927, 7.

100. "Editor's Secrets," *Monster*, 25 June 1927, 7; and "A Watch If You Watch," *Monster*, 4 June 1927, 7.

101. "A Watch for Watching," *Monster*, 18 June 1927, 7.

102. "Editor's Secrets," *Monster*, 23 July 1927, 7.

103. "Editor's Secrets," *Monster*, 25 June 1927, 7.

104. "Editor's Secrets," *Monster*, 9 July 1927, 7.

105. "Editorial," *Golden*, 17 September 1927, 2. The first story in this iteration of the series was Netley Lucas, "Anthony Grex," *Golden*, 17 September 1927, 2.

106. "Editor's Secrets," *Monster*, 16 July 1927, 7.

107. "Editor's Secrets," *Monster*, 1 October 1927, 7.

108. Netley Lucas, "Anthony Grex," *Golden*, 31 December 1927, 6.

109. Frank Fischer, *Democracy and Expertise: Reorienting Policy Inquiry* (Oxford: Oxford University Press, 2009); David Edgerton, *Warfare State: Britain, 1920–1970* (Cambridge: Cambridge University Press, 2006), 15–39; and James Vernon, *Hunger: A Modern History* (Cambridge, MA: Harvard University Press, 2008).

110. Cyril Burt, *The Young Delinquent* (London: University of London Press, 1925); William Norwood East and W. H. de B. Hubert, *Report on the Psychological Treatment of Crime* (London: HMSO, 1939); William Norwood East, *An Introduction to Forensic Psychiatry in the Criminal Courts* (London: J. and A. Churchill, 1927); Nigel Morland, *Fingerprints: An Introduction to Scientific Criminology* (London: Street and Massey, 1936); and Henry Rhodes, *The Criminal in Society* (London: L. Drummond, 1939). See Neil Davie, *Tracing the Criminal: The Rise of Scientific Criminology in Britain, 1860–1918* (Oxford: Bradwell Press, 2005); and David Garland, "Of Crimes and Criminals: The Development of Criminology in Britain," in *The Oxford Handbook of Criminology*, 3rd ed., ed. Mike Maguire, Rod Morgan, and Robert Reiner (Oxford: Oxford University Press, 2002).

111. *Criminal Paris*, xi–xii. Michel Mazévet, *Edmond Locard: Le Sherlock Holmes Français* (Brignais, France: Editions des Traboules, 2006).

112. "Sociology," *Times Literary Supplement*, 10 June 1926, 399.

113. Basil Thomson, "Three Prison Books," *Times Literary Supplement*, 19 March 1925, 186.

114. Mathew Thomson, *Psychological Subjects: Identity, Culture and Health in Twentieth-Century Britain* (Oxford: Oxford University Press, 2006).

115. John Goodwin, *Crook Pie* (London: Alston Rivers, 1927), 9–10; John Goodwin, *Sidelights on Criminal Matters* (London: Hutchinson, 1923); John Goodwin, *Insanity and the Criminal* (London: Hutchinson, 1923); and John Goodwin, *The Soul of a Criminal* (London: Hutchinson, 1924).

116. John Goodwin, *The Zig-Zag Man* (London: Hutchinson, 1925), 108.

117. *Crooks: Confessions*, v–vii.

118. Goodwin, *Crook Pie*, 108–9.

119. "Review," *Scotsman*, 25 January 1926, 2.

120. Joseph, *Autobiography of a Journalist*, 228–29.

121. "Crime and Criminals in Britain To-day," *Pictorial Weekly*, 30 April 1927, 418; and Netley Lucas, "Manchester's 'Crook Janes,'" *Pictorial Weekly*, 14 May 1927, 516.

122. Netley Lucas, "How Liverpool Fights the Lawbreaker," *Pictorial Weekly*, 7 May 1927, 449; and Netley Lucas, "Bigamists of Bradford," *Pictorial Weekly*, 21 May 1927, 28.

123. Netley Lucas, "London's Motor Bandits," *Pictorial Weekly*, 9 July 1927, 319.

124. N. Lucas, "How Liverpool Fights the Lawbreaker," *Pictorial Weekly*, 7 May 1927, 449.

125. Netley Lucas, "Cardiff's Amazing Crimes," *Pictorial Weekly*, 28 May 1927, 66.

126. Netley Lucas, "Hull's 'Young Offenders,'" *Pictorial Weekly*, 18 June 1927, 195.

127. N. Lucas, "How Liverpool Fights the Lawbreaker," *Pictorial Weekly*, 7 May 1927, 449.

128. Netley Lucas, "Cleaning Up Sheffield," *Pictorial Weekly*, 25 June 1927, 230–31.

129. N. Lucas, "Bigamists of Bradford," *Pictorial Weekly*, 21 May 1927, 27.

130. Ibid., 28.

131. N. Lucas, "Manchester's 'Crook Janes,'" *Pictorial Weekly*, 14 May 1927, 518.

132. Netley Lucas, "Why Crooks Pass Leeds," *Pictorial Weekly*, 2 July 1927, 278–79.

133. TNA, MEPO/3/268B: Netley Lucas to CI Cooper (23 July 1927).

134. Goodwin, *Crook Pie*, 311.

135. "With a Skirmishing Party in Flanders" (1915), *BFI Screenonline*, accessed 9 September 2013, http://www.screenonline.org.uk/film/id/583402/index.html.

136. Nicholas Reeves, *Official British Film Propaganda during the Great War* (London: Croom Helm, 1986), 175; *The Kinematograph Year Book 1926* (London: Kinematograph Publications, 1926), 224; and "Frederick Walderman Engholm," *News on Screen*, accessed 9 September 2013, http://bufvc.ac.uk/newsonscreen/search/index.php/person/270.

137. Goodwin, *Crook Pie*, 311. As well as filming Hawker and Grieves's *Trans-Atlantic Flight* (1919), Engholm worked for the London and North Eastern Railway and the *Daily Mail*'s Ideal Homes Exhibition. See "Frederick Engholm," *Kine Year Book 1925* (London: Kinematograph Publications, 1925), 252; " 'Daily Mail' Film in US," *Daily Mail*, 25 May 1929, 12; and "Help British Film Photographers," *Daily Mail*, 15 February 1926, 8.

138. " 'Everyday Frauds' Filmed," *Daily Mail*, 20 January 1927, 5.

139. Ibid.; and "Everyday Frauds," *Kinematograph Weekly*, 20 January 1927, 81.

140. " 'Everyday Frauds' Filmed," *Daily Mail*, 20 January 1927, 5.

141. "Everyday Frauds," *Kinematograph Weekly*, 20 January 1927, 81.

142. Goodwin, *Crook Pie*, 311; "'Everyday Frauds' Filmed," *Daily Mail*, 20 January 1927, 5; and "Everyday Frauds," *Kinematograph Weekly*, 20 January 1927, 81.

143. "Everyday Frauds," *Kinematograph Weekly*, 27 January 1927, 18.

144. "The Lighter Side," *Nottingham Evening Post*, 30 March 1926, 4.

145. "Crooks' Secrets on the Screen," *Singapore Free Press*, 22 February 1927, 3.

146. "Crooks' Secrets on the Screen," *Evening News*, 17 January 1927, 3.

147. "Crooks' Secrets on the Screen," *Singapore Free Press*, 22 February 1927, 3.

148. "'Everyday Frauds' Filmed," *Daily Mail*, 20 January 1927, 5.

149. "Everyday Frauds," *Kinematograph Weekly*, 27 January 1927, 18; and "Everyday Frauds," *Kinematograph Weekly*, 20 January 1927, 81.

150. "Entertainments," *Derby Daily Telegraph*, 26 March 1928, 4; and "Entertainments," *Angus Evening Telegraph*, 30 May 1927, 2.

151. TNA, HO/45/14276: Birmingham Cinema Enquiry Committee, Reports of Visits to Cinemas (15 May 1931).

152. *Crook Janes*, 13, 9.

153. Ibid., 38.

154. Ibid., chaps. 29 and 20.

155. "Books and Their Writers," *Dundee Courier*, 20 November 1926, 8.

156. "Reviews and Notices of Books," *British Journal of Inebriety* 25, no. 1 (July 1927): 23.

157. *London and Its Criminals*, frontispiece. I have a photograph of this copy of the book in my possession. J. M. Cameron, "Camps, Francis Edward (1905–1972)," rev. K. D. Watson, *ODNB*, accessed 10 June 2013, http://www.oxforddnb.com/view/article/30896.

158. Frank Crane, "Checking Crime," *San Antonio Light*, 16 October 1926, editorial page.

159. *Criminologist* 1, no. 1 (15 May 1927); HRC: Netley Lucas to P.E.N. (21 March 1927); and TNA, MEPO/3/268B: Lucas to CI Cooper (23 July 1927).

160. Dr. Bernard Hollander, "The Criminal from Brain Disease," *Criminologist* 1, no. 1 (15 May 1927): 3–4. Frances Hedderly, *Bernard Hollander: Pioneer, Reformer and Champion of Dr Francis Joseph Hall* (London: British Phrenological Society, 1965). Hollander's work included Bernard Hollander, *The Psychology of Misconduct, Vice and Crime* (London: Macmillan, 1923); and Bernard Hollander, *The Female Mind* (Loughborough, UK: J. Corah and Son, 1927).

161. Daniel Vyleta, *Crime, Jews and News: Vienna, 1895–1914* (New York and Oxford: Berghahn, 2007), 19–20; and Ian Burney, "Our Environment in Miniature: Dust and the Early Twentieth-Century Forensic Imagination," *Representations* 121, no. 1 (2013): 31–59.

162. Professor C. J. S. Thompson, "Poisoned Clothes," *Criminologist* 1, no. 1 (15 May 1927): 13–14. See also C. J. S. Thompson, *Poison Mysteries in History: Romance and Crime* (London: Scientific Press, 1923); and C. J. S. Thompson, *Poisons and Poisoners* (London: Harold Shaylor, 1931).

163. H. Ashton-Wolfe, "Languages and the Criminal," *Criminologist* 1, no. 1 (15 May 1927): 8–9; and Ashton-Wolfe, *Invisible Web*, xvii.

164. Ashton-Wolfe, *Warped in the Making*, frontispiece.

165. Lieutenant Colonel Edwin Richardson, "Bloodhounds as Man-Trackers," *Criminologist* 1, no. 1 (15 May 1927): 14–15. See Edwin Richardson, *Forty Years with Dogs* (London:

Hutchinson, 1918); and Edwin Richardson, *British War Dogs: Their Training and Psychology* (London: Skeffington and Son, 1920).

166. J. M. Kenworthy, "Commonsense versus Capital Punishment," *Criminologist* 1, no. 1 (15 May 1927): 6–7. See J. M. Kenworthy, *Sailors, Statesmen and Others: An Autobiography* (London: Rich and Cowan, 1933).

167. "Detectives," *Criminologist* 1, no. 1 (15 May 1927): 1.

168. Cerberus, "Potpourri of Crime," *Criminologist* 1, no. 1 (15 May 1927): 2.

169. F. A. Mackenzie, "Is Crime Made Too Fascinating?" *Daily Mirror*, 19 May 1927, 6.

170. Shani D'Cruze, " 'Dad's Back': Mapping Masculinities, Moralities, and the Law in the Novels of Margery Allingham," *Cultural and Social History* 1, no. 3 (2004): 256–79; Martin Wiener, *Reconstructing the Criminal: Culture, Law, and Policy in England, 1830–1914* (Cambridge: Cambridge University Press, 1990), 214; and John Carter Wood, " 'The Third Degree': Press Reporting, Crime Fiction and Police Powers in 1920s Britain," *Twentieth Century British History* 21, no. 4 (2010): 464–85.

171. Goodwin, *Crook Pie*, 311.

172. Emile Laurent, "Criminal Paris of To-day," *Criminologist* 1, no. 1 (15 May 1927): 5–6; and Dr. Edmond Locard, "Evolution of the Motor-Bandit," *Criminologist* 1, no. 1 (15 May 1927): 11–12.

173. Netley Lucas, "Innocent Murderers?" *Criminologist* 1, no. 1 (15 May 1927): 10–11.

174. "The Underworld of Books," *Criminologist* 1, no. 1 (15 May 1927): 19.

175. Netley Lucas, "How Criminals Use Motor Boats," *Motor Boat*, 18 September 1925, 260–61.

176. Holepicker, "Crook Life on the Screen," *Criminologist* 1, no. 1 (15 May 1927): 20.

177. HRC: Lucas to P.E.N. (21 March 1927).

178. John Gray, *Gin and Bitters* (London: Jarrolds, 1938), 296.

179. TNA, MEPO/3/268B: Netley Lucas to CI Cooper (23 July 1927).

180. "The Prince of Wales on Crime and Punishment," *Criminologist*, 15 May 1927, 4.

181. Joseph, *Autobiography of a Journalist*, 229.

182. See Mark Benney, *Low Company: Describing the Evolution of a Burglar* (London: Peter Davies, 1936); Mark Benney, *The Truth about English Prisons* (London: Fact, 1938); Mark Benney, *Charity Main: A Coalfield Chronicle* (London: Allen and Unwin, 1946); and Mark Benney, A. P. Gray, and R. H. Pear, *How People Vote: A Study of Electoral Behaviour in Greenwich* (London: Routledge, 1956).

183. Mike Ashley, *The Age of the Storytellers: British Popular Fiction Magazines, 1880–1950* (London: British Library and Oak Knoll Press, 2006), 15.

CHAPTER FIVE

1. "Editor's Secrets," *Golden*, 4 June 1927, 7; and "Editor's Secrets," *Monster*, 28 April 1927, 7.

2. The story began with Basil Vaughan, "Sons of the Sea," *Monster*, 18 June 1927, 2, and ran until "Sons of the Sea," *Monster*, 27 August 1927, 3. Netley Lucas's series began with "The Desert Watchers," *Monster*, 12 February 1927, 6, and ended with "The Desert Watchers," *Monster*, 11 June 1927, 2.

3. "Editor's Chuckle," *Monster*, 27 August 1927, 7.

4. Ibid. The story began with Basil Vaughan and Netley Lucas, "East at War with the West," *Monster*, 3 September 1927, 3, and ran until "East at War with the West," *Monster*, 3 December 1927, 3.

5. LMA, LJ/SR/602: County of London Quarter Sessions (27 July 1920); "Apprehensions Sought," *Police Gazette*, 2 July 1920, 1; and *Crooks: Confessions*, 13.

6. *My Selves*, 106–8, 162.

7. "Get-Rich-Quick Scheme That Failed," *Glasgow Weekly News*, 4 October 1924, 10.

8. "Undesirables Deported," *News of the World*, 28 September, 1924, 9.

9. *My Selves*, 188; and HL, MS/ENG/796 (82): Richard Dent to James B. Pinker (28 February 1925).

10. *My Selves*, 160; Netley Lucas, "Life at Wormwood Scrubs," *Detective*, 23 May 1924, 11; and Netley Lucas, "My Life in Borstal," *Detective*, 8 May 1925, 1259–64.

11. Netley Lucas, "On Trial," *Detective*, 13 February 1925, 650.

12. Lucas, "Pearls and the Woman," *Detective*, 15 August 1924, 601, 637–42.

13. *My Selves*, 163.

14. Dearden's work included R. L. Dearden, *Christopher Parkins, RN* (London: T. Fisher Unwin, 1925); R. L. Dearden, *Jim of the* Valfreya (London: A. and C. Black, 1925); R. L. Dearden, *Maiden Voyage* (London: Herbert Jenkins, 1938); and R. L. Dearden, *Care of the Commander* (London: Herbert Jenkins, 1939).

15. *My Selves*, 185–86; and "A Swindler's Own Life Story," *Daily Mail*, 7 January 1925, 4.

16. R. L. Dearden, from material supplied by Netley Lucas, *The Autobiography of a Crook* (New York: Lincoln MacVeagh / Dial Press, 1925).

17. "Villainy of a Very Sordid and Petty Kind," *New York Times*, 9 August 1925, BR8.

18. Winthrop Lane, "Making a Criminal," *Saturday Review*, 11 September 1926, 104.

19. "Evelyn Graham's Dupe," *Daily Mail*, 3 December 1930, 16.

20. "Life Story of a 'Crook,'" *Daily Express*, 1 September 1933, 18.

21. "Women the 'Best Criminals,'" *Daily Express*, 16 December 1925, 3.

22. *My Selves*, 187.

23. H. G. Castle, *Case for the Prosecution* (London: Naldrett Press, 1956), vii.

24. *Crooks: Confessions*, 13–14, 15.

25. Ibid., xi, 222, 254.

26. "Advert," *Popular*, 18 April 1925, 391, 404; and "Two Crooks Confess," *Popular*, 25 April 1925, 415.

27. "Two Crooks Confess," *Popular*, 16 May 1925, 9–13; and "Two Crooks Confess," *Popular*, 23 May 1925, 55–59.

28. *Crooks: Confessions*, 13–14.

29. *My Selves*, 186–87.

30. Ibid., 187.

31. Sir Basil Thomson, "Three Prison Books," *Times Literary Supplement*, 19 March 1925, 186.

32. "A Swindler's Own Life Story," *Daily Mail*, 7 January 1925, 4.

33. "Review," *Scotsman*, 17 June 1926, 2.

34. "Criminal Paris," *Queenslander*, 21 August 1926, 8.

35. "Sociology," *Times Literary Supplement*, 2 December 1926, 891.

36. "Bob-Haired Bandits," *Register* (Adelaide), 23 April 1927, 4.

37. Herbert Gorman, "Paris Is What You Will," *New York Times*, 27 February 1927, BR5. "Imported Sin," *Saturday Review*, 26 June 1926, 889.

38. "Women Who Make Mischief," *Dundee Courier*, 26 October 1926, 4.

39. Algernon Blackwood, "Detective Systems," *Time and Tide*, 20 August 1926, 756–57. David Hendy, "Painting with Sound: The Kaleidoscopic World of Lance Sieveking, a British Radio Modernist," *Twentieth Century British History* 24, no. 2 (2013): 169–200, provides an alternative perspective on the porous boundaries between cultural forms and media between the wars.

40. Netley Lucas, "How Bicycles Are Stolen," *Cycling*, 21 August 1925, vii.

41. R. Thurston Hopkins, *Famous Bank Forgeries, Robberies and Swindles* (London: Stanley Paul, 1936), 156.

42. *My Selves*, 110, 162, 188.

43. Miles Orvell, *The Real Thing: Imitation and Authenticity in American Culture, 1880–1940* (Chapel Hill: University of North Carolina Press, 1989), xv, xxiii; Christopher Hilliard, *To Exercise Our Talents: The Democratization of Writing in Britain* (Cambridge, MA, and London: Harvard University Press, 2006), 176–77; and K. K. Ruthven, *Faking Literature* (Cambridge: Cambridge University Press, 2001), chap. 4.

44. H. M. Paull, *Literary Ethics: A Study in the Growth of the Literary Conscience* (London: Thornton Butterworth, 1928), 187–88. On the process of ghosting, see, e.g., Trevor Allen, *Underworld: The Biography of Charles Brooks, Criminal* (London: Grant Richards, 1931); Alexander McArthur and H. Kingsley Long, *No Mean City: A Story of the Glasgow Slums* (London: Longmans, 1935); James Spenser, *Limey: An Englishman Joins the Gangs* (London: Longmans, 1933); Andrew Davies, *City of Gangs: Glasgow and the Rise of the British Gangster* (London: Hodder and Stoughton, 2013), 298–300; John Galsworthy, "Conscience" (1922), in *Caravan*, 818–23 (London: William Heinemann, 1927); Herbert John, *My Literary Adventures* (London: W. and G. Foyle, 1925), 73–81; Violet Powell, *A Substantial Ghost: The Literary Adventures of Maude Ffoulkes* (London: Heinemann, 1967); and Claire Squires, "Ghostwriting," in *The Oxford Companion to the Book*, ed. Michael Suarez and H. R. Woudhuysen (Oxford: Oxford University Press, 2010).

45. Sydney Moseley, *Short Story Writing and Freelance Journalism* (London: Isaac Pitman 1926), 72–106.

46. Sydney Moseley, *The Truth about a Journalist* (London: Isaac Pitman, 1935), 268, 272, 276.

47. Ibid., 272, 275.

48. Andrew Davies, "The Scottish Chicago? From 'Hooligans' to 'Gangsters' in Interwar Glasgow," *Cultural and Social History* 4, no. 4 (2007): 512; and Chris Waters, "Beyond 'Americanization': Rethinking Anglo-American Cultural Exchange between the Wars," *Cultural and Social History* 4, no. 4 (2007): 453.

49. Harold Herd, *The Making of Modern Journalism* (London: George Allen and Unwin, 1927), 10–11.

50. TNA, J/54/2130/2245: Statement of Claim (13 November 1931).

51. "Verdict for Josephine O'Dare," *Straits Times*, 17 April 1933, 19.

52. "Story of Her Life," *Irish Times*, 14 March 1933, 18.

53. TNA, J/54/2130/2245: Statement of Claim (13 November 1931).

54. "Miss Josephine O'Dare's Libel Action," *Times*, 14 March 1933, 4; "Miss Josephine O'Dare on Her Life in Mayfair," *Evening Standard*, 13 March 1933, 5; and A. M. Sullivan, *The Last Serjeant: The Memoirs of Serjeant A.M. Sullivan, QC* (London: Macdonald, 1952).

55. "Verdict for Josephine O'Dare," *Straits Times*, 17 April 1933, 19.

56. "Miss Josephine O'Dare's Libel Action," *Times*, 14 March 1933, 4; and "Josephine O'Dare's Duel with KC," *Daily Mirror*, 14 March 1933, 2.

57. "Exploiting the Gallows," *Saturday Review*, 30 August 1924. Patrick Collier, *Modernism on Fleet Street* (Aldershot, UK: Ashgate, 2006), 1.

58. "Miss Josephine O'Dare's Libel Action," *Times*, 14 March 1933, 4.

59. "Verdict for Josephine O'Dare," *Straits Times*, 17 April 1933, 19.

60. "Awarded £500 for Libel," *Scotsman*, 15 May 1929, 20; and "Two More Actions by Mr Morriss," *Guardian*, 15 May 1929, 6.

61. "Josephine O'Dare's Brother," *Scotsman*, 15 February 1929, 11.

62. "Story of Her Life," *Irish Times*, 14 March 1933, 8; and "Irish Woman Sues London Journal," *Irish Independent*, 14 March 1933, 14.

63. "Crowded Sensations in the Great Stella Maris Murder Trial," *Reynolds's*, 28 November 1926, 1; and "Lifestory of One of London's Worst Women," *Reynolds's*, 29 August 1926, 8.

64. "Josephine O'Dare's Duel with KC," *Daily Mirror*, 14 March 1933, 2; "One Farthing Damages for Josephine O'Dare," *Daily Express*, 15 March 1933, 7; and TNA, J/54/2130/2245: Further and better particulars of defence (14 April and 3 May 1932).

65. Moseley, *Truth about a Journalist*, 267, 272. While Wray has left little archival trace, there are hints in *Census Returns of England and Wales, 1901*, class RG13, piece 2306, folio 15, p. 1; and *Census Returns of England and Wales, 1911*, class RG14, piece 2395—accessed 13 March 2015, www.ancestry.co.uk.

66. "Miss Josephine O'Dare's Libel Action," *Times*, 14 March 1933, 4.

67. TNA, J/54/2130/2245: Further and better particulars of defence (14 April and 3 May 1932).

68. Ibid.

69. "Irish Woman Sues London Journal," *Irish Independent*, 14 March 1933, 15; "Josephine O'Dare's Duel with KC," *Daily Mirror*, 14 March 1933, 2, 4; "Josephine O'Dare's Life in Mayfair," *Daily Mail*, 14 March 1933, 6; and "Miss Josephine O'Dare on 'Cutting Off from the Past,'" *Evening Standard*, 14 March 1933, 4.

70. "Story of Her Life," *Irish Times*, 14 March 1933, 8.

71. "Miss Josephine O'Dare's Libel Action," *Times*, 14 March 1933, 4.

72. "Story of Her Life," *Irish Times*, 14 March 1933, 8.

73. "Miss Josephine O'Dare's Libel Action," *Times*, 14 March 1933, 4.

74. Paul John Eakin, *How Our Lives Become Stories: Making Selves* (Ithaca, NY: Cornell University Press, 1999), 43.

75. "Miss Josephine O'Dare on Her Life in Mayfair," *Evening Standard*, 13 March 1933, 5; and "Some New Books," *Century* (1925): 767.

76. "Verdict for Josephine O'Dare," *Straits Times*, 17 April 1933, 19; and "Josephine O'Dare's Life in Mayfair," *Daily Mail*, 14 March 1933, 6.

77. Philippe Lejeune, *On Autobiography*, trans. Katherine Leary (Minneapolis: University of Minnesota Press, 1989), ix.

78. Lord Riddell, "Psychology of the Journalist," in *Journalism, by Some Masters of the Craft* (London: Isaac Pitman, 1932), 56.

79. "Verdict for Josephine O'Dare," *Straits Times*, 17 April 1933, 19.

80. "Miss Josephine O'Dare's Libel Action," *Times*, 15 March 1933, 4.

81. "View of Miss Josephine O'Dare," *Daily Express*, 14 March 1933, 7.

82. TNA, J/54/2000/230: William Hobbs vs. C. T. Tinling (December 1928); TNA, J/54/2000/36: Hobbs vs. *Nottingham Journal* (December 1928); and Angus McLaren, *Sexual Blackmail: A Modern History* (Cambridge, MA: Harvard University Press, 2002), chap. 6. On libel, see Samuel Hyde, "'Please Sir, He Called Me "Jimmy"!' Political Cartooning before the Law: 'Black Friday,' J.H. Thomas and *The Communist* Libel Trial of 1921," *Contemporary British History* 25, no. 4 (2011): 521–50; and Leslie Treiger-Bar-Am, "Defamation Law in a Changing Society: The Case of Youssoupoff v Metro-Goldwyn Mayer," *Legal Studies* 20, no. 2 (2006): 291–319.

83. TNA, J/54/2002/1779: Alfonso Smith vs. National Magazine Co. (November 1930); TNA, J/54/2311/1394: Smith vs. Everybody's Publications (December 1937); and TNA, MEPO/3/614: Solicitors in a libel action seek police evidence about client's earlier history (1926–37).

84. TNA, J/54/2119/2059: Hayley Morriss vs. Baines and Co. (December 1932–January 1933); TNA, J/54/2109/743: Morriss vs. Sir Charles Hyde (November–December 1932); TNA, J/54/2016/2309: Morriss vs. *News of the World* (May 1929); TNA, J/54/2016/2363: Morriss vs. *London Express Newspaper* (May 1929); TNA, J/54/2016/1106: Morriss vs. United Newspapers (April 1929); TNA, J54/2016/1980: Morriss vs. *London Express Newspaper* (May 1929); TNA, J/54/2094/614: Morriss vs. *Bristol Times and Mirror* (May 1932); and "Apology to Hayley Morriss," *People*, 2 June 1929, 1.

85. "Miss O'Dare Awarded Farthing Damages," *Daily Mail*, 15 March 1933.

86. Sydney Moseley, *The Private Diaries of Sydney Moseley* (London: Max Parrish, 1960), 276.

87. TNA, LCO/2/3060: Law of Libel Committee, Memorandum of Arnold Maplesden (1939).

88. "Hotels and Shops Defrauded by Boy," *Register* (Adelaide), 30 October 1920, 10.

89. TNA, J/54/2130/2245: Claim (13 November 1931); TNA, J/54/2002/1779 (November 1930); TNA, J/54/2000/230 (December 1928); TNA, J54/2000/36 (December 1928); TNA, MEPO/3/1088: "William Hobbs and Edmond O'Connor" (1935–42); A. Sullivan, *Last Serjeant*, 309; and Angus McLaren, "Smoke and Mirrors: Willy Clarkson and the Role of Disguises in Inter-war England," *Journal of Social History* 40, no. 3 (2007): 597–618.

90. TNA, MEPO/3/441: Respecting "Trixie" Skyrme (May 1926), 3–4.

91. TNA, LCO/2/3060: Memorandum submitted by the Institute of Journalists.

92. "The Law of Libel," *Times*, 2 October 1936, 10; and "Freedom and Influence of the Press," *Scotsman*, 15 September 1936, 11.

93. Edward Wooll, *A Guide to the Law of Libel and Slander* (London: Blackie and Son, 1939).

94. "Freedom of the Press," *Times*, 5 November 1936, 9. "Law of Libel," *Times*, 24 September 1936, 6; "Abuses of Libel Law," *Times*, 23 January 1937, 14; and "The Newspaper Society," *Scotsman*, 4 May 1932, 12.

95. TNA, LCO/2/3058: List of Persons and Societies (30 March 1939); and TNA, LCO /2/3065: Law of Libel Committee (1939).

96. Wooll, *Guide to the Law of Libel*, 9–10.

97. TNA, LCO/2/3060: Richard Willies (15 May 1939).

98. Political and Economic Planning, *Report on the British Press* (London: Political and Economic Planning, 1938), 37; *Report of the Royal Commission on the Press, 1947–8* (London: HMSO, 1948), 166, 170; and H. Montgomery Hyde, *Their Good Names: Twelve Cases of Libel and Slander with Some Introductory Reflections on the Law* (London: Hamilton, 1970), 14–15.

99. Wooll, *Guide to the Law of Libel*, 3.

100. Charles Pilley, *Law for Journalists* (London: Isaac Pitman, 1924), 7.

101. "Miss O'Dare to Pay Her Own Costs," *Daily Express*, 16 March 1933, 7.

102. "Miss O'Dare's Farthing," *Straits Times*, 4 April 1933, 6.

103. H. P. Lansdale-Ruthven, *The Law of Libel for Journalists* (London: Blandford Press, 1934), 107–8.

104. Ibid., 138.

105. Pilley, *Law for Journalists*, 44.

106. *My Selves*, 197.

107. "Broadmoor Sensation," *Sunday News*, 10 July 1927, 1. See TNA, MEPO/3/259: Murder of Major Miles Seaton by Lieutenant Colonel Rutherford (1919); and TNA, HO/144/22266: Lt. Colonel Cecil Rutherford: Found Guilty but Insane on a Charge of Murder (1919–29).

108. TNA, MEPO/3/268B: Murder of Frances Buxton; and Minute 1a: C. I. Stoneham to Superintendent (23 July 1927).

109. *My Selves*, 197. The police file supports this narrative: TNA, MEPO/3/268B (1920–27).

110. "New Chelsea Murder Hunt," *Sunday News*, 24 July 1927, 1.

111. C. F. Carr and F. E. Stevens, *Modern Journalism: A Complete Guide to the Newspaper Craft* (London: Isaac Pitman and Sons, 1931), vii; and Joel Wiener, "Get the News! Get the News! Speed in Transatlantic Journalism, 1850–90," in *Anglo-American Media Interactions, 1850–2000*, ed. Joel Wiener and Mark Hampton, 48–61 (Houndmills, UK: Basingstoke, Palgrave Macmillan, 2007).

112. TNA, MEPO/3/268B: Cooper to Superintendent (26 July 1927).

113. Ibid: Lucas to Cooper (23 July 1927).

114. "Trying to Bluff the Yard?," *People*, 24 July 1927, 11.

115. "Murder Mystery Hoax," *John Bull*, 6 August 1927, 13.

116. Ibid.

117. Ibid.

118. "Bank Plot by Four Forgers," *Daily Mirror*, 20 December 1927, 2.

119. "Boulogne Mystery," *Sydney Morning Herald*, 14 March 1927, 11.

120. "A Holiday Ordeal," *Liverpool Echo*, 2 September 1927, n.p.; and TNA, MEPO/3/268B: Minute 2a, Cooper to Superintendent (5 September 1927).

121. "Bank Plot by Four Forgers," *Daily Mirror*, 20 December 1927, 2; "Conspiracy to

Forge," *Times*, 20 December 1927, 6; and "Sued for Libel He Wrote of Himself," *Guardian*, 20 December 1927, 20. O'Connor's arrest was reported in "Nurse Daniels," *Evening News*, 29 August 1927, 1.

122. TNA, MEPO/3/268B: Minute 2a, Cooper to Superintendent (5 September 1927).

123. "Trying to Bluff the Yard?," *People*, 24 July 1927, 11.

124. TNA, MEPO/3/268B: Cooper to Superintendent (26 July 1927).

125. Ibid., Minute 2a, Cooper to Superintendent (5 September 1927).

126. Ibid.

127. Ibid.: Lucas to Cooper (23 July 1927).

128. "Murder Mystery Hoax," *John Bull*, 6 August 1927, 13.

129. *My Selves*, 198; and "New Hunt for Chelsea Murder," *Star*, 23 July 1927, 1.

130. TNA, MEPO/3/268B: Minute 2a, Cooper to Superintendent (5 September 1927).

131. "Trying to Bluff the Yard?," *People*, 24 July 1927, 11.

132. Pilley, *Law for Journalists*, 151.

133. Moseley, *Truth about a Journalist*, 187.

134. Political and Economic Planning, *Report on the British Press*, 153–54.

135. Hamilton Fyfe, *Press Parade: Behind the Scenes of the Newspaper Racket and the Millionaires' Attempt at Dictatorship* (London: Watts, 1936), 112–13, 120.

136. *My Selves*, 198.

137. Ibid., 196–97.

138. Ibid., 198.

139. "British Passengers Embarked at the Port of Liverpool, SS *Aurania*" (17 December 1927), accessed 13 March 2015, http://search.findmypast.co.uk/record?id=tna%2fbt27%2f116 4000010%2f00095.

140. NFSA, title 642150: Macquarie Broadcasting Service, Production Report "Episode 45: Netley Lucas" (22 August 1955), 10–11.

141. *My Selves*, 207.

142. Ibid., 202.

143. "Criminologist to Wed Woman Criminal," *New York Herald Tribune*, 4 January 1928, 17.

144. May Churchill Sharpe, *Chicago May: Her Story* (New York: Macaulay, 1928).

145. BAN, 72/227c, box 13: Berkeley Police Records: May Sharpe to August Vollmer (10 December 1927, 13 December 1927).

146. Ibid., Sharpe to Vollmer (23 November 1927, 30 November 1927, 19 December 1927, 13 December 1927, 9 January 1928, 4 January 1928, 28 January 1928, 9 February 1928). See Nuala O'Faolain, *The Story of Chicago May* (London: Michael Joseph, 2005).

147. BAN, 72/227c, box 13: Berkeley Police Records: Sharpe to Vollmer (9 January 1928).

148. *My Selves*, 205–6.

149. Netley Lucas, *Ladies of the Underworld: The Beautiful, the Damned, and Those Who Get Away with It* (New York: J. H. Sears, 1927).

150. "Famous Criminologist Marries the Greatest Living Woman Thief," *San Antonio Light*, 22 January 1928, 8.

151. Ibid.

152. *My Selves*, 202.

153. *Crook Janes*, 73, 79.

154. *London and Its Criminals*, 32–33.

155. See also *Crooks: Confessions*, 27–29, 61. "Potpourri of Crime," *Criminologist*, 15 May 1927, 2, included a paragraph on Churchill's recovery from a "serious operation" in Detroit.

156. *My Selves*, 200.

157. Ibid., 207–8.

158. *My Selves*, 208. See, e.g., "Chicago May to Wed," *Daily Express*, 5 January 1928, 9; "Chicago May Churchill," *Los Angeles Times*, 10 January 1928, A12; and "May—and Orange Blossom," *People*, 8 January 1928, 5.

159. *My Selves*, 207–8.

160. The phrase is the title of chap. 18 of *My Selves*.

161. "His Badness a Myth," *New York Times*, 5 January 1928, 22.

162. Ibid. On the interview as "democratic" and "aggressive," see J. Wiener, "Get the News!," 48–61.

163. "Fiancé Intrigued by 'Chicago May,'" *New York Evening Post*, 5 January 1928, 4.

164. Ibid.

165. "Famous Criminologist Marries the Greatest Living Woman Thief," *San Antonio Light*, 22 January 1928, 8.

166. Ibid. See also "Criminologist to Wed Woman Criminal," *New York Herald Tribune*, 4 January 1928, 17; "To Wed Crime Expert," *Indiana Weekly Messenger*, 2 February 1928, 6; and "Noted Woman Criminal Will Marry Author," *Detroit Free Press*, 4 January 1928, 1.

167. "'Chicago May' Soon Will Be a Bride," *New York World*, 4 January 1928, 4.

168. "Fiancé Intrigued by 'Chicago May,'" *New York Evening Post*, 5 January 1928, 4.

169. "Underworld Romance," *News of the World*, 8 January 1928, 15.

170. "They're to Wed," *Decatur (IL) Herald*, 10 January 1928, 12; and "To Wed Crime Expert," *Indiana Weekly Messenger*, 2 February 1928, 6.

171. "Chicago May and Young Writer to Wed," *Chicago Daily Tribune*, 6 January 1928, 40.

172. "'Chicago May's' New Romance," *Sunday News*, 8 January 1928, 2; and "Author and Siren to Marry," *Evening Post* (New Zealand), 20 April 1928, 13.

173. "May—and Orange Blossom," *People*, 8 January 1928, 5; and "Eddie Guerin Confesses," *People*, 8 January 1928, 5.

174. "'Chicago May's' New Romance," *Sunday News*, 8 January 1928, 2.

175. "Chicago May to Marry a Reformed Crook," *Empire News*, 8 January 1928, 7.

176. "Chicago May," *Chicago Sunday Tribune*, 15 January 1928, S2.

177. BAN, 72/227c, box 13: Sharpe to Vollmer (4 January 1928).

178. Ibid., Sharpe to Vollmer (28 January 1928).

179. *My Selves*, 209; and "'Chicago May' to Wed Cherubic Villain," *New York Times*, 4 January 1928, 2.

180. "'Chicago May' to Wed Cherubic Villain," *New York Times*, 4 January 1928, 2.

181. "His Badness a Myth," *New York Times*, 5 January 1928, 22.

182. Ibid.

183. Churchill's biographers have been unable to decide whether Lucas could claim a criminal past. See O'Faolain, *Chicago May*, 264–75.

184. "Not Investigating Lucas," *New York Times*, 6 January 1928, 23.

185. "His Badness a Myth," *New York Times*, 5 January 1928, 22.

186. "Returns of Passengers, SS *Aquitania*" (13 January 1928), accessed 13 March 2015, www .findmypast.com. Three weeks later Graham was followed by Richard Dent. See "Returns of Passengers, SS *Albertic*" (6 February 1928), accessed 13 March 2015, www.findmypast.com; and *My Selves*, 212.

187. See above, p. 163.

188. The first installment was published as Netley Lucas, "Crime Club," *Monster*, 7 May 1927, 7, and ran under his name until "The Secret Society," *Monster*, 11 February 1928, 7.

189. Netley Lucas, "Monster's Adventurers Succeed," *Monster*, 17 December 1927, 6; Netley Lucas, "Convict Murdered in Cell," *Monster*, 24 December 1927, 6; Netley Lucas, "Fugitive Jewel Thieves' Car Leaps River Parapet," *Monster*, 31 December 1927, 6; Netley Lucas, "Darky Returns to the 'Underworld,'" *Monster*, 7 January 1928, 6; Netley Lucas, "Darky Kemp and Two 'Operatives' Kidnapped on Atlantic Liner," *Monster*, 14 January 1928, 7; and Netley Lucas, "The Stolen Guns," *Monster*, 21 January 1928, 2.

190. "The Fire Raisers," *Monster*, 28 January 1928, 7; Netley Lucas, "Julia in Prison," *Monster*, 4 February 1928, 7; and Netley Lucas, "The Secret Society," *Monster*, 11 February 1928, 7.

191. Frank Mort, *Capital Affairs: London and the Making of the Permissive Society* (New Haven, CT: Yale University Press, 2010), 16.

192. Pilley, *Law for Journalists*, 152.

193. Martin Conboy, *The Press and Popular Culture* (London: Sage, 2002), 93.

194. Political and Economic Planning, *Report on the British Press*, 156.

195. "Mr Hayley Morriss's Libel Action," *Times*, 7 April 1937, 4.

CHAPTER SIX

1. "His Pen of Deceit," *News of the World*, 27 September 1931, 6; and Percy Smith, *Plutocrats of Crime: A Gallery of Confidence Tricksters* (London: Frederick Muller, 1960), 187.

2. "News and Views of Literary London," *New York Times*, 25 August 1929, BR7.

3. *My Selves*, 220–21, 267.

4. Carol Helstosky, "Giovanni Bastianini: Art Forgery and the Market in Nineteenth-Century Italy," *Journal of Modern History* 81, no. 4 (2009): 793–823; K. K. Ruthven, *Faking Literature* (Cambridge: Cambridge University Press, 2001), 2; Aviva Briefel, *The Deceivers: Art Forgery and Identity in the Nineteenth Century* (Ithaca, NY, and London: Cornell University Press, 2006), 2; Anthony Grafton, *Forgers and Critics: Creativity and Duplicity in Western Scholarship* (London: Collins and Brown, 1990); and Anne Stevens, "Forging Literary History: Historical Fiction and Literary Forgery in Eighteenth-Century Britain," *Studies in Eighteenth-Century Culture* 37 (2008): 217–32.

5. I draw here on Anna Clark, *Scandal: The Sexual Politics of the British Constitution* (Princeton, NJ: Princeton University Press, 2006); and James Epstein, *Scandal of Colonial Rule: Power and Subversion in the British Atlantic during the Age of Revolution* (Cambridge: Cambridge University Press, 2012).

6. William Kuhn, *Democratic Royalism: The Transformation of the British Monarchy, 1861–1914* (Houndmills, UK: Macmillan, 1996), 79.

7. Frank Prochaska, *Royal Bounty: The Making of a Welfare Monarchy* (New Haven, CT: Yale University Press, 1995), 184.

8. Ibid., 140-41; Kenneth Rose, *King George V* (London: Weidenfeld and Nicolson, 1983), 7, 141, 224; and Philip Williamson, "The Monarchy and Public Values, 1910-53," in *The Monarchy and the British Nation, 1780 to the Present*, ed. Andrzej Olechnowicz, 223-57 (Cambridge: Cambridge University Press, 2007).

9. Alexis Schwarzenbach, "Royal Photographs: Emotions for the People," *Contemporary European History* 13, no. 3 (2004): 263, 267-68; Laura Mayhall, "The Prince of Wales versus Clark Gable: Anglophone Celebrity and Citizenship between the Wars," *Cultural and Social History* 4, no. 4 (2007): 532-39; David Cannadine, "The Context, Performance and Meaning of Ritual: The British Monarchy and the 'Invention of Tradition' c. 1820-1977," in *The Invention of Tradition*, ed. Eric Hobsbawm and Terence Ranger (Cambridge: Cambridge University Press, 1983); Frank Mort, *Capital Affairs: London and the Making of the Permissive Society* (New Haven, CT: Yale University Press, 2010), chap. 1; and Hilary Sapire, "Ambiguities of Loyalism: The Prince of Wales in India and Africa, 1921-2 and 25," *History Workshop Journal* 73 (2011): 37-65.

10. K. Rose, *King George V*, 229. Frank Mort, "Love in a Cold Climate: Letters, Public Opinion, and Monarchy in the 1936 Abdication Crisis," *Twentieth Century British History* 25, no. 1 (2014): 30-62.

11. Kingsley Martin, *The Magic of Monarchy* (London: Nelson, 1937), 10-13, 94, 103, 112; Ernest Jones, "The Psychology of Constitutional Monarchy," *New Statesman*, 1 February 1936; Humphrey Jennings and Charles Madge, eds., *May the Twelfth: Mass-Observation Day-Surveys, 1937* (1937; repr., London: Faber and Faber, 1987); Harold Laski, *Parliamentary Government in England* (London: Allen and Unwin, 1938), 388-96; and Andrzej Olechnowicz, "Britain's 'Quasi-Magical' Monarchy in the Mid-twentieth Century," in *Classes, Cultures and Politics: Essays on British History for Ross McKibbin*, ed. Clare Griffiths, James Nott, and William Whyte, 70-84 (Oxford: Oxford University Press, 2011).

12. David Sinclair, *Two Georges: The Making of the Modern Monarchy* (London: Hodder and Staughton, 1988), 2. Chandrika Kaul, "Monarchical Display and the Politics of Empire: Prince of Wales and India, 1870s-1920s," *Twentieth Century British History* 17, no. 4 (2006): 478, is an exception.

13. Dan LeMahieu, *A Culture for Democracy: Mass Communication and the Cultivated Mind in Britain between the Wars* (Oxford: Clarendon Press, 1988), 3, 99.

14. On mass culture and monarchy as antithetical, see Ryan Linkof, " 'The Photographic Attack on His Royal Highness': The Prince of Wales, Wallis Simpson and the Pre-history of Paparazzi," *Photography & Culture* 4, no. 3 (2011): 277-92.

15. Jon Lawrence, "Paternalism, Class and the British Path to Modernity," in *The Peculiarities of Liberal Modernity in Imperial Britain*, ed. Simon Gunn and James Vernon (Berkeley: University of California Press, 2011), 147; and Thomas Hajkowski, *The BBC and National Identity in Britain, 1922-53* (Manchester, UK: Manchester University Press, 2010).

16. Sinclair, *Two Georges*, 136.

17. Jeffrey Richards, "The Monarchy and Film," in *The Monarchy and the British Nation, 1780 to the Present*, ed. Andrzej Olechnowicz, 258-79 (Cambridge: Cambridge University Press, 2007); Rachel Brunt, "The Family Firm Restored: Newsreel Coverage of the British Monarchy, 1936-45," in *Nationalising Femininity: Culture, Sexuality and British Cinema in the Second*

World War, ed. Christine Gledhill and Gillian Swanson, 140–51 (Manchester, UK: Manchester University Press, 1996); Tom Fleming, ed., *Voices out of the Air: The Royal Christmas Broadcasts, 1932–1981* (London: Heinemann, 1981); and Luke McKernan, "The Finest Cinema Performers That We Possess: British Royalty and the Newsreels, 1910–37," *Court Historian* 8 (2003): 59–71. On the abdication crisis, see Philip Zeigler, *King Edward VIII* (Stroud, UK: Sutton, 2001); and Philip Williamson, *Stanley Baldwin: Conservative Leadership and National Values* (Cambridge: Cambridge University Press, 1999), 326–29.

18. Jon Lawrence, *Electing Our Masters: The Hustings in British Politics from Hogarth to Blair* (Oxford: Oxford University Press, 2009), chap. 4; Laura Beers, *Your Britain: Media and the Making of the Labour Party* (Cambridge, MA: Harvard University Press, 2010); Helen Mc-Carthy, "Democratising British Foreign Policy: Rethinking the Peace Ballot, 1934–5," *Journal of British Studies* 49, no. 2 (2010): 358–87. On philanthropy, see Eve Colpus, "*The Week's Good Cause*: Mass Culture and Cultures of Philanthropy at the Interwar BBC," *Twentieth Century British History* 22, no. 3 (2011): 321–22; Ellen Boucher, "Cultivating Internationalism: Save the Children Fund, Public Opinion and the Meaning of Child Relief, 1919–24," in *Brave New World: Imperial and Democratic Nation Building in Britain between the Wars*, ed. Laura Beers and Geraint Thomas, 141–70 (London: Institute of Historical Research Press, 2012); and Scott Anthony, *Public Relations in Britain: Stephen Tallents and the Development of a Progressive Media Profession* (Manchester, UK: Manchester University Press, 2011).

19. Priya Satia, "Interwar Agnotology: Empire, Democracy and the Production of Ignorance," in *Brave New World: Imperial and Democratic Nation Building in Britain between the Wars*, ed. Laura Beers and Geraint Thomas (London: Institute of Historical Research Press, 2012), 182. See also David Vincent, "Government and the Management of Information, 1944–2009," in *The Peculiarities of Liberal Modernity in Imperial Britain*, ed. Simon Gunn and James Vernon, 165–81 (Berkeley: University of California Press, 2011); David Vincent, *The Culture of Secrecy: Britain, 1832–1998* (Oxford: Oxford University Press, 1998); and Peter Hennessy, "Searching for the 'Great Ghost': The Palace, the Premiership, the Cabinet and the Constitution in the Postwar Period," *Journal of Contemporary History* 30, no. 2 (1995): 211–31. My argument about the culture/politics distinction draws on Patrick Joyce, "What Is the Social in Social History?" *Past and Present* 206, no. 1 (2010): 236.

20. "Royal Names in Pages of a Bluffer," *Empire News*, 27 September 1931, 3.

21. "News and Views of Literary London," *New York Times*, 25 August 1929, BR7. See Evelyn Graham, *Princess Mary, Viscountess Lascelles: An Intimate Life-Story* (London: Hutchinson, 1929); Evelyn Graham, *The Queen of Spain: An Authorised Life-Story* (London: Hutchinson, 1929); Evelyn Graham, *Albert, King of the Belgians* (London: Hutchinson, 1929); and Sir George Aston and Evelyn Graham, *His Royal Highness the Duke of Connaught and Strathearn* (London: Harrap, 1929).

22. Evelyn Graham, *Lord Darling and His Famous Trials* (London: Hutchinson, 1929); and Evelyn Graham, *Fifty Years of Famous Judges* (London: Long, 1930).

23. Sir George Aston, *Secret Service* (London: Faber and Faber, 1930). The book was serialized beginning with "Best Kept Secrets of the War," *Sunday Dispatch*, 26 January 1930, 2, and running until "Secret of the Fifth Army," *Sunday Dispatch*, 6 April 1930, 2. For Graham and Aston's collaboration, see RMM, ASTON/5/10: "Memorandum of Agreement between

Sir George Aston and Faber and Faber" (17 July 1929); "Memorandum of Agreement between Aston and Associated Press" (n.d. [July 1929?]); KCLMA, ASTON/3/8: "Notes, correspondence, and newspaper cuttings from the *Sunday Dispatch* for article on Secret Service" (November 1929–February 1930); and KCLMA, ASTON/3/9: "Papers including correspondence for article on Secret Service" (October–November 1930). Margaret Prothero, *The History of the Criminal Investigation Department* (London: Herbert Jenkins, 1931).

24. *My Selves*, 212.

25. Christopher Hilliard, *To Exercise Our Talents: The Democratization of Writing in Britain* (Cambridge, MA, and London: Harvard University Press, 2006), 12. Billie Melman, *Women and the Popular Imagination in the Twenties: Flappers and Nymphs* (Houndmills, UK: Palgrave Macmillan, 1988); Jay Dixon, *The Romance Fiction of Mills & Boon, 1909–1990s* (London: UCL Press, 1999); Mary Hammond, *Reading, Publishing, and the Formation of Literary Taste in England, 1880–1914* (Aldershot, UK: Ashgate, 2006); Joseph McAleer, *Popular Reading and Publishing in Britain, 1914–1950* (Oxford: Oxford University Press, 1992); and Philip Waller, *Writers, Readers, and Reputations: Literary Life in Britain* (Oxford: Oxford University Press, 2008).

26. "Royal Names in Pages of a Bluffer," *Empire News*, 27 September 1931, 3.

27. Kathleen Woodward, *Queen Mary of England* (London: Hutchinson, 1927); Lady Cynthia Asquith, *HRH the Duchess of York* (London: Hutchinson, 1927); and Hon. Mrs. Frances Lascelles, *Our Duke and Duchess* (London: Hutchinson, 1932).

28. *My Selves*, 212–13.

29. Ibid., 215.

30. H. M. Paull, "Literature and Money," *Author*, January 1930, 6–7.

31. "Herbert Jenkins Autumn Books," *Bookman*, December 1930, 85; and Evelyn Graham, *The Life Story of King Alfonso XIII* (London: Herbert Jenkins, 1930).

32. "Company Meeting," *Daily Mail*, 28 August 1926, 3. Mike Ashley, *The Age of the Storytellers: British Popular Fiction Magazines, 1880–1950* (London: British Library and Oak Knoll Press, 2006), 15; Stefan Collini, "Always Dying: The Ideal of the General Periodical," in *Common Reading: Critics, Historians, Publics*, 221–35 (Oxford: Oxford University Press, 2008); Kate Jackson, *George Newnes and the New Journalism in Britain, 1880–1910: Culture and Profit* (Aldershot, UK: Ashgate, 2001), chap. 2; and David Reed, *The Popular Magazine in Britain and the United States, 1880–1960* (Toronto: University of Toronto Press, 1997).

33. *My Selves*, 284.

34. Ashley, *Age of the Storytellers*, 223–30.

35. Evelyn Graham, "Pets of Royal Personages," *Windsor*, May 1929, 673–79.

36. Evelyn Graham, "Edward P.," *Windsor*, June 1929, 2–20; July 1929, 127–42; August 1929, 255–69; and September 1929, 383–402.

37. See, e.g., Evelyn Graham, "HRH Princess Mary Viscountess Lascelles," *Pearson's*, March 1929, 263–69; Evelyn Graham, "Our Radiant Duchess," *Pearson's*, April 1929, 390–95; Evelyn Graham, "The Fourth Lady in the Land," *Pearson's*, May 1929, 516–21; Evelyn Graham, "The Beautiful Princesses of Spain," *Pearson's*, May 1929, 636–40; Evelyn Graham, "The Crown Princess of Belgium," *Pearson's*, July 1929, 80–84; Evelyn Graham, "Five Princesses of Europe," *Pearson's*, August 1929, 186–91; Evelyn Graham, "Chapters of Royal Life," *My Home*,

December 1930, 58–62; and Evelyn Graham, "Chapters of Royal Life: The House of Windsor," *My Home*, January 1931, 28–30, 79. Graham's work on the Duke and Duchess of York included the series that began with Evelyn Graham, "Intimate Pictures from Home Life of the Duke and Duchess of York," *Hartford Courant*, 19 August 1929, 10. This was reworked as Evelyn Graham, "At Home with the Duke and Duchess of York," *Modern Home*, October 1930, 40–45; and Evelyn Graham, "Bringing Up Princess Elizabeth," *Modern Home*, November 1930, 40–41, 99.

38. D. Kilham Roberts, "The Literary Agent," in *The Book World: A New Survey*, ed. John Hampden (London: Thomas Nelson and Sons, 1935), 39, 42–48; and Mary Ann Gillies, *The Professional Literary Agent in Britain, 1880–1920* (Toronto: University of Toronto Press, 2007).

39. Mark Meredith, ed., *Who's Who in Literature* (Liverpool, UK: Literary Year Books Press, 1925), xi.

40. *My Selves*, 215–17.

41. "Next Monday's *Daily Mail*," *Daily Mail*, 25 September 1928, 13; "Princess Mary," *Daily Mail*, 1 October 1928, 12; and "Princess Mary's Life Story," *Daily Mail*, 28 September 1928, 13.

42. *My Selves*, 215–17.

43. Ibid., 217. See, e.g., "The Story of Princess Mary," *Evening Citizen*, 1 November 1928, 1. The *Washington Post* serialization began with Evelyn Graham, "The Life Story of Princess Mary," *Washington Post*, 16 December 1928, SM5, and ran for nineteen weeks until Evelyn Graham, "The Life Story of Princess Mary," *Washington Post*, 21 April 1929, SM4.

44. HRC, box 29, folder 5: Graham to William Bradley (12 November 1928).

45. Aston and Graham, *Duke of Connaught*. The series began with Evelyn Graham and George Aston, "The Duke of Connaught's Life Story," *Daily Chronicle*, 7 October 1929, 9, 11, and ran daily until Evelyn Graham and George Aston, "The Duke of Connaught's Life Story," *Daily Chronicle*, 18 October 1929, 11. "Best Selling Books during March," *Publisher and Bookseller*, 4 April 1930, 750. For the price of Graham's books, see, e.g., "Biography," *Times Literary Supplement*, 5 December 1929, 1034; and "Bar and Buskin," *Times Literary Supplement*, 1 May 1930, 360.

46. "Biography," *Times Literary Supplement*, 12 September 1929, 705. Christopher Hilliard, "The Twopenny Library: The Book Trade, Working-Class Readers, and 'Middlebrow' Novels in Britain, 1930–42," *Twentieth Century British History* 25, no. 2 (2014): 199–220, is an excellent introduction to patterns of book borrowing and buying.

47. Evelyn Graham, *Edward P.: A New and Intimate Life Story of HRH the Prince of Wales* (London: Ward Lock, 1929). See the series beginning Evelyn Graham, "The Authorized Life Story of the Prince of Wales," *Register* (Adelaide), 3 September 1928, 9, and concluding Evelyn Graham, "Authorized Life Story of the Prince of Wales," *Register*, 19 September 1928, 11.

48. "The Outstanding Biography of the Year," *Publisher and Bookseller*, 8 November 1929, 950.

49. "Don't Grieve Girls," *Clearfield (PA) Progress*, 31 October 1929, 1; and "Wales Doesn't Want a Woman to Boss Him," *Portsmouth (OH) Daily Times*, 1 November 1929.

50. "Books of the Day," *Illustrated London News*, 28 December 1929, 1130.

51. "Edward P.," *Scotsman*, 2 December 1929, 2; and "Our London Letter," *Malayan Saturday Post*, 28 December 1929, 16.

52. "Books of the Day," *Guardian*, 16 December 1929, 5.

53. "Two Kings," *Times Literary Supplement*, 12 December 1929, 1044.

54. "Character of King Alfonso," *Daily Mirror*, 24 October 1930, 7.

55. "King Alfonso XIII of Spain," *New York Times*, 1 February 1931, BR11.

56. "Princess Mary," *Queenslander*, 4 September 1930, 49.

57. "Advert," *Illustrated London News*, 25 May 1929.

58. "Advert," *Daily Express*, 1 May 1929, 19; and "Advert," *Illustrated London News*, 20 April 1929, XVI.

59. Evelyn Graham, "The First Lady in the Land," *Britannia and Eve*, May 1929, 27–29; Evelyn Graham, "The Queen with a 'Human Touch,'" *Britannia and Eve*, July 1929; Evelyn Graham, "HM the Queen of Spain," *Britannia and Eve*, September 1929, 32–33; Evelyn Graham, "Why the Prince Does Not Marry," *Britannia and Eve*, November 1929, 17–21; and Evelyn Graham, "Royal Romances," *Britannia and Eve*, June–July 1930.

60. Evelyn Graham, "Our Gracious Queen Mary," *Illustrated London News*, 6 July 1929, 28; and *My Selves*, 285.

61. *My Selves*, 219–20.

62. "'Evelyn' as a Name," *Canberra Times*, 5 February 1929, 4. "Miss Evelyn Graham" appears in "Two Royal Lives," *Saturday Review*, 26 October 1929, 4.

63. RA, PS/PSO/GV/PS/MAIN/48600: Graham to Sir Bryan Godfrey-Faussett (23 April 1929).

64. Ibid.

65. Ibid., Godfrey-Faussett to Graham (25 April 1929).

66. *My Selves*, 267.

67. Ibid., 265–67.

68. Ibid., 267–69.

69. "Names and Descriptions of British Passengers Arriving on the SS *Largs Bay*" (21 April 1928), accessed 13 March 2015, www.ancestry.co.uk.

70. "Names and Descriptions of British Passengers Arriving on the *Gloucester Castle*" (10 July 1930), accessed 6 June 2014, www.findmypast.com; and "Names and Descriptions of British Passengers Arriving on the *Dunluce Castle*" (23 July 1930), accessed 13 March 2015, www .ancestry.co.uk.

71. *My Selves*, 281–82.

72. "Returns of Passengers, SS *Largs Bay*," accessed 21 April 1928, www.findmypast.co.uk.

73. RA, PS/PSO/GV/PS/MAIN/48600, Graham to Lord Stamfordham (21 August 1928).

74. TNA, J/13/12151: Proceedings against Albert Marriott Ltd., Memorandum C.22, Statement of Affairs (24 November 1930).

75. *The Blue Guide: Muirhead's London and Its Environs* (London: Macmillan, 1922), 11, 15, 17; and LMA, LCC/MIN/4386: agenda papers (8 July 1931).

76. "Names and Descriptions of British Passengers Arriving on the *Gloucester Castle*" (11 July 1930), accessed 6 June 2014, www.findmypast.com; and *My Selves*, 270, 220–21.

77. "Returns of Passengers: *Dunluce Castle*" (23 July 1930), accessed 6 June 2014, www .findmypast.com.

78. See the business card for "Mr Leslie Graham, ~~Journalist~~" in RA: EVIIIPWH/PS /MAIN/2004 (undated).

79. RA, EVIIIPWH/PS/MAIN/2004: Graham to Thomas (19 February 1929); RA, PS/PSO/GV/PS/MAIN/48600: Graham to Godfrey-Faussett (23 April 1929); and "Flats and Chambers," *Times*, 16 March 1928, 2.

80. TNA, J/13/12151: Statement of Affairs (24 November 1930); and Order Made at the High Court of Justice (31 March 1932).

81. "Hiller, Park, May and Rowden," *Times*, 21 January 1929, 24; RA, EVIIIPWH/PS/MAIN/2004: Marriott to Private Secretary (5 May 1928), and Marriott to Thomas (24 July 1928).

82. TNA, J/13/12151: Statement of Affairs (24 November 1930); "Personalia," *Publishers' Circular*, 21 September 1929, 337; and "Notes and News," *Publisher and Bookseller*, 20 September 1929, 516.

83. Stanley Unwin, introduction to *The Book World: A New Survey*, ed. John Hampden (London: Thomas Nelson and Sons, 1935), 9–10.

84. "A New Era in Publishing!," *Publishers' Circular*, 20 July 1929, 52.

85. Walter Townsend and Leonard Townsend, *The Biography of His Holiness Pope Pius XI* (London: Marriott, 1930); and A. M. K. Watson, *The Biography of President von Hindenburg* (London: Marriott, 1930).

86. William Mackay, *Ex-Soldier: We Are Dead* (London: Marriott, 1930), vii, ix; and "New Books and Reprints," *Times Literary Supplement*, 16 October 1930, 840.

87. Dora Macy, *Ex-Mistress* (London: Marriott, 1930); and Anonymous, *Ex-Husband* (London: Marriott, 1930).

88. Otto Nückel, *Destiny: A Novel in Pictures* (London: Marriott, 1930).

89. Donald Sinderby, *Mother-in-Law India* (London: Marriott, 1929); "Review," *Times Literary Supplement*, 18 December 1930, 1089; and Mrinalini Sinha, *Specters of Mother India: The Global Restructuring of an Empire* (Durham, NC: Duke University Press, 2006). Marriott's other publications included Evadne Price, *Meet Jane* (London: Marriott, 1930); Eleanor Elsner, *The Airway to See Europe: A Woman round the Airways of Europe* (London: Marriott, 1930); Norman Hill, *The Intimate Life of the Queen of Sheba* (London: Marriott, 1930); Norman Hill, *The Italian Artists as Men* (London: Marriott, 1931); William Logan, *Dress of the Day: A War-and-After Novel of the British Navy* (London: Marriott, 1930); and Prudence O'Shea, *Famine Alley* (London: Marriott, 1930).

90. Walter Townsend and Leonard Townsend, *The Biography of H.R.H. the Prince of Wales* (London: Marriott, 1929).

91. *My Selves*, 288–89.

92. "Best Selling Books during October," *Publisher and Bookseller*, 8 November 1929, 962; "Best Selling Books in November," *Publisher and Bookseller*, 6 December 1929, 1120; and "Best Selling Books during March," *Publisher and Bookseller*, 4 April 1930, 750.

93. TNA, J/13/12151: Proof of debt submitted by Leonard Townsend (1931).

94. Ibid., Statement of Affairs (24 November 1930).

95. *My Selves*, 290–92.

96. Ibid., 293.

97. David Foster, *Self Portraits* (Canberra: National Library of Australia, 1991), 112; and NLA: "Evadne Price interviewed by Hazel de Berg," 13 May 1977, accessed 1 March 2012, http://nla.gov.au/nla.oh-vn1479641.

98. Helen Zenna Smith, *Not So Quiet on the Western Front: Stepdaughters of War* (London: Marriott, 1930), 134–35.

99. "Marriott," *Publisher and Bookseller*, 11 April 1930, 799; and "Best Selling Books during April," *Publisher and Bookseller*, 2 May 1930, 968.

100. Foster, *Self Portraits*, 111–14; and TNA, J/13/12151: Affidavits of Evadne Fletcher (16 May and 12 June 1931).

101. "Not So Quiet," *Publishers' Circular*, 15 February 1930, 162; and *My Selves*, 293–94.

102. "Albert Marriott," *Illustrated London News*, 12 April 1930, 609.

103. *My Selves*, 297.

104. George Harrap, *Some Memories, 1901–1935* (London: Harrap, 1935), 120, 123.

105. W. G. Taylor, "Publishing," in *The Book World: A New Survey*, ed. John Hampden (London: Thomas Nelson, 1935), 68.

106. TNA, J/13/12151: Statement of Affairs (24 November 1930) and Bill of Costs of Messrs Denton Hall and Burgin (1931); "Albert Marriott," *Saturday Review*, 22 March 1930, 371; "Albert Marriott," *Saturday Review*, 24 May 1930, 664; and "Albert Marriott," *Illustrated London News*, 12 April 1930, 609.

107. Foster, *Self Portraits*, 114. "Some Coming War Books," *Publishers' Circular*, 1 February 1930, 103; "Not So Quiet," *Publishers' Circular*, 15 February 1930, 162; and "Result of £10 'Not So Quiet' Competition," *Publishers' Circular*, 12 July 1930, 36.

108. TNA, J/13/12151: Proof of Debt submitted by Morrison and Gibb Ltd (1931).

109. Ibid., Albert Marriott, Trading Account (1 January–24 November 1930).

110. W. Taylor, "Publishing," 70, 68.

111. "Notes of the Week," *Publishers' Circular*, 12 July 1930, 31.

112. "Albert Marriott," *Publishers' Circular*, 16 November 1929, 686–87; and "The Most Interesting Book of the Season," *Publisher and Bookseller*, 13 September 1929, 472.

113. "Marriott Books Mean SALES!," *Publisher and Bookseller*, 27 June 1930, 1333; and "Publicity Pays!," *Publishers' Circular*, 26 April 1930, 528.

114. "Notes and News," *Publisher and Bookseller*, 22 August 1930, 412.

115. "Albert Marriott," *Publishers' Circular*, 16 August 1930, 234; and "Book Display Competition," *Publisher and Bookseller*, 15 August 1930, 374. The company also offered a ten-pound prize for "the best 100-word criticism" of *Not So Quiet*, providing a "special display card" to advertise the competition. "£10 for 100-Word Criticism," *Publishers' Circular*, 10 May 1930, 625; and "Result of £10 'Not So Quiet' Competition," *Publishers' Circular*, 12 July 1930, 36.

116. "Free Press Publicity," *Publishers' Circular*, 12 October 1929, 509.

117. Frank Swinnerton, "Authorship," in *The Book World: A New Survey*, ed. John Hampden (London: Thomas Nelson and Sons, 1935), 14.

118. Jeremy Aynesley and Kate Forde, *Design and the Modern Magazine* (Manchester, UK: Manchester University Press, 2007), 8; and Alice Staveley, "Marketing Virginia Woolf: Women, War, and Public Relations in Three Guineas," *Book History* 12 (2009): 295–339.

119. W. Taylor, "Publishing," 63, 66.

120. Swinnerton, "Authorship," 23, 35. On the "battle of the brows," see Rosa Maria Bracco, *Betwixt and Between: Middlebrow Fiction and English Society in the Twenties and Thirties* (Melbourne, AU: History Department, University of Melbourne, 1990); Erica Brown and Mary Grover,

eds., *Middlebrow Literary Cultures: The Battle of the Brows, 1920–1960* (Basingstoke, UK: Palgrave Macmillan, 2011); Melissa Sullivan and Sophie Blanch, "The Middlebrow within or without Modernism," *Modernist Cultures* 6, no. 1 (2011): 1–17; Nicola Humble, *The Feminine Middlebrow Novel, 1920s to 1950s: Class, Domesticity and Bohemianism* (Oxford: Oxford University Press, 2001); and John Carey, *The Intellectuals and the Masses* (London: Faber and Faber, 1992).

121. TNA, J/13/12151: Statement of Affairs (24 November 1930). See also Christopher Hilliard, "The Provincial Press and the Imperial Traffic in Fiction, 1870s–1930s," *Journal of British Studies* 48, no. 4 (2009): 653–73; Simon Potter, "Webs, Networks and Systems: Globalization and the Mass Media in the Nineteenth- and Twentieth-Century British Empire," *Journal of British Studies* 46, no. 3 (2007): 621–46; and Simon Potter, *News and the British World: The Emergence of an Imperial Press System, 1876–1922* (Oxford: Clarendon Press, 2003).

122. TNA, J/13/12151: Albert Marriott, Trading Account (1 January–24 November 1930) and Order Made at the High Court of Justice (31 March 1932).

123. *My Selves*, 222.

124. Ibid., 225, 228.

125. Ibid., 229.

126. Graham, *Queen of Spain*, 17, 18, 190.

127. Ibid., 28.

128. Ibid., 277.

129. Osbert Burdett, "The King in His Beauty," *Saturday Review*, 7 November 1931, 594.

130. David Cannadine, "From Biography to History: Writing the Modern British Monarchy," *Historical Research* 77, no. 197 (2004): 289; and Andrzej Olechnowicz, "Historians and the Modern British Monarchy," in *The Monarchy and the British Nation, 1780 to the Present*, ed. Andrzej Olechnowicz (Cambridge: Cambridge University Press, 2007), 11.

131. "An Impertinent Biography of the Queen," *Daily Mail*, 11 April 1930, 13.

132. Charlotte Cavendish, *The Biography of H.M. Queen Mary* (London: Marriott, 1930), 88.

133. Ibid., 88; and Graham, *Edward P.*, 126.

134. Cavendish, *Queen Mary*, 243.

135. "Royal Names in Pages of a Bluffer," *Empire News*, 27 September 1931, 3; and Mayhall, "Prince of Wales," 529–43.

136. Evelyn Graham, "Chapters of Royal Life," *My Home*, December 1930, 58–62.

137. *Homes and Haunts of Famous Authors* (London: Wells, Gardner, Darton, 1906).

138. Marie Stopes, *Married Love: A New Contribution to the Solution of Sex Difficulties* (London: G. P. Putnam, 1918), 15.

139. Alison Light, *Forever England: Femininity, Literature and Conservatism between the Wars* (London and New York: Routledge, 1991).

140. Paddy Scannel and David Cardiff, *A Social History of British Broadcasting* (Oxford: Oxford University Press, 1991), 280–81; Olechnowicz, "Britain's 'Quasi-Magical' Monarchy"; and Williamson, "Monarchy and Public Values," 223–57.

141. H. Jennings and C. Madge, *May the Twelfth*, 92.

142. Ernest Jones, "The Psychology of Constitutional Monarchy" (1936), in *Essays in Applied Psychoanalysis*, vol. 1 (London: Hogarth Press, 1951); and Ross McKibbin, "Mass-Observation in the Mall," in *After Diana: Irreverent Elegies*, ed. Mandy Merck (London: Verso, 1998), 20.

143. Evelyn Graham, "Our Radiant Duchess," *Pearson's*, April 1929, 390–95; and Evelyn Graham, "Chapters of Royal Life," *My Home*, December 1930, 58–62.

144. Evelyn Graham, "At Home with the Duke and Duchess of York," *Modern Home*, October 1930, 40–45. On the feminization of monarchy, see Margaret Homans, *Royal Representations* (Chicago: University of Chicago Press, 1998); Simon Schama, "The Domestication of Majesty: Royal Family Portraiture, 1500–1850," *Journal of Interdisciplinary History* 17, no. 1 (1986): 155–83; and Clarissa Campbell Orr, "The Feminization of the Monarchy, 1780–1910: Royal Masculinity and Female Empowerment," in *Monarchy and the British Nation, 1780 to the Present*, ed. Andrzej Olechnowicz, 76–107 (Cambridge: Cambridge University Press, 2007).

145. *My Selves*, 231.

146. Evelyn Graham, "Bringing Up Princess Elizabeth," *Modern Home*, November 1930, 40–41, 99.

147. Evelyn Graham, "HRH Princess Mary Viscountess Lascelles," *Pearson's*, March 1929, 263–69; Richard Speaight, *Memoirs of a Court Photographer* (London: Hurst and Blackett, 1926); and Linkof, "'Photographic Attack,'" 277.

148. Susanna Brown, "Cecil Beaton and the Iconography of the House of Windsor," *Photography & Culture* 4, no. 3 (2011): 293–308; and Schwarzenbach, "Royal Photographs," 255–80. While images of female royals emphasized beauty and glamour, those of the Prince of Wales depicted public roles, military uniform, or state ceremonial. See Evelyn Graham, "Why the Prince Does Not Marry," *Britannia and Eve*, November 1929, 17–21.

149. Graham, *Princess Mary*, 15–16.

150. F. Lascelles, *Our Duke and Duchess*, 19.

151. Aston and Graham, *Duke of Connaught*, 5.

152. Graham, *Princess Mary*, 245–46.

153. Graham, *Edward P.*, 11.

154. Ibid., 12.

155. Ibid., 35.

156. Graham, *Princess Mary*, 163.

157. TNA, J/13/12151: Statement of Affairs (24 November 1930).

158. RA, EVIIIPWH/PS/MAIN/2004: Walter and Leonard Townsend to Officer Commanding, 1st Battalion, Grenadier Guards (12 May 1928).

159. Unattributed [Evelyn Graham], *Albert the Brave* (London: Hutchinson, 1934), 54–57.

160. Graham, *Edward P.*, 39.

161. Cavendish, *Queen Mary*, 195.

162. Graham, *Princess Mary*, 152–53.

163. "Victoria of Spain," *San Antonio Light*, 2 December 1928, 1.

164. Richard Dent, "Why Prince of Wales Has Not Fallen in Love," *Collier's*, 23 November 1928, 7–8, 42.

165. Richard Dent, *The Life Story of King George V* (New York: E. P. Dutton, 1930), 291–92.

166. "A Literary Fabricator," *Truth*, 24 June 1931, 1027.

167. "A King's Daughter," *Scotsman*, 6 September 1929, 8.

168. "Notes on Recent Books," *Bookman*, January 1930, 245.

169. See, e.g., Hilliard, "Twopenny Library," 215–20; Light, *Forever England*, passim; and

Nicola Beauman, *A Very Great Profession: The Woman's Novel, 1918-39* (London: Persephone Books, 2008). Thanks to Chris Hilliard for suggesting these comparisons.

170. Evelyn Graham, "The Story of Princess Mary," *Daily Mail*, 18 October 1928, 5. The correction was included in Graham, *Princess Mary*, 44.

171. "The New Princess," *Truth*, 27 August 1930, 1.

172. "Royalty on Gossip Writers," *Truth*, 14 May 1930, 822.

173. Michael Saler, " 'Clap If You Believe in Sherlock Holmes': Mass Culture and the Re-enchantment of Modernity, c. 1890-c. 1940," *Historical Journal* 46, no. 3 (2003): 599-622; and Jennie Taylor, "Pennies from Heaven and Earth in Mass Observation's Blackpool," *Journal of British Studies* 51, no. 1 (2012): 149.

174. Evelyn Graham, "Things They've Neither Done Nor Said," *Woman's Journal*, December 1930, 16-17, 117, 118, 121, 122, 125.

175. Ibid., 121.

CHAPTER SEVEN

1. RMM, ASTON/5/10: Memorandum of Agreement between Sir George Aston and Evelyn Graham, and George Harrap (7 February 1929). The contract with United Newspapers for serial rights to the *Duke of Connaught* included similar provisos. RMM, ASTON/5/10: Memorandum of Agreement with United Newspapers (4 March 1929).

2. "Mr Murray's Christmas Books," *Publisher and Bookseller*, 7 November 1930, 1052.

3. David Cannadine, "From Biography to History: Writing the Modern British Monarchy," *Historical Research* 77, no. 197 (2004): 295; Andrzej Olechnowicz, "Historians and the Modern British Monarchy," in *The Monarchy and the British Nation, 1780 to the Present*, ed. Andrzej Olechnowicz (Cambridge: Cambridge University Press, 2007), 11; and Harold Nicolson, *Diaries and Letters, 1930-64* (Harmondsworth, UK: Penguin, 1984), 334. Quasi-official lives included Sir George Arthur, *King George V* (London: Cape, 1929); Sir Lionel Cust, *Edward VII and His Court* (London: John Murray, 1930); Lady Cynthia Asquith, *God Save the King* (London: Chapman and Hall, 1935); and Gertrude Lascelles, *Our King and Queen* (London: Hutchinson, 1937).

4. Kenneth Rose, *King George V* (London: Weidenfeld and Nicolson, 1983), 225.

5. William Kuhn, "Arthur John Bigge, Baron Stamfordham," *ODNB*, accessed 6 August 2012, http://ezproxy.ouls.ox.ac.uk:2117/view/article/31883; Frank Prochaska, "Clive Wigram, first Baron Wigram," *ODNB*, accessed 6 August 2012, http://ezproxy.ouls.ox.ac.uk:2117/view /article/36890; David Sinclair, *Two Georges: The Making of the Modern Monarchy* (London: Hodder and Staughton, 1988), 135-36; and Kenneth Rose, *Kings, Queens and Courtiers* (London: Weidenfeld and Nicolson, 1985), 167-69, 265-69, 280-82.

6. Duff Hart-Davis, *In Royal Service: The Letters and Journals of Sir Alan Lascelles, 1920-1936*, vol. 2 (London: Hamish Hamilton, 1989), x-xi, 2-3; Frank Prochaska, "Sir Alan Lascelles," *ODNB*, accessed 6 August 2012, http://ezproxy.ouls.ox.ac.uk:2117/view/article/31334; and V. V. Badeley, rev. Marc Brodie, "Sir Lionel Halsey," *ODNB*, accessed 6 August 2012, http:// ezproxy.ouls.ox.ac.uk:2117/view/article/33661.

7. John Plunkett, *Queen Victoria: First Media Monarch* (Oxford: Oxford University Press, 2003).

8. K. Rose, *King George V*, 226; and Donald Spoto, *The Decline and Fall of the House of Windsor* (New York: Simon and Schuster, 1995), 169.

9. Hart-Davis, *In Royal Service*, 17–19, 28; and Chandrika Kaul, "Monarchical Display and the Politics of Empire: Prince of Wales and India, 1870s–1920s," *Twentieth Century British History* 17, no. 4 (2006): 478.

10. RA, EVIIIPWH/PS/MAIN/2004: Marriott to Thomas (18 May 1928).

11. Ibid., Sir Godfrey Thomas memorandum (25 May 1928).

12. Ibid., Private Secretary to Graham (14 July 1928).

13. Ibid., Graham to Thomas (6 July 1928); and Private Secretary to Graham (14 July 1928).

14. Ibid., Private Secretary to Graham (14 July 1928).

15. Ibid., Graham to Thomas (2 July 1928). See also RA, EVIIIPWH/PS/MAIN/2004: Marriott to Thomas (20 June 1928); Private Secretary to Marriott (18 June 1928); Graham to Thomas (13 June 1928); and Private Secretary to Graham (4 June 1928).

16. RA, PS/PSO/GV/PS/MAIN/48600: Marriott to H.M. the King (3 September 1928); and Graham to Stamfordham (21 August 1928).

17. Ibid., Stamfordham to Graham (23 August 1928).

18. RA, EVIIIPWH/PS/MAIN/2004: Wigram to Thomas (12 November 1929).

19. RA, PS/PSO/GV/PS/MAIN/48600: Stamfordham to Marriott (5 September 1928).

20. RA, EVIIIPWH/PS/MAIN/2004: Hutchinson to Thomas (23 August 1928); Kathleen Woodward, *Queen Mary of England* (London: Hutchinson, 1927); and Lady Cynthia Asquith, *HRH the Duchess of York* (London: Hutchinson, 1927).

21. RA, EVIIIPWH/PS/MAIN/2004: Private Secretary to Hutchinson (24 August 1928).

22. Ibid., Hutchinson (27 August 1928).

23. Ibid., Private Secretary to Harry Golding (4 July 1929).

24. Ibid.

25. Ibid., Golding to Thomas (5 July 1929).

26. Evelyn Graham, "Edward P.," *Windsor*, June 1929, 2–20; Evelyn Graham, "Edward P.," *Windsor*, July 1929, 127–42; Evelyn Graham, "Edward P.," *Windsor*, August 1929, 255–69; and Evelyn Graham, "Edward P.," *Windsor*, September 1929, 383–402.

27. RA, EVIIIPWH/PS/MAIN/2004: Golding to Thomas (3 December 1929).

28. Ibid., E. L. Skinner to A. F. Lascelles (12 February 1929).

29. Ibid., A.L. to Skinner (14 February 1929).

30. Ibid., Skinner to Lascelles (15 February 1929).

31. RA, PS/PSO/GV/PS/MAIN/48600: Private Secretary to Wigram (6 November 1929).

32. RA, EVIIIPWH/PS/MAIN/2004: Graham to Thomas (19 February 1929).

33. "The Prince of Wales," *Publishers' Weekly*, 14 December 1929, 1031; and cutting: "The Most Interesting Book of the Year," *Publishers' Circular*, 14 September 1929, 306.

34. RA, EVIIIPWH/PS/MAIN/2004: dust jacket for W. and L. Townsend, *The Biography of H.R.H. the Prince of Wales* (n.d.).

35. Ibid., Private Secretary to Graham (23 July 1928).

36. Ibid., Marriott to Thomas (24 July 1928).

37. Ibid., Golding to Thomas (4 October 1929); and "The Book about the Prince," *Publishers' Weekly* (October 1929).

38. RA, EVIIIPWH/PS/MAIN/2004: GT handwritten memo (n.d.).

39. Ibid., Marriott to Private Secretary (4 January 1930); Private Secretary to Marriott (6 January 1930); Private Secretary to Marriott (17 January 1930); and Marriott to Thomas (30 January 1930).

40. RA, PS/PSO/GV/PS/MAIN/48600: cutting from dust jacket (n.d.); prospectus for *The Biography of His Majesty King George V* (n.d.); "Do You Know—?," *Publishers' Circular*, 11 January 1930, 29; and "Advert: Home Magazine," *Publisher and Bookseller*, 14 February 1930, 347.

41. RA, PS/PSO/GV/PS/MAIN/48600: Stamfordham to Marriott (24 February 1930).

42. The serial began with Major C. F. L. Kipling, "Life of His Majesty King George V," *Home*, February 1930, 516–19, 572–74, and ran monthly until Major C. F. L. Kipling, "Life of His Majesty King George V," *Home*, August 1930, 514–17, 564, 571.

43. RA, EVIIIPWH/PS/MAIN/2004: Golding to Halsey (31 May 1929); Golding to Thomas (28 June 1929); and Private Secretary to Golding (4 July 1929). On the control of images of Princesses Elizabeth and Margaret, see RA, ADYH/MAIN/071: Lady in Waiting to Marcus Adams (20 January 1931).

44. RA, EVIIIPWH/PS/MAIN/2004: Graham to Thomas (7 September 1928); and Comptroller to Graham (26 September 1928).

45. Ibid., Private Secretary to Golding (4 July 1929).

46. RA, PS/PSO/GV/PS/MAIN/48600: Halsey to Stamfordham (26 September 1928).

47. RA, PS/PSO/GV/PS/MAIN/43520: Raymond Savage to Stamfordham (26 June 1928).

48. RA, PS/PSO/GV/PS/MAIN/48600, Stamfordham to Thomas (12 September 1928); and Halsey to Stamfordham (26 September 1928).

49. RA, EVIIIPWH/PS/MAIN/2004: Lady Helen Graham to Thomas (21 May 1928).

50. Ibid., Thomas to Helen Graham (23 May 1928); and Graham to Thomas (27 May 1928).

51. RA, PS/PSO/GV/PS/MAIN/43520: Stamfordham to Thomas (5 February 1930).

52. Ibid., Thomas to Stamfordham (6 February 1930); and Mitchell to Wigram (10 January 1930).

53. RA, EVIIIPWH/PS/MAIN/2004: Marriott to Private Secretary (4 January 1930).

54. RA, PS/PSO/GV/PS/MAIN/48600: John Murray to Stamfordham (11 December 1929).

55. Ibid., Stamfordham to Murray (11 December 1929); and Murray to Stamfordham (12 December 1929).

56. RA, EVIIIPWH/PS/MAIN/2004: Golding to Thomas (3 December 1929).

57. RA, PS/PSO/GV/PS/MAIN/48600: Stamfordham to Manager, Hatchards (22 February 1930); and E. W. Shepherd to Stamfordham (22 and 24 February 1930).

58. Ida May, *The Elizabeth Gift Book* (London: Marriott, 1931), 12, 23, 39.

59. RA, ADYH/MAIN/071: Comptroller to Marriott (8 July 1930).

60. Ibid., Marriott to Sir Basil Brook (9 July 1930).

61. Ibid., Comptroller to Marriott (10 July 1930).

62. "Princess Elizabeth Book," *Morning Post*, 2 October 1930, n.p.

63. The editor of the *Morning Post* was closely associated with Sir William Joynson-Hicks, the Conservative home secretary. In 1929 the director of public prosecutions took action against Norah James's book *Sleeveless Errand* after the editor tipped off Joynson-Hicks. Thanks to Chris Hilliard for drawing this to my attention. See TNA, DPP/192: Partridge, E.H., obscene publication, *Sleeveless Errand* (1929).

64. RA, PS/PSO/GV/PS/MAIN/48600: Louis Greig to Wigram (n.d.). See also RA, PS/PSO/GV/PS/MAIN/48600: George Sutton to Wigram (24 February 1929).

65. RA, PS/PSO/GV/PS/MAIN/48600: Sutton to Wigram (20 February 1929).

66. Ibid., Sutton to Wigram (29 April 1929).

67. Ibid., Wigram [?] handwritten note (n.d.).

68. K. Rose, *King George V*, 314–15.

69. RA, PS/PSO/GV/PS/MAIN/43520: Wigram to Greig (6 July 1932).

70. RA, PS/PSO/GV/PS/MAIN/48600: handwritten note, Alexander Hardinge (24 April 1929).

71. "The King 'Home' Again," *Morning Post*, 16 May 1929, 13; and "Girls Shower Roses on the King," *Daily Chronicle*, 16 May 1929, 3.

72. RA, PS/PSO/GV/PS/MAIN/48600: Sutton to Wigram (6 May 1929).

73. RA, PS/PSO/GV/PS/MAIN/43520: enclosed and highlighted cutting: "Royal Biography Sensation," *Star*, 16 May 1929, 1.

74. "Royal Biography Sensation," *Star*, 16 May 1929, 1.

75. Ibid.

76. "Book on the King Stopped," *Daily Chronicle*, 17 May 1929, 3.

77. "Official Ban on King's Life Story," *Irish Times*, 17 May 1929, 7; "King George V's Biography Withheld from Public," *New York Times*, 17 May 1929, 1; and "Book on the King Stopped," *Daily Chronicle*, 17 May 1929, 3.

78. "Life Story of the King," *Daily Telegraph*, 17 May 1929, 14; and "Biography of the King," *News of the World*, 19 May 1929, 4.

79. "A Life of the King," *Morning Post*, 18 May 1929, 12.

80. "A Life of the King," *Morning Post*, 17 May 1929, 11.

81. RA, EVIIIPWH/PS/MAIN/2004A: telegram (22 May 1930).

82. Ibid., Alice Head to Thomas (24 May 1930).

83. Ibid., Private Secretary to Head (26 May 1930).

84. Ibid., Head to Thomas (27 May 1930); and RA, PS/PSO/GV/PS/MAIN/48600: EGA (27 April 1930).

85. RA, EVIIIPWH/PS/MAIN/2004A: Graham to Sir Ernest Benn (20 May 1930); Benn to Thomas (21 May 1930); and Thomas to Head (26 May 1930).

86. Ibid., Thomas to Benn (22 May 1930).

87. "Fake War Diary of the Prince," *Daily Express*, 18 July 1930, 1; and "Royal War Diary Offered," *New York Times*, 18 July 1930, 8.

88. "Faking the Prince's 'War Diary,'" *Truth*, 23 July 1930, 136.

89. RA, EVIIIPWH/PS/MAIN/2004A: Thomas to Benn (22 May 1930).

90. RA, PS/PSO/GV/PS/MAIN/48600: Graham to H.M. the Queen (7 September 1928).

91. Ibid., Stamfordham to Graham (8 September 1928).

92. RA, EVIIIPWH/PS/MAIN/2004: Thomas to Helen Graham (23 May 1928). On the politics of privacy and secrecy, see Deborah Cohen, *Family Secrets: Living with Shame from the Victorians to the Present Day* (London: Viking, 2013).

93. RA, PS/PSO/GV/PS/MAIN/43520: Mitchell to Wigram (10 January 1930). For similar concerns, see RA, EVIIIPWH/PS/MAIN/2004: Halsey to Stamfordham (26 September 1928).

94. RA, PS/PSO/GV/PS/MAIN/43520: Richard Dent to Private Secretary, HM the King (28 May 1929).

95. Ibid., Wigram [to Dent?] (1 June 1929).

96. RA, EVIIIPWH/PS/MAIN/2004A: Head to Thomas (24 May 1930).

97. RA, PS/PSO/GV/PS/MAIN/48600: Murray to Stamfordham (12 December 1929).

98. RA, EVIIIPWH/PS/MAIN/2004A: Private Secretary to Head (26 May 1930).

99. *My Selves*, 249.

100. *My Selves*, 250; and RA, PS/PSO/GV/PS/MAIN/43520: Malcolm Murray to Stamfordham (28 June 1928). For Savage's relationship with the royal household, see RA, PS/PSO/GV/ PS/MAIN/43520: Stamfordham to Savage (28 June 1928); Savage to Stamfordham (12 November 1925); Stamfordham to Savage (13 November 1925); Savage to Stamfordham (14 November 1925); Savage to Stamfordham (26 June 1928); and Stamfordham to Murray (27 June 1928).

101. *My Selves*, 250.

102. RA, PS/PSO/GV/PS/MAIN/43520: Thomas to Stamfordham (6 February 1930).

103. RA, EVIIIPWH/PS/MAIN/2004A, Thomas to Benn (22 May 1930).

104. Evelyn Graham, "Things They've Neither Done Nor Said," *Woman's Journal*, December 1930, 125.

105. "The Bulow Memoirs," *Publishers' Circular*, 16 May 1931, 632. The book in question was Bernhard von Bulow, *The Memoirs of Prince von Bulow* (London: Putnam, 1930–31).

106. TNA, J/13/12151: Order Made at the High Court of Justice (31 March 1932); and Bill of Costs of Messrs Denton Hall and Burgin (1931).

107. M. M. Knappen, "The Abdication of Edward VIII," *Journal of Modern History* 10 (1938): 248–50. The book was published in the United States as Geoffrey Dennis, *Coronation Commentary* (New York: Dodd, Mead, 1937).

CHAPTER EIGHT

1. "Royal Biography Sensation," *Star*, 16 May 1929, 1.

2. Lytton Strachey, *Eminent Victorians* (London: Chatto and Windus, 1918); and Laurel Brake, *Subjugated Knowledges: Journalism, Gender and Literature in the Nineteenth Century* (Houndmills, UK: Basingstoke, Macmillan, 1994), 190–94.

3. Marjorie Bowen, "Human Appeal," *Bookman*, December 1931, 53; and Charles L. Ponce de Leon, *Self-Exposure: Human Interest Journalism and the Emergence of Celebrity in America, 1890–1940* (Chapel Hill and London: University of North Carolina Press, 2002).

4. Osbert Burdett, "A Tory to the Life," *English Review*, August 1931, 346.

5. Ian Hunter, *Nothing to Repent: The Life of Hesketh Pearson* (London: Hamish Hamilton, 1987), 122.

6. Hesketh Pearson, *Thinking It Over: The Reminiscences of Hesketh Pearson* (London: Hamish Hamilton, 1938), 203–4, 290.

7. Harold Nicolson, *The Development of English Biography* (London: Hogarth Press, 1933), 11, 142; Lord David Cecil, introduction to *An Anthology of Modern Biography* (London: Thomas Nelson, 1936); Lord David Cecil, ed., *Modern Biography* (London: Thomas Nelson, 1938), xvi; "The Rights of the Dead," *New Statesman*, 24 January 1931, 459–61; Charles Whibley, "The

Indiscretions of Biography," *English Review*, December 1924, 769–72; and A. G. Gardiner, "Art of Biography," *Star*, 23 July 1931, 6.

8. H. M. Paull, *Literary Ethics: A Study in the Growth of the Literary Conscience* (London: Thornton Butterworth, 1928), 270.

9. Ibid., 272.

10. Ibid., 274.

11. Ibid., 272. For these debates, see, e.g., Jacob Omnium, "Under Cover," *Publisher and Bookseller*, 4 January 1929, 20; and "Flesh and Blood History," *Truth*, 14 January 1931, 68.

12. Pearson, *Thinking It Over*, 294; and D. Cecil, *Modern Biography*, ix. Max Jones, " 'National Hero and Very Queer Fish': Empire, Sexuality, and the British Remembrance of General Gordon, 1918–72," *Twentieth Century British History* (first published online 13 October 2014, accessed 6 April 2015, doi:10.1093/tcbh/hwu050), offers a different perspective on the limits of Strachey's influence. For unease around modernism, see Stefan Collini, *Absent Minds: Intellectuals in Britain* (Oxford: Oxford University Press, 2006); Michael Saler, *The Avant-Garde in Interwar England: Medieval Modernism and the London Underground* (Oxford: Oxford University Press, 1999); and Christopher Hilliard, "Modernism and the Common Writer," *Historical Journal* 48, no. 3 (2005): 769–87.

13. Charlotte Cavendish, *The Biography of H.M. Queen Mary* (London: Marriott, 1930), 148.

14. "New Stories of the Queen's Life," *Daily Chronicle*, 16 April 1930, 9.

15. "The Queen's Part in Royal Romance," *Evening Standard*, 16 April 1930, 21.

16. Annotated copy of Charlotte Cavendish, *Biography of H.M. Queen Mary* (1930), Royal Collection Trust, accessed 29 July 2014, http://www.royalcollection.org.uk/collection/1054640 /the-biography-of-hm-queen-mary-by-charlotte-cavendish-ie-netley-lucas.

17. "The Queen," *Daily Mail*, 10 April 1930, 12.

18. "An Impertinent Biography of the Queen," *Daily Mail*, 11 April 1930, 13.

19. Ibid.

20. Ibid.

21. Nick Groom, *The Forger's Shadow: How Forgery Changed the Course of Literature* (London: Picador, 2002), 63.

22. "The Impertinent Biography," *Daily Mail*, 12 April 1930, 11. See also Harold Nicolson, "Authors Must Learn Sincerity," *Daily Express*, 10 April 1930, 8.

23. "Bachelor Princes," *Daily Mirror*, 10 April 1930, 3; and "The Queen and a Biography," *Daily Mirror*, 11 April 1930, 4.

24. "The Queen and a Biography," *Daily Mirror*, 11 April 1930, 4.

25. "New Biography of the Queen," *Star*, 10 April 1930, 2.

26. "Notes and News," *Publisher and Bookseller*, 21 March 1930, 649.

27. "The Real Queen Mary," *Daily Express*, 12 April 1930, 11. See also "The Real Queen Mary," *Evening Standard*, 12 April 1930, 9; and "Four Great Sunday Features," *Daily Express*, 26 April 1930, 2. The serialization began with "Queen Mary's Playmates as Her Suitors," *Daily Express*, 10 April 1930, 3, and ran until "How the Queen Rules Her Family," *Daily Express*, 18 May 1930, 13.

28. "The Real Queen Mary," *Daily Express*, 12 April 1930, 11; "Best Selling Books during

April," *Publisher and Bookseller*, 2 May 1930, 968; and "Best Selling Books in 1930," *Publisher and Bookseller*, 16 January 1931, 80–81.

29. "Marriott Limited," *Publishers' Circular*, 5 April 1930, 463.

30. "Publicity Pays!" *Publishers' Circular*, 26 April 1930, 528.

31. RA, EVIIIPWH/PS/MAIN/2004: Thomas to Sir Harry Verney (14 April 1930).

32. "The Queen and a Biography," *Daily Mirror*, 11 April 1930, 4; and RA, PS/PSO/GV/PS/MAIN/4860: Dent to Stamfordham (2 May 1930). As the controversy expanded, the Home Office pathologist, Sir Bernard Spilsbury, forced Marriott to abandon plans to publish Leonard Townsend and Walter Townsend's *Sir Bernard Spilsbury's Famous Case Book*. See "Sir Bernard Spilsbury and a Book," *Daily Mail*, 21 April 1930, 9; "Sir B. Spilsbury and a Book," *Star*, 21 April 1930, 22; "Spilsbury Book Storm," *Daily Chronicle*, 23 April 1930, 1; "Spilsbury Book Withheld," *Daily Mail*, 24 April 1930, 8; and "Legal Action to Stop a Book," *Daily Chronicle*, 21 April 1930, 1. The book was hastily revised as W. Townsend and L. Townsend, *Black Cap: Murder Will Out* (London: Marriott, 1930), the "true story of every famous murder for the last 50 years." On Spilsbury, see Ian Burney and Neil Pemberton, "Bruised Witness: Bernard Spilsbury and the Performance of Early Twentieth-Century Forensic Pathology," *Medical History* 55, no. 1 (2011): 41–60; and Ian Burney and Neil Pemberton, "The Rise and Fall of Celebrity Pathology," *British Medical Journal* 341, no. 3 (2010): 1319–21.

33. "Smash and Grab Memoirs," *Daily Chronicle*, 22 April 1930, 6.

34. Jacob Omnium, "Under Cover," *Publisher and Bookseller*, 16 May 1930, 1065–66.

35. Ibid.

36. "The Mystery of Evelyn Graham," *Daily Mail*, 1 December 1930, 13.

37. Ibid.

38. Ibid.

39. "Evelyn Graham Unmasked," *Daily Mail*, 2 December 1930, 11.

40. "The Amazing Case of Evelyn Graham," *Daily Mail*, 5 December 1930, 9.

41. "Netley Lucas's Eight Names," *Daily Mail*, 4 February 1931, 3.

42. "Netley Lucas Again," *Daily Mail*, 31 December 1930, 7.

43. "The Amazing Case of Evelyn Graham," *Daily Mail*, 5 December 1930, 9.

44. "Evelyn Graham Unmasked," *Daily Mail*, 2 December 1930, 11.

45. Ibid.

46. "Netley Lucas Again," *Daily Mail*, 31 December 1930, 7.

47. "The Mystery of Evelyn Graham," *Daily Mail*, 1 December 1930, 13.

48. Ibid.

49. "Evelyn Graham Unmasked," *Daily Mail*, 2 December 1930, 11. I draw on K. K. Ruthven, *Faking Literature* (Cambridge: Cambridge University Press, 2001), 2, 4.

50. " 'Evelyn Graham,' " *Ottawa Evening Citizen*, 1 December 1930, 20.

51. "Netley Lucas's Eight Names," *Daily Mail*, 4 February 1931, 3. NLA, Evadne Price, interviewed by Hazel de Berg, 13 May 1977, accessed 1 March 2012, http://nla.gov.au/nla.oh-vn1479641.

52. *My Selves*, 298.

53. Ibid., 300.

54. Ibid., 308–9.

55. Ibid., 306.

56. "Evelyn Graham Flees the Country," *Daily Mail*, 9 December 1930, 13.

57. "Netley Lucas Again," *Daily Mail*, 31 December 1930, 7. I discuss Graham and his wife's presence on the *Dunluce Castle* above (see p. •••).

58. *My Selves*, 312.

59. "Netley Lucas," *Daily Mail*, 22 January 1931, 9.

60. "Netley Lucas's Eight Names," *Daily Mail*, 4 February 1931, 3.

61. "Netley Lucas," *Daily Mail*, 3 February 1931, 7.

62. "Netley Lucas's Eight Names," *Daily Mail*, 4 February 1931, 3.

63. *My Selves*, 314.

64. Ibid., 319.

65. Ibid.

66. Evelyn Graham, "At Home with the Duke and Duchess of York," *Modern Home*, October 1930, 40; Evelyn Graham, "Bringing Up Princess Elizabeth," *Modern Home*, November 1930, 40-41, 99; Evelyn Graham, "The Prince as Favourite Uncle," *Modern Home*, December 1930; and Unattributed [Evelyn Graham], "The Duchess of York as Housemaker," *Modern Home*, January 1931, 21.

67. "Evelyn Graham's Waterloo," *Truth*, 30 September 1931, 507.

68. *My Selves*, 286.

69. Ruthven, *Faking Literature*, 35-39; and Groom, *Forger's Shadow*, 55.

70. See Ava Briefel, *The Deceivers: Art Forgery and Identity in the Nineteenth Century* (Ithaca, NY: Cornell University Press, 2006), 176.

71. TNA, J/13/12151: Albert Marriott, Trading Account (1 January-24 November 1930); Order Made at the High Court of Justice (31 March 1932); Bill of Costs of Messrs Denton Hall and Burgin (1931); and "More Light on Evelyn Graham's Life," *Daily Mail*, 24 December 1930, 11.

72. NLA, "Evadne Price," accessed 1 March 2012, http://nla.gov.au/nla.oh-vn1479641.

73. TNA, J/13/12151: Statement of Affairs (24 November 1930).

74. "News and Views of Literary London," *New York Times*, 4 January 1931, BR5; TNA, J/107/62: Registrars' Notes, Albert Marriott (1930); TNA, J/13/12151: Affidavit of R. R. H. Hazell (22 November 1930); "Winding-Up Orders," *London Gazette*, 12 December 1930, 8068; "Winding-Up Order," *Daily Mirror*, 9 December 1930, 6; "Evelyn Graham Flees the Country," *Daily Mail*, 9 December 1930, 13; and "Albert Marriott," *Publishers' Circular*, 20 December 1930, 862.

75. "More Light on Evelyn Graham's Life," *Daily Mail*, 24 December 1930, 11.

76. TNA, J/13/12151: Order Made at the High Court of Justice (31 March 1932).

77. Ibid.

78. "First Meetings," *London Gazette*, 12 December 1930, 8609; "Notice of Appointment of Liquidator," *London Gazette*, 30 January 1931, 739; "Notice of Intended Dividend," *London Gazette*, 25 December 1931, 8382; "Notice of Dividend," *London Gazette*, 26 January 1932, 623; TNA, J/107/62 (1930); TNA, J/13/12151: Bill of Costs of Messrs Denton Hall and Burgin (1931); and TNA, J/13/12151: Statement of Affairs (24 November 1930).

79. "Best Selling Books during December," *Publisher and Bookseller*, 9 January 1931, 52; "Best Selling Books in 1930," *Publisher and Bookseller*, 16 January 1931, 80-81; and "Best Selling Books in January," *Publisher and Bookseller*, 13 February 1931, 306.

80. Jacob Omnium, "Under Cover," *Publisher and Bookseller*, 16 May 1930, 1065–66.

81. "From Gaol to Grub Street," *Truth*, 16 December 1930, 949.

82. Ibid.

83. Jacob Omnium, "Under Cover," *Publisher and Bookseller*, 16 May 1930, 1065–66.

84. Marion, "Woman's Way," *Worker*, 21 January 1931, 18.

85. Ibid.

86. Christopher Hilliard, *To Exercise Our Talents: The Democratization of Writing in Britain* (Cambridge, MA, and London: Harvard University Press, 2006), 13.

87. "The Society's Quarterly Record," *Author* (Spring 1931): 116. The society's dealings with shark publishers can be traced in BL, SOA: vol. 382, Add MS 56956: C. D. Medley to D. K. Roberts (8 October 1930); vol. 383, Add MS 56957: Medley to Roberts (2 February 1931) and Medley to Roberts, "Report of the legal matters for the year 1930–31" (5 January 1932); vol. 384, Add MS 56958: Medley to Roberts, "Comments on annual report on legal matters for 1932–33" (6 January 1933); vol. 385, Add MS 56959: Medley to Roberts (23 November 1933); and Add MS 56972: "Complaints and cases against Arthur Stockwell" (1920–45).

88. "Elections," *Author* (January 1929): 67.

89. BL, SOA: vol. 382, Add MS 56956: Medley to Roberts (5 December 1930). For the society's work for Pilcher, see BL, SOA: vol. 382, Add MS 56956: Medley to Roberts (1 December 1930) and Field Roscoe to Roberts (8 December 1930); vol. 383, Add MS 56957: Medley to Roberts (16 June 1931), and Medley to Roberts (18 June 1931).

90. TNA, J/13/12151: Order Made at the High Court of Justice (31 March 1932) and Affidavit of Hugh Pilcher (22 June 1931).

91. RMM, ASTON/5/10: Memorandum of Agreement between Sir George Aston and Evelyn Graham, and George Harrap (7 February 1929). For Aston's correspondence with the society, see RA, PS/PSO/GV/ PS/MAIN/48600, Aston to Wigram (16 December 1930).

92. RMM, ASTON/5/10: D. Kilham Roberts to Aston (29 October 1930).

93. RA, PS/PSO/GV/PS/MAIN/48600: Aston to Wigram (26 January 1931) and Wigram to Aston (29 January 1931).

94. Ibid., Aston to Wigram (2 February 1931).

95. "Contemporary Comment," *Author* (Summer 1930): 138.

96. "Shark Publishers and the Colonies," *Author* (June 1929): 128; "Publisher Sharks," *Publishers' Circular*, 13 April 1929, 421; and "A Warning to Authors," *Author* (Winter 1931): 84.

97. "Scamps," *Publishers' Circular*, 11 July 1931, 25.

98. Two belated articles advised members whose publishers went bankrupt: E. J. Macgillivray, "Insolvent Publishing Companies," *Author* (Autumn 1931): 10–12; and Winifride McConnell, "Author's Rights against a Publishing Company in Liquidation," *Author* (Autumn 1931): 13–14.

99. RA, PS/PSO/GV/PS/MAIN/48600: Wigram to Mitchell (2 December 1930) and Mitchell to Wigram (3 December 1930).

100. Ibid., Wigram to Aston (4 December 1930), Aston to Wigram (16 December 1930), Wigram to Aston (17 December 1930), Aston to Wigram (26 January 1931), Wigram to Aston (29 January 1931), and Aston to Wigram (2 February 1931).

101. RA, EVIIIPWH/PS/MAIN/2004A: Thomas to James Brown (16 December 1930).

102. Ibid., Brown to Thomas (9 December 1930).

103. "A Literary Fabricator," *Truth*, 24 June 1931, 1027; and "Evelyn Graham Again," *Truth*, 8 July 1931, 52.

104. "Week-end Gossip," *Empire News*, 5 July 1931, 8; "Evelyn Graham Again," *Daily Mail*, 6 July 1931, 11; "Evelyn Graham's New Tricks," *Daily Mail*, 7 July 1931, 11; and "Evelyn Graham," *Daily Mail*, 8 July 1931, 7.

105. "18 Months for Evelyn Graham," *Morning Post*, 23 September 1931, 5.

106. *My Selves*, 323.

107. "Author in Court," *News of the World*, 26 July 1931, 14.

108. "Says Writer Stole in Reform School," *New York Times*, 11 October 1931, 22.

109. "Author in Court," *News of the World*, 26 July 1931, 14.

110. "Evelyn Graham's New Tricks," *Daily Mail*, 7 July 1931, 11.

111. Mark Meredith, ed., *What Editors and Publishers Want* (Liverpool: Literary Year Books Press, 1924), 9; Mary Ann Gillies, *The Professional Literary Agent in Britain, 1880–1920* (Toronto: University of Toronto Press, 2007), 7, 88–89, 90, 93, 99; and James Hepburn, *The Author's Empty Purse and the Rise of the Literary Agent* (Oxford: Oxford University Press, 1969), 57, 63.

112. Gillies, *Professional Literary Agent*, 170.

113. International reports included "Biographer of Royalty Held on a Fraud Charge," *Chicago Daily Tribune*, 19 July 1931, 3; "Mythical Lady," *Otautau Standard*, 1 September 1931, 3; and "Our London Letter," *Straits Times*, 17 August 1931, 6. For reports of Graham's arrest in Britain, see, e.g., "Evelyn Graham in Court," *Morning Post*, 20 July 1931, 12; "Evelyn Graham, the Author, Arrested," *Evening Standard*, 18 July 1931, 3; "Evelyn Graham in the Dock," *Sunday Pictorial*, 19 July 1931, 2; "Author Arrested," *News of the World*, 19 July 1931, 3; "Bail Refused for Royal Biographer," *Empire News*, 19 July 1931, 1; and "Netley Lucas in Court," *Sunday Dispatch*, 19 July 1931, 3.

114. Percy Smith, *Plutocrats of Crime: A Gallery of Confidence Tricksters* (London: Frederick Muller, 1960), 190.

115. Depositions and transcripts of evidence do not survive, but there are useful details in LMA, PS/BOW/A01/135: Bow Street Police Court Register (18, 24, and 28 July 1931); and LMA, ACC/2385/179: Central Criminal Court, Calendar of Prisoners (21 and 22 September 1931).

116. "Author Sent to Prison," *Guardian*, 23 September 1931, 1.

117. "Names on Pad at Author's Address," *Empire News*, 2 August 1931, 6; "Evelyn Graham Committed," *Morning Post*, 29 July 1931, 12; and "Evelyn Graham on Fraud Charges," *Morning Post*, 22 September 1931, 12.

118. "Puzzle of 'Lady Angela Stanley,'" *Daily Express*, 29 July 1931, 7; and "Author in Court," *News of the World*, 26 July 1931, 14.

119. "Author in Court," *News of the World*, 26 July 1931, 14.

120. "Royal Names in Pages of a Bluffer," *Empire News*, 27 September 1931, 3.

121. "Netley Lucas Sent for Trial," *Daily Mirror*, 29 July 1931, 5.

122. "Says Writer Stole in Reform School," *New York Times*, 11 October 1931, 22.

123. "Bail Refused for Royal Biographer," *Empire News*, 19 July 1931, 1; "Evelyn Graham in the Dock," *Sunday Pictorial*, 19 July 1931, 2; LMA, PS/BOW/A01/135 (18, 24, and 28 July 1931); and LMA, ACC/2385/179 (21 and 22 September 1931).

124. P. Smith, *Plutocrats of Crime*, 190.

125. "Persons in Custody Who May Be Wanted Elsewhere," *Police Gazette*, 12 August 1931, 3.

126. "Netley Lucas in Court," *Sunday Dispatch*, 19 July 1931, 3; and "Evelyn Graham," *Sunday Dispatch*, 26 July 1931, 9.

127. "Persons in Custody Who May Be Wanted Elsewhere," *Police Gazette*, 12 August 1931, 3; and "Bail Refused for Author," *Reynolds's*, 19 July 1931, 9.

128. "Bail Refused for Royal Biographer," *Empire News*, 19 July 1931, 1.

129. "Royal Names in Pages of a Bluffer," *Empire News*, 27 September 1931, 3.

130. "His Pen of Deceit," *News of the World*, 27 September 1931, 6.

131. This quotation is a composite taken from "Evelyn Graham in Court," *Evening Standard*, 24 July 1931, 3; "Evelyn Graham Case," *Scotsman*, 25 July 1931, 10; "Charges against an Author," *Times*, 25 July 1931, 7; "Netley Lucas Sent for Trial," *Evening Standard*, 28 July 1931, 10; "Netley Lucas Alleged Fraud," *Daily Express*, 25 July 1931, 7; and "Evelyn Graham in Court," *Morning Post*, 25 July 1931, 11.

132. "Literary Agent Defrauded," *Times*, 23 September 1931, 7.

133. "Pseudonyms," *Publisher and Bookseller*, 26 September 1930, 633; and "Dictionary of Anonymous and Pseudonymous English Literature," *Publishers' Circular*, 29 June 1929, 755.

134. "Evelyn Graham Again," *Daily Mail*, 6 July 1931, 11.

135. "Author Sent for Trial," *Scotsman*, 29 July 1931, 15.

136. John Mullan, *Anonymity: A Secret History of English Literature* (London: Faber and Faber, 2007), 297. See also Stefan Collini, "Plain Speaking: The Lives of George Orwell," in Stefan Collini, *Common Reading: Critics, Historians, Publics*, 72–83 (Oxford: Oxford University Press, 2008); Stephanie Newell, *The Power to Name: A History of Anonymity in Colonial West Africa* (Athens: Ohio University Press, 2013); and Carmela Ciuraru, *Nom de Plume: A (Secret) History of Pseudonyms* (New York: Harper, 2011).

137. P. Smith, *Plutocrats of Crime*, 185.

138. "From Gaol to Grub Street," *Truth*, 16 December 1930, 949; and "Evelyn Graham's Waterloo," *Truth*, 30 September 1931, 507.

139. "His Pen of Deceit," *News of the World*, 27 September 1931, 6.

140. *My Selves*, 248–49.

141. "Evelyn Graham at Old Bailey," *Evening Standard*, 21 September 1931, 5.

142. "Re-convictions," *Police Gazette*, 26 September 1931, 8.

143. "Literary Agent Defrauded," *Times*, 23 September 1931, 7; "Author's Fraud Unmasked," *Daily Express*, 23 September 1931, 11; "The Amazing Career of Evelyn Graham," *Daily Mail*, 23 September 1931, 9; and "Eighteen Months for Evelyn Graham," *Morning Post*, 23 September 1931, 5.

144. "Author's Fraud Unmasked," *Daily Express*, 23 September 1931, 11.

145. "Evelyn Graham's Waterloo," *Truth*, 30 September 1931, 507. For reports of Graham's conviction, see also "Imprisoned for Fraud," *Argus* (Melbourne), 25 September 1931, 9; "Evelyn Graham Gets 18 Months," *Evening Standard*, 22 September 1931, 4; "Evelyn Graham Sentenced to 18 Months," *Daily Mirror*, 23 September 1931, 5; "Gaol for Author," *Straits Times*, 23 September 1931, 14; and "18 Months for Evelyn Graham," *Morning Post*, 23 September 1931, 5, 11.

146. "Literary Agent Defrauded," *Times*, 23 September 1931, 7. On Wild's literary pretensions, see Alec Craig, *Suppressed Books: A History of the Conception of Literary Obscenity*

(London: World Publishing, 1963); and Robert Blackham, *Sir Ernest Wild, K.C.* (London: Rich and Cowan, 1935).

147. "Royal Names in Pages of a Bluffer," *Empire News*, 27 September 1931, 3.

148. "Literary Agent Defrauded," *Times*, 23 September 1931, 7.

149. *My Selves*, 218.

150. "His Pen of Deceit," *News of the World*, 27 September 1931, 6.

151. "Author Sent to Prison," *Guardian*, 23 September 1931, 1.

152. Ethelreda Lewis, "Literary Hoaxes," *Author* (October 1929): 14–15; "A Literary Hoax," *Publishers' Circular*, 4 May 1929, 505; and "Important Announcement," *Publisher and Bookseller*, 3 May 1929, 800.

153. Cleone Knox, *The Diary of a Young Lady of Fashion, 1764–65* (London: Thornton Butterworth, 1925); and "Cleverest Hoax of the Century," *Daily Express*, 4 June 1926, 1. See also "A Blow for the Highbrows," *Truth*, 4 February 1931, 171; "Newspaper Hoaxes," *Truth*, 12 February 1930, 260; "An Impudent Pirate," *Author* (January 1930): 30; and "Bogus Baroness's Secret Microphone," *John Bull*, 15 November 1930, 13.

154. See Hesketh Pearson, *Hesketh Pearson by Himself* (London: Heinemann, 1965), chap. 10; and Hunter, *Nothing to Repent*, 111–20. Pearson's trial is reported in, e.g., "The Whispering Gallery," *Daily Mail*, 27 January 1927, 6; "The Whispering Gallery," *Daily Mail*, 29 January 1927, 6; "An Author in the Dock," *News of the World*, 5 December 1926, 6; "Withdrawn Book," *News of the World*, 12 December 1926, 1; "Hesketh Pearson Wins," *News of the World*, 30 January 1927, 6; "Whispering Gallery Withdrawn," *Evening News*, 20 November 1926, 1; "Bonfire of the Whispering Gallery," *Evening News*, 22 November 1926, 7; "Editorial: Enough Whisperings," *Evening News*, 23 November 1926, 6; "The Unmasking of a Fake," *Evening News*, 23 November 1926, final edition; and "Acquittal of Pearson," *Reynolds's*, 30 January 1927, 9. For the *Daily Mail*'s translation of the case into a talking point, see "The Scandal of Faked Memoirs," *Daily Mail*, 19 November 1926, 8; "A Scandalous Fake Exposed," *Daily Mail*, 19 November 1926, 9; "The Daily Mail Exposure Succeeds," *Daily Mail*, 22 November 1926, 9; Lord Birkenhead, "Trifling with Reputations," *Daily Mail*, 23 November 1926, 9; "Reputations and Writers," *Daily Mail*, 24 November 1926, 8; "Real People in Fiction," *Daily Mail*, 24 November 1926, 9; Arnold Bennett, "Trifling with Reputations," *Daily Mail*, 25 November 1926, 8; "The Publishers' Responsibility," *Author* (April 1927): 92–94; and "TP's Table Talk," *T.P.'s and Cassell's Weekly*, 11 December 1926, 259. The case is discussed in Max Saunders, *Self Impression: Life-Writing, Autobiografiction, and the Forms of Modern Literature* (Oxford: Oxford University Press, 2010), 222–24.

155. "An Address Delivered at Harrogate," *Publisher and Bookseller*, 5 June 1931, 1110–13.

156. I draw on Ari Adut, *On Scandal: Moral Disturbances in Society, Politics and Art* (Cambridge: Cambridge University Press, 2008), 27.

157. See, e.g., Virginia Woolf, *Flush: A Biography* (London: Hogarth Press, 1933); and Saunders, *Self Impression*, passim. Robert Graves and Alan Hodge, *The Long Week-End: A Social History of Great Britain, 1918–39* (London: Faber and Faber, 1940), 298, reflects on this process.

158. Ruthven, *Faking Literature*, 4; and Melissa Sullivan and Sophie Blanch, "Introduction: The Middlebrow within or without Modernism," *Modernist Cultures* 6, no. 1 (2011): 1.

159. Paull, *Literary Ethics*, 39. See also Henry Rhodes, *The Craft of Forgery* (London: John Murray, 1934), chap. 15.

160. Aviva Briefel, *The Deceivers: Art Forgery and Identity in the Nineteenth Century* (Ithaca, NY, and London: Cornell University Press, 2006), 175.

161. Nicki Hitchcott, "Calixthe Beyala: Prizes, Plagiarism and 'Authenticity,'" *Research in African Literatures* 37, no. 1 (2006): 106–7; Ruthven, *Faking Literature*, 72; and Mark Jones, ed., *Why Fakes Matter: Essays on Problems of Authenticity* (London: British Museum Press, 1992), 9.

162. Ruthven, *Faking Literature*, 47, 3; and Miles Orvell, *The Real Thing: Imitation and Authenticity in American Culture, 1880–1940* (Chapel Hill: University of North Carolina Press, 1989), xv. See also the emphasis on "Ruling in and ruling out" elaborated in Nicola Humble, "Sitting Forward or Sitting Back: Highbrow v. Middlebrow Reading," *Modernist Cultures* 6, no. 1 (2011): 42–51.

163. *My Selves*, 236.

164. J. M. Golby and A. W. Purdue, *Kings and Queens of Empire: British Monarchs, 1760–2000* (Stroud, UK: Tempus, 2000), 9.

CHAPTER NINE

1. LMA, ACC/3444/PR/01/197: Wandsworth Prison, register (July 1931–September 1932), 51–52.

2. "Crook Lived and Died in a Blaze," *Empire News*, 7 July 1940, 2.

3. I draw on Kali Israel, *Names and Stories: Emilia Dilke and Victorian Culture* (Oxford: Oxford University Press, 2002), 7.

4. "Publishers Cancel Book by Mr Evelyn Graham," *Daily Express*, 9 August 1933, 1.

5. RA, PS/PSO/GV/PS/MAIN/48600: Sir George Aston to Clive Wigram (15 July 1933).

6. Ibid., Edwin Shepherd (12 July 1933).

7. Ibid., Keeper of the Privy Purse to Wigram (13 July 1933).

8. Ibid., Wigram to Shepherd (13 July 1933); Wigram to Arthur Barker (18 July 1933); and Wigram to Aston (17 July 1933).

9. Ibid., Aston to Wigram (15 July 1933).

10. Ibid., Barker to Private Secretary (13 July 1933).

11. Ibid., Barker to Wigram (18 October 1933).

12. "Evelyn Graham Tells What Is in His Banned Book," *Daily Express*, 10 August 1933, 3. On Society gossip, see Sarah Newman, "The Celebrity Gossip Column and Newspaper Journalism in Britain, 1918–1939" (DPhil thesis, University of Oxford, 2012).

13. RA, PS/PSO/GV/PS /MAIN/48600: Graham to Wigram (26 August 1933).

14. Ibid., Wigram to Manager, Unicorn Press (28 August 1933).

15. Ibid., Hunter to Wigram (31 August 1933); Wigram to Hunter (2 September 1933); and Hunter to Wigram (6 September 1933).

16. Ibid., Barker to Wigram (18 October 1933).

17. "I Was a Crook," *Angus Evening Telegraph*, 18 June 1934, 7; Netley Lucas, "Unblushing Confessions of a Versatile Rascal," *San Antonio Light*, 12 November 1933, 3–4, 22; 19 November 1933, 3–4, 20, 22; 26 November 1933, 3–4, 18, 19; and 3 December 1933, 3–4, 20.

18. *My Selves*, 156–57.

19. Ibid., 212.

20. Ibid., 1.

21. See above. pp. 187–90.

22. *My Selves*, 23.

23. Ibid., 269, 279, 294–96.

24. Ibid., 222–23.

25. Ibid., 267–68.

26. Ibid., 270.

27. Ibid., 271. Another footnote to a silence: there is no obvious record of this incident in the registers of the Marylebone court. Thanks to Sim Koole for checking these records for me.

28. *My Selves*, 319.

29. Ibid., 273.

30. Ibid.

31. Ibid., 332, 354–55.

32. Ibid., 2, 4, 317. On ideas of ancestry, see Stephen Kern, *A Cultural History of Causality: Science, Murder Novels, and Systems of Thought* (Princeton, NJ: Princeton University Press, 2004), chap. 1.

33. *My Selves*, 6.

34. Ibid., 317.

35. Ibid., 58.

36. Ibid., 156.

37. Ibid., 157.

38. Ibid., 156.

39. William Matthews, *British Autobiographies: An Annotated Bibliography of British Autobiographies Published or Written before 1951* (Berkeley and Los Angeles: University of California Press, 1955), 188, 308.

40. SHC, 606/2/1/1/53: Western Surrey Coroner's Papers, No. 33, Netley Lucas (25 June 1940) and Mavis Lucas (23 June 1940).

41. "Obituary," *British Medical Journal* (25 June 1949): 1142–43; and "Obituary," *Lancet* (1949): 1122. See Sir James Purves-Stewart, *The Diagnosis of Nervous Diseases* (London: Arnold, 1906); Sir James Purves-Stewart and Arthur Evans, *Nerve Injuries and Their Treatment* (London: H. Frowde, 1916); Sir James Purves-Stewart, *A Physician's Tour in Soviet Russia* (London: George Allen and Unwin, 1933); Sir James Purves-Stewart, *Sands of Time: Recollections of a Physician in Peace and War* (London: Hutchinson, 1939); and Stephen Casper, "Trust, Protocol, Gender, and Power in Interwar British Biomedical Research: Kathleen Chevassut and the 'Germ' of Multiple Sclerosis," *Journal of the History of Medicine and Allied Sciences* 66, no. 2 (2010): 180–215.

42. *My Selves*, vii.

43. Ibid., vii. On multiple personalities, see Hillel Schwartz, *The Culture of the Copy: Striking Likenesses, Unreasonable Facsimiles* (New York: Zone Books, 1996), 80–87; and Ian Hacking, *Rewriting the Soul: Multiple Personality and the Sciences of Memory* (Princeton, NJ: Princeton University Press, 1998).

44. *My Selves*, vii.

45. Sir James Purves-Stewart, *The Diagnosis of Nervous Diseases* (London: Arnold, 1920), 360–61.

46. *My Selves*, vii–viii.

47. Purves-Stewart, *Diagnosis of Nervous Diseases* (1920), 364–65.

48. Ibid., 364.

49. Ibid.

50. Ibid., 362.

51. Ibid., 363.

52. *My Selves*, 317.

53. Ibid., viii–ix.

54. "Our London Letter," *Straits Times*, 23 August 1933, 6.

55. "Faking Made Him £20,000," *Daily Express*, 1 July 1940, 5.

56. "Trickster Prince's Fate in Fire," *News of the World*, 30 June 1940, 2.

57. "Netley Lucas Denies Agency 'Ramp,'" *Singapore Free Press*, 20 July 1936, 3. The term *ramp* is a British expression for a confidence trick.

58. CHAR, 8/502A: Allan Eidenow to Winston Churchill (1 June 1935); and "Netley Lucas Denies Agency 'Ramp,'" *Singapore Free Press*, 20 July 1936, 3.

59. Allan Eidenow, "A Job Which Nobody Seems to Want," *Straits Times*, 11 June 1932, 10; Allan Eidenow, "American Presidents," *West Australian*, 19 November 1932, 4; Allan Eidenow, "Frenzied Money Making Drama on 'The Floor,'" *Daily Mirror*, 22 June 1933, 10; Allan Eidenow, "How American Women Face the Crisis," *Daily Mirror*, 31 August 1933, 10; and Allan Eidenow, "A Man of Courage," *Daily Mirror*, 30 January 1934, 10.

60. Reina Lewis, *Rethinking Orientalism: Women, Travel and the Ottoman Harem* (London: I. B. Tauris, 2004); and Reina Lewis and Nancy Micklewright, eds., *Gender, Modernity and Liberty: Middle Eastern and Western Women's Writings* (London: I. B. Tauris, 2006), chap. 10. Grace Ellison's published work included Melek Hanoum and Grace Ellison, *Abdul Hamid's Daughter: The Tragedy of an Ottoman Princess* (London: Methuen, 1913); Grace Ellison, *An Englishwoman in a Turkish Harem* (London: Methuen, 1915); Grace Ellison, *The Disadvantages of Being a Woman* (London: A. M. Philpot, 1924); and Grace Ellison, *Turkey To-day* (London: Hutchinson, 1928).

61. RA, EVIIIPWH/PS/MAIN/2004A: Godfrey Thomas (27 November 1934).

62. "The Girlhood of the Duchess," *Observer*, 30 December 1934, 4; and Grace Ellison, *The Authorised Life Story of Princess Marina* (London: Heinemann, 1934).

63. RA, EVIIIPWH/PS/MAIN/2004A: Thomas (27 November 1934).

64. RA, PS/PSO/GV/PS/MAIN/4860o: Richard Tracy to Private Secretary (4 December 1934); Private Secretary to Tracy (6 December 1934); and Wigram to Brigadier Henry Tomkinson (6 December 1934).

65. RA, PS/PSO/GV/PS/MAIN/4860o: R. Cameron to Wigram (12 February 1935); Wigram to Manager, London United Press (13 February 1935); Cameron (14 February 1935); and RA, EVIIIPWH/PS/MAIN/2004A: Cameron to Thomas (13 February 1935).

66. "Action against the Aga Khan Fails," *Guardian*, 3 December 1935, 18.

67. Allan Eidenow to Paul Robeson (3 April 1935), quoted in Paul Robeson Jr., *The Undiscovered Paul Robeson: An Artist's Journey, 1898–1939* (New York: Wiley, 2001), 354.

68. Dan LeMahieu, *A Culture for Democracy: Mass Communication and the Cultivated Mind in Britain between the Wars* (Oxford: Clarendon Press, 1988).

69. CHAR, 8/502A: Eidenow to Churchill (16 April 1935); and Eidenow to Churchill (25 May 1935).

70. Ibid., Churchill to Eidenow (30 May 1935); Eidenow to Churchill (28 May 1935); and Eidenow to Churchill (1 June 1935). Peter Clarke, *Mr Churchill's Profession: Statesman, Orator, Writer* (London: Bloomsbury, 2012).

71. CHAR, 8/502A: Eidenow to Churchill (6 June 1935).

72. Ibid., Churchill to Eidenow (4 June 1935).

73. Ibid., Churchill to Eidenow (7 June 1935).

74. Ibid., Churchill to Eidenow (7 June 1935); Eidenow to Churchill (12 June 1935); and Churchill to Eidenow (21 June 1935).

75. Ibid., Eidenow to Churchill (16 April 1935).

76. "Unwritten Articles," *Evening Post* (NZ), 7 January 1936, 16. See also "Verdict Is Given for the Aga Khan," *Montreal Gazette*, 4 June 1936, 10; "Suit against Aga Khan Fails," *Times of India*, 14 December 1935, 14; and "Aga Khan in Lawsuit," *Daily Mirror*, 3 December 1935, 9.

77. "Unwritten Articles," *Evening Post* (NZ), 7 January 1936, 16.

78. Ibid.

79. "Alleged Breach of Contract," *Times*, 3 December 1935, 5.

80. "Unwritten Articles," *Evening Post* (NZ), 7 January 1936, 16.

81. "Alleged Breach of Contract," *Times*, 3 December 1935, 5.

82. "Bankruptcy," *Times*, 8 July 1936, 4; and "Netley Lucas Denies Agency 'Ramp,'" *Singapore Free Press*, 20 July 1936, 3.

83. "Netley Lucas Denies Agency 'Ramp,'" *Daily Mail*, 9 July 1936, 5. For the formal record of bankruptcy proceedings, see "First Meetings and Public Examinations," *London Gazette*, 13 December 1935, 8093; "Receiving Orders," *London Gazette*, 13 December 1935, 8091; "Adjudications," *London Gazette*, 3 January 1936, 112; "Appointments of Trustees," *London Gazette*, 7 January 1936, 217; "Day Appointed for Proceeding with Public Examination," *London Gazette*, 5 June 1936, 3640; "Adjudications," *London Gazette*, 14 February 1936, 1038; and "Appointments of Trustees," *London Gazette*, 18 February 1936, 1124.

84. MRC, GB/0152/MSS.334/3/1/93: Eidenow to Mann (14 April 1936). On L. V. Reece-Jones, who defended Eidenow's acquaintance Martin Coles Harman against charges of fraud, see "L.V. Reece-Jones," *London Gazette*, 17 April 1931, 2528; on S. W. Laker-Wright, see "Laker Wright and Co.," *London Gazette*, 30 September 1930, 5971.

85. "Alleged Conspiracy to Defraud," *Times*, 23 July 1938, 7; and "Court of Criminal Appeal," *Times*, 29 November 1938, 5.

86. "Alleged Conspiracy to Defraud," *Times*, 27 July 1938, 4. Born in Trinidad, de Verteuil published fiction and scientific commentaries as John Dellbridge, Freddy Bannister, and Francis Vere. See, e.g., Frederick de Verteuil, *Fifty Wasted Years* (London: Chapman and Hall, 1938); John Dellbridge, *The Moles of Death* (London: Diamond Press, 1927); John Dellbridge, *Revolution in India* (London: Morley and M. Kennerley, 1930); John Dellbridge, *The Lady in the Wood: A Hambledon Story* (London: Hurst and Blackett, 1950); and Francis Vere, *The Piltdown Fantasy* (London: Cassell, 1950).

87. "Harman Worked for Two Years to Trap Disbarred Barrister," *Daily Express*, 28 July 1938, 4. On Guylee, see George Robb, *White-Collar Crime in Modern England: Financial Fraud and Business Morality, 1845–1929* (Cambridge: Cambridge University Press, 1992), chap. 4. TNA, HO/144/21424: Edward Guylee, Obtaining Money by False Pretences (1936–40).

88. "Alleged Conspiracy to Defraud," *Times*, 23 July 1938, 7

89. "Libel Action by Mr Martin Coles Harman," *Times*, 28 April 1939, 4.

90. "Alleged Conspiracy to Defraud," *Times*, 22 July 1938, 11; "Alleged Conspiracy to Defraud," *Times*, 23 July 1938, 7; "Alleged Conspiracy to Defraud," *Times*, 26 July 1938, 4; "Alleged Conspiracy to Defraud," *Times*, 27 July 1938, 4; "Convict Says Ex-Lawyer Asked for £3000 to Stop Case," *Daily Express*, 3 June 1938, 7; "De Verteuil Witness Weeps in Box," *Daily Express*, 22 July 1938, 7; "De Verteuil in Box," *Daily Express*, 26 July 1938, 5; and "Harman Worked for Two Years to Trap Disbarred Barrister," *Daily Express*, 28 July 1938, 4. See also TNA, HO/144/21624: Frederick de Verteuil, Obtaining Money by False Pretences (1938–42); TNA, CRIM/1/1024: Frederick de Verteuil and Frank Whelan, Obtaining Money by False Pretences (12 July 1938); and TNA, DPP/2/477: de Verteuil and Whelan, Conspiracy and False Pretences (1937).

91. Robb, *White-Collar Crime*, chap. 4.

92. Percy Smith, *Plutocrats of Crime: A Gallery of Confidence Tricksters* (London: Frederick Muller, 1960), 191, 190.

93. Unattributed [Evelyn Graham], *Albert the Brave* (London: Hutchinson, 1934).

94. Evelyn Graham, *Edward P.* (London: Ward Lock, 1936).

95. Netley Lucas and Evelyn Graham, *Moi et Moi* (Paris: Gallimard, 1939).

96. Patrick Mouze, "Daumal après le Grand Jeu," *Amis de l'Ardenne* 21 (2008); and Alain Virmaux, review of Roger Gilbert-Lecomte and Leon Pierre-Quint, *Correspondence, 1927–1939*, in *Europe: Revue Litteraire Mensuelle* 87, no. 961 (2009): 366. On Daumal, see Kathleen Rosenblatt, *René Daumal: The Life and Work of a Mystic Guide* (New York: SUNY Press, 1999).

97. Sarah Maza, *Violette: A Story of Murder in 1930s Paris* (Berkeley and Los Angeles: University of California Press, 2011), 177–84, chap. 8; and David Walker, *Outrage and Insight: Modern French Writers and the Faits Divers* (Oxford: Berg, 1995), chap. 3.

98. *My Selves*, 165–66.

99. "Netley Lucas Denies Agency 'Ramp,'" *Singapore Free Press*, 20 July 1936, 3.

100. TNA, J/77/3698/9814: Cedric Hill vs. Dorothy Hill (1936).

101. TNA, J/77/3711/3087: Elsie Lucas vs. Netley Lucas otherwise Leslie Evelyn Graham: Matrimonial Causes where wife is a poor person (30 November 1936); Lucas vs. Lucas, Original Petition for Dissolution of Marriage (15 January 1937); and "122 Decrees Made Absolute," *Times*, 3 May 1938, 6.

102. TNA, J/77/3711/3087: Original Petition (15 January 1937); and Matrimonial Causes (30 November 1936). TNA, J/77/3698/9814 (1936).

103. "Mavis Cox and Netley Lucas, Certified Copy of an Entry of Marriage Given at the General Register Office, Application Number 1388088-1," *England and Wales Civil Registration Indexes*, vol. 1a, p. 1221 (13 December 1938), accessed 4 July 2009, www.ancestry.com; "Names and Descriptions of British Passengers, SS *California*" (16 April 1935), accessed 3 June 2012, www.ancestry.com; "Baptisms Solemnized at St James's Church, Calcutta," *British India Office, Births and Baptisms* (18 October 1913), accessed 13 March 2015, http://search.findmypast.co.uk/record?id=bl%2fbind%2fb%2f601684; and "Trickster Prince's Fate in Fire," *News of the World*, 30 June 1940, 2.

104. SHC, 606/2/1/1/53: Netley Lucas (25 June 1940); and "Trickster Prince's Fate in Fire," *News of the World*, 30 June 1940, 2.

105. SHC, 606/2/1/1/53: Dr. Easton (23 June 1940).

106. Ibid., P.S. Smith (23 June 1940).

107. Ibid., Dr. Easton (23 June 1940).

108. Ibid., P.S. Smith to G. Wills Taylor, H.M. Coroner (23 June 1940).

109. Ibid., P.C. Collis (23 June 1940); Donald Winter-Moy (23 June 1940); and Dr. Easton (23 June 1940).

110. Ibid., Mavis Lucas (23 June 1940).

111. Ibid.

112. Ibid.

113. Ibid., Dr. Easton (23 June 1940).

114. Ibid., Eric Gardner (23 June 1940). On the tools of postmortem investigation, see Jan Margaret Ross, *Post-mortem Appearances* (Oxford: Oxford University Press, 1937).

115. SHC, 606/2/1/1/53: Eric Gardner (23 June 1940); and Netley Lucas, certified copy of an entry of death, Epsom and Leatherhead (28 June 1940), no. 91: General Register Office application no. 1390838-1. I draw on Ian Burney, "Our Environment in Miniature: Dust and the Early Twentieth-Century Forensic Imagination," *Representations* 121, no. 1 (2013): 31–59; and Ian Burney, *Bodies of Evidence: Medicine and the Politics of the English Inquest, 1830–1926* (Baltimore: Johns Hopkins University Press, 2000).

116. SHC, 606/2/1/1/53: Dr. Easton (23 June 1940); and Reinhart Koselleck, *The Practice of Conceptual History: Timing History, Spacing Concepts* (Stanford, CA: Stanford University Press, 2002), 102.

117. "Faking Made Him £20,000," *Daily Express*, 1 July 1940, 5; "Fake Author Had 'Mania for Fires,'" *Daily Mail*, 1 July 1940, 3; "Crook Lived and Died in a Blaze," *Empire News*, 7 July 1940, 2; and "Hoaxer's Death," *Sunday Times* (Perth), 15 December 1940, 4.

118. "Trickster Prince's Fate in Fire," *News of the World*, 30 June 1940, 2.

119. NFSA, title no. 642150: Macquarie Broadcasting Service: Production Report "Episode 45: Netley Lucas" (22 August 1955); and "Advert: 3UZ," *Argus* (Melbourne), 7 May 1956, 12.

120. NFSA, title no. 642150: Macquarie Broadcasting Service: Production Report "Episode 45: Netley Lucas" (22 August 1955), 2.

121. Ibid., 3–6.

122. Ibid., 8.

123. Ibid.

124. Ibid., 14.

125. Ibid., 14–15.

126. Ibid., 16.

127. "The Rogue Who Made Cash out of Fake Royal Secrets," *Winnipeg Free Press*, 9 January 1953, 8; and P. Smith, *Plutocrats of Crime*, 184–92.

128. H. G. Castle, *Case for the Prosecution* (London: Naldrett Press, 1956), xi. H. G. Castle, *The Boy's Book of Sailing* (Rockliff, UK: Guilford Press, 1956). See also H. G. Castle, *The Boy's Book of Motor Racing* (Rockliff, UK: Guilford Press, 1954); H. G. Castle, *Britain's Motor Industry* (London: Clerke and Cockeran, 1950); and H. G. Castle and Edward Mortelmans, *Spion Kop* (London: Almark, 1976).

129. H. Castle, *Case for the Prosecution*, vii.

130. Ibid, vii, ix. Lucas played a similar role in Gertrude Lythgoe, *The Bahama Queen: The Autobiography of Gertrude "Cleo" Lythgoe* (Mystic, CT: Flat Hammock Press, 2007), 57–58, 156. Here Lythgoe also challenged Lucas's account of their meeting in *Crooks: Confessions*; *My Selves*, 89–96; and Netley Lucas, "Unblushing Confessions of a Versatile Rascal," *San Antonio Light*, 12 November 1933, 3–4, 22; 19 November 1933, 3–4, 20, 22; 26 November 1933, 3–4, 18, 19; 3 December 1933, 3–4, 20.

131. Alun Munslow, *A History of History* (London and New York: Routledge, 2012); Alun Munslow, "Why Should Historians Write about the Nature of History (Rather Than Just Do It)?," *Rethinking History* 11, no. 4 (2007): 623; Jeremy Popkin, *History, Historians, and Autobiography* (Chicago: University of Chicago Press, 2005), chap. 2; Israel, *Names and Stories*; and Carolyn Steedman, "Cries Unheard, Sights Unseen: Writing the Eighteenth-Century Metropolis," *Representations* 118, no. 1 (2012): 28.

COOLING OUT

1. Mavis was living in a flat in Kensington when she died at the Royal Marsden Hospital in Chelsea. See Mavis Jessie Lucas, certified copy of an entry of death, Metropolitan Borough of Chelsea (12 October 1962), no. 341: General Register Office application no. 6373504-1.

2. "Mayfair Fell for That 'Irish Lilt,'" *Daily Mirror*, 12 September 1951, 5; and "Sleep Drug Overdose," *Daily Mail*, 27 August 1951, 5.

3. SHC, 606/2/1/1/53: Western Surrey Coroner's Report, no. 33, Netley Lucas (23 June 1940).

4. "Trickster Prince's Fate in Fire," *News of the World*, 30 June 1940, 2; and "Faking Made Him £20,000," *Daily Express*, 1 July 1940, 5.

5. William Sewell, *The Logics of History: Social Theory and Social Transformation* (Chicago: University of Chicago Press, 2005), 183–84; and Christopher Hilliard, "'Is It a Book That You Would Even Wish Your Wife or Your Servants to Read?' Obscenity Law and the Politics of Reading in Modern England," *American Historical Review* 118, no. 3 (2013): 653–78.

6. NFSA, 642150: Macquarie Broadcasting Service, Production Report "Episode 45: Netley Lucas" (22 August 1955). For the other episodes, see NFSA, 641749, 642552, 642553: "Scripts and Production Reports" (1955–56).

7. Harold Nicolson, *King George the Fifth: His Life and Reign* (London: Constable, 1952).

8. Marion Crawford, *The Little Princesses* (London: Cassell, 1950); and Hugo Vickers, "Crawford, Marion Kirk (1909–1988), in *ODNB*, accessed 17 July 2012, http://ezproxy.ouls .ox.ac.uk:2117/view/article/59443. Crawford's career ended in scandal when her ghosted column in *Woman's Own* was exposed as fraudulent in 1955.

9. Gillian Swanson, "Serenity, Self-Regard and the Genetic Sequence: Social Psychiatry and Preventative Eugenics in Britain, 1930s–1950s," *New Formations* 60 (2007): 50.

10. Terry Castle, *The Apparitional Lesbian: Female Homosexuality and Modern Culture* (New York: Columbia University Press, 1993); Swanson, "Serenity, Self-Regard and the Genetic Sequence," 65; and Sewell, *Logics of History*, 183–84.

11. Hugo Vickers, "Alexandra, Princess, Duchess of Fife (1891–1959)," *ODNB*, accessed 18 July 2012, http://ezproxy.ouls.ox.ac.uk:2117/view/article/30376; Hugo Vickers, "Arthur of Connaught, Prince (1883–1938)," *ODNB*, accessed 18 July 2012, http://ezproxy.ouls .ox.ac.uk:2117/view/article/30461; Neville Laski, "Darling, Charles John, First Baron Darling

(1849–1936)," rev. G. R. Rubin, *ODNB*, accessed 18 July 2012, http://ezproxy.ouls.ox.ac.uk:2117 /view/article/32714; and G. K. S. Hamilton-Edwards, "Mary, Princess Royal (1897–1965)," *ODNB*, accessed 18 July 2012, http://ezproxy.ouls.ox.ac.uk:2117/view/article/36654. Other citations of Lucas's work include Compton Mackenzie, *The Windsor Tapestry* (London: Rich and Cowan, 1938), 580; Hans von Hentig, *The Criminal and His Victim* (New Haven, CT: Yale University Press, 1948), 386, 415; and J. Arthur Hoyles, *The Treatment of the Young Delinquent* (London: Epworth Press, 1952), 57, 60–61, 69–70.

12. Judith Halberstam, *The Queer Art of Failure* (Durham, NC: Duke University Press, 2011), 11–12; and Lee Edelman, *No Future: Queer Theory and the Death Drive* (Durham, NC: Duke University Press, 2004).

13. Paul Ricoeur, *Time and Narrative*, vol. 1, trans. Kathleen McLaughlin and David Pellauer (Chicago and London: University of Chicago Press, 1984), 52.

14. Thanks to Seth Koven for suggesting this comparison.

15. See, e.g., Erving Goffman, *The Presentation of Self in Everyday Life* (New York: Anchor Books, 1959).

16. Anthony Grafton, *The Footnote: A Curious History* (London: Faber and Faber, 1999), 232, 235. On the historian as trickster, see Natalie Zemon Davis, *A Passion for History: Conversations with Denis Crouzet* (Kirksville, MO: Truman State University Press, 2010), 11.

INDEX

Page numbers in italic refer to figures.